Software Engineering 1990

THE BRITISH COMPUTER SOCIETY CONFERENCE SERIES

Editor: P. HAMMERSLEY

The BCS Conference Series aims to report developments of an advanced technical standard undertaken by members of The British Computer Society through the Society's conference organization. The series should be vital reading for all whose work or interest involves computing technology. Volumes in this Series will mirror the quality of papers published in the BCS's technical periodical *The Computer Journal* and range widely across topics in computer hardware, software, applications and management.

British Computer Society Conference Series 1

SE90

Proceedings of Software Engineering 90,
Brighton, July 1990

Edited by

Patrick A.V. Hall
Brunel University

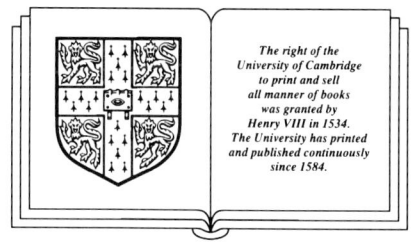

Published by
CAMBRIDGE UNIVERSITY PRESS
on behalf of
THE BRITISH COMPUTER SOCIETY
Cambridge
New York   Port Chester   Melbourne   Sydney

Published by the Press Syndicate of the University of Cambridge
The Pitt Building, Trumpington Street, Cambridge CB2 1RP
40 West 20th Street, New York, NY 10011, USA
10 Stamford Road, Oakleigh, Melbourne, Australia

© British Informatics Society Ltd 1990

First published 1990

Printed in Great Britain at the University Press, Cambridge

Library of Congress cataloging in publication data available

British Library cataloguing in publication data available

Contents

Preface ix

Quality 1
Software Engineering, QA friend or foe? Maurice Resnick (invited paper) 3

CASE and IPSE Databases 13
Method Support needs an OMS, M. Lemoine and S. Pascaud 15
A Comparison of Databases for Software Engineering, P. Hitchcock & A.W. Brown 27

Metrics 65
The Use of Metrics for the Early Detection of Software Design Errors, M. Shepperd & D. Ince 67
The relative software complexity metric: a validation study, J. Munson & T. Khoshgoftaar 89

Requirements Engineering 103
Capturing and Analysing User Problems: separating the 'why' from the 'what', D. Bustard, M. Norris & B. van Toen 105
Presenting an Entity model using hierarchical abstraction, D. Flynn & H. Yue 121

CASE, IPSE and AI 143
Evaluating Tool Support Interfaces, F. Long & M. Tedd 145
Towards a Convergence in Knowledge-based and Conventional Software Engineering: Tools, Methods, Techniques, L. Hickman 161

Verification and Validation 183
Providing a foundation for rigorous software development: issues of language specification and compiler validation, J. Souter & M. Woodman 185
Methods and Tools for Testing-in-the Large, R. Franck, A. Spillner & J. Herrmann 209

Formal approaches 223
Adding Structure and Formality to the Physical Design Stage of SSADM, H. Edwards, J. Thompson & P. Smith 225

Z Specifications and Modal Logic, E. Fergus & D. Ince   255

Knowledge Based Methods   269
An Integrated Approach to Expert System Development, Project Organization, and Project Management, K. Kurbel   271
CONCH: A life-cycle model of knowledge-based systems development, R. Taylor   282

Verification and Validation 2   303
Software Testing: Human-Computer Interaction concepts, and Testing, D.R. Graham   305
Software Verification and Testing Tools: Availability and Uptake, D.R. Graham (written paper only)   335
Defect Removal Models: Theory and Practice, M. Coleman & J. Allan   372

Analysis and Design   385
Designing Systems with Objects, Processes and Modules, B. Kirk   387
The Synthesis of Object-Oriented Designs from the Products of Structured Analysis, P. Sully & D. Ince   405

Resources   433
Managing Key Resources During Systems Engineering, R. Barker   435
Implications of Assessing Software as a Financial Asset, P. Rigby and M. Norris   455

HCI / Reuse   465
User Centred Design: Experience from a Commercial Project, D. Browne, H. Mylam & A. Woods   467
Specification Reusability: Why Tutorial Support is Necessary, A. Sutcliffe & N. Maiden   489

Technical Futures   511
The Systems Engineering approach within British Telecom, A. Fawthrop   513
Technology Prediction in Software Engineering, R. Higham, M. Norris and H. Chapman   529

Reuse 541
Towards a generic and extensible reuse environment,. Th. 543
  Moineau, J. Abadir & E. Rames
PRACTITIONER: Pragmatic Support for the Reuse of Concepts 574
  in Existing Software, C. Boldyreff, P. Elzer, P. Hall, U.
  Kaaber, J. Keilmann & J. Witt

PREFACE

This is the proceedings of the British conference on Software Engineering held in Brighton in July 1990. The theme of the conference was software engineering in the 1990s: this theme was more strongly marked by the various keynote and invited papers. These were:

    Brian Gladman, MoD *Safety and Quality Issues*
    Brian Oakley, Logica Cambridge. *Research directions*
    Maurice Resnick, SD-SCICON (Invited speaker)*Software Engineering, QA friend or foe?*
    Steve Matheson, *User needs and priorities in software development: Poacher turned Gamekeeper*
    Alan Laing, *Current legal challenges facing the software industry.*
    Ranald Robertson, *Product liability and its implications for safety critical computer products*
    Ian Thompson, CCTA , *Methodologies for the 1990s*
    Martyn Thomas, Praxis. *Software Engineering in the 1990s*

Of these, only the paper by Maurice Resnick is included in the proceedings.

We had a large number of papers offered to us on the basis of abstracts, and from these the programme committee have put together a strong programme covering most key issues. The one disappointing gap was the limited coverage of technology prediction. While clearly software will become more and more pervasive, with society relying more and more upon computers, the form of these applications may surprise us. Looking back over the last decade we have seen considerable changes in the application of computers, with the advances in the underlying hardware leading to the establishment of relational databases for information storage, and bit-map graphics to highly interactive graphical interfaces. Aspects of Artificial Intelligence has become achievable. All this has led to a broadening of the concerns of software engineering, as is seen in the papers at this conference. But where will the next ten years lead us?

My thanks go to the considerable help that has been given to me in putting together this programme:
- Martyn Thomas (Praxis), overall chairman of the conference,
- Simon Holloway (DCE) the treasurer,
- the programme committee,
  - Richard Barker (Oracle Corporation UK Ltd.)
  - Alan Bundy (Edinburgh University)
  - Ken Croucher (SD-Scicon)
  - John Cullyer (University of Warwick)
  - David Hannaford (BIS, Birmingham)
  - Jill Hill (Rolls Royce Associates, Derby)
  - David Iggulden (ANSA, Cambridge)
  - Manny Lehman (Independent consultant, London)
  - Willy List (Peat Marwick McLintock, London)
  - John McDermid (University of York)
  - John Nicholls (PRG, Oxford)
  - Bill Olle (Independent consultant, London)
  - Ranald Robertson (Stevenson Harwood, London)
  - Rosemary Rock-Evans (DCE, London)
  - Mike Tedd (University College of Wales)
  - Ian Thompson (CCTA, Norwich)
  - Rob Witty (Rutherford Appleton Laboratories)
- the staff of BISL, notable Karen MCartney and Karen O'Sullivan who have handled to administration of the conference, and
- Jean Phillips at Brunel who has carried the major burden of the secretarial and administration work associated with obtaining the papers from the authors, for patiently progress chasing everybody to ensure that we met our many deadlines.

Pat Hall, 8 May 1990

Quality

Software Engineering, QA friend or foe? Maurice Resnick
   (invited paper)

Software Engineering : QA Friend or Foe

M. RESNICK

1 INTRODUCTION

This paper examines the goals and approaches of software quality assurance and software engineering, and explores the convergence of the approaches leading to mutual advantages for both communities and in turn the promotion of improved quality and productivity in the software production process.

It is my belief that the ultimate objectives of both software engineering and software quality assurance are identical, that is, to consistently produce software of a known quality, to known costs and within known timescales.

However, the methods employed by the two communities to promote these objectives were, until recently, difficult to reconcile as they relied on different infrastructures.

2 APPROACHES

Software engineering, for instance, leans heavily on the software development life cycle and many methodologies and tools specifically address elements or combinations of elements of the life cycle.

Quality assurance, on the other hand, operates through the Quality Management System, often set up in a manner which complements the requirements of military or civil national quality system standards, which are not particularly related to either software development or life cycles.

For instance, the current British Standard on quality systems applicable to development, manufacturing and maintenance, BS 5750 Part 1, which since 1987 has been identical to the intentional standard ISO 9001, specifies its requirements in 20 sections, as follows.

Quality system requirements

- Management responsibility
- Quality system
- Contract review
- Design control
- Documont control
- Purchasing
- Purchaser supplied product
- Product identification and traceability
- Process control
- Inspection and testing
- Inspection measuring and test equipment
- Inspection and test status
- Control of nonconforming product
- Corrective action
- Handling, storage, packaging and delivery
- Quality records
- Internal quality audits
- Training
- Servicing
- Statistical techniques.

As you will doubtless have noticed, the sequencing of requirements is very loose and there is an implicit bias towards both hardware and manufacture.

So much so that some Quality Management systems, set up within software development environments supplying to customers who request compliance with such standards, have had difficulty linking the benefits of those quality systems with the successfulness of the software produced.

Small wonder that there has been a reluctance on the part of software engineering to fit into such systems.

The reluctance, of course, is not all one-sided. The heavy emphasis on improved productivity as a major selling feature by methods and tools producers has generated an instinctive adverse reaction from traditional QA people, to whom improved productivity has often meant cutting corners on reviews and testing.

It seems a pity that the genuine elements which contribute to apparent improved productivity, that is consistency, completeness and the matching of interfaces, are not promoted more visibly. These, after all, are some of the components of getting it right first time, now recognised as a major element in achieving both improved quality and productivity.

3 RECONCILIATION

Having briefly considered the two approaches, how can they be reconciled? Many of you will doubtless be aware of the comments made in the DTI report on Quality Management Standards for Software (1988) regarding the need for synergy between quality management and software engineering.

Some two years before that report, however, work had already started on an initiative which now provides a major component to bridging the gap between software engineering and quality assurance.

This was the production by a working group of the Computing Services Association (CSA) of guidelines on implementing a quality system for software, firmly based on the software life cycle.

These guidelines addressed Quality System Elements, that is, activities which are part of any phase of the life cycle, and Quality Control Elements, activities which relate to only one phase of the life cycle.

The contents list of the final document, published in 1988, was as follows:

Introduction

Desired Effects

Quality System Elements
- Implementing and Maintaining a Quality System
- Managing the Organisation and its Interfaces
- Reviewing
- Documenting Projects and Products
- Recruitment, Training and Staff Development
- Configuration Management
- Back-up, Security and Archiving
- Quality System Reviews and Audits
- Procurement
- Progress Monitoring and Reporting

Quality Control Elements
- Identify Task
- Prepare Proposal
- Initiate Project
- Analyse Requirement and Specify System
- Produce High Level Software Design
- Produce Detailed Software Design
- Code and Unit Test
- Integrate and System Test
- Perform Acceptance Test
- Handover/Release
- User Training
- Storage and Shipment
- Deliver and Install
- Maintain and Enhance
- Phase Out Product

CSA Software Project Life Cycle

Public Domain Standards

Incidentally, no specific life cycle model was identified, although for illustrative purposes an expanded version of the STARTS life cycle was used.

Around the same time, and quite unknown to the British computing or quality assurance fraternity at large, an international initiative had begun on producing a companion document to ISO 9001, the international quality systems standard. This new document was to specify quality system requirements for software and the initial versions were a section by section terminological softwarisation of the existing quality system requirements in ISO 9001.

British interests at the early meetings were discharged by a BSI observer representing the Consumers Association!

However, once the significance of this work became apparent, a BSI group was set up to support a software QA representative to this international committee. The BSI group had members from supplier, procurer and user organisations, who through their ISO representative were instrumental in turning the ISO document from a list of requirements structured in accordance with ISO 9001 into a set of guidelines on quality systems for software, based on the software development life cycle.

This document is currently at the Draft for Public Comment stage and its contents include:

Quality system - framework
- Management responsibility
- Quality system
- Internal quality system audits
- Corrective action

Quality System - life cycle activities
- Contract reviews
- Purchasers requirements specification
- Development planning
- Quality planning

- Design and implementation
- Testing and validation
- Acceptance
- Maintenance

Quality system - supporting activities
- Configuration management
- Document control
- Quality records
- Measurements
- Rules, practices and conventions
- Tools and techniques
- Purchasing
- Included software product
- Training.

With the appearance of these documents, there is now a major drive from the quality assurance side towards quality systems based on the software development life cycle.

An opportunity window would therefore appear to be opening for a close harmonisation of quality assurance and software engineering.

One way in which this could be addressed would be to further develop this quality system/development life cycle theme, whereby in each phase the methods and controls are not only related to quality and productivity, but also contain 'hooks' to which methods and tools are attached, so demonstrating where they sit on a universal model and the value that they add.

This approach could be implemented at a variety of levels.

Within companies developing software, it could be both a feature of project quality plans, where the methods, tools, procedures, standards, etc must be explicitly declared as part of the project development life cycle, while at company level it would exist as a documented expression of the company preferred methods and tools, with options, again as an integral part of the quality assured development life cycle.

Within the industry, generic guidelines could be developed for implementing such an approach, perhaps under the auspices of a joint BCS/IQA/IEE committee, with representation from procuring, supplier and user groups.

The output should not just define requirements for a system but should offer practical and pragmatic guidelines on implementing such a system.

4 BENEFITS

The benefits of this system, in which both quality assurance and software engineering are actively involved, should accrue on both sides.

Quality assurance would get real help in identifying what methods and tools are of value in promoting quality and at which points in the life cycle. It would also ensure that software engineering is viewed as an integrated partner in quality systems and that QA can and should utilise its power.

Software engineering should likewise derive benefit from quality assurance experience in introducing standards and procedures, basic elements of many methods and tools.

For instance, there is still a widely held belief that the obvious advantages of a method mean that it can be introduced easily and everyone works to it.

However, the extensive QA experience with in-house standards does not support this view.

Standards do not get adopted or operate effectively for a variety of reasons

- overly detailed for the user

- documents the knowledge which the author wishes to impart, rather than the information which the user seeks

- obscure style of writing making it difficult to understand
- format strictures making accessibility to information poor

- long introductions or interspersed theory or background information in 'how-to' standards

- ownership problems

- excessive cross-referencing or 'clever' technical authoring.

Many of these problems are of course people related, and solutions have been mainly addressed through consideration of the people effect.

For instance, where possible, in-house standards should be written and reviewed by users or practitioners.

The author should identify and write to the user audience.

'How-to' standards should start the instructions on the first page and ruthlessly exclude anything which does not assist the progression of the activity. With 'how-to' standards, small is beautiful.

Document structuring requirements should be minimal and flexible. Nobody reads a set of company standards like a novel so there is no real requirement that adjacent standards should look alike.

Clever technical authoring can be dispensed with by publishing what is written, after suitable peer review. This also helps promote ownership. External requirements standards, often viewed as 'theirs' not 'ours', should be fitted into the in-house standard structure, tailored where necessary in terms of terminology and cultural interpretation.

What has this to do with software engineering? Well, many of the above problems in adopting or using in-house standards translate into adopting or using methods and tools.

For example, user-friendly - an overused and poorly defined phrase - is, in relation to methods and tools, about understandable and accessible information at the level of the user audience.

Ownership, i.e. where does it fit in 'our' culture, is also a live issue in companies adopting methods and tools.

The abandonment of parts of a methodology is sometimes because the lack of an automated tool makes the process tedious, but it is also sometimes because the rigidity of the procedures are perceived as limiting the legitimate creativity of the user.

These and other people problems have already been addressed with some success by quality assurance and the solutions should be tapped by software engineering, thus negating a need to reinvent the wheel.

5 CONCLUSIONS

In conclusion, it would appear that a convergence path is now possible between the current approaches of software quality assurance and software engineering, based on the software development life cycle and the newly emergent software quality management systems.

The intiative needs to be taken up at both company and industry level if real benefits in improved quality and productivity are to realised by the combined efforts of both quality assurance and software engineering.

6 REFERENCES

BS 5750 Part 1/EN 29000/ISO 9001 : Specification for design/development, production, installation and servicing.

DTI Report : Quality Management Standards for Software (1988)

CSA Report : Quality Systems for Software (1988)

ISO DP 9001/2 : Guidelines for the Application of ISO 9001 to the Development, Supply and Maintenance of Software.

CASE and IPSE Databases

Method Support needs an OMS, M. Lemoine and S. Pascaud
A Comparison of Databases for Software Engineering, P. Hitchcock & A.W. Brown

Method Support needs an OMS.

M. LEMOINE and S. PASCAUD[1]

ONERA-CERT
Département d'Etudes et de Recherches en Informatique
2, avenue E. Belin
31055   Toulouse CEDEX France

1   The ToolUse project

1.1   The DEVelopment lAnguage

The general objectives of the ToolUse project[2][Hor85], [JJL+89] are to provide active assistance in the various activities of software development through the formalization, and the support, of development methods. Thus we have designed and implemented a development language DEVA [SWdGC88], the purposes of which being:

- the ability to express formally developments [CJLM89].

  The use of a **formal** development language has as major consequence that important mathematical properties can be ensured. Among them, the proof that a program satisfies its specification is certified.

- the ability to express development methods.

  A second step in the DEVA design has been to integrate concepts allowing to take into account what are usually called methods. As soon as we are able to formalize a method we are able to express it as set of meta–rules which act upon the rules (transformations, behavior, etc) of the chosen method.

- finally, the reuse of formal developments.

  The expression of formal developments allows to derive new developments and new programs in an assisted manner from the reuse of formal ones as it is experimented in REPLAY, the DEVA companion project.

---

[1] Now at SYSECA Company - 315 Bureaux de la Colline, 92213 St. Cloud Cedex-F
[2] ToolUse and REPLAY are partially supported by the ESPRIT Programme (#510 and #1651).

These requirements have led to a language which is a synthesis of λ–calculus, natural deduction and constructive logic systems. A consequence of this technical direction is that the same framework is able to express both specifications, programs and developments.

1.2 Formalizing Developments and Methods

DEVA is independent on any method. It is generic enough to allow to express either formal developments or methods when they are formalizable and formalized.

1.2.1 DEVA as a support of formal developments

A formal development with DEVA is written in defining and handling DEVA components directly translated from the elements of the chosen method.
For instance in the JSP method [Jac83], the Jackson's trees are treated as regular expressions. The program construction rules are translated into inferences rules seen at this level as transformation rules. All these translations correspond to DEVA programs. A hand-made mapping has been done between JSP components and DEVA components.
A 1st example based on the formalization of the JSP method has allowed several developments. Nevertheless, two main drawbacks do exist:

- from an implementation point of view, the DEVA evaluator interprets statements that are usually treated once at compiling time in a classical environment. Consequently the performance is slow.

- from a conceptual point of view, the DEVA evaluator has to support operations which are not necessarily close to its expression power. For instance, DEVA is well suited for the expression of dynamic properties between two components but not really adequate at all for expressing the completion of other properties.

1.2.2 DEVA as a support of formal methods

We do not define precisely what is called a method. Nevertheless we consider a method as acting at two different levels:

- At the 1st one (predicative or passive level), the system has only to check that method components satisfy (or not) some relations and (mathematical) properties.

- At the 2nd level (predictive or interactive level), the system has to guide the user and must allow (or forbid) him to realize some available operations depending on a chosen method.

In a 2nd large example based on VDM, it has been exhibited that DEVA suffers from expressive power about the behavioral aspects of the method. These drawbacks lead us to complement the DEVA interpreter with other tools giving to the DEVA Support Environment (DSE) more power. These tools concern:

- the Man Machine Interface (MMI) problem studied in [Gab88]

- specific theorem prover for intuitionistic logic [Bit88]

- sophisticated pattern matcher [DH88]

- and of course at the kernel of the DSE, the evaluator (more or less an inference engine) and an Object Management System.

In the rest of the paper we will concentrate on the main purposes of the DEVA OMS.

2 An OMS Definition

Informally an OMS is a DBMS which has some knowledge[3] about the objects it handles. Thus it should be able to treat some of the syntactic features and (part of) the semantic capabilities they support.
As described in [LP88] we formally define an OMS by a model that includes objects, relations and semantic operations.

2.1 Objects

Objects are basic entities which compose any software project. For instance *program module, requirements, formal specification, documentation* are software objects. They are not supposed to be atomic since they can be decomposed. Indeed a part of program modules such as a *procedure* can be considered as an object itself. Objects are classically decomposed into:

- a content: it supports information which is significant for the user and at various level for the OMS.

- attributes : they represent some additional information about the object which allows the OMS to *know* more about it. The attributes can support part of syntax and/or semantics.

An object may be instanced. This means that the user may introduce some instances of objects with specific values of attributes.

---
[3]Knowledge is meant according to its linguistic aspect

example: The object *variable* owns the *name* and *type* attributes and its content is its *value*. The *VAR* variable is an instanc[23 iation of the variable object with the name attribute containing *VAR* and the type attribute containing *integer*.

2.2 Relations

They constitute the dependency links between the objects and the type of these links. They contribute to the semantics of the software development process.

example: The *is_declared_in* relation links a *variable* object with a *module* object. In this case the relation supports semantics.

2.3 Semantic Operations

They are decomposed into:

- constraints: they are the validity conditions on relations and attributes.

- actions: they define the procedures to be applied when constraints are violated.

The operations will allow to support the semantics of a formalized method.

example : We can imagine the action *link_to_declaration* which is activated when the user introduces a variable (constraint). This action must link the object variable with the module where it was declared (if it exists) with the *is_declared_in* relation.

3 The OMS role in the context of ToolUse

In the ToolUse context, the main role of the OMS is to support as far as possible the operations that software development processes require and that should not be directly supported by the DEVA primitives.

3.1 Levels of actions

The ToolUse OMS can act at 2 different levels:

- At a basic level the OMS is only concerned with DEVA objects themselves. It treats part of the semantics of DEVA. In other words, the OMS considers the DEVA objects and their relationships without any reference to a method. It must be recalled that DEVA is in no ways a method but a linguistic framework to express either formal developments or methods.

- At a method level, the OMS takes into account the objects depending on a formalized method. This time it is more concerned with the semantics of a specific software development process that the implemented method supports.

3.2 Level 1: Managing DEVA objects

DEVA includes two classes of objects and some formation rules:

1. **Texts**, which may describe developments. Each text has a type which is itself a text. The type of a text describing a development is a text expressing the result of this development. The type system of DEVA is stratified starting from the untypable text constant: **primal**.

2. **Contexts**, which describe theories on which the developments are based. Contexts are used also to introduce modularity.

3. **formation rules** for DEVA objects are: **context abstraction** over a text or a context (composition), **application** of context abstraction or of text, **judgement** of a text by a text. All of them are concerned with the DEVA evaluation.

The evaluator processes a program , e.g. a text or a context, which constitutes a whole. That means that all the importations, which allows to refer to some already existing contexts, must be satisfied before evaluation. In order to shift the responsibility of the DEVA evaluator with such problems (indeed in this case modularity is language independent), we have attached to the DEVA OMS as first objective to act as a Data Base Management System at a basic level. Thus the **import** relation is directly supported by the OMS.
Of course the OMS is also responsible of managing in the classical sense all the DEVA objects.
From a behavioral point of view the DEVA objects are kept in some object base. Evaluating a DEVA program needs first of all build up a local base in which many operations will be undertaken such as interpretation of a DEVA program, modification of some objects, testing, and so on. The OMS plays the main role e.g. it is responsible for building up the local base, loading the objects, saving them and insuring the consistency of manipulated basis. In the following we restrict ourselves to manipulations about objects without regarding the classical operations on object basis.

3.2.1 Definition of the DEVA objects

The attributes for a DEVA object are defined and gathered [Pas89] as follows:

1. **identification**

    - *name*

      It allows to identify the object. The identifier is unique both for the DEVA programmer and for the OMS.

    - *type*

      Each object has a type such as **text, context definition, other context.**

2. **levels of representations**

    - *source program*

      The input source program as written and eventually modified by the DEVA programmer.

    - *program at D-level*

      The D-level corresponds to an abstract syntax level in which a 1st transformation has been realized.

    - *program at S-level*

      The S-level is more concrete than the D-level, many transformation have been achieved such as the β-reduction for instance.

3. **versioning**

    For simplicity reasons, a UNIX-like versioning system has been adopted.

    - *Base*

      The base name the object belongs to.

    - *version number*

      Several versions may exist.

    - *mother version number*

      From which the current version has been created.

    - *date of creation, comments, author*

    - *access rights*

      Only one level: read, write (which includes read) or no access at all, for the owner and other users.

4. **path**

   Denotes all the linked objects and locates them.

5. **consistency**

   - *global validation*

     correctness of the object according the DEVA type-checking.

   - *forced validation*

     Attribute set by the user when the global validation fails. Consequently the OMS will accept to save it into the object base.

   - *revalidation*

     Set up when any linked object (see the *import* relation or other) has been modified.

3.2.2 Relations

Two main relations are considered:

- **importation**

  Only the valid objects of type *context definition* may be imported at run time. This has a drastic consequence: only the bottom up approach should be available for the construction of DEVA objects. In order to avoid this strong requirement, the *forced validation* under the user's responsibility has been introduced. Thus both bottom up and top down approaches are allowed.

  The *importation* may also be seen as a kind of inheritance mechanism as introduced in Object Oriented Programming. The dynamic binding is solved at the construction of a local base in which all the links are satisfied by the OMS before the DEVA interpretor may operate.

- **Method defined relations**

  Other kind of relations may exist. They are meaningless for the basic DEVA OMS and of course meaningful for the OMS method level. Indeed these relations are used a lot to support the method level.

3.2.3 Method independent consistency checks

As written before the main role of the basic DEVA OMS is to keep the base safe or consistent. For a base of objects built independently of any method, this means:

- the object base must contain only *valid* objects according to the DEVA type-checking. At saving time *forced validation* is considered as *global validation*.

- all the relations between objects must be satisfied.

What happens at saving time?
Many checks are performed by the OMS according to the following constraints:

- Handling of DEVA objects must be conform to their access rights.

- Any object is declared as valid iff all the objects it imports are valid.

- Each modified object is declared as not valid. It is to be revalidated and all the objects using it as well.

- For any object the transitive closure of the **import** relation must not contain any cycle.

- An object will be put in an object base iff:
  1. it is valid by construction or set as valid by the user
  2. all the relations it uses are satisfied

- any modified and valid object is put in the object base as a new version.

The corresponding semantic actions are:

- for any action on object, check of the access rights

- before storing an object, check on the valid attribute (global or forced)

- removing an object needs:
  1. computing the subgraph of descendants (or sons)
  2. informing the user of the list of objects to be removed
  3. deleting (or not) the objects according to the user's answer

- altering an object needs:
  1. updating the validation attribute
  2. updating the revalidation attribute for all its ancestors
  3. informing the user of the list of objects to be revalidated.

The so defined OMS is both a DBMS and a consistency checker.

3.3 Level 2: Managing Method Dependent Objects

As soon as we regard a method as being a means to organize a development and to guide the user, all the power of an OMS appears.

For instance, let us suppose we are interested by all the information concerning what has been done and what is to be done, which is classicaly known as *development graph and agenda*. The suggested model of the OMS should allow to express in a very easy way both what is the current state of the development and what are the next actions the user may undertake.

In the former, the OMS acts as a classical DBMS. Its response gives a snapshot of the current state of the development. In the latter, the OMS checks that the allowed operations such as introduction of a new step or of new objects are consistent with all the rest of the object base. It will accept or reject any operation according to the semantic rules attached to the chosen method.

The first definition of a method based OMS we made was about the VDM method [Jon86]. This method is very predicative. It has as main consequence that the OMS helps the user verify his development. In the following we develop this approach.

3.3.1 The VDM objects and relations

It is not our purpose to introduce the VDM method and the way a development can be conducted according to the method. Nevertheless we may briefly describe what kind of objects does VDM consider. A simplified view [Per89] of VDM objects is:

- at the abstract level:

    an abstract object, also called a specification, consists of:

    - a global state which is a collection of abstract data types or typed variables.
    - a set of operations acting upon these variables. An operation is either a program or part of a program.

- at the concrete level:

    an implementation, also called a representation, which is nothing else than a more concrete specification.

A development will consist of a hierarchy of specifications from a very abstract level to a very concrete one. Of course at each step the current specification is refined down to the implementation level is reached.

Two successive representations are linked according to 2 main relations:

- the *Data reification* which refines variables.
- the *operation decomposition* which refines the operations.

The consistency of any development is guaranteed by the establishment of proofs obligation both on data and operations. These proofs are introduced through some functions insuring that the data reification and the operation decomposition preserve the semantics of the initial specification.

3.3.2 Managing the VDM objects

A VDM object is seen as a set of DEVA texts and contexts including some specialized relations as *method defined relations*. They allow to represent both the mapping between VDM objects and DEVA objects, and the constraints linked to the VDM method. More precisely:

- to a VDM *global state* corresponds a *DEVA context definition* which is the most appropriate for declarations and definitions.
- at the VDM *data reification phase*, a DEVA text is introduced in order to support the proof of the adequation between the 2 corresponding VDM objects.
- to an *operation* is associated a *DEVA text* since a text supports algorithms. This text may include the result rule and the domain rule which are obtained when decomposing.
- Finally, to the hierarchy of VDM objects corresponds a DEVA text which must include the consistency proof of the representation of the considered object.

A few comments are to be added:

- it is the responsibility of the VDM assistant, a specialized tool, to translate a VDM object into DEVA texts and contexts and to build inside the DEVA texts, the method dependent relations
- a refinement in VDM generates at the DEVA level a text and at least a constrained relation which will guarantee the validity of the development.

The above mapping of VDM objects into several DEVA objects is justified by the predicative nature of VDM. Indeed the DEVA OMS for VDM works in a proof checker way e.g. verifications are made a posteriori.

3.3.3 A DEVA OMS for VDM

The 1st DEVA OMS for VDM has been used as presented above. At any step of the development, the associated VDM-DEVA OMS has shown what was wrong, what VDM rule was violated. Of course only small pieces of software have been developed. Nevertheless the clear distinction between the evaluator and the OMS has allowed us to work in parallel and sometimes independently on 2 different tools: on one hand the DEVA evaluator, on the other one on methods and on the way to formal[23 ize them in the DEVA language.

4 Conclusion

In this paper is shown the ability to transfer part of the semantics of a language to an associated tool which can more easily support some important semantic operations. The experiments conducted in and around methods such as JSD and VDM have proved the feasibility of such an approach. Nevertheless, if a method independent development language (DEVA) has been designed and implemented, the formalization of methods is not yet achieved. A considerable amount of work is nee[23 ded in order to formalize methods and to make them available on support environments.

References

[Bit88]   O. Bittel. TILT–a theorem prover for the intuitionistic logic based on tableau calculus in the DEVA support environment. Task–S report, GMD, 1988.

[CJLM89] J. Cazin, R. Jacquart, M. Lemoine, and P. Michel. Manipulation of formal developments expressed in DEVA. In *Proceedings of the SEE 89*. Ellis Horwood, April 1989.

[DH88]   C. Duprat and A. Hunot. Introduction d'heuristiques dans un 'Pattern-Matcher' du second ordre. In *Congrès Génie Logiciel 4*, October 1988.

[Gab88]   R. Gabriel. The automatic generation of graphical user interfaces. In *System Design: Concepts, Methods and Tools*. IEEE–COMPEURO 88, 1988.

[Hor85]   H. Horgen. TOOLUSE: an advanced support environment for method-driven development and evolution of packaged software. In CEC-GDXIII, editor, *ESPRIT'85: Status Report*, pages 545–562. North-Holland, 1985.

[Jac83]   M. Jackson. *JSP & JSD: The Jackson Approach to Software Development.* IEEE Computer Society Press, 1983.

[JJL+89]   J.Cazin, R. Jacquart, M. Lemoine, P. Maurice, and P. Michel. Method driven programming. In G. X. Ritter, editor, *Information Processing 89.* Elsevier Science Publishers B.V., August 1989.

[Jon86]   C. B. Jones. *Systematic Software Development–A Rigorous Approach.* Prentice–Hall Int., 1986.

[LP88]   M. Lemoine and L. Pommier. Role and design of a software engineering data base in the context of an advanced support environment. In *Proc. of Software Engineering and its Application to Avionics,* 1988. AGARD, CESME–Turquie.

[Pas89]   S. Pascaud. Formalisation et développement d'un système de gestion d'objets. Master's thesis, Université Paul Sabatier, June 1989.

[Per89]   E. Perrichon. Essai de définition d'un SGO spécificique à la méthode VDM. Technical report, ENSAE, 9 1989.

[SWdGC88] M. Sintzoff, M. Weber, Ph. de Groote, and J. Cazin. Definition 0.1 of the approximation deva.0 of a development language. Technical report, UCL, ToolUse.TD.deva01.DD88a, 1988.

A Comparison of Databases for Software Engineering

Peter Hitchcock and Alan W Brown

Department of Computer Science
University of York

Abstract This paper compares the data definition and data manipulation facilities of four database management systems that are candidates for the data management component of an Integrated Project Support Environment (IPSE). The four systems are: an implementation of SQL, the Object Management System of the Portable Common Tool Environment, Iris - a prototype implementation of an object oriented database and GemStone - an object oriented system based on Smalltalk. The comparison is made using small examples under the headings of logical data independence, physical data independence, data definition constraints, representation and access to the meta-schema, flexibility and the complexity of application programs.

1. INTRODUCTION

It is now recognised that developing large, complex software systems not only requires that significant *technical* problems are overcome, it also requires many *managerial* issues to be addressed in organising, monitoring, and controlling project development to ensure its continued progress. Unfortunately, automated support for large scale software engineering projects has concentrated heavily on the technical aspects of the project. Typically, software projects are supported by some form of computerised development environment with automated tools to help with the application and use of a particular method, language, or notation. In many cases this consists of no more than the file store of the computer's host operating system as a persistent data repository, with some *ad hoc* collection of software tools to help with some of the development tasks. For many software developers a text editor, programming language compiler, and object code debugger form their everyday software development environment. In addition, systems analysts may have tools which help automate the construction of designs in a particular structured design notation.

Helpful as these individual tools are, there are a number of important aspects of software development which receive very little support from development environments formed from loose collections of individual tools. These include:

Management Visibility. A major problem associated with large system development is that the current state of the project must be continually reviewed to ensure its progress. It is very difficult to maintain management control over a project when individual developers use disparate tools, producing information in different formats buried within files.

Developer Communication. A software developer rarely works in isolation It is inevitable that one developer will rely on the results of another developer's work for their input, and must be constrained in what they do by the requirements of some further developer's needs.

Information Sharing. The strong relationships which exist between different phases of the software development life-cycle imply that common interfaces must be defined between different pieces of work. For example, the systems analyst must rely on the requirements document being correct and up to date. Whenever changes to the requirements are necessary, the information must be shared between systems analyst and requirements analyst.

The need for a more supportive environment in which software can be developed has long been recognised. One of the most important approaches which is currently being investigated is to develop an infrastructure of common services which can be used as the basis of a software development environment. Such environments are called *Integrated Project Support Environments (IPSE's)*. Other alternative terms which are commonly used include Software Engineering Environment (SEE) and Computer-Aided Software Engineering (CASE) Environment. These terms are treated as synonymous for the purposes of this discussion.

A project currently taking place at the University of York is aimed at examining the data management facilities which form the heart of an IPSE system, and is investigating a number of possible Database Management Systems (DBMS's) as candidates for this service. While there are a large number of factors which will affect a DBMS's suitability as an IPSE data management system, in this paper we concentrate on the data modelling aspects of the candidate database systems and on the data definition and data manipulation languages. It is planned that future papers will describe results of the comparisons in other database areas (concurrency, recovery, performance, and so on).

2. INTEGRATED PROJECT SUPPORT ENVIRONMENTS

The architecture of an IPSE was initially guided by work carried out to define requirements for an Ada Programming Support Environment (APSE), reported in the Stoneman document [2]. Here, to support the development of large Ada programs, the need for automated support of the program development process led to the definition of a set of requirements which outline the basic architectural components of an APSE. To summarise, the basis of any APSE must be a database which records data items and their relationships in a structured and accessible form. The database provides a set of core services for tools that communicate through this structured repository for data. A Kernel Ada Programming Support Environment (KAPSE) is then defined as the database together with communication and run-time support to allow a set of Ada programs to be executed. With the addition of a minimal set of tools to support the creation and maintenance of Ada programs, a Minimal Ada Programming Support Environment (MAPSE) results. Finally, an Ada Programming Support Environment (APSE) is constructed by extending the MAPSE to provide support for different programming methodologies and techniques.

An important feature of the architecture is the interface between the KAPSE and MAPSE. Essentially, this interface provides access to the set of services provided by the KAPSE to the tools implemented as part of the MAPSE and APSE. In this sense it is equivalent to what is often called a Public Tool Interface (PTI) [3].

2.1 Software Development is a Database Application

In recent years much attention has been focussed on the requirements for software development environments. It has been found that a key element in providing effective support is the *integration* that is provided within the software development environment. The concept of integration can manifest itself in a number of different ways within the development environment. For example, we could interpret integration as meaning one or more of the following:

1. Each tool has the same set of constructs at the user interface. Hence, tool users would find it very simple to move between tools as the ways in which a user interacts with tools is standardised.

2. The environment has been constructed to support a single software development methodology. For example, the Perspective system [4] was designed for supporting the development of real-time embedded avionics software systems. It provides a tool for capturing system requirements in the CORE notation [5] and semi-automatically generates software to implement those requirements in an extended form of the Pascal programming language. In addition, Host-Target debugging tools are provided for the object code this

language produces. The result is a development environment which is well integrated in the sense that the tools work together with a common understanding of the software development life cycle supported.

3. To allow tools to share data a common data format can be defined. The most obvious example of this is the Unix development environment [6] in which all data is assumed to be in the form of a simple steam of bytes. Tools can be combined very easily as a data consumer tool (eg. a printer driver) can expect the output from a data producer (eg. a text processor) to arrive in a predefined form.

4. The environment may be aimed at a single programming language. A number of programming support environments have been constructed which provide very strong support for software developed in a particular language [7]. These environments can provide structured editors, optimising compilers, and symbolic debuggers for the chosen language. A generalisation of this approach is to provide tool-generating tools for a given language syntax. For example, tools are available to generate a lexical analyser and parser from a definition of the syntax of the given language. This approach has been enhanced to allow a complete suite of tools to be generated for a given language definition [8].

While all of the above provide interpretations of the term *integrated* with respect to a software development environment, we can also adopt a somewhat more general notion of this term, equating it to the view of software development as a data processing activity. In particular, a recognised way of providing this integration is through building support tools around a shared data storage facility which reduces the need for maintaining multiple copies of the same data, provides a general language for data definition and manipulation, enforces some measure of consistency within the data, is self-describing (allowing you to query the repository to find out what kind of data it contains), and includes some mechanisms for controlled data sharing. These are the facilities which are typically provided by existing Database Management Systems (DBMS).

The principle advantage of DBMS's are that they provide (logically) centralised control of the users' operational data [9]. That is, the data which is of interest is no longer embedded and distributed throughout the applications which use the data. Instead it is maintained as an independent resource with controlled redundancy and sharing. While the general advantages of the database approach to maintaining large amounts of data have been often described, [9, 10] it is useful to examine the particular advantages of using a database for maintaining software development data.

In this paper we will look at four database management systems that are candidates for the data management component of an IPSE. These are Empress [11] (a commercially available implementation of the relational language SQL), the Object Management System of the PCTE [12], a prototype object oriented system (Iris [13]) and a Smalltalk based system (GemStone[14]). In this paper we are restricting our comparison to the data definition and data manipulation facilities of each.

3. SAMPLE PROBLEM FOR SE DATABASES

We will be using the following example as the basis for the comparison of the data definition and data manipulation languages of the four different systems. It is based on the Document Management System that was developed in the Comprehensive Introduction to PCTE produced by the SFINX consortium[15]. In particular, we will look at the facilities provided to support logical and physical data independence, the ability of the schema to capture constraints, how close it is to the statement of the problem as an Entity-Relationship diagram, how readily information in the schema can be accessed, and the complexity of the programs which will access the schema.

We give an Entity-Relationship diagram of the schema, the notation is to be interpreted as follows:

a) A document is always inside many locations. A location may contain a number of documents

b) A document may be defined by a number of keywords. A keyword may define a number of documents.

c) A person may write a number of documents. Each document must be written by one person.

d) A person may hold a number of documents. Each document may be held by a number of people.

e) Each document my be provided by one person. A person may provide a number of documents.

f) A person may belong to one specific group. Each group may include a number of people.

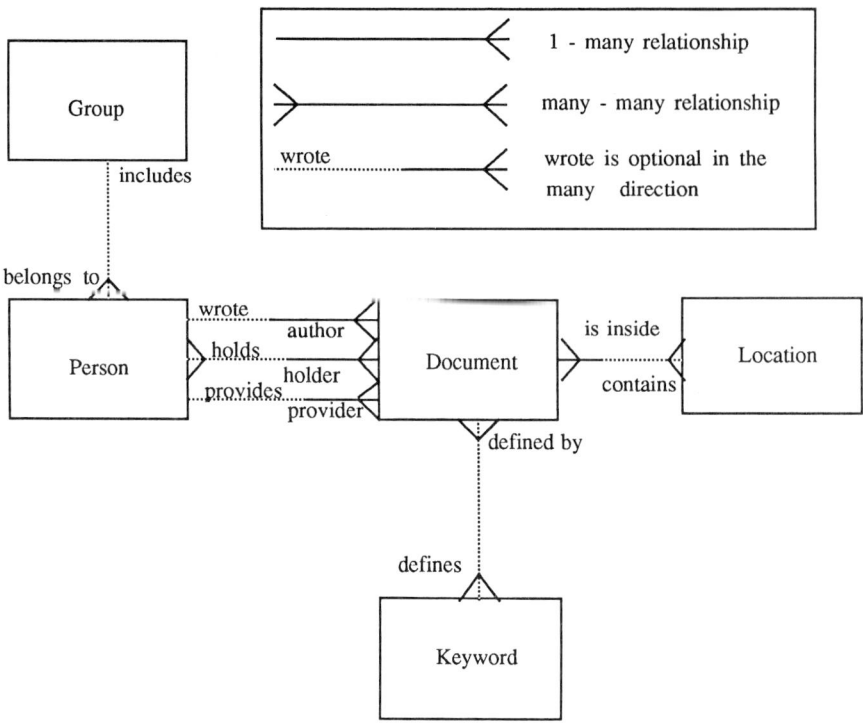

We will examine this example under a number of headings. We will look at:

1) The representation of the schema in each system. In particular, we will consider how it is achieved, how well logical and physical data independence can be maintained and how well integrity rules can be centrally defined and maintained.
2) How the schema information, or metadata, can be queried. In particular, we will develop a tool to display the relationships that each entity type can participate in.
3) How the information base can be manipulated. In particular, we will look at a tool that will create a document with an identification number that is one higher than the highest number already in the database, set access privileges, give values to its attributes and link it to its author.
4) How the database may be used for queries. In particular, we will

develop tools that will print the document identification number, version number and title for each document in the database, that will list all people in the database and which will give the set of documents related to a given set of keywords.

4. ANALYSIS OF DATABASE SYSTEMS

4.1 SQL

SQL has been chosen as typifying the relational systems that are commercially available. This would be the obvious beginning for a software engineering database if no new technology were to be developed. It has the advantage that it is a mature product, available across operating systems and has the status of an ISO standard. It already forms the basis for some commercially available Computer Aided Software Engineering (CASE) tools.

4.1.1 Schema Representation

The E-R diagram maps naturally into SQL tables. The tables can be considered to be of two types, those that represent the entity types and those that represent the relationships between entity types. The tables follow, with the key attributes for each table underlined. This is done for clarity; it is not possible to maintain the uniqueness of these keys, called *entity integrity*, directly in SQL.

Entity tables

Location:	location-id, name
Document:	document-id,version-number, title, publication-date, status, type, contents
Person:	person-id, name, code-proj
Group:	group-id, name
Keyword:	keyword

Relationship tables

Contains:	location-id, document-id,version-number
Defines:	keyword,document-id,version-number
Author:	document-id,version-number,person-id
Holder:	document-id, version-number, person-id
Provider:	document-id, version-number, person-id
Belongs-to:	person-id,group-id

This has given the logical description of the tables. The actual SQL commands that are issued would all follow the pattern given for the Document table.

>
> create Document
> (document-id   integer   not null,
> revision-number integer not null,
> title char(50),
> publication-date date,
> status char(10),
> type char(10),
> contents   text(60,60,300));

The implementation of SQL that we are using is Empress[11]. We are thus able to use integers, character strings, date and text data types. The text data type is implemented in the following manner. The first 60 characters of the document contents are stored in the document table and will be printed out in the results of queries. The remainder of the document is divided into 300 character pieces which are stored in a separate overflow area.

In this implementation of SQL we are able to define a number of integrity constraints on the values of attributes. For example we can restrict the valid values for the status of a document.

>
> create range check on Document.status
> set 'draft', 'approved', 'published', 'withdrawn';

In addition we can restrict references to values in other tables to those that exist (*referential integrity*).

>
> create referential on Author(document-id, version-number)
> insert Document (document-id, version-number);

This ensures that we cannot insert value pairs for document-id, version number into the Author table unless they first exist in the Document table.

Conversely we must guard against deleting values from the Document table that are referred to in the Author table.

>
> create referential Document (document-id,version-number)
> delete Author (document-id,version-number);

We will need to define two referential constraints in a similar way between Author.person-id and Person.person-id, making four constraints on the Author table. Each of the relationship tables should have four referential constraints defined in a similar way.

4.1.2 Accessing Metadata

Most implementations of SQL, and Empress is no exception, hold information about their tables in system defined tables which can be queried in the same way as any others. In Empress the relevant tables are:

    sys_tables: tab_name, tab_number, ...
    sys_attrs: attr_name, attr_number, attr_tabnum, ...

To find out the relationships in which an entity type participates, and in particular the Document entity, we would ask the following SQL query:

    select tab_name from sys_tables, sys_attrs
        where attr_name = 'document_id'
        and attr_tabnum = tab_number

This enables us to find out the required information, because of the way in which we have defined and named tables and attributes. In no sense are we querying the E-R schema which has been implemented. This is a short coming of SQL which is being remedied by the Information Resource Dictionary System (IRDS)[16]. IRDS is at the stage of a draft ISO standard and, among other things, will enable E-R schemas to be held together with the mappings to the tables that implement them.

4.1.3 Manipulation of the Information Base

The objective is to create a document with a document-id which has been internally generated to be one bigger that the largest used so far and with a revision number of zero. We must also make allowance for the initial case where the document table is empty. We can then give values to the attributes of the document and make the linkage to the author of the document.

The SQL language is not computationaly complete. It will often be used embedded in a host programming language and this might simplify the following example. In this case however, we are able to solve the problem in SQL directly. We will use three temporary tables. Buffer will hold the values of the attributes for the document that we are going to create with the exception of the document-id. Temp1 and Temp2 are used to find the maximum document-id so far. We will assume that the tables have already been defined. We start by ensuring that they are empty.

empty Buffer;
empty Temp1;
empty Temp2;

We now insert the number of documents in the database into Temp1. This is zero if the Document table is empty and will always be less than or equal to the maximum document-identifier. This is followed by entering the maximum document-identifier. This is empty if the Document table is empty. Temp1 will therefore contain either zero or two numbers. The maximum value is inserted into Temp2.

    insert into Temp1(document-id) select count(*) from Document;
    insert into Temp1(document-id) select max(document-id)
        from Document;
    insert into Temp2(document-id) select max(document-id) from Temp1;

We now insert the values of the attributes of the document into Buffer.

    insert into Buffer
    set rev-number to 0,
        title to '..........',
        publication date to ....
        etc.

We must now join the contents of Buffer with the new document-id and insert it into the Document table.

    insert into Document
        select document-id + 1, rev-number, ...
        from Temp2, Buffer;

The final action is to link the document to its author where we are given the author's name as a parameter.

    insert into Author
        select person-id, document-id+1, 0
        from Person, Temp2
        where Person.name = 'name';

The integrity check that the named Person exists does not need to be explicitly carried out because of the referential integrity rules that have already been defined.

4.1.4 Use of the Information in the Information Base
The first task was to list the document identifiers, version numbers and titles of all the documents in the system.

        select document-id, version-number, title
        from Document;

The next was to list all the people who are in the database.

        select * from Person;

Finally we must find all the documents which are defined by at least all the keywords in a given set.

We will assume that the given keywords are held in the table Search.

Although this is a text book problem in SQL, the solution may need some explanation. The solution is:

```
1.      select document-id,version-number
2.      from Defines Defines1
3.      where not exists
4.          (select *
5.          from Search
6.          where not exists
7.              (select * from Defines
8.               where  Defines.document-id =
9.                      Defines1.document-id
10.              and    Defines.version-number =
11.                     Defines1.version-number
12.              and    Defines.keyword =
13.                     Search.keyword ))
```

The predicate "not exists" is true if its argument is the empty set. In line 2, Defines1 is declared as an alias for Defines.

A row from Defines1 will appear in the result of the select statement in line 1 if the result of the select statement in line 4 is empty. Assume that the contents of this row are <d,v,k>. The result of the select in line 4 will be empty if for every keyword s in Search the predicate in line 6 is false, i.e. the select statement in line 7 returns at least one result. This will happen if the where clause in lines 8 to 13 is true i.e. if <d,v,s> is a row in the table Defines.

4.1.5 Discussion

It is not possible to use SQL directly to impose access controls at the level of individual entries in a table. There are two solutions to this problem. Read and write privileges can be granted to a user at the level of individual tables. Views of underlying relations can be defined to present a user with a table of those documents that are read-only and another table of those documents where read and write access are allowed. The alternative, and probably more realistic, solution is to construct a superstructure to handle version libraries and their associated publication mechanism as was carried out by the Aspect project [17].

In the current problem, there is only a single author to a document. The changes needed if there were to be multiple authors would be minimal. There would be no change to the data definition and the part of the create document transaction which links a document to its author would minimally change in the following way:

Assume that the set of names for authors of a document is in the table Names.

```
insert into Author
    select person-id, document-id+1,0
    from Person,Temp2
    where Person.name in
        (select (*) from Names);
```

It is also possible to define indexes on various fields in tables in order to speed up access. This tuning will not cause the application programs to be rewritten in any way.

4.2 PCTE Object Management System

PCTE is the Portable Common Tool Environment[23]. The Object Management System is an example of a DBMS specially developed for use in UNIX based support environments. It is most closely an example of the network type of database management system. The emphasis is on navigating from object to object rather than dealing with sets of objects as in the relational model. The PCTE is receiving strong support for standardization within Europe.

The subsequent work in this section is essentially taken from Annex B of [15].

4.2.1 Schema Representation
The PCTE notation used to represent the schema is as follows:

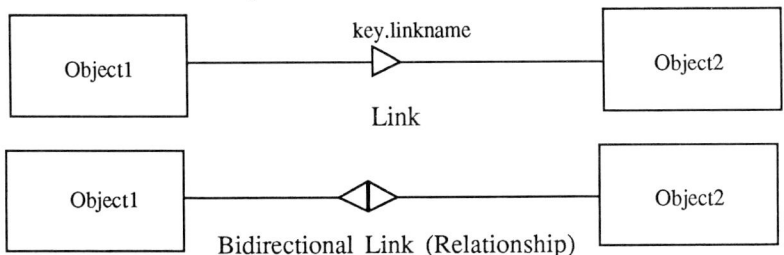

The schema for our example is implemented thus:

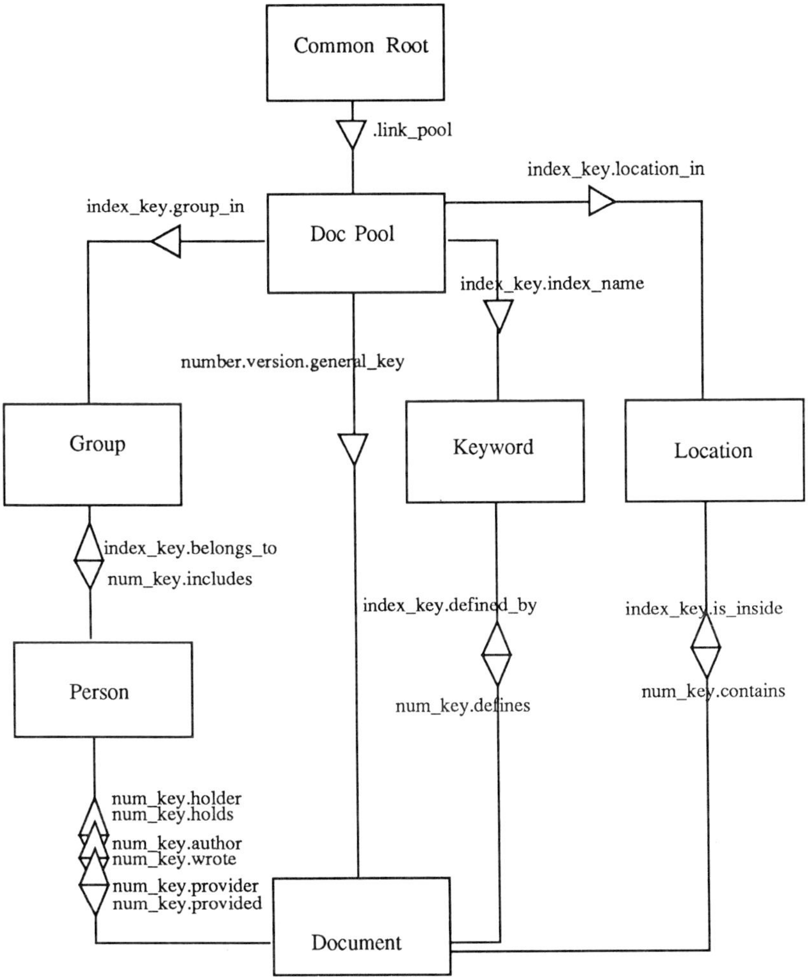

This is a direct implementation of the original E-R diagram. The entities are mapped onto PCTE objects and the relationships are represented by bidirectional links or PCTE relationships. There are some extra entities and links that are necessitated by the data model of PCTE. Firstly, there is a unique common root which provides the only entry point into the database. One proceeds from this point by navigation. This is linked to the object Doc_Pool which provides a focus for the objects in the Document Management System. The system needs to hold information about Groups, Keywords, Locations and Documents as independent objects and so these are made accessible from the Doc_Pool object by indexed links. The link to Document objects, called general_key, is indexed by a pair consisting of number and version.

The logical description of the DDL is :

```
keyword:subtype of sys-object;

document:subtype of sys-file
with attribute
        title: string
        public_date:string;
        status:string;
        gen_key:string;
        type_code: string;
end document;

relationship(
defines : reference link (num_key) to document;
defined_by: reference link (index_key) to keyword);

location : subtype of object;

relationship(
        is_inside: reference link (index_key) to location;
        contains : reference link (num_key) to document);

person:subtype of object
        with attribute
        name : string;
        code_proj : string;
end person;
```

```
relationship(
        author : reference link(num_key) to person;
        wrote: reference link (num_key) to document);

relationship (
        provider : reference link (num_key) to person;
        provides : reference link ( num_key) to document);

relationship(
        holder: reference link(num_key) to person
        holds : reference link (num_key) to document);

group : subtype of object;

relationship (
        belongs_to : reference link (index_key) to group;
        includes: reference link(num_key) to person);

doc_pool: subtype of object
with link
        general_key : link ( general_number : integer;
                             general_version : integer)
                    to document;
        group_in : link (index_key) to group;
        location_in : link(index_key) to location;
        index_name : link (index_key) to keyword;
end doc_pool;

        extend sys-common_root
        with link
                link_pool: link to doc_pool;
        end common_root;
```

The actual PCTE commands that are issued would follow the pattern given below.

Firstly there is some preamble to initialise the object base. We must then construct the Schema Definition Set (SDS) which is an application's view of the information base. Two basic object types are imported as the objects "document" and "keyword" are subtypes of these. The identifiers for these definitions are held in the storage areas given by buf[0] and buf[1]. These are then used to create the new object types "document" and "keyword" whose identifiers are held in buf[2] and buf[3].

```
sdsimpdef("doc","sys","object","object",&buf[0]);
sdsimpdef("doc","sys","file","file",&buf[1]);

sdscrobj("doc","document",&buf[1],&buf[2]);
sdscrobj("doc","keyword",&buf[0],&buf[3]);
```

We now have to create an attribute, in this case "title" and apply it to the "document" object type.

The variables O_ATTR and V_STRING are masks whose values are defined in a system header file to indicate that we are creating an attribute for an object and that its type is string.

```
sdscrattr("doc","title",O_ATTR + V_STRING,NULL,&buf[4]);
sdsapattr("doc",&buf[4],&buf[2]);
```

Similarly for all the other attributes.

We must also create two attributes index_key (buf[10]) and num_key (buf[11]). These are the key attributes used in relationships. In this case we will define the relationship between "keyword" and "document". We set the necessary parameters for the call by putting the link names "defined_by" and "defines" into an array called "links", set an array called "d_kinds" to contain the masks which describe the links in each direction to be of reference link type with a reverse reference and a cardinality of many and an array called "keyattrs" to hold the list of key attributes of each of the links. Each list must be terminated by NULL. Finally we define an array to hold the identifiers for the links that have been created.

```
strcpy(link1,"defined_by");
strcpy(link2, "defines");
links[0] = &(link1[0]);
links[1] = &(link2[0]);
.......
.......
newdefids[0] = &(buf[15]);
newdefids[1] = &(buf[16]);
```

We are now in position to create the relationship and to apply the link by stating that it is applied to the "document" and that it has "keyword" as a destination. Because we have defined a relationship, the reverse link from "keyword" to "document" is automatically included.

```
sdscrrel("doc", links, d_kinds, keyattrs, newdefids);
sdsaplink("doc", &(buf[15]),&(buf[2]));
sdsextdest("doc", &(buf[15]),&(buf[3]));
```

This sequence needs to be repeated for each relationship.

4.2.2 Accessing Metadata

We outline a tool which will take as input parameters an object type and the name of a schema definition set and which will list the link types which start from the given object type.

We start by finding the internal identifier which corresponds to the type name that is passed as a parameter. This is returned in "of_def".

```
sdsdefid(sdsname,obj_type, &of_def);
```

The function "sdscan" is called repeatedly to find the internal names of the links associated with the object, and the corresponding external names are found. The parameters to "sdsscan" are the "sdsname", a system defined mask to say we are looking at links, the internal name of the object type, the current link being looked at, an array to hold the internal identifiers of the link that is found and the number of "next" links to be returned. "Sdsdefname" returns up to 50 characters of the external name in the variable "link_type".

```
resul = sdsscan(sdsname,D_LINK_SET,&of_def,0,list,1);
while (resul > 0)
    {
    sdsdefname(sdsname,&list[0],link_type,50);
    print (link_type);
    resul = sdsscan(sdsname, D_LINK_SET, &of_def,
        &list[0],list,1);
    }
```

In an similar way, "sdsscan" can be repeatedly called with a different mask, D_ATTR_SET, to find the attributes associated with a particular object type.

4.2.3 Manipulation of the Information Base

We are given the title, publication date, status type code for a document and the group name, person name and code_proj of its author. Firstly we must create a new instance of the document object and then link it to the author, having first checked that he or she exists in the information base.

In the Object Management System of PCTE, objects are found by following a navigation path from a unique root entry point. The main origin for the Document Management System is the object doc_pool. The path name to this object from root is _ /.link_pool. It is possible to designate the doc_pool by the pathname ".1" by creating a reference object.

        chrefobj("_/.link_pool",".1");

First the new document object instance is created. The first parameter is the origin for the link to this object. The second parameter is the name of the link instance. This has a pair of integers for the key and is followed by the name of the type of the link. ++ can be used for the value of the first integer, this is taken to mean the highest existing value + 1. The second integer is zero, signifying the first version. The third parameter gives the type of object to be created and the final parameter is a mask which indicates the protection levels for the object. This could have been written using the predefined system constants: R_OWNER + W_OWNER + R_GROUP + R_OTHERS.

        crobj(".1","++.0.generalkey","document",0644);

The attributes must now be set. We also record the path to this new object. The convention + for a key gives the highest key value. The value of the title attribute is in the variable title. Surprisingly, we have to give the type of the attribute, in this case a variable string using the predefined constant V_STRING, even though this was given when the document type was declared in the SDS.

        strcpy(path, ".1/+.0.general_key");
        d_kind = V_STRING;
        setattr(path,"title",title,d_kind);

There is similar code for all the other attributes. The authors of [15] have also defined a redundant attribute "gen_key" which simplifies many operations on the information base. This is a copy of the status information about the link to the new object, which must be the closest that PCTE has to the identifier for an object. It is returned in a structure called "buf" the relevant part of which is "l_key", the key of the link.

>   getlinkstat(".1","+.0.general_key",&buf);
>   setattr(path, "gen_key",buf.l_key,d_kind);

We must now verify that the author exists and build the pathname to the author and then link the new document and this author. Again we have to navigate to the required group object by following a path from root and using the fact that the links are distinguished by the index key "group name". Once we are at the required group object, we must repeatedly obtain the includes links that leave this object and for each of them compare the name and code_proj values of the objects at the end of them with the person_name and code_proj values that have been given as parameters. If both match, then we have found the required author. It is then straightforward to set up the links in both directions between the document object denoted by path and the person object denoted by person_path. The links are both given a numeric key that is one greater than the highest existing one.

Firstly, we define the path to the appropriate group object.

>   strcpy(group_path,".1/");
>   strcat(group_path,"group_name");
>   strcat(group_path,".group_in");
>   chrefobj(group_path,".2");

Next we look at the attributes of the persons linked to this group in turn, until a match is found. The parameters to lslinks are the path to the object, the name of the link, the current link, the number of links to be returned in the result and finally, the list to hold the result. This is a structure and we are interested in the l_key part. Attribute names are prefixed by the SDS name "doc".

>   resul = lslinks(".2","includes", 0,1,lsget);
>   while (resul > 0)
>   {
>   strcpy(person_path,".2/");
>   strcat(person_path,lsget[0].l_key);
>   strcat(person_path,".includes");
>   getattr(person_path,"doc-name",25,buf1,&d_kind);
>   getattr(person_path,"doc-code_proj",10,buf2,&d_kind);

```
            if /* these attribute values are equal to the given
                    parameters*/
            then resul = -10;
            else resul = lslinks(".2","includes",&lsget[0],1,lsget);
            }
```

Finally, having found the author we can link it to the document, generating an identifier for the links in each direction at the same time.

```
            crlinkr (path,"++.author",person_path, "++.wrote");
```

4.2.3 Manipulation of the Information Base

There is no query language defined in the PCTE specifications and so queries must be constructed by scanning the information base in a similar way to that in which the appropriate author was found in the previous section.

The tool to list all documents in the information base can be sketched as:

```
            chrefobj(pool_path,".1");
            resul = lslinks(".1","general_key",0,1,lsget);
            while (resul > 0)
                    {
                    /*get attributes "lsget[0].general_key" and print them*/
                    resul = lslinks(".1","general_key",&lsget[0],1,lsget);
                    }
```

This example worked because all documents were accessible directly from the doc_pool object.

The next example is to list all people who are stored in the data base. This requires a nested loop. We start from doc_pool and find all the groups, and from these groups list all the people whom this group includes.

```
            chrefobj(pool_path,".1");
            nb_gr = lslinks(".1","group_in",0,20,l_grp);
            /* this assumes no more than 20 groups in the base
            nb_gr contains the number of links effectively read*/
            for ( i = 0; i < nb_gr; i ++);
                    {
                    /* build path".1/l_grp[I].group_in" and define as ".2"*/
                    res = lslinks (".2","includes",0,1,l_pers);
```

```
        while (res > 0)
                {
                /* get attributes "l_pers[0].includes" and print them */
                res = lslinks(".2","includes",&l_pers[0],1,l_pers);
                }
        }
```

The final example is a tool which lists the documents that are related to all the keywords in a given list.

We will not give this program in quite as much detail as the others, but merely sketch the plan of attack.

> Find the path to the first keyword in this list from doc_pool.
> Find all the documents that are linked to this keyword via the "defines" link.
> For each of these documents access the keywords attached to it via the "defined_by" link.
>> For each of these keywords check to see if it occurs in the given keyword list. If this is so then increment sum by 1.
>> if sum is equal to number of keywords in the list then this document is linked to all the given keywords and can be listed.

4.2.5 Discussion

The Object Management System of the PCTE is a language at a lower level than SQL and the object oriented languages that we will be looking at. This is principally due to its underlying network model which navigates from single object to single object and is not concerned with higher level constructs such as tables or sets of objects and so by the very nature of the language the programs will be longer and much more complex. This is highlighted if we were to change the problem to allow many authors for a document and then to look at the impact on the program to insert a new document. However, the two points that we would like to make are independent of the level of the language but are a result of its particular use of the navigational model.

Firstly, the structure of the schema which defines the access paths is intimately built-in to the structure of the accessing programs. There is no insulating layer analogous to the view mechanism in SQL. This leads to very reduced logical data independence.

Secondly, there is no concept of an identifier for an object, *object identity,* other than the path name to that object from the root. The introduction of extra indices, or paths to objects must be explicitly declared at the logical level and their use coded into programs. This drastically reduces physical data independence.

4.3 Iris

The Iris database system is a research prototype under development at Hewlett-Packard Laboratories in Palo Alto [18]. One of the most interesting features of the Iris system is the evolutionary approach that is being taken. In particular, the Iris database consists of an Object Manager which is built on top of a relational database system (HP-SQL) which acts as the Storage Manager for the system. This design has a number of advantages. In particular, all Iris queries and functions are converted into an intermediate form of an extended relational algebra. It is at this level that query optimisation can take place based on well defined relational algorithms.

The Iris Object Manager supports an object-oriented data model, providing facilities for schema definition, data manipulation, and query processing. These facilities are accessed through a number of different interfaces. In addition to embedded C and Lisp interfaces, a graphical interface and an (extended) SQL interface have been provided. This later interface is particularly interesting, as the interactive language interface has been designed based on extending the SQL language towards object-based manipulation. The result is a language called Object-SQL (OSQL) [19]. As it has many similarities to the basic SQL language, users of Iris should have few problems in moving to it from traditional relational database systems which use SQL. Similarly, it may be possible to convert many existing applications from relational databases to Iris without undue effort.

While we shall concentrate our attention on the OSQL language which forms the primary interface to the Iris system, it is useful to note the following additional points about the Iris system:

- One function definition can make calls to any other defined function. This arbitrary nesting of functions provides a powerful abstraction mechanism.

- For computational completeness, functions may be implemented in a programming language such as C. These are called *foreign functions*. This greatly increases the flexibility of Iris, for example allowing users to define their own storage structures for specialised applications.

- A rule mechanism is available through the definition of derived functions.

- Simple version control facilities are provided. An object can be made versionable, and can then only be accessed through *checkout* and *checkin* commands which create the next version of the object. Controlled sharing of versions requires the user to explicitly define a lock when checking out a version.

- Many of the basic database management facilities (such as transactions, recovery, indexing, and locking) are not explicitly defined, but are available through using the relational database system HP-SQL as the underlying Storage manager.

The OSQL language extends SQL in three main ways:

Object Identity. Every object is given a unique, system generated identifier. The system does not explicitly reveal identifier values, however, end users can make use of their existence as unique object handles. In particular, direct reference can be made to objects rather than by posting foreign keys. This enforces referential integrity.

User Defined Functions. It is possible for end users to define their own functions on data and then use those functions within queries. The function can be defined extensionally (by explicitly defining the result of the query for particular input parameters) or intentionally (by writing a query as the body of the function).

Syntactic Changes. A number of syntactic changes to the language are made to try to enforce a new way of thinking about the language. For example, *create table* is replaced by *create type*.

4.3.1 Schema Representation
The E-R diagram of our example schema can easily be defined in OSQL in an analogous way to the SQL example given earlier. The main data definitions

could be as shown below:

Entity Types:

> create type Location
> (location-id char(10) required unique,
>   name char(20));
>
> create type Document
> (document-id integer required unique,
> revision-number integer required unique,
> title char(50),
> publication-date date,
> status char(10),
> type char(10),
> contents text);
>
> create type Person
> (person-id integer required unique,
> name char(20),
> code-proj integer);
>
> create type Group
> (group-id integer required unique,
> name char(20));
>
> create type Keyword
> (keyword char(20) required unique);

Relationship Types:

The OSQL model provides the flexibility to record relationships in three different ways: As a <u>relationship type</u>, analogous to the approach in SQL. For example, the **Author** relationship could be defined by a new type definition with appropriate attributes.

> create type Author
> (doc Document,
> written-by Person);

As a <u>set-valued attribute</u>. For example, the **Author** relationship could be held as a set-valued attribute of Document.

> create type Document
> (...
> author set of Person);

As a user defined function. For example, the **Author** relationship could be defined as a function which, given a Document identifier, returns the set of authors of that document.

> create function author_of(Document) --> set of Person;

This flexibility in OSQL means that the most 'natural' approach can be chosen, aiding user comprehension of the schema.

An additional concept which could be introduced in the OSQL implementation is subtyping. For example, if we wished to introduce the idea that documents have reviewers, we could create a subtype of Person which inherits the attributes of Person and additionally has information about a reviewer's area of expertise. Assuming the type Topic has been defined, we could have:

> create type Reviewer subtype of Person
> (expertise set of Topic);

4.3.2 Accessing Metadata

In the Iris system a predefined type hierarchy has been defined. Then, all new type and function definitions can be seen as extending that hierarchy. In fact, an operation such as

> create type Document
> (...);

is exactly equivalent to the operation

> create type Document subtype of UserType
> (...);

As a result, all types are consistently represented, including types recording metadata. Thus, as in SQL, the same operators can be used to query both user data and metadata.

4.3.3 Manipulation of the Information Base

As OSQL can be seen in many ways as a superset of SQL, the OSQL query to create a document with a new document-id and revision number of zero could be constructed in an analogous way to the SQL example shown earlier. Alternatively, as <u>foreign functions</u> can be written in a programming language, we could also write this operation as a small piece of programming language code.

4.3.4 Discussion

OSQL shares with SQL the conciseness of programs due to the higher level data model being used. In addition, the flexibility of alternative representations for objects and their attributes could mean a much simpler way of constructing programs. For example, the **Defines** relationship could be held as a set valued attribute of **Document**. An operator for **is-subset-of** would provide an immediate and easily comprehended solution to the query that we are studying. This flexibility can be a two-edged sword however. It makes it very easy to answer this query, but would make the symmetrical query, "What keywords does this set of documents have in common" much more complex. We are biasing the schema towards various applications which can again cut down on logical data independence. Again, a view mechanism can provide this presentation bias so that each application gets the view of data that it needs without compromising the underlying basic schema.

4.4 GemStone

GemStone is the first product of the Servio Logic Corporation [14, 20, 21]. The basic approach taken has been to examine the Smalltalk language and system, and to identify a number of requirements with regard to making Smalltalk a database system. The result is the language OPAL which manipulates persistent data objects controlled by a disk-based storage manager [1].

There are two main components to the GemStone architecture.

Stone provides persistent object management, concurrency control, authorisation, transaction, and recovery services.

Gem augments the Stone services by providing compilation mechanisms for OPAL programs, user authorisation control, and monitoring of user sessions. In particular, Gem provides the predefined set of OPAL classes and methods which are available in a GemStone system.

Other notable features of GemStone include:

- Concurrency control is provided through implementing both pessimistic and optimistic concurrency control schemes, which are alternately used depending on which is likely to provide better performance.
  For the optimistic scheme a shadow copy of the user workspace is taken at the start of a transaction. When the transaction commits, a check is made for possible conflicts with transactions which have committed since this transaction began. In the absence of any conflicts, the shadow copy replaces the original. This approach ensures deadlock can never occur, and has minimum transaction overhead. Of course, when conflicts are detected, the whole transaction must be rolled back and replayed.
  In the pessimistic scheme, a traditional two-phase locking protocol is employed.

- Authorisation is based on the notion of a user *segment*. Each user controls at least one segment, and all objects are owned by at least one segment. Authorisation is on a per segment basis.

- Support for large persistent objects is provided so that one object can span many physical disk pages. Such an object can be manipulated by bringing only a subset of the pages into a user workspace at any one time.

- Collections of OPAL objects may be indexed to speed up associative access to those objects. A form of *select* statement is used for making associative queries. For example, to obtain all the libraries which contain a particular module, an OPAL query may have the form:

    Library select:
    [aLib | aLib.contains.name = "SomeModuleName"]

    To make use of any indices on the paths used, the user must explicitly replace the spare brackets with curly ones:

    Library select:
    { aLib | aLib.contains.name = "SomeModuleName" }

- Schema modification primitives are provided so that changes to a class definition can be made with automatic conversion of existing class instances to comply with the new class definition.

- The OPAL language is heavily influenced by the Smalltalk language. Hence, users define classes of objects in many different categories. An initial class hierarchy is provided including classes for objects, sets, bags, lists, and so on.

4.4.1 Schema Representation
Entity Types:

To create "record types" we must define new classes which are subtypes of the class **Object**. To do this we send the message *subclass* to the **Object** class and define the instance variables for that class. We can think of these as attributes of the object class.

Hence, we could define the schema for our example as below:

>Object subclass: 'Location'
>>instVarNames: #['location-id', 'name']
>>constraints: #[#[#location-id, String],
>>>#[#name, String]].

>Object subclass: 'Document'
>>instVarNames: #['document-id', 'revision-number', 'title', 'publication-date', 'status', 'type', 'contents']
>>constraints: #[#[#document-id, Integer],
>>>#[#revision-number, Integer],
>>>#[#title, String],
>>>#[#publication-date, Date],
>>>#[#status, String],
>>>#[#type, String],
>>>#[#contents, Text]].

>Object subclass: 'Person'
>>instVarNames: #['person-id', 'name', 'code-proj']
>>constraints: #[#[#person-id, Integer],
>>>#[#name, String],
>>>#[#code-proj, Integer]].

>Object subclass: 'Group'
>>instVarNames: #['group-id', 'name']
>>constraints: #[#[#group-id, Integer],
>>>#[#name, String]].

>Object subclass: 'Keyword'

               instVarNames: #['keyword']
               constraints: #[#[#keyword, String]].

Relationship Types:

We have the same three choices of representations for relationships in OPAL as we had for OSQL. Hence, using the example of the Author relationship as an example, we could define it in one of the following three ways:
By defining a new object class 'Author' which references both Person and Document.

               Object subclass: 'Author'
                       instVarNames: #['doc', 'written-by']
                       constraints: #[#[#doc, Document],
                               #[#written-by, Person]].

Using set-valued attributes we could amend the definition of Document to include an Author attribute. Note also that we need to create a set of objects, which we call **PersonSet**, and we constrain the elements of that set to be of the class **Person**. This allows us to make the link between **Document** and **Person** by giving **Document** a set-valued attribute. This gives the flexibility that a document may be authored in the future by a set of people.

               Set subclass: PersonSet
                       constraints: Person.

               Object subclass: Document
                       instVarName: #[..., 'author']
                       constraints: #[...
                               ...
                               ...
                               #[#author, PersonSet]].

By defining a new *method* (ie. function) which returns a set of Person as the result of the appropriate message being sent to a Document instance (we give an example of a method definition later).

4.4.2 Accessing Metadata
As we said for OSQL, the GemStone system has a predefined class hierarchy, which is extended when a user defines a new class. Hence, users are able to look at the metadata in the same way as they examine their own data.

4.4.3 Manipulation of the Information Base
Unlike SQL and OSQL, OPAL does not have a predefined algebra of operations. Hence, we must define the operators we want specifically for each different object class by defining appropriate **methods**.

However, having said that, each of the predefined GemStone classes has a number of methods available which are inherited by any sub-classes that a user defines. For example, the **Set** class has a method 'select' which retrieves members of a Set based on a predicate. A message to invoke the method has the general form:

> select: [:X | <code involving X which returns true or false>]

When a message of this form is sent to an object O which is a subclass of **Set**, it has the effect of returning a new object (also a subclass of **Set**) that is the set of all objects in O for which the body of the select operation returns true.

To encode the example of creating a new document with identifier one greater than the maximum already used, we would have no problems in OPAL defining such a method as the 'insertDocument' method as OPAL provides a computationaly complete language.

4.4.4 Use of the Information in the Information Base
The first of the examples we wish to encode was to list the document identifiers, version numbers, and titles of all documents in the system. We would use a 'select' method to cycle through all documents in the set **Documents** and examine the appropriate instance variables.

Similarly, to list all the people in the database we would use 'select' to cycle through each element of the set **Documents** and print the names etc.

Finally, to obtain all documents with a given keyword, let us assume that each document has a list of keywords associated with it via an instance variable 'keywords'. Also, assume the keywords we are searching for are in set object **SearchKeywords**. We could create an empty set of documents as:

> DocsIncludingKeywords := Document new

Assuming we have defined an 'insert' method for **DocsIncludingKeywords**, then we could get all the documents using the 'do' method which applies a block of code to each element of a given set:

```
SearchKeywords do:
    [ :s |
    Documents do:
        [ :d |
        (( d getKeywords) testFor: s )
            ifTrue: [ DocsIncludingKeywords insert: d ]
        ]
    ]
```

5. CONCLUSIONS

We have compared four candidate database systems from the point of view of their data models as typified by their data definition and data manipulation languages. Further papers will look at the other functional needs of Software Engineering databases such as version control, library management and support for long transactions in a design environment. The example used throughout was a rather simple one in that it exhibited little time dependence and showed no history. Essentially it captured a snapshot in time of the relationships between the objects involved. Typically the example would be enhanced by replacing several of the one to many relationships by many to many relationships which are then distinguished by their start and end times. It could be further enhanced by considering different versions of the objects used. It would be interesting to see if our conclusions were then any different. However, by analysing the simple example we used, we are able to raise the following points:

5.1 Logical Data Independence

Databases, and software engineering databases are no exception, are large shared objects which will evolve over time. This means that the underlying schema will change as new needs become apparent. Systems will show good data independence if these changes to the schema cause minimal changes to the application programs, or tools, which are accessing the schema. In our example we have used the example of a document changing from having one author to having many authors. SQL scores highly in this regard. Not only does the set orientation of the language make such changes almost transparent, but it also has a view mechanism which can often present tables in their original form even though the underlying schema may have changed. This feature will be shared by Iris based as it is on an underlying relational database. Most other object oriented languages, as typified by GemStone, do not have such a view mechanism although the idea is under investigation [22]. The

PCTE does not score very high on the logical data independence front. Although the notion of schema definition sets can give a subset of the underlying schema, this is not really a view mechanism. One cannot change the basic shape or access paths of the schema when presenting a view to a tool. One is merely restricted to see part of the schema.

5.2 Physical Data Independence
Databases will also evolve in that the accessing requirements of the tools may change over time or need to be changed as new tools appear. If application programs do not need to be changed as the database system is tuned at the physical level then there is a high level of physical data independence.

Both SQL and Iris allow indexes to be built on the objects that they are concerned with. These will speed up access times to individual objects in a completely transparent fashion. No changes to the application programs are required. By contrast, in the PCTE such tuning of access paths has to be made explicit at the logical level of the schema and their use explicitly coded into programs. This provides very little physical data independence. In Gem-Stone it seemed necessary to replace square brackets with curly ones if an index is to be used. Again, there is a reduction in data independence.

5.3 Data Definition Constraints
If constraints on data values can be held centrally as part of the data definition language then they will be consistently enforced by the DBMS and the corresponding checks need not be coded into application programs. Fundamental consistency constraints are entity integrity (a guarantee that an entity occurrence is unique) and referential integrity (that relationships can only occur between entities that exist). Further basic mechanisms would include range checks on the values of attributes.

The particular implementation of SQL that we are using can support all three basic constraints mentioned above, and so can the Iris system. It is very difficult to support entity integrity in the PCTE although by the very nature of the way a link is constructed it must necessarily support referential integrity. There is no mechanism in PCTE for the definition of range constraints. Gem-Stone, by the nature of its rich set of data types can support range constraints. Object oriented systems exhibit object identity which is a very similar concept to entity integrity, and referential integrity comes if relationships are modelled as first class objects.

5.4 The Meta Schema

Access to the meta schema was possible in all the systems. In SQL it depended on representing the Entity-Relationship diagram in a disciplined way and making use of a consistent naming convention. There is no support in the language for the notions of entity and relationship. By contrast, the PCTE represents the E-R diagram almost directly although it has to be expanded to include extra access paths so that every independent entity can be reached from the root. The object oriented systems enable the appropriate constructs to be directly defined.

5.5 Flexibility

Object oriented systems offer a richer set of data constructs than those of either SQL or the PCTE. This can mean that the most suitable construct for a particular tool can be chosen but with the caveat that this can possibly impair data independence.

5.6 Complexity of Application Programs

The language of the PCTE is at a lower level than those of either SQL or the object based languages. It is also necessary to navigate to each object from the root. Direct access is not possible. As is apparent from the examples the PCTE programs are much more complex. The SQL programs may not be always obvious either and it is here that the richer set of data structures and operations of the object based models should start to show advantages.

5.7 Summary

Comparisons between systems are always difficult, it is tempting to compare advanced prototypes with commercial implementations which by their very nature will always be behind in the technology used.

PCTE is being proposed as a standard IPSE framework within Europe. We feel that this is premature. It appears to offer few advantages over the use of SQL in the areas which we have studied. Fundamental advances in database technology such as the move away from navigation and the recognition of the need for object identifiers, or surrogates, have not been incorporated by the PCTE designers.

SQL is a mature language which has been in widespread use for some years. As our studies have shown it offers many advantages over PCTE. The major advantage being the high level query language which dramatically reduces the complexity of the application programs. Its principal disadvantage is that it does not implement the E-R design model directly, but this is being remedied by the proposed IRDS standard, itself being defined in SQL. IRDS is likely to form the integrating focus for CASE tools in the area of commercial data processing.

The two other systems that we studied, Iris and GemStone, fall into the category of advanced prototypes. Their principal advantages are the increased flexibility that object-oriented techniques will bring.

Finally, it is worth remembering that standardising the framework of an IPSE is only half the problem. It is still necessary to standardise the data structures that tools will share which will then be implemented in this common framework. This level of detail is being studied for the IRDS but is being left to various tools implementations such as PACT (PCTE Added Common Tools) [24] for the PCTE.

REFERENCES

[1]   J.D. Ullman, Principles of Database and Knowledge Base Systems, Computer Science Press, 1989.

[2]   Requirements for APSE - STONEMAN J. N. Buxton, February 1980, US Department of Defence.

[3]   T.G.L. Lyons, The Public Tool Interface in Software Engineering Environments, Software Engineering Journal, **1**, 6, November 1986, 254-258.

[4]   Systems_Designers, DEC/VAX Perspective Technical Overview, November 1984.

[5]   G. Bate, Mascot3 : An Informal Introductory Tutorial, Software Engineering Journal, **1**, 3, May 1986, 95-102.

[6]   B.W. Kernighan, J.R. Mashey, The UNIX Programming Environment, IEEE Computer, 14, 4, April 1981.

[7]   T. A. Standish R. N. Taylor, Arcturus: A Prototype Advanced Ada Programming Environment, ACM SIGPLAN Notices, **19**, 5, 57-64, May 1984.

[8]   T. Teitelbaum T. Reps, The Cornell Program Synthesizer: A Syntax-Directed Programming Environment, ACM SIGPLAN Notices, **14**, 10, 75-87, October 1979.

[9]   C.J. Date, An Introduction to Database Systems - Volume I, Addison-Wesley, 1986, Vol1.

[10] A.W. Brown, Database Support for Software Engineering, Kogan Page Ltd, October 1989.

[11] Empress V 2.4, Rhodnius Incorporated, Toronto, Canada.

[12] PCTE Functional Specification 4th ed., Bull, GEC, ICL, Nixdorf, Olivetti, Siemens, 1987.

[13] D.H. Fishman et al, An Overview of the Iris DBMS, in Object-Oriented Concepts, Databases, and Applications, ed. W. Kim and F.H. Lochovsky, 219-250, Addison-Wesley, 1989.

[14] R. Bretl and Others, The GemStone Data Management System, in Object-Oriented Concepts, Databases, and Applications, eds. W. Kim and F.H.Lochovsky, Addison-Wesley, 1989.

[15] SFINX Consortium, A Comprehensive Introduction to the Portable Common Tool Environment, SFGL(F), CAP(UK), CRI (D), CSATA(I), ERIA (E). March 1988.

[16] Information Resource Dictionary System, Working Draft, ISO/IEC JTC1 / SC21 / WG3 N752, Jan 1989.

[17] P. Hitchcock, R.P. Whittington, Information Base of the Aspect Integrated Project Support Environment, Information and Software Technology, **30**, 6, July/August 1988

[18] P. Lyngbaek, W Kent, A data modeling Methodology for the Design and implementation of information systems, in International Workshop on Object-Oriented Database Systems, eds. Klaus Dittrich and Umeshwar Dayal, IEEE, September 1986.

[19] D. Beech, A Foundation for Evolution from Relational to Object Databases, in Extending Database Technology '88, Springer Verlag, 1988.

[20] D. Maier and J. Stein, Development and Implementation of an Object-Oriented DBMS, in Research Directions in Object-Oriented Programming, eds. B Shriver and P Wegner, MIT Press, 1987, 355-392

[21]   D.J. Penney and J. Stein, Class Modification in the GemStone Object-Oriented DBMS, Proceedings of the 2nd ACM Conference on Object-Oriented Programming Systems, Languages and Applications, 1987.

[22]   G. Wiederhold, Views, Objects, and Databases, IEEE Computer, December 1986.

[23]   G. Boudier et al, An Overview of PCTE and PCTE+, ACM SIGPLAN Notices, **24**, 2 (February 1989).

[24]   PACT Consortium, The PCTE Added Common Tool Environment, Louveciennes, France.

Metrics

The Use of Metrics for the Early Detection of Software Design Errors,
  M. Shepperd & D. Ince
The relative software complexity metric: a validation study, J. Munson
  & T. Khoshgoftaar

The Use of Metrics for the Early Detection of Design Errors

MARTIN SHEPPERD

Wolverhampton Polytechnic

DARREL INCE

Open University

ABSTRACT

This paper considers the important topic of identifying structural errors in a software system architecture, at design time when corrections are relatively inexpensive. A taxonomy of structural errors is proposed which encompasses both functional and data aspects of software design. This taxonomy is then used as a yardstick against which to assess six representative design metrics. All metrics are found wanting in at least one respect, and it is therefore argued that a combination of metrics is necessary to adequately evaluate a system architecture for structural errors. It is further argued that the majority of metrics emphasise the structural or syntactic aspects of design and that there is a pressing need for more research into metrics that attempt to capture the semantics of a design, without which one is restricted to the identification of possible symptoms of design errors rather than the underlying problems themselves. The paper concludes, that despite these very real problems there is still much benefit to be obtained from the use of at least some existing metrics for the early detection of structural design errors.

1. INTRODUCTION

Over recent years there has been considerable interest in the application of software metrics in quality assurance. Such metrics: numerical measures of quality extracted from a software product such as a specification or test plan, enable the project manager and quality assurance staff to monitor and control large projects. Normally, metrics are used in a rather loose predictive capacity; for example to gauge delivered system reliability, or more indirectly as project standards - but not always to great effect. Two principles have, however, emerged. The first is that the earlier measurement occurs the greater the "leverage" it offers the project manager. The second is that well defined measurement objectives lead to the more successful applications of metrics, whilst ventures to employ the illusive pan-software engineering metric to predict all characteristics of all software systems for all circumstances have foundered - see for example [Shep88] on McCabe's metric [McCa76] or the work of Basili and Rombach on the need for measurement goals [Basi88].

This paper addresses an important application of a particular class of measures: system design metrics. Such metrics can be applied during the early stages of design to measure significant architectural properties including module coupling, cohesion and information flows. The paper describes an application of detection of structural errors at an early stage of the software project. Because of the mounting body of empirical evidence concerning the relationship between design decisions and quality factors of the ensuing software system (e.g. [Kafu87], [Romb87], [Ince89], [Shep90b]), we feel that this is an important and under-exploited application for metrics. System architectures should be reviewed with the above in mind prior to implementation, that is whilst design changes are still relatively inexpensive.

Our concern is with structural design errors. Clearly other types of error are also of concern, such as verification errors where the design does not meet the specification, but these are beyond the scope of this work. We are interested in the usually very large number of possible designs that in some sense could be made to "work", but with differing consequences upon the resulting software system. The paper first describes an eightfold classification of structural design errors. These cover aspects of functional design - the more frequent habitat of the software engineer - *and* data design - rather more sparsely populated and usually regarded as the province of an alien species, the database worker! This is an unfortunate dichotomy since both aspects are closely interleaved. Although similar in aim, we argue that our approach is more comprehensive than the pioneering work of Stevens *et al* [Stev74] on module cohesion and coupling.

Next, we attempt a formal set of rules to enable the unambiguous identification and assignment of design errors to the appropriate error class. This requires the existence of adequate specification and design notations (e.g. module hierarchy charts, data flow diagrams and relational data models) together with some notion of requirements traceability from specification to design. We then describe how system design metrics, derived from the above notations, can be formally related to these errors. We belive this approach to be essential since without a clear understanding of software design errors we cannot expect great success in using metrics to help identify them.

We then describe how this framework can be employed to evaluate design metrics and their ability to locate structural errors in the above taxonomy. Our analysis demonstrates that all the design metrics surveyed (Yin and Winchester's C'_i metric [Yin78], Kafura and Henry's Information Flow metric [Kafu81], Card and Agresti's metric [Card88], Ince and Shepperd's IF4 [Ince89] and Shepperd's "work" metric [Shep89]) were wanting in at least one respect: their ability to detect all classes of design error that we have identified. Nonetheless, we find that a combination of some of the metrics provides an excellent coverage.

The paper proceeds to report on the application of these ideas to a number of small to medium sized software systems. The distribution of error by type and severity is found to display significant clustering, in particular around the middle levels of the system design hierarchy. Furthermore, some systems were notably more error prone than others.

For quality assurance, at the design stage, to be a practical proposition, the software developer requires a measurement or set of measurements capable of detecting *all* classes of structural error. The paper concludes by addressing this issue and describes how our ideas may be melded with current software design practice - that design methodologies which are relatively strong on qualitative evaluation criteria are somewhat deficient in terms of quantitative criteria. Thus, demonstrating that software quality metrics have a major part to play in current and future software development.

2. PRE-AMBLE: NOTATIONS AND DEFINITIONS

It is appropriate to first consider what we mean by design, especially as there are probably more definitions than there are software engineers. Our area of concern is sometimes known as high level or system architecture design - that is the decision making process to create a structure that partitions a given problem into a number of communicating components or modules. This communication is accomplished via data objects that may also be structured in a hierarchical fashion. The data objects may be passed as arguments between modules or the design may allow for shared access. It is noteworthy that such a definition does not incorporate any element of algorithmic design (i.e. low level or detailed design).

What then is a module? A module must have the following properties: be called by name, return control to the caller after elaboration and have clearly defined boundaries (e.g. BEGIN END statements). Obviously such a definition permits many possible implementations depending upon the programmer and the programming language. Thus programs, procedures, and paragraphs can all be viewed as modules. Structural design is not, though, concerned with details of implementation.

Likewise, what is a data object? We view a data object as any data that is shared between at least two modules (i.e. is not local, and therefore not private to a single module). Data objects may be stored permanently, for example as a file, or may be temporary, for example as an array. Also, data objects may be complex - hierarchically composed from other data objects - or may be primitive.

This type of information is readily available from notations such as module hierarchy charts [Stev74] [Your79], which also describe the module interfaces with the rest of the system. Unfortunately, this information tends only to be syntactic in nature whereas the meaning of the components is implicit within the choice of the module or data object name. This is a serious problem, as the identification of structural errors often requires semantic information. Consequently, the following additional information is required.

First, it is necessary to understand the functional requirements that the design is intended to satisfy. These may be depicted as a functional requirements hierarchy where individual requirements are structured together to form higher level, or more abstract requirements. The primitive functional requirements should always available. To assume otherwise implies that design is a random activity, since we do not know what we are trying to achieve, against such a background, the notion of an error must be somewhat academic. The isolation of structuring information may be less straightforward. Some specification notations (e.g. Yourdon [deMa78]) already embody the notion of hierarchy. Likewise, natural language specifications may be organised hierarchically with requirements numbered 1.3, 1.3.1, 1.3.2 and so forth. However, in many circumstances this may not be the case, nevertheless there do exist techniques for constructing a hierarchy from a base set of primitive requirements by using cluster analysis algorithms based upon the sharing of data objects - a similar approach has been demonstrated by Karimi and Konsynski [Kari88]. Functions that have no data objects in common will be placed further apart in a hierarchical structure.

Second, it is necessary to understand the traceability of functional requirements from the specification to the system architecture. This helps interpret the meaning of a module hierarchy chart as it indicates which functional requirements each module satisfies. There are four possible cases for a module:

> - it may satisfy exactly one functional requirement;
> - it may partially satisfy a requirement (i.e. the requirement maps to several modules);
> - a combination of the above;
> - it may satisfy no requirements (in principle this ought never occur!).

Third, we require additional information concerning the data objects identified in the design. Relational data modelling [Codd70] [Kent83] is a popular method to describe potentially exceedingly, complex data objects, at a conceptual level. If this is supplemented by knowledge of the mapping from the conceptual data model to its intended physical realisation, then a basis is provided to identify potential design errors that are related to data objects.

Even by restricting the area of concern to structural errors, quite sophisticated design notations are required, if our understanding is not to be restricted to a merely syntactical level. Furthermore, it is necessary to have a concern for issues of data design as well as of functional design. This is a necessary foundation if metrics are to be effective in detecting the full range of possible errors whilst the software development is still at the design stage.

There have been proposed a considerable number of design metrics (see for instance [Ince88] for a survey). We have selected six metrics as being reasonably representative of the work currently being undertaken within this field. The metrics fall into four general categories.

An example of a design metric based upon the module calling structure is the Yin and Winchester C metric [Yin78]. This metric captures the graph impurity of the calling structure so that each time a module is re-used this has the effect of incrementing the metric by one. The definition can also be extended to incorporate shared data objects. In practice it would seem that the C metric is a proxy for design size, since as designs increase in size there tends to be more scope for module re-use and data object sharing.

The information flow metrics (Henry and Kafura's metric [Henr81] and Shepperd's IF4 [Shep90a]) attempt to capture connections between modules and their environments. This is important because it is indicative of the degree to which a software engineer can work on one module, or area, of a software system without reference to other modules. Furthermore, information flows are the means whereby unwanted side-effects propagate through a system as a consequence of a maintenance change. Information flows can occur either via parameterised communication between two modules, or via shared data objects when one module updates and the other module retrieves from the data object. The metrics although superficially similar, differ in three important respects. The Henry and Kafura metric penalises module re-use, the use of parameterised communication as opposed to global data objects, and has a somewhat capricious definition of an additional class of information flow known as an indirect flow; such flows are not incorporated into IF4.

The next category, interface based design metrics includes two approaches: the Card and Agresti metric [Card88] and Chapin's Q metric [Chap79]. Card and Agresti explicitly identify total design complexity as comprising of intermodular or structural complexity plus the sum of all the intra-modular or local complexity. The structural complexity is given as the sum of the squares of individual module fan-outs, thus modules with many subordinates will score highly. The fan-in is disregarded as previous empirical work [Card86] has shown it to be insignificant, coupled with the problem that counting it penalises module re-use. Local complexity for a module is the number of imported and exported variables, divided by the fan-out plus one. The rationale for this, is that the greater the number of arguments, the greater the module workload. On the other hand, the greater the module fan-out the greater the proportion of this workload that this distributed to other modules.

Adopting, a slightly different approach, though still based upon interface measurements, is Chapin's Q metric. In this case he not only identifies the inputs and outputs to each module, but also attempts to give a weighting factor dependent on the purpose of the data since this influences the complexity of the module interface. The following types of data are identified:

> 'P' data - inputs required for processing;
> 'M' data - inputs that are modified by the execution of the module;
> 'C' data - inputs that control decisions or selections;
> 'T' data - through data that is transmitted unchanged.

In addition a weighting factor is included to indicate the complexity of the control structure to invoke the module.

The last category is based upon requirements traceability from a specification to the design and is exemplified by the "work" metric [Shep90b] which attempts to capture the workload of each module in a design. Modules can perform two types of work, they may satisfy primitive functional requirements directly or they may perform scheduling working based upon the inheritance of requirements satisfaction up the module hierarchy. Obviously many modules can perform both types of work.

3. DESIGN ERRORS

Having considered how software designs might be represented we now progress to problem of classifying structural design errors, bearing in mind that we are not addressing what might be termed a verification issue of whether the design meets the specification. The classic approach to design evaluation has been based upon the notions of module coupling (i.e. the strength of inter module relationships) and module cohesion (i.e. the strength of internal module relationships). Stevens *et al* [Stev74], amongst others have argued that the designer should minimise coupling and maximise cohesion. These ideas have been extremely influential amongst software engineers and indeed have formed the basis for many of the design metrics described above. Although we belive that these concepts form an important platform from which to develop notions of design errors, they are lacking in three respects.

First, coupling and cohesion are the consequences, or symptoms of design errors. They are not errors in themselves. This is significant because it means that they indicate underlying problems with a design but do not directly suggest a solution. Worse, still the same symptom may be the consequence of several possible design errors. For example, high coupling between modules might indicate that there exists a problem of multiple functionality within one module, split functionality between the two modules, a misplaced module or inappropriately shared data objects. It is not, however, immediately clear which is the problem.

Second, coupling and cohesion tend to emphasise the functional aspects of a software design and thus they are insufficiently comprehensive.

Finally, coupling and cohesion are vulnerable to the criticism that they are rather subjective in application. This observation has been one of the primary motivations for research in the field of design metrics *viz.* to quantify these design evaluation criteria. It is one of the aims of this work, albeit a rather ambitious one, to render the process of error identification a little less arbitrary.

To summarise we propose a development of the work of Stevens *et al* to yield an eightfold classification of structural design errors. Briefly these are:

> missing levels of functional abstraction;
> multiple functionality;
> split functionality;
> misplaced functions;
> duplicate functionality;
> inadequate data object isolation;
> duplicate data objects;
> over-loaded data objects.

The first five classes are essentially shortcomings in the functional design, whilst the remaining three classes are errors of data design. As with any classification there are certain difficulties, particularly where several structural errors appear related. It may be that in future the classification will be subject to refinement and improvement. However, for the present we will deal with each of these classes in turn.

(a) Missing levels of functional abstraction

This type of error occurs when lower level modules are not grouped together to provide useful higher level, or more complex, services or functions. As a consequence whenever the higher level function is required, the software engineer must understand how it is provided in terms of the lower level modules and the necessary control mechanisms. It would preferable to shield this detail from the software engineer by encapsulating in a higher level module, often referred to as a functional or procedural abstraction.

Figure 1 presents an example of where such an abstraction is absent. The module hierarchy chart gives the architecture of part of a transaction processing system in which a transaction is obtained, and if valid used for some calculations and then applied to an existing MASTER-FILE. All updates to the MASTER-FILE are simultaneously recorded in a LOG-FILE. All erroneous transactions are recorded in an ERROR-FILE. Such a design exemplifies the structural error of missing levels of function abstraction. Consider the modules UPDATE-MASTER-FILE and UPDATE-LOG-FILE; whenever the system needs to update the MASTER-FILE the software engineer has to be aware that two modules must be invoked. Furthermore, they must be invoked in a particular order otherwise different parts of the system will behave inconsistently. The solution is, of course, to introduce a higher level module, say WRITE-VALID-TRANS, which in turn invokes the two lower level modules UPDATE-MASTER-FILE and UPDATE-LOG-FILE (see Figure 1a). Module WRITE-VALID-TRANS provides a more abstract service or function that is missing from the original structure.

The empirical study referred to the next section suggests that this type of error is rather commonplace. This is disturbing because these structures may potentially cause a number of problems. First, they hinder the re-use of higher level services in a software system. Second, they are maintenance "time bombs". Suppose the system is modified at some subsequent stage and an additional transaction update of the MASTER-FILE is required, the maintainer has the added burden of having to remember to also update the LOG-FILE and in the correct order. Such oversights are the stuff of embarrassing and costly system faults. Third, they make the system harder to understand since they place the task of inferring the service provided by groups of lower level modules upon the software engineer.

Having considered what is meant by missing level of function abstraction we must now turn to the problem of identifying such errors. Unfortunately, reference to module hierarchy charts only yields indicators, or symptoms of this type of problem. The classic symptoms are either a module with an usually large number of subordinates, in this case the module PROCESS-TRANS has six subordinate modules, or a number of modules that all invoke the same set of subordinates implying that this subordinate set represents some useful function.

Since all the metrics under consideration, bar one, are derived from module hierarchy charts this means that they cannot define this type of structural design error, only highlight symptoms. To be able to define the error more information is required concerning the actual functions each module carries out and the relationship between these functions. This is available as a functional requirements hierarchy and a mapping from this hierarchy to the module hierarchy. The requirements hierarchy for the system in Figure 1 is:

```
SYSTEM process transactions      (PT)
   1 obtain transaction       (FT)
   2 check transaction        (PT)
       2.1 validate transaction for errors    (VT)
       2.2 record erroneous transaction       (RET)
   3 perform calculations     (CNT)
   4 store valid transaction  (PT)
       4.1 update master file    (UMF)
       4.2 update log file       (ULF)
```

The module abbreviations in parentheses indicate the module which implements the functional requirement. From this we observe that although the low level functions 4.1 (update master file) and 4.2 (update log file) each map to low level modules. The next level of abstraction 4 (store valid transaction) is less straightforward; it is only satisfied by the top level module (PT) since it is only at this level that the functions 4.1 and 4.2 are both available and may be combined. However, the same module, PT also satisfies a yet more abstract requirement, namely the entire system (process transactions), thus one module satisfies more than one level of abstraction of function as defined by the functional requirements hierarchy, and this indeed is our definition of a missing level of functional abstraction within a software design.

(b) Multiple functionality

The class of structural design error, multiple functionality indicates, as the name suggests, that a module implements more than one function. This related to the concept of low module cohesion [Stev74] where the various parts of a module are unrelated in terms of the service or functions that they provide. Because it is a comparatively well understood problem it is often disguised. Figure 2 shows the architecture of part of a menu driven system to control user-ids which allow access to some computer system, including options to add, remove and list user-ids. At first glance this appears a very plausible design, unfortunately, the module PROCESS-MENU contains a number of functions including displaying a menu, obtaining a response, validating the response, displaying an error message if appropriate and then selecting the required menu facility. Does this matter? The answer is an emphatic yes - as the design stands PROCESS-MENU is harder to understand due to the interleaving of several functions within a single module. Furthermore, re-use of these functions is almost impossible. And the corollary of such a strategy is the duplication of functions through the system, such as displaying menus and fetching responses, with the consequent maintenance "time bombs".

How may such errors be detected? Mere use of a module hierarchy chart is insufficient, since it reveals few symptoms of multiple functionality other than a possible increase in the number of information flows into and out of a module. Recourse to requirements traceability again provides us with a definition and therefore a means of identifying all occurrences of this class of error. Whenever more than one primitive (i.e. leaf) requirement maps to a single module then the module exhibits multiple functionality. As a consequence the five module hierarchy based design metrics would seem ill equipped to detect this class of error, an observation bourne out by an empirical study of an information flow based design metric [Shep90a] that showed that the metric performed poorly for architectures with very large (multiple function) modules.

(c) Split functionality

This type of error is in many ways the antithesis of multiple functionality as it involves a single function being distributed amongst several modules. Figure 3 provides an example of split functionality where the functional requirement to validate a part number is distributed over three modules in a highly arbitrary fashion. It is hard to belive that software engineers would set out to deliberately create such a design, rather it is our belief that such designs arise for one of three reasons. First, the original design is inadequate in that it failed to anticipate the complexity of a particular function and so effectively the design is left to the coder. An extreme example might be the inclusion of a single module DO-COMPANY-ACCOUNTS in a design! Second, the coder might be subject to standards concerning module size, for instance a module must not exceed 40 lines of code, leading to arbitrary partitioning of the module. Third, the design might be subject to maintenance changes. Our experimental evidence of software maintenance [Shep90c] suggests that few software engineers are prepared to make significant structural changes to an existing system.

This class of error is undesirable since it inhibits function re-use, and makes a system significantly harder to understand. As *per* the previous two error categories it cannot be detected without knowledge of the functions that modules perform. The only symptoms manifested on a module hierarchy chart are possible increases in levels of coupling or information flow between the modules concerned. Again we suggest that these errors cannot be easily detected using the five module hierarchy based metrics. It is defined to occur whenever a primitive requirement is only partially satisfied by individual modules in the system architecture.

(d) Misplaced functions

Misplaced functions are a class of structural errors where functionally related modules are placed unnecessarily far apart by the system architecture leading to a proliferation of information flows, parameters and modules that have little purpose other than to route information. Such an example is given by Figure 4 where the module HANDLE-COMMAND-ERROR is misplaced since it is closely related to the module VALIDATE-COMMAND. Clearly, a solution would be to move the module to become a subordinate of the module, VALIDATE-COMMAND.

The consequences of misplaced functions are threefold. First, these type of structures severely inhibit the possibilities of function re-use. Second, this provides great scope for unwanted "side effects" if maintenance changes occur. Third, such structures present considerable barriers to comprehension.

Yet again, this type of structural problem cannot be directly detected purely by measurements extracted from a module hierarchy chart. Possible symptoms are additional information flows to and from the misplaced modules, however, requirements traceability is necessary to define this class of structural error. A module is deemed to be misplaced if there exist modules within the scope of a given requirement X that satisfy functions not subordinate to X in the functional requirement hierarchy.

(e) Duplicate functionality

The final functionally related class of structural design error is duplicated functionality. Since it is hard to imagine that this would ever be an intentional design objective, duplicated functions are normally disguised, frequently by the use of synonyms for module names (e.g. FETCH-COMMAND and GET-COMMAND). Where duplicate functionality occurs in combination with other structural problems such as multiple functionality it may be even harder to isolate as the module name may reflect another function which it satisfies. Potential maintenance problems are the main problem with this type of error.

There are few, if any symptoms for duplicate functionality in a module hierarchy chart and so the error can only be detected when using additional requirements traceability information. Obviously, duplication occurs whenever a functional requirement is independently satisfied by two or more modules, or sets of modules.

(f) Inadequate data object isolation

Inadequate data object isolation is the first of three structural error categories that concerns data objects, although the definition of data object should be generalised to include devices. Avoiding such structural errors has been one of the prime motivations behind the object-oriented approaches [Booc86], yet despite being a relatively widely understood principle our empirical analysis would suggest is not well adhered to. Maintenance activities may well be one of the reasons for a breakdown of data object isolation. The other explanations are poor communication within a development project and multiple functionality so that data object access routines are packaged with other functions inhibiting re-use.

Figure 5 illustrates a partial system architecture where many modules all access the same data object, ACTIVITIES-TABLE. A better solution is to restrict access to ACTIVITIES-TABLE to the minimal set of primitive functions, possibly ADD, DELETE and FETCH and use these as building blocks to construct the more complex operations. As the architecture stands it may lead to a number of problems. First, since the structure of ACTIVITIES-TABLE may be complex this will make the software harder to comprehend and with an increase in the probability of committing errors as the processing details for manipulating the object cannot be separated from the remainder of a module's functionality. Second, introducing data integrity checks will prove to be difficult and result in much duplication of functionality. The usual consequence of this type of system structure is to treat it as a powerful disincentive to build in any such integrity features. Third, sharing the data object in this fashion effectively couples many modules together with a resultant increase in the probability of side effects.

Symptoms for this class of error are a high level of accesses to a data object which may be observed from a module hierarchy diagram. To fully define a lack of data object isolation one needs information concerning the actual functions of the modules concerned and this available from the functional requirements hierarchy and the requirements traceability. Strictly speaking, this error is particular case of multiple functionality for a set of modules that all share a given data object. We choose to make this error a special class since, the error would appear commonplace and is given special emphasis in the literature (see for example [Parn72] [Stev74] [Parn79]).

(g) Duplicate data objects

The duplication of parts or all of a data object is seldom considered to be an issue by software engineers, however, it may have considerable impact upon a design and consequently upon a range of quality factors of the resultant implementation. Synonyms often disguise duplication particularly if a system has had a long maintenance history. Apart from the possibilities of data inconsistency, duplicate data objects lead to unnecessarily complex software and a loss of maintainability. Traditionally, this has been regarded as the domain of the database worker, and it is therefore no surprise that the six design metrics under review have no notion of data object duplication. The remedy is to make use of techniques such as relational data modelling [Codd70] [Kent83] which highlight any duplication. Parenthetically, we note that there situations when one might deliberately build in duplication due to other considerations such as efficiency, however, software engineers ought at least be aware that such a situation prevails.

(h) Over-loaded data objects

Our final class of structural design error derive from over-loaded data objects, that is where a data object is used by more than one module and assigned more than one meaning. In the example given by Figure 6, the two unrelated modules CHECK-INPUT and DISPLAY-MESSAGE both share the same data object FLAG although they use it for different purposes, in other words FLAG is over-loaded with two meanings. This is an undesirable state of affairs as this allows for potentially disastrous side effects, and makes the system harder to understand and maintain.

This over-loading of data object cannot be detected without knowledge of the meaning of the data, something not present in a module hierarchy diagram nor in functional requirements hierarchies. It is the mapping from the conceptual data model to its physical realisation that indicates the presence of this class of error. Where two or more conceptual errors map to a single physical data object this implies the existence of over-loading. Since none of our six design metrics are concerned with data models, conceptual or otherwise, they are not capable of detecting this class of error.

Thus, after somewhat extensive preliminaries, we are now able to assess the extent to which our six selected design metrics might be able to help the software engineer highlight structural design errors. In addition, we also consider deviation from Third Normal Form (TNF) which can be regarded as a metric if one employs dynamic programming to derive the minimum number of distinct operations (e.g. split a relation) to transform a given relational model into its equivalent TNF [Ince90]. The results are summarised in Table One.

The table entries were assigned on the following basis. In a situation where a structural error may be fully defined in terms of a metric, a 'defines' is allocated. For example, multiple functionality may be defined using the "work" metric as occurring whenever more than one primitive functional requirement maps to a single module in a module hierarchy. By contrast, the Henry and Kafura Information Flow metric is only able to detect symptoms suggestive of a missing level of functional abstraction, in the form of increased number of information flows. However, such a circumstance might also arise if there is a lack of data object isolation, thus, it is not possible to define the error missing level of abstraction by the Henry and Kafura metric, and so the metric is considered to be 'suggestive' of the error. Where the symptomatic evidence is weak, as in the case of Chapin's Q metric for identifying split functionality (since it will probably only result in a slight increase in total module interface size) the metric is deemed to be weakly suggestive of the structural error. If the metric is independent of the a structural error as in the case of IF4 and duplicate data objects, the metric is said to be neutral. Finally, if the metric masks the structural error, for example the Yin and Winchester metric penalises re-use of modules and therefore encourages the duplication of functionality, it is considered to be positively misleading.

Error type	Y&W	H&K	Q	C&A	IF$_4$	Work	TNF
Missing level of abstraction	-	S	WS	S[1]	S	D	-
Multiple functionality	-	WS	WS	WS	WS	D	-
Split functionality	-	WS	WS	WS	WS	D	-
Misplaced functionality	-	WS	WS	WS	WS	D	-
Duplicated functionality	M	M	-	-	-	D	-
Lack of D.O. isolation	WS	WS	-	-	S	D	-
Duplicate D.O.'s	M	-	-	-	-	-	D
Over-loaded D.O	WS	-	-	-	WS	-	D

D = defines error
S = suggestive
WS = weakly suggestive
- = neutral
M = misleading

Y&W = Yin and Winchester C' metric [Yin78]
H&K = Henry and Kafura Information Flow metric [Henr81]
Q = Chapin's Q metric [Chap79]
C&A = Card and Agresti metric [Card88]
IF$_4$ = Ince and Shepperd information flow metric [Ince89]
Work = Shepperd "work" metric [Shep90]
TNF = Third Normal Form relational data model [Codd70]

Table 1: Relationship between design metrics and design errors

Recall that our objective is to apply design metrics for the early detection of software design errors. Table 1 makes it abundantly clear that no single metric provides anything near to full coverage of the eight classes of design error. However, between the "work" metric and measures derived from a conceptual and physical relational data model it is possible to define, and therefore identify, all the classes of structural error that we have discussed. It is interesting to note that none of the metrics derived purely from the design structure notation of a module hierarchy chart are able to do anything other than pinpoint symptoms that are to a greater or lesser extent indicative of an underlying error. Nevertheless, this table should not be interpreted as suggesting that all further work on the first five metrics be abandoned forthwith!

---

[1] The inter-modular part of the metric is suggestive of this type of error but the intra-modular part acts as a misleading indicator and therefore, the two parts of the metric ought not be agglomerated.

Firstly, the fact that a metric is not effective in detecting a particular type of structural error does not imply that is ineffectual for all software engineering objectives. For example, although the Yin and Winchester metric highlights few design error symptoms, it is useful for indicating the degree of component re-use within a software system.

Secondly, there are problems associated with requirements traceability and therefore the "work" metric. In many environments the necessary information may not be accessible, also there may be problems constructing a functional requirements hierarchy in an objective fashion, despite some of the techniques discussed earlier. Furthermore, this is a very under-developed field of software metrics research. The same may be said for data model based metrics as software engineers have tended to strongly emphasise the functional aspects of software design ([Geri77] and [Ince90] are rare exceptions). Consequently, the retention of at least the information flow metrics would seem to be highly desirable, given their ability to pinpoint problem areas, if not exactly identify the type of structural design error.

4. EMPIRICAL OBSERVATIONS

We now briefly review an empirical analysis of 13 small to medium sized, interactive, software systems (14 to 33 modules and 313 to 983 executable lines of Pascal code) to assess the incidence and distribution of the eight classes of structural design errors identified by this paper. The systems were implemented by teams of three to four second year computer science students. The distribution of errors is given in Table 2.

Error type	Frequency	No. of systems affected (out of 13)
Missing level of abstr'n	13 (22%)	12
Multiple functionality	7 (12%)	5
Split functionality	5 (8%)	5
Misplaced functionality	6 (10%)	4
Duplicated functionality	5 (8%)	4
Lack of D.O. isolation	20 (34%)	7
Duplicate D.O.'s	0 (0%)	0
Over-loaded D.O	3 (6%)	2
Total	59	

Table 2: Distribution of structural design errors

These findings should be viewed more as a case study rather than as having widely applicable results, because the systems are small, have not been subjected to any maintenance changes, and manipulate relatively simple data objects. The latter observation probably explains the fact that duplicate and over-loaded data objects only account for 6% of all errors. The systems were designed, at least in theory, according to object oriented principles, so it was somewhat disconcerting to note that lack of data object (or device) isolation was the most commonplace type of structural error. However, this error clustered around 7 out of the 13 systems whilst the next most common problem, a missing level of functional abstraction was almost evenly distributed amongst all bar one design. The probable explanation is that some project teams enforced a data hiding discipline and thereby prevented the problem altogether, whilst the more anarchic teams failed to do so and it could thus occur a number of times. None of the project teams had much awareness concerning the problem of missing levels of abstraction and therefore it was widespread. Certainly, it is not an issue that is directly addressed by object oriented design methodologies.

Our other major observation from this investigation is that the structural errors showed a particular tendency to cluster in the non leaf modules of the system architecture. Of the 59 design errors, 43 or 73% of them, occurred in non-leaf modules. This strongly suggestive that software engineers are fairly competent at designing the lowest levels of a system architecture, but are not always effective at combining modules into higher level structures. Such an observation, particularly if it is repeated by other empirical analyses, has implications upon the choice of design methodology and where effort should concentrated for design evaluation.

5. CONCLUSIONS

In this paper we have reviewed the possibilities of using metrics for the early detection of structural design errors. We have argued that this goal is an important one because of the considerable impact of the design upon such quality factors as the reliability and maintainability of the delivered software product. We have examined more closely the term structural design error, and suggested an eightfold classification. This approach is an improvement upon the classic work of Stevens *et al* [Stev74] on module coupling and cohesion, because it addresses specific underlying problems, rather than mere symptoms which might be the consequence of any one or none, of a range of possible explanations. The advantage for the software engineer is that understanding the underlying problem greatly facilitates the process of design improvement. The other feature of our classification is that it is considerably more comprehensive than existing approaches which tend to neglect data aspects of system architectures. This classification, still needs further refinement and in particular a formal definition of each error class, thereby allowing the software engineer to unambiguously identify structural error types. We are currently investigating an axiomatic approach to this problem.

An analysis of six design metrics indicates that no single metric is able to detect all of the types of structural error. Furthermore, five of the metrics which are derived from module hierarchy diagrams are restricted to identifying features possibly symptomatic of some the structural errors. Of these metrics, those that are information flow based seem to perform most effectively at highlighting error symptoms. This conforms with current empirical evidence, for instance [Kafu87] and [Romb87].

The explanation for the inability of these five metrics to define any of the classes of structural error is that they are measures of structural or syntactic aspects of a design, and therefore have no notion of the semantics of either the data objects or modules contained in the design. Indeed they have very weak notions of even structural aspects of data objects. The sixth metric, "work" [Shep90b] is a measure based both upon design structure and also upon the traceability of functional requirements onto a design and the hierarchical relationship between individual requirements.

All six design metrics have a strong functional bias and to overcome this software engineers will need to pay considerably more attention to the data modelling facets of the design process. Until this occurs the use of metrics will always paint an incomplete picture of structural design errors.

Notwithstanding, the above problems, we believe that combinations of metrics (e.g. information flow and "work" may be used to considerable effect - *vide* [Shep90b]) particularly for systems that might be characterised as function oriented, and for which the data objects are comparatively straightforward. Design metrics do seem to have some success at identifying features of system architectures that are suggestive of underlying structural problems. The difficulty is, at present, that the burden remains entirely upon the software engineer to establish precisely what the underlying problem is, and how it may best be dealt with.

REFERENCES:

[**Basi88**] Basili, V.R. Rombach, H.D. 'The TAME Project: Towards Improvement-Oriented Software Environments'. *IEEE Trans. on Softw. Eng.* 14(6) pp758-773. 1988.

[**Booc86**] Booch, G. 'Object-oriented design' *IEEE Trans.on Softw. Eng.* 12(2) pp211-221. 1986.

[**Card86**] Card, D.N. Church, V.E. Agresti, W.W. 'An Empirical Study of Software Design Practices'. *IEEE Trans. on Softw. Eng.* 12 pp264-271. 1986.

[**Card88**] Card, D.N. Agresti, W.W. 'Measuring software design complexity' *J. of Sys. & Softw.* 8, pp185-197. 1988.

[**Codd70**] Codd, E.F. 'A relational model of data for large data banks' CACM 13(6) pp377-387. 1970.

[**Geri77**] Geritsen, L. 'On some metrics for databases or what is a very large database?' *ACM SIGMOD Record* pp50-74, June 1977.

[**Henr81**] Henry, S. Kafura, D. 'Software metrics based on information flow.' *IEEE Trans. on Softw. Eng.* 7(5) pp510-518. 1981.

[**Ince88**] Ince, D.C. Shepperd, M.J . 'System design metrics: a review and perspective.' *Proc. IEE / BCS Conf. Software Engineering '88* July 12- 15, Liverpool University, pp23-27. 1988.

[**Ince89**] Ince, D.C. Shepperd, M.J. 'An empirical and theoretical analysis of an information flow based design metric'. *Proc. European Software Eng. Conf.*, Warwick, England. Sept. 11-16, 1989.

[**Ince90**] Ince, D.C. Shepperd, M.J. 'The measurement of data designs'. Open University Tech. Rep. May 1990.

[**Kafu87**] Kafura, D. Reddy, G.R. 'The use of Software Complexity Metrics in Software Maintenance'. *IEEE Trans. on Softw. Eng.* 13(3) pp335-343. 1987.

[**Kari88**] Karimi, J. Konsynski, B.R. 'An automated software design assistant'. *IEEE Trans. on Softw. Eng.* 14(2) pp194-210, 1988.

[**Kent 83**] Kent, W. 'A simple guide to five normal forms in the relational database theory'. *CACM* 26(2) pp120-125. 1983.

[**McCa76**] McCabe, T.J. 'A complexity measure' *IEEE Trans. on Softw. Eng.* 2(4), pp308-320. 1976.

[**Parn72**] Parnas, D.L. 'On the criteria to be used in decomposing systems into modules'. CACM 15(2) pp1053-1058.

[**Parn79**] Parnas, D.L. 'Designing software for ease of extension and contraction'. *IEEE Trans. on Softw. Eng.* 5(2) pp128-138. 1979.

[**Romb87**] Rombach, H.D. 'A controlled experiment on the impact of software structure on maintainability.' *IEEE Trans. on Softw. Eng.* 7(5) pp510-518. 1987.

[**Shep88**] Shepperd, M.J. 'A critique of cyclomatic complexity as a software metric' *Softw. Eng. J.* 3(2) pp30-36. 1988.

[**Shep89**] Shepperd, M.J. 'Specification: a new perspective on design metrics'. *Wolverhampton Polytechnic, School of Computing and Information Technology, Technical Report 89/01.* (Also accepted for publication *The Computer J.*). 1989.

[Shep90a] Shepperd, M.J. 'An empirical study of design measurement'. *Softw. Eng. J.,* Jan. 1990.

[Shep90b] Shepperd, M.J. Ince, D.C. 'The multi-dimensional modelling and measurement of software designs'. *Proc. Annu. ACM Comp. Sci. Conf.,* Washington DC, Feb.20-22, 1990.

[Shep90c] **Shepperd, M.J.** 'An experimental investigation into the relationship between design metrics and software maintenance' *Wolverhampton Polytechnic, School of Computing and Information Technology, Technical Report 90/02.*

[Stev74] Stevens, W.P. Myers, G.J. Constantine, L.L. 'Structured design' *IBM Sys. J.* 13(2) pp115-139. 1974.

[Yin78] Yin, B.H. Winchester, J.W. 'The establishment and use of measures to evaluate the quality of software designs' *Proc. ACM Softw. Qual. Ass. Workshop* pp45-52. 1978.

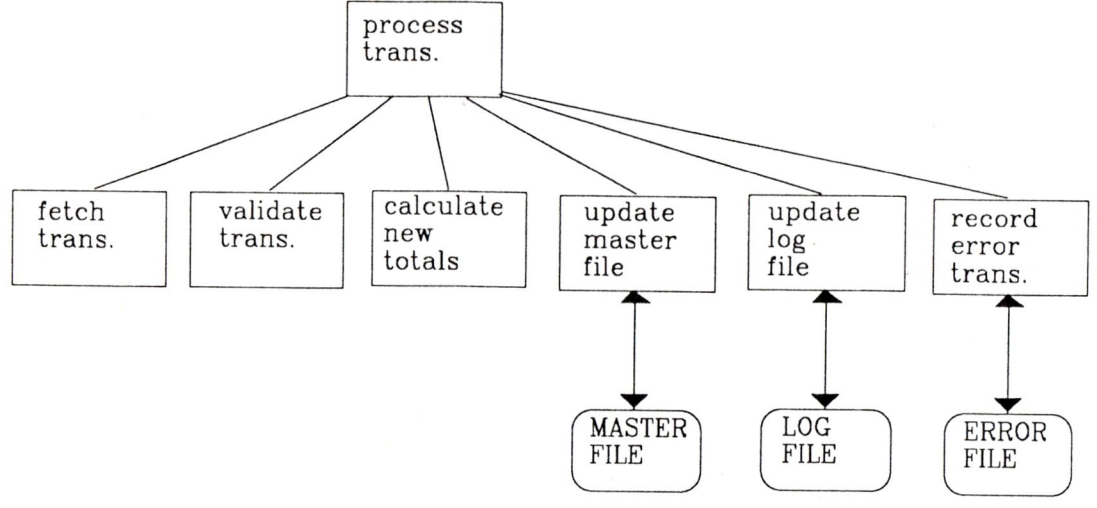

Figure 1: An example of a missing level of abstraction

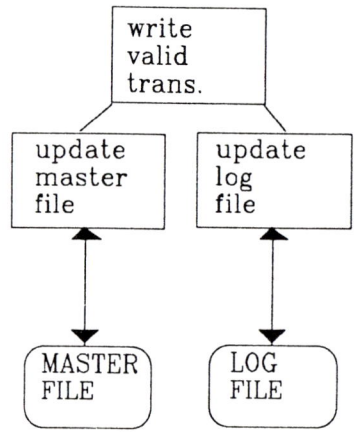

Figure 1a: Introduction of missing abstraction

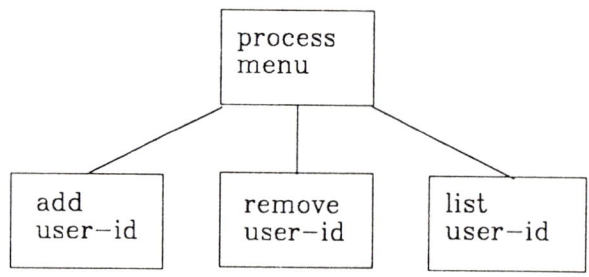

Figure 2: Multiple functionality

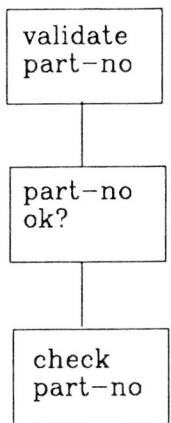

Figure 3: Split functionality examples

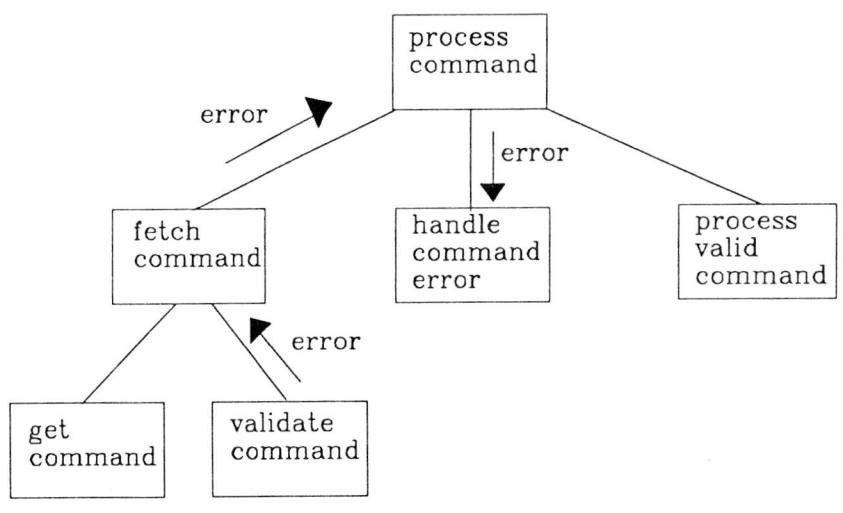

Figure 4: Misplaced function example

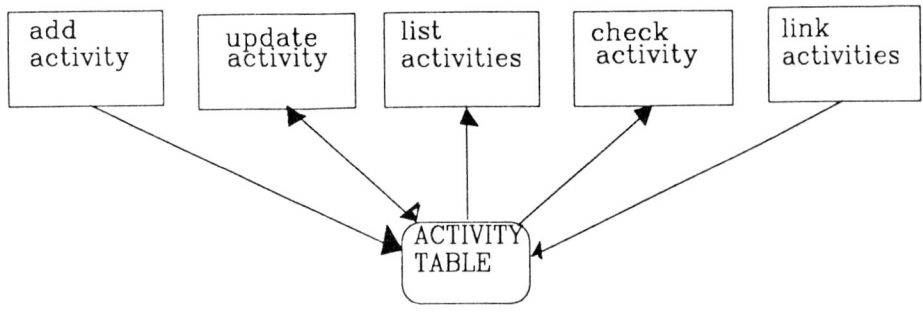

Figure 5: Lack of data object isolation

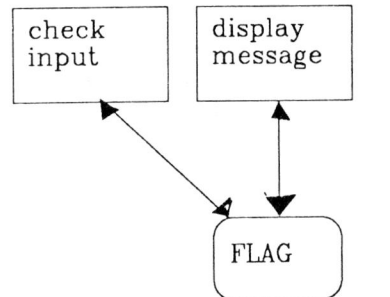

Figure 6: Over-loaded data objects

The Relative Software Complexity Metric: A Validation Study

John C. Munson

University of West Florida

Taghi M. Khoshgoftaar

Florida Atlantic University

ABSTRACT

Many software metrics have been developed for the purpose of evaluating certain characteristics of computer programs. These complexity metrics do provide substantial information on the distinguishing differences among the elements of software systems. Attempts to use these software metric data have met with questionable success in program development scenarios. This is largely due to the inherent overlap and shared variance of these metrics. In this paper, a new approach to the use of complexity metrics is explored. A method is presented for the construction of a linear combination of existing metrics to form a single relative complexity metric C_r. The particular focus is on the validation of this metric concept in regards to its stability in terms of samples drawn from with replacement from a known population.

1 INTRODUCTION

There are currently over 90 distinct software complexity metrics available to researchers in the area of software engineering. Many of these metrics are simple linear compounds of other metrics. From the founding father of software science, we have a simple example of this idea. Halstead's metric of program vocabulary, η, is the sum of η_1, unique operator count, and η_2, unique operand count [5]. If we have the two measures of η_1 and η_1 on a program module, there is not additional source of variability described by their sum. There is no new information contributed by η.

There is considerable overlap among the set of metrics as to what each is measuring. Consider the case of the two metrics of lines of code and statement count. Clearly, the more lines of code a program has the more program statements it will contain. In the case of some languages, this correspondence is one to one. While there appears to be a large number of complexity metrics for measuring differing phenomena, these metrics may be seen to be linear compounds of a small number of orthogonal complexity domains. Some effort has been devoted to organizing the many metrics into various taxonomic categories in a effort to understand the nature of the underlying complexity domains[4]. For example, there are two distinctly different classes of metrics in terms of those that measure static program attributes, such as lines of code, and those that measure dynamic program attributes such as the number of times a particular control structure is executed at run time.

The relative success of the use of complexity metrics is predicated on the ability of these metrics to describe all aspects of program variability. Also, problems have arisen in the past in the application of complexity metrics to predictive models for software development in that different program modules would have substantially different values of these metrics. In response to the felt need to compare programs one to another based on their complexity, we have developed a realistic measure of relative complexity that will reflect the contribution of each program module to the total complexity of a software system.

The concept of relative program complexity is a derivative of our recent explorations into the dimensionality of program complexity using the statistical technique of factor analysis [10]. Factor analysis is a useful tool in the reduction of the complexity metric space to a set of orthogonal complexity dimensions. These orthogonal dimensions provide the basis for a conceptual model of software complexity. Based on our recent work in this area, such a conceptual model would consist, perhaps, of the independent complexity domains of Control, Size, Modularity, Effort or Information Content, and Data Structure. Any program might be seen to have characteristic measures on each of these orthogonal domains.

2 THE CONCEPT OF RELATIVE COMPLEXITY

A major problem, in the past, with the application of complexity metrics in the task of prediction or for comparative purposes among program modules is that different program modules would have substantially different sets of values of these metrics. There were no direct means of comparing these program constituents. For example, program module A might have many lines of code (LOC) and low cyclomatic complexity ($V(G)$) whereas program module B might have a low LOC and high $V(G)$. These modules are clearly different in their complexity but are not comparable in some relative sense. When it is desirable to compare program modules directly in terms of their relative complexity we have developed a realistic measure of relative complexity that will reflect the contribution of each program module to the total complexity of a programming system. This relative complexity has proven quite useful both for classifying program modules into categories of varying complexity and also for comparing them as well.

The role of relative complexity in software engineering research is best understood in terms of this classification process. Through the use of the relative complexity metric, individual programs and program modules may be arranged and grouped by this single measure. Complex programs are known to require a disproportionate amount of development effort and are also known to contain a disproportionate number of errors [1,3]. The value of complexity metrics in software development management has also been established [11]. The relative complexity metric provides a simple mechanism of aggregating the many similar complexity metrics into one single metrics that is a linear compound of the variance components of the set of metrics used to describe a program or a set of programs.

The problem of the proliferation of software complexity metrics can be reduced and eventually eliminated through validating a set of metrics via the statistical techniques called factor analysis. An example of the application of factor analysis to the field of software complexity metrics may be seen in the authors' recent study [10]. The most important conclusion that can be drawn from this investigation is that the domain of complexity measures does not appear to be unrestricted. There are many software complexity metrics in the literature, but there are relatively few dimensions in the complexity measure space. It would appear perfectly reasonable to characterize the complexity of a program with a simple function of a small number of variables. In the case of program complexity, there are many measures of complexity, but factor analysis has shown that all of these metrics map onto a small number of complexity domains.

The essential purpose of factor analysis is to describe, if possible, the covariance relationships among variables in terms of a few underlying, but understandable, random quantities called factors. Basically, the factor model is motivated by the following argument. Suppose variables can be grouped by their correlations. That is, all variables within a particular group are highly correlated among themselves but have relatively small correlations with variables in a different group. It is conceivable that each group of variables represents a single underlying construct, or factor, that is responsible for the observed correlations. Factor analysis can be considered as an extension of principal component analysis [6]. Both can be viewed as attempts to approximate the covariance matrix, Σ. However, the approximation based on the factor analysis model is more elaborate. The primary question in factor analysis is whether the data are consistent with a prescribed structure.

The initial objective of the factor analysis was to achieve a reduction in the dimensionality of the problem. This factor analytic technique also has another benefit. One of the products of a factor analysis is a factor score coefficient matrix, $\mathbf{F}$. This matrix is constructed to send an associated matrix of standardized complexity metrics, $\mathbf{z}$, onto the underlying orthogonal factor dimensions. From these new orthogonal measures of program complexity we have derived our concept of the relative program complexity measure, C_r. For each program a raw data vector of complexity measure is input to the factor analysis. This raw data vector is converted to a new standard score vector, $\mathbf{z}$. Then, for each data vector a new vector of factor scores, $\mathbf{f}$, is calculated: $\mathbf{f} = \mathbf{zF}$, where $\mathbf{F}$ is the factor score coefficient matrix and $\mathbf{z}$ is the vector of standardized values of the variables that have been factor analyzed.

The matrix $\mathbf{F}$ is then used to map a matrix of standardized complexity metrics, $\mathbf{z}$, onto the identified orthogonal factor dimensions. Thus the relative complexity, C_r, of the factored program modules may be represented as follows:
$$\mathbf{C}_r = \mathbf{zF}\Lambda^T = \mathbf{f}\Lambda^T$$
where Λ is a vector of eigenvalues associated with the specific factor dimensions. From the vector $\mathbf{C}_r$ of relative complexity metrics, the ith entry C_{r_i} represents the relative complexity of the ith program module or program in a program set.

From a statistical perspective, the underlying distribution of the C_{r_i}'s is both interesting and tractable. These represent observations from a normally distributed population with a mean of zero and a variance of
$$V(C_r) = \sum_{i=1}^{j} \lambda_i^2,$$
where j represents the number of factors in the rotated factor pattern, and λ_i is the eigenvalue associated with the ith factor. Each of the relative complexity metrics, C_{r_i}, represents a weighted linear compound of the constituent raw complexity metrics as follows:
$$C_{r_i} = \sum_k (\sum_j z_{ij} F_{jk}) \lambda_k,$$
where z_{ij} is the standardized value of the jth metric for the ith program and F_{jk} is the factor score coefficient for the jth metric on the kth factor. In this context, the relative complexity metric represents each raw complexity metric in proportion to the amount of unique variation contributed by that complexity metric.

3 AN EMPIRICAL ANALYSIS

The relative complexity metric has demonstrated value in that it may be used to classify program modules into categories of varying complexity and for providing a mechanism for ordering them as well. None of the other single complexity metrics can be used for this classification on all aspects of the complexity domains simultaneously. In this study we will show the application of the relative complexity metric to data derived from actual programming systems to discuss notions of applicability and validity of the concept of relative complexity. The data to be analyzed were obtained from a set of 202 programs whose characteristics were measured by Jensen and Vairavan [7]. These programs were written in Pascal. The complexity metrics were obtained using a Pascal lexical scanner. These programs were independent components of an existing building automation system. They constituted a representative sample from the complete set of real-time programs in this application.

The specific complexity metrics developed included Halstead's software science metrics, McCabe's [9] cyclomatic complexity $V(G)$, and Belady's [2] *Band* metric. The Halstead metrics are derived from the four measures of η_1 the unique operator count, η_2 the unique operand count, N_1 the total operator count, and N_2 the total operand count. From these four measures the metrics program vocabulary (η), program length (N), program volume (V), effort (E), difficulty (D), and intelligence content (I) computed as follows:

$\eta = \eta_1 + \eta_2$
$N = N_1 + N_2$
$V = N \log_2 \eta$
$E = V(\eta_1/\eta_2)(N_2/2)$
$D = V/(\eta \log_2 \eta)$
$I = \eta \log_2 \eta$.

Two additional estimates for program length were computed. These were $\hat{N}$ and N_F computed as follows:

$\hat{N} = \eta_1 \log_2 \eta_1 + \eta_2 \log_2 \eta_2$
$N_F = \log_2 \eta_1! + \log_2 \eta_2!$.

McCabe's cyclomatic complexity was computed according to the formula,

$V(G) = e - v + 2$

where e and v represent the number of edges and vertices in a directed graph that in turn represents the control flow within a program. The *Band* metric was developed by Belady based on the notion that it is more difficult to create programs with deeply nested control structures than those with less nesting. The *Band* of a program is defined as follows:

$B = (\Sigma i L(i))/n$

where $L(i)$ is the number of nodes at level i and n is a count of the nodes in the control graph.

Correlation coefficients for the 202 programs were computed to show the bivariate relationship among these metrics. These coefficients are presented in Table 1 below. Some of these values are very high. For example, the correlations between the estimator N_F and operand counts are all greater than 0.90. There is a substantial amount of shared variance among these measures.

Table 1. Correlation Coefficients among the Complexity Metrics

	η_1	N_1	η_2	N_2	$\hat{N}$	N_F	I	V	D	E	$V(G)$
N_1	.69										
η_2	.69	.89									
N_2	.66	.97	.90								
$\hat{N}$	.70	.89	.99	.91							
N_F	.69	.89	.99	.91	.99						
I	.48	.78	.93	.78	.92	.92					
V	.67	.99	.91	.99	.91	.91	.79				
D	.79	.88	.71	.88	.72	.71	.51	.86			
E	.59	.92	.74	.93	.75	.76	.58	.94	.86		
$V(G)$	.55	.83	.66	.78	.66	.66	.58	.80	.74	.75	
Band	.54	.78	.63	.72	.62	.62	.56	.74	.69	.67	.97

To show the underlying structure of the complexity domains that these twelve metrics have in common, principal components factor analysis was employed to reduce the dimensionality. The emergent factor structure was subsequently rotated using the varimax orthogonal rotation method. The rotated factor matrix from this analysis is shown in Table 2 below. From the twelve original metrics a total of three distinct factors emerge. These factors, in turn, account for approximately 95% of the total variance. The resulting eigenvalues are also shown in Table 2.

Table 2 Varimax Factor Pattern of the Complexity Metrics

Metric	Factor 1 Volume	Factor 2 Control	Factor 3 Effort
I	**.935**	.285	.115
η_2	**.860**	.303	.400
N_F	**.851**	.300	.420
N	**.848**	.300	.426
V	**.643**	.535	.520
N_2	**.634**	.520	.532
N_1	**.602**	.577	.526
Band	.288	**.892**	.236
$V(G)$	.313	**.889**	.284
η_1	.323	.179	**.835**
D	.289	.499	**.789**
E	.417	.569	**.588**
Eigenvalues	4.78	3.43	3.16

Table 3. Raw Complexity Metrics for 15 Sample Programs

PGM	η_1	N_1	η_2	N_2	$\hat{N}$	N_F	I	V	D	E	$V(G)$	Band
1	9	29	16	21	92	62	39	232	5	1371	3	1.8
2	13	57	37	76	240	175	56	750	13	10022	3	2.0
3	13	72	52	81	344	258	91	921	10	9329	4	2.7
4	9	22	15	21	87	58	31	197	6	1242	5	3.1
5	12	169	54	131	353	265	124	1813	14	26394	10	6.0
6	11	110	45	98	285	211	100	1207	12	14468	12	6.9
7	6	13	9	10	44	27	27	89	3	300	1	1.0
8	13	263	87	271	608	472	175	3547	20	71833	15	8.2
9	12	91	51	97	332	248	98	1123	11	12824	5	3.3
10	10	122	50	114	315	236	122	1394	11	15892	11	5.5
11	10	49	33	52	199	144	69	548	7	4318	2	1.3
12	12	95	31	75	196	141	63	922	14	13391	7	3.6
13	7	27	19	29	100	69	49	263	5	1406	1	1.0
14	12	48	23	50	147	103	38	482	12	6037	6	3.3
15	10	73	46	86	287	213	98	923	9	8631	4	2.3

The three factors presented in Table 2 may be labeled in terms of the metrics associated with each of these factors. Based on our earlier exploratory work with the underlying complexity domains, we suggest that Factor 1 may be called a **Volume** domain in that the associated metrics have a common element of the size or volume of a program. Factor 2 consists of Belady's *Band* metric and McCabe's cyclomatic complexity, $V(G)$, that are concerned with the **Control** structure of the program. Factor 3 consists of those metrics related to Halstead's concept of the conceptual **Effort** needed to construct a program.

From the standpoint of the practical application of the concept and for the purposes of validating the stability of our notion of relative complexity, a random sample of fifteen programs were drawn from the total set of 202 programs. For illustrative purposes, the raw complexity metrics for each of these fifteen programs is shown in Table 3 below. It is quite clear, from an inspection of this table, that these fifteen programs differ substantially on all of the twelve metrics. The problem is that there is no single metric that will permit these fifteen programs to be ordered. For example, the Halstead effort, E, for Program 5 is greater than that of Program 6. However, Program 6 has a greater value of McCabe's cyclomatic complexity than that of Program 5. This makes for an impressive, though incomprehensible, table for just the fifteen selected programs. An inspection of this table does not permit the comparison or the classification of these programs in that the range of metric values are not the same across all programs.

4 THE STABILITY OF THE RELATIVE COMPLEXITY METRIC

When the dimensionality of the complexity metrics has been reduced through the use of factor analysis, it is possible to obtain factor scores for each of the programs by multiplying the matrix of standardized complexity metrics, $\mathbf{z}$, by the factor score coefficient matrix, $\mathbf{F}$ as was discussed above. This will send the twelve metrics for each program onto the three orthogonal dimensions of **Volume, Control,** and **Effort**. The factor scores for the fifteen programs randomly selected above are shown in Table 4 below. The factor scores presented in this table are far more comprehensible, if for no other reason than there are fewer metrics. It is still not possible to compare or classify these programs.

When the relative complexity measure, C_r, is computed for the fifteen programs shown in Table 4, there is one resulting number. On the basis of this relative complexity measure we can see that the Program 7 of this table is the least complex of the fifteen programs in a relative sense because it has the smallest value in the table. On the other hand, Program 8 has the largest value of the fifteen programs and is thus the most complex. The relative complexity values for this set of fifteen programs, however, are derived from the total set of 202 programs from the factor score coefficient matrix derived for all programs. The relative complexity values for these fifteen programs are in relation to the complete population of 202 programs.

Table 4. Factor Scores and Relative Complexity for 15 Sample Programs

	Factor 1 Volume	Factor 2 Control	Factor 3 Effort	C_r
Program 1	-0.89040	-0.2785	-0.3968	-6.4674
Program 2	-0.62030	-0.8261	0.7379	-3.4674
Program 3	0.09880	-0.8418	0.2172	-1.7313
Program 4	-1.06650	0.0599	-0.4758	-6.3970
Program 5	0.15790	0.2455	-0.1820	1.0220
Program 6	-0.23450	0.6448	-0.5816	-0.7465
Program 7	-0.88830	-0.1834	-0.9444	-7.8630
Program 8	1.13540	0.5957	-0.0368	7.3561
Program 9	0.10714	-0.5453	0.0160	-1.3097
Program 10	0.19541	0.4125	-0.8076	-0.2041
Program 11	-0.30570	-0.6837	-0.2122	-4.4801
Program 12	-0.81420	-0.1040	0.3735	-3.0674
Program 13	-0.58720	-0.3736	-0.7736	-6.5366
Program 14	-1.13240	-0.1921	0.4187	-4.7478
Program 15	0.16280	-0.5321	-0.4216	-2.3826

We are now concerned about the stability and the statistical robustness of this new relative complexity measure. To this end, we wish to compare values of the relative complexity metrics for the fifteen programs as derived from sample subsets of the 202 programs of the population. That is, if we take a sample of 40 programs from the remaining 187 programs, always including the same fifteen programs from the original sample, the relative complexity measures for the fifteen programs should be fairly stable regardless of the sample chosen. Within the set of 55 programs the relative complexities of the fifteen programs should not vary and the relative order of these fifteen programs should remain essentially the same across all samples.

To test this conjecture, a total of twenty such samples of 40 programs were drawn, with replacement, from the set of 187 programs. Each sample ultimately consisted of 55 programs, 15 test cases and 40 programs from the set of 187. For each of the 20 such samples drawn, relative complexity values, C_{r_i} were calculated for the 15 test programs. A mean for C_{r_i} for each of the fifteen programs was computed together with the standard deviation for this mean. These values are shown in Table 5 below, together with the values of the C_{r_i} for each of the fifteen programs from the complete set of 202 programs.

Table 5. Sampling Estimates of C_r from a Known Population

	N	SAMPLE MEAN	STD DEV	POP. MEAN
Program 1	20	-6.541	0.801	-6.467
Program 2	20	-3.046	0.639	-3.467
Program 3	20	-1.354	0.618	-1.731
Program 4	20	-6.367	0.869	-6.397
Program 5	20	2.157	1.060	1.022
Program 6	20	0.127	1.007	-0.746
Program 7	20	-8.166	1.027	-7.863
Program 8	20	9.665	2.123	7.356
Program 9	20	-0.774	0.651	-1.309
Program 10	20	0.606	1.030	-0.204
Program 11	20	-4.432	0.583	-4.480
Program 12	20	-2.394	0.655	-3.067
Program 13	20	-6.727	0.836	-6.536
Program 14	20	-4.340	0.699	-4.747
Program 15	20	-2.090	0.611	-2.382

The vector of sample means was compared to the corresponding vector of population means with a Hotelling T^2 test. With $T^2 = 11.362$ the null hypothesis was not rejected at the a priori criterion of **p < .05**. In this case, H_0 would have been rejected if $T^2 > 57 F_{(.05;5,15)}$. (A brief discussion of the relationship between the T^2 statistic and the F statistic is included in the Appendix.) Thus, the means of the samples are not distinctly different from the total means. From this we may conclude that values obtained for the individual relative complexity metrics, C_{r_i}, are quite stable and not too sensitive to variation in the associated set of programs.

As a by-product of this sampling process, it is possible to study the relationships among the fifteen sample programs based on the variation in relative complexity of each program between samples. These correlation coefficients are presented in

Table 6 below. In essence, program pairs with relatively high correlations varied in a similar fashion across the twenty samples. These correlation coefficients, then, might be regarded as indices of similarity among the programs. For example, the program pairs 13 and 7 were quite similar in terms of the variation between samples of C_r where the pairs 8 and 7 were inversely related. When these observations are examined against the raw complexity metric data of Table 3, it would appear that the programs with the consistently lowest indices of similarity, such as program 8, also represent the extremes in terms of the values of the individual complexity metrics.

Table 6. Correlation Matrix of C_r of 15 Programs

	\multicolumn{14}{c}{Program Number}													
	1	2	3	4	5	6	7	8	9	10	11	12	13	14
2	.54													
3	.28	.83												
4	.98	.46	.24											
5	.08	.30	.68	.17										
6	.36	.27	.55	.47	.92									
7	.96	.31	.08	.95	.01	.30								
8	-.25	.09	.54	-.17	.93	.75	-.30							
9	.30	.68	.94	.31	.87	.78	.14	.73						
10	.27	.21	.56	.37	.95	.98	.24	.83	.80					
11	.88	.78	.66	.83	.33	.46	.78	.02	.64	.43				
12	.68	.80	.76	.70	.66	.75	.51	.39	.81	.67	.81			
13	.97	.41	.23	.95	.11	.38	.98	-.20	.28	.32	.86	.60		
14	.86	.82	.57	.85	.28	.46	.70	-.04	.53	.34	.87	.89	.75	
15	.54	.60	.82	.55	.80	.81	.45	.60	.92	.84	.80	.82	.58	.60

5 SUMMARY AND CONCLUSIONS

A primary objective of this study has been to explore some aspects of the statistical viability of the concept of relative program complexity. From the results of this investigation, we conclude that the relative complexity measure, C_r, is both a stable and a reasonable statistical tool for the comparison and the classification of programs. Unlike other metrics, the relative complexity metric combines, simultaneously, all attribute dimensions of all complexity metrics. Our previous work in this area has shown that software complexity metrics are stable measures throughout the software life cycle. We have established that software complexity metrics, and the subsequently relative complexity metric, are closely associated with measures of program quality [8]. By combining the set of complexity metrics for each phase of the life cycle into a single, comprehensive metric, it is possible to determine quality measures for a final program product using complexity measures from the design or possibly even the specification phases.

Perhaps the most important feature of the relative complexity metric is that it is a tool that is generalizable in a forward direction. As more complexity metrics are developed, they may be incorporated into the formulation of the relative complexity metric. We have concluded that there are relatively few dimensions in the complexity problem space. If raw complexity metrics are suitable chosen to reflect all aspects of the underlying complexity domains, then the concept of relative complexity should provide a reasonable means of ordering programs as to their complexity.

In practice, project management and control of software development projects have had to rely on the individual expertise of a software project manager as the sole arbiter of the quality control process. This research suggests that software complexity metrics will serve as useful tools in the determination of software quality and also in the software maintenance function. Unlike other metrics, the concept of relative complexity will permit complex programs and program modules to be identified and monitored during development and maintenance activities. The unnecessarily complex programs and program modules are those that will consume the most resources in these activities.

Altogether too often, software complexity metrics have been employed, without refinement, in large project management scenarios. The naive use of software complexity metrics can lead to two unpleasant conclusions. The first conclusion would establish that the complexity metrics are worthless. The second conclusion would be the unhappy result that software managment decisions were made based on weak software measures. Software complexity metrics are still research tools whose nature is imprecisely understood. The lack of statistical sophistication in the application of metrics as tools can only lead to questionable results. This paper represents a step in the direction of refinement process that will ultimately permit the use of metrics as reliable tools in the field of software engineering.

APPENDIX

The Hotelling T^2 test is the multivariate analogue of Student's t statistic. In quadratic form the T^2 statistic is defined as follows:
$$T^2 = \mathbf{d}' \Sigma^{-1} \mathbf{d},$$

where **d** represents a vector of mean differences $\bar{x}_1 - \bar{x}_2$ for two groups of observations. The matrix, Σ is the common covariance matrix. Assuming a multivariate normal distribution of **d** with a zero mean vector and covariance matrix estimated by Σ, the distribution of T^2 may be expressed in terms of the F distribution as follows:

$$T^2 = n_e \, p \, F / (n_e - p + 1),$$

where n_e represents the degree of freedom for error. In this case the F statistic has p degrees of freedom in the numerator and $n_e - p + 1$ in the denominator. Thus we would fail to reject the null hypothesis, **d** = 0 if the computed value for

$$T^2 < F_{(\alpha; p, n_e - p + 1)}.$$

REFERENCES

[1] Albrecht, A. J. and Gaffney, Jr., J. E. (1983) "Software function, source lines of code, and development effort prediction: A software science validation," *Transactions on Software Engineering*, SE-9, 639-648.

[2] Belady, B. L. A. (1980) "Software geometry," *Proceedings of the 1980 International Computer Symposium*, Taipei.

[3] Basili, V. R. and T. Phillips (1981) "Evaluating and comparing software metrics in the software engineering laboratory," *Performance Evaluation Review*, 10, 95-106.

[4] Cote, V., P. Bourque, S. Oligny, and N. Rivard (1988) "Software metrics: an overvies of recent results," *Journal of Systems and Software*, 8, 121-131.

[5] Halstead, M. H. (1977) *Elements of Software Science*. Elsevier, New York.

[6] Dillon, W. R. and M. Goldstein (1984) *Multivariate Analysis: Methods and Applications*, John Wiley & Sons, New York.

[7] Jensen, H. A., and K. Vairavan (1985) "An experimental study of software metrics for real-time software," *IEEE Transactions on Software Engineering*, Vol. SE-11 (2), 231-234.

[8] Khoshgoftaar, T. M. and J. C. Munson (1989) "The use of a relative complexity metric to compare software designs: an empirical investigation," *Proceedings of the ISMM International Conference on Intelligent Distributed Processing*.

[9] McCabe, T. (1976) "A complexity measure," *IEEE Transactions on Software Engineering*, SE-2 (4), 308-320.

[10] Munson, J. C. and Khoshgoftaar, T. M. (1989) "The dimensionality of program complexity," *Proceedings of the 11th Annual International Conference on Software Engineering*, 245-253.

[11] Sonohara, R, A. Takano, K. Vehara, and T. Ohkawa (1981) "Program complexity measures for software development management," *Proceedings of the Fifth IEEE International Conference on Software Engineering*, 100-106.

Requirements Engineering

Capturing and Analysing User Problems: separating the 'why' from the what', D. Bustard, M. Norris & B. van Toen

Presenting and Entity model using hierarchical abstraction, D. Flynn & H. Yue

Capturing and Analysing User Problems: separating the 'why' from the 'what'

DW Bustard, Department Of Computer Science
The Queen's University of Belfast, Belfast, BT7 1NN, Northern Ireland

MT Norris & B Van Toen, British Telecom Research Laboratories
System and Software Engineering Division
Martlesham Heath, Ipswich, IP5 7RE, England

Abstract
In very broad terms, the systems analysis activity yields three definitions: that of a *current* situation, that of a more desirable *target* situation and that of the means by which the former can be transformed into the latter. The purpose of this paper is to consider how the first of these definitions, that of a current situation, might be produced. The approach taken is to identify and analyse the *problems* in the current situation that prompt the need for change. Techniques for analysing problems are proposed and a prototype tool, SOP (Statement of Problem), embodying the proposals, is presented and discussed.

1. INTRODUCTION
It is widely agreed that the requirements of a computing system should be expressed as *goals* rather than *solutions*; that is, to state *what* a system should do rather than *how* it should do it [e.g. 1, 2]. In this way, the implementors can focus on the purpose of the proposed system and so have a greater chance of meeting the client's needs. However, the goals are not the starting point for system development. Before that, the client will have noticed *problems* that will have driven him or her to seek a computing solution. A problem may be an opportunity for improvement or a deficiency in an existing way of working or, in more general terms, "a situation in which there is perceived to be a mismatch between 'what is' and what might, or could or should be" [22]. The purpose of this paper is to consider how such problems can be clarified and documented, giving particular emphasis to problems that represent difficulties in a current situation. The main objective of the paper is to draw a clear distinction between *problems* and *goals*; that is, to separate the reasons *why* a system change is

needed from a consideration of *what* can be done to satisfy some or all of that need.

The separation between problems and goals can be enforced through a suitable model of systems analysis. The one that is used here suggests that analysis strives to produce three definitions:

1. a specification of the *current situation*, in which problems reside;
2. a specification of the *target situation*, intended to meet a stated set of goals (usually encompassing some or all of the identified problems); and
3. a specification of how the current situation can be transformed into the target situation.

In this model, it is intended that the three definitions should be produced in the order listed. This is a controversial point. Most analysis techniques tend to be goal-driven [e.g. 7, 8, 15], encouraging the analyst to "develop positive statements" rather than dwell on problems [9]. Also strategic goals are often defined by the client before analysis starts. Nevertheless, the authors believe that it is beneficial to gain a full understanding of the current situation and the problems that it poses, before moving on to consider how improvements can be made. The main reasons for this belief are:

- it is usually necessary to have some knowledge of the current situation before considering the target situation whereas the current situation can be explored in isolation;
- it is easier to set (or analyse) goals once the current situation and its difficulties have been expressed;
- focusing on problems before goals tends to reduce the risk of adopting solutions during analysis;
- by starting with goals there is a danger of considering only those problems that act as constraints on the business objectives; problems are arguably issues in their own right and so should be processed as such.

In the computing field very little work has been done on problem analysis. Most software development methods make no mention of the documentation of problems and instead start, or move quickly, to a consideration of the requirements for a computing system [e.g. 3, 4, 5, 6]. Where problems are treated explicitly, the procedure is usually to list them in note form, as in CORE [7, 8]. CORE suggests that problems be used as an informal cross-check on goals but are otherwise ignored.

This paper proposes that problems be analysed using an approach based on Gilb's impact analysis technique [2]. Three main types of analysis are suggested:

- *inconvenience analysis*
  Here a table is constructed of the problems and those whom they affect. An attempt is made to assess the degree of inconvenience caused by each problem for each individual (or group) involved. The problems can then be prioritised according to the the total assessed inconvenience. Those affected can, similarly, be put into a priority order according to the extent to which they experience inconvenience.

- *quality analysis*
  Any system, involving computing equipment or not, can be examined with respect to a basic set of quality attributes [e.g. 10, 11, 12], such as efficiency, reliability, learnability and so on. This gives another way of looking at problems in the current situation. Once again a table is used, this time relating problems to quality attributes. Through this analysis the problems that have the most severe impact on quality become evident as do those quality attributes that are most affected.

- *interaction analysis*
  Problems are rarely independent, so attempting to solve any one problem will tend to contribute to the solution of one or more others. In some cases, solving one problem may make others worse! Once again a table can be used to clarify the inter-relationships that are present and estimates made of the dependency involved. This gives a means of identifying problems that can be tackled in isolation and grouping those that need to be treated collectively.

The first section of this paper discusses each type of analysis with respect to a video library example. The second section then describes a prototype tool, SOP, (Statement Of Problem), built using HyperCard [13, 14], which can be used to construct the analysis tables. The concluding section evaluates the work and suggests where it might proceed in the near future.

2. ANALYSIS OF PROBLEMS

Before an analysis of the problems in a current situation can begin the situation needs to be described in sufficient detail to enable the context of each problem to be understood fully. The description can be split into two parts: a brief overview of the situation, followed by a more detailed account that fills in the necessary background for the problems concerned. For example, in the case of a video library the overview might take the form:

A video library maintains a collection of video cassettes for rental to customers registered to use the library.
• Each new video cassette purchased is registered for inclusion in the library.
• Anyone may join the library on proof of identity. There is no charge to join.
• Video cassettes are usually rented for one evening and returned the following day. The fee for this period is charged at the time of rental. Videos may be retained at a reduced daily charge.
• Customers may attempt to reserve a video for a particular evening. This service is not guaranteed, however, because of the unpredictability of the returns.

This overview captures the essence of the situation and prepares the way for further detail, thus (it isn't necessary to read all of it!):

Video Registration
Each new video cassette purchased is registered for use in the library.
Registration entails:
1. allocating a unique *Video Registration Number*; these are allocated sequentially and are not re-used;
2. printing the *Video Registration Number* on the video cassette; and
3. making an entry in the *Video Registration Book*, recording the allocated number and the name of the video concerned.

Customer Registration
Anyone may join the library on proof of identity. There is no charge for registration.
Registration entails:
1. allocating a unique *Customer Registration Number*; these are allocated sequentially and are not re-used;
2. making an entry in the *Customer Registration Book*, recording the name, address, telephone number and *Registration Number* of the customer;
3. issuing a *Membership Card*, containing the *Registration Number*; and
4. preparing a *Rental Card*, holding the customer's name and *Registration Number*; the card has space for rental entries.

Rental
Video cassettes are usually rented for one evening and returned the following day. The fee for this period is charged at the time of rental. Videos may be retained at a reduced daily charge.
Rental entails:
1. locating the customer's *Rental Card*;

2. making an entry in the *Rental Card*, recording the date and *Video Registration Number*;

3. making an entry in the *Rental Book*; recording the date and the *Customer* and *Video Registration Numbers*;

4. supplying the video cassette;

5. filing the *Rental Card*;

6. receiving the returned video;

7. locating the customer's *Rental Card*;

8. charging for any additional rental incurred;

9. drawing a line through the rental entries in the customer's *Rental Card* and the *Rental Book*;

10. filing the *Rental Card*.

Reservations

Customers may attempt to reserve a video for a particular evening. This service is not guaranteed, however, because of the unpredictability of the returns.

Reservation entails:

1. making an entry in the *Reservation Book*, recording the *Customer Registration Number* and the video name;

2. checking each returned video against the entries in the *Reservation Book* and retaining it if it is needed that day.

Stocktaking

The *Rental Book* is checked once a week to identify late returns. An attempt is made to contact the defaulters by telephone and if this fails a letter is issued. If no response is made to the letter the manager is informed. General stocktaking is performed every three months, and the *Video Registration Book* adjusted accordingly.

Having built up this picture, each problem can then be clearly presented.

Problems are experienced by those in the problem situation, the *actors*. In the video library example there are three different roles to consider:

1. the library *owner* who runs the business and commissions the analysis;

2. the library *assistants* who implement the library procedures, and

3. the *customers* who rent videos.

Those in each role will identify different types of problem though interview or survey. Below are seven problems of the type that might be offered in the case of the video library:

1. the owner needs more information on rental patterns to decide on the number of copies of each video to hold;

2. the owner considers that staff-turnover rate is too high;

3. the assistants find the rental procedure tedious because it is error-prone and time-consuming;
4. some assistants would prefer more sociable library opening hours;
5. the assistants and most customers consider the video booking service to be much too unreliable;
6. customers would like ready access to information on what videos are in stock, to avoid a fruitless search of the library shelves; and
7. customers would like to be able to return videos at any time.

At this stage all problems have equal status and, in particular, no preference is given to those for which a computing solution seems likely.

Although each problem will tend to be associated with the actor that feel strongest about it, it is desirable to obtain, or at least assess, the effect of every problem on every actor in order to determine the full impact of each problem. Such an analysis will yield a large amount of information. This needs to be organised carefully if it is to be managed intellectually [16]. Figure 1 shows one approach, where the information is recorded in a tabular form, constituting what is described here as an *inconvenience analysis*.

	1	2	3	4	5	6	7	|Σ|
Owner	5	7	3	-5	3	2	-4	29
Assistants	1	6	6	5	7	3	-2	30
Customers	1	2	2	-4	6	6	6	27
Σ	7	15	11	-4	16	11	0	

Figure 1: Inconvenience Analysis

Problems are numbered across the top of the table and actors in the problem situation identified down the left hand side. Cells in the grid hold values on a scale -9 to +9 (say). The magnitude of a value is a measure of the strength of opinion expressed. Thus a value of zero represents a neutral position. These values are determined by the analyst in consultation with the actors (as far as is practical). A positive value indicates that a particular problem affects a particular actor. A negative value indicates that an actor is unaffected by a problem *and* believes that an attempt to solve the problem *may* have a detrimental effect. It could be argued that it would be better to record a zero in such cases because negative values tend to presuppose particular solutions. For example, with problem 4 (the unsociable working hours of the library) the assumption is that the opening hours need to be changed, an option which neither the owner nor the customers would welcome. An alternative approach, however, might be for the owner to pay more to the assistants for particularly unpopular working periods, a solution which the owner may find unsatisfactory but which would have no effect on customers.

Despite such difficulties, however, the use of negative values in the table does have the advantage of enabling potential conflicts to be recorded explicitly. All assumptions relating to the concerns expressed must, of course, be noted at the same time so that, if necessary, the entries can be revised when a greater understanding of the current situation (and possible target situations) is developed. Indeed, every value in the table must be accompanied by a detailed justification so that decisions made on the basis of the values present can be explained.

At the right hand side, the absolute values in each row have been summed to identify those who have expressed the strongest feelings. At the bottom of the table the columns have been summed to show the combined feelings of the actors about each problem. These values serves as an aid to comparing problems and putting them into a priority order. Note, however, that the sums only provide a rough guide for the analyst. They should not and, indeed, can not be used as the sole basis for decision taking. The difficulties to appreciate are:

1. In general, summed values in a decision table cannot be used to identify a priority order *unless* the entities being compared are independent [23]. This is not true of problems (as discussed later) and is also not true of the actors. For example, any problem experienced by an assistant or a customer *should* also be a problem for the owner in that the success of his or her business depends on their level of satisfaction.
2. The summations assume that all problems and all actors are equally important. This is not true of problems and probably less true of actors.
3. The table, by averaging the opinions of assistants and customers, diminishes their contribution to the problem sums and so diminishes the importance of their opinions.

Given these limitations it might be argued that the sums are not worth producing! In practice they do provide a useful way of highlighting those problems that appear to be important but ultimately it is the values in the body of the table that matter most. Together these values capture the situation as it is perceived at present and serve as a basis for discussion on how improvements might be made. Problems for which there is consensus are likely to be processed quickly, with rather more attention given to those cases where conflict has been detected, such as problems 4 and 7 in the video library example.

Another complementary way of analysing problems is to consider that they reflect a lack of quality in the current situation. By subdividing quality into a set of standard attributes [e.g. 10, 11, 12] it is possible to highlight those aspects of quality that are particularly lacking. Figure 2, for example, shows such a *quality analysis* for the video library.

	1	2	3	4	5	6	7	$|\Sigma|$
Reliability	0	3	4	0	9	2	0	18
Stability	0	8	0	0	0	0	0	8
Recoverability	0	2	2	0	9	5	0	18
Efficiency	3	7	7	1	9	8	1	36
Availability	2	3	1	2	4	0	9	21
Learnability	-2	1	1	0	2	-3	0	9
Modifiability	-1	0	0	7	0	-2	-1	11
Security	0	4	0	2	0	1	-2	9
Σ	2	28	15	12	33	11	7	

Figure 2: Quality Analysis

The table has the same structure as that described for the inconvenience analysis, with actors replaced by quality attributes. The meaning of the quality attributes is given as follows:

Reliability
   The frequency with which errors occur in a system - the lower the frequency the greater the reliability.
Stability
   The frequency of changes to the structure and/or operation of a system - the lower the frequency the greater the stability.

Recoverability
   The ease with which a recovery can be made following the occurrence of an error.
Efficiency
   The ratio of useful work done to the effort expended.
Availability
   The ratio of the time the system is operation to the time when it is inoperable.
Learnability
   The ease with which a system can be understood.
Modifiability
   The ease with which a system can be changed.
Security
   The extent to which a system is protected from malicious interference.

The cells in the quality analysis table (like those in the inconvenience analysis table) hold values in the range -9 to 9. Positive values are a measure of the extent to which a particular quality attribute is affected by a particular problem. Negative values indicate that (in the opinion of the analyst) any attempt to fix the problem concerned will have an adverse affect on the identified quality attribute. As with the inconvenience analysis, a full explanation of each value cited must be recorded.

The right hand column of the table gives an indication of the level of concern for each quality attribute. Efficiency is the most significant area of concern, with reliability, recoverability and availability also being worthy of attention. Note that in the case of "learnability" the current situation could become more complicated when the problems identified have been resolved.

The bottom row of the table in Figure 2 shows the relative effect of each problem on quality. The order of problem priority suggested by the quality analysis is almost the same as that emerging from the inconvenience analysis. While this is true of the video library example, major differences can occur, in general, if there are problems identified that have no significant impact on quality, such as "lack of profit". Sometimes, however, a different priority order will highlight a contradiction which the analyst must then resolve.

Problems are not independent and their linkage must be clearly understood before an attempt is made to resolve them. Some problems may have to be treated collectively while others may require ingenious solutions to prevent existing problems being aggravated or new problems appearing. Figure 3 shows an *interaction analysis* for the video library example. Only the lower triangle of the table is used as it is the link between problems that is being examined. Consequently only one sum is produced.

	1	2	3	4	5	6	7
1	*	*	*	*	*	*	*
2	0	*	*	*	*	*	*
3	0	2	*	*	*	*	*
4	0	5	1	*	*	*	*
5	0	3	0	0	*	*	*
6	5	0	0	0	2	*	*
7	0	2	0	-4	3	0	*
|Σ|	5	12	3	10	13	12	9

Figure 3: Interaction Analysis

Zero entries in the table indicate that the two problems concerned are independent. Positive values are a measure of problem affinity and negative values estimate the extent to which solving one or other problem will tend to aggravate the linked problem. In the example, there is only one negative case, that indicating the potential conflict between assistants wanting to work more sociable hours and customers wanting to return videos at any time. As with the other analyses, all values must be accompanied by details of any assumptions made. For example, if customers could return videos by posting them through the library letterbox this would have little effect on the assistants but an extension of the library opening hours is much less acceptable to them.

The values at the bottom of the table give the sum of the magnitudes of the links between each problem and every other one. Absolute values are summed because attraction and repulsion among problems are considered equally important linkages. The lower a sum the easier it is for that problem to be tackled in isolation, whereas problems with high ratings will usually have to be treated in groups.

The next section describes a prototype tool, SOP, that can be used to build and maintain the problem analyses tables discussed in this section.

3. SOP: STATEMENT OF PROBLEM TOOL

HyperCard [13, 14] is an application that is currently supplied free with each Apple Macintosh computer. Its principal use would appear to be as a tool for prototyping applications. It provides a means of managing textual and graphical data and of constructing interfaces through which other applications can be launched. Data is stored on *cards* (screens) that may be linked as desired. Data is held in either a graphical form (MacPaint style) or as text in *fields*. Actions, such as movement from one card to another are usually achieved by the selection of *buttons* whose effect is programmed in HyperTalk [13]. The HyperTalk language has the expressive power of a typical imperative programming language.

The SOP (Statement of Problem) prototype tool uses five cards to hold:
1. a summary, in English, of the current situation;
2. the *inconvenience* analysis table, maintaining details of the impact of each problem on those affected;
3. the *quality* analysis table, maintaining details of the effect of each problem on the defined range of quality attributes; and
4. the *interaction* analysis table, maintaining details of the inter-dependence of the set of problems identified;
5. a comparative summary of the inconvenience, quality and interaction tables.

Each card has the format shown in Figure 4.

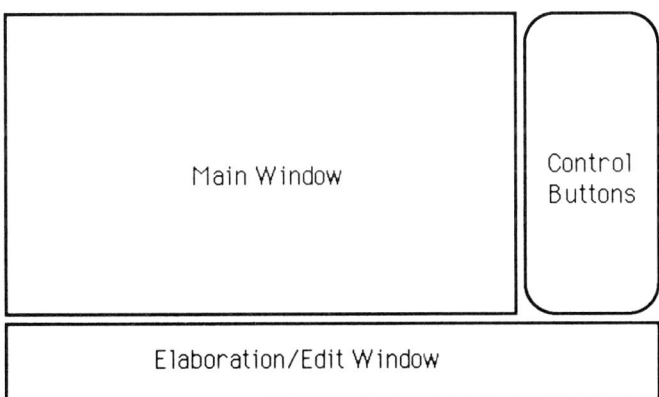

Figure 4: SOP Card Format

The screen is divided into three parts:

1. The *main window*, either contains a grid for the analysis tables or a scrolled field for the summary of the current situation.
2. The elaboration/edit window is used to hold a description of each screen and provide information on items that are selected on the screen. The principle items are the cells of each table. By selecting a cell the value stored is presented, together with an explanation of that value. Once elaborated the value and text can then be edited as required.
3. The control buttons are used to select from a range of operations including moving to a particular screen, printing the full current situation description and obtaining help on the use of SOP.

Figure 5 shows the actual appearance of the card providing the current situation overview.

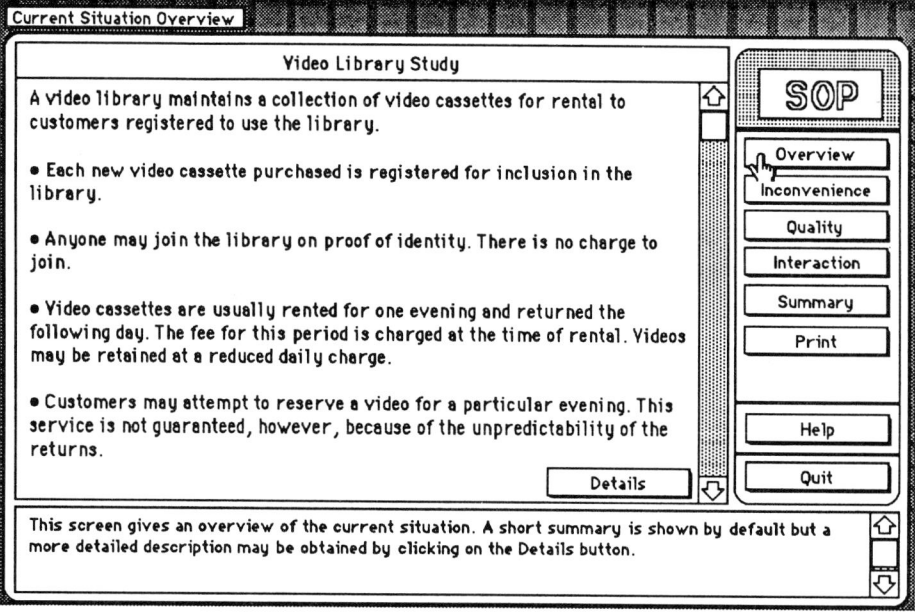

Figure 5: Current Situation Overview Screen

The summary and details of the current situation are accessed through the same card. The summary is shown by default and the details obtained by selecting the button at the bottom right hand side of the main window. When the details are revealed, the button at the bottom of the main window is replaced by one named "Summary". When this is selected the card reverts to its initial state. The elaboration/edit window at the bottom of the card is used solely to provide a description of the purpose of the card. The text in any of the windows may be edited directly.

Figure 6 shows the actual appearance of the quality analysis card. On this or any of the analysis cards, individual cells in the table can be selected for elaboration. Figure 6, for example, shows the case where the efficiency estimate for problem 6 has been chosen. The quality attributes, problems and summation signs can also be selected for explanation. The control button "Calculate" when selected produces the sums on the right hand side and bottom of the table.

The inconvenience, interaction and summary cards have a similar form and operate in the same way. The summary card contains the sums (in normalised form) that appear at the bottom of the three main analysis tables.

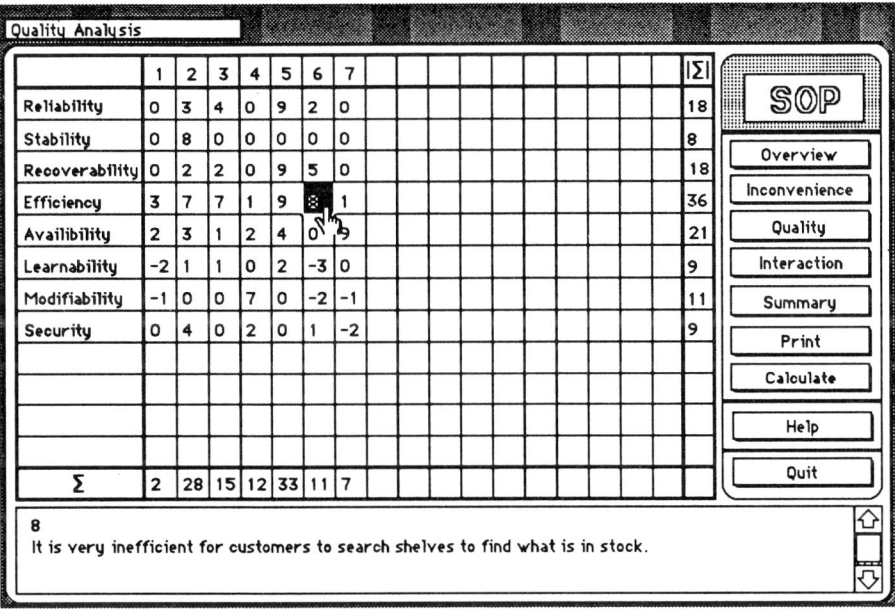

Figure 6: Quality Analysis Screen

4. CONCLUSIONS

This paper has suggested an approach to systems analysis in which emphasis is placed on gaining a full understanding of the problems in a current situation before considering the requirements of a desirable target situation. The nature of problems varies enormously and while most are technical, some are social and others are political [17]. All problems, regardless of their type, require full analysis before improvements can be made. The analysis proposed here covers three relationships: the inconvenience of problems to those whom they effect, the impact of problems on the quality of the current situation and the interdependence among problems. Such a treatment produces a substantial amount of information which has to be managed effectively if it is to be of value to those taking decisions. SOP is introduced as an example of a tool that can help with this process. The approach it supports is consistent with the growing trend towards increased quality [e.g. 18] and formality [21] in Systems and Software Engineering.

The discussion has been illustrated through the analysis of the operation of a video library and the problems that it presents. The experience of developing the library example, and other similar exercises, has convinced the authors of the benefit of analysing systems in this way.

The initial impetus for the work was a concern to improve rigour in the requirements capture and analysis phase of software development - the phase that is often crucial to the ultimate success or failure of a project [19]. The technique suggested here makes progress in that direction. The approach also has wider application in that it can be used in any context where inter-dependent facts need to be documented and analysed [e.g. 20]. It has been applied, for example, to the task of prioritising research objectives and is currently being used to help assess project selection.

The basic objective of the paper, to suggest an approach to systems analysis that separates the reasons *why* a system change is needed from a consideration of *what* can be done to satisfy that change is not fully met. In all three analysis tables the influence of possible solutions is felt even though the solutions are not usually addressed explicitly. It remains to be seen whether any further separation is possible or desirable. The fundamental difficulty is that the articulation of a problem often carries with it the concept of (or belief in) a solution and the two may not always be distinguishable. Nevertheless, the approach suggested enforces a systematic investigation of a current situation and yields a detailed description that gives a firm platform from which to launch an attack on the definition of a more favourable state of affairs - the target situation. It seems likely that this situation can be analysed in a similar way to that described for problems and work is continuing in that direction.

Acknowledgements
The authors of this paper would like to thank the director of the British Telecom Research Laboratories for permission to publish the paper. The authors are also

very grateful to numerous other people in British Telecom who have commented on the ideas presented here, especially Gino Martin and Huw Roberts. Dave Bustard is particularly grateful to Alan Stoddart and Charles Jackson of British Telecom, for arranging the research fellowship during which the work described was undertaken. This is part of a larger, long-term project at British Telecom, investigating ways of automating the requirements capture and analysis process.

References

1   Cohen, B., Harwood, W.T. and Jackson, M.I.: *The Specification of Complex Systems*, Addison-Wesley, 1986
2   Gilb, T.: *Principles of Software Engineering Management*, Addison Wesley,. 1988
3   Brackett, J.W.: *Software Requirements*, SEI Curriculum Module SEI-CM-19-1.0, Software Engineering Institute, Dec 1988
4   Longworth, G.: *Realistic User Requirements*, NCC Publications, 1983
5   *The STARTS Guide*, 2nd ed., Chapter 4, NCC Publications, 1987
6   Dubois, E. et al: *A Data Model for Requirements Engineering*, Proc. 2nd International Conference on Data Engineering, IEEE, 1986
7   Mullery, G.: *CORE - a method for controlled requirements specification*, Proc. 4th International Conference on Software Engineering, 1979
8   Mullery, G.: *Acquisition - Environment*, in Paul, M. and Siegert, H. (eds): *Distributed Systems: methods and tools for specification*, Lecture Notes in Computer Science 190, Springer-Verlag, 1985
9   Smith, M.J. and Kokotovich, N.M.: *Documenting an Organisation's Computer Requirements*, Wiley, 1985
10   Roman, G.C.: *A Taxonomy of Current Issues in Requirements Engineering*, Computer, Vol 18, No. 4, pp 14-21, 1985
11   Meyer, B.: *Object-oriented Software Construction*, Prentice-Hall, 1988
12   Kitchenam, B.A. and Walker, J.G.: *The Meaning of Quality*, Proc. Software Engineering 86, Peter Peregrinus, 1986
13   Shafer D.: *HyperTalk Programming*, Hayden Books, Indianapolis, 1988
14   Apple Corporation: *Hypercard User's Guide*, 1988
15   Arthur Young Ltd: *Information Engineering Methodology*, 1989
16   Millar, G.A.: *The Magical Number Seven Plus or Minus Two: some limits on our capacity for processing information*, The Psychological Review, Vol. 63, pp. 81-97, 1956
17   RACE Project 1023: BEST, a methodological approach to system specification.
18   Rigby, P., Stoddart, A. & Norris, M.T.: *Assuring Quality in Software - practical experience of attaining ISO 9001*, BT Engineering Journal, Vol. 8,

Part 4, 1990

19 Boehm, B., *Software Engineering Economics*, Prentice Hall International, 1981

20 Foster, J.: *Priority Control in Software Maintenance*, Proc. 7th International SETSS Conference, Bournmouth, 1989

21 McDermid, J.: *The Role of Formal Methods in software development* Journal of Information Technology vol 2 no 3, 1987

22 Checkland, P.: *Systems Thinking, Systems Practice*, Wiley, 1981

23 French, S.: *Decision Theory*, Ellis Horwood 1988

Presenting an Entity model using hierarchical abstraction

D J FLYNN and H K H YUE

Department of Computation
University of Manchester Institute of Science and Technology
Sackville Street
Manchester
M60 1QD
UK

1 INTRODUCTION

Although Entity models have been used successfully for some time now as an aid to user communication during systems development, there are still problems concerned with the size and complexity of typical Entity model diagrams (Vermeir 1983, Bryce and Hull 1986).

We describe a Presentation framework which, using an existing Entity model, allows for the display of different levels of detail of the model, using a graphical and textual interface. The framework has been implemented in software which adopts a browsing approach, and aims, through the use of abstraction, to assist users to manage model complexity. We have extended the expressive power of the model to allow for the aggregation of entities into higher-level entities, and have emphasised a hierarchical structuring which modularises the model into levels of detail. There are three elements to our Presentation framework approach:

(1) Two basic levels of detail are defined, based on common Entity model abstractions. The Overview level allows users only to see entities and entity relationships, while the Detailed level shows attributes, entity generalisation hierarchies, and relationship names and functionality.

(2) The Overview level is itself abstracted into higher level entities, based on an approach in (Feldman and Miller 1986).

(3) In addition to the facilities for the reduction in complexity, we have also provided, in a limited way, for information on the Detailed level to be presented from a "fact-based" viewpoint as well as from the more orthodox "entity-based" viewpoint (Kent 1986).

The context in which the framework might be used is that of a designer or a user validating an Entity model, or a programmer requiring knowledge about a system represented in the model in order to perform a maintenance activity.

Section 2 introduces terminology and concepts relating to the Entity-Relationship model and then examines these with respect to their potential for hierarchical structuring of a given Entity model. Section 3 then discusses the need for more than one level of entity to permit additional hierarchical structuring, and the work of Feldman and Miller is then considered in Section 4, who propose two such additional levels of entity. The ER model is extended to allow the additional typed entities by providing an aggregation abstraction operator.

Section 5 describes the functional requirements of our Presentation framework, while Section 6 gives a description of the main aspects of the tool, with diagrams showing the user interface. The tool is implemented in Pascal on an Apollo DN3000 graphic workstation. Section 7 briefly discusses related work. Finally, Section 8 contains a discussion with problems raised, future work, and conclusions.

2 CHARACTERISTICS OF THE ENTITY MODEL

2.1 Introduction

We use the term *ER (Entity-Relationship) model* to refer to a modelling language, typically based on the concepts of *entity*, *attribute*, and *relationship*, which is used to describe objects of interest in an application domain. The description is expressed in a form (usually diagrammatic) which we term an *Entity model* and which forms part of the specification of a desired system.

Since the ER model was first defined (Chen 1976), there have been many attempts to extend it to capture wider application aspects (Navathe and Pillalamarri 1988). The ER model considered here is one which is in common use within the domain of commercial Information systems, in that it does not distinguish between strong and weak entities, it excludes attributes of relationships, and is extended to allow for generalisation. Generalisation is an abstraction whereby similar object types are viewed as a single, higher level, object type. For example, we may generalise the entity types aircraft, land vehicle, and boat into the more generic entity type vehicle.

2.2 Requirement for a model overview

Aims - we are concerned with an application of the notion of **abstraction** to an Entity model, to provide improved diagrammatic presentation facilities for different types of users. By the term abstraction we mean the process of hiding insignificant detail, although we will also employ the term as a noun, where it refers to a higher-level object which refines into lower-level detail.

Traditionally, an Entity model has been held in one, diagrammatic form only. However, the advent of CASE tools has made it practicable to maintain a central, machine-readable version of the Entity model, giving the freedom to map this central model into many different forms.

Existing Entity model - a 'raw' Entity model is a rather flat diagram, as only one level of detail is available. This may not be appropriate for every need, and we have taken a pragmatic approach to the problem by identifying (at least) two levels of detail which are required when inspecting an Entity model.

Firstly, there is the requirement to view detailed information concerning all the entities, attributes, and relationships in the Entity model. This is the current situation for almost all CASE tools. We term this level the **Detailed** level.

Secondly, in contrast to the first requirement, there is a need for more of an overview of the diagram. This might show only entities and entity relationships, and would hide lower level detail. We term this level the **Overview** level.

The improvement offered by this second requirement is that diagram complexity is reduced. This makes it easier to search for and understand the information that is required. The use of such an overview might be to understand how a given entity in one area of an organisation relates to entities in other areas. For example, a maintenance programmer may need to estimate the impact of a proposed change to an entity. Another example is that of a departmental manager who needs to check that the key entities within his or her department are present.

Levels of detail available - the possibilities for more than one level of detail within the ER model are three-fold, using the abstractions that already exist in many models. A discussion of these abstractions may be found in (Urban and Delcambre 86, Navathe and Pillalamarri 88). Firstly, the *entity* may be viewed as an **aggregation** abstraction with respect to its attributes, and so we may regard entity attributes as being on a lower level of detail. We may often want to know, for example, which entities are related to a particular entity, without being concerned with the entity attributes.

Secondly, *relationships* between entities may possess relationship names, cardinalities, and optionalities, all of which may be regarded as being on a lower level of detail, with respect to the relationship itself. For example, we may simply wish to know about the existence of relationships between a given entity and other entities, leaving the detail of the relationships until later.

Thirdly, a given *entity* may be both a **generalisation** abstraction of lower-level entities (possessing subtypes), as well as being a part of such an abstraction itself (having supertypes). When we are on the Detailed level, focusing on a particular entity, we may need to see all the related entities within the hierarchy. However, on the Overview level, it may be sufficient to show only the topmost entity in the hierarchy.

In the first element of our approach, we provide both the Overview and the

Detailed levels for an Entity model. However, in addition, to reduce the extent of complexity on the lower level, we allow, for an entity as the unit of focus, the entity attributes, relationships, and generalisation hierarchy to be displayed separately in full detail. Thus, a user who wishes only to see the detail of attributes for an entity is not bothered by relationship or generalisation hierarchy detail.

Existence of multiple viewpoints - when browsing through an Entity model, the construct which is normally the centre of focus is the entity. Attributes are regarded as being related to "their" entity, and relationships emanate from entities radially, like spokes from the hub of a wheel. This approach is thus based on an entity viewpoint. We regard this as rather restrictive, and in our framework we have allowed a relationship to be selected as the focus of enquiry. This approach shows the related entities from the viewpoint of the relationship, rather as "attributes" of the relationship. These two views correspond approximately to the "entity-based" and "fact-based" views discussed in (Kent 86).

3 LEVELS OF ENTITY

3.1 The need for different levels of entity

The types of abstraction described in the previous section are helpful, but they are not enough. The problem is that the Overview level is based on the entity as the fundamental unit, and an Entity model may contain several hundreds of entity types. Opinions differ as to the upper limit on numbers of objects for comprehensibility of a single diagram, ranging from 20 (Vermeir 1983) to 100-200 (Bryce and Hull 1986).

To reduce the complexity of such models, we may apply a further abstraction operation which will operate on entity types themselves. This will be different to the generalisation operation discussed above.

The general effect of such an operation is to produce an abstraction which we may term a "abstract" entity type, and instances of this type will therefore be "ordinary" entity types. A high level Entity model will then consist of several of these abstract entity types, with their inter-relationships. Such a model will be simpler to understand as it will contain fewer objects than the lower level model. This principle is well-known in the Data flow diagram approach, where a top level process is elaborated in terms of its more detailed components.

We may further apply the abstraction operation to the abstract entity types, and so on, until we create enough levels of abstraction to provide the required degrees of overview. The Entity model will thus consist of a multi-level hierarchy, with ordinary entity types on the lowest level and abstract entity types on higher levels, with each level (excepting the lowest) being an abstraction of its lower level.

The ability to understand such an abstract model depends in part on the abstract entity types possessing semantics, in the same way that ordinary entity types are assigned names, and it would be an additional task in the Entity model construction process to identify abstract object types in the application that were meaningful and to use these as candidates for abstract entity types. The user views which emerge during the construction process may be considered as a possibility.

3.2 Uses of a multi-level Entity model
The most obvious way for the model to be used would be:

(1) for a user to select the abstract entity that contains the detail required. The entities into which this refines will be presented, and the user may then select, for example, a related group of these entities for more detailed examination. The higher level thus acts as a navigational aid or map, in this example.

(2) for a user to obtain an overview of, for example, a part of the organisation by selecting the level required, and then viewing the abstract entities and their relationships with entities in other parts of the organisation. These relationships represent relationships between lower level entities.

The presence of abstract entity types in such a multi-level Entity model has also **added** to the information we have captured about the target system, as they are units into which the organisation groups its entity types. We may also see more clearly the situation where an "ordinary" entity is a refinement of two or more abstract entities.

4 ABSTRACTIONS OF FELDMAN AND MILLER

4.1 Introduction

Subject area and Information area - the notion of abstract entity (we omit the term type now for brevity) may be seen in recent work (Feldman and Miller 1986) in the forms of the Subject and Information areas. An Information area is an abstraction of ordinary entities, and it is formed by grouping together ordinary entities which have a property in common. Similarly, a Subject area is an abstraction of information areas which possess a common property.

They thus propose a three-level ER model, where, broadly, the top level consists of Subject areas, the middle level consists of Information areas, and the lowest level consists of ordinary entities. However, certain ordinary entities, termed major entities, may appear on any level in the diagrammatic representation.

The semantics of their Subject area and Information area abstractions (the semantics of the relationship between the abstraction and its constituent entities) may be expressed in a term such as "part of", or "belonging to". For example, in figure 1, Stock handling is an Information area which is an abstraction of entities including Region, and Region may be said to "belong to" Stock handling.

Diagrammatic representation - to reduce diagrammatic complexity of the Entity model, they suggest that the middle and lower level diagrams should be partitioned. The middle level consists of a set of disjoint diagrams, one diagram for each Subject area, with each diagram containing the Information areas of the Subject area. Similarly, the lowest level consists of a set of disjoint diagrams, with one diagram for each Information area, each diagram containing the "ordinary" entities of the information area. Major entities may appear on any level.

Each lower level diagram corresponds to an abstract entity on the next higher level diagram, as that abstract entity is the abstraction of the objects represented in the lower level diagram. The set of diagrams representing the Entity model thus consists of a tree, where the root node is the diagram (termed 'High level view') containing Subject areas, the middle nodes are diagrams containing Information areas, and the leaf nodes are diagrams containing ordinary entities.

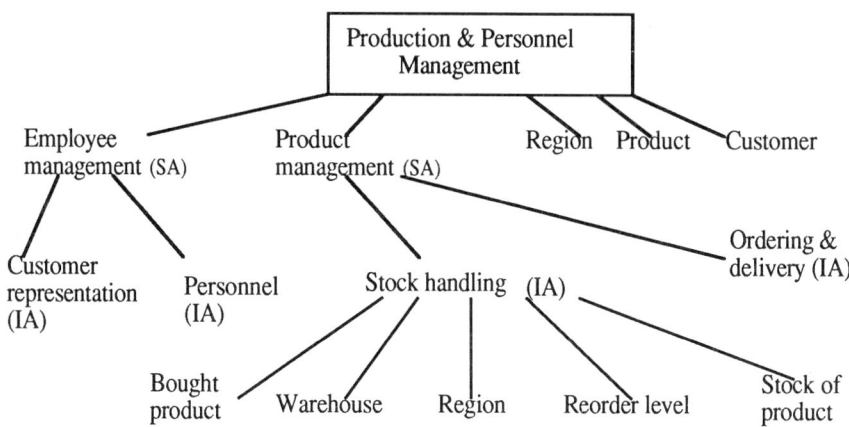

Figure 1. Structured Entity model entities forming example

4.2 Determination of Information and Subject areas

Distinction between major and minor entities - a preliminary step is to distinguish major entities from among ordinary entities, and the main determinant of a major entity is that all its relationships to other entities should be 1:N (N ≥ 1). That is, an instance of the major entity type can be uniquely identified from an instance of any related entity type. In addition, a major entity must appear in more than one Information area. Entities which are not major are minor, and cannot appear in more than one Information area.

Determination of Information areas - the main step in determining Information areas is to find the "logical horizon" of each entity. The "logical horizon" of an entity encloses itself and those entities which can be uniquely identified from that entity. Thus, it can be established from the chain of N:1 (N ≥ 1) relationships emanating from the entity.

The logical horizons which result (not all entities will have logical horizons) thus contain entities clustered on the basis of identifying another entity. Information areas are now determined by selecting those logical horizons whose entities do not overlap (or do not overlap by much) with other logical horizons. Where entities (minor) do overlap, they must be assigned to only one Information area. Major entities emerge more clearly from this process and will appear in several Information areas.

Determination of Subject areas - using the Information areas and major entities determined, an Entity model is drawn, showing relationships between major entities and entities within an Information area as entity-Information area relationships. Logical horizons are drawn and Subject areas determined in similar fashion to Information areas.

Limitations on entity clustering - using the clustering method described above does not result in a set of disjoint Information areas. There are two reasons for this. Firstly, major entities are, in effect, entities which are so important that they cannot be clustered within any one Information area. Major entities are thus shown in all the Information areas in which they occur.

Secondly, although minor entities only belong to one Information area, they will often have relationships to entities in other Information areas. This is due to the fact that clustering takes place on entities only, and doesn't include entity relationships.

4.3 Extending the Entity model

We may informally extend the ER model to allow explicitly for the abstraction of Information area (and further similar abstractions) by providing an *aggregate* constructor, as, from the discussion concerning the semantics of the area abstractions, it is evident that **aggregation** abstraction is involved. Hence, assuming we have defined types *major* and *minor* entity:

type information area = *aggregate* (information area name)

    information area name : string;
    major entities : SET OF major entity;
    minor entities : SET OF minor entity;
    relationships :   SET OF entity relationships;
end

5 REQUIREMENTS AND SOFTWARE

5.1 Requirements

The main requirement was for a presentation framework to allow an Entity model to be viewed on several levels of detail. A secondary requirement was to allow for more than one viewpoint of the model. Finally, the framework had to allow for users wanting detailed information of a small part of the model.

We decided to implement, for demonstration purposes, a four-level model, consisting of Subject area, Information area, Overview, and Detailed levels. We have thus combined the two-level model of Section 3 with the three-level model of Feldman and Miller in Section 5, by splitting their bottom level into Overview and Detailed levels.

5.2 Architecture

The Presentation framework software has a simple architecture, which is composed of three parts, and may be seen in figure 2. The Presentation interface handles all the interaction between the users and the Inquiry functions, and is designed in icon and menu form. It allows for the display of different levels of an Entity model with a graphics as well as a textual interface.

The Inquiry functions generate different forms of queries concerning the Entity model. The user can make a query through the Presentation interface to initiate a particular inquiry function on the desired Entity model and obtain the relevant information in textual or graphical form. The Entity model database contains the Entity models (in machine-readable form) which are to be viewed. The software is implemented in Pascal and Apollo Dialogue and GMR packages on an Apollo DN3000 workstation.

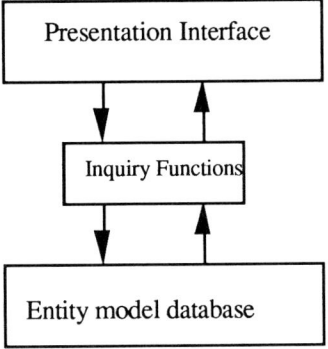

Figure 2. Presentation framework architecture

5.3 Inquiry functions

The inquiry functions which have been implemented are:

(a) Show High-level view - the user has a global view of the structured Entity model. The Subject areas, major entities, and their inter-relationships are shown.

(b) Select Subject area - the user may select the Subject area of interest and the relevant major entities, Information areas, and inter-relationships are shown.

(c) Select Information area - Information areas consist of major entities, appropriate minor entities, their inter-relationships, and relationships to other Information areas. All these objects may be shown.

The user is able to view the full detail of any object on the Detailed level by selecting the object required using the viewing facilities described next.

(d) Viewing facilities - the viewing facilities allow a user to view a diagram, or part of a diagram, in which the user is interested on a lower level of detail. When used on entities within an Information area, this allows a view of the Detailed level. The facilities may also be used within the High-level view and

Subject areas, to control the amount of detail presented.

(1) Show attributes - the user may view the attributes of any entity by indicating the entity which is the focus of interest.

(2) Show generalisation hierarchy - by indicating the relevant entity, the user may view its generalisation hierarchy, in both graphical and textual form. Different kinds of hierarchy, such as network or tree, may be displayed.

(3) Show relationship details - the user may view all the relationships between any **two** entities, graphically and textually, by indicating the required entities. The order in which the entities are indicated affects the roles of the relationships that are displayed. Self-related entities may also be indicated.

(4) Show inter-relationships between entities - the user may view all the relationships between **two or more** different entities by indicating the relevant entities. To avoid over-complexity in graphical display, the maximum number of entities that can be indicated is four. In the graphical display, the number of different relationships that exist between each pair of related entities is shown. The detail of these relationships may be shown in textual form.

(5) Show related entities - the user may see all related entities and relationships to a given entity by indicating that entity. The maximum number of related entities shown is limited to eight. Where there are more than eight entities, a new display is generated. Numbering exists in the graphical displays to indicate the number of relationships that exist between each pair of entities.

(6) Show common relationships - the user may see all the entities involved in a relationship by supplying the name of the relationship required (the "fact-based" view). A use for this would be to check on entity relationships spanning Information areas, as the relationship name would be an entity name.

Scrolling facilities are available as, for a large model, the windows may not be large enough to cope with the required information.

6 PRACTICAL EXAMPLE

6.1 Example Entity model

This section will describe the use of some of the main Inquiry functions, and will also serve to illustrate the Presentation interface. The Entity model on which it is based is shown in figure 1 (drawn partially from Feldman and Miller). This shows two Subject areas, Employee management and Product management, with three major entities, Region, Product and Customer. Product management contains two Information areas, Ordering & delivery, and Stock handling, which contains the minor entities Warehouse, Reorder level, and Stock of product.

Figure 3- High level view. This refers to the highest level of the structured Entity model. The major entities and the Subject area abstract entities are shown as rectangular boxes in the Entity-list window (bottom window of figure 3). The default mode of the Presentation framework is entity mode, and the list of entities is always given as soon as a viewing area (High level, Subject area, Information area) is selected. To list the relationships of the chosen viewing area, the rectangular box containing the string 'Relationships' at the top of the right-hand side of the Entity-list window is selected with the cursor and mouse button.

The figure also shows the inter-relationships of the entities Region, Customer and Employee management, obtained by selecting the 'Show inter-relationships' Inquiry function, and then selecting these entities.

Figure 4- Information areas: Show attributes. The attributes of the entities Bought product, Stock of product, Warehouse and Ordering & delivery are listed textually with the symbol "#" attached to identifying attributes. For Information area entities (shown by an *) attribute-value pairs (concerning contained entities) are shown. One entity only may be selected if desired.

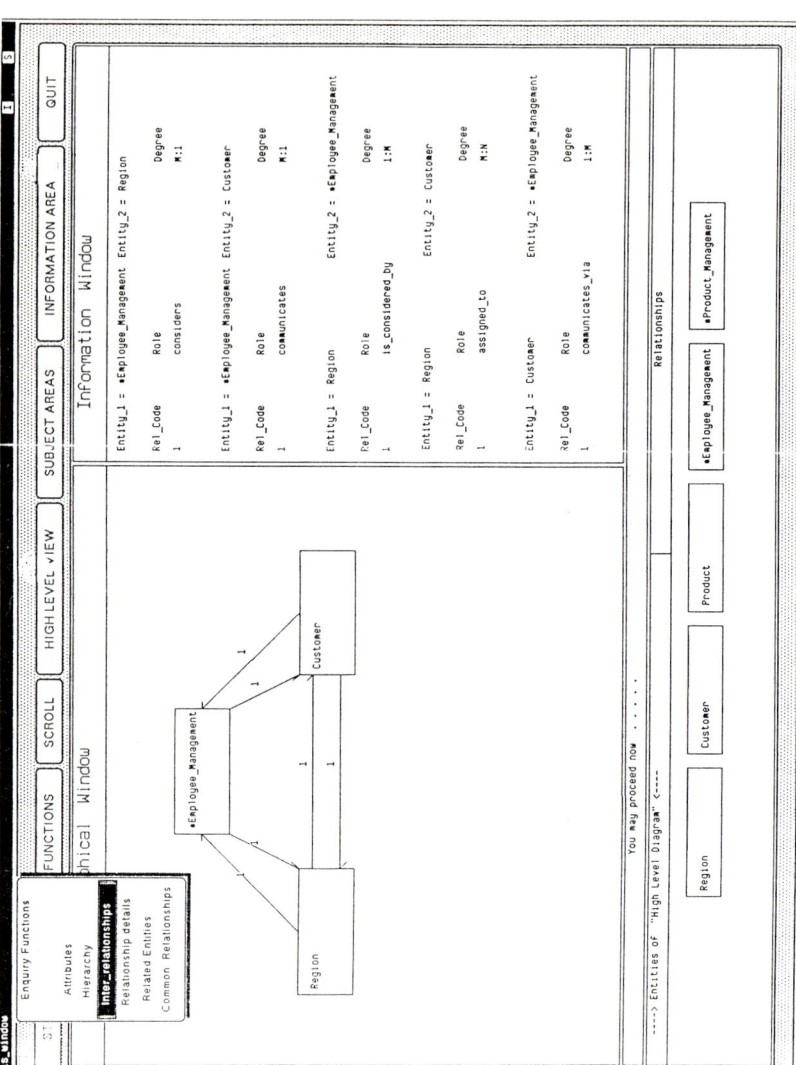

Figure 3. High level view

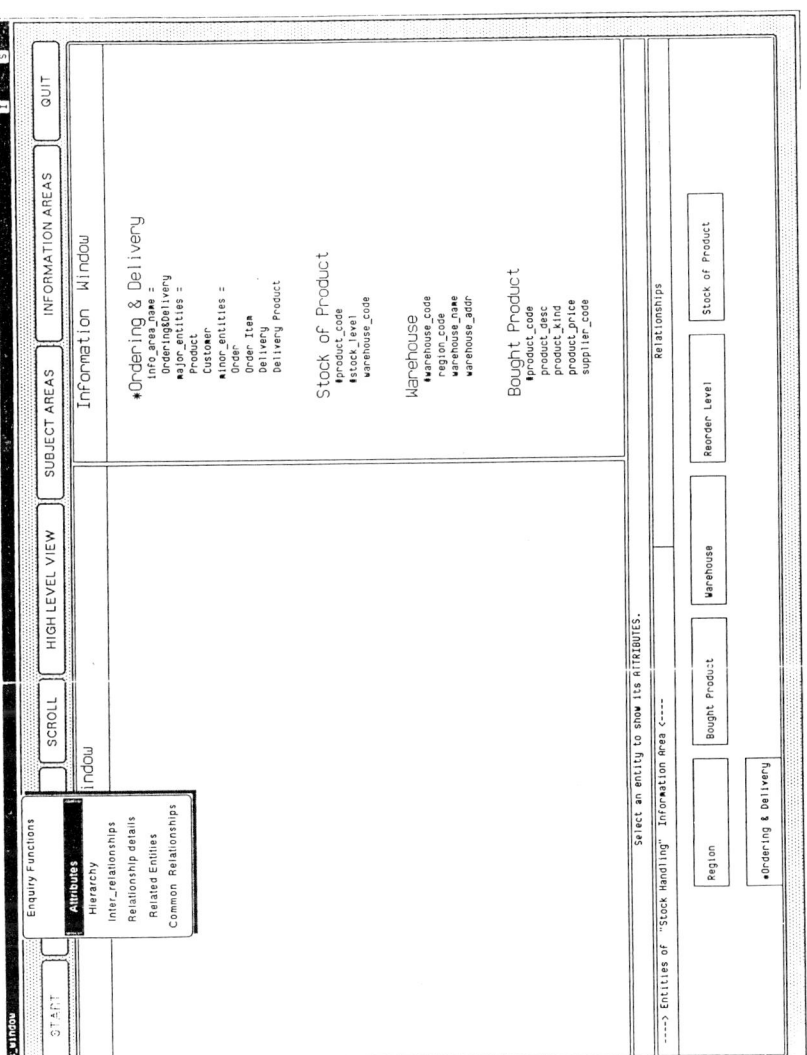

Figure 4. Stock handling Information area - show Attributes

Figure 5- Show hierarchy. The indicated entity is Bought Product, and the standard graphical convention is followed whereby higher objects are supertypes and lower objects are subtypes.

7 COMPARISON TO RELATED WORK

Related work in the main combines a browsing function with other activities such as model design, query specification, and query retrieval, especially using graphical interfaces to databases. For example, the SNAP system (Bryce and Hull 1986) allows browsing on a central graphical model which can be scrolled to show different sections, and which permits generalisation hierarchy edges to be shown or hidden. They also provide a brief survey of earlier, related literature. In SKI (King and Melville 1984), as well as ISIS (Goldman et al 1985) and "Living in a database" (LID) (Fogg 1984), access may also be had to an underlying database of type instances represented in the model, and SKI provides a graphical interface to the selection of individual objects, where detail may be refined into attributes and subtypes.

ISIS and LID allow navigation through a model from one entity-like object to another, with detail being presented as an object is viewed, rather than under user control. All the above systems also have model design facilities. The ERDDS system (Springsteel and Chuang 1988) is a database design system which provides a limited amount of pop-up detail for specified objects.

None of the above systems has facilities for structuring the model with abstract entity types such as Information or Subject area, and so their complexity is scarcely reduced. This is probably due to the fact that the systems are mainly oriented to query specification. Although a scheme for model modularisation is described in (Vermeir 1983), which partitions a model into "scopes", no facilities for abstracting the scopes or showing levels of detail are discussed. In addition, SNAP does not hide relationships or attributes, SKI omits relationship-centred views, and ISIS and LID, presumably assuming knowledge of a whole model, do not provide help for determining the model context in which a user is trying to navigate. Finally, a different, more interpretive approach to entity clustering

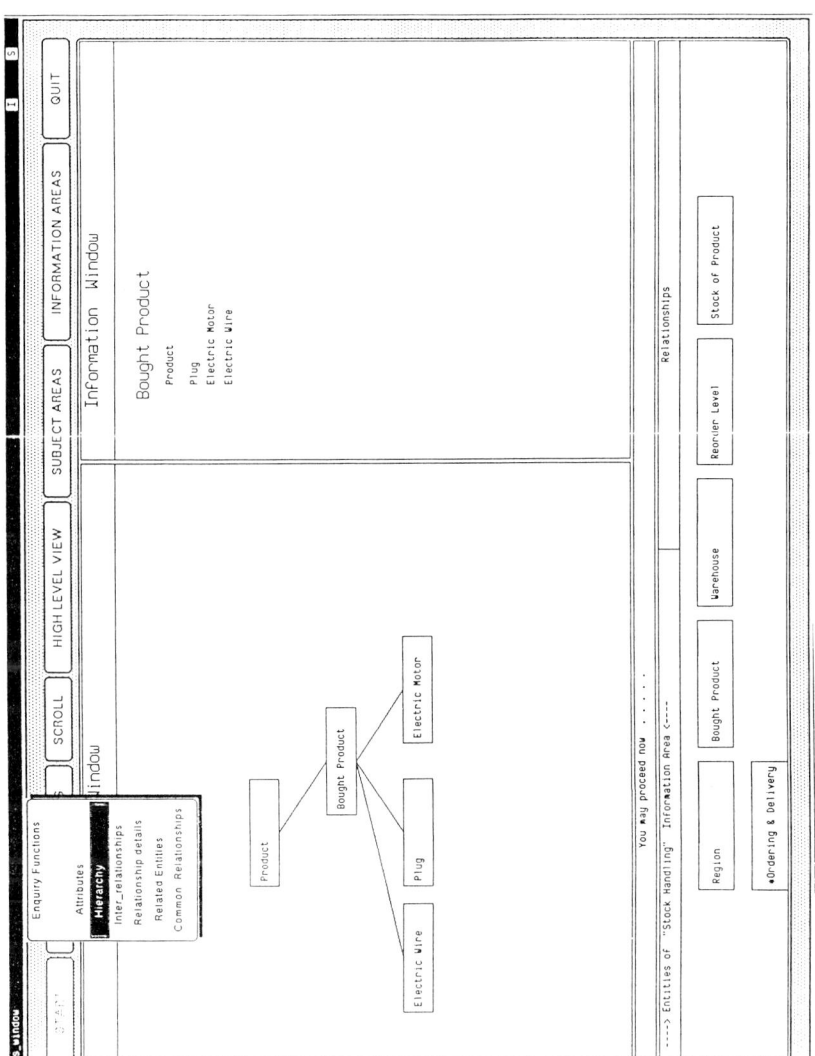

Figure 5. Stock handling Information area - show Hierarchy

which has not been implemented may be found in (Teorey et al 1989).

8 DISCUSSION

8.1 Summary

We have described an approach to structuring an Entity model using the principle of abstraction. The approach has three main elements. Firstly, we outlined two basic levels of detail for displaying the Entity model, based on common abstractions occurring in the ER model. On the Overview level, users were presented with only entities or entity relationships, so that their understanding should not be obscured by the detail available on the Detailed level.

On the Detailed level, full detail was available, but in such a way that the user had control over the extent of the detail. An individual entity could be selected, and its attributes, generalisation hierarchy, or relationships could be displayed separately or at the same time. In addition, a relationship (or relationships) could be selected, and role names, cardinality and related entities displayed.

Secondly, a relationship could also be selected as the unit of focus, this facility presenting a "fact-based" viewpoint of the information that differs to the normal entity-centred view.

The third element of the approach was to define two higher levels of abstract entity within an ER model, based on ideas from Feldman and Miller, using the aggregation abstraction, and a presentation tool framework based on an example Entity model containing four levels was implemented as a prototype for demonstrating the concepts.

8.2 Future work

One may form abstractions with different semantics, and it would obviously be possible to have different sets of Subject and Information areas based upon different properties which lower level entities had in common. For example, an organisation with a matrix structure may combine a view consisting of Subject and

Information areas based upon organisational functions, such as that used in the example in this paper, with a view based upon a product or service. This would require the introduction of such abstract entities into the model.

It may be noted that the effect of generalisation hierarchies on the clustering method of Feldman and Miller was not considered by them, and, where such hierarchies exist amongst minor entities, it may be more difficult to apply the method due to the fact that entity hierarchies may span Information areas if subtypes have relationships with other entities. An advantage of their method is that it is reasonably algorithmic, and could be made more so. An implementation of a tool for entity clustering based on modifications to the Feldman and Miller approach is presently underway.

We provided the ability to generate a restricted "fact-based" view, although it was incidental to our main aim of complexity reduction, as it came virtually for free with the software we produced. However, we may develop this aspect more in the future, perhaps extending it to abstract entities, so that a library of different views is available.

The general problem of drawing an unrestricted Entity model was encountered, and the limited time available for implementation meant, in our case, that the drawing algorithm could not be as sophisticated as we would have liked.

8.3 Conclusions

The ability of the framework to browse through a model on different levels of detail may be useful on completed models (for example, for maintenance programmers) or within individual views to assist in, for example, query specification. Although we have used an Entity model for our example, the principle may be applied to other semantic models. Very often, the notion of different views implies different levels of detail, and so the framework might also assist in view definition. Some further suggestions are made in (Urban and Delcambre 1987).

We see the main use of the Presentation framework as being for model validation, where it may help to clarify requirements. To use the framework effectively, however, we feel that it must be situated within an overall context of validation procedures. Although little research has been done on how users validate Entity models, there is more general empirically-based work, for example, (Flynn et al 1990), which is attempting to form the broad outline of the validation process.

Hierarchical structure may be built in to Entity models either at construction time, or later, and experimentation is required to develop effective structuring methods. However, in order to validate effectively, it is clearly necessary to identify a structuring method, as an additional activity, which should take place within the model construction process.

REFERENCES

(Bryce and Hull 1986)
D Bryce and R Hull. SNAP: a graphics-based schema manager. *Proceedings of the International Conference on Data Engineering*, Los Angeles, California, Feb 5-7, 1986. IEEE Computer Society, 1986, pp 151-164.

(Chen 1976)
P P Chen. The entity-relationship model: towards a unified view of data. *ACM Transactions on Database Systems*, **1**, 1, March 1976, pp 9-36.

(Feldman and Miller 1986)
P Feldman and D Miller. Entity model clustering: structuring a data model by abstraction. *The Computer Journal*, Vol 29, No 4, 1986, pp 348-360.

(Flynn et al 1990)
D J Flynn, R Warhurst, M Gibson, D Browne, and R Summersgill. An empirical study into the process of validating a specification. Submitted to *3rd IFIP Conference on Human-Computer Interaction (Interact '90)*, Cambridge, UK, 27-31 August 1990.

(Fogg 1984)
D Fogg. Lessons from a "Living in a database" graphical query interface. *Proceedings of the ACM SIGMOD International Conference on Management of Data*, B Yormark (ed), Boston, Massachusetts, Jun 18-21, 1984, pp 100-106.

(Goldman et al 1985)
K J Goldman, S A Goldman, P C Kanellakis, S B Zdonik. ISIS: interface for a semantic information system. *Proceedings of the ACM SIGMOD International Conference on Management of Data*, S Navathe (ed), Austin, Texas, May 28-31, 1985, pp 328-342.

(Kent 1986).
W Kent. The realities of data: basic properties of data reconsidered. *Database Semantics (DS-2)*, T B Steel, Jr and R Meersman (eds). Amsterdam, Elsevier, 1986, pp 175-188.

(King and Melville 1984)
R King and S Melville. Ski: a semantics-knowledgeable interface. *Proceedings of the 10th International Conference on Very Large Data Bases*, Singapore, Aug 27-31, 1984, pp 30-33.

(Navathe and Pillalamarri 1988)
S B Navathe and M K Pillalamarri. OOER: toward making the E-R approach object-oriented. *Proceedings of the 7th International Conference on Entity Relationship approach*, Rome, Italy, Nov 16-18, 1988. IEEE Computer Society, 1988, pp 55-76.

(Springsteel and Chuang 1988)
F N Springsteel and P J Chuang. ERDDS: the intelligent E-R-based database design system, yielding normal forms under extended regularity. *Proceedings of the 7th International Conference on Entity Relationship approach*, Rome, Italy, Nov 16-18, 1988. IEEE Computer Society, 1988, pp 211-230.

(Teorey et al 1989)
T J Teorey, G Wei, D L Bolton, and J A Koenig. ER model clustering as an aid for user communication and documentation in database design. *Communications of the ACM*, 32, 8, Aug 1989, pp 975-987.

(Urban and Delcambre 1986)
S D Urban and L M L Delcambre. An analysis of the structural, dynamic, and temporal aspects of semantic data models. *Proceedings of the International Conference on Data Engineering*, Los Angeles, California, Feb 5-7, 1986. IEEE Computer Society, 1986, pp 382-389.

(Urban and Delcambre 1987)
S D Urban and L M L Delcambre. Perspectives of a semantic schema. *Proceedings of the 3rd International Conference on Data Engineering*, Los Angeles, California, Feb 3-5, 1987. IEEE Computer Society, 1986, pp 485-492.

(Vermeir 1983)
D Vermeir. Semantic hierarchies and abstractions in Conceptual schemata. *Information Systems*, Vol 8, No 2, 1983, pp 117-124.

CASE, IPSE and AI

Evaluating Tool Support Interfaces, F. Long & M. Tedd
*Towards a Convergence in Knowledge-based and Conventional
   Software Engineering: Tools, Methods, Techniques,* L. Hickman

Evaluating Tool Support Interfaces

F.W. LONG & M.D. TEDD

Department of Computer Science
University College of Wales, Aberystwyth

Abstract

In 1985 we were awarded a grant by the British Ministry of Defence to study the practicability of tool support interfaces for the APSE. The project involved building a prototype implementation of the Common APSE Interface Set (CAIS) and evaluating it, both objectively, by measuring its performance, and subjectively, by assessing its usability.

This work led to our involvement in the ESPRIT funded Sapphire Project in which we evaluated the tool support interface PCTE and compared it with CAIS and, later, with CAIS-A.

This paper summarises our evaluations of these two TSI's and presents some conclusions from our evaluation and implementation work.

1 Introduction

During the development of the Ada Programming Language it was recognised in the Stoneman report [1] that modern software development should be given substantial support from the software environment (then referred to as an Ada Programming Support Environment, or APSE). Such environments later became known as Integrated Project Support Environments (IPSEs). Different organisations will require different software tools in their IPSE to support their own methods and practices, so we cannot expect a standard IPSE.

However, standards for tool portability and interoperability must be developed to encourage the software tool industry to build better and more sophisticated tools. It was realised that an IPSE could be built round a kernel which provided support for commonly used facilities like database utilities, process management, interprocess communication, distribution and user interface. The interface to this kernel could be standardised, so that tools written to this interface could be ported and used in different environments built on the standard kernel. Such kernel interfaces became known as Tool Support Interfaces (TSI's).

In the US, the Ada Joint Program Office set up the KAPSE Interface Team and KAPSE Interface Team in Industry and Academia (KIT/KITIA) to define a TSI called the Common APSE Interface Set (CAIS) [2]. This original version was always recognised as an interim definition with a number of 'deferred topics' which could not be addressed with the resources available. A revised version, CAIS-A [3], has been developed by a contractor to meet the requirements defined by KIT/KITIA in the "Requirements and Design Criteria for the Common APSE Interface Set" (RAC) [4].

In Europe, the ESPRIT Programme led to the development of a large number of software tools. In order to encourage portability of these tools, one of the first ESPRIT projects was to define a TSI for use by other ESPRIT projects. This project was called "A Basis for a Portable Common Tool Environment" and the interface it defined is known as PCTE. The PCTE interface specifications have been through a number of revisions but are now stable and available as C interfaces and as Ada interfaces [5, 6, 7].

PCTE has been further developed under the aegis of the Independent European Programme Group of NATO nations, Technical Area 13, into an enhanced TSI called PCTE+. This is also published as C and Ada interfaces and Issue 3 is now available [8].

2 Evaluation of CAIS

2.1 Implementation Work

The project has successfully implemented a prototype of the CAIS. Our work started in 1985, and so was based on the proposed MIL-STD-CAIS version dated 31 January 1985. However, cognisance has been taken of later versions of the CAIS and, where appropriate, the implementation described here has taken account of later versions. However, there has been no systematic attempt to bring the whole of this implementation up to the 1987 CAIS-1 standard (DOD-STD-1838).

Those parts of the CAIS that have not been implemented are mandatory and discretionary access control and the input/output packages associated with scroll terminals, form terminals, magnetic tape and file export.

Our CAIS prototype consists of a tool interface, which must be linked into every tool which uses the interface, and four separate, continuously running processes or "daemons". These four processes we call the Node Manager, the Process Manager, the Process Controller and the Queue Manager. The architecture of the prototype and the possible interactions between its components are shown in figure 1.

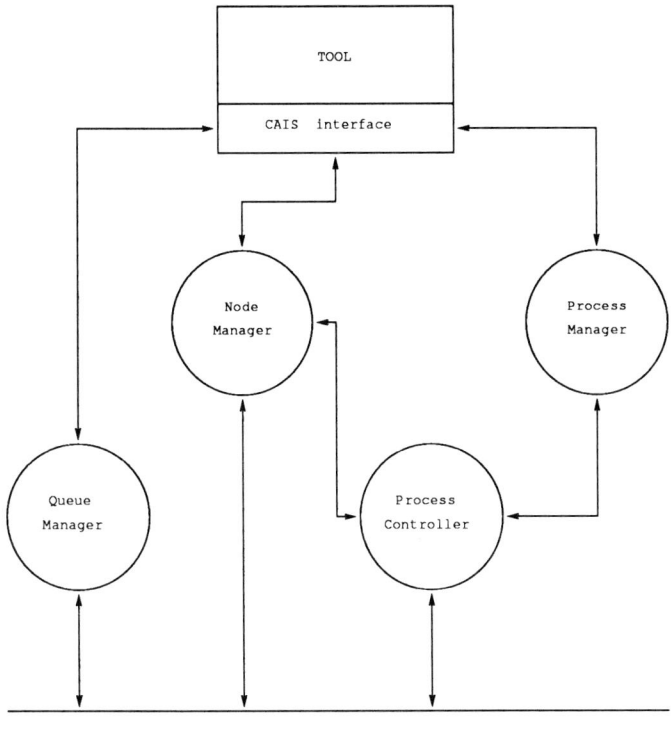

Figure 1: The KITE prototype architecture.

The "Manager" daemons are responsible for creating, looking after and deleting the CAIS entities after which they are named. The Process Controller is responsible for tactical control (*e.g.*, suspend and resume) of the CAIS processes.

Our prototype was implemented on a Sun 3/160 workstation on top of the Unix[1] BSD 4.2 (Sun v.3.4) operating system. The work took about three man years, 98% was coded in Ada and the remaining 2% in C. Most of the development work was done using the Verdix Ada Development System (ending up using version 5.41). However, when we came to run our prototype for any length of time we encountered a "heap creep" problem, so we switched to using the Alsys Ada System (version 3.2). Our timings were done on a Sun 3/50 workstation (using the Sun operating system v.3.5) with 4Mbytes of main memory and a Maxtor XT-4380S 300Mbyte disc. The manufacturers claim that the disc drive has an average seek time of 16 milliseconds and a

---

[1] Unix is a trademark of Bell Laboratories

transfer rate of better than 4Mbytes per second.

The port from Verdix to Alsys took about five man weeks. We encountered no real problems in the port which says much for the portability of Ada programs. The code sizes for the various components of our prototype are given in Table 1. For comparison, we give the Verdix code sizes as well as the Alsys sizes although these are not precisely comparable because development of the Alsys code continued after that of the Verdix.

Module	Statements	LOC	Alsys Executable (kbytes)	Verdix Exec. (kbytes)
Tool Interface	11,153	29,559	499	950
Node Manager	13,386	35,252	770	1040
Process Manager	3,551	9,430	344	352
Process Controller (C)	284	793	49	-
Queue Manager	3,158	9,200	286	400

Table 1: Code sizes.

In conclusion, we have shown that CAIS-1 (DOD-STD-1838) is implementable on top of Unix. Our experience has been such as to cause us to believe that CAIS-1 could be implemented on a wide range of operating systems (but see the remarks below on performance). A prototype implementation of most of CAIS-1 can be implemented in 3 man years. Although it is difficult to extrapolate from this, we believe that a production quality version would take somewhere between ten and twenty man years to complete.

2.2 Evaluation

In order to measure the performance of our prototype CAIS our implementation has been very heavily instrumented.

The instrumentation was designed to measure the amount of CPU time and disc activity performed within the prototype and the number of times sections of code were executed. The measurement of time was both the amount of time actually used by the CPU, and the elapsed time, as seen by the user of the prototype. Measurements were taken when the computer was otherwise "quiet".

The prototype was instrumented such that it was possible to make a detailed analysis right down to the individual routine, although the time taken to run the instrumentation also had to be taken into account when dealing with such fine granularity. When required, the accumulated statistics could be sent to log files.

From this instrumentation we have been able to calculate the resources required by the various parts of the CAIS and we have identified bottlenecks and potential problem areas. A summary of these findings is presented at the end of this section.

So that we could evaluate the CAIS more generally we designed the following five typical tasks or "scenarios" which one might wish to carry out using the CAIS.

Configuration Management Scenario. This scenario is a stylised configuration management tool-set which concentrates on recording derivations and solving the problems associated with bug tracing and system building. It is referred to as "CM" below.

CELT - Compile, Edit, Link & Test Tool. CELT simulates the actions performed by a compile, edit, link and test tool used during the development of Ada programs when bug fixing. Compile or test errors result in the edit phase being re-run, the cycle continuing until all detectable bugs are removed.

Conference Management Scenario. The object of this scenario was to produce a tool which would allow two or more users to confer with one another. This is a bit like the UNIX "talk" facility, except that this tool would not restrict the number of users to two.

Window Management System. This scenario simulates a "Window Manager" process. This process gives the ability for other processes to be run with output directed to windows (*i.e.*, specific areas) on the user's screen and input taken from the user's mouse and keyboard when appropriate (*i.e.*, when the window corresponding to the process is "active").

Design Editor. This scenario is a highly simplified version of a design editing tool. The tool is intended to assist users in the program or system design process, by allowing them to define objects and their relationships.

These scenarios were first designed in a stylised, task oriented manner and then they were mapped onto the CAIS. An evaluation was made of the ease of this mapping, of features of CAIS which helped with or hindered this mapping, of any "missing" features which would have been useful and of the performance of the final system.

The detailed results of the evaluation of each scenario could not be included in this paper but the conclusions are summarised here.

All our scenarios mapped quite easily onto CAIS, which feels like a nice "clean" interface to the toolwriter. We found no glaring omissions, apart from the lack of transactions, and the different facilities are certainly appropriate.

The node model of CAIS supported the design of the tools' data structures in a natural way. The integration of the node and process models was of particular help to the tool writer where data needed to be associated with particular processes.

The inter-process communication mechanisms (queues) provided by CAIS are quite high-level, so it was a pleasure to discover that these facilities were totally appropriate for our purposes.

Moreover, one of our researchers found a fairly simple CAIS tool on the network which he was able to install on top of our implementation with about two hours effort. This suggests that the CAIS will meet its primary objective, that of providing a portable tool interface.

At a more detailed level, the following points are worthy of note.

One aspect of CAIS that we found to be very good was the modelling of processes within the node model. We have fed this experience to the PCTE+ project and are pleased to see it being acted upon in PCTE+ version 2.

CAIS version 1.4 was expressed in terms of Ada packages in the worst possible way. That is, the combination of two different styles, parallel packages and one big package. (Parallel packages are a number of packages side by side). This problem was subsequently addressed by the CAIS team and the current CAIS-1 (MIL-STD-1838) has a much better way of presenting such an interface, using parallel packages, which we adopted.

As to the more detailed evaluation, careful instrumentation and measurement is essential in order to gain an understanding of what is happening within something as complex as our CAIS prototype.

Our feeling is that the performance figures for the scenarios are about a factor of ten away from being acceptable. This is also true for primitive operation times where, for example, our prototype takes approximately twelve seconds to create a process while we would expect an acceptable time for process creation to be no more than one second. (However, we understand that well known operating systems can take as much as six seconds to start a process.)

It is hard to prove, but we have few doubts that this factor of ten could be achieved in a production quality implementation which would cache a lot more information, as well as generally tuning the code.

2.3 Summary of Conclusions

This section looks at what the Aberystwyth KITE research team has learned from implementing and evaluating a prototype of CAIS.

From the analysis of our performance figures we conclude that our CAIS prototype is quite large and very slow. It is disc bound and still uses a substantial amount of CPU. 60% of its time is spent in CPU activity and the other 40% in disc activity.

The 60% CPU utilisation breaks down as follows:

    30% instrumentation
     6% inter-process communication
     6% LIST_UTILITIES
    18% rest of code

(LIST_UTILITIES is a CAIS package which manages lists. All attributes in CAIS are expressed as lists, even when they have a single value.)

In order to provide acceptable performance, a production quality CAIS would have to be about ten times faster than our prototype. By removing the instrumentation, using clever caching techniques to minimise disc activity and by using faster, optimising compilers, we believe that this factor of ten increase in speed is feasible.

In conclusion, we believe that modern tool support interfaces, such as CAIS, provide facilities which are useful for the tool writer and should enable software engineering tools to be produced more easily and more reliably.

Layered implementations of tool support interfaces (that is, implementing the interface strictly on top of a host operating system), are feasible now and will become even more acceptable as the underlying hardware becomes faster.

3 Evaluation of PCTE

We also became involved in the ESPRIT Sapphire Project. The main aim of this project was to port the Emeraude implementation of PCTE (Portable Common Tool Environment) to a number of computer hardware bases. However, part of the project was to be an evaluation of PCTE and a comparison of PCTE and CAIS.

3.1 Introduction

The motivation behind this experimentation was to provide an objective evaluation of the two tool support interfaces. We mapped three of the scenarios used in our CAIS evaluation onto PCTE, namely the Configuration Management, CELT and Conference Management scenarios. This enabled us to compare CAIS and PCTE both from the subjective point of view of the ease of mapping and unhelpful or missing features and from the more objective performance of the completed systems (although we were not able to instrument PCTE in the same way that we had with CAIS).

The instrumentation was confined to the Ada binding on top of PCTE and was designed to measure the amount of elapsed and CPU time consumed and the frequency at which key sections of code were executed. As for the KITE work the scenarios were all run on a Sun 3/50 with 4Mb of physical memory and a Maxtor XT-4380S 300Mbyte disc.

For further comparison we built a second implementation of CAIS, this time on top of PCTE. It may seem strange to implement a TSI with reduced functionality on top of one with more functionality. However, by so doing, we could compare the performance of our KITE CAIS prototype, which was a layered implementation on top of Unix, with that of the Sapphire CAIS prototype on top of PCTE, which could take advantage of Emeraude's hooks into the Unix kernel. Also, in implementing CAIS on PCTE, we learned a lot about PCTE. The CAIS on PCTE prototype was also believed to be useful from a tool portability perspective, raising the possibility of running CAIS-1 tools on PCTE implementations, without having to recode them to run directly on PCTE.

3.2 An Overview of the Second CAIS-1 Prototype

The following is a brief overview of the Sapphire CAIS-1 prototype. The purpose of this section is to give the reader some insight into the implementation of the prototype so that he/she will appreciate the differences between this and the KITE prototype.

Unlike the KITE prototype daemons were not used. Instead the entire interface code was linked into each tool requiring access to CAIS. The basic strategy was to define a machine independent, low level interface, onto which it would be quite straightforward to map CAIS, and also quite straightforward to map this interface onto PCTE (see figure 2). This gives three levels of interface, level one being CAIS, level 2 being the machine independent interface and level three being PCTE. With the exception of the package CAIS_TEXT_IO, all the CAIS implementation is expressed in terms of the facilities offered in level two.

In this implementation of CAIS we controlled concurrent database access at the PCTE level by the judicious use of protected locks. Transaction activities were also used to envelop atomic CAIS operations.

The layering offers a natural way of instrumenting the CAIS prototype. All the interface subprograms in levels one and three were instrumented, and only those subprograms in level two which were judged to be important enough were instrumented. Thus three levels of instrumentation are provided.

3.3 Scenario Performance on CAIS-1 on PCTE

The three scenarios used in this evaluation were run on this version of CAIS-1 in the same manner as they had been on the original CAIS-1 and detailed

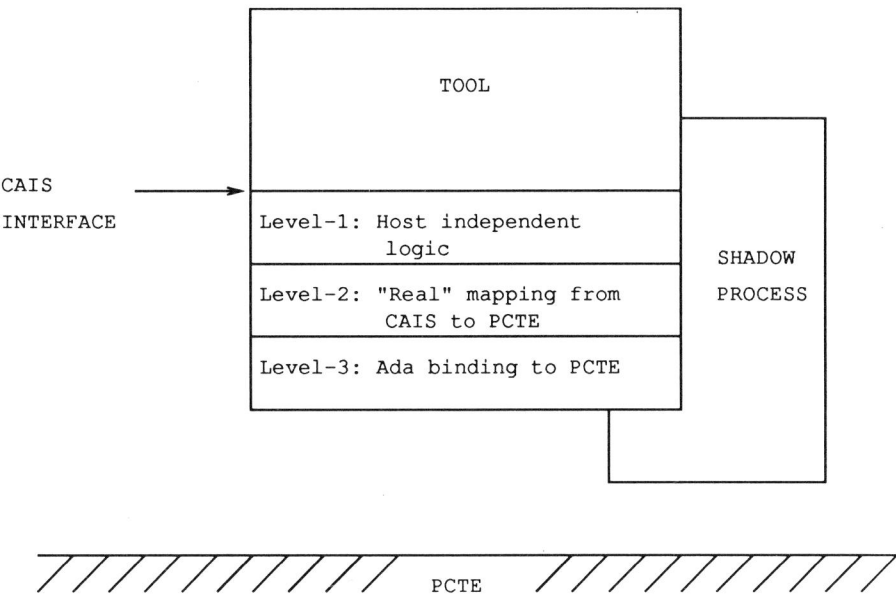

Figure 2: The Sapphire prototype architecture.

performance figures collected. These figures are directly comparable with those produced in the first evaluation. They are summarised in section 4.

3.4 Scenario Performance on PCTE

The three scenarios used in the evaluation of the second CAIS-1 prototype were also mapped directly onto PCTE. This gave us the opportunity to compare the facilities offered by the two tool support interfaces from the tool writers point of view. We also collected detailed performance measurements, as before, and these are also summarised in section 4.

4 Comparison of Performance Statistics

Tables 2 and 3 summarise the elapsed and CPU time (respectively) taken for each of the scenarios on each of the three TSI's.

Scenario	KITE CAIS	Sapphire CAIS	PCTE
Configuration Manager	42.33	111.42	3.95
CELT	151.94	100.62	8.20
Conferencing Manager	209.50	779.96	15.24

Table 2: Summary of elapsed times in seconds.

In addition to the figures derived from the scenarios we also ran ran a number of simple bench mark tests, each test being based on a particular CAIS-1

Scenario	KITE CAIS	Sapphire CAIS	PCTE
Configuration Manager	28.53	69.36	2.15
CELT	80.71	74.70	5.90
Conferencing Manager	115.96	298.62	2.84

Table 3: Summary of CPU times in seconds.

function. These tests were run on the KITE CAIS prototype and the Sapphire CAIS prototype.

Table 4 shows average elapsed and CPU times from running tests on a selection of "commonly" used CAIS-1 functions. Each operation was performed N times, where N was in this case 20.

The figures for spawning a process include creating the process node, setting up required relationships and attributes, and starting the new process.

CAIS-1838 Operation	KITE CAIS		Sapphire CAIS	
	CPU	Elapsed	CPU	Elapsed
OPEN (by path 1 element)	0.31	0.40	3.78	6.14
CLOSE	0.11	0.19	1.12	1.86
GET_NODE_ATTRIBUTE (user)	0.22	0.29	0.24	0.24
SET_NODE_ATTRIBUTE (user)	0.24	0.36	0.47	0.49
CREATE_NODE_ATTRIBUTE (user)	0.06	0.11	0.31	0.33
CREATE_NODE (structural)	1.60	2.93	2.65	4.46
CREATE_SECONDARY_RELATIONSHIP	0.19	0.23	1.19	2.34
SPAWN_PROCESS	—	6.62	—	23.65

Table 4: Bench mark results (seconds)

5 Discussion

Two major questions can be asked:

- Why was the KITE prototype more efficient than the Sapphire prototype?

- Why did the scenarios run so much faster on PCTE than on either of the other two CAIS prototypes?

5.1 KITE CAIS versus Sapphire CAIS

As stated in the Introduction, we started this project with the belief that CAIS on PCTE would be more efficient than CAIS on Unix. The PCTE OMS is designed around the entity, relationship and attribute model as is the CAIS database. As such the mapping of CAIS on top of PCTE should be far easier than CAIS on top of Unix; efficient facilities should already be there. As a direct result, detailed implementation work such as scheduling and caching is required less in the Sapphire prototype, there being more reliance on the quality of the Emeraude code. From the figures in the last section, both from running bench marks, and from the scenarios, it can be seen that we were wrong; CAIS on PCTE is substantially less efficient than CAIS on Unix.

From table 4 it can be seen that, overall, the Sapphire bench marks were ten times slower (CPU) than the equivalent KITE bench marks, when it was expected that they would be better. The difference between total CPU times for the three scenarios is much less, the Sapphire prototype being approximately two to three times as slow for the Configuration Manager and Conferencing Manager scenarios.

For CELT, the Sapphire prototype is faster than the KITE prototype. This is because the timings for CELT on the KITE prototype are dominated by TEXT_IO times which are much faster on the Sapphire prototype.

The question remains as to why the bench marks and scenario results should be so different, since the scenarios changed only slightly when ported to the Sapphire prototype.

The probable answer is that bench marks are an artificial means of measuring performance, performing the same function many times in succession, and allowing caching if caching is provided. The KITE prototype was able to do a substantial amounts of caching whereas the Sapphire prototype was not. Also, the number of system operations performed to (say) open a node handle, is greater in the Sapphire prototype than in KITE; there are approximately twice as many system operations, including the necessary use of transactions. Furthermore, more tuning could be done in the Sapphire prototype to reduce the number of system operations required for some of the CAIS operations.

Even after removing transactions, which it should be said only influence some of the above CAIS operations, the times were still slower for the Sapphire bench marks. For example to open a node handle without transactions takes on average 2.48 sec cpu time and 2.87 of elapsed time, a drop of over a second from the times with transactions, but still substantially more than the same operation on the KITE prototype.

Why does the Sapphire prototype need more system operations than the KITE prototype? Table 5 lists the operations required to open a node handle via a pathname of one element, e.g. 'USER(CWL) .

For this CAIS operation the Sapphire prototype calls nearly six times as many system operations and is twelve times slower. Each of the operations is repeated in order to open the current process node. In the KITE prototype this is done by accessing cached information, so system operations are not required. By tuning the Sapphire prototype the number of operations could

Sapphire Prototype	KITE Prototype
lock node × 3	open details file
get intents attribute × 3	close details file
start transaction × 3	open details file
create handle link × 2	close details file
delete handle link × 1	
write intents to link × 2	
write intents to object × 3	
end transaction × 3	
unlock object × 3	

Table 5: A comparison of system operations.

be reduced, firstly by not opening the current process node properly, but simply peeping at the intents set on it to check for locking, and secondly by putting intents only within the object and not also on the handle link. After extensive tuning the number of operations could potentially be whittled down from 23 to six for the Sapphire prototype. The KITE prototype could also be easily tuned further, for example by opening the *details* file only once, so there would still be three times as many operations. Indeed the potential for optimisation is greater in the KITE prototype, as far more process information could also be cached. The question remains, why are there more operations?

The probable answer is that the Sapphire prototype is forced to write intents to objects representing nodes being opened, so that other CAIS tools can find out what intents are currently set on the node, to determine whether it is locked or not. This was not a problem in the KITE prototype as there was a central daemon process which would cache such information, and serialise access to the database, thus removing the need for concurrency locks. The situation is worse, as it is also necessary to associate opened nodes with the processes that have opened them, so that if a process dies without all its handles being closed, a *supervisor* process is able to find out which nodes were opened and to then close them. This association is achieved by having *handle* links from objects representing process nodes, to each node opened.

This detailed discussion has really shown one thing — that an efficient implementation needs shared data in main store, as is achieved by the daemons used in the KITE prototype. The "natural" implementation of CAIS on PCTE used in the Sapphire prototype lacks this shared data, and so causes a great deal of disc traffic.

Clearly, one could use a KITE-like daemon approach on top of PCTE, but then one would be taking little advantage of the main features of PCTE.

The overall conclusion is that KITE has daemon processes which cache, whereas the Sapphire prototype sits directly on PCTE. As a consequence, although a PCTE implementation could cache at a lower level, it cannot possibly know about high level CAIS concepts. We believe that the potential for even further optimisation in KITE would speed the prototype up by a factor of ten.

5.2 CAIS vs. PCTE

The second question asked was why the scenarios ran so much faster on PCTE than on either implementation of CAIS? The CM and CELT scenarios were 13 times faster on PCTE than KITE CAIS and the Conferencing Scenario was 40 times faster. Why should there be such differences when there are so many similarities between the KITE and Emeraude interfaces? After all one is simply CAIS sitting on Unix and the other PCTE "on top of" Unix.

As stated in the last section we believe KITE could be speeded up by a factor of ten. The CM and CELT scenario times would then be almost equivalent. However Conferencing Scenario times are more than ten times greater on KITE. The probable reason is that there are some substantial differences between the two implementations. The first is that Emeraude PCTE has hooks into the underlying Unix kernel, and therefore potential for optimisation in key areas; it is not a black box implementation like KITE. The second major difference is that in CAIS, processes are part of the database, and remain in the database after process termination; PCTE has processes that are not represented in the database. However we feel that it is with processes that the greatest optimisation could be achieved in the KITE prototype.

5.3 Conclusions

On the whole, PCTE was found to provide facilities which are useful and appropriate. Problems encountered were the lack of a type lattice (*i.e.*, no multiple inheritance) and the lack of a representation of a running process in the OMS. The PCTE access control and queue facilities were also found wanting. When we came to run the scenarios on PCTE we found the performance to be much better than on our CAIS prototype. This indicates that the implementation of PCTE that we were using (Emeraude) has acceptable performance. However, we were concerned with the reliability and efficiency of the transaction mechanism in this implementation.

Essentially, we found that the CAIS node model mapped easily onto the PCTE OMS but there was a mismatch between the two process models which made the mapping in this area rather convoluted. Further, our expectation that Emeraude's kernel hooks would make the Sapphire CAIS prototype more efficient than the KITE CAIS prototype turned out to be quite wrong. In the KITE prototype we were able to cache information about open nodes and this led to far fewer system calls than in the Sapphire prototype. The mismatch between the process models of the two interfaces contributed to this problem.

From our experience of the CAIS and PCTE TSI's, we consider that layered implementations are feasible and provide a better solution than kernel implementations.

6 CAIS-A/PCTE Comparison

The original CAIS, DOD-STD-1838, was recognised to be an interim standard, to be superceded by a much more ambitious TSI, known as CAIS-A [3].

Stable drafts of the CAIS-A specifications were not available until our projects were well advanced, and prototype implementations of CAIS-A are only starting to appear now (early 1990). So, when a small extension to the Sapphire project was approved, in 1987, it was natural to extend our work to CAIS-A, but we could only embark on a paper study since neither time and budget, nor software availability, allowed anything more ambitious.

Our study had three parts:

- subjective evaluation of CAIS-A,
- comparison between CAIS-A and PCTE,
- study of the feasibility of bridging tools between CAIS-A and PCTE.

To facilitate the first two parts of the study, we first defined a Data Definition Language (DDL) for CAIS-A. Before we did this, CAIS-A schemas were only defined as database structures, making it arduous to define schemas, and making it very hard to compare with PCTE SDS's.

Our *subjective evaluation* was conducted by designing how our scenarios would be supported by CAIS-A. The designs were quite straightforward. The CAIS-A database is well thought out; the type lattice (multiple inheritance) was particularly useful. The channel/port structure was a natural mechanism to use for input/output; however the lack of multiple readers and writers on channels will lead to proliferation of channels.

Our *comparison of PCTE and CAIS-A* concentrated on the database typing mechanisms of the two interfaces. At first sight the two mechanisms are very different; the very different ways of representing type information obscure attempts at comparison. However, in designing our DDL for CAIS-A, we were able to bring out the similarities by adopting a DDL style very similar to that for PCTE. There are many differences of detail, but one is struck by this essential similarity of concept, and indeed of many details.

Our study of *bridging between CAIS-A and PCTE* was quite encouraging. Mapping schemas either way should not present too many problems. Tools can be written, with a degree of automatic generation, to convert bulk data. The tools themselves can be moved with the aid of some source conversion, given a little manual help, and some judicious use of libraries. To a surprising degree, the differences of detail between the two TSI's can be handled; for example the lattice of PCTE composition links can be represented satisfactorily in CAIS-A, which has a tree of primary relationships. While it is certainly true that tools can be written, relying on detailed subtleties of one TSI, which will not easily port to the other TSI, we believe that, in practice, sensibly written tools will port without too much effort.

This realisation leads us to conclude that it no longer makes *technical* sense to attempt early convergence between CAIS-A and PCTE. The converged interface would be unlikely to present significantly smaller bridging problems, between it and either PCTE or CAIS-A, than we have between PCTE and CAIS-A. If both PCTE and CAIS-A themselves were to survive the existence of a converged TSI, we would be faced by three bridges rather than just the one between PCTE and CAIS-A.

7 Main Conclusions

The overall conclusions resulting from our study are:

- PCTE provides facilities which are useful and appropriate to the tool builder;

- the Emeraude implementation of PCTE has acceptable performance;

- it is feasible to construct implementations of Tool Support Interfaces layered on top of native operating systems;

- implementing Ada interfaces to PCTE was straightforward, allowing us to use Ada very successfully for most of our work on PCTE;

- it is feasible to implement CAIS-1 on top of PCTE (we have done it) but there are severe performance penalties;

- PCTE and CAIS-A are sufficiently similar that it will be feasible to bridge between them;

- any short-term convergence between CAIS-A and PCTE+ no longer makes technical sense.

Acknowledgements

This work was carried out by C.W. Loftus, F.W. Long, H.E. Oliver, M.D. Tedd and P.F. Warren, with some part being done by a Ph.D. student, K.M. Warren-White.

The KITE project was funded under contract No. 2110/17 RSRE of the Ministry of Defence. The Sapphire Project was partly funded by the Commission of the European Community under its ESPRIT programme, as project number 1229 (1277).

References

[1] Buxton, J.N., *STONEMAN: Requirements for Ada Programming Support Environments*, United States Department of Defense, Washington, 1980.

[2] *Military Standard DOD-STD-1838 Common APSE Interface Set (CAIS)*, United States Department of Defense, Washington, October 1986 (actually published in 1987).

[3] *Military Standard DOD-STD-1838A Common APSE Interface Set (CAIS) (Revision A)*, United States Department of Defense, Washington, April 1989.

[4] *Requirements and Design Criteria for the Common APSE Interface Set (CAIS)*, United States Department of Defense, Ada Joint Program Office, Washington, October 1986.

[5] *PCTE Specifications: Version 1.5, C Interfaces, Volume 1*, Commission of the European Communities, Brussels, November 1988.

[6] *PCTE Specifications: Version 1.5, C Interfaces, Volume 2*, Commission of the European Communities, Brussels, November 1988.

[7] *PCTE Specifications: Version 1.5, Ada Interfaces, Volume 1*, Commission of the European Communities, Brussels, November 1988.

[8] *PCTE+ Specifications (Ada & C) Issue 3*, NATO, Independent European Programme Group, TA 13, Brussels, October 1988.

Towards A Convergence In Knowledge-Based And Conventional Software Engineering: Tools, Methods, Techniques

L.J.Hickman, Ph.D

INTRODUCTION

For the past several decades, there has been too little discussion between AI developers and other software engineers. AI developers were often engaged in independent work, which until recently had little commercial impact. Lack of dialogue and divisions between the two groups was sustained by the specialised terminology each used, e.g. the term "knowledge engineer."

As knowledge-based systems (KBS) increasingly become more integrated into business practices, the need for convergence of KB and conventional software engineering becomes a high priority. The trend for using KB for business applications is increasing at a rapid rate. A 1987 survey by Feigenbaum found 2,000 production systems based on KBS technology in the US alone. Some estimates place market growth of KBS at 30% per year currently.

THE PROBLEM

The introduction of the new KBS technology in an organisation has often been in a "standalone" manner. The lack of integration with other existing systems has been the standard situation with a resulting divergence from the structured systems development which many organisations have been adopting. This paper will explore the means of creating convergence through a common software engineering approach. In particular, the requirements for integrating the use of CASE tools, a structured methodology, systems development techniques such as prototyping, and KB/database management systems will be described.

Some of the issues facing KBS developers currently are similar to ones which have been addressed by other software engineers earlier. In the area of CASE tools, for example, KBS developers lag behind. There are very few tools which provide computer-assisted system engineering in the KBS environment. Knowledge acquisition tools to automate the process of entering knowledge to create rules are needed. Much of the process is currently manual. Another example of CASE tools currently used by software engineers are data dictionaries. There is a growing demand for a similar facility for KBS development. In addition, system managers working towards system integration, will require tools which can span both types of development.

The lack of structured methods for KBS development has resulted in the same types of problems which preceded the movement towards a structured systems life cycle development method for conventional systems. As more KBS are brought into the business routines, it has been observed that end-users' needs have often not been adequately met. The isolated development process of KBS is similar to the type of system development which occurred prior to the introduction of structured methods. Methods which emphasized the need for system analysts to interview end-users as a part of development contributed to better overall systems development.

Techniques for development can be gainfully exchanged between AI and conventional software engineers. For example the concept of prototyping is firmly embedded in the approaches to KBS development and can be used for both types of system developments.

The area crucial for convergence will be in knowledge base/database management systems. As businesses adopt KBS, the need to use data on operational databases as well as knowledge in a knowledge base will drive the two technologies closer together. Business needs will be one source of the demand for tighter coupling, but the performance requirements unique to each system now can be reduced by solutions which seek utilization of both technologies in an advanced form of knowledge base/database management systems.

OVERVIEW

The paper will discuss the topic in four sections. First, operational definitions will be provided. In the second section, the common requirements for tools, structured methods, techniques, KB/database management systems for KBS and conventional systems will be presented. The third section will outline the proposed convergence for tools, structured methods, techniques, etc. Finally, the fourth section will suggest future directions for implementing convergence in KB and conventional software engineering.

1. OPERATIONAL DEFINITIONS

> What's in a name? that which we call a rose
> By any other name would smell as sweet
> Romeo & Juliet, Shakespeare

Unfortunately, the poetic ideal does not provide a sound basis for good communications. One of the reasons AI developers and other software engineers have often gone down separate development paths is due to the lack of understanding in the terminology used by each. There is always a danger in a newly emerging field, e.g. AI within computing, of many different new terms coined for similar ideas. It is necessary, therefore, to clarify and make explicit the operational definitions used for this current paper.

1.1. Knowledge-based system

The term knowledge-based system (KBS) has been used increasingly as a synonym for expert system. Emphasizing "knowledge" of the system rather than the "expertise" of the system provides a generalised hierarchy (knowledge - information - data) that fits more easily with the concepts already in use in systems development. The literature contains many attempts to define "knowledge-based system". For an operational definition which may help distinguish KB from other systems, the following definition of KBS will be used in the paper:

> a software system able to perform tasks which would be performed by human experts who have accumulated the required (specific) knowledge.
>
> (Sellis, 1989)

In contrast, a conventional system does not require domain knowledge, and instead embodies procedures which have been pre-determined, often by a standard algorithm.

Two systems representing the two approaches show the differences: In the first, a conventional sales system created for tracking sales, a standard monthly sales report by region may be generated (perhaps using a control-break algorithm or other standard reporting procedure.)

In the second, a KBS, a system for fault diagnosis, the domain knowledge regarding potential causes for specific faults (as in equipment maintenance) needs to be known.

1.2. Goals, Facts and Rules

How are KBS related to other software systems? They should be considered just another type of application system - albeit with important differences in the actual computing process. Conventional programs written in procedural languages embed control structures in the code and the programmer creates the control structures e.g. IF x = 1 THEN GO TO END.

In contrast, in a KBS, the inference engine, which can be considered a logic module, is coded to search for conclusions (goals): a fact(s) not (yet) proven, and the path for the search is not pre-determined by the programmer. Indeed, given varying combinations of facts and rules there is considerable variation in the path taken for a search for a conclusion. It is this richness and complexity which permits emulation (within a limited range) of human expertise by utillizing knowledge. The knowledge base (KB) holds facts and rules.

> Facts = assertive knowledge e.g. TOWN, IS A ...
> Rules = operating knowledge indicating the way facts are to be used e.g. IF TOWN ... THEN

In the case of the fault diagnostic system, the rules for potential faults would be checked against the observed and known run-time facts and values of the rule variables.

1.3. Control Strategies

Within the logic module, or inference engine of a KBS, different control strategies may be chosen depending upon the type of application:

Backward chaining - hypothesises a particular conclusion and then works backwards to see whether its premises are true.

Forward chaining - begins with known facts and attempts to establish conclusions from a particular set of given data.

Breadth-first search - In a hierarchy of rules or objects, the strategy is to examine all of the rules on objects on the same level before any of the rules on objects on the next level are checked.

Depth-first search - In a hierarchy of rules on objects, the strategy in which one rule or object on the highest level is examined and then the rules or objects immediately below are examined - as in a single branch - until the end, whereupon the search continues from the highest level of the next branch.

Thus, in a KBS, a control strategy is predetermined, but the run-time search depends upon the actual facts and rules for the run.

DATA, INFORMATION, KNOWLEDGE

```
DATA + DATA + DATA  ⟶  INFORMATION + CONTEXT  ⟶  KNOWLEDGE
```

Distinctions between KBS and conventional systems exist not only in programming the control and logic, but also, very importantly, in the essential base for computing. In 3rd GE computing, systems dealt exclusively with DATA, **raw facts and discrete values, e.g. "PRODUCT CODE"**. The emphasis was on large-scale data manipulation especially "number crunching" tasks. Access to the data was usually quite restricted and determined by the design of the file structure and the program code. The inaccessibility to data which was stored in fixed formats gave rise to the development of relational databases which permitted storage and access to related data.

In the 4GE systems the computing basis became INFORMATION **or related data e.g. "PRODUCT - ORDER"**. The techniques of ENTITY - RELATIONSHIP MODELLING provided a basis for designing a relational database, mapping the entities, things of significance about which information is held, and the type of relationships between entities.

Information is used differently depending upon context, however. The semantics of the data and information need to be available. Thus, in 5th GE systems, KNOWLEDGE, **or the meaning and significance of given data,** is the basis for computing. For example, with Product-Order: how changing the specifications of an order can affect product configuration. Meaning of data comes from viewing it in a context which is individual (e.g. experts' rules-of thumb) or collective experience (e.g. laws and principles).

In a KBS rules and facts are stored in a knowledge base while in a conventional system, the data is stored in a database, and in the case of a relational database, data and information is held.

2. COMMON REQUIREMENTS for
TOOLS, STRUCTURED METHODS, TECHNIQUES, KB/DBMS
2.1. CASE Tools for development - Requirements

Developing software, either KBS or conventional requires tools for analysing, designing and building the system. The key tasks requiring CASE Computer-Aided-Software-Engineering support:

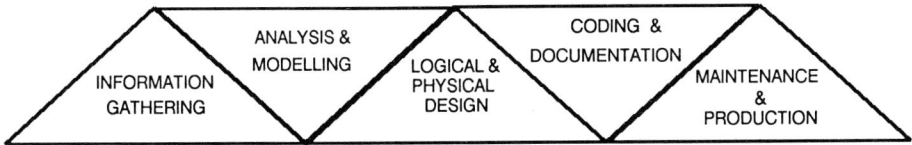

2.2. In KBS the CASE support requirements by task:

Interviews with domain expert(s) to determine rules and facts - the KNOWLEDGE ACQUISITION *Requirements:* automated storage, interactive elicitation, dictionary.

Analysis of rules and modelling of the logical relationship e.g. decision trees
Requirements: rule paradigms, decision trees, dictionary

Developing a design for the rule sets and knowledge base (or with links to a shell)*
Requirements: automating the rules generation, dictionary

Coding of rules and necessary coding for the logic (inference engine in a shell)
Requirements: Rule documentation, rule generation, meta-rules for rule consistency and rule checking, dictionary

Maintenance of rule base - modification of rules, additions, changes, deletions, revisions of certainty factors, variables, etc.
Requirements: dictionary, impact analysis, tracing rules fired, version and change control

As a complex requirement, consider the problem of integrating a number of knowledge bases for use by various applications and maintaining the rules and use of rules for an integrated KBS supported system. A very powerful dictionary is required.Increasingly the support of a central repository, dictionary, is needed for multiple KBS.

> * EXPERT SYSTEM SHELL: a software package "tool" to assist in the developemnt of expert system applications. Shells provide an inference engine (the logic element), knowledge-base structure, and a user-interface to create a knowledge base.

2.3. CASE TOOLS for development - Requirements

In conventional systems development:

Interviews with management and users to determine entities, relationships, processes, functions, information requirements

Requirements: automated storage, interactive elicitation, dictionary

Analysis of information requirements and E-R modelling, (meta-rules about modelling using embedded knowledge of database modelling)

Requirements: graphics for modelling, interactive modelling, automated defaults

Logical and physical designs for the system requirement (translating logical to physical)

Requirements: automated default design, dictionary, error checking, sizing and performance analysis

Generation of code to meet design specifications

Requirements: extending automated application code generation, dictionary, system and user documentation

Maintenance of the system and data - updates, additions, deletions, changes to system

Requirements: dictionary, impact analysis, version and change control

How feasible is it now to meet all of the above requirements? Consider E-R modelling: If human experts now make decisions and if the basis (rules and heuristics) for the rules can be extracted and recorded in a KB then intelligent CASE tools can be created.

In comparing the CASE tool needs for both types of systems, a commonality of functions is readily apparent. In the third section the convergence requirements will be discussed more fully.

2.4. STRUCTURED METHODS

The lack of structured methods for KBS development and particularly the lack of a common structured method for developing either type of system has led to fragmented development. The problems software developers inevitably face in an unstructured development environment are: a lack of complete understanding of the system requirements, lack of knowledge about users' needs, and a multitude of prototypes which fail to reach the production stage. This is due to inadequate design, or failure to match requirements to actual needs. Seldom are the systems failures in terms of not being able to produce system goals, e.g. expert evaluation of a domain problem.

Just as conventional software developers had to learn of the need for structured development - so, too, do KBS developers. The CASE*Method, as one example of a top-down structured approach, outlines 7 stages of development with specific tasks and deliverables for each. Using such a top-down methodology provides the basis for a sound strategic model for proposed systems.

Similarities in KBS development stages have remained unnoted. At the current time, each KBS developer proposes a slightly different set of "phases in development" and there is no standard for an approach. Without a standardised approach it can be argued, the CASE tools for KBS cannot be developed easily. Structured methods and the supporting tools are integrally related.

2.5. TECHNIQUES

Techniques used for both types of systems can be adapted to the advantage of all developers. Developers' techniques such as knowledge elicitation used by KBS engineers can be gainfully used by conventional system analysts. Structured interview techniques are needed for all systems development. Due to the critical necessities of accurate and complete knowledge in building rule-sets for KBS, much attention has been focussed on interviewing and knowledge elicitation by knowledge engineers. Currently there is not one, but many approaches, some of which have been evaluated as more effective than others, for example, structured rather than unstructured interviews yield a higher amount of information (Hoffman, 1987). Documenting critical cases is another approach with high benefits. Repertory Grid analysis has been used and automated by some KBS developers and it could be modified for use as an interview technique for system analysts.

2.6. PROTOTYPING

The use of prototyping in developing KBS is widely practiced. Prototypes provide an opportunity for faster results and in-depth evaluation before the production version. The need to gain sponsor and user commitment is often cited as one use of the prototypes. With 4GE tools, conventional software developers can adopt the use of prototypes throughout the development process to achieve the same quick results and provide users with prototypes for more detailed evaluation and feedback. There is also the possible advantage of more controlled testing with the prototypes.

2.7. KB/DBMS

No issue looms larger currently in KBS development than the need for larger KB storage and better performance. Lengthy searches, resource inefficiencies, lack of integrity controls are just several of the main problems. The potential for convergence in using RDBMS technology is very positive. The relatively independent development of KBS has led to a surprising lack of knowledge or use of RDBMS technology. RDBMS likewise can benefit from the use of KB technology. The key features that a knowledge base and a database could provide in a complementary fashion are listed below. The advantages of developing tightly coupled systems becomes apparent.

COMPARATIVE FEATURES

KNOWLEDGE BASE	RELATIONAL DATABA
rule-based reasoning	data security
"expressiveness"-semantics	integrity control
explicit interpretation	aggregate computation
heuristic search	dictionary functions
	rapid search

2.8. SUMMARY OF COMMON REQUIREMENTS

There are important parallelisms in the development of both types of systems. In the area of CASE tools, the tasks and supporting tool requirements as outlined above, show significant similarities throughout the life cycle. The needs, from automated support for information gathering, intelligent modelling, and design of knowledge-bases and databases based on meta-rules, rule and code generation, to maintenance of rules and data in a dictionary throughout the development cycle, are remarkably similar.

To date, there has been an articially imposed separateness in tool development. On the one hand, KBS knowledge acquisition and shell tools have been created exclusively for KBS. Meanwhile, conventional CASE tool developments have neglected KBS technology requirements. The future of CASE development needs to be re-examined and use the commonality as a guide for CASE enhancements and new tools.

Likewise, the need for a structured method for development stages and to overcome problems, such as determing the detailed requirements for the User's business environment, are similar for both types of systems.

An examination of commonality in techniques shows the extensive use of prototyping as a development technique by KBS builders, and the increased use of prototyping by other software engineers could be extended.

The future integration of KB/DBMS seems an inevitable evolutionary path. The strengths of each could complement. By adding the semantic expressiveness of a KB to a RDBMS, a higher performance in a coupled system of a KB and an RDBMS could be attained.

The need and opportunity for greater convergence between KBS and other software developers should be apparent from the foregoing description of commonality of requirements for tools, structured methods, and techniques. Defining the need is only the first step. The next section will propose means for greater convergence drawing especially upon the experience of developing a KB system which interfaces with an Oracle relational database (as well as having the system goal of operating with another Oracle RDBMS)

3. PROPOSED CONVERGENCE

3.1. Developers

The first area for convergence is to bring the developers together in teams on projects. The plethora of stand-alone projects and separate AI or KB departments, although fashionable, needs to be checked. The differences in technology have been greatly exaggerated by the isolation of developments. While specialisation provides an environment of concentration, the effect of bringing specialists together creates a natural synthesis and synergy. Thus, first bring the two groups together to explore the commonalities that are shared.

A panel at the 1989 IJCAI (International Joint Conference on Artificial Intelligence, 1989) debated the lack of greater penetration in industry of AI techniques. An academic spokesman from M.I.T. complained of the lack of business awareness. Prominent industry representatives from DEC, SHELL and other organisations made the point that businesses could accept the technology. The solution seems obvious - to communicate more often and work together - not only researchers and industry but then at the development level KBS and other software engineers.

3.2. CASE Tools

There is a commonality of the tools required as well as the opportune advantages of embedding KBS technology within CASE tools - all of which suggests the potentials for eventual convergence.

In outlining common requirements, the question was posed, is it feasible? The level of feasibilty is, in fact, enhanced through convergence. KBS development tools based on CASE software technology can be more rapidly developed and facilities in CASE tools for conventional software development can be greatly expanded by utilizing KBS technology. From the perspective of the author who is an experienced user of CASE tools and a KBS developer, such convergence is urgently needed to advance both fields.

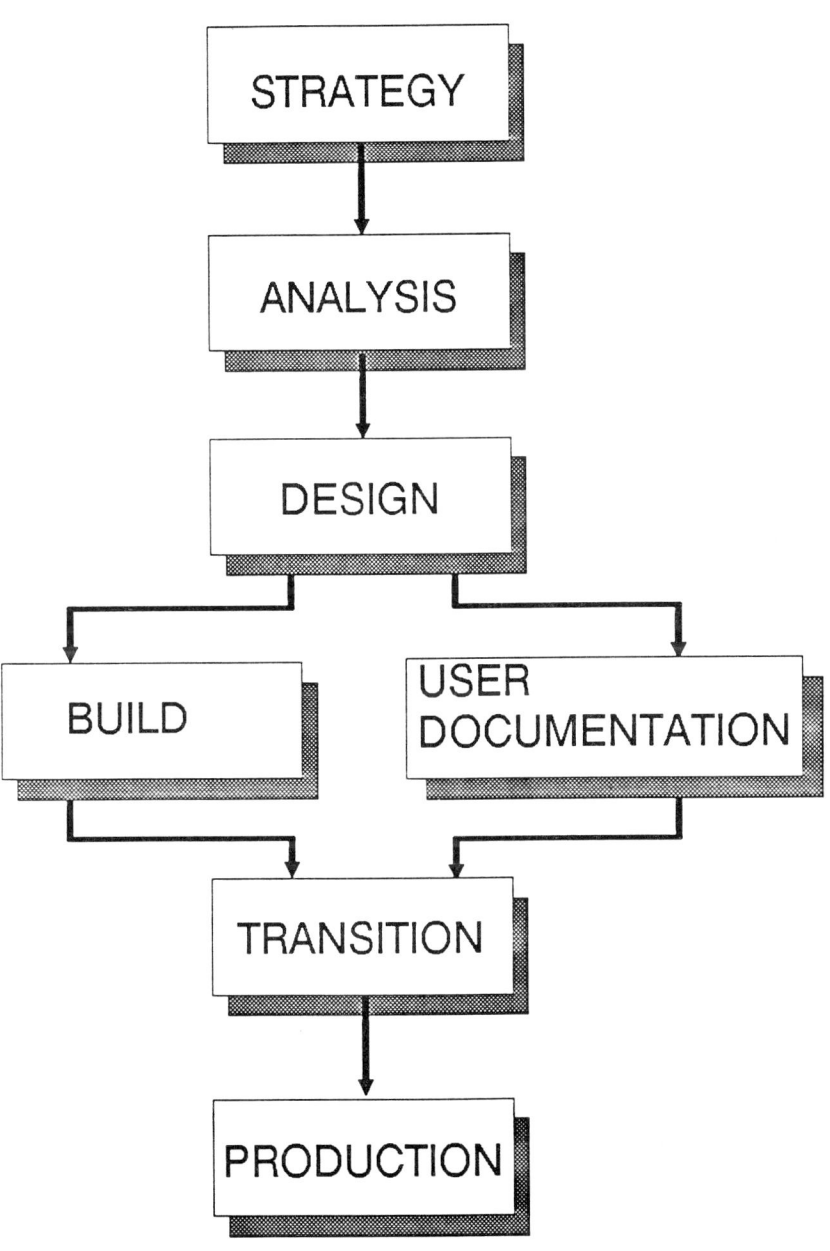

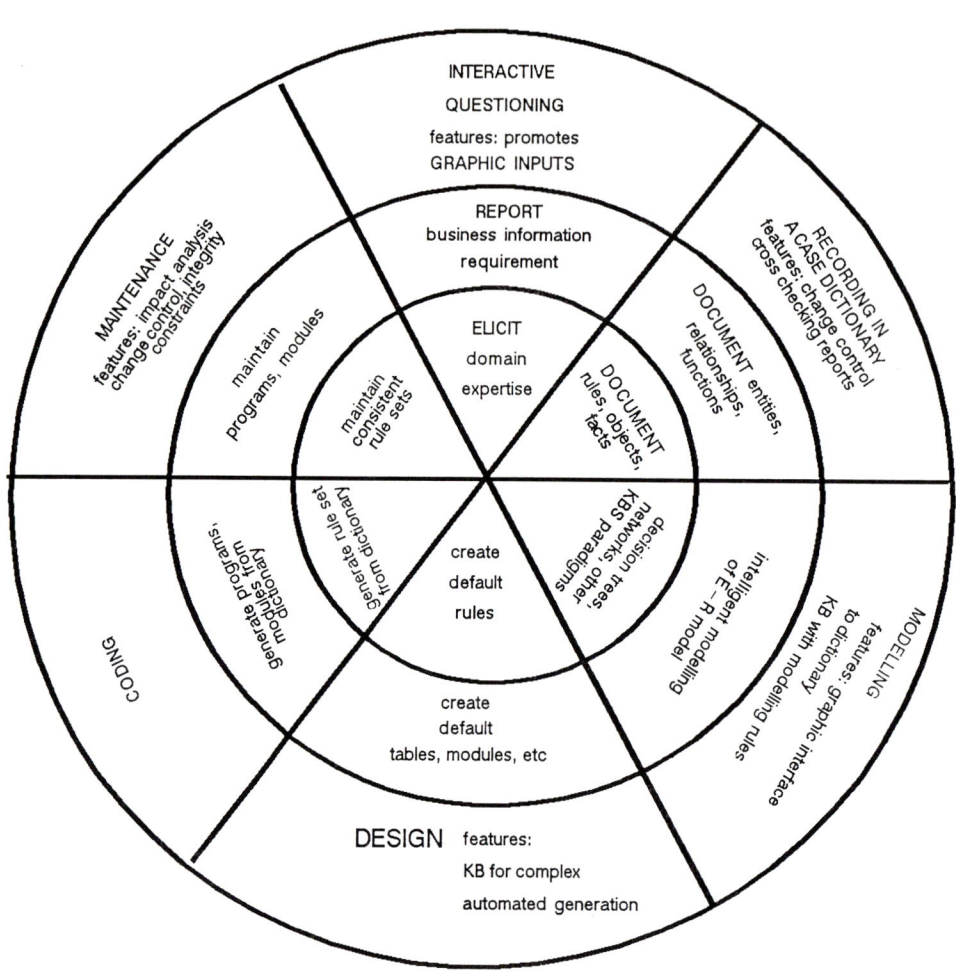

Converged Scheme Of CASE Tools

The proposed technical developments in CASE tools which are needed to support the joint requirements of KBS and conventional systems are outlined in the following two diagrams. In the first, features are listed which can satisfy the development requirements described previously. The second is a converged scheme of CASE tools showing on the outer circle the support by development stage; The middle circle represents features especially for conventional systems while the inner circle depicts the CASE assistance for KBS development.

3.3. PROPOSED CONVERGENCE
STRUCTURED METHODS

KBS developers have much to gain by incorporating structured methods in KBS development. Some of the problems were outlined above. Basically, the prime issue in all software development is to have a framework which enables project estimating, project control, analysis and design to have a context in order to produce systems meeting the needs of the user environment. Conversely, software engineers need to embrace KBS systems within structured methods at all stages. Looking at a structured life cycle path, using the CASE*Method example, the stages are:

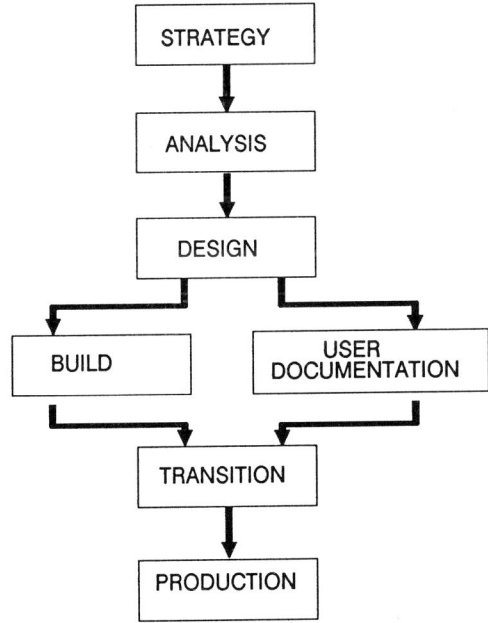

STRATEGY

Beginning at the first stage of the structured life cycle development path, the strategy stage, KBS applications need to be considered . At the strategy stage, methods can incorporate questions of feasibility to determine if the organisation's information requirements extend to KBS within application areas. The greatest potential for all systems in the 1990's will be in areas where KBS technology will be embedded in applications so that "intelligent applications" will be created.

For that concept to be implemented, requirement analysis must be expanded to include questions asked to determine KBS feasibility. Most importantly, the analysis of KBS should not be outside the scope of the enterprise modelling of the information model.

The strategy stage creates a model of the information requirements at the enterprise level. Consistent with that scope, any requirement for KBS applications should be documented and become a part of the I.T. strategy plan. Within strategy analysis an attempt to determine when a KBS may be required leads to adding feasibility analysis in order to determine, for example:

- ° is heuristic knowledge necessary for problem solving? (example: are there rules to determine discounts)
- ° is there staff experience/knowledge which needs to be preserved in the system (example: are there individuals with expertise which needs to be documented?)
- ° are there places where human expertise is not readily available, but the expertise can be duplicated? (example: senior credit analysts cannot cope with the high volume of applications - their expertise can be duplicated in a KBS)
- ° are there repetitive situations requiring senior staff involvement (example: training insurance adjustors in difficult forms)
- ° can human error result with an overload of information? (example: in monitoring applications)
- ° are there complex decisions involved which may be more efficiently processed by computer (example: complex logistical scheduling)

These represent typical questions which might lead to further feasibility analysis for KBS within an application area.

As soon as KBS are included in the original IT strategy there is a natural convergence towards using the organisation's database in an integrated manner in coupled systems. As the aim of I.T. strategy planning is for integrated systems, the goal can be reached at an even higher level than previously.

ANALYSIS

Detailed requirements for systems can be extended to include KBS details. The techniques of knowledge acquisition would be adapted at this stage.

DESIGN

Extension of tasks to include architecture using design criteria currently used by software engineers.

BUILD

Building rule sets and coding conventional applications requires procedures for conforming to design specifications and for system testing. At this stage, too, prototyping for all developments can be adapted. Structured methods defining the tasks and deliverables can, thus, be used for KBS as well as modified to include KBS architecture.

TRANSITION

The preparation for conversion to a new system begins at the analysis stage and very similar constraints and issues require identification for KBS and conventional.

PRODUCTION

Maintenance during production requires structure and is a particular weakness in KBS methods which have few tools or methods for maintenance. The end-user structured use of feedback sessions, for example, would improve the feedback to KBS developers. The CASE tools which are used by software engineers are urgently needed for KBS maintenance.

Each of the life cycle stages needs to be extended in all structured methods to incorporate KBS development.

TECHNIQUES

Convergence has been suggested in adopting the use of rapid prototyping techniques for KBS and conventional systems.

Due to the new technology of KBS, prototyping has been commonly used as a development technique. Shorter timescales and lower initial investment in the commitment of resources coupled with rapid evaluation has been especially attractive for KBS sponsors. Existing guidelines within structured methods for prototyping can also be used for KBS.

Rapid prototyping tools in 4GE, forms, menus, etc, for conventional systems may be used for KBS also. In one expert system (with over 200 rules) developed within ORACLE SQL*FORMS and SQL*MENU were coupled with an expert system shell to develop a rapid prototype within a month.

KB/DBMS

The convergence of KB/DB technology is already occurring more and more frequently. The advantages of better performance for KB using an RDBMS are obvious to developers familiar with each. The reciprocal advantage is for an RDBMS to gain KB capabilities in coupled systems. The features were outlined above.

It is beyond the scope of this paper to describe in detail the design and architecture of loosely or tightly coupled systems or to suggest the design requirements for a complete KB/RDBMS system. Researchers developing POSTGRES have suggested some of the potential paths in the future.

FUTURE DIRECTIONS

A natural evolution is occurring with the convergence of KBS and conventional software engineering. There is good evidence supporting common requirements for tools, methods and techniques. What has to be done to accomplish better integration?

A common dialogue must begin. One purpose of the paper is to contribute to the basis for such dialogues. Terms which are specialized need to become de-mystified and then used in a general manner by software engineers of all types of systems.

A common understanding of how all types of systems are used to support the information and knowledge requirements of an organisation needs to be shared. The history of software development in most organisations shows a lack of integrated systems resulted until structured methods emphasizing enterprise models were introduced. The proliferation of non-integrated systems will continue and increase if the KBS are kept separate also.

These are the non-technical tactics for creating convergence. The goal will be to provide better software engineering by supporting user requirements.

Proposed technical developments provide the potential for convergence of CASE tools and Methods. The enhanced tools would promote the ease of developing integrated systems based on KB and conventional technology.

Imagine a future software development project scenario.

A project team is assembled with specialists in KB and 4GE technology.

During the STRATEGY study, the strategic business analysts use CASE tools to interactively elicit information from key decision makers in the organisation. As responses are recorded in the dictionary, a KB embedded in the tool assists in intelligently modelling of the entity-relationships and functions (processes) for the enterprise model. Links to the strategic objectives and the organisation's requirements are generated automatically.

In one business area, rules are needed to intelligently determine discounts (which are currently based on complex factors).The rules are elicited through an interactive CASE dialogue then recorded in the CASE dictionary. During ANALYSIS the decision trees of the rules are reviewed on the screen to determine from the point of view of the senior discount specialist if the tree matches an "expert" decision process.

On a broader scale, the graphic enterprise model (E-R and functions) is used for a feedback session with the users to determine correctness and completeness. Later, the graphic model is used to elicit detailed requirements from users.

After automated and user cross-checks are completed, a default DESIGN for the KB of discount rules is completed by the CASE tool. The default DESIGN for the organisation database is also generated and then reviewed prior to the automated application generation.

The BUILD stage (using prototyping) of the "intelligent discount application" will require an expert system shell with an interface to an RDBMS or it may be more tightly coupled, and the KB/RDBMS will include the rules and data storage/manipulation/retrieval as well as a logic module. The customer, product, price, etc. information in the database must be linked integrally with the rules for discounts. It is a large database, and due to performance issues, the discount application was not feasible without an integral RDBMS link.

TRANSITION to the application system will use documentation from CASE tools to train and support end-users. The intelligent discount system will undergo acceptance testing by the users and cross-checking for rule consistency as the system goes live.

The system enters the PRODUCTION stage and inevitably changes to rules and the application will occur as time passes. The CASE impact analysis reports, change and version control, integrity constraints will all help to maintain a concurrent, consistent model of the "intelligent discount system". An intelligent system engineered using converged tools, methods and techniques.

REFERENCES

Barker, Richard, Editor, CASE*Method: Tasks and Deliverables, (Chertsey: Oracle Corporation UK Ltd), 1988.

Boose, John and Shaw, Mildred, "Knowledge Acquisition for Knowledge-Based Systems", ref. SA6, IJCAI 1989.

Proceedings of the Eleventh International Joint Conference on Artificial Intelligence, 20-25 August 1989, Detroit, Michagan USA.

Fiegenbaum, Edward, McCorduck, Pamela, and NIIM, H. Penny, THE RISE OF THE EXPERT COMPANY (London: Macmillan) 1988.

Harmon, Paul, Editor, "Expert Systems Strategies", Vol. 5, No. 8 monthly newslatter, (Salem, MA: Cutter Information Corp.)

Harmon, Paul and Maus, Rex, and William, Morrisey, EXPERT SYSTEMS TOOLS AND APPLICATIONS, (New York: John Wiley & SONS), 1988.

Hoffman, Robert R., "The Problem of Extracting the Knowledge of Experts from the Perspective of Experimental Psychology", AI Magazine, Vol. 8, No. 2, 1987 pp. 53-67.

Sellis, Timos, "Artificial Intelligence and Database Systems," Codd and Date Seminar, London 1989.

Stonebraker, M. and L.A. Rowe, "The Design of POSTGRES", Proc. ACM SIGMOD International Conference on Management of Data, Washington, D.C., May 1986, 340-355.

Verification and Validation

Providing a foundation for rigorous software development: issues of language specification and compiler validation, J. Souter & M. Woodman

Methods and Tools for Testing-in-the Large, R. Franck, A. Spillner & J. Herrmann

Providing a Foundation for Rigorous Software Development: Issues of Language Specification and Compiler Validation

JOHN SOUTER

BSI Quality Assurance, Software Engineering Department

MARK WOODMAN

Open University, Computing Department

ABSTRACT

The last decade has seen a shift towards formal methods of software development, with standards such as the Draft Interim Defence Standard 00-55 for safety critical software effectively defining the state of the art. As a result, researchers and developers have concentrated on introducing rigour into software development. Rigorous methods and supporting tools have been designed for the early stages of development, and are based on the assumption that rigour can continue to applied in later stages using well-defined and properly implemented programming languages.

However, the specification of languages, and the validation of their compilers still present many obstacles in the way of achieving rigour throughout development. This paper describes problems with current language specifications and defines what quality means in the context of language implementations. It airs some of the issues of specifying for quality and validation. In particular, it reports on recent experience in the specification of Modula-2 and in developing tests for different classes of Modula-2 compilers.

1. INTRODUCTION

Rigorous software development must be built on sound foundations. A rigorous method of software development must be complimented by a standardized language and a validated implementation of that language; see Souter (1989).

Indeed, here is little point in employing development methods for an aircraft control system, for example, if the aircraft crashes due to a bug in the compiler used to implement the control system. This is recognized in the defence standard for safety critical software, MoD (1989), which demands that implementation languages be block-structured, have strong typing, and have well-defined semantics. Unfortunately, the software industry has not embraced such languages wholeheartedly, and when a software developer has chosen one, the implementation has been inadequate; often they exhibit surprising ignorance of the 'well-defined' semantics. We provide some explanation of this situation by describing the current state of language specifications and how implementors react to them. We do this by examining a selection of language standards and how implementations fall short of the quality which rigorous development and software portability demand.

Another aspect of the defence standard 00-55 which relates to programming languages and rigorous software development is the use of static analysis tools for checking source code. The usefulness of these tools cannot be denied, but the question of whether they precisely match the semantics of the language for which they are intended is moot. When we combine this uncertainty with the failure of compilers to provide the semantics of the language they implement (see Horton (1989) for example), the need to progress language technology becomes urgent.

Throughout the paper we draw on lessons learnt from specifying particular languages and from validating implementations of them. We frequently refer to the development of Modula-2 which has attempted to avoid the problems of earlier languages. (Also, Modula-2 is an appropriate choice for analysis because it is particularly suited to the programming of embedded systems and is being increasingly being used in safety critical applications.) In this context we consider some compiler validation issues and the use of formality in language specification

We begin by defining terms which are needed to establish conceptual models of language specifications and implementations.

2. DEFINITION OF TERMS
Terminology and taxonomy are important in young disciplines. They are especially important in areas where problems exist but are generally unacknowledged by those professionals involved in the discipline; this is the case in the area of programming languages, which models of software development do not properly address. In order to develop appropriate models for language specification and implementation, the terminology must be adequate. Without a

sufficiently expressive and precise terminology, the confusion surrounding languages and their implementations will continue to have a deleterious effect on standardizers, procurement managers and software project teams.

Work has been done in this area: an international cross-language working group (ISO/IEC JTC1/SC22/WG10) has produced guidelines on the specification of programming languages, ISO (1989). However, some of the definitions suggested in ISO (1989) have proved inadequate for the complexities of modern languages. A case in point is Modula-2 whose standardization committee, although influenced by ISO (1989), has found it necessary to develop a more sophisticated formal model, using VDM-SL, CEC (1989)

We single out four key terms for attention, as follows.

2.1 Error

This is a very abused term, which often leads to unnecessary confusion. To illustrate this, consider the following three definitions. The first is taken from the ISO Pascal standard, ISO (1983); the second and third are given, as alternatives, in the ANSI/IEEE Glossary of Software Engineering Terminology, ANSI (1983).

> Error — A violation by a program of the requirements of this standard that a processor[1] is permitted to leave undetected.

> Error — A discrepancy between a computed, observed, or measured value or condition and the true, specified or theoretically correct value or condition.

> Error — Human action that results in software containing a fault.

The first definition (from the Pascal Standard) is inadequate in that it does not distinguish between static and dynamic situations. These are fundamentally different: a static fault always manifests itself, whereas a dynamic fault may not exhibit itself and, in general, needs greater effort to detect. The abuse of the term 'error' in the Pascal has been widely acknowledged; see Sale (1983)

The ANSI/IEEE standard is describing data and human faults respectively. The two ANSI (1983) definitions are too vague to be helpful in constructing a model for languages and their implementations.

---

[1] A processor is a language implementation in this context.

These definitions cover a wide spectrum, from which the software industry has contentedly picked-and-mixed elements. Our preferred definition is the one we have used in the draft Modula-2 standard, BSI (1989):

> Error — This term refers to a construct in a program which is in violation of the syntax or static semantics of the language, thus preventing meaning being ascribed to any text containing the construct. (For example an 'expression' which includes a plus operator between two arrays is an error.) Thus an error prevents valid execution and must be detected by an implementation.

Note that the Modula-2 draft standard describes a compile-time event, whereas the Pascal standard can be interpreted as describing a semantic fault (i.e. essentially a run-time event).

2.2 Exception

An exception is a run-time event; it is a semantic condition to which an implementation may or may not react. This notion has been well established in Ada, ISO (1987).

As we have seen, the Pascal Standard overloads the term error and uses it to mean exception. The ANSI/IEEE standard defines exception thus:

> Exception — An event that causes suspension of normal program execution.

The problem with these definitions stem from two sources: confusion with (compile-time) errors and confusion with the events that may or may not be *caused* by exceptions. The latter point is concerned with exception *handling* which must be viewed as distinct from the semantic condition that leads to it.

Furthermore, the second definition is flawed because it assumes a predictable action (suspension of normal program execution) which requires the event to be detected. There are several types of exception which are rarely detected by production implementations (for example, accessing the value in an unassigned variable is rarely detected). Unfortunately, standards have addressed neither this point nor the distinction between an exception, its detection, and any handling of it.

Once again, we prefer the draft Modula-2 standard definition:

> Exception — an exception is the violation by a program of the dynamic semantics of the language, or of a library module. It is a run-time occurrence which invalidates the normal semantics of an executing program. (For example, dereferencing a pointer variable whose value is NIL, is an exception.)

> An exception in a program may be detected and reported by an implementation, in which case this International [Modula-2] Standard defines the semantics of the program, thus:
>
> - either exceptional termination shall occur, or
> - the program shall provide a procedure to handle the exception...
>
> If an implementation does not detect an exception, or if, for other reasons, an implementation permits execution to continue after an exception has occurred, no meaning is given to the program by the standard. The Modula-2 standard requires that certain exceptions be detected by an implementation in some mode of its use.

The Modula-2 definition clearly separates the event of violating the semantic rules of the language from the choices an implementation has of detecting or reporting them. It also specifies that for a program to have standard semantics after an exception, it must either terminate or handle the exception.

2.3 Implementation-defined

For performance, commercial, and other reasons, language implementations must often be closely coupled with the architecture of the hardware and operating system for which they produce code. Thus whole numbers will be represented by a small multiple (often 1) of the word size of the machine, and procedure call parameter evaluation will be carried out in an order which matches the conventional use of registers. The term implementation-defined is used to describe those aspects of an implementation which may be varied in this way.

The Ada, C, Modula-2 and Pascal standards are in harmony over this; we quote the Modula-2 definition:

> Implementation-defined — this term is used to refer to a feature of the language or standard library whose behaviour may be constrained by an implementation or whose attributes (i.e. the range of values of a type) may be chosen by an implementor. (For example the range of values of the integer type is implementation-defined.)
>
> An implementation-defined language feature must be supplied in an implementation; an implementation-defined library feature must be supplied if the library module which contains it is supplied. Implementation-defined behaviour must be predictable, and implementation-defined attributes must always be available in an implementation. The Modula-2 standard requires that such features be fully documented by an implementor (and may therefore be validated).

Note that implementation-defined features must be provided by a language implementation, and that they are fixed (i.e. predictable) for a given implementation.

While implementation-defined features tend to be features relating to capacity or complexity, implementation-*dependent* behaviour tends to be less predictable.

2.4 Implementation-dependent

Many people seem to think that 'implementation-definedness' is the only concept needed to deal with those things that language standards leave open to the implementor. In fact this is not so; we need one more concept and related term: 'implementation-dependent'. Our preferred (Modula-2) definition is:

> Implementation-dependent — This term is used to refer to a feature of the language or standard library whose precise behaviour is at the discretion of an implementor. (For example the order of evaluation of operand in an expression is implementation-dependent.)
>
> An implementation-dependent language feature must be supplied in an implementation; an implementation-dependent library feature must be supplied if the library module which contains it is supplied. Implementation-dependent behaviour is not necessarily predictable.

The C draft standard ANSI (1989) also allows for 'undefined behaviour', which admits the possibility of a feature not being implemented at all. This is a simply a failure to confront hard decisions by the standardizers of that language (and a weakness which also undermines the much-vaunted portability of C).

3. RELEVANCE OF STANDARDS

Amongst all possible information technology applications, it can be argued that standards have the greatest relevance to programming languages. Without standards (and in this context standard has the widest possible meaning) we would have no high-level languages and the world's programmers would be exclusively using assemblers which, of course, are proprietary.

3.1 Standardizing Products

Initially, standardizers (whether they were the inventors of a language, or formal committees, within or outside the ISO framework) thought the language specification they were writing had only to define 'standard' *programs*. Indeed, early attempts (e.g. FORTRAN, as defined by ISO (1980)) concentrated heavily on what standard programs should look like (their syntax) rather than what they meant (their semantics). This approach does not assist either implementor or programmer. Such standards are necessarily rather abstract and contain no requirements that can be applied to real-world products. Of course, the significant products in the programming language sense are the language implementations (compilers, cross-compilers, interpreters etc.) — not standard programs.

During the 1980s there have been considerable efforts to produce requirements for implementations (for some languages anyway), and this turns out to be the key aspect determining the relevance and usefulness of a language standard. In fact, experience across the broad spectrum of product standardization indicates that if conformance to a standard is not verifiable, then that standard is probably worthless.

The meta-standards for standardization which have been published by BSI, ISO, and other standards bodies assert this point strongly. The standard for British Standards, BSI (1987), requires that product standards contain clear and unambiguous requirements clauses, backed up by precise methods of test. Thus a standard on safety helmets, say, is expected to specify both the characteristics of its products and the methods for testing them; programming language standards have singularly failed to specify the test methods for the products to which it relates.

The Pascal Standard, ISO (1983) is still probably the best example of this, as its requirements clauses for implementations[2] have stood up to eight years of intensive compiler testing without any major bugs having been found in the standard (which is more than we can say for the Pascal implementations!).

3.2 Deviance testing

The Pascal standard requires that a conforming implementation:

> ...be able to determine whether or not a program violates any requirements of this standard...

This facilitates what we call *deviance* testing, in which test programs containing subtle errors are used to check that conforming implementations reject them. Empirical evidence by Wichmann (1973) suggests that we will find twice as many genuine bugs in compilers using deviance tests as with more traditional conformance tests. Thus, not only is it a powerful test tool for determining conformance, but it is also modelling those situations where we would like the compiler to protect us from our own mistakes.

This test technique is used in the Modula-2, Pascal and Ada validation suites, described in BSI (1988), Wichmann (1983), and AJPO (1983) respectively. However, deviance testing cannot be used for either COBOL or FORTRAN (which are still by far the most commonly used languages) — since the relevant language standards, ISO (1985) and ISO (1980), do not have requirements clauses that legitimize them. This is a major weakness, and may go some way to explaining two phenomena:

---

[2]Implementations are called processors in the Pascal Standard.

- COBOL and FORTRAN implementations are commonly of poor quality;

- many information technology practitioners are still not convinced about the relevance of standards, since the standards with which they ought to be most familiar are simply not delivering the results they want or need.

If we move on to look at other cases of programming language standards that have not delivered the goods, we will see that there are other lessons to be learnt.

3.3 Exemplars of programming language standards

In the case of Pascal, we have a small, elegant language that cried out for standardization in the late 1970s. Initially, implementations tended to be fairly close to each other (in terms of syntax and semantics) across dissimilar architectures, because the form of the 'standard' was an implementation: Professor Wirth, the inventor of Pascal, made the source code of his compiler freely available, and so there was a model for all to follow.

In general, however, an implementation used as an oracle is a poor form of standard, since any bugs in the implementation will generally be faithfully replicated across all products based upon them, and such bugs will be harder to see than in a more stylized representation of what the language is supposed to be. Model implementations are also inadequate from the point of view of balance of control (good standards are made with the consensus of all interested parties: users, suppliers and those with academic interests).

Unfortunately, the small size (in terms of facilities) of Standard Pascal turned out to be its biggest weakness. For complex political rather than compelling technical reasons, the standard was published in 1982 before the work was really complete. In a sense, it was sufficiently complete to publish, and few argued against publishing at the time, but with hindsight we can say that the lack of a type-secure module feature, no syntax for logical to physical file binding, no support for direct access (as opposed to sequential) i/o and no real string handling meant that Standard Pascal's success was not as great as it might have been. In particular, portability (which for the standard language is very strong) suffers badly once you reach for implementation-specific extensions. We can conclude that although well specified (the semantics are expressed in a heavily stylized form of English), the Pascal standard was too narrow in scope.

In contrast, the portability of Ada suffers from being inadequately specified (partly as a result of the huge scope of the language). Despite the popular belief that Ada implementations are essentially equivalent, the standard, ISO (1987), leaves a surprising amount to the implementor, and this has lead to difficulties with which Ada standardizers are still wrestling; see Wichmann (1989). This is probably due to the fact that the Ada standard followed the Pascal model, and although semantics expressed in natural language worked for Pascal, it doesn't seem to have been adequate for Ada.

As a final example we refer to PL/1 ISO (1979). Here, the language standardizers used a formal notation (VDM) and specified the full scope of a large, general purpose language. Many millions of pounds went into the standardization of PL/1, and yet standard PL/1 is barely used. Why? The reason is that the wrong language was standardized; or rather, the standardization committee and user community did not succeed in bringing standard PL/1 and IBM PL/1 together. The result is a well specified language, of full scope, which almost no-one uses.

It is depressing to observe that no standard language yet exists that would meet the sort of software engineering criteria that as a profession we are struggling to apply to applications software. This is particularly so at a time when the new Draft Interim Defence Standard for safety critical software MoD (1989) has been heralded as a lead to industry for the 1990s. That document contains sound requirements in the area of software implementation, which cannot currently be met. Unfortunately, as we argue in this paper, the foundations needed for the implementation requirements are only beginning to be established.

The most recent procedural language standardization effort is that for Modula-2, BSI (1989). The standardization committee has attempted to learn the lessons of the earlier mistakes by formally defining the language using VDM-SL, CEC (1989), by specifying implementation requirements which can be verified, and by not shying away from extending the language or its libraries in order not to specify a language too limited to be useful.

In view of the current state of standards, we would argue that the relevance of standards should be judged by what can be achieved, rather than what has been achieved in the past.

4. IMPLEMENTATION QUALITY AND RIGOROUS DEVELOPMENT
One of the problems in establishing the use of rigorous methods of software development is the notation gulf between specification and implementation languages. This gulf must be bridged by a development method (e.g. VDM, Jones (1990)). There is a widespread assumption that the choice of an appropriate programming language alone greatly lessens the problem: the choice of Pascal over FORTRAN, for example, would generally be held to be 'better' for

developing software using formal or rigorous methods. However, the choice of language is only a partial solution to the problem of the notation gulf; an examination of programming language standards and language implementations by Horton (1989) reveals a plethora of poor-quality implementations which undermine rigorous development, invalidate proofs, and frustrate testing.

In this section we provide evidence of these low-quality implementations and suggest how standards should address the issues which encourage the production.

4.1 Quality of language implementations

To discuss the relationship between quality and the implementation of languages requires a common understanding of 'quality' in this context. A textual definition would be insufficient, and so the main characteristics of high-quality implementations are given.

The first characteristic is that of *complexity*. Arguably, it is the most important, since it limits the achievement of the others. Here, complexity refers to the complexity of the source code which an implementation must correctly process; i.e. which an implementation must accept as input and for which it must generate correct code. This complexity is not synonymous with well-formedness or semantic correctness; it is relatively easy to construct valid, standard programs which implementations cannot process; see Wichmann (1989)

Obvious, but rare, characteristics are completeness and correctness. By *complete*, we mean that within its complexity limits an implementation will accept all source texts which are well-formed according to the definition of the language. Unfortunately incompleteness is common. All programmers know about 'missing features' (the ones which are coming *real-soon-now*).

For a language implementation to be *correct*, it must generate code which implements the semantics defined for well-formed source code — that is, subject to the complexity constraints already described. Again, incorrect implementations are common; many critical systems have failed because of incorrect object code, rather than because of a failure in the development process.[3] Worse, many high-integrity systems are currently being programmed using non-validated implementations, some of which are known to generate incorrect object code; see Horton (1989). Despite this, very few model implementation have been written:

---

[3]The most notorious example of this is the US F16 fighter aircraft that suffered from a bug in the sine function of an implementation used to produce the flight control software; the bug allegedly caused to the aircraft to invert as it crossed the equator.

Pascal (Welsh (1986)) and Ada[4] model implementations exist, and a C model implementation is being tested.[5]

Clearly the usefulness of rigorous development and of formal proofs is undermined when a language implementation is not correct.

As well as these important characteristics of quality, there are those which are immediately accessible to the programmer and, indeed, to marketing executive and the advertising copy writer. These include: speed of object code, efficient use of storage, reclamation of storage, documentation and program development environments (such as language sensitive editors, debuggers, etc.). While these are important and relevant to the non-functional goals of software development, we omit them from this discussion.

The final characteristic of a high-quality language implementation is the level of exception detection it provides. Exception detection is essential to the development of high-integrity systems as without it, testing may be futile. By implication, if not explicitly, the specification of most languages define exceptional dynamic behaviour in which the semantics of an executing program are lost. Obviously, if a language implementation does not generate code to check for exceptions, no amount of testing of the object code of a system will detect them. The absence of error detection may remove the point of unit testing and, more importantly, emasculates system and acceptance testing.

To summarize: software development ultimately relies on language implementations. The most important quality characteristics of an implementation are the ability to process complex programs, completeness, correctness, and the level of exception detection. We next look at the failure of standards to address issues of quality and what steps can be taken to correct this situation. Exception detection is discussed separately.

4.2 Quality aspects of language standardization

Most of the current programming language standard shy away from the quality aspects of language implementations. (In general, the older the standard, the less it will include concerning quality.)

One reason for this state of affairs is that many languages were invented and standardized at a time when hardware resources were expensive and scarce, and

---

[4]The model Ada implementation is the New York University Ada Interpreter.
[5]Knowledge Software, Farnborough, Hants., has produced the model compiler for C.

when there was considerable resistance to high-level languages for speed-critical or resource-consuming applications. A culture thus grew in which the both compilation speed and execution speed of object code became of paramount concern. Quality of object code became synonymous with this one aspect of quality. Consequently, implementors have gone to great lengths to produce fast code but have ignored those aspects of languages which are difficult or 'expensive' to implement. ('Expensive' often means speed-reducing in this context.) As argued before, the quality of language implementations should be primarily determined by their ability to handle complex programs, by their completeness, correctness and error detection capabilities.

A more subtle reason is the misunderstanding of the writers of standards as to the purpose of language standards and the consequent confusion in which quality issues are badly handled or omitted entirely. We contend that a programming language standard must provide two specifications:

1. A standard must define the form and meaning of a standard program, no matter how complex or demanding of the resources of the target machine. (By implication this defines an ideal implementation — one which can correctly handle programs of any complexity.)

2. A standard must define how an implementation may be less than ideal — how it can be incomplete, or the degree to which must accept complex programs, and how implementation-defined limits or implementation-dependant behaviour must be documented.

Without these clear goals, language requirements and implementation requirements have been confused. The most common example of this confusion is where a standard specifies execution semantics when defining a *language* construct. Many instances of this is to be found in the draft ANSI C standard.

This is not good practice, since such semantics, especially when expressed in natural language, will probably be ambiguous or non-portable, or both.

While a standard should not mislead by implying that all standard programs will be accepted by all implementations, it should not use implementation semantics. Clearly standards should identify those parts of a language which are prone to portability problems, and not just stay silent.

In general, quality-related *language* features are relevant to rigorous software development, and quality-related *implementation* features are relevant to portability (we postpone issues relating to portability until later). Of the language features the most important is the subject of exceptions — their detection, reporting and handling

4.3 Exception detection

There are two ways in which exceptions are detected: 'for free' by hardware or host operating system, and at a cost by code generated by an implementation. If it was not for that cost, all implementations would provide exception detection. (Although some programmers would occasionally prefer exception detection to be disabled, we assume that software engineers would prefer to know of any failure in their development process.)

Of course, in order for the designers of language implementations to provide exception detection, they must be informed of the exceptional states which programs can reach. Consequently language standards must at least record what exceptions can occur. The Pascal standard did this; it listed 59, and one or two compilers detect over 50, and far too many detect less than 10.

Ideally, therefore, standards should also require the detection of the exceptions it lists. However, because of the aforementioned cost of detection, standardizers may feel obliged to relax the requirement to detect certain exceptions. This pragmatic view has been taken during the standardization of Modula-2.

In the Modula-2 draft standard, BSI (1989), 47 exceptions have been listed —28 in the language and system modules, and the rest in separate library modules. (A list of Modula-2 exceptions is given in Annexe A.) The draft standard has proposed that for all but three of the exceptions detection should be mandatory in some mode of use. The exceptions for which detection is not mandatory are:

- Variable is undefined
- Access to inactive component of variant record
- Attempt to access non-existing variable

The reason for relaxing the requirement for these three is that their cost is held to be too high by most implementors. It is claimed that even if an implementation generated code (albeit complex and slow) to detect these exceptions, programmers would always choose a mode of use[6] which would disable the detection of the particular exceptions. Despite this argument, there is a strong counter-argument

---

[6]Language implementations can ususally run in different modes of use. Compiler directives can be employed to choose different sorts of code generation.

that even these should be detected in some mode of use because the programmer can always choose another mode.

5. IMPLEMENTATION QUALITY AND PORTABILITY

The portability of a program is directly related to the cost of re-implementing it using another implementation of the same language; highly portable software is inexpensive to rewrite for a different implementation. For high-level languages the cost *should* always be low. Woodman et al (1989).have shown that this is not the case. Proliferation of implementations before a precise standard, failure to upgrade implementations in line with hardware development, complacency as a result of captive markets, as well as confusion over requirements, have all led to deficiencies in many implementations of languages which should otherwise assist the software developer.

For example, while it is probably obvious that the range of values in whole number types will vary significantly among implementations, it is less obvious that some implementations of Pascal, for example, allow only 5 procedures to be nested; others permit 15; others have no practical limit. Ada implementations can also vary considerably; one implementation allows up to 250–343 different types to be declared, while another allows at least 1000 different types.[7]

While nesting limits will not cause problems for many applications, low limits on the number of procedures in a compilation unit (as low as 127) would. Similarly a limit of 64k bytes in a program (as in UCSD Pascal, see Clark (1982)) would be a severe handicap when re-implementing many systems.

As a result of such restrictions, in particular because of inadequate implementation of set types in Modula-2 compilers, it is proposed that the forthcoming Modula-2 Standard BSI (1989) will specify certain minima. These include minimum largest values for whole numbers, a minimum for any size restricting set cardinality, and minimum maxima for nesting data structures or procedures. (See Annexe B for further examples.)

Languages which support features such as concurrency or object-oriented structures will have corresponding limits for which minima should be specified. For example, the forthcoming Modula-2 standard is likely to specify a minimum for the maximum size of a coroutine workspace. An object-oriented language might impose a limit on the number of sub-classes of an object.

---

[7] The lack of precision is due to the method by which the Ada Evaluation System determines certain limits.

6. VALIDATION ISSUES

In this paper we have discussed quality as it relates to rigorous software development and as it relates to portability. To a large extent the former is tested using a *validation* suite for a language, while the latter is tested by an *evaluation* suite. As languages become more complex and implementors strive to produce high-quality systems, the task of validating and evaluating compilers becomes more difficult.

6.1 Evolving validation techniques

While it is appealing to assume that evaluation suites will evolve in line with compiler technology and that validation suites becomes frozen soon after a language's standardization (because the language has become frozen), this is not the case. Most language standards have paid scant regard to the needs of validation. This has resulted in continuing post-standardization work on ways in which test implementations. Also, our understanding of languages and their implementations is evolving, resulting in changes to the conceptual model of what a language specification and what an implementation is. In the case of Pascal, for example, this has lead to ten (annual) releases of the Pascal Validation Suite (PVS). Each release has exposed new problems in Pascal implementations — even those which have been certified to a high level with a previous release initially fail to reach the same level when validated to a later release of the suite.

In early releases of the PVS attempts were made to establish that validated compilers provided 'reasonable' lower limits for capacity and complexity; see Wichmann (1983). However, this was considered to be unsatisfactory because, without lower limits specified in a language standard, the tests were somewhat arbitrary. Also, the validating authority could not consider the failure to pass these non-mandated 'quality tests' in the validation report. Consequently, the quality tests were dropped from the validation suite and incorporated in an evaluation suite.[8] Capacity and complexity limits of the type described in §5 are determined by including a limit test generator and program generator Wichmann (1989) respectively.

Two problems with language design still present problems for validation which have yet to be solved. Both are present in Modula-2, but are not, in concept, peculiar to that language. The first is the provision of 'language' functionality through libraries. The second problem is that certain compiler analysis or code generation strategies may result in a compiler being able to handle the 'full'

---

[8]A Pascal Evaluation Service is run by BSI Quality Assurance.

language in some way; single-pass Modula-2 compilers cannot process programs which refer to identifiers in statements before they are declared. Both these problems are discussed below.

6.2 Validating libraries

In common with languages such as Ada and C, certain functions in Modula-2 are not provided in the language but through libraries. For example, Modula-2 does not provide either i/o functions or mathematical functions, but most Modula-2 implementations provide sets of modules for both. The Third Working Draft Modula-2 Standard, BSI (1989), describes both these libraries, and in general they could be validated in similar ways that Pascal i/o and mathematical functions are validated by the PVS.

It can be noted in passing that without the built-in exception handling feature of the Ada and proposed Modula-2 standards, it would be difficult, if not impossible to work out what is happening when an exception arises due to failure to meet the post-conditions of library semantics.

The situation for Modula-2 is more complex than has been indicated: the i/o and mathematics libraries are collections of modules which are not required to be present in an implementation (embedded systems do not need text or file i/o, for instance). These modules are simply called *separate* modules. Another class of module is the *required* separate module. An example of this is the module for creating and manipulating storage directly. It is required because the language has two built-in procedures (NEW and DISPOSE) which directly access such a module. It is separate because the programmer may choose to import different versions of the Storage module, and this means that validation must explicitly check the linking process and version control in general.

A third class of module is *system* modules: these are ones which the compiler 'knows' about. Arguably, Modula-2 system modules are those parts of the language which are not intended for casual use (e.g. facilities for accessing storage directly) and which are made less easily accessible using module *syntax*. However, it is possible that system modules could be implemented separately from the main translator in an implementation. Validation must deal with this type of language design.

6.3 Validating subset implementations

Many Modula-2 implementations process source code in a single-pass. Therefore they cannot process programs in which identifiers are used in statements before they have been declared. Multi-pass compilers, on the other hand, can process such programs. The draft Modula-2 standard accommodates both by considering implementations which insist on declaration-before-use as implementations whose ability to handle certain complex programs has been limited.[9] Thus, a Modula-2 validation suite would have to be capable of processing implementations which provide what could be considered to be a subset of the language.

The main implication for validation due to this type of language design (which in essence is not dissimilar from the Level 0/Level 1 split in Standard Pascal) is that deviance tests for the 'subset' may be, in fact, conformance tests for the full language. Thus, often a test which confirms that a multi-pass (use-before-declaration) implementation conforms to the language specification will confirm that a single-pass (declare-before-use) implementation deviates from the full language specification but conforms to the 'subset' specification.

Unwarranted complexity in validation, such as this is, inevitably leads us to question the wisdom of language designs from which the complexity derives.

---

[9] A predicate in the formal definition determines what semantics are applied to a given compiler.

7. USE OF FORMALITY IN LANGUAGE SPECIFICATION

It is ironic that nearly all programming languages have been either specified or standardized informally, in the sense that they have relied upon natural language specification of the semantics. This is not just a phenomenon of the past, there are many active projects where natural language is still being used, as the following table illustrates:

ISO Working Group	Language	Specification Method
WG2:	Pascal	Natural Language
	Extended Pascal	Natural Language
WG3:	APL	Semi-Formal
	Extended APL	Semi-Formal
WG4:	COBOL	Natural Language
WG5:	FORTRAN	Natural Language
	FORTRAN-8X	Natural Language
WG7:	PL/1	Meta-4
WG8:	BASIC	Natural Language
	Minimal-BASIC	Natural Language
WG9:	Ada	Natural Language
	Ada-9X	Natural Language
WG13:	Modula-2	VDM-SL
WG14:	C	Natural Language
WG16:	Lisp	Undecided
WG17:	Prolog	Logic

The heavily stylized English of the Pascal and Extended Pascal standards is occasionally augmented by the use of pre- and post-conditions. When natural language is not sufficient in the draft C standard, it describes what it expects to be implemented: effectively it provides execution semantics. The semi-formal notation referred to in the table is based on APL (it is thus based on mathematics) but has itself not been fully defined. Only PL/1 and Modula-2 have fully embraced a formal notation (Meta-4 and VDM-SL, respectively), although an attempt to specify Prolog using itself is in progress.

Experience with Modula-2 standardization has been very favourable. The use of a formalism has encouraged the construction of a number of formal models for consideration, rejection and revision; the ability to 'throw away' failed models cannot be afforded by standardizers who use natural language specification.

Having a formal model exposes many problems and has assisted the Modula-2 committee in devising solutions. A practical consequence of the use of formalism is that the ability to debate semantic issues is greatly enhanced. An unexpected bonus has been the ease with which exceptions have been identified and analyzed.

8. CONCLUSIONS AND RECOMMENDATIONS

As the software industry produces increasing numbers of high-integrity systems, its customers have demanded that the quality of the software be assured by various methods. A variety of methods — structured, rigorous and formal — have been invented and refined in order to facilitate the progression from a customer's statement of requirements to delivered, executable software. All these methods ultimately rely on robust implementations of languages and the ability to verify programs through the use of static analysis and dynamic testing.

In this paper we have exposed aspects of the poor state of programming language technology and thereby the weakness in the foundations which underpin all development methods:

- There is confusion in the terminology. If implementors and programmers do not understand fundamental aspects of their tools, how can they demand improvement?

- Compiler writers and the designers of language implementations are not using common or even consistent models of languages in their products. There is a need for standards which they must adopt.

- For too long the quality of language implementations has been determined by appealing advertising hyperbole rather than the less well provided capabilities for handling complex programs and error detection, not to mention completeness and correctness.

- Program portability is not well-served by current technology. The limits on complexity and capacity restrictions of implementations can have costly consequences for re-implementing high-level programs.

- In the past programming language standards have not explicitly required implementations to achieve certain quality minima.

In order to improve the basis of rigorous software development the supporting technology must be improved in the following ways:

1. Languages should be formally defined and all exceptions specified.

2. Standards must separate language and implementation requirements and specify minimum levels of quality in implementations. Programming language standardization must take into account the validation of implementations, and the evaluation of their qualities.

3. Validation and evaluation systems for assessing the quality of language implementations and associated static analysis tools must continue to be developed. Once operational, such systems must undergo continuous appraisal and improvement.

REFERENCES

AJPO (1983) *The Ada Compiler Validation Capability*, AJPO.

ANSI (1983) ANSI/IEEE Std 729-1983 *Glossary of Software Engineering Terminology*, ANSI, 1983.

ANSI (1989) ANSI X3.159-1989, *Programming Language C*, 1989

ISO (1983) ISO, *ISO 7185: Computer Programming Language Pascal*, 1983

BSI (1987) BSI, *BS0:1987 A Standard for Standards*, 1987

BSI (1988) *The Modula-2 Validation Suite*, BSI Quality Assurance, 1988

BSI (1989) *Third Working Draft Modula-2 Standard D106/N336*, BSI, 1989.

CEC (1989) *VDM Proto standard*, CEC, Brussels, 1989

Clark (1982) R. Clark and S. Koehler, *The UCSD Pascal Handbook*, Prentice-Hall, Englewood Cliffs, 1982

Horton (1989) M. Horton, *A Validation Report for Seven Pascal Compilers for IBM PCs and Compatibles under MS-DOS*, BSI Quality Assurance, 1989.

ISO (1979) *ISO 6160:1979 Programming Language PL/1*, 1979

ISO (1980)   ISO 1539 *Programming Language FORTRAN*, 1980

ISO (1985)   *ISO 1989:1985 Programming Language COBOL*, 1985.

ISO (1987)   ISO, ISO 8652:1987 *Ada Programming Language*, 1987

ISO (1989)   ISO/IEC JTC1/SC22/WG10, *Guidelines for the Preparation of Programming Language Standards*, ISO, 1989.

Jones (1990)   C.B. Jones, *Systematic Software Development Using VDM*, 2nd Edition, Prentice-Hall, London, 1990.

MoD (1989)   *Draft Interim Defence Standard 00-55*, 1989

Sale (1983)   A.H.J. Sale, Second Thougts on the Validation Suite in B.A. Wichmann and Z.J. Ciechanowicz (eds), *Pascal Compiler Validation*, Wiley, Chichester, 1983.

Souter (1989)   J. Souter, *Choosing a Compiler: An Approach to Reducing Risk*, Proceedings SafetyNet Conference, Malvern, October 1989.

Welsh (1986)   J. Welsh and A. Hay, *A Model Implementation of Standard Pascal*, Prentice-Hall, London, 1986

Wichmann (1973) B.A. Wichmann, *Some Validation Tests for an Algol Compiler*, National Physical Laboratory Report NAC 33, 1973

Wichmann (1983) B.A. Wichmann and Z.J. Ciechanowicz (eds), *Pascal Compiler Validation*, Wiley, Chichester, 1983.

Wichmann (1989) B.A. Wichmann and M. Davies, *Experience with a Compiler Testing Tool*, National Physical Laboratory Report DITC 138/89, 1989

Wichmann (1989) B.A. Wichmann, *Insecurities in the Ada Programming Language*, NPL Report DITC 137/89, 1989

Woodman et al (1989)   M. Woodman, R. Griffiths, J. Souter and M. Dacies, *Portable Modula-2 Programming*, McGraw-Hill, London, 1989.

ANNEXE A — MODULA-2 EXCEPTIONS

The formal definition of Modula-2 contains a number of instances of the auxiliary function *exception*. These instances are points at which violations of the dynamic semantics occur. It shall be required in the Modula-2 standard that certain exceptions shall be detected (and reported) when a conforming implementation is in some mode. Five lists of exceptions, together with an indication of whether detection of them is mandatory, follow: language exceptions, exceptions in the modules for coroutines, mathematics and i/o.

Language exceptions

Cause of Exception	Detection Mandatory?
Missing return statement in function procedure	Y
Assignment value out of range of target	Y
Tag value out of range	Y
Returned result of a function is out of range	Y
Case selector out of range	Y
Array indexed out of range	Y
Access to inactive component of variant record	N
Attempt to access non-existing variable	N
Attempt to dereference nil	Y
Real overflow	Y
Real division by zero	Y
Whole number overflow	Y
Whole number division (/) by zero	Y
Whole number remainder by zero	Y
Whole number division (DIV) by negative or zero value	Y
Whole number modulo by negative or zero value	Y
Variable is undefined	N
Set values out of range of set type	Y
Value to be excluded does not belong to the base type	Y
Value to be included does not belong to the base type	Y
Given protection is not equal to the current protection	Y
Expression cannot be converted to the new type	Y
There is not previous protection in the protection stack (i.e. Call of LEAVE without corresponding call of ENTER.)	Y
Attempt to use invalid procedure variable	Y

Coroutines Module Exceptions

Cause of Exception	Detection Mandatory?
Size of the supplied workspace is smaller than the minimum size required	Y
The caller is not attached to a source of interrupts	Y

Storage Module Exceptions

Cause of Exception	Detection Mandatory?
Value of the variable passed to DEALLOCATE is NIL	Y
Variable points to unallocated storage location	Y
Area to be unallocated is not the same as the currently allocated area	Y

Mathematical Modules Exceptions

Cause of Exception	Detection Mandatory?
Value of the argument to sqrt is negative	Y
The value of the argument to the natural logarithm is zero or negative	Y
The absolute value of the argument to arcsin is greater than 1.0	Y
The absolute value of the argument to arccos is greater than 1.0	Y
The value of the argument to the power function is zero or negative	Y

I/O Library Exceptions

Cause of Exception	Detection Mandatory?
Output operation called for on a channel that does not currently support output operations.	Y
Input operation called for on a channel that does not currently support input operations.	Y
Operation called for on the nil channel	Y
Open called for a channel that is already open.	Y
A device specific operation called for on a channel that is not open to that device.	Y
Random access file position cannot be expressed using given chunk size.	Y
Random access file position closer to start of file than number of storage units to move back by.	Y
Random access file length cannot be expressed using given chunk size.	Y
Text operation called for on a channel that does not currently support text operations.	Y
Direct operation called for on a channel that does not currently support direct operations.	Y
String not in required format for numeric conversion operation.	Y

ANNEXE B: PROPOSED MINIMA FOR MODULA-2 IMPLEMENTATIONS

The following minima have been proposed for Modula-2.[10]

Minimum lexical values:
- maximum length of an identifier (e.g. 32)
- maximum length of a string literal (e.g. 255)

Minimum maxima for simple types:
- maximum cardinality of set types (e.g. 255)
- value of maximum whole number type (e.g. 32767)
- maximum number of values in the character type (e.g. 127)

Minimum maxima for structured types:
- maximum number of components of an array (i.e. number of values in an index type (e.g. 65535)
- maximum (static) nesting of parentheses in an expression (e.g. 16)
- maximum (static) nesting of record types (e.g. 8)
- maximum number of variants in record types (e.g. 8)
- maximum (static) nesting of array types (e.g. 8)
- maximum size (in terms of storage) of a structured type (e.g. 128k bytes)

Minimum maxima for statements:
- maximum static nesting of statements (e.g. 8)
- maximum number of case alternatives (e.g. 255)

Minimum maxima for procedures:
- maximum number of parameters in a procedure (e.g. 16)
- maximum (static) nesting of procedures (e.g. 8)
- maximum local storage for a procedure (e.g. 64k bytes)
- maximum size of code generated for a procedure (e.g. 64k bytes)
- maximum size of a variable parameter's type or of a function result type (e.g. 64k bytes)

Minimum maxima for i/o:
- maximum number of i/o streams which may be open simultaneously (e.g. 16)

---

[10] The values for these minima have not yet been decided.

Methods and Tools for Testing-in-the-Large

R. Franck, A. Spillner, J. Herrmann

University of Bremen - Fachbereich Mathematik/Informatik
Federal Republic of Germany

Abstract

Testing is the most important practical technique to assure the quality of a program. The test methods developed up to now can primarily be applied to small programs or parts of them. There do not yet exist procedures for testing huge modular systems taking into account the decomposition of the system and concentrating on the evaluation of the interface behaviour between its single parts.

In this paper static and dynamic test methods developed for testing-in-the-small are applied to the situation of integrating large systems. Some classes of errors which cannot be found by isolated module testing are pointed out. A corresponding tool to support integration testing is sketched.

1 THE NEED OF INTEGRATION TESTING METHODS

Software systems are growing more and more complex. The construction of large systems is only feasible by decomposition into subsystems and modules until these parts are small enough to be successfully implemented and tested. In the past many methods and tools supporting all the early activities in the development of software systems have been evolved, i.e. requirements definition, design, decomposition, specification and implementation of modules. It is generally accepted that a modularization of huge systems is necessary and there is agreement about the desirable criteria and properties of software modules [Parnas/Clements/Weiss 85]. Corresponding module constructs have been integrated into more recent programming languages like ADA and Modula-2.

There is however a lack of methods and tools to support the integration testing of large systems [Beizer 84]. Usually the only aspects discussed in the literature are integration strategies e.g. top-down, bottom-up or some combinations of them like sandwich or jo-jo integration [Myers 79, Yourdon/ Constantine 79].

This deficiency regularly shows up in software projects during the integration phase: the integration team starts with some modules which happen to be ready; these are tied together and then tested in the same way as if they were a single module - and everybody hopes that this procedure can be continued till the system is finished. But usually one does not succeed that way. One major source of the resulting problems is the fact that the existing test methods are only suited for testing smaller programs, i.e. isolated modules of a system. These fail however when applied to a huge system or a program torso which grows more and more complex.

The methods developed for module testing fail when applied to components and subsystems of growing size during integration because they do not take into consideration the decomposition of the system decided upon before. The same divide-and-conquer strategy used for this decomposition should be applied to reduce the complexity while integrating and testing a growing part of the whole system.

To improve the situation the following strategy is proposed:

- All modules are tested in isolation before integration. The results of module testing are available for integration testing.

- Integration testing takes place on a more abstract level: the atoms to be evaluated during integration are the modules and their interactions.

- The main interest is on the interface relations between the modules: as long as a module shows the specified interface behaviour it is assumed to be correct - trusting in the module testing performed before.

For testing-in-the-small there have been some different and complementary methods developed: each of them is useful in revealing a certain class of errors. Applying several of them to the same test object augments the probability of detecting errors. The same holds for integration testing as well: one cannot expect to develop a single, exhaustive test method revealing all errors during the integration of a large system.

In the sequel the well-known test methods of static analysis and dynamic execution are investigated in order to see in which way they can be adapted to integration testing, i.e. to evaluate the interfaces of modules:

- It is described which new results can be derived, i.e. which class of errors may be found which cannot be detected before by testing single modules.

- In order to be able to perform the coupling analysis one needs some information about the interfaces which is hidden in the source code of modules and obtained during module testing. We derive some additional requirements for isolated module testing the outcomes of which will later be used for integration testing.

- Furthermore a tool for supporting these methods is described.

2 STATIC ANALYSIS

This method comprises all static investigations, i.e. all knowledge which can be gained about a program without its execution [Miller/Howden 78/81 Section 3]. The results of these investigations are usually presented as lists and graphs : the use of program objects is investigated (type, structure and liveness), the wrong static usage of program objects (mainly those of variables) and unreachable code can be detected. The outcome of static analysis normally includes program graphs and procedure call graphs [Muchnik/Jones 81]. A special kind of static data flow analysis [Fosdick/Osterweil 76] detects the following read/write anomalies: reading a data object without a valid value (undefined reference) or the missing reading of a data object with a valid value (dead definition).

Similary during integration testing many interface investigations can be done without the execution of the system. Anomalies (if they exist) can be uncovered and the structure of the system can be described:

- The syntactical correctness of interfaces is checked, e.g. a wrong number of parameters or a mismatch of parameter types. (Compilers or linkers of languages like Modula-2 and Ada guarantee such consistencies.)

- In [Osterweil/Fosdick 76] interface data (used global variables, actual/formal parameter lists) are classified into input or output data (or both). This allows abstraction from the detailed data flow along the possibly great number of paths through the procedure. Transferring this idea leads to the development of a method for uncovering interprocedural and intermodular data flow anomalies [Herrmann/Spillner/Franck 90]. One example of an indication of a possible error which can be detected this way is the following situation (see example 1): an external (imported) procedure with a result (output) parameter is called and immediately after this call there occurs an assignment to this parameter (example of a dead definition).

Example 1:

```
MODULE A;                                   MODULE B;
    EXPORT P;                                   IMPORT P;
    ...                                         ...
    PROCEDURE P (VAR out : INT)                 BEGIN
    ...                                             ...
        BEGIN                                       P(outcome);
            ...                                     outcome := x;
            out:=result;                            ...
        END P;                                  END B
    ...
END A
```

The following investigations give an indication of the quality of the system structure:

- [Myers 75] has defined a six step hierarchy of coupling (relationship) between modules: modules are strongly coupled if they communicate by global variables; a loose coupling is the exchange of data via parameters, but where the complexity of the data structure of the parameters is also taken into account. The strength of coupling influences the understanding, changing and the testing of a program system: the stronger a system is coupled the more difficult these activities are.

  The relationships between the single parts of the system and its overall architecture become clear and can be compared with the specified design decisions.

- Relationships are detected which can not be seen readily from the source program: if two modules (A,B) communicate via a global variable, which is exported by a third module (C), this coupling is not always evident: if one module is changed this dependency may easily be overlooked. Hence it is necessary to compute and to analyze the transitive closures of global variable couplings (see figure 1).

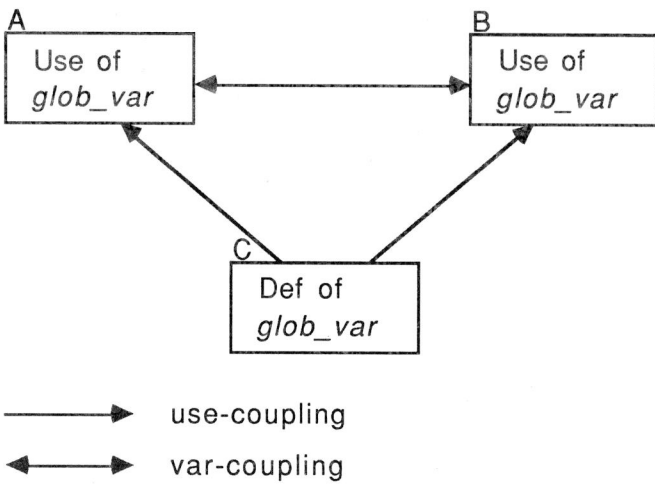

Figure 1: Coupling via global Variables

The information collected this way is a good documentation of the architecture of the system and in combination with the classification of module couplings yields important support for the maintenance phase: consequences of desired changes can be calculated more exactly.

– Another aspect of static investigations is to provide knowledge for the following dynamic test, e.g. by helping to find input values for the execution of certain program paths.

3 DYNAMIC EXECUTION

Dynamic testing is the normal activity of running a program to see what happens. A test bed must exist which allows the execution of a module or a system: the tester has to provide input data and the expected program output; the program behaviour and the input-output relations are documented.

As part of the specification of a module should exist at least rough input/output descriptions of test cases; they should prove the desired functionality of the test object [Howden 80, 87]. Additionally, a test should include data which are within and outside the range of legal input data domains [Goodenough/Gerhard 75]. The results of static investigations are used for instrumenting the test object and for gaining hints to supplementary test cases of interest.

A possible criterion for the development of test cases is to execute all statements or branches of the test object at least once [Miller 77]. A dual aim is to exhaust the legal values of all of its data objects [Rapps/Weyuker 85]. For regression testing and maintenance purposes it is important to collect statistics while carrying out the test cases. This is usually supported by an automatic instrumentation of the test object.

Dynamic integration testing concentrates on checking the couplings between modules and should yield the following results:

- A weaker form of transferring the usual control flow coverage is to demand that a collection of test cases for integration testing should invoke every interface procedure of the system at least once: i.e. all exported procedures of all modules must be called once during the execution of the test suite. It is possible that such a check has to be delayed because some interfaces of a module already integrated are only used by parts of the system which are still missing.

- A more rigid coverage demand would be the aim that a set of test cases activates all external references (i.e. all import sites) within a module, especially within the last module being added to the already integrated subsystem. Clearly this stronger coverage implies the weaker form above.

In both cases the information about the intermodular interfaces and their activation within a module is necessary and should be a result of module testing which is stored and used for this sort of interface checking during integration testing.

- The data which should be covered by integration testing are the interface data. Test cases which lead to extreme or boundary values of interface data should be included. During module testing such boundary values often cannot be checked because of the limited functionality of stubs.

- The functionality of each module and interface has to be checked. Indeed this is the most important aspect of integration testing. It is the first and in general only chance during the development to detect interface misunderstandings between different (teams of) developers. ([Basili/Pericone 84, p. 46] report that statistically about 50% of all errors are unexpected functional behaviours of modules.)

  An example of such an error is the following: a module offers an interface which functionally sorts a list in ascending order. But in the coded program the ordering is done in reverse. If during the module testing this function is checked by a stub written by the same developers it will contain the ordering which was expected but which is wrong. This is one of those typical errors which can only be found during integration testing.

- There are often certain restrictions on the order in which the interface operations of a module or component may be activated. This mostly applies to programs or modules with internal states. A concrete example is a stack where the first access must not be a read operation. In a good design one will try to localize these restrictions within one module. But e.g. for reasons of complexity one may be forced to subdivide this component further. In such a case checks must be made on all sequences of interface activations possible in the system to check that they do not violate the specified constraints.

4 DESIGN AND IMPLEMENTATION OF AN INTEGRATION TESTING TOOL

Due to the great number of specifications, source files, test cases and other documents integration teams have to deal with, there is an urgent need for support by an appropriate tool. Taking into account that a great deal of the sketched integration testing will often be repeated during the maintenance of a system, machine support becomes a must. As well as a speed-up the access to desired information, an appropriate tool should assure the provision of up-to-date information. This will help to prevent maintainers from trying to repair today's errors while having in mind yesterday's structure of the system.

A tool for integration testing must have access to all information about the implementation of the system (specification of modules and interfaces, description of the system architecture and especially all results of module testing). Different information is needed for different testing methods and stages. An adequate testing tool must be able to offer only the desired information in an appropriate manner; it should help to split up the overall integration testing process into a sequence of small and manageable tasks. These goals become even more urgent when one takes into account the fact that there is often not enough effort and time reserved for integrating the system in the project planning. In addition to this integration tends to take place in a situation where nearly everybody can see that the project is going to be late anyway.

The research described above has been developed within a project funded in part by the National Research Foundation of the Federal Republic of Germany (Deutsche Forschungsgemeinschaft). From the beginning, an integral aim of the project has been to demonstrate the usefulness of the integration testing methods by developing a prototype for a corresponding tool.

The principal aim of the integration testing tool we have designed is to incorporate and support the integration test methods described above. We did not aim at supporting the management of all data and files necessary for test and integration teams, even though we are aware of the fact that this is often their most urgent problem. This must be solved by services of a specialized project library, a software development environment or programming support environment [PSDE 87]. Nevertheless we laid stress on an adequate user interface supporting a quick and comfortable access to the information which the tester wants to see.

In the following we will describe the user interface of our prototype and summarize the state of our implementation.

<u>User Interface.</u> For different testing situations different forms of interaction and representation of information will be adequate. The knowledge about the test object will be offered in three different ways:
- as graphical representation,
- by a query interface answering user requests
- and in the usual way as text documents.

Modern workstations made it possible and popular to use pictures for visualizing algorithmic models and states. Such graphical means can also heavily support the task of an integration team. In order to help immediate understanding such pictures must not be too complex; in particular, they should not be overloaded with details. Keeping graphics simple and providing all information relevant for integration testing means defining a clear hierarchy of information layers and providing good functions for zooming and abstracting.

The highest level represents a general view of the system's architecture. If a tester asks for more information about an interface which shows up in a list of external references of the interesting module, he should be guided to the concrete source code level of the exporting module. Thinking about the effect of a change one needs quite another picture to demonstrate all the applied occurrences of the interface or module under consideration.

Often the tester needs only quite restricted information about the test object; but mostly he is forced to extract this out of a bunch of documents. The query interface exploits a knowledge base. It will help the tester and reduce the effort of searching. E.g. the following queries are possible:
- Where is the global variable *overflow* used/written/read?
- Which are the call environments and actual parameters of the function *control_output* in the modules *printer* and *terminal* ?
- Which coupling relations exist in the system?

Searching manually for this kind of information, one has a good chance of overlooking data and neglecting or even introducing errors. An appropriate algorithm guarantees the correctness, completeness and up-to-dateness of the gained information.

Our integration test support offers the graphic and query interface in parallel: the graphic interface shows the abstract relationships between modules and the query interface answers concrete questions about details omitted in the picture and/or refering to the implementation.

Looking at the piles of documents being produced during the development of a system and stored in a project library, one should have some automatic support for browsing through these documents, extracting information relevant for a specific data item or procedure etc. In integration testing some data is also produced which has to be integrated in the project documentation, such as the integration strategy, the order in which modules/procedures have been added, the test cases and traces which support regression testing. Clearly this information should be provided by the same user interface and using the same graphic means and queries as for the rest of the documentation.

Development of a Prototype. Any test tool providing support beyond the administration of test cases and results will very soon become languagedependent. In particular, the analysis and instrumentation of test objects directly depend on the syntax of the language of the test objects. For pragmatic reasons we chose Modula-2: we have good compilers available; we have experience with this language; there are language constructs which strongly support modularization such that the compiler guarantees the syntactic consistency of the module interfaces; we expected that this would facilitate the necessary analysis of programs so that there would be more time left to concentrate on integration testing methods.

Our prototype is implemented on a Sun workstation 3/50. There are several implementation languages and packages: the lexical and syntactic analysis of the test objects is done by a parser written in C and relying on the UNIX-tools LEX and YACC. The results of the analysis are stored as Prolog facts. In this way the semantic analysis of interest can be performed by applying corresponding rules using the Prolog interpreter. This representation of the syntactic skeleton of a program can also be viewed as the knowledge base on which we build our query interface. We use a graphics package EDGE written in C++ [Newbery 89] to construct the diagrams for a graphic visualization of facts. An example of the user interface of the prototyp is given in figure 2.

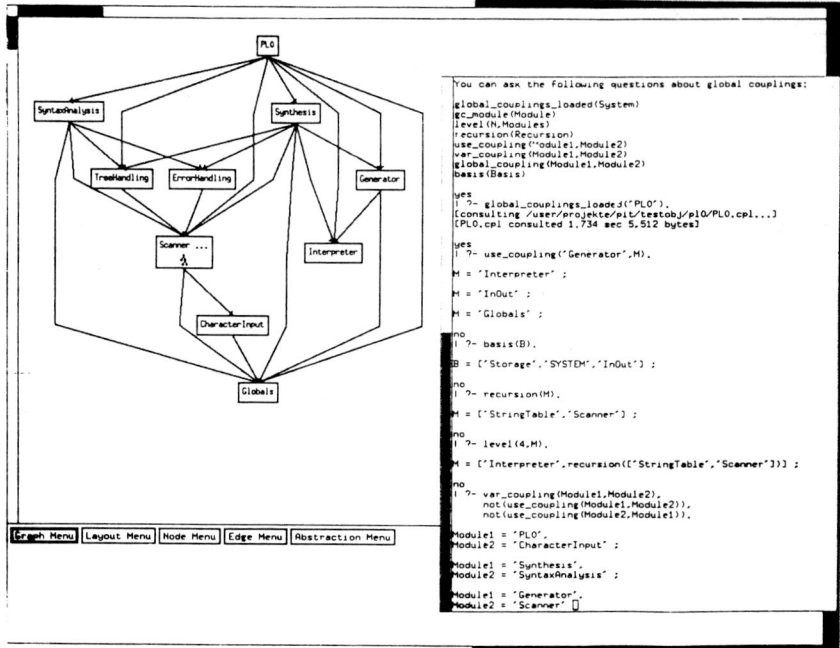

Figure 2: User interface of the prototyp

5 CONCLUSION

We had a number of discussions with representatives of industrial organisations: all of them agreed that it would be desirable to have a tool available providing the services outlined above for their quality assurance team. Therefore we are going to start the design of a comparable tool for systems written in C.

Another recent confirmation of our research occured during the last conference on testing and validation: the development of integration testing support was mentioned among the most important directions for the future (c.f. 'White Paper' mentioned on p. 56 in [TAV3 89]). So we hope that our results can contribute to the development of a generally accepted methodoloy of integration testing and interface evaluation.

LITERATURE

[Basili/Perricone 84] Basili, V.R.; Perricone, B.T.: *Software Errors and Complexity: An Empirical Investigation.* Communication of the ACM, Vol. 27, No. 1, 1984, pp 42-52

[Beizer 84] Beizer, B.: *Software System Testing and Quality Assurance.* Van Nostrand Reinhold Company, NY, 1984, 357 p.

[Fosdick/Osterweil 76] Fosdick, L.D.; Osterweil, L. J.: *Data Flow Analysis in software reliability.* ACM Computing Surveys, Vol. 8, No. 3. 1976, pp 305-330

[Goodenough/Gerhart 75] Goodenough, J.B.; Gerhart, P.L.: *Toward a Theory of Test Data Selection.* IEEE Transactions on Software Engineering, Vol. SE-1, No. 2, 1975, pp 156-173

[Herrmann/Spillner/Franck 90] Herrmann, J., Spillner, A., Franck, R.: *Statischer Integrationstest.* to appear as Fachbericht Informatik, Fachbereich Mathematik/Informatik, Universität Bremen, 1990

[Howden 80] Howden, W.E.: *Functional Program Testing.* IEEE Transactions on Software Engineering, Vol. SE-6, No. 2, 1980, pp 162-169

[Howden 87] Howden, W.E.: *Functional Program Testing & Analysis.* McGraw-Hill, NY, 1987, 175 p.

[Miller 77] Miller, E.: *Program Testing: Art Meets Theory.* Computer, July 1977, pp 42-51

[Miller/Howden 78/81] Miller, E.; Howden, W.E. (eds): *Tutorial: Software Testing & Validation Techniques.* 1st/2nd Ed., IEEE Cat. No. EHO-138-8/180-0, 1978/81, 425/454 p.

[Muchnick/Jones 81] Muchnik, S.S., Jones, ND. (eds): *Program Flow Analysis: Theories and Applications.* Prentice-Hall, Englewood Cliffs, NJ., 1981, 418 p.

[Myers 75] Myers, G.J.: *Reliable Software Through Composite Design.* Petrocelli/Charter, NY 1975, 163 p.

[Myers 79] Myers, G.J.: *The Art of Software Testing.* John Wiley & Sons, NY, 1979, 177 p.

[Newbery 89] Newbery, F.J.: *Edge Concentration: A Method for Clustering Directed Graphs.* Software Engineering Notes, Vol 17, No 7, November 1989, pp 76-85

[Osterweil/Fosdick 76] Osterweil, L.J.; Fosdick, L.D.: *DAVE - A Validation Error Detection and Documentation System for Fortran Programs.* Software - Practice and Experience, Vol 6, No 4, 1976, pp. 473-486

[Parnas/Clements/Weiss˘85] Parnas, D.L, Clements, P.C., Weiss, D.M.: *The Modular Structure of Complex Systems.* IEEE Transactions on Software Engineering, Vol SE-11, No 3, March 1985, pp 259-266

[PSDE 87] Proc. *Software Engineering Symposium on Practical Software Development Environments,* ACM SIGPLAN Notices, Vol 22, No 1, January 1987, 227 p.

[Rapps/Weyuker 85] Rapps, S.; Weyuker, E.J.: *Selecting Software Test Data Using Data Flow Information.* IEEE Transactions on Software Engineering, Vol. SE-11, No. 4, 1985, pp 367-375

[TAV3 89] Proc. *3rd Symposium on Testing and Validation,* ACM Software-Engineering Notes, Vol 14, No 8, December 1989, 229 p.

[Yourdon/Constantine 79] Yourdon, E.; Constantine, L.: *Structured Design.* Prentice Hall, Englewood Cliffs, NJ, 1979, 493 p.

Formal approaches

Adding Structure and Formality to the Physical Design Stage of SSADM, H. Edwards, J. Thompson & P. Smith

Z Specifications and Modal Logic, E. Fergus & D. Ince

Adding Structure and Formality to the Physical Design Stage of SSADM

H.M.EDWARDS, J.B.THOMPSON AND P.SMITH

Sunderland Polytechnic.

ABSTRACT

SSADM(version 3) is extended to explicitly consider the requirements of the program design phase of the system development life cycle. The extended physical design phase is specifically targeted at the JSP program design method (since this is frequently used in conjunction with SSADM for systems development). In the physical design phase the processing is considered in the Program Specification stage and this is structured into a series of steps and tasks (supported by systems design techniques) which define the form and contents of the (modular) programs. The products of the stage facilitate JSP program design.

The first part of the paper describes the procedure of the Program Specification stage. In the second part the formalisation of this procedure, using the basic concepts of category theory, is outlined.

KEYWORDS: SSADM, JSP, Formalism, Category Theory.

1 INTRODUCTION

In the UK the two design methods, SSADM (Structured Systems Analysis and Design Method) [LONG86] and JSP (Jackson Structured Programming) [JACK75] [THOM89] are frequently used during systems development projects [EDWA88] [NCC87]. SSADM competently addresses the analysis and logical design stages of systems development whilst JSP provides a rigorous and systematic method for detailed program design. However, both methods have their inadequacies: in SSADM(version 3) the approach to physical design lacks depth and breadth in terms of both structure and formalism [EDWA88a,b,c] and JSP fails to provide a general method for decomposing programs into modules. Therefore, the authors have designed an interface [EDWA89d] which optimises the benefits gained by using both methods and overcomes their shortcomings.

In the interface the physical design stage of SSADM(version 3) is replaced by a three-staged physical design phase. These replacement stages are: Physical Data Design, Program Specification and Completion of the Minor Tasks (where the tasks covered in the minor steps of the current stage six can be executed in parallel with the other two stages). The revised structure of SSADM is shown in Figure 1 and the three stages of the replacement phase are described fully in [EDWA89d].

This paper focuses on the Program Specification stage which impacts most upon the subsequent Program Design and Implementation phase of the software life cycle. The stage is structured into a series of steps and tasks, (supported by well established systems design techniques) which are used to define the form and contents of the (modular) programs. The products of the stage facilitate the production of well defined JSP-designed programs.

In system and program development consistency of design is a primary concern and since the preservation of structures is the underlying concept of category theory [GOLD84] [BURS88] this is particularly suited to such applications. The procedure in the Program Specification stage is formalised by a category theoretic underpinning. The techniques used to develop the program specifications and designs are defined categorically [TSE87]. Within each of these categories the development of a program design is validated by the existence of arrows between one version of a diagram and the next. Furthermore, by defining functors between categories the form of the program design in one technique can be mapped into another thus assuring consistency of design.

In this paper Section 2 gives an overview of the Program Specification stage and its output. Sections 3 to 5 provide detail for the tasks and techniques which add structure to the physical design. Section 6 gives an overview of the role of category theory in the method, then Sections 7 8 and 9 consider the categories and functors used and the resultant formal -ism of the stage. Finally, Section 10 considers future developments of the formalised method.

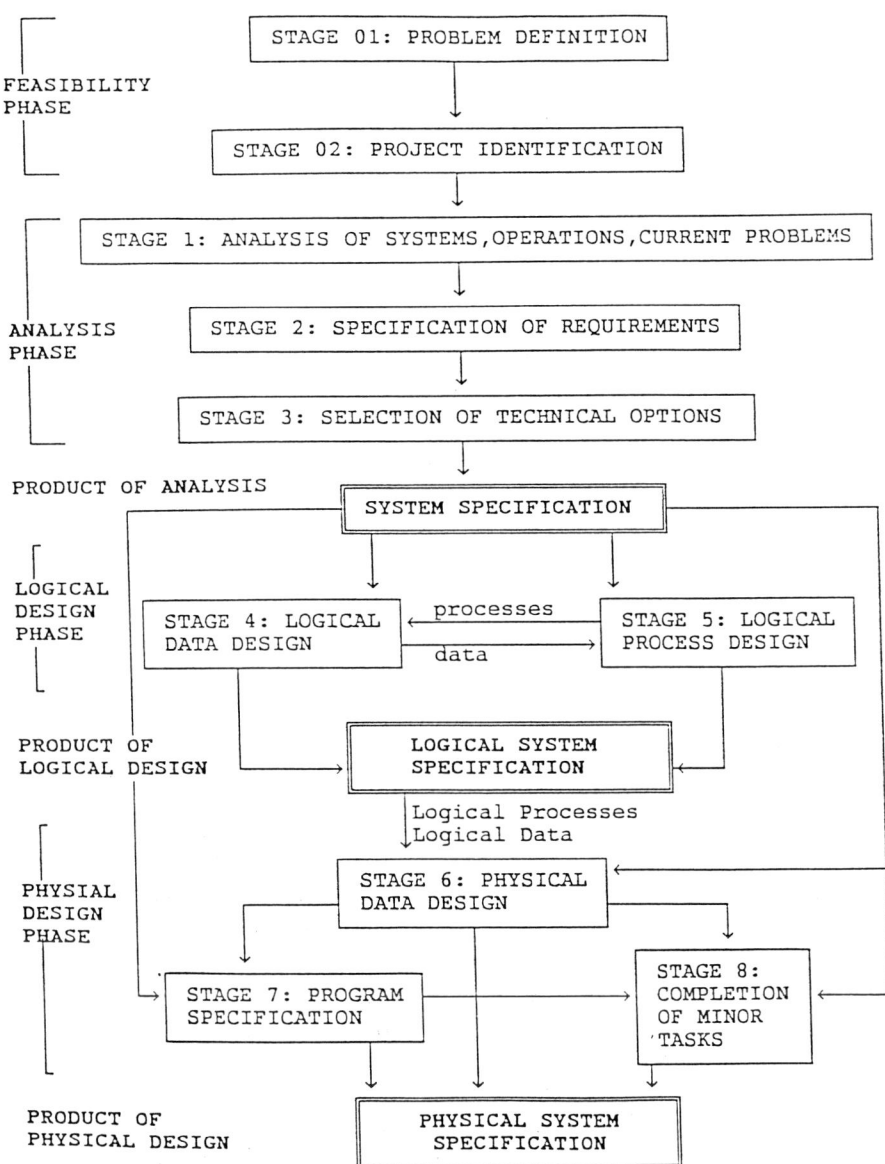

Figure 1: PROPOSED REVISED STRUCTURE FOR SSADM

2 OVERVIEW OF THE PROGRAM SPECIFICATION STAGE

The Program Specification stage has two main parts (and First and Second Cut Modular Design) and one major output.

2.1 First Cut Modular Design

The programs in the system are identified and their basic modular structures are defined (this is largely independent of implementation considerations).

2.2 Second Cut Modular Design
The modular program structures are assessed and modified in relation to the installation standards and rules to give the detailed program specifications which are the output of the stage.

2.3 Output of the Stage: The Program Specifications
The products of this stage are detailed and unambiguous specifications for the programs within the system. Several of the items listed in the program specifications may be references to installation standards and procedures. A program specification has two possible frameworks [EDWA89d]. The first is used where the program is small and non-modular, therefore, all the information is contained within the specification. The second is used for large modular programs where the program specification contains general information needed for all modules and references to the specification of all modules within the program. Detailed specifications are then produced for each module within the program.

The steps and techniques of the stage are shown in Figure 2.

3 PRODUCING THE FIRST CUT MODULAR DESIGNS
The functional areas addressed by the programs within the system are determined from products of the analysis and logical design phases of SSADM. The functions, defined in the catalogues, consist of one, or more, processes recorded on the lowest levels of the DFD sets. The Physical Process Specifications, PPSs, (derived from the Stage 5 Logical Process Outlines, POs) are allocated to these functions. For those functions which do not affect the central data design (and so have no PPSs allocated to them) the constituent processes of the functions must be identified and their corresponding PPSs and data created. Thereafter all functions are treated in the same manner.

Each function is examined to determine whether any further processes are required to support it. The processes identified in the PPSs (and the data processed) are used in the construction of the Program Data Flow Diagrams (PDFDs); any further processes and data streams that are identified as missing are documented. For such processes PPSs are constructed and for the data the necessary external files are defined.

The initial PDFD sets for each functional program group is used to determine which, if any, processes need to be combined or decomposed further.

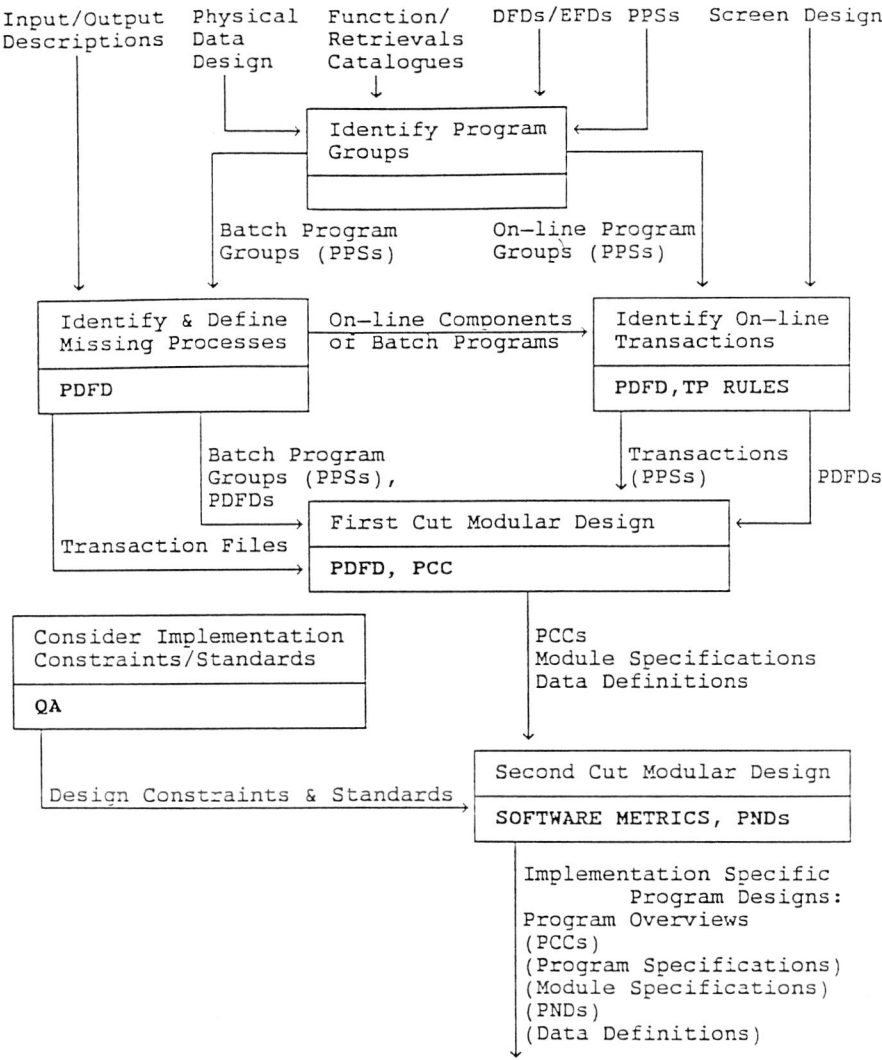

Figure 2: PROGRAM SPECIFICATION STAGE

The PDFD is modified until it adequately reflects the processes (and their data) in the functional group. Then using the Transform and Transaction Analysis procedures [YOUR78] [MYER78] [STEV81] the initial modular program structures are derived. First Cut Modular Design (FCMD) is complete when the programs have been developed into fully modular structures (Program Composition Charts, PCCs).

4 PROCEDURES AND TECHNIQUES OF FIRST CUT MODULAR DESIGN

4.1 Program Data Flow Diagrams

The Program Data Flow Diagrams (PDFDs) show the processes and annotated dataflows of programs. Two symbols are used to explicitly show the coexistence and selection of data flows. ⊗ between data flows into, or out of, a process implies that whenever the process is executed all of the flows are consumed or produced (Coexistence). ⊕ implies that whenever the process is executed only one of the flows is consumed or produced (Selection). The form of a PDFD is shown in Figure 4-1.

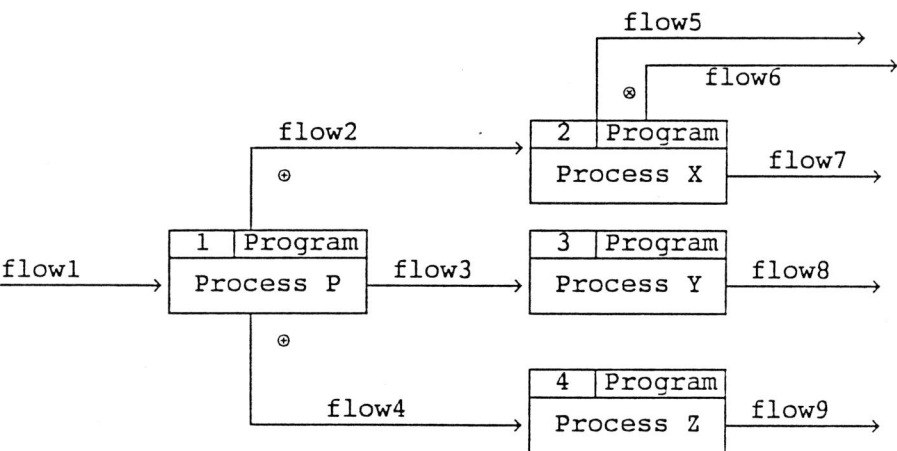

Figure 4-1: EXAMPLE OF A PDFD

4.2 Program Composition Charts (PCCs)

Program Composition Charts (PCCs) show the modular structure of programs (they have some similarities to Yourdon Structure Charts [YOUR78]). The chart shows how superordinate modules call sequences or selections of modules or coexistent modules (where the modules on the subordinate level have no data transferred among them). The parameters passed from one module to another are shown by annotated arrows. The form of a PCC (without any data flows) is shown in Figure 4-2.

In Figure 4-2:
Module A calls a sequence of modules B, C, and D.
Module C calls subordinate modules where a slectin of F or G is involved.
Module F calls coexistent subordinate modules H, I and J.

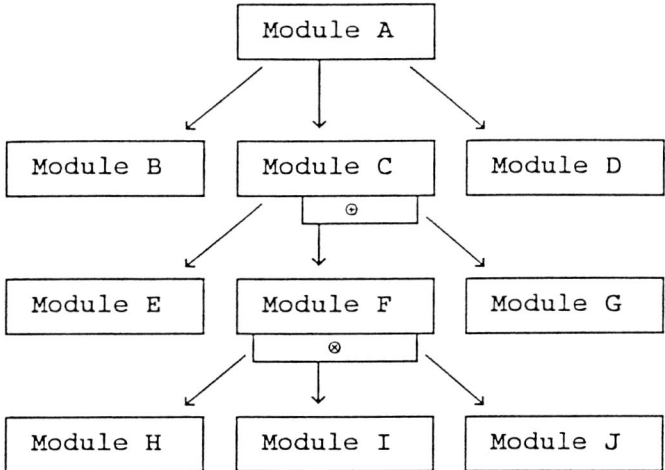

Figure 4-2: EXAMPLE OF A PCC

4.3 Transform Analysis Procedure

In Transform Analysis the PDFD form of a program is structured into a balanced hierarchy of modules, which is shown in a Program Composition Chart (PCC). This is achieved by first defining the inflow and outflow data streams of the PDFD, and then the Central Transforms of the program can be identified. The PDFD is then converted into a balanced PCC with inflow, outflow and central transform branches. The main module of the program is an "executive" module which controls the subordinate modules. The contents of the inflow, outflow and transform branches of the program are then developed; during this process modification of the modules identified in the PDFD may be necessary. A detailed description of Transform Analysis is given in [YOUR78] chapter 10.

Not all programs will have the most suitable structure when decomposed into strictly inflow and outflow branches, however, this approach is used to give the initial modularization of the program.

4.4 Transaction Analysis Procedure

Transaction Analysis is used to develop programs with PDFDs which exhibit the form shown in Figure 4-3.

Process P of Figure 4-3 is termed a "Transaction Centre" since it accepts a data flow (transaction) and then, depending upon the detail of the information in the data flow, outputs a specific type of data flow, x,y or z, for further processing.

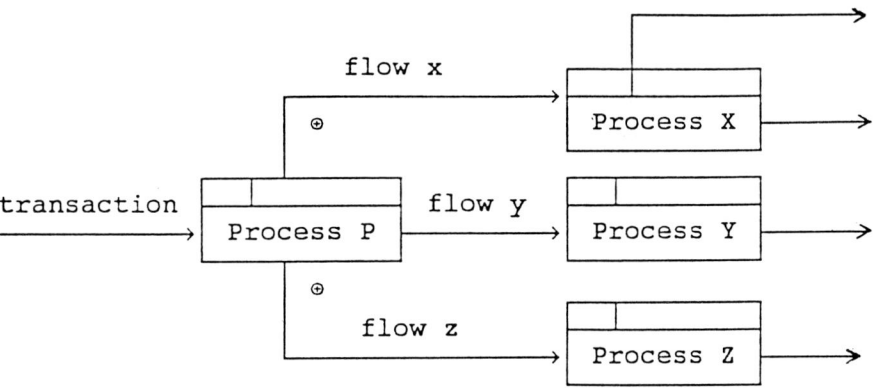

Figure 4-3: A TRANSACTION-CENTRED PDFD

The modular decomposition of a transaction centre has a basic, four-level, structure of the type shown in Figure 4-4. As the figure shows modules at the action and detail level may be shared by the superordinate transaction modules. A detailed description of Transaction Analysis is given in [YOUR78] chapter 11.

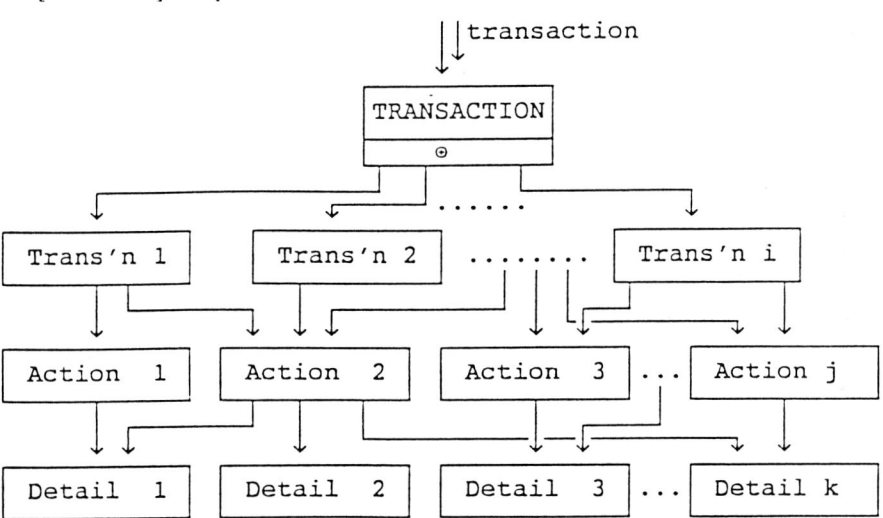

Figure 4-4: A TRANSACTION CENTRED PCC

In general a transaction centre can occur anywhere within a transform-based program structure; therefore, Transaction Analysis may be combined with Transform Analysis during the development of the structured modular form of a program.

5 PRODUCING THE SECOND CUT MODULAR DESIGNS

The Second Cut Modular Designs (SCMDs) are produced from the First Cut Modular Designs (FCMDs), which were developed using Transform and Transaction Analysis. In SCMD the program specifications and structures are tailored to conform to each installation's standards and rules. Where these are wholly or partly unknown they must defined, documented and quality assured.

As the nature of each module is defined the detail on each PCC is extended. Each module is assessed in relation to its position in the program and according to its characteristics (module type). During this process the structure of the PCC may be modified: modules can be decomposed into subordinate modules or amalgamated into superordinate modules. The characteristics of each module must be identified before the programming phase since the type specification specified will affect the program and module design and implementation. Modules can be classed into the main types described below.

5.1 Independent Modules

There are two types of independent modules: external subroutines and internal subroutines. External subroutines are called by other modules and only pass and/or receive data parameters. An internal subroutine is simply a segment within a module or program; however, this is explicitly identified in the module specification. Both of these module types are indicated on the PCC by module boxes with small annotated arrows to show the flow of data where necessary.

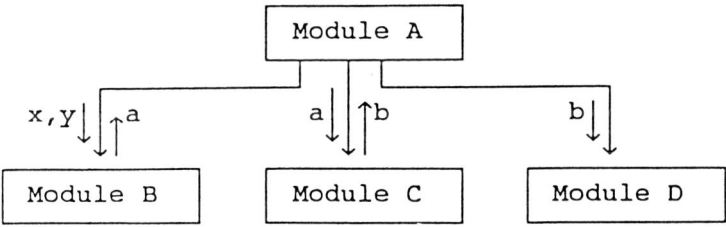

Figure 5-1: EXAMPLE OF A PCC WITH INDEPENDENT MODULES

5.2 Dependent Modules

Dependent subroutines are called by other modules but, since their actions are in part dependent upon their past history, have control information parameters are always passed and/or received (these are indicated on a PCC by double-headed arrows).

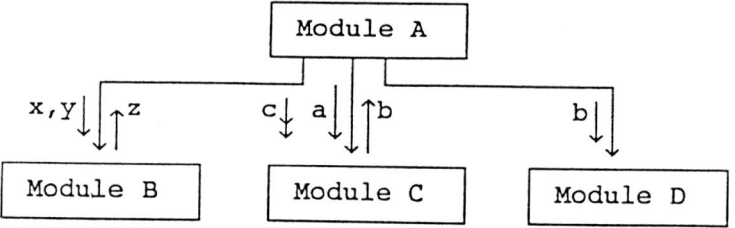

Figure 5-2: EXAMPLE OF A PCC WITH A DEPENDENT MODULE

5.3 Coroutines

A coroutine is a special type of dependent module. Coroutines occur in pairs, where one is the calling module and the other the called. Their actions are in part dependent upon their past history, furthermore, the actions of the coroutine pairs must be synchronized. State variables are used to facilitate the synchronization; these are either passed by the calling coroutine as control information or are resident in the called coroutine. Inversion, a standard JSP technique, is specifically designed to deal with coroutines and their synchronization [THOM89].

Since a module may be a coroutine with more than one other module coroutine pairs are denoted on a PCC by "cn" (n = 1,2...). "cn" is placed in the lower portion of the calling coroutine and in the upper portion of the called coroutine. The state variable only shown on a PCC if it is passed between the coroutines; it is then shown as a control information arrow.

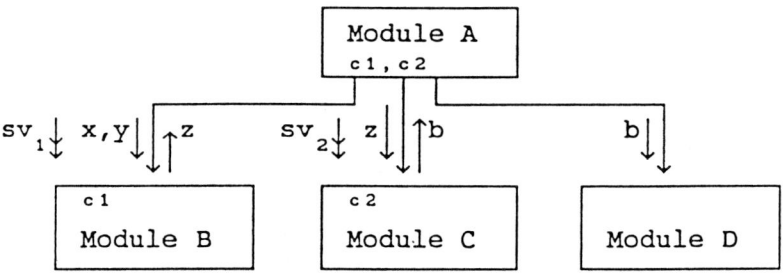

Figure 5-3: EXAMPLE OF A PCC WITH COROUTINES

5.4 Process Network Diagrams

A Process Network Diagram (PND) is included as part of the detailed specification form each module. It shows the data streams consumed or produced by a module: input streams are shown to the left of the diagram and output streams to the right. The data streams may be files, databases, screens, parameter lists or internal tables. The parameters between modules are termed an "Intermediate File (IMF)" and are indicated by an oval.

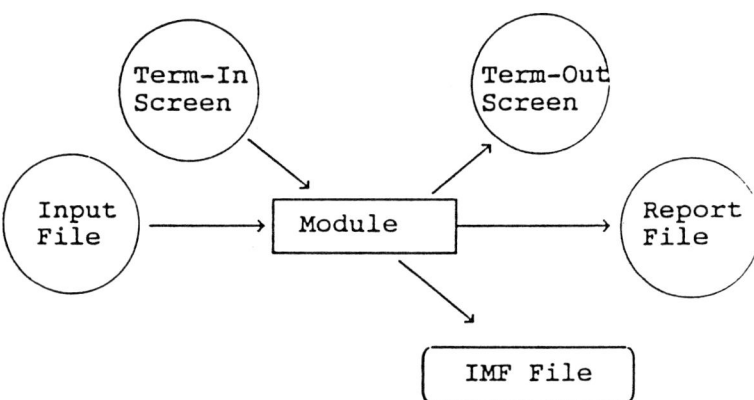

Figure 5-4: EXAMPLE OF A PND FOR A MODULE

6 OVERVIEW OF THE USE OF CATEGORY THEORY

The extension of SSADM aims to improve the physical design of systems and therefore, requires the consistent and full design of programs. Such consistency is ensured by considering both the program modular design and the detailed module design from a category theoretic viewpoint.

The four categories defined and used in the interface between SSADM and the Program Design phase are **PDFD**, **PCC**, **JSC** and **STRT**. The first two categories correspond to design techniques used within the Program Specification stage; **JSC** is used in the subsequent Program Design and Implementation phase. Category **STRT**. acts as the bridge between the others categories to ensure this consistency. This bridging is effected through the use of functors from each of the design categories to **STRT** and vice versa (see Appendix B).

In Sections 7 and 8 the categories and functors used to formalise the Program Specification stage are described (their detailed definitions are given in Appendices A and B). Then in Section 9 the formalisation of the Program Specification stage is outlined.

7 THE CATEGORIES USED

Every category is composed of objects and arrows (the relationships between objects). Therefore, **PDFD**, **PCC**, **JSC** and **STRT** are briefly described in terms of their objects and arrows in this section; they are formally defined in Appendix A along with the definition of a category.

7.1 The Objects of the Categories

The objects of **PDFD** are formalised Program-DFDs (PDFDs). In a formalised PDFD the diagram consists of sequences of elementary components and of closed loops (whenever selection or coexistence is used). Only a single data flow is permitted into, or out of, an elementary component or a closed loop.

These rules are demonstrated below: in Figure 7-1 an example of an unformalised PDFD is given, the formalised version is shown in Figure 7-2.

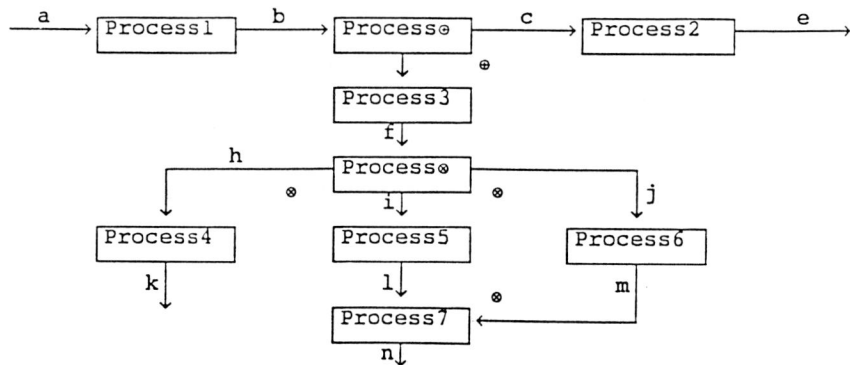

Figure 7-1: AN EXAMPLE PDFD (UNFORMALISED)

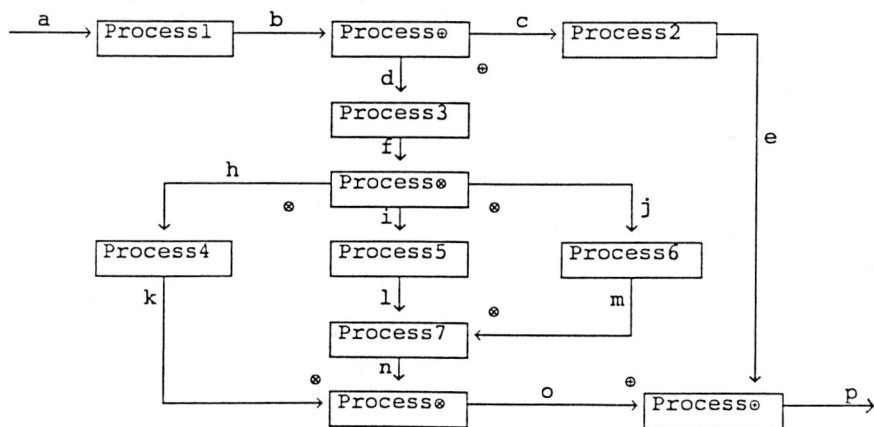

Figure 7-2: THE EXAMPLE PDFD (FORMALISED)

The objects of **PCC** are valid Program Composition Charts (PCCs) where each level on a PCC is restricted to one type (so a level may not have sequence and selection modules mixed as in Figure 4-2). They are composed entirely of combinations of elementary, sequence, selection and coexistent levels. For each valid level the associated data and control information of each component is part of that level.

JSC has as its objects valid Jackson Structure Charts (JSCs) composed entirely of combinations of elementary, sequence, selection and iteration levels. The charts show either the logical structure of each data stream which is to be processed in a program (or module) or the structure of the program (or module) itself. A valid JSC is hierarchical with elementary nodes decomposing no further, and any non-elementary node decomposing into a series of lower level nodes each of which has the same type. The valid levels are elementary, sequence, selection, and iteration.

The objects in **STRT** are Structured Tasks and these are defined in set-theoretic terms (see Appendix A). Structured Tasks are composed of a combination of sub-tasks which are themselves composed of sets of flows. There are five types of Sub-tasks: elementary, sequence, selection, coexistence and iteration.

7.2 The Arrows of the Categories

The arrows for each of the design technique categories are the rules which ensure that one diagram is a valid development of another. Therefore, if diagram A is developed into diagram B there must be an arrow, f say, mapping A into B (f:A$\rightarrow$B). The arrows are defined as compositions of refinements, where each refinement maps an elementary component/level into one of the permitted component/level types. Similarly, for **STRT** the arrows are defined as compositions of refinements of the sub-tasks (where a refinement, r, maps an elementary sub-task into one of the five possible sub-tasks).

7.3 The Dual Categories

In the design procedure of the SSADM Program Specification stage and the subsequent Program Design phase first the modular form of each program is developed and then the detailed structure of each module. This procedure makes use of both refinements and abstractions of the diagrams (an abstraction of a diagram occurs when modules are merged). Therefore, the procedure requires both the four categories already defined (which map objects via refinements) and additionally the dual of each (to map objects via abstractions).

One result of category theory states that every category has a unique dual (or opposite) category. Both categories have the same objects, and for each arrow between two objects, f:A$\rightarrow$B say, in a category there is a corresponding arrow, f:B$\rightarrow$A, in the dual, furthermore, these are the only arrows in the dual. Therefore, for each of the categories, **PDFD, PCC, JSC** and **STRT** there are dual categories **PDFD**^{op}, **PCC**^{op}, **JSC**^{op} and **STRT**^{op}. In the

8.2 The Pair of Functors Between PCC and STRT₁.

The pair of functors are: G:**PCC**→**STRT₁** and G':**STRT₁**→**PCC**. These can be defined in a a similar fashion to F and F'.

G maps formalised PCCs into their corresponding structured task form in **STRT₁** such that the compositions of the Structured task are the same as those for the composition of the PCC in **PCC**.

elementary level → elementary sub-task
sequence level → sequence sub-task
selection level → selection sub-task
coexistence level → coexistence sub-task

Each arrow in **PCC** maps into a corresponding arrow in **STRT₁** such that the refinements in these arrows in **STRT₁** correspond exactly to the refinements in the arrows in **PCC**.

The functor G' is defined in a similar way but acts from **STRT₁** to **PCC**.

8.3 The Pair of Functors Between JSC and STRT₂.

The pair of functors are: H:**JSC**→**STRT₂** and H':**STRT₂**→**JSC**. H maps JSCs into their corresponding structured task form in **STRT₂** such that the compositions of the Structured task are the same as those for the composition of the JSC in **JSC**.

elementary level → elementary sub-task
sequence level → sequence sub-task
selection level → selection sub-task
iteration level → iteration sub-task

Each arrow in **JSC** maps into a corresponding arrow in **STRT₂** such that the refinements in these arrows in **STRT₂** correspond exactly to the refinements in the arrows in **JSC**.

The functor H' is defined in a similar way but acts from **STRT₂** to **JSC**.

8.4 Functors and the Dual Categories.

During the program specification and design procedure the individual diagrams of the design techniques may be developed via refinement, abstraction, or combinations of both. Therefore, to preserve the consistency of the design functors must exist both between the three design technique categories and **STRT** (when refinements of a diagram occur) and also between the duals of these categories and the dual of **STRT** when abstractions occur).

One of the results of category theory states that for any functor between two categories, F:**X**→**Y** say, there is a dual functor, F^{op}:X^{op}→Y^{op}, which maps the objects in X^{op} to objects in Y^{op} and the arrows in X^{op} to arrows in Y^{op} [BURS88] therefore, since dual categories have been defined for each of original categories the arrows are compositions of refinements, therefore, the arrows in the dual categories are compositions of abstractions, $f^{op}:B \to A$ and an abstraction a ($a:A'' \to A'$), is the inverse of a refinement r ($r:A' \to A''$).

8 THE FUNCTORS BETWEEN THE CATEGORIES

A functor between two categories has properties which ensure that the objects and arrows in one category map into objects and arrows in the other such that the relationships and structures of the first category are preserved in the second. Thus functors provide the mechanism by which the continuity and consistency of the program design is ensured.

Three pairs of functors are defined between the three design technique categories (**PDFD, PCC** and **JSC**) and the categorical bridge, **STRT**. In each pair one functor maps a design technique category to a subcategory of **STRT**, the other maps the subcategory to the design technique category. Subcategories of **STRT** are used since the objects of **STRT** have more types of constituent components than any of the individual design technique categories. In the first, $STRT_1$ there is no construct of iteration in the permitted types of subtasks and in the second, $STRT_2$ there is no construct of coexistence.

It is only in **STRT** that a complete program design can be explicitly defined; since the objects of **PDFD** and **PCC** hold the form of the modular composition of programs and the objects of **JSC** hold the detailed design of the modules. The three pairs of functors used in the formalised procedure are outlined in this section and are defined explicitly in Appendix B.

8.1 The Pair of Functors Between PDFD and $STRT_1$

The pair of functors are: $F:PDFD \to STRT_1$ and $F':STRT_1 \to PDFD$. F maps formalised PDFDs into their corresponding structured task form in $STRT_1$ such that the compositions of the structured task are the same as those for the composition of the PDFD in **PDFD**.

elementary component → elementary sub-task
sequence component → sequence sub-task
selection component → selection sub-task
coexistence component → coexistence sub-task

Each arrow in **PDFD** maps into a corresponding arrow in $STRT_1$ such that the refinements in these arrows in $STRT_1$ correspond exactly to the refinements in the arrows in **PDFD**.

The functor F' is defined in a similar way but acts from $STRT_1$ to **PDFD**.

the four categories (**PDFD, PCC, JSC** and **STRT**) the duals of these functors exist and have been implicitly defined by F, F', G, G', H and H'.

9 FORMALISING THE PROGRAM SPECIFICATION STAGE

To formalise the program modularization procedure each PDFD and PCC is partitioned into three. The three parts correspond to the inflow, central transform, and outflow components of the program. Then PDFD = {$PDFD_I$, $PDFD_C$, $PDFD_O$} where $PDFD_I$ is the diagram of the inflow branch (including the inflow element), $PDFD_C$ is the diagram of the central transforms branch (including the inflow and outflow elements) and $PDFD_O$ is the diagram of the outflow branch (including the outflow element). Figure 9-1 shows how a PDFD splits into these three component parts and Figure 9-2 then shows the formalised components of the PDFD.

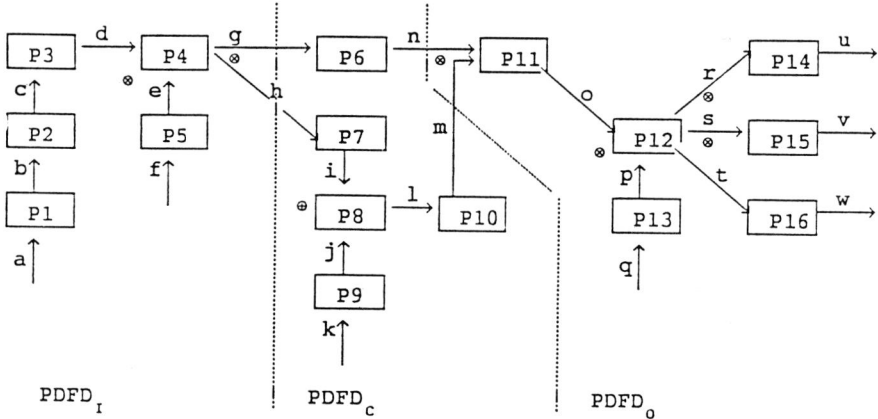

Figure 9-1: EXAMPLE OF A PDFD WITH ITS THREE COMPONENTS

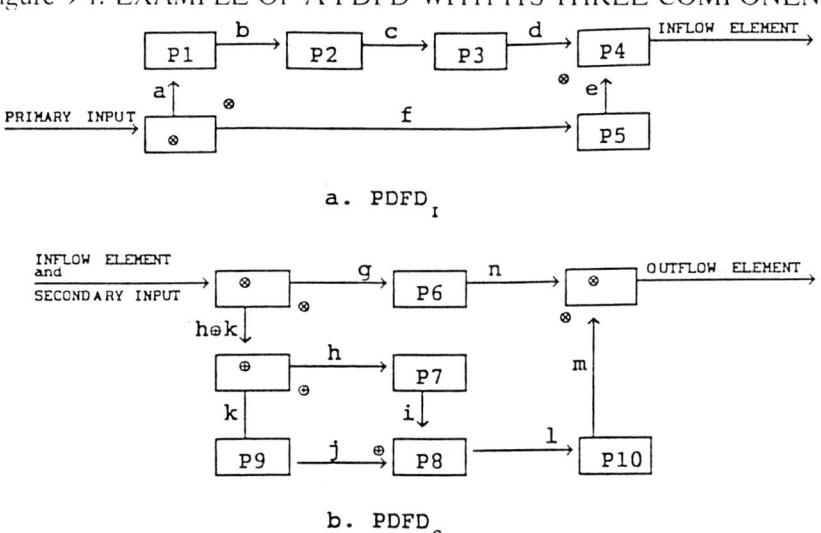

a. $PDFD_I$

b. $PDFD_C$

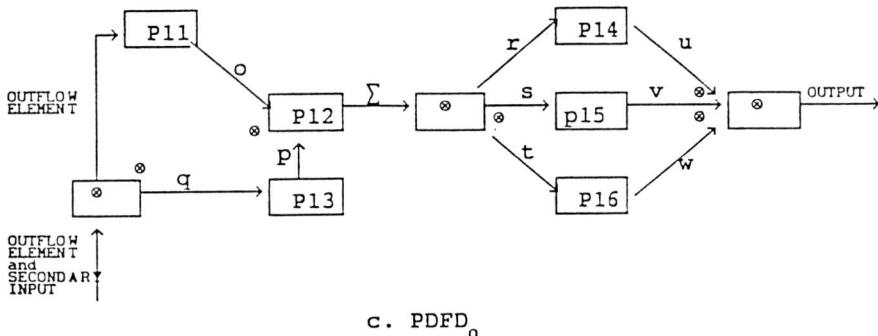

c. PDFD$_o$

Figure 9-2: THE FORMALISED COMPONENTS OF FIGURE 9-1

9.1 Formalising the Conversion of the PDFD to PCC Form.

Once the PDFD has been formalised it can be converted to its structured task form and hence to the PCC form. This conversion process ensures that the consistency of the design is maintained (through the use of the functors F and G') thus assuring the validity of the resulting PCC.

Each valid PDFD component is mapped into an object in **STRT**$_I$ via F (F:**PDFD**→**STRT**, such that $STRT_i = F(PDFD_i)$. The examples in Figure 9-3 show the $STRT_i$ which result after F is applied to the $PDFD_i$ of Figure 9-2.

{<PRIMARY INPUT,t,<a,f>>, <f,P5,e>, <a,P1,b>, <b,P2,c>, <c,P3,d>, <<d,e>,P4,<INFLOW ELEMENT>}

a. STRT$_I$

{<INFLOW ELEMENT with SECONDARY INPUT,t,<g,hsk>, <g,P6,n>, <hsk,s,<h,k>, <h,P7,i>, <k,P9,j>, <<i,j>,P8,l>, <l,P10,m>, <<n,m>,t,OUTFLOW ELEMENT>}

b. STRT$_C$

{<OUTFLOW ELEMENT with SECONDARY INPUT,t,<OUTFLOW ELEMENT,q>>, <q,P13,p>, <OUTFLOW ELEMENT,P11,o>, <<o,p>,P12,rst>, <rst,t,<r,s,t>>, <r,P14,u>, <s,P15,v>, <t,P16,w>, <<u,v,w>,t,OUTPUT>}

c. STRT$_O$

Figure 9-3: THE STRUCTURED TASK FORM OF FIGURE 9-2.

The design is continued by converting the $STRT_i$ corresponding to the $PDFD_i$ into PCC_i (objects in **PCC**).This conversion is achieved via the functor G' (G':**STRT**→**PCC** such that $PCC_i = G'(STRT_i))$. At this stage the three PCC_i correspond exactly to the three $PDFD_i$. Figure 9-4 shows the PCC_i which result after G' is applied to the $STRT_i$ of Figure 9-3.

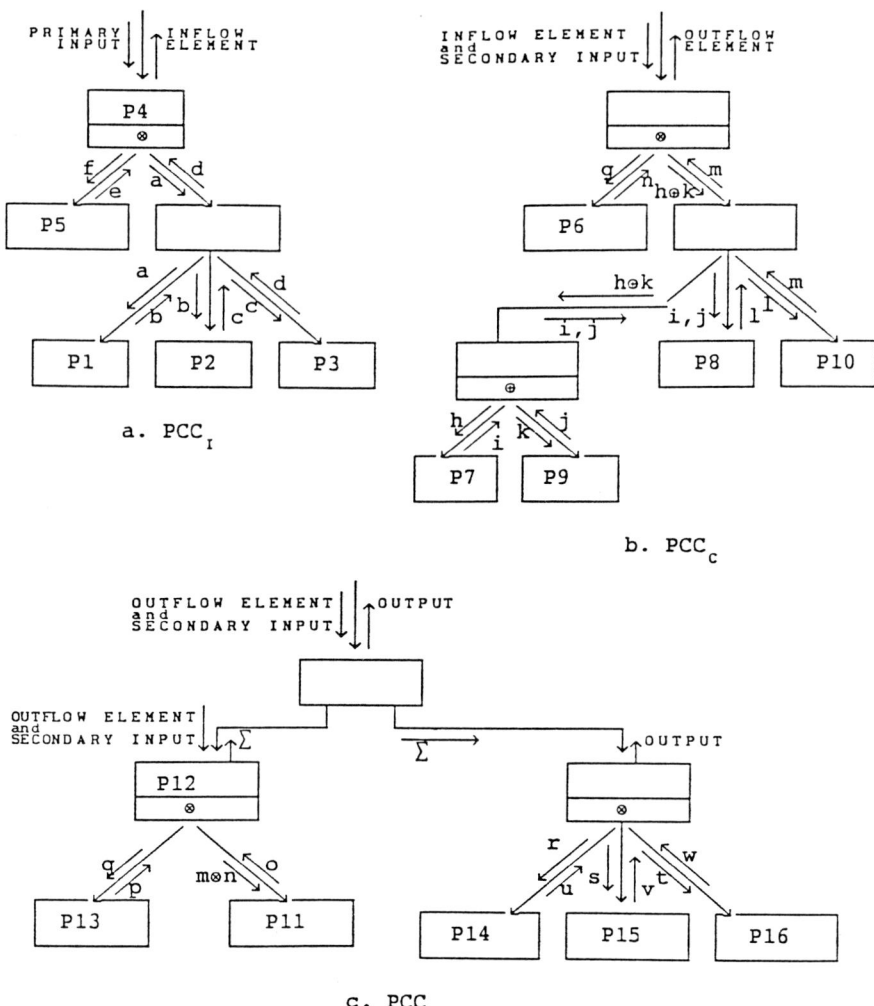

Figure 9-4: THE PCC FORM OF FIGURE 9-3

System inputs and outputs are not shown on the diagrams for the formalised PCC_i. Their use and production are noted in the processing detail of the Physical Process Specifications (PPSs). Therefore, for the PCC_I the top level of the diagram is an inflow module (this may just be an executive module) with the inflow element as its outward data. For PCC_O the top level of the diagram is an outflow module (again this may be just be an executive module) with the outflow element as its inward data. For PCC_C the top level of the diagram is always an executive control module. This has the inflow element as it inward data and the outflow element as its outward data. The formalised forms of the PCC_i in Figure 9-4 are shown in Figure 9-5 where the system inputs (a, f, k and q) and the system outputs (u, v, w) have been removed from the diagram.

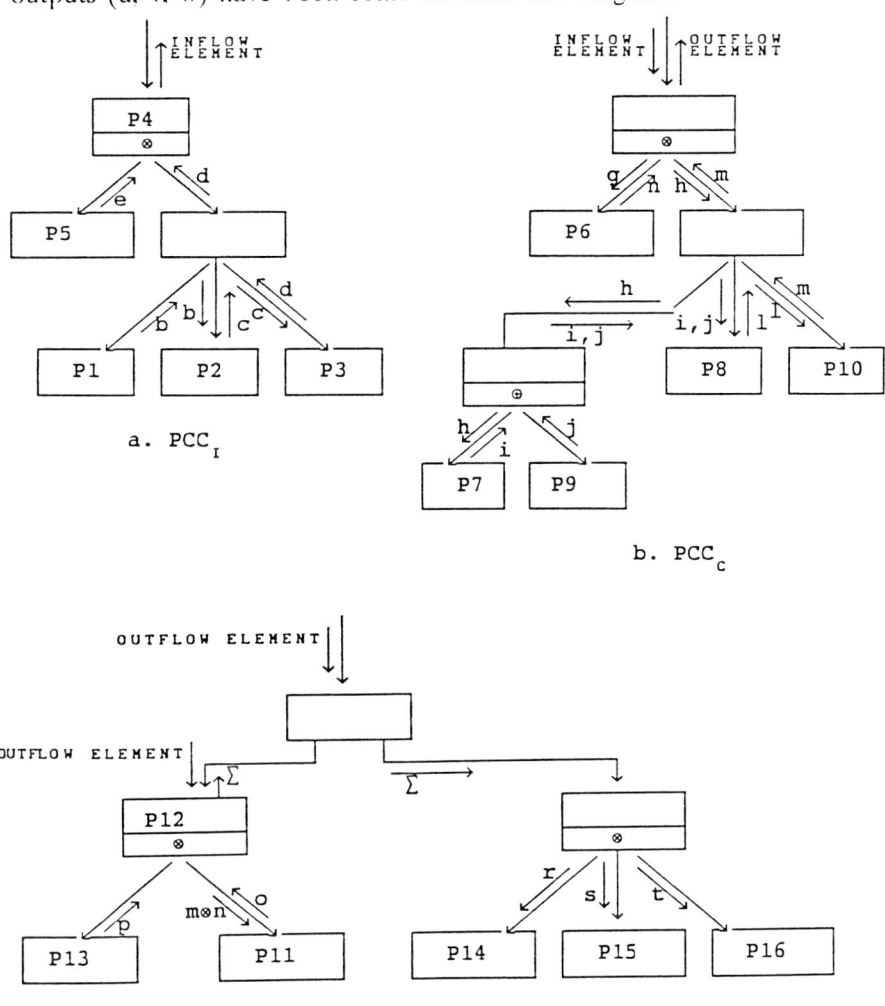

Figure 9-5: THE FORMALISED COMPONENTS OF FIGURE 9-4

9.3 Development of the Formalised PCC

Each component PCC is now developed by the designer until the modular form of the design is felt to be satisfactory (this occurs in both FCMD and SCMD). The development may consist of refinement of levels, abstraction of levels, or a combination of the two. (That is, the arrows between the PCC and the developed PCC are composed of refinements in **PCC** or abstractions in **PCC**^{op}, or both).

For instance, Figure 9-6 shows that PCC_1 is developed into PCC_2 via refinements and abstractions. X is an intermediate PCC which can be reached by refinement from both PCC_1 and PCC_2. The arrows in the diagram can be expressed as $f = r_3 \circ r_2 \circ r_1$, $f \in$ **PCC**. and $g^{op} = a_1$, $g \in$ **PCC** ($g^{op} \in$ **PCC**^{op}).

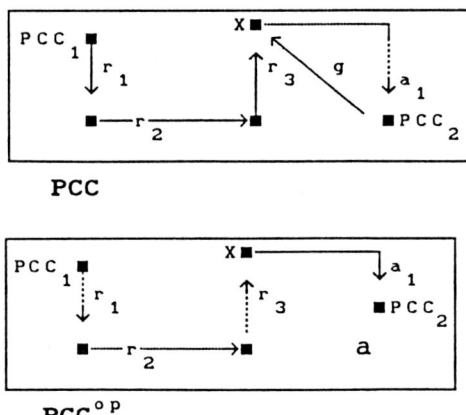

Figure 9-6: RELATIONSHIPS OF THE ARROWS IN **PCC** AND **PCC**^{op}

The separate PCC_i are mapped into $STRT_1$ (G:**PCC** $\rightarrow$ **STRT**$_1$) Thus the $STRT_1$ objects $G(PCC_i)$ and $F(PDFD_i)$ can be compared. If consistency of design has been preserved then there is an object X and arrows f and g in $STRT_1$ such that $f:F(PDFD_i) \rightarrow X$ and $g:G(PCC_i) \rightarrow X$.

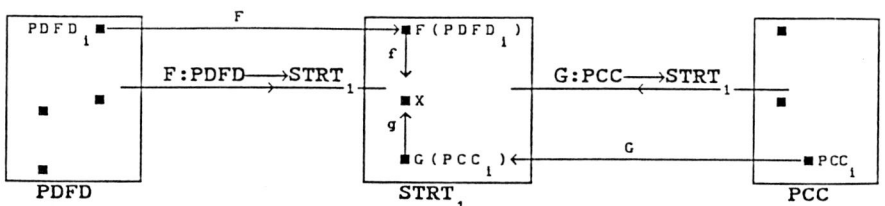

Figure 9-7: THE RELATIONSHIPS AMONG THE OBJECTS IN **PDFD**, **STRT** AND **PCC**

If no such X can be found then the consistency of the design has been lost. At this point the designer must evaluate both forms of the program structure and accept one as the valid design (this would normally be the design held in PCC form). The other design must be either modified accordingly or some documentation must be kept to reference the noted discrepancy.

The full PCC is formed from the PCC_i components such that the first level is an elementary level (the executive module) with inflow and outflow data elements feeding in and out of it: PCC = {Executive Module, PCC_I, PCC_C, PCC_O}.

9.4 Formalising the Detailed Module Design

The detailed design for each module specified on a PCC is developed individually using JSP. Therefore, the continued consistency checking of each program design can be continued by the formalising the detailed program design in the Program Design and Implementation phase. The category **JSC** and the functors H and H' between it and $\textbf{STRT}_2$ allow validation of the consistency of the design. Since the JSCs hold the detailed design for each module the full program design (modular structure and module detail) can be expressed in **STRT**.

10 CONCLUSIONS

This paper has outlined the authors' replacement procedure for the physical design stage of SSADM(version 3). It improves the physical design phase by the provision of a structured Program Specification stage which uses established techniques and procedures. By using the basic concepts of category theory a formalism has been added to the stage to allow validation and consistency checking of the procedure.

The authors are extending this work into the Program Design and Implementation phase of the life cycle (for JSP designed programs). This extension not only covers the use of Jackson Structure Charts (and the **JSC** category) but also considers the role of Schematic Logic and its categorical representation. Therefore, it will be possible to verify the consistency of a design from the physical system design stage of Program Specification up to the production of the Schematic Logic.

This approach to full program design has the potential for automation, whereby the underlying formalism of the procedure achieved through the use of category theory would be hidden from the system developers. This would facilitate the use of the design procedure, accessing its techniques, whilst the tool supporting the process would translate the diagrammatic forms of the design into structured task representations for formal evaluation and consistency-checking. Such automation would offer an improvement in the quality of systems design and provide a level of confidence in the consistency of the design which is at present lacking in many of the popular systems development methods.

REFERENCES

[BURS88] BURSTALL,R.M and RYDEHEARD,D.E. Computational

Category Theory. Prentice-Hall, New Jersey (1988).

[EDWA88] EDWARDS,H.M. THOMPSON,J.B. and SMITH,P. A Survey of the Use of SSADM in the Commercial and Government Sectors. Keith London Associates, Welwyn (1988).

[EDWA89a] EDWARDS,H.M. THOMPSON,J.B. and SMITH,P. "Experiences in the Use of SSADM:A Series of Case Studies. Part 1: First Time Users" Inf. Soft. Technol. Volume 31 No 8 (October 1989) pp411-419.

[EDWA89b] EDWARDS,H.M. THOMPSON,J.B. and SMITH,P. "Experiences in the Use of SSADM:A Series of Case Studies. Part 2: Experienced Users" Inf. Soft. Technol. Volume 31 No 8 (October 1989) pp420-428.

[EDWA89c] EDWARDS,H.M, THOMPSON,J.B and SMITH,P. SSADM (Version 3) Stage Six: Physical Design - A Critical Appraisal. School of Computer Studies and Mathematics, Occasional Report No 89-8 (1989).

[EDWA89d] EDWARDS,H.M. THOMPSON,J.B and SMITH,P. A Proposed Replacement for Stage Six of SSADM: Physical Design. School of Computer Studies and Mathematics, Occasional Report No 89-9 (1989).

[GOLD84] GOLDBLATT,R. Topoi: The Categorial Analysis of Logic. North-Holland, Amsterdam (1984).

[JACK75] JACKSON,M.A. Principles of Program Design. Academic Press, London (1975).

[LONG86] LONGWORTH,G and NICHOLS, D. The SSADM Manual. NCC Publications, Manchester (1986).

[MYER78] MYERS,G.J. Composite/Structured Design. Van Nostrand Reinhold Co, New York (1978).

[NCC87] NCC Members Survey 1987. NCC Publications, Manchester, (1987).

[STEV81] STEVENS,W.P. Using Structured Design, How to Make Programs Simple, Changeable, Flexible and Reusable.
Wiley-Interscience, New York (1981).

[THOM89] THOMPSON,J.B. Structured Programming with COBOL and

JSP Vols 1 and 2. Chartwell-Bratt, Bromley (1989 and 1990).

[TSE87] TSE,T.H."Integrating the Structured Analysis and Design Models: A Category-Theoretic Approach." Austral. Comp. Journal Volume 19 No 1, (1987) pp25-31.

[YOUR78] YOURDON,E and CONSTANTINE,L.L. Structured Design, Fundamentals of a Discipline of Computer Program and Systems Design. Prentice-Hall, New Jersey (1978).

APPENDIX A: CATEGORIES

A1 DEFINITION OF A CATEGORY
A Category, **X**, consists of
i) a class of objects $|X|$, and
ii) a set of arrows for each pair of objects $A, B \in |X|$.
Arrows must satisfy the following properties and laws:
a) Composition: for each pair of arrows $f:A \to B$ and $g:B \to C$ $\exists$ the composite arrow $g \circ f : A \to C$
b) Associative Law: for any arrows $f:A \to B$, $g:B \to C$ and $h:C \to D$ then $h \circ (g \circ f) = (h \circ g) \circ f$.
c) Existence of Identities: for each object $A \in X$ $\exists$ an identity arrow $i_A : A \to A$
d) Identity Law: for any arrow $f:A \to B$ $f \circ i_A = i_B \circ f = f$

A2 DEFINITION OF THE CATEGORY PDFD
The Objects of **PDFD** are valid Program-DFDs (PDFDs) composed of combinations of four valid component types.
i) Elementary component

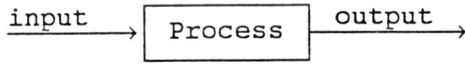

ii) Sequence component

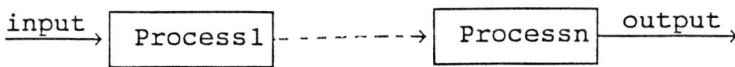

iii) Selection component (generally there may be more than two paths).

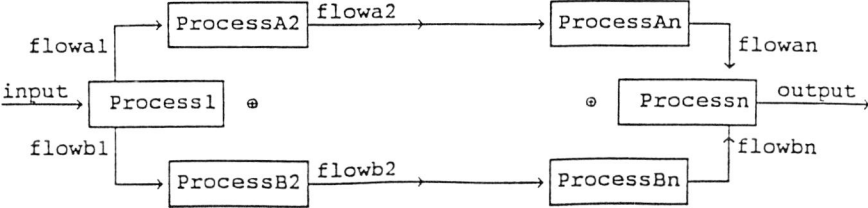

iv) Coexistent component (generally there may be more than two paths).

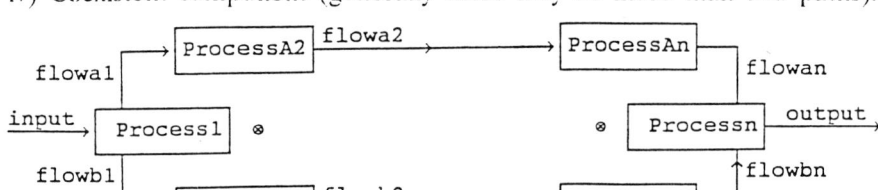

An arrow in **PDFD** is defined as a composition of refinements; therefore, $f:A \rightarrow B$ iff $f = r_n \circ r_{n-1} \dots r_1$ where r_i are refinements. A mapping, r, between two objects A and B, $r:A \rightarrow B$, is a refinement iff $\exists$ an elementary component in A and a valid component in B such that:

i) an elementary component in A is mapped into a valid component in B, and

ii) any other valid component in A is mapped into the same valid component in B

The refinement, $e:A \rightarrow B$, is defined such that
i) an elementary component in A is mapped into the same elementary component in B, and
ii) any other valid component in A is mapped into the same valid component in B
(every valid component in A is mapped into the same valid component in B. Therefore, $A = B$).

A3 DEFINITION OF THE CATEGORY PCC

The objects of **PCC** are valid Program Composition Charts (PCCs). Any PCC must be composed of combinations of four valid levels. The associated data and control information of each component is part of its level, however, in the definitions below these are shown in the first case only.

i) Elementary level: an elementary component uses no subordinate modules.

$a \downarrow \uparrow z$

| COMPONENT A |

ii) Sequence level: an elementary component uses a number of subordinate modules in a sequence (N.B. there may be only one module in a sequence level).

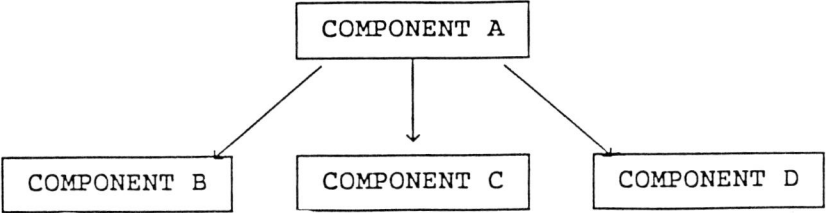

iii) Selection level: an elementary component uses one module from a number of possible modules.

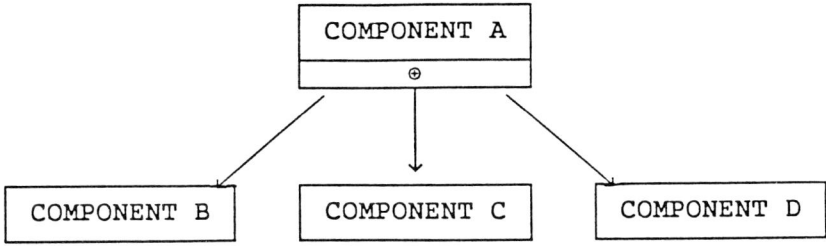

iv) Coexistence level: an elementary component uses all the subordinate modules in the level, but these subordinate modules are independent of each other.

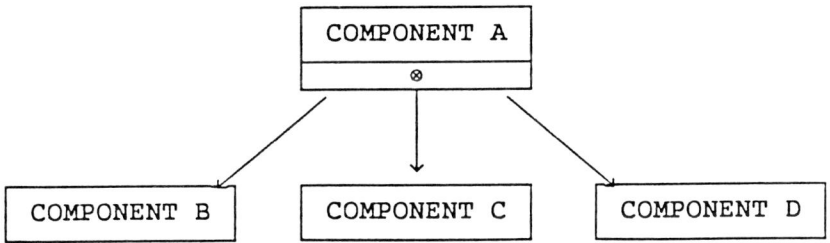

The arrows between the objects of **PCC** are the rules which ensure that one chart is a valid development of another. They are defined in terms of refinements of valid levels. An arrow in **PCC** is defined as a composition of refinements; therefore, $f:A \rightarrow B$ iff $f = r_n \circ r_{n-1} \circ ... r_1$ where r_i are refinements. A mapping, r, between two objects (PCCs), A and B, $r:A \rightarrow B$, is a refinement iff $\exists$ an elementary level in A and a valid level in B such that:
i) an elementary level in A is mapped into a valid level in B, and
ii) any other valid level in A is mapped into the same valid level in B.

The refinement, $e:A \rightarrow B$, is defined such that
i) an elementary level in A is mapped into the same elementary level in B, and

ii) any other valid level in A is mapped into the same valid level in B. (every valid level in A is mapped into the same valid level in B. Therefore, A = B).

A4 DEFINITION OF THE CATEGORY JSC

Jackson Structure Charts, JSCs, are used in the Program Design and Implementation Phase of the development life cycle rather than in the proposed Program Specification stage of SSADM. However, the category of **JSC** is needed to validate that the program design is consistent both in its structural form and its detailed design. Jackson Structure Charts, JSCs, are used in program design to show either the logical structure of each data stream which is to be processed in a program (or module) or the structure of the program (or module) itself.

The objects of **JSC** are valid Jackson Structure Charts A valid JSC is hierarchical: elementary nodes are those which decompose no further, any non-elementary node must decompose into a series of lower level nodes each of which has the same type, either:- sequence, selection or iteration.

i) Elementary level: a node is decomposed no further.

| COMPONENT A |

ii) Sequence level: a node is decomposed into a level containing a finite number of sequence nodes. (Sequences operate strictly from left to right).

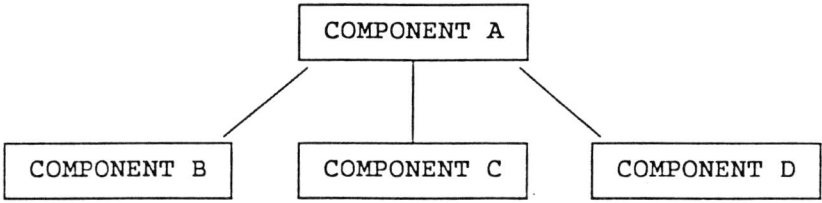

iii) Selection level: a node is decomposed into a level with a finite number of selection nodes (denoted by "o" in the top right corner of the box).

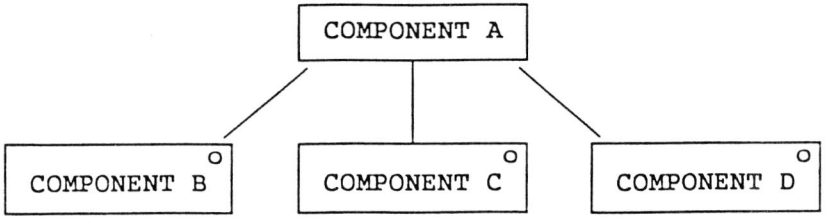

iv) Iteration level: a node is decomposed into a level of one iteration node (denoted by "*" in the top right corner of the box).

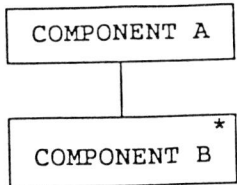

The arrows between the objects are the rules which ensure that one chart is a valid development of another. They are defined in terms of refinements of valid levels. An arrow is defined as a composition of refinements; therefore, $f:A \rightarrow B$ iff $f = r_n \circ r_{n-1} \circ ... r_1$ where r_i are refinements. A mapping, r, between two objects (JSCs), A and B. $r:A \rightarrow B$, is a refinement iff $\exists$ an elementary level in A and a valid level in B such that:
i) an elementary level in A is mapped into a valid level in B, and
ii) any other valid level in A is mapped into the same valid level in B.

The refinement, $e:A \rightarrow B$, is defined such that
i) an elementary level in A is mapped into the same elementary level in B, and
ii) any other valid level in A is mapped into the same valid level in B.
(every valid level in A is mapped into the same valid level in B. Therefore, A = B).

A5 DEFINITION OF THE CATEGORY STRT

The category of Structured Tasks, **STRT**, forms the bridge between the design technique categories used in the SSADM program specification stage and JSP program design phase.

The objects in **STRT** are Structured Tasks and these are defined in set-theoretic terms. Structured Tasks are composed of tasks which are themselves composed of sets of flows. These terms are defined below.

A5.1 Flows and Processes

A flow $<<s_{11},s_{12},...s_{1m}>,p,<s_{21},s_{22},...s_{2n}>>$ has a process p, input states s_{1i} $i=1....m$ and output states s_{2i} $i=1....n$.
i) a flow for a standard process, p, which has only one input state s_1, and one output state s_2, is $<s_1, p, s_2>$
ii) a flow for a decision process, $\oplus$, which has one input state and one of two (or more) possible output states is $<s_1,\oplus,<s_{21},s_{22}...>>$.
iii) a flow for a collection process, $\oplus$, which has two (or more) possible input states and only one output state is $<<s_{11},s_{12}...>,\oplus,s_2>$.
iv) a flow for a fork, $\otimes$, which has one input state and two (or more) output states is $<s_1,\otimes,<s_{21},s_{22}..>>$.

v) a flow for a join, ⊗, which has two (or more) possible input states and one output state is $<<s_{11},s_{12}...>,\otimes,s_2>$.

A5.2 Tasks

A task is a set of zero, one or many flows: that is,
$T = \{ flow_1, flow_2,..., flow_n \}$.

Sub-tasks are composed of elementary tasks. There are five types of Sub-tasks: elementary, sequence, selection, coexistence and iteration. A Structured Task is composed of a combination of Sub-tasks. The types of Sub-tasks are defined below.

i) Elementary Task: $T(s_1,s_2) = \{<s_1, p, s_2>\}$.
(this set contains one and only one flow).

ii) Sequence of Tasks: for $T_1(s_1,s_2)$ and $T_2(s_2,s_3)$
$(T_1 \circ T_2)(s_1,s_3) = T_1(s_1,s_2) \cup T_2(s_2,s_3)$

iii) Selection of Tasks: for $T_1(s_1,s_2)$ and $T_2(s_3,s_4)$
$(T_1 \oplus T_2)(s_5,s_6) = \{<s_5,\oplus,<s_1,s_3>>\} \cup T_1(s_1,s_2) \cup T_2(s_3,s_4)$
$\cup \{<<s_2,s_4>,\oplus,s_6>\}$

iv) Coexistence of Tasks: for $T_1(s_1,s_2)$ and $T_2(s_3,s_4)$
$(T_1 \otimes T_2)(s_5,s_6) = \{<s_5,\otimes,<s_1,s_3>>\} \cup T_1(s_1,s_2) \cup T_2(s_3,s_4)$
$\cup \{<<s_2,s_4>,\otimes,s_6>\}$

v) Iteration of a Task: $T(s_1,s_2)$
$T(s_3,s_4) = \{<<s_3,s_2>,\oplus,s_5>\} \cup T(s_1,s_2) \cup \{<s_5,\oplus,<s_1,s_4>>\}$

The arrows for the category are defined in terms of refinements of the sub-tasks. An arrow in **STRT** is defined as a composition of refinements; therefore, $f:A \rightarrow B$ iff $f = r_n \circ r_{n-1} \circ ... r_1$ where r are refinements.
A mapping, r, between two objects (STRTs), A and B , $r:A \rightarrow B$, is a refinement iff $\exists$ an elementary Sub-task, $\{<s_1, p, s_2>\}$, in A and a Sub-task, T, in B such that:
i) the single flow $<s_1, p, s_2>$ in A is mapped into a flow of T in B , and
ii) any other flow in A is mapped into the same flow in B.

The refinement $e:A \rightarrow B$ is such that:
i) the single flow $<s_1, p, s_2>$ in A is mapped into the single flow
   $<s_1, p, s_2>$ in B, and
ii) any other flow in A is mapped into the same flow in B.

(That is: any flow in A is mapped into the same flow in B. Hence A=B).

APPENDIX B: FUNCTORS

B1 THE DEFINITION OF A FUNCTOR
For any functor, $F:X \rightarrow Y$, between categories **X** and **Y** the following properties must hold:
i) each object $A \in |X|$ is related to one (and only one) object $F(A) \in |Y|$, and
ii) each arrow $f:A \rightarrow B$ in **X** is related to one (and only one) arrow $F(f):F(A) \rightarrow F(B)$ in **Y**.
The property of composition and the laws of associativity and identity of the arrows must be preserved in both categories, that is:
a) if $h = g \circ f$ then $F(h) = F(g \circ f) = F(g) \circ F(f)$
b) $F(i_A) = i_{F(A)}$

B2 THE PAIR OF FUNCTORS BETWEEN PDFD AND STRT$_1$
These functors are $F:\textbf{PDFD} \rightarrow \textbf{STRT}_1$ and $F':\textbf{STRT}_1 \rightarrow \textbf{PDFD}$.

B2.1 Functor F.
i) For any $A \in \textbf{PDFD}\ \exists\ F(A) \in \textbf{STRT}_1$ such that the compositions of A are the same as those for the composition of $F(A)$. That is:

$$\begin{array}{rcl}
\text{elementary component} & \rightarrow & \text{elementary sub-task} \\
\text{sequence component} & \rightarrow & \text{sequence sub-task} \\
\text{selection component} & \rightarrow & \text{selection sub-task} \\
\text{coexistence component} & \rightarrow & \text{coexistence sub-task}
\end{array}$$

ii) For each arrow $f:A \rightarrow B$, $f \in \textbf{PDFD}$, $\exists$ an arrow $F(f) \in \textbf{STRT}_1$, $F(f):F(A) \rightarrow F(B)$, such that $f = r_n \circ r_{n-1} \circ ... r_1$ and $F(f) = F(f = r_n \circ r_{n-1} \circ ... r_1)$
$r_i \in \textbf{PDFD}$ where r_i and s_i are refinements: $s_i = F(r_i)$ since component types map to corresponding subtasks.

B2.2 Functor F'.
i) For any $A' \in \textbf{STRT}_1\ \exists\ F'(A') \in \textbf{PDFD}$ such that the compositions of A' are the same as those for the composition of $F'(A')$ and
ii) For each arrow $f':A' \rightarrow B'$, $f' \in \textbf{STRT}_1$, $\exists\ F'(f') \in \textbf{PDFD}$. $F'(f'):F'(A) \rightarrow F'(B)$, such that $f' = s_n \circ s_{n-1} \circ ... s_1$ and $F'(f') = F'(s_n \circ s_{n-1} \circ ... s_1)$

B3 THE PAIR OF FUNCTORS BETWEEN PCC AND STRT$_1$
These functors are: $G:\textbf{PCC} \rightarrow \textbf{STRT}_1$ and $G':\textbf{STRT}_1 \rightarrow \textbf{PCC}$.

B3.1 Functor G
i) For any $A \in \textbf{PCC}\ \exists\ G(A) \in \textbf{STRT}_1$ such that the compositions of A are the same as those for the composition of $G(A)$. That is:

elementary level → elementary sub-task
sequence level → sequence sub-task
selection level → selection sub-task
coexistence level → coexistence sub-task

ii) For each arrow $f:A \to B$, $f \in$ **PCC**, $\exists$ an arrow $G(f) \in$ **STRT$_1$**, $G(f):G(A) \to G(B)$, such that $f = f = r_n \circ r_{n-1} \circ \ldots r_1$ and $G(f) = G(r_n \circ r_{n-1} \circ \ldots r_1)$ $r_i \in$ **PCC** where r_i and s_i are refinements: $s_i = G(r_i)$ since levels map to corresponding subtasks.

B3.2 Functor G':
i) For any $A' \in$ **STRT$_1$** $\exists$ $G'(A') \in$ **PCC** such that the compositions of A' are the same as those for the composition of $G'(A')$, and
ii) For each arrow $f':A' \to B'$, $f' \in$ **STRT$_1$**, $\exists$ $G'(f') \in$ **PCC**, $G'(f'):G'(A) \to G'(B)$, such that $f' = s_n \circ s_{n-1} \circ \ldots s_1$ and $G'(f') = G'(s_n \circ s_{n-1} \circ \ldots s_1)$

B4 THE PAIR OF FUNCTORS BETWEEN JSC AND STRT$_2$
These functors are H:**JSC**→**STRT$_2$** and H':**STRT$_2$**→**JSC**.

B4.1 Functor H
i) For any $A \in$ **JSC** $\exists$ $H(A) \in$ **STRT$_2$** such that the compositions of A are the same as those for the composition of $H(A)$. That is:

elementary level → elementary sub-task
sequence level → sequence sub-task
selection level → selection sub-task
iteration level → iteration sub-task

ii) For each arrow $f:A \to B$, $f \in$ **JSC**, $\exists$ an arrow $H(f) \in$ **STRT$_2$**, $H(f):H(A) \to H(B)$, such that $f = r_n \circ r_{n-1} \circ \ldots r_1$ and $H(f) = H(r_n \circ r_{n-1} \circ \ldots r_1)$
$r_i \in$ **JSC** where r_i and s_i are refinements: $s_i = H(r_i)$ since levels map to corresponding subtasks.

B4.2 Functor H'
i) For any $A' \in$ **STRT$_2$** $\exists$ $H'(A') \in$ **JSC** such that the compositions of A' are the same as those for the composition of $H'(A')$ and
ii) For each arrow $f':A' \to B'$, $f' \in$ **STRT$_2$**, $\exists H'(f') \in$ **JSC**, $H'(f'):H'(A) \to H'(B)$, such that $f' = s_n \circ s_{n-1} \circ \ldots s_1$ and $H'(f') = H'(s_n \circ s_{n-1} \circ \ldots s_1)$

Z Specifications and Modal Logic

E.FERGUS,
Liverpool Data Research Associates Ltd.
D.INCE,
The Open University, Milton Keynes

1   ABSTRACT

The standard presentation of a Z specification makes use of a rather limited classical logic in the statement of system dynamics. The notational limitations cause serious difficulty when specifying temporal relationships. A significant improvement can be achieved by employing a modal logic. This paper discusses the use of non-classical logic in the Z specification of the dynamic properties of two communication protocols, and demonstrates how the properties of such systems such as liveness, fairness and termination can be reasoned about. The solution involves replacing the state-space adjacency relationship of the usual Z treatment with a more general reachability relationship.

2   INTRODUCTION

A Z specification [ABR87] is based on a general system model known as an abstract machine. It consists of a state (in the sense of [MIN72]) and one or more actions that modify that state. A Z specification contains one or more variables which constitute the various components of the state, and an invariant which specifies the static laws of a system.

One of the authors is currently engaged in teaching formal methods to staff in the defence industry as a preparation for Defence Standard 0055. Based on this experience, and the application of Z and VDM to concurrent processing case studies, we feel that such augmentation of Z is necessary for the standard to be successful.

Although Z is widely thought of as a fundamentally sequential notation, the need for a concurrent Z has been recognised. In work due to be published shortly, Morgan and Woodcock of the Oxford Programming Research Group establish (via a weakest-precondition calculus) a formal link between Z schema predicates and the CSP process algebra. In this paper we take a simpler approach. A concurrent system may be specified in Z as a collection of sequential systems which are coupled by means of their input and output streams: two components A and B operate concurrently if the outputs of A are the inputs of B. This device is well established in the area of protocol specification (eg. [BRAND83]).

For Z to be a useful notation for concurrent processing, it must enable the analyst/specifier to express and reason about several dynamic properties such as correctness, liveness, termination, absence of unspecified stimuli, absence of race hazards, and fairness. It is possible to make some progress in the standard Z notation by explicitly introducing counters of events. However, for all but very simplest systems the use of such counters rapidly becomes more complex than the application which is the main interest of the specification effort: the counter initialisation conditions are frequently troublesome, and it may become necessary to keep track of combinations of counters. This view is strongly supported by the experience of [DEL89].

However, it is not necessary to record the progression of time explicitly. Rather, it is required to state that events will occur *sometime* in the future. That is, that events will be separated by some interval which is unknown but finite. This can be achieved by replacing the state-space adjacency relationship of the usual Z treatment with a more general reachability relationship. This is modelled using temporal logic.

3   TEMPORAL LOGIC

Temporal logic is an example of modal logic, formally identical to first-order predicate calculus. A good introduction to the subject can be found in [MAN81]. It discusses changes due to the passage of time by treating a process as a sequence of execution states and examining the transformation of one state into another.

Consider a classical scheme of constants, variables, quantifiers, propositions, and predicates. Consider also a formula $F(Q,R)$ of at least two arguments, where one of the arguments Q takes discrete values. One can then write the formula F with one explicit argument R and one implicit argument Q. The distinct values of Q are known as *modes* or *worlds*. In each such mode $F(R)$ has an unambiguous first-order interpretation: an assignment of values to its arguments such that the truth value of $F(R)$ can be evaluated. The interpretation of $F(R)$ may differ in different modes.

A modal formula is constructed from the classical symbols and operators above, and from the modal operators invariance (■), eventuality (♦), precedence (U), and sequence (●). The universe of a modal formula F consists of a (finite or infinite) *set of modes*, an *accessibility relation* stating which mode can be reached from which other mode, and a *distinguished* or *starting* mode, but always within the constraints of the accessibility relation.

For stating the dynamic properties of protocols, the temporal invariance operator conveniently states the safety properties, for example, *the undesirable event X will never happen*, or *the desirable Y will always hold*, while the eventuality operator conveniently states liveness: *the desirable property X will eventually happen*.

The value of temporal logic has been commented on by other authors. [DUB89] distinguishes between static and dynamic constraints (the latter depending in some way on "time" or on progress through a defined procedure) and adopts an extended temporal logic as an appropriate formulation of passing time. Related to the use of temporal logic in this paper is the approach of [KOO89] where temporal logic is used in conjunction with VDM [JON86] to specify the interfaces to a system of concurrent modules. But whereas [KOO89] is interested in separating the statements of the interleaved operations, here we are more concerned to achieve an abstract definition of an event sequence whose members are separated by indefinite intervals. The separate statement of these sequences is a welcome by-product, but of essentially secondary interest: in a more elaborate example one could contemplate modelling race hazards by means of interfering sequences.

Two examples illustrate the usefulness of temporal logic: the 2-phase commit protocol, and a simple user-server protocol.

4 THE 2-PHASE COMMIT PROTOCOL

Figure 1 shows the states of the well-known 2-phase commit protocol [SKE83].

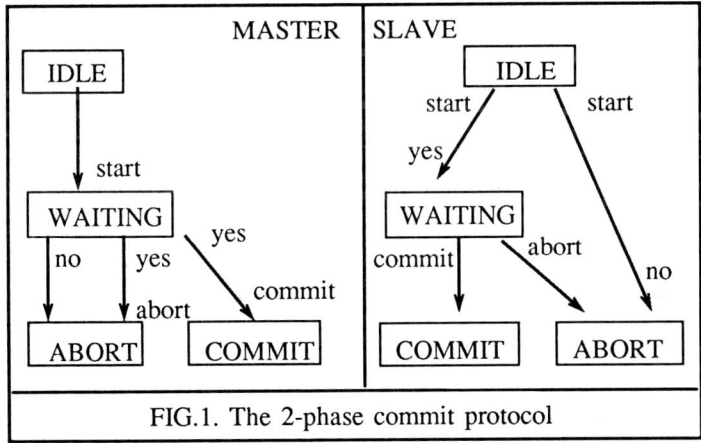

FIG.1. The 2-phase commit protocol

The approach here is to use the Z statics to describe the structure of the protocol (i.e. communicating partners, legal signals, etc.), and to use Z substitutions to describe the protocol state transitions.

The protocol is specified in terms of two communicating components - a *master* and a *slave*. The following basic sets of Z objects are of interest in this specification:
1. the legal states of master and slave: state-m, state-s
2. the legal input signals to master and slave: input-m, input-s
3. the legal output signals the master and slave: output-m, output-s
4. a set of environment conditions for master and slave: environment-m, environment-s

One must remove the decision ambiguities which arise in two ways: non-specific input, and ambiguous decisions. A non-specific input is demonstrated by the master in state *idle*: the input signal is unspecified. An ambiguous decision is demonstrated by the master receiving *yes* in state *waiting*, and then deciding either to commit or abort. One must take into account the circumstances of the communicating applications which enable the protocol partners to make unambiguous decisions, and then encode these conditions as the guarding predicates of pre-conditioned Z substitutions. (Note that the static invariant is an implied term in all preconditioned substitutions.) This is a fundamental feature of any communication protocol and is independent of the particular specification technique adopted. The application circumstances are

> AM1 master wants to communicate
> AM2 master wants to continue
> AM3 master wants to abort
> AS1 slave agrees to communicate
> AS2 slave refuses to communicate

One permissible ambiguity is the undefined output (eg. the master receives *no* in state *waiting*) which does not lead to decision ambiguity, but merely raises the possibility of unobservable states.

Four variables are needed to denote the instantaneous value of the master's state, input, output and environment (ms,mi,mo,me), and four similar variables for the slave (ss,si,so,se).

─── Master ───────────	─── Slave ───────────
ms: state-m	ss: state-s
mi: input-m	si: input-s
mo: output-m	so: output-s
me: environment-m	se: environment-s
state-m = {idle,waiting,abort,commit}	state-s = {idle,waiting,abort,commit}
input-m = {no,yes}	input-s = {start,abort,commit}
output-m = {start,abort,commit}	output-s = {no,yes}
environment-m = (AM1,AM2,AM3)	environment-s = (AS1,AS2}

The static invariant simply requires that no inputs, outputs, or states other than those above may appear during the operation of the protocol. This is simply a restatement of set membership.

4.1 Protocol state transitions

The initial state and the protocol actions of the master and slave are specified by the following schemas. (Note the interpretation of the pre-conditioned substitution: if the substitution is applied when the pre-condition is false, then a fatal error results.

```
┌─── Initialise master ────────
│ Master
├──────────────────────────────
│ ms = idle
└──────────────────────────────
```

```
┌─── Initialise slave ─────────
│ Slave
├──────────────────────────────
│ ss = idle
└──────────────────────────────
```

```
┌─── Master transition 1 ──────
│ ΔMaster
├──────────────────────────────
│ ms = idle
│ me = AM1
│ ms',mo! := waiting,start
└──────────────────────────────
```

```
┌─── Slave transition 1 ───────
│ ΔSlave
│ i? : input-s
├──────────────────────────────
│ ss = idle
│ se = AS1
│ i = start
│ ss',so! := waiting,yes
└──────────────────────────────
```

```
┌─── Master transition 2 ──────
│ ΔMaster
│ i? : input-m
├──────────────────────────────
│ ms = waiting
│ i = no
│ ms',mo! := abort,undefined
└──────────────────────────────
```

```
┌─── Slave transition 2 ───────
│ ΔSlave
│ i? : input-s
├──────────────────────────────
│ ss = idle
│ se = AS2
│ i = start
│ ss',so! := abort,no
└──────────────────────────────
```

```
┌─── Master transition 3 ──────
│ ΔMaster
│ i? : input-m
├──────────────────────────────
│ ms = waiting
│ me = AM2
│ i = yes
│ ms',mo! := commit,undefined
└──────────────────────────────
```

```
┌─── Slave transition 3 ───────
│ ΔSlave
│ i? : input-s
├──────────────────────────────
│ ss = waiting
│ i = commit
│ ss',so! := commit,undefined
└──────────────────────────────
```

```
┌─── Master transition 4 ──────
│ ΔMaster
│ i? : input-m
├──────────────────────────────
│ ms = waiting
│ me = AM3
│ i = yes
│ ms',mo! := abort,abort
└──────────────────────────────
```

```
┌─── Slave transition 4 ───────
│ ΔSlave
│ i? : input-s
├──────────────────────────────
│ ss = waiting
│ i = abort
│ ss',so! := abort,undefined
└──────────────────────────────
```

4.2 Protocol properties

For practical reasons, one wishes to go further and to state and demonstrate certain desirable properties of the protocol. [SPI89] [WOO89a] argue convincingly that this proof facility is an important motivation for, and an integral part of, the mathematical approach to specification. The dynamic properties of concurrent systems involve events which are separated by indefinite time intervals (or more precisely, indefinitely long sequences of events). The standard Z notation [SPI89] for describing such time-dependent changes appears to be weak and a full temporal logic scheme appears to be a practical alternative.

The following general procedure allows one to incorporate dynamic protocol properties in the Z specification. The property is formulated using whatever dynamic notation is convenient. (In this case, we will use temporal logic.) The property is then ANDed with the static invariant to add another term to the overall system invariant. The overall system invariant is therefore the logical conjunction of the (strictly) static invariant and all the predicates (temporal, in our case) which express the protocol properties of interest. It is static in the Z sense that no protocol action may violate it, but it expresses both static and dynamic aspects of the protocol behaviour.

4.3 Correctness

The correctness of the protocol is stated by listing the sequence of state pairs which indicate correct progression of the negotiation, and then asserting that this sequence occurs. The following state sequences (where the prefixes "m-" and "s-" indicate master and slave states respectively) characterise correct behaviour.

1	(m-idle,s_idle),(m-waiting,s-waiting),(m-commit,m-abort)	
2	(m-idle,s_idle),(m-waiting,s-waiting),(m-abort,s-abort)	
3	(m-idle,s_idle),(m-waiting,s-abort),(m-abort,s-abort)	

The master and slave can always be initialised to the *idle* state. (More formally, for all instants reachable from the current instant, the expression ... will eventually become true.)

Eq-1   ■◆(m-idle <u>and</u> s-idle)

Reinitialisation is guaranteed by asserting that the initialisation condition becomes true infinitely often (i.e. the protocol cycles infinitely).

After initialisation, one of the following state pairs always results. (More formally, from the initialisation condition either ... or ... eventually becomes true.)

Eq-2   m-idle <u>and</u> s-idle) ⊃ ◆(m-waiting <u>and</u> s-waiting) <u>or</u>
◆(m-waiting <u>and</u> s-abort)

From the above intermediate stages, one of three termination conditions always results.

Eq-3   (m-waiting <u>and</u> s-waiting) ⊃ ◆(m-commit <u>and</u> s-commit) <u>or</u>
◆(m-abort <u>and</u> s-abort)

Eq-4   (m-waiting <u>and</u> s-abort) ⊃ ◆(m-abort <u>and</u> s-abort)

The complete statement of correctness is the conjunction of E1-4. This assertion can then be conjoined to the static invariant (which is trivially true in this example) to yield the overall system invariant.

4.4 Liveness

It is quite straightforward to state in temporal terms the condition which guarantees freedom from deadlock. Observe that both the master and the slave must start in state *idle* and both must progress either to commit or to abort.

Eq-5   (m-idle <u>and</u> s-idle) ⊃ ◆((m-commit <u>and</u> s-commit) <u>or</u>
(m-abort <u>and</u> s-abort))

By [MAN81] the eventuality operator can be distributed over <u>or</u> to give the intuitive result Eq-6 that eventually either (1) both master and slave commit, or (2) both master and slave abort.

Eq-6   (m-idle <u>and</u> s-idle) ⊃ ◆(m-commit <u>and</u> s-commit) <u>or</u>
◆(m-abort <u>and</u> s-abort)

5 A SIMPLE USER-SERVER PROTOCOL

Figure 2 shows the states of a simple user-server protocol used by [BRAND83].:

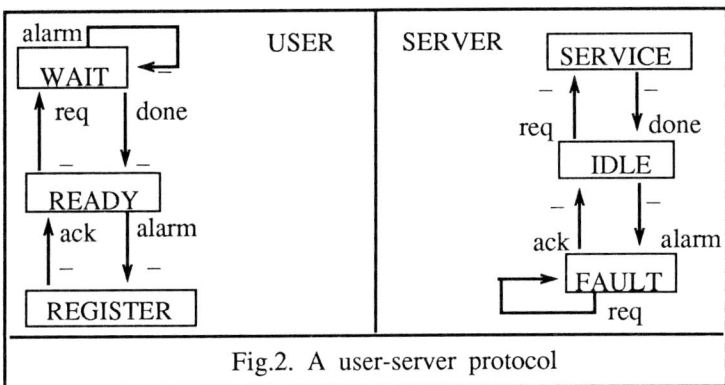

Fig.2. A user-server protocol

The protocol is specified in terms of two communicating components - a *user* and a *server*. The following basic sets of Z objects are of interest in this specification:
1. the legal states user and server: state-u, state-s
2. the legal input signals to user and server: input-u, input-s
3. the legal output signals the user and slave: output-u, output-s
4. a set of environment conditions for user and slave: environment-u, environment-s

As before, one removes decision ambiguity by taking into account the circumstances of the communicating applications which enable the protocol partners to make unambiguous decisions. These are:

> AU1 user wants service
> AU2 user acknowledges a remore fault
> AS1 server completes the service request
> AS2 server develops fault

Four variables are needed to denote the instantaneous value of the user's state, input, output and environment (us,ui,uo,ue), and four similar variables for the server (ss,si,so,se). The static invariant is trivially true, and requires simply that no illegal inputs, outputs, or states may appear during the operation of the protocol.

```
┌──── User ─────────────
│ us : state-u
│ ui : input-u
│ uo : output-u
│ ue : environment-u
├───────────────────────
│ state-u = {wait,ready,register}
│ input-u = {alarm,done}
│ output-u = {req,ack}
│ environment-u = {AU1,AU2}
└───────────────────────
```

```
┌──── Server ───────────
│ ss : state-s
│ si : input-s
│ so : output-s
│ se : environment-s
├───────────────────────
│ state-s = {service,idle,fault}
│ input-s = {req,ack}
│ output-s = {alarm,done}
│ environment-s = {AS1,AS2}
└───────────────────────
```

6   The protocol state transitions

The initial state and dynamic actions of the user and server are specified by the following schemas Again, if the substitution is applied when the pre-condition is false, then a fatal error results.

```
┌─── Initialise user ──────────────
│ User
├──────────────────────────────────
│ us = ready
└──────────────────────────────────
```

```
┌─── Initialise server ────────────
│ Server
├──────────────────────────────────
│ ss = idle
└──────────────────────────────────
```

```
┌─── User transition 1 ────────────
│ ΔUser
├──────────────────────────────────
│ us = ready
│ ue = AU1
│ us',uo! := wait,req
└──────────────────────────────────
```

```
┌─── Server transition 1 ──────────
│ ΔServer
├──────────────────────────────────
│ ss = service
│ se = AS1
│ ss',so! := idle,done
└──────────────────────────────────
```

```
┌─── User transition 2 ────────────
│ ΔUser
│ i? : input-u
├──────────────────────────────────
│ us = wait
│ i = alarm
│ us',uo! := wait,undefined
└──────────────────────────────────
```

```
┌─── Server transition 2 ──────────
│ ΔServer
│ i? : input-s
├──────────────────────────────────
│ ss = idle
│ i = req
│ ss',so! := service,undefined
└──────────────────────────────────
```

```
┌─── User transition 3 ────────────
│ ΔUser
│ i? : input-u
├──────────────────────────────────
│ us = wait
│ i = done
│ us',uo! := ready,undefined
└──────────────────────────────────
```

```
┌─── Server transition 3 ──────────
│ ΔServer
├──────────────────────────────────
│ ss = idle
│ se = AS2
│ ss',so! := fault,alarm
└──────────────────────────────────
```

```
┌─── User transition 4 ────────────
│ ΔUser
│ i? : input-u
├──────────────────────────────────
│ us = ready
│ i = alarm
│ us',uo! := register,undefined
└──────────────────────────────────
```

```
┌─── Server transition 4 ──────────
│ ΔServer
│ i? : input-s
├──────────────────────────────────
│ ss = fault
│ i = req
│ ss',so! := fault,undefined
└──────────────────────────────────
```

```
┌─── User transition 5 ────────────
│ ΔUser
├──────────────────────────────────
│ us = register
│ ue = AU2
│ us',uo! := ready,ack
└──────────────────────────────────
```

```
┌─── Server transition 5 ──────────
│ ΔServer
│ i? : input-s
├──────────────────────────────────
│ ss = fault
│ i = ack
│ ss',so! := idle,undefined
└──────────────────────────────────
```

7 Correctness

The correctness of the protocol is stated by listing the sequence of state pairs which indicate correct progression of the negotiation, and then asserting that this sequence occurs. The following state sequences (where the prefixes "u-" and "s-" indicate user and server states respectively) characterise correct behaviour.

> 1 (u-ready,s-idle), (u-wait, s-service), (u-ready,s-idle)
> 2 (u-ready,s-idle), (u-register, s-fault), (u-ready,s-idle)

The master and slave can always achieve the initial state

Eq-7   ■◆(u-ready and s-idle)

There are two circumstances of interest. The first is a correctly handled transaction request, and the second is a correctly acknowledged fault report. Exactly one of these two must result from the initialisation condition.

Eq-8   (u-ready and s-idle) ⊃ ◆(u-wait and s-service) or
                                ◆(u-register and s-fault)

The complete statement of correctness is the conjunction of E1-7 and 8. This assertion can then be conjoined to the static invariant (which is trivially true in this example).

8 Liveness

The freedom from deadlock is expressed by asserting that the user and server will succeed in cycling endlessly i.e. no delay will last forever. The state achieved immediately after initialisation is denoted by

Eq-9   ●(u-ready and s-service)

From this state we require the initial state to be recovered eventually

Eq-10   (u-ready and s-service) ⊃ ◆●(u-ready and s-service)

9 Conclusions and future work

The standard Z first-order notation for describing time-dependent changes imposes a significant restriction on the specification of system dynamics. This view is strongly supported by the expericnce of [DEL89]. A temporal logic scheme appears to be a practical alternative. Although temporal logic is formally identical to first-order predicate calculus, the notation for making statements about events which are separated by indefinitely long intervals is invaluable. The invariance and eventuality operators are ideally suited to expressing the correctness and liveness properties that frequently occur in concurrent systems.

The Z specification technique has been extended significantly by the addition of a schema calculus, a structuring mechanism which permits a schema to appear in any expression where a predicate is acceptable. The temporal expressions illustrated in this paper contain only simple terms, but it is easy to construct more elaborate examples containing predicate terms. It seems reasonable to require that predicates should be equally acceptable in both temporal expressions and standard first-order expressions. However, the full implications of schema structuring have not yet been considered in detail.

A promising area of further development is the combination of predicate-based description techniques such as Z with specification techniques which are more obviously designed for concurrent systems, for example, process algebras. A recent international workshop [WOO89b] discussed the possibility of combining Z and CSP. This is a particularly interesting combination, given (1) that the LOTOS [BRI87] technique has been adopted as the basis of an international standard technique for specifying telecomms applications, and (2) the large degree to which CSP concepts have contributed to LOTOS. However, the use of temporal logic in conjunction with other techniques (eg. finite-state) also figured prominently in the above discussion. It is clear that there is a significant overlap in the capabilities and areas of application of the many specification techniques currently available. Indeed [WOO89a] indicates that work is already proceeding on extending the original goals of Z to accommodate concurrent systems in a more obvious manner.

10   References

ABR87   A.Abrial, C.Morgan, "Formal software specification and provable design", EWICS TC7 seminar, 4-7/May, 1987

BRI87   E.Brinksma, "A tutorial on LOTOS", in *"Proc. IFIP workshop on protocol specification, testing and verification"*, ed. M.Diaz, pp.73-84, North-Holland, 1987

BRAND83   D.Brand, P.Zafiropulo, "On communicating finite-state machines", JACM, **30**, N2, April 1983

DEL89   N.Delisle, D.Garlan, "Formally specifying elcotronic instruments", in *Proc. 5th Intl. Conf. on Software Specification and Engineering*, ACM SIGSOFT Engineering Notes, **14**, N3, May/1989, pp.242-248

DUB89   E.Dubois, "A logic of action for supporting goal-oriented elaborations of requirements", in *Proc. 5th Intl. Conf. on Software Specification and*

	Engineering, ACM SIGSOFT Engineering Notes, **14**, N3, May/1989, pp.160-168
JON86	C.Jones, "*Systematic software development using VDM*", Prentice Hall, 1986
KOO89	M.Kooij, "Interface specification with temporal logic", in *Proc. 5th Intl. Conf. on Software Specification and Engineering*, ACM SIGSOFT Engineering Notes, **14**, N3, May/1989, pp.104-110
MAN81	Z.Manna, A.Pneuli, "Verification of concurrent programs: the temporal framework", in *"The correctness problem in computer science"*, eds. R.Boyer and J.Strother-Moore, International Lecture Series in Computer Science, Academic Press, 1981, pp.215-273
MIN72	M.Minsky, *"Computation: finite and infinite machines"*, Prentice-Hall, 1972, ISBN 0 13 165449 7
SKE83	D.Skeen,D.Stonebraker, "A formal model of crash recovery in a distributed system", IEEE trans Soft. Eng., **SE-9**, No.3, May 1983
SPI89	J.Spivey, "An introduction to Z and formal specifications", Soft.Eng.J., **4**,N1, January 1989
WOO89a	J.Woodcock, "Structuring specifications in Z", Soft.Eng.J., **4**, N1, January 1989
WOO89b	J.Woodcock, "Formal techniques and operational specifications", Summary of the session at the 5th Intl. Conf. on Software Specification and Engineering, ACM SIGSOFT Engineering Notes, **14**, N3, May/1989, pp.41-42

Knowledge Based Methods

An Integrated Approach to Expert System Development, Project Organization, and Project Management, K. Kurbel

CONCH: A life-cycle model of knowledge-based systems development, R. Taylor

An Integrated Approach to Expert System Development, Project Organization, and Project Management

K. Kurbel, Münster (FRG)

1 INTRODUCTION

Expert systems are different from conventional software systems in many ways [5]: They apply to rather ill structured problems, they have to cope with incomplete or uncertain knowledge, they have to combine general domain knowledge with knowledge on problem dependent exceptions, they do not always create correct solutions (just as human experts are not infallible) etc.

Hence expert system development and maintenance are also different. It is not appropriate to employ approaches to development methodology, project organization, and project management which are based upon a conventional software development life cycle model (SDLC). The SDLC approach to software development has proved useful when

- problems are well structured,

- development personnel and users have experience with similar solutions and problems,

- requirements can be specified early and comprehensively,

- requirements are stable, i.e. there are no fundamental changes during the development process.

Expert system development does not comply with most of those assumptions. One important objection against life cycle models is that the basic idea of development phases to be executed one *after* another is incompatible with the observation that expert system development is primarily an evolutionary process [1]: in most cases expert systems grow in small steps, and development "phases" such as knowledge acquisition and knowledge implementation are heavily intertwined. It should be noted that even in "conventional" software development practical users do not execute phases strictly one after another; they nearly always run in some parallel or iterative manner.

Conventional project organization and management depending on the SDLC model are not appropriate for expert systems because the SDLC model itself is not suitable for expert systems. It should be noted, however, that circumstances may change. A formerly ill structured problem will be better understood when more experience is gained with the problem domain. "Problem structure evolves as the state of knowledge increases" [12]. Hence an expert system might be the best choice for the time being, but after a while a procedural software system might turn out to be more appropriate.

2 APPROACHES TO EXPERT SYSTEM DEVELOPMENT

Different approaches to expert system development have been taken by researchers and practitioners so far. Prototyping often plays an important role. A life-cycle model based upon prototyping has been proposed by a CAS working group, for example [1].

Approaches to expert system development may be classified into three but not necessarily disjunct categories:

Experimental development
Many expert systems have been developed by using heuristics and "trial and error". Starting with a first knowledge base, further pieces of knowledge are extracted from the expert, added to the knowledge base, and validated with the help of the expert [3, 4, 11].

Rapid prototyping
Expert system development is costly and time consuming, and potential benefits are often not obvious in advance. Therefore, a prototype system may be developed first [6]. The prototype system is then used to gain experience with the area of knowledge, to find out whether developing a real system is profitable, to elaborate and refine requirements, or for other purposes. One possible conclusion may also be that a 3GL or 4GL solution is preferable.

Model based development
A basic principle of software engineering is to separate the specification of a program from its implementation. An analogous approach to expert system development would mean that a model of the expertise is constructed first and afterwards translated into an executable representation. For example, such models have been proposed by Freiling [5] and Iwashita et al. [7]. The most elaborate

approach so far is probably the KADS methodology (Knowledge Acquisition Documentation and Structuring) [2, 13]. In many cases model based development implies in principle that all of the domain knowledge is acquired from the expert and represented within the knowledge model prior to being implemented in a "real" software system which can be validated.

3 EVOLUTIONARY DEVELOPMENT OF EXPERT SYSTEMS

Pure experimental or model based development as well as rapid prototyping show severe drawbacks. Therefore, an approach to expert system development is proposed which combines basic ideas of those three approaches.

The development method focuses on the main activities during expert system development: *acquiring* knowledge from the expert (or other sources) and *representing* knowledge in a formalized manner. Knowledge representation may be performed on different levels. For the purpose of this paper, two distinct levels are considered as shown in figure 1:

- a *conceptual level* where the acquired knowledge is modeled and represented in a conceptual knowledge model,

- an *implementation level* where the conceptual knowledge model is described in an executable representation.

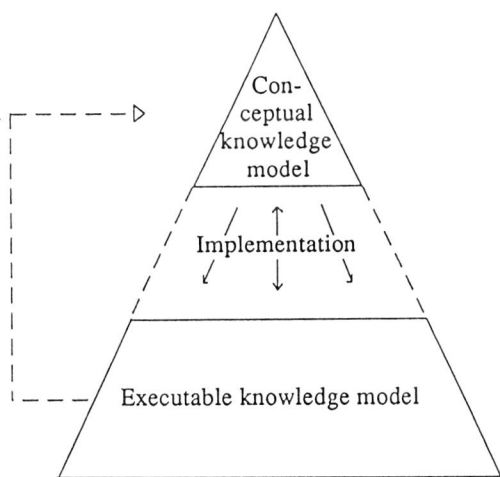

Fig. 1: Levels of knowledge representation

The *conceptual knowledge model* will thus not be an executable model. Although automatic translation might be considered useful, it is not yet sufficiently supported by the state of the art of knowledge engineering tools. Most available tools do not support knowledge modeling on a higher abstraction level, or if they do, no interpreter for the knowledge model is provided.

Furthermore, too early formalization may also impede comprehensive and adequate representation of knowledge. In software engineering much effort has been devoted to formalized specifications of software systems. Although applicable to small problems, abstract specifications have not yet been successful as far as large real world problems are concerned. Expert system technology is less well understood than conventional software technology, thus formalized adequate specifications of expert behaviour which can be translated automatically do not appear to be practical up-to-date.

If expert system development is regarded as an evolutionary process, then knowledge acquisition and knowledge representation are not sequential stages but they have to be performed several times throughout the development cycles. Figure 2 illustrates that several versions of an expert system are produced. Major steps are the following:

Knowledge acquisition
Domain knowledge is acquired from the expert and recorded. A conceptual knowledge model is constructed, extended and/or revised. It is binding for the present cycle.

Knowledge implementation
The knowledge model is expressed by means of a language or some other software tool, e.g. an expert system shell. Implementation is performed incrementally: Parts of the knowledge model are added to the knowledge base and validated step by step. If shortcomings or inconsistent knowledge units are detected feed-back is given to the knowledge acquisition step.

Acceptance test
The result of the implementation stage is a version of the expert system. It will be checked and validated against specific quality measures which were established at the beginning of the cycle. Shortcomings will be recorded in a report.

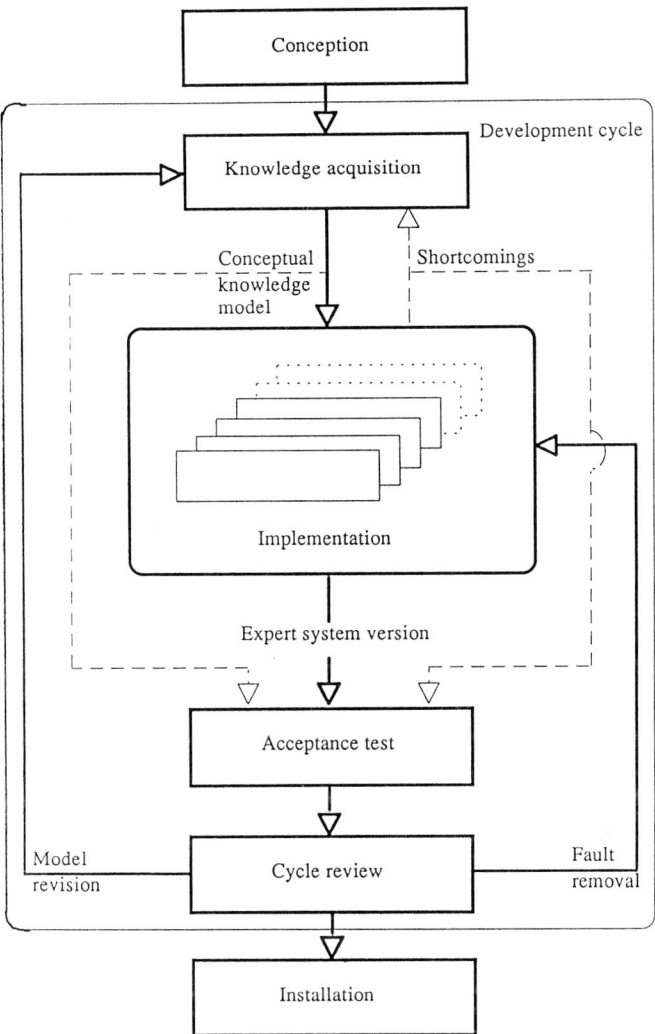

Fig. 2: Expert system development cycles

Cycle review

Results and experience gained within the cycle as well as reported shortcomings are discussed. A decision is made as to which faults can be removed within the current cycle ("fault removal") and which faults call for revision of the conceptual knowledge model. The latter ones will be considered within the knowledge acquisition stage of the next cycle. A change of the software tool may be considered if it proved to be inadequate. Within the cycle review step it will also be examined whether the time schedule for the activities of the current cycle was appropriate. Conclusions may be applied to the next cycle.

Validation and *testing* are performed at various points of the development model. During knowledge acquisition the conceptual knowledge model is analyzed by the expert. During knowledge implementation working sessions with the expert are held where the knowledge base is evaluated continously. Acceptance testing includes checking the performance of the expert system such as: does it solve typical problems as expected? or: how many percent of difficult problems does it solve satisfactorily etc.?

Two important prerequisites for *quality assurance* of an expert system are documentation and change control [1]. A conceptual knowledge model as proposed above is a structured semi-formal description of the knowledge on a high abstraction level ("paper model"). It is implementation independent and does serve the purpose of documenting the knowledge very well. The conceptual knowledge model also supports change control. It is established or revised, respectively, in each cycle before implementation starts, and it is used as a binding "specification" for that cycle. If modifications are necessary, they are reported during implementation or acceptance testing.

Evolution of an expert system during a development project usually requires several cycles [9]. We propose at least three cycles:

- an *initialization cycle* where the primary objective is to make system developers familiar with basic problems and problem solving strategies in the application domain; some characteristic parts of the knowledge model will be constructed and implemented fast,

- a *reorientation cycle* where experience from the first cycle is employed for thorough revision and extension of the conceptual knowledge model; now the bulk of the knowledge model can be implemented.

- a *stabilization cycle* where shortcomings of the conceptual knowledge model which could not be corrected during the second cycle are removed and system tuning is performed.

In large projects or in projects dealing with complex problem domains more than three cycles may be required. A start-up cycle in the beginning and a stabilization cycle at the end will be useful in any case.

The idea of evolutionary development may have to be continued on a further level. If an expert system is to be integrated into an existing data processing environment, or if it has to cooperate with other expert systems, a prototyping approach will often prove useful. Merging systems may require several cycles, and feed-back may lead to changes of the conceptual knowledge model and thus imply further iterations.

4 EXPERT SYSTEM PROJECT ORGANIZATION

Project organization should be chosen in accordance with activities of the development cycles in order to be efficient. Therefore only few roles of conventional software projects may be adopted for expert system development. In particular, project organization should support fundamental activities such as knowledge acquisition and implementation, based on a conceptual knowledge model. Furthermore, we strongly argue that the person(s) performing knowledge acquisition should not be identical with the person(s) implementing the knowledge model.

Those two roles often pursue different goals: One who is responsible for knowledge acquisition will primarily try to cover all of the relevant domain knowledge, no matter which implementation restrictions might exist. But on other hand, anyone who is in charge of implementing the knowledge will probably try to make the implementation as efficient as possible by means of the chosen software tool. He or she will also often discover that parts of the knowledge cannot be implemented satisfactorily.

If knowledge acquisition and implementation roles are not separated from each others a severe drawback often occurs: Representation problems (e.g. difficulties resulting from restrictions of the software tool) already affect the way knowledge acquisition is performed, and knowledge which does not lend itself to a particular formalization may be inadequately recorded or even left out. Thus compromises between efficient implementation and adequate elaboration of domain knowledge are not subject to an explicit decision, e.g. by the project head; they are rather made implicitly by the knowledge engineer. On the contrary, if the separation is made, conflicts become transparent because they have to be carried out between different persons.

In figure 3 a possible structure of a large expert system project is illustrated where acquisition and implementation roles are further refined with regard to particular tasks. They may be filled by one or more persons. For example, one of the knowledge acquisition roles may cover elicitation and analysis of the expertise, whereas the other one is in charge of the conceptual knowledge model. Implementation roles may focus on software-based knowledge representations appropriate for the particular domain and, respectively, on transforming the conceptual model into executable code.

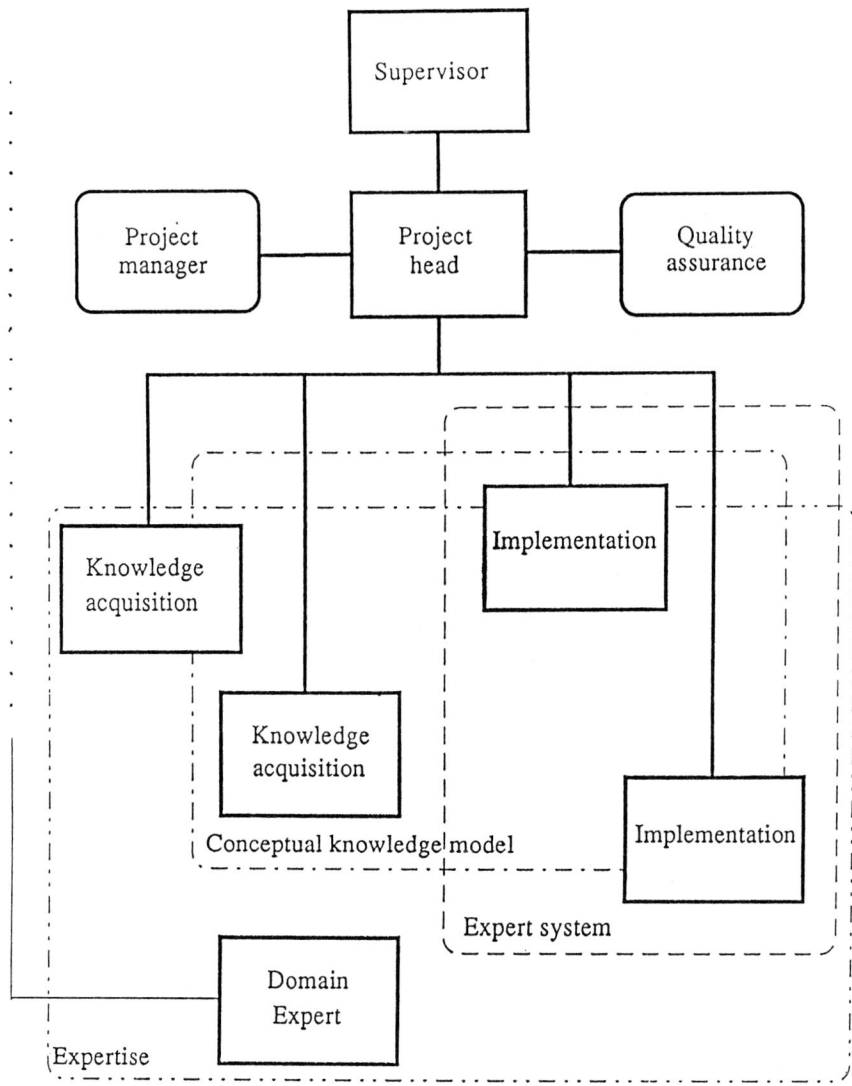

Fig. 3: Organization of an expert system project

The roles on top of figure 3 - supervisor, project head, project manager, quality assurance - are similar to those of conventional software projects. Timetables are set up by the project head and the project manager. The former one decomposes the whole development process into cycles with rough starting and finishing dates whereas the latter one is in charge of detailed scheduling of activities.

The quality assurance role establishes specific quality standards at the beginning of each cycle. Cycle results are evaluated with respect to those standards. That role is also responsible for preparing the acceptance test and the cycle review. A cycle review is partly based upon a list of faults detected during accceptance testing. When those faults are removed (after "fault removal" or "model revision", see figure 2) the quality assurance role is in charge of accepting or rejecting the modifications.

5 PROJECT MANAGEMENT SYSTEMS

Expert system projects are more difficult to control than conventional software projects because in many cases it is impossible to establish detailed requirements specifications in advance. Furthermore, requirements may change during the development process, and often it does not become clear what can be achieved at all until a prototype system is developed. Therefore project planning and control must provide for great flexibility, e.g. they must allow project plans to be modified continously according to development needs.

Experience with computer based project management systems has shown that those systems are inappropriate for expert system development. Often they do not even adequately support the needs of SDLC projects because in many cases they have originated from industrial manufacturing. They are too rigid to provide the high amount of flexibility needed in the development of expert systems. In particular, the number and shape of development cycles, the activities within a cycle, and the time it takes to perform a particular activity are neither fixed nor even predictable with sufficient certainty in advance. Activities of the third cycle such as stabilization and tuning steps, for example, heavily depend on the outcome of the first two cycles.

Subsequently a possible structure of a flexible project management system is outlined. It has been designed to support evolutionary software development, particularly expert system development. Three project management levels are distinguished for this purpose:

- Top level activities include strategic decisions with regard to the project plan, e.g. how many and which cycles should be performed, which are major milestones etc.

- On an intermediate level, the project structure is determined with respect to concrete activities within a particular development cycle.

- Low level project management deals with short term tasks such as planning the daily work of the project members. But responsibility for project control and coordination of every day activities is left to the project members to a great deal.

On each level a different view of an expert system project is appropriate. Therefore the software tools have to support different views of project management. For example, top level tools include tools for flexible modification of the project structure, for resource planning, etc. whereas low level tools will make intelligent recommendations to project individuals of what to do next etc. They also support communication among the project team which is very important if project members themselves are in charge of low level coordination as suggested above.

A flexible project management system supporting three levels of project planning and control is under development at the University of Dortmund. It is part of a research project sponsored by the major German researchers' association, Deutsche Forschungsgemeinschaft (DFG). A prototype system including a project knowledge base will be completed in 1990. The project management system may be "customized" to a specific project. Different views of a project according to the three level structure and tools for the respective levels will be provided [10].

6 CONCLUSIONS

SDLC models and project management concepts based upon those models do not provide enough flexibility for expert system development. Furthermore, development methodology, organization, and management of expert system projects cannot be treated separately. Expert systems require an integrated approach to all three issues. One central concept of the integrated view is the conceptual knowledge model. It is part of the development process, it is referred to by each role of the project organization, and it is an important document for project management and quality assurance.

References

[1] Born, G. (ed.): Guidelines for Quality Assurance of Expert Systems, CSA Working Group on QA and Expert Systems, Working Paper, Issue 1.1. London: Computer Services Association, November 1988.

[2] Breuker, J., Wielinga, B., van Someren, M., et al.: Model-Driven Knowledge Acquisition: Interpretation Models. Deliverable task A1, Esprit Project 1098, VF Project Knowledge Acquisition in Formal Domains, Department of Social Science Informatics, University of Amsterdam, 1987.

[3] Buchanan, B.G.: Expert Systems: working systems and the research literature. Expert Systems, January 1986, pp. 32-51.

[4] Buchanan, B.G., Barstow, D., Bechtal, R., et al.: Constructing an Expert System, in: Hayes-Roth et al. (eds.): Building Expert Systems. London, Amsterdam: Addison-Wesley 1983, pp. 127-167.

[5] Freiling, M., Alexander, J., Messick, S., et al.: Starting a Knowledge Engineering Project: A Step-by-Step Approach. The AI Magazine, Fall 1985, pp. 150-164.

[6] Harmon, P., King, D.: Expert Systems - Artificial Intelligence in Business. West Sussex: John Wiley & Sons 1985.

[7] Iwashita, Y., et al.: Knowledge Acquisition and Learning in Case Studies of Expert Systems Development. ICOT TR-0204, 1986.

[8] Kurbel, K.: Entwicklung und Einsatz von Expertensystemen - Eine anwendungsorientierte Einführung in wissensbasierte Systeme. Berlin, Heidelberg, New York: Springer 1989.

[9] Kurbel, K., Pietsch, W.: Projektmanagement bei einer Expertensystementwicklung; Information Management, No. 1, 1988, pp. 6-13.

[10] Kurbel, K., Pietsch, W.: Projektmanagementebenen bei evolutionärer Softwareentwicklung, in: Kurbel, K., Mertens, P., Scheer, A.-W. (eds.), Interaktive betriebswirtschaftliche Informations- und Steuerungssysteme. Berlin, New York: de Gruyter 1989, pp. 261-285.

[11] Shortliffe, T., Davis, R.: Some Consideration for the Implementation of Knowledge-Based Expert Systems. ACM Sigart Newsletter, No. 55, December 1975, pp. 9-12.

[12] Sviokla, J.J.: Business Implications of Knowledge Based Systems. Data Base, Fall 1986, pp. 5-16.

[13] Wielinga, B.J., Breuker, J.A.: Models of Expertise, in: Du Boulay, B., Hogg, D., Steels, L. (eds.): Advances in Artificial Intelligence - II. Elsevier Science Publishers 1987, pp. 497-509.

CONCH: A Life-Cycle Model of Knowledge-Based Systems Development

Robert M Taylor

The Knowledge-Based Systems Centre,
Touche Ross Management Consultants

Abstract

This paper describes a life-cycle model (LCM) for the development and management of knowledge-based systems (KBS). The life-cycle model is called CONCH (Client-Oriented Normative Control Hierarchy). CONCH is part of the KADS methodology for KBS development, developed under ESPRIT project 1098. CONCH has two layers of description; the "model layer" focuses on the output results of development activity (documents and models), whilst the "control layer" details the phases, stages and activities involved in KBS development and management. The control layer features a hierarchy of parallel spiral LCMs as an important view of the iterative development process.

Key words: risk-driven, spiral LCM, results-oriented, KADS methodology.

1 THE KBS LCM IN THE KADS METHODOLOGY

KADS [Hesketh 89, Wielinga 89, Hickman 89a] is the name of what is almost certainly the principal methodology for KBS development available today. KADS has been developed under a series of ESPRIT-sponsored projects (notably projects 12 and 1098) and is gaining subscribers in Europe and North-America at an ever-increasing rate.

In KADS we take the view that the KBS development process is essentially a transformation of models. Thus, a conceptual model of the knowledge in the domain in question is built and subsequently transformed into design models of the target system, and, eventually, into software and a working system to service its function. For our purposes here, the software that is developed can also be regarded as a model: an 'active' model (whereas the other models are paper-based).

KADS prescribes the phases and activities involved in KBS development [Barthelemy 87, Killin 89], gives details of milestone deliverables and also adds the discipline of requirements engineering to KBS development practice. In these ways, KADS has been made structurally similar to conventional software development methodologies, whilst retaining a *detailed* configuration and a modelling language especially adapted to the particular concerns that present themselves in knowledge engineering.

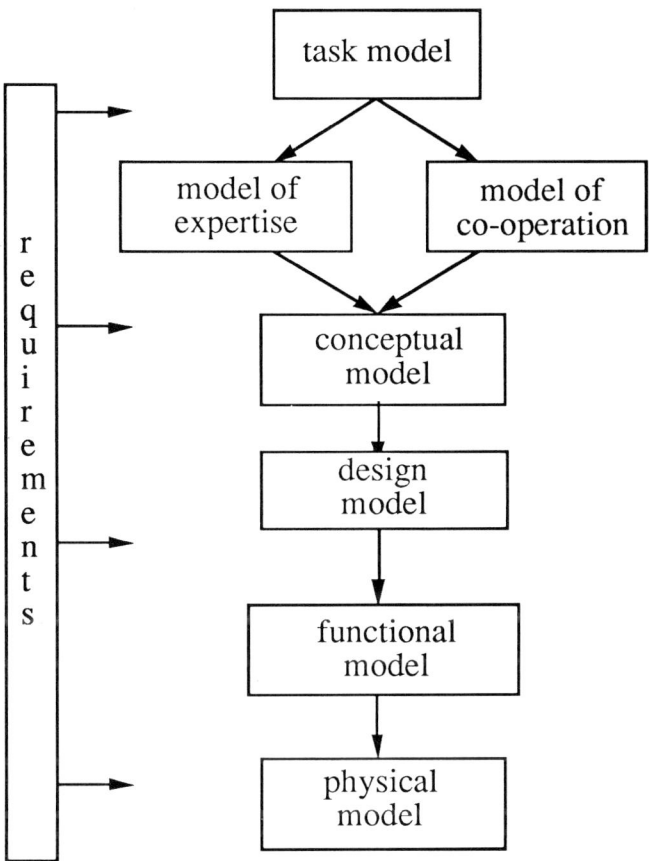

Figure 1 Transformation of models in KADS
[Hickman 89a & 89b; adapted from Wielinga 89]

A large number of general forms of the systems development LCM have been evaluated for adoption by KADS [Barthelemy 86, Taylor 89]. The discussion as to their suitability is not the subject of this paper. Initially a waterfall version of the KBS LCM was developed for KADS [Barthelemy 87].

This general form of the KBS LCM has been used with considerable success in a number of experiments carried out under ESPRIT project 1098 as well as in commercial development projects. By and large, the success has been repeated in each of the four European countries participating in P1098. The provision of a KBS LCM is an innovation of KADS: There really is no well-developed precursor. Early use of the KADS waterfall LCM, therefore, made many new benefits available to KBS developers. These benefits will not come as news to the software engineering community, and so they are not dwelt on here. However, it is important to note that they *were* news to the KBS community which largely believed (as some practitioners still do) that, due to the special problems of uncertainty inherent in the knowledge engineering domain, the only appropriate systems development paradigm was the rather experimental "rapid prototyping" approach.

The initial KADS LCM illustrated how the process could at last be *managed*. However, with increasing experience it became clear that there were some deficiencies in this form of the LCM:

- it was incomplete (there was a detailed lower-level view of the analysis phase but there were not similar detailed views of phases other than analysis);

- it was found to be wrong in many points of detail (the SADT notation used is really far too precise for our level of understanding of the process, and, consequently, there must be vastly more interpretation than guidance in the practical application of the LCM);

- it tends to describe only knowledge engineering activities, and ignores project management activities (such as planning; in CONCH we take the view that the primary aim of the LCM is to support planning) and client involvement;

- as a waterfall LCM it was old-fashioned in software engineering terms, suffering from the many, and well-documented, faults of that representation [Boehm 88, Gilb 85, Spinrad 85, Gladden 82, McCracken 82, Hughes 86, Balzer 83];

- it gave an inadequate account of the role of prototyping in KBS development (a topic that we must turn to next).

CONCH [Taylor 89, Hickman 89b] is an attempt to address these problems in the light of increased experience in the methodological development of KBS.

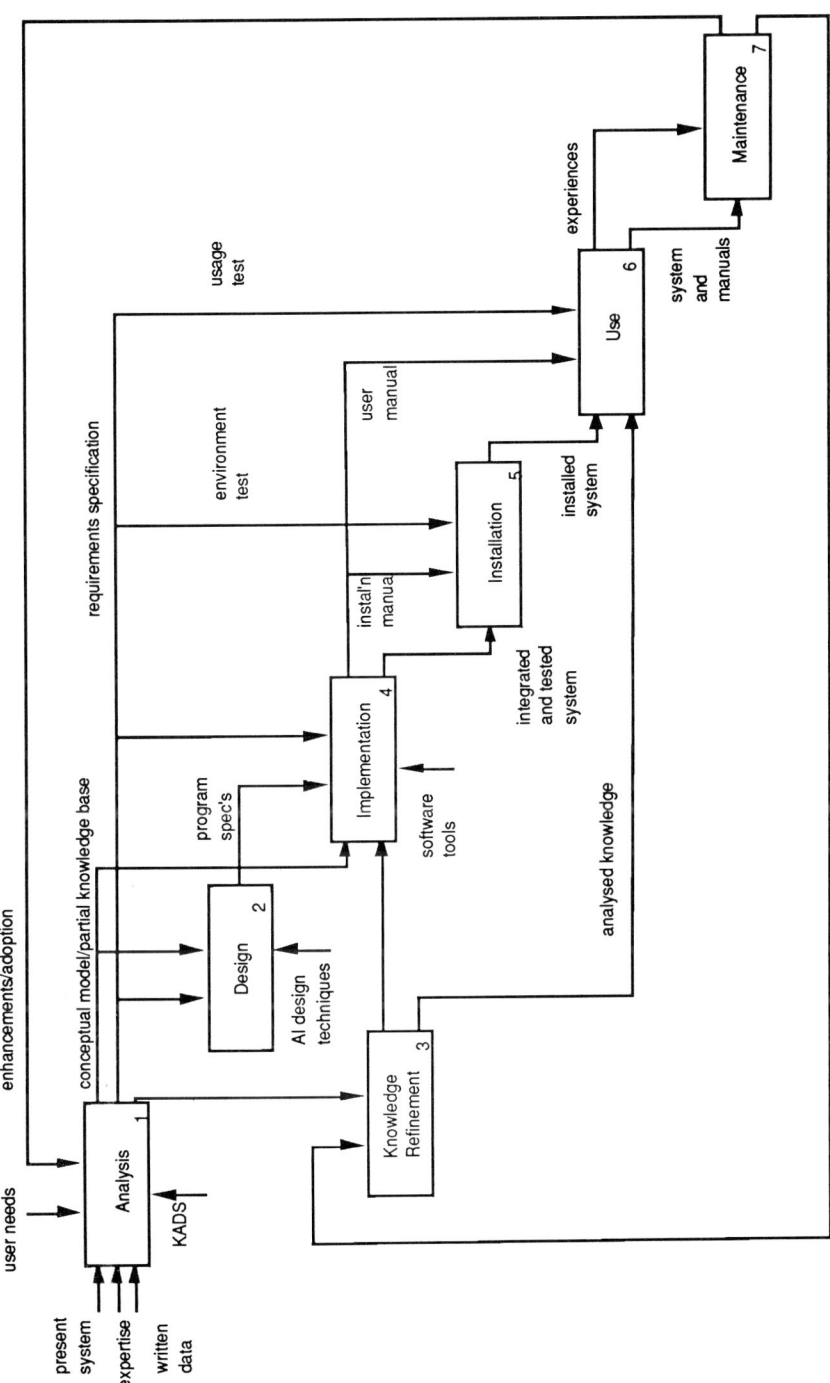

Figure 2 The waterfall LCM for KADS. [Hickman 89, based on Barthelemy 87]

2 THE ROLE OF PROTOTYPING IN KBS DEVELOPMENT

KADS has emerged as an alternative to the prevalent development paradigm in KBS which we call 'rapid prototyping'. The methodological approach is an alternative that is gaining more and more adherents as the advantages it offers (in terms of planning and control) over more 'experimental' approaches are realised. However, the precise and proper role of prototyping in serious KBS development has, until recently, been something of a problem for KADS, which rejected the iterative development of software performance prototypes in favour of the iterative development of paper models of expert competence [Nobis 88]. [Born 88] has suggested how greater control can be brought to the rapid prototyping development paradigm through applying quality management procedures with pre-set objectives and review criteria. We suggest, however, that whilst these innovations were much needed in KBS development, a wholesale rejection of the rapid prototyping paradigm was called-for on the grounds of it being insufficient to the problems of serious system development. There is no need to discuss this further for the present audience, though the curious reader is referred to the discussion of the issues in [Hickman 89a, Taylor 89].

Since the LCM is a concept in the methodology domain, it can hardly have any credible existence before KADS. Indeed, little thought had been given to such issues as KBS maintenance and decommissioning in the heyday of rapid prototyping; It was all too easy! Expert systems shells meant that code was "self-documenting" and, therefore, easily maintainable, and, in any case, expert systems were thought to be cheap and quick to develop. Whilst this thinking may have been fine for very small, experimental systems, it is manifestly not good enough when we come to tackle more significant bodies of knowledge that themselves have a life-cycle.

In the early days of KADS, when there was a need to make an obvious break from rapid prototyping, the case against prototyping may have been overstated. This appears to be the case since people are often incredulous to find proponents of KADS talking about prototyping: Some even appear to feel vindicated in holding on to the old methods. Actually, nothing has changed in KADS' stance towards prototyping except our ability to explain it. It is the new form of the KADS LCM, CONCH, that has clarified the proper role of prototyping. KADS is not a prototyping methodology, but it *does* accommodate prototyping as a technique that can be used in risk management activities (this is explained later). Prototyping is not advised as a development paradigm, though it is a technique we can use:

- to test a particular method, algorithm, piece of software or hardware (for instance, for performance metrics);

- as an aid to elicit requirements;

- to reinforce client confidence (sadly, often called-for);

- to test aspects of the knowledge-base;

- in user interface development (which is still a fairly haphazard business, even in the view of the specialists).

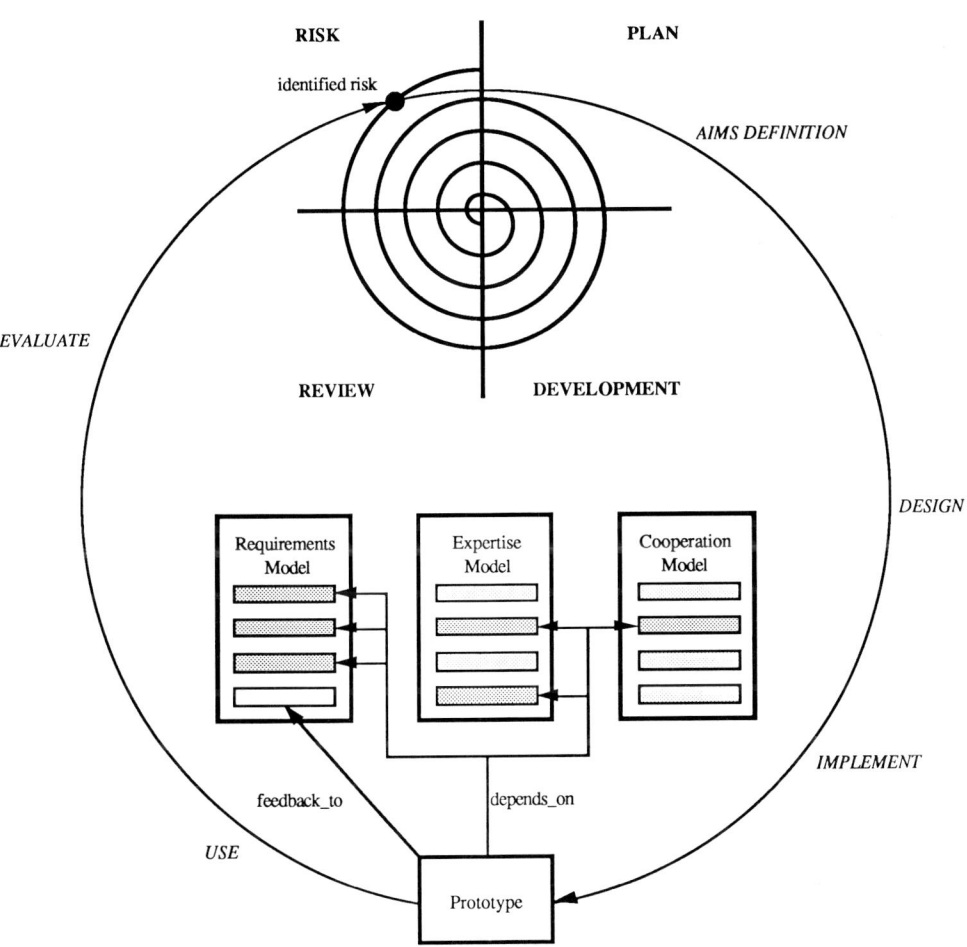

Figure 3 Prototyping in CONCH for risk management

From the CONCH point-of-view the important things are to:

- know what the objective of the prototyping is, and how it will be evaluated;

- perform the exercise to plan with absolute discipline;

- review the activity regularly according to the evaluation criteria and objectives;

- feed the *results*, and not the *artifact* (the software) back into the main development.

The last point is the most important: We prototype in order to answer definite questions. It is the answers to the questions that we require from the prototyping exercise and not the software that is developed: that way lies the path of the iterative development of prototypes with all the inherent risks of taking that development path.

The 'new' KADS view on prototyping is expounded by [Porter 89] and how this fits into CONCH is shown in his contribution to [Taylor 89] (Figure 3, above)

3 CONCH: CLIENT-ORIENTED NORMATIVE CONTROL HIERARCHY

3.1 A definition of CONCH
CONCH is the KADS KBS LCM. CONCH has two layers of description; the *control layer* and the *model layer*. The control layer is illustrated by a spiral model for the stages and by PERT charts for phase decomposition and scheduling, whilst the model layer consists of a series of frame-based representations of knowledge to do with the production of the individual models and other document objects in system development and management.

3.2 Phases in the control layer
The process of building KBS entails modelling the knowledge involved (analysis), transforming that model of knowledge so that it can be implemented on a computer (design) and writing the software (implementation). Together, analysis, design and implementation are known as the *development phases* of the life-cycle. The *later phases* of the life cycle are installation, use, maintenance and decommissioning. CONCH aims to describe the whole of the KBS life-cycle, though it is bound to concentrate more on the development phases as this is where the support an LCM can give is most relevant to system developers. It is also because KBS developers have less experience of the later phases of the life-cycle.

The diagram below expresses the scheduling of the phases of the KBS LCM. From the start to the end of the life cycle some phases contain activities that are normally carried out in parallel, whilst there are others that are more likely to be sequential to one another. These two kinds of relationships are shown in the diagram below and the others like it, which are simplified PERT charts.

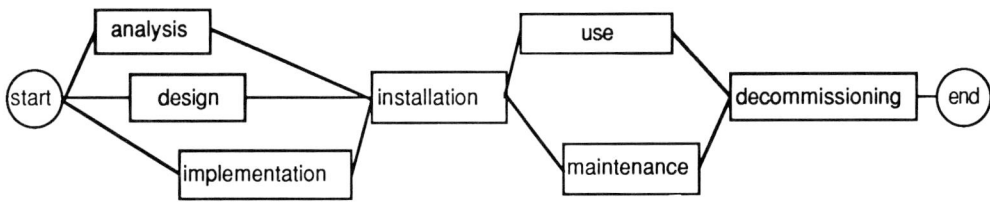

Knowledge-based systems life-cycle model

Figure 4 Phases in the CONCH KBS LCM control layer

During the analysis phase these models are built; abstract models of the problem-solving knowledge (expertise model) and the task (cooperation model; from modality analysis) in question, and a definition of the client's requirements.

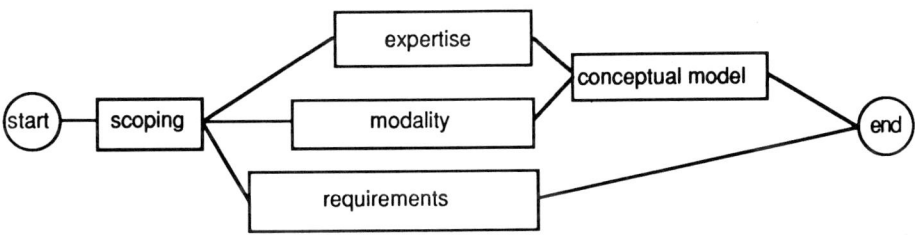

Analysis phase

Figure 5 Sub-phases of analysis in CONCH

This is a level one decomposition of analysis showing the three parallel streams of model development during that phase. The development of each model is influenced by and influences the pattern and direction of development of the other two models. This is achieved by holding joint review meetings and by the circulation of documents between personnel involved in the separate model developments.

The CONCH control layer also includes similar PERT views of the sub-phases of the other phases in the LCM. These are most fully expounded in [Taylor 89].

3.3 Stages in the CONCH control layer: The spiral model

Activities in every phase of the life-cycle fall into an iterative pattern of four stages. This iteration around stages is described by the spiral model at the control layer of CONCH. The actual filling of the spiral model varies according to the phase and model in question, though the general form is always the same at every level of control.

The four stages in the CONCH LCM are named: review, risk, plan and develop.

Figure 6 Stages in the CONCH spiral

The stages ought not to be confused with activities. Any one stage must be seen as a *packet* of several activities. For example, in model-driven knowledge acquisition, the develop stage includes interviewing, transcription, protocol analysis and model building. It is important to remember that the spiral model is a very general description of the iterative process of system development.

There now follows a general account of each of the CONCH stages.

Review stage

In the review stage the basic questions that may be asked are "Where are we? How much of all that we need have we got? What else have we got? What is the situation? How well are we doing? What is the nature of the problem we are tackling?".

Review will always occur after some development activity is completed. Although the plan must include formal reviews there are also informal reviews which may not be explicitly indicated in the plans (certainly at the higher levels, although they may be in evidence at the lower levels). Formal reviews include project steering group (PSG) meetings, and informal reviews include knowledge acquisition team meetings, for example. Formal reviews will also feature inputs from the quality management & control activities.

Risk stage
The risk stage is a packet of activities which include the following:
- feasibility assessment;
- risk assessment & reduction (risk management);
- objectives setting;

The output of this stage includes feasibility and risk reports and, possibly, reports on prototyping exercises.

Plan stage
In this stage project plans are drawn up. The plans are mainly concerned with model development activities, though the plan must include review activities and the production of risk-stage deliverables such as feasibility reports. Plans are updated throughout development as more is learned about the special needs of that development and as the constraints and context change. Every plan is a plan for the whole development project (at its own level), and each plan will specify a number of review points (internal meetings and PSG meetings). However, after every review there is a reassessment of priorities ("risk" stage) and a new plan is devised *for the total remaining effort and time*. Evidently, this means that there is a *"planning horizon"* which is as far ahead as you can reliably plan. Sometimes it may be possible to have a far horizon; meaning that it is possible to plan more than one review ahead with a high degree of surety that subsequent development will follow a predictable path. More usually in a field with a high degree of risk and uncertainty involved, however, like KBS, the horizon will be close and it will be necessary to replan frequently as more is learned. This should be pointed out to the client (management) early on and included in any contract. This is another good reason for adopting an LCM with iterative reviewing and planning, like CONCH, for KBS development.

Develop stage
This stage is to do with activities connected with developing models and also with other activities that form a logical "packet" such as scoping and installation. When one comes to consider the later phases of the LCM the term "develop" is a less relevant title for this stage. Essentially, "develop" is concerned with the actual progress-making activities; whether in the modelling or operationalisation of the system. The proper description of the develop stage comprises of the description of the model involved, its form and role and its development process (including tools, techniques and activities). Refer to the individual models and to the KADS literature for these details. (As has been suggested above, the develop stage is so named as this is the stage that accounts for the progress-making activities, namely model-building, during the development phases of the life-cycle. Once we are in the later phases, and hence out of the

modelling universe, it may make more sense to name this stage after the phase concerned: Hence; install, use, maintain, decommission).

3.4 The CONCH hierarchy of spirals
During the planning stage it may be possible to identify distinct areas of the work that can be delegated to individual members or sub-groups of the development team to be carried out in parallel.

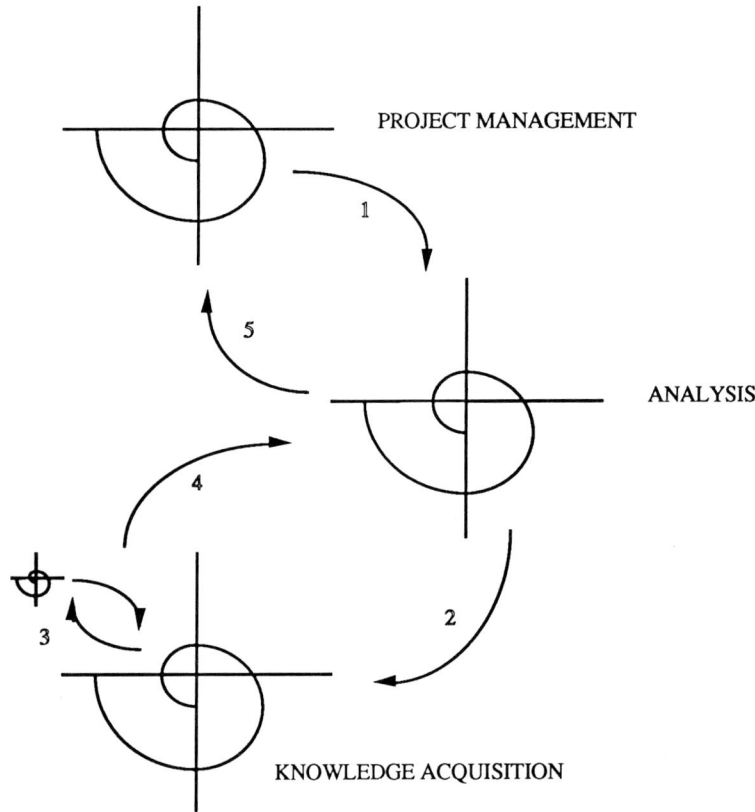

Figure 7 Delegation of control through the hierarchy of spirals

Where planning for part of a development is delegated to a lower level it is as if someone else is the manager of a smaller project with more constrained goals. As such, all of their activities and concerns, at that lower level, can be described by another copy of the spiral model: They too have to be concerned with reviewing, assessing risk, planning and developing models (or carrying out activities). It is as if you have *passed them the CONCH,* except that you have kept it yourself as well since the two **CONCH** models are kept separate at different levels and the lower one is part of the higher one. The lower one is not smaller than the higher one though, since, although it concerns a smaller area of the total development enterprise, it will contain a greater amount of detail about it: CONCH is a fractal model with the property of being self-similar. Lower levels of control can be regarded as black boxes at the higher levels.

If there are parallel sub-plans then the controlling plan arc must be seen as the process of co-ordinating and agreeing the sub-plans, which is a process of negotiation between the planners in which the project manager is the arbiter (and has to engage in the "external" negotiation with the client). If the project manager happens also to be the leader of one of the sub-plans, then this is described at the sub-plan layer and not at the controlling layer: The person has two roles, project manager and task leader, and it is purely incidental that the two roles are filled by the same person.

3.5 Putting the two levels together: The parallel, hierarchical spiral model

The diagram below (figure 8) uses the PERT-view of the control layer, together with the spiral view, to express how the control hierarchy works. The project manager has an overview of the whole life-cycle (or, at least, certainly the development phases). This is the top-level plan. As its coverage is much greater than any sub-plan it is, consequently, less detailed in the minutiae. In the plan depicted, control over maintenance has been delegated to a sub-plan. If the project manager should call a review then he can put all current phases, models and activities under review if he so chooses. This means that the review stages of all invoked spirals (the plans) at all levels of alignment can be brought into overall alignment. It is best that this is planned ahead so that dates for overall reviews can be percolated down through the lower plans and included in any appropriate layers. Dates of formal reviews at the top level can prompt informal, internal reviews in the lower levels in time to queue corrective development work before the formal review. The diagram also illustrates the relationship between the two layers of CONCH: The control layer is applied to the models and document objects in the model layer whilst the nature of the particular model under consideration constrains the nature of the control exerted.

3.6   The model layer

The CONCH model layer describes the objects (models) in the KADS LCM and activities related to their development and operationalisation. In KBS terms, the models in the model-layer of CONCH play a role loosely analogous to that of domain knowledge in an expert-systems shell: Whilst the detail of the control layer (in the precise selection and ordering or the phases, for example) instantiates the CONCH LCM *specifically* to KBS to some extent, this is really achieved by the filling of the model-layer with KADS models.

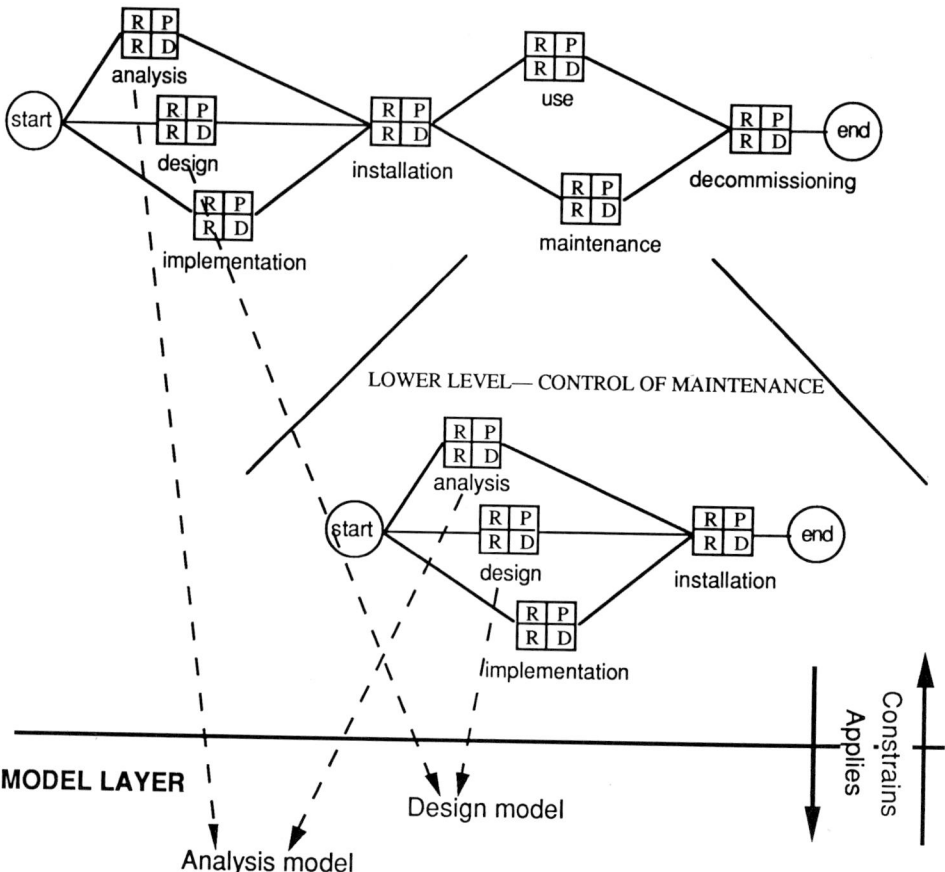

Figure 8 Hierarchical control in CONCH

3.7 Model specifications

Models in CONCH are specified in a frame of slots holding knowledge about the development process for each model. The slots in the standard frame include one for each stage in CONCH; review, risk, plan & develop.

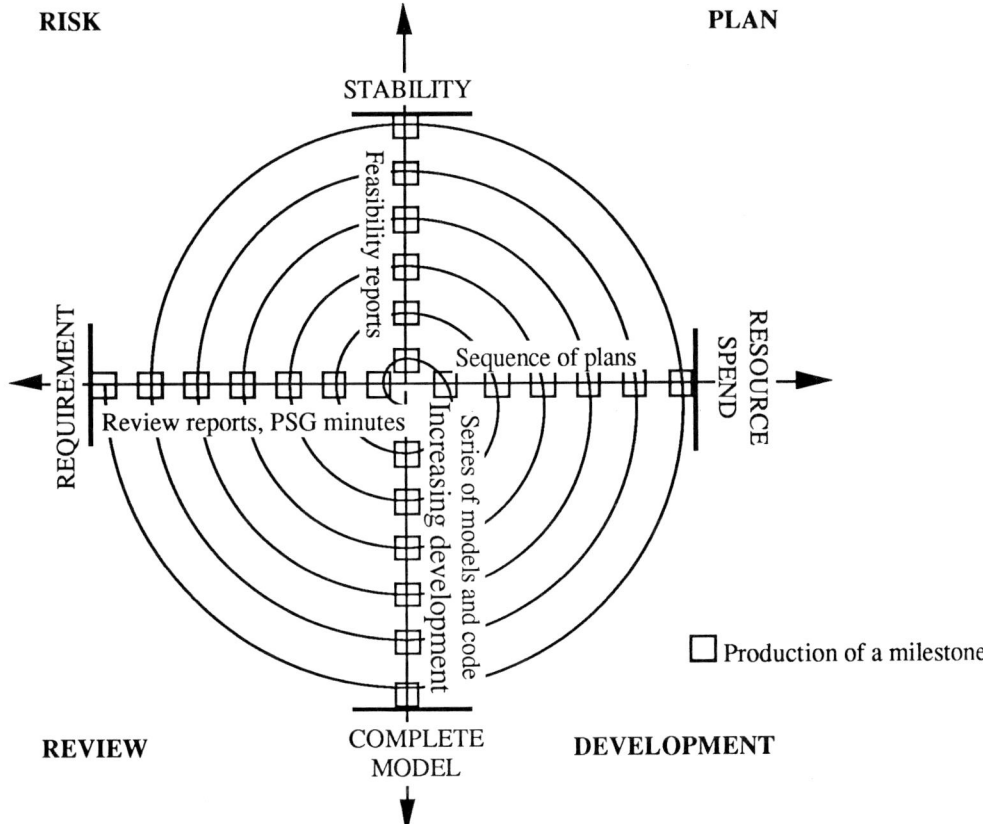

Figure 9 Models and document objects in the stages of the CONCH spiral

As the diagram above shows, different kinds of models and other document objects are associated with the various stages of the spiral model (They are all model-layer entities). The main analysis and design models are, of course, products of the develop stage of their own phase. The spiral model again accounts for the various other reports and notes that are produced during each phase of the systems' life-cycle.

4 THE DEVELOPMENT OF CONCH

The CONCH spiral is a development of the spiral LCM of [Boehm 86, 88] in the light of the KADS experience. In the diagram below we compare our interpretation of the spiral to a simplified version of the original. It will be immediately obvious that, whilst we have basically the same stages as [Boehm 88], we have reinterpreted their meaning and, therefore, rearranged them.

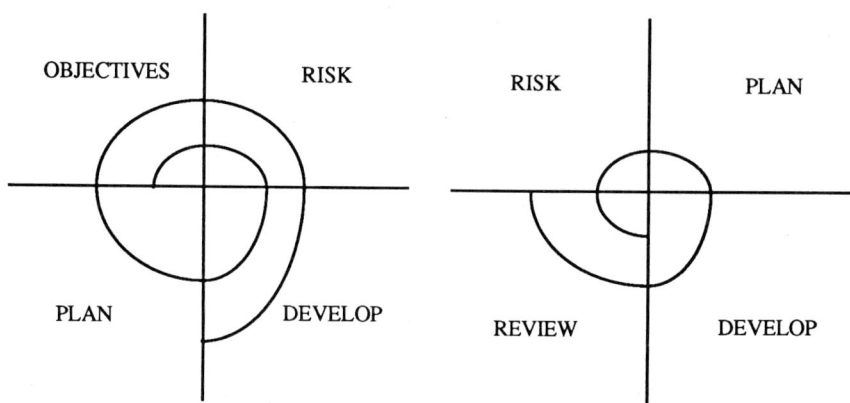

Left: the spiral LCM of Boehm, and, right: CONCH

Figure 10 A comparison of Boehm's spiral LCM and CONCH

The path of the spiral indicates how, in system development, one continually iterates around a cycle of basic stages. One never goes back as such, though the way of achieving that effect is to cycle around the stages again.

It seemed to us that one needed to plan before carrying out any development, review all development work immediately afterwards, and re-plan on the basis of the new risk position. Furthermore, it seemed to be the case that one always starts and ends in a review: Review is the basic starting point and it is necessary to have a fully satisfactory review in order to stop any development work (or else a review that decides not to go on any further). For these reasons, we have altered the arrangement of the spiral model from [Boehm 88].

Even though CONCH is now quite different to the original source for the spiral model, we have, nonetheless, introduced its essential principles (the iterative stage pattern and the risk-driven control) into KBS development, which was a key reason in choosing this representation.

5   OTHER WORK ON THE KBS LCM

There is currently some considerable interest in the KBS LCM. This is evidenced by (a) the interest shown in CONCH and, (b) the recent IEE seminar on the issue (Expert systems lifecycle, IEE, 18th December 1989). To the CONCH developers there are two main points of interest in other work on the LCM:

- similar work by [Iivari 87] and others;

- GEMINI [Duffin 89].

Late on in the development of CONCH we came across the work of J.Iivari who also envisages Boehm's spiral model replicated in a hierarchy similar to ours (though he goes even further in suggesting a notation for expressing the interrelationships between spirals). We also know of some work going on, independently of CONCH (although we have communicated), in large-scale engineering in the USA where Boehm's model has been applied to KBS development (though, in this case, without the innovation of a hierarchy).

GEMINI (General Expert Systems Methodology Initiative) is a collaborative KBS methodology development between UK industry and government, and is still in its early stages. GEMINI has the main aim of integrating KBS methodology and conventional methodology. We might guess that GEMINI will borrow many of its LCM concepts from methodologies like SSADM; concepts such as phases, stages and steps; and well-defined cross-validation review techniques and precise formality in the production of documents. We hope that GEMINI will borrow views and techniques from, and will have something of the flavour of KADS. It is easy to see how CONCH might be adapted to this save in one respect: That CONCH is explicitly open-endedly iterative whereas SSADM tends to suggest (no more than that) a more predictable development path from the start. It will be interesting to see if CONCH, the waterfall LCM, or some other LCM is favoured by GEMINI.

One aim of GEMINI must be to simplify KBS development. Some experienced KADS users have been confused by CONCH (which is puzzling). However, the experience on two training courses for non-KADS-literate systems developers is that the spiral view, in particular, is a great aid to understanding the application of KADS techniques. It may be that, for more experienced KADS users, the ordering of the stages becomes seamless and all stages occur simultaneously, such that they are unable to perceive their distinction any more. If this is so, then it is a quite acceptable interpretation of CONCH. Furthermore, it tends to suggest that an appropriately higher level of support is provided by the spiral model in CONCH for new users than for the more experienced.

6 FURTHER WORK

Whilst progress has been made in the development of the LCM, new avenues of exploration have been opened up. The following are some suggestions for further work in the area of KBS LCMs:

- The proposed framework should be challenged and clarified by application to a large number of systems.

- There is further KADS theory, which was work ongoing in parallel with this

LCM research, to be integrated. This includes:
- quality assurance theory;
- metrication theory;
- design theory.

- Practical guidance on LCM configuration, project planning and other aspects of management using this model should be given.

- Tools support for CONCH should be investigated, including;
  - the use of existing tools;
  - the possibility and desirability of developing specific tools for CONCH.

- The full four-layer knowledge-based model of the KBS life-cycle could be developed. Principally, this concerns the further separation of the two layers of CONCH. We believe that the current model is half-way to a KADS model of expertise for knowledge engineering (at least in form if not in content).

- In all respects there is infinite scope for refinement of the LCM: in the phase and sub-phase structuring and in the detailing of the stages and models. Specifically;
  - the work done under P1098 on activity-specification (Task C10) could be integrated;
  - the precise filling of the frame-based structure of the models in the model-layer leaves a lot to be desired.

ACKNOWLEDGEMENTS

The author would like to acknowledge the work of CONCH co-developers in P1098: David Porter, Frank Hickman (both of Touche Ross), Karl-Heinz Streng (of NTE NeuTech), Guillaume Dorbes (of Cap Sesa Innovation) and Stewart Tansley (of STC Technology), and also to thank Clive Hayball, Marco de Alberdi (both of STC Technology), Lise Land, Tim Mulhall (both of Touche Ross), Reinhard Nobis, Diederich Wermser (both of NTE NeuTech) and Alexandre Wallyn (of Cap Sesa Innovation) for their contributions. The partners in Phase 2 of ESPRIT Project 1098, under which CONCH was developed, were; the University of Amsterdam, K.B.S.C. Ltd (later The Knowledge-Based Systems Centre of Touche Ross Management Consultants), STC Technology Ltd, SD-SCICON Ltd, Cap Sogeti Innovation (later Cap Sesa Innovation) and NTE NeuTech Gmbh.

Contact address: Robert M Taylor, The Knowledge-Based Systems Centre, Touche Ross Management Consultants, Hill House, 1 Little New Street, London EC4A 3TR, England. Tel. 01 936 3000

REFERENCES

[Balzer 83]
    Balzer, R., Cheatham, T., Green, C, *Software technology on the 1990s: Using a new paradigm*, IEEE Computer, pp 39–45, November 1983.

[Barthélemy 86]
    Barthélemy, S., Edin, G., Toutain, E., Becker, S., Nobis, R., Schachter-Radig, M., Siegfried, T., Wermser, D, *An assessment of software development life-cycle models for KBS*, ESPRIT P1098, Deliverable Y8, Cap Sogeti Innovation, 1986.

[Barthélemy 87]
    Barthélemy, S., Edin, G., Toutain, E., Becker, S., *Requirements analysis in KBS development*, ESPRIT P1098, Deliverable D3, Cap Sogeti Innovation, 1987.

[Boehm 86]
    Boehm, B., *A spiral model of software development and enhancement*, ACM Sigsoft Software Engineering Notes, Vol. 3, No. 4, August 1986.

[Boehm 88]
    Boehm, B., *A spiral model of software development and enhancement*, IEEE Computer, May 1988.

[Born 88]
    Born, G., *Guidelines for quality assurance of expert systems*, CSA Working Group on QA and ES, Working Paper Issue 1.1, Computing Services Association, 1988.

[Duffin 89]
    Duffin, P., *GEMINI: Government Expert system Methodology Initiative*, OECD Conference, Paris, May 1989.

[Gilb 85]
    Gilb, T., *Evolutionary design versus the "Waterfall Model"*, ACM Sigsoft Software Engineering Notes, Vol. 10, pp 49–61, July 1985.

[Gladden 82]
    Gladden, G., *Stop the lifecycle – I want to get off*, ACM Software Engineering Notes, Vol. 7, No. 2, pp 35–39, 1982.

[Hesketh 89]
    Hesketh P., T Barrett, *An introduction to the KADS methodology*, ESPRIT P1098, Deliverable M1, 1989, STC PLC

[Hickman 89a]
Hickman, F., Killin, J., Land, L., Mulhall, T., Porter, D., Taylor, R., *Analysis for knowledge-based systems*, Ellis Horwood, 1989

[Hickman 89b]
Hickman, F., *Knowledge-based systems life-cycle models within the KADS methodology* IEE meeting on Expert systems lifecycle, 18th December, 1989.

[Hughes 86]
Hughes, A., *An overview of the ASPIS project*, in *ESPRIT 86: results and achievements*, Elsevier Science Publishers, 1986.

[Iivari 87]
Iivari J., *A hierarchical spiral model for the software process: notes on Boehm's spiral model*, ACM Sigsoft software engineering notes Vol 12, No 1 p35, Jan 87

[Killin 89]
Killin J., D Porter, S Becker, T Vietze, *Output and results 1&2*, ESPRIT P1098, Task C10, Touche Ross & Co., 1989

[McCracken 82]
McCracken D., Jackson, M., *Lifecycle concept considered harmful*, ACM Software Engineering Notes, Vol. 7, No. 2, pp 28–32, 1982.

[Nobis 88]
Nobis, R., Siedka-Bauer, H., *Prototyping and the LCM*, ESPRIT P1098, Deliverable NTE-G13-PR-001, NTE NeuTech, September 1988.

[Porter 89]
Porter, D., *Integration of Prototyping into the life-cycle model*, ESPRIT P1098, Task G9, Working Paper T6, The Knowledge-Based Systems Centre of Touche Ross Management Consultants, June 1989.

[Spinrad 85]
Spinrad, M., Abraham, C., *The wild-west lifecycle (WILI)*, ACM Sigsoft Software Engineering Notes, Vol. 10, No. 3, July 1985.

[Taylor 89]
Taylor, R.(ed), D Porter, F Hickman, K-H Streng, S Tansley, G Dorbes., *System evolution–Principles and methods*, ESPRIT P1098, Deliverable G9, The Knowledge-Based Systems Centre of Touche Ross Management Consultants, 1989.

[Wielinga 89]
    Wielinga B., G Schreiber, P de Greef, *Synthesis report*, ESPRIT P1098, deliverable Y3, University of Amsterdam, 1989

Verification and Validation 2

Software Testing: Human-Computer Interaction concepts, and Testing, D.R. Graham
Software Verification and Testing Tools: Availability and Uptake, D.R. Graham (written paper only)
Defect Removal Models: Theory and Practice, M. Coleman & J. Allan

Software Engineering, Human-Computer Interaction concepts, and Testing

D. R. GRAHAM

Independent Software Engineering Consultant
Grove Consultants, Grove House,
40 Ryles Park Road, Macclesfield,
Ches. SK11 8AH U.K. Tel. 0625 - 616279

ABSTRACT

Software Engineering can benefit from being open to relevant research from other disciplines, but it is worrying that some of the most applicable areas appear to be regarded as irrelevant or unimportant. This paper describes some aspects of possible influence from cognitive psychology in two areas: general software engineering including tool design, and software testing.

Software development cannot escape the fact that it is ultimately a human-intensive activity, in the development not only of software itself but also in the development of underlying methodologies, models, methods and tools. Failing to take into account the relevant research ideas from the human sciences will ultimately impoverish the software engineering discipline. The contributions of the Human-Computer Interface discipline are particularly relevant to software development at the beginning (requirements and design) and end (testing) of software development, but are also applicable to the development processes carried out by the (human) software designers.

Software testing is an area which relies heavily on human insight into the identification, causation, prevention, and removal of software anomalies; cognitive concepts can elucidate the areas of software construction where human fallibilities cause the most serious problems, and can also aid in identifying the most effective software engineering techniques for overcoming them.

Software Engineering, Human-Computer Interaction concepts, and Testing

D. R. GRAHAM

Independent Software Engineering Consultant
Grove Consultants,
Grove House,
40 Ryles Park Road,
Macclesfield, Ches. SK11 8AH U.K.
Tel. 0625 - 616279

1. INTRODUCTION

1.1. Software engineering and other disciplines

At the 2nd European Software Engineering Conference in Coventry, September, 1989, there seemed to be a common thread in the reaction of a number of software engineers to ideas from other disciplines. Although ideas from some neighbouring disciplines were readily accepted, [Boehm] ideas from others were not only rejected but were regarded as unimportant, even though they involved issues which affect every software system at the beginning and end of development as well as the processes which occur throughout software development.

The purpose of this paper is to inform and justify to software engineers the relevance of concepts from the discipline of cognitive psychology, using an example of cognitive research which is applicable to several areas of software engineering, and an area of software engineering where the author has found cognitive concepts to be relevant and useful.

1.2. Mathematical foundations of software engineering

The term "software engineering" was coined over 20 years ago, partly to encourage the take-up of ideas from other engineering disciplines. At the time, software development was a rather haphazard process, proceeding without disciplined procedures, and without mathematically based foundations.

Software engineering has developed into much more of a scientific discipline in recent years, although the actual cross-over of ideas or techniques from mechanical or electrical engineering has been limited. One example is Inspection, carried over from mechanical/electrical engineering by M.E. Fagan; Fagan's Inspection remains the most cost-effective manual verification and validation technique today. [Fagan]

Computer science theory is based in mathematics, and software development practice is being encouraged to develop in more rigourous ways through the use of formal specification methods. Certainly the mathematical basis for software engineering is justified [Baber]; the use of mathematical models is essential for any scientific engineering discipline. However they should only be used for areas where they are applicable and appropriate.

1.3. Non-mathematical areas.

1.3.1. Legitimacy of study

There are many areas of software engineering which are not amenable to being modelled in mathematical terms, however; those areas where human beings are extensively involved. There can be no mathematical model for users, for example, because human beings are highly complex entities which cannot be adequately described by straight-forward mathematical expressions. Similarly, there can be no mathematical model of the human system designer, although some of the processes which the designer performs can be modelled mathematically, as can some user processes. The human being involved is much more than the simple processes which are modelled, however.

Because human beings cannot be contained in simple mathematical models does not, however, infer that they cannot be studied, not does it infer that such study is unimportant. What does follow is that the study of human beings is necessarily not the same as the study of say circuit diagrams or formal specification languages e.g., a statistical approach or even an introspective approach rather than a formal analytical approach. The study of the human mind, cognition, is therefore necessarily a "soft" science rather than a "hard" (i.e. mathematical) science, because the object of study is not quantifiable in mathematical rules. This does not mean that such study is not a valid scientific endeavour.

1.3.2. Definitions of terms from cognitive psychology

The processes of the mind are called called "cognition" or "cognitive" processes, such as acquiring, storing and using knowledge, attention, perception, learning, memory, and problem solving; the study of cognition is called "cognitive psychology".[Lindsay & Norman] [Wærn] [Smyth et al]. Not all of the areas of study of cognitive psychology are directly relevant to software engineering.

The study of human beings at work is called "ergonomics" (Europe) or "human factors" (U.S.) [Curtis], which includes the fitting of workstation layouts to the human anatomy, for example. Not all of the areas of ergonomics are directly relevant to software engineering.

A more recent area of specialisation of cognitive psychology is that of "cognitive ergonomics", defined as:

> "A science aimed at developing knowledge about the interaction between human information-processing capacities and limitations and technical information-processing systems." [Wærn]

It is this area which is the most likely to be directly relevant to software engineering, but which many software engineers seem to be unaware of as yet.

1.3.3. HCI Organisations and Events

There are conferences and seminars organised often under the title of "Human Computer Interaction" (HCI); there is also a BCS Human Computer Interaction Special Interest Group. HCI is the term which has replaced the now out-of-date term MMI (Man-Machine Interface). A special issue of the BCS Computer Journal dealt with HCI issues in software engineering [Damodaran]. A free network called "HICOM" [HICOM] provides e-mail and printed information in HCI, including an extensive bibliography of over 250 books and articles in the field, some of which are also reviewed. There is a "Psychology of Programming Interest Group [PPIG]

1.4. Problems of non-formal disciplines.

Just as there are difficulties in mathematical expression and proof, there are other difficulties in the study of non-formal disciplines such as cognitive ergonomics.

1.4.1. Lack of experimental "control" subject

The main difficulty from scientific viewpoint is that although there can be controlled studies, there is no standard-issue "control" human being against which experiments can be performed. No two people are the same; they may react differently to identical input. In fact no one person is exactly the same at different times; one may react differently to the same input at different times or under different conditions (e.g. under stress such as an emergency).

1.4.2. The Hawthorn Effect

When human subjects are studied, their behaviour is modified simply by the fact that they are being studied; this is called the "Hawthorn effect", after experiments which showed that productivity increased when changes were made to the working environment, even when the changes were the reverse of changes which had previously raised productivity.

1.4.3. Subjectivity

Results of study into the working of the human mind can only be reported by the human subjects; although behaviour can be studied objectively, there is no way of observing mental processes directly. This causes unavoidable subjectivity in some cognitive results. However, that does not mean that the human-computer interface cannot be measured; an assessment of four prototypes used a combination of subjective and objective techniques to evaluate not only technical issues, but also job factors, task factors, and the match to cognitive characteristics. [Jagodzinski & Clarke]

1.4.4. Scale of studies

Cognitive studies tend to be rather small-scale and limited; in order to gather analysable data, only a small task or a small number of subjects is often studied.

The limitations of cognitive study do not invalidate the conclusions of such studies, however. Knowing that people actually do different things than they say they are doing can have a profound effect on the design of a system. If the system is designed to cope only with the way people say they work, it will not be successful in actual use when people want to use the system or software tool in other ways. Even a study of a few people on a limited task can give information which may make the difference between a successful and unsuccessful software product.

2. THE RELEVANCE OF COGNITIVE CONCEPTS TO SOFTWARE ENGINEERING

2.1. Importance

2.1.1. Relevance

Every software system has three areas where human beings interface to that system: the initial idea for the system, the eventual users or operators of the system, and the people who actually construct the software and associated documentation, including those who elaborate and specify system requirements, those who design and build the system (hardware-software division, architectural software structure, detailed software design, the production of code, if not done by a 4GL, and the testing of the system).

The results which have come from cognitive research, particularly into computer-related tasks, can have a great impact on the development of software, both for the software development process and the software products developed. Cognitive results which affect the process of software development are outlined in this section.

2.1.2. Effect on software products

For software products, the "usability" of a developed software product can often make the difference between an expensive white elephant and a product which is well-liked and well-used. This is particularly important for safety-related systems; after recent accidents in nuclear power plants, "as much attention has been paid to the operators' perception of the situation as to the behaviour of engineered systems". [Mayfield & Wells]

The "maintainability" of a product, which is related to the cognitive effort required to change it, can make the difference between a short-lived disaster and a long-lived adaptable flexible system. The quality attributes of systems are more related to cognitive issues than to technical function, yet often cause systems to fail. [Gilb]

Failed systems are often developed according to good software engineering techniques, yet they are not accepted by users. User sabotage, political manoeuvring, hostility, frustration, conflict and passive avoidance are all too common reactions to systems. [Hirschheim & Newman]

2.1.3. Resistance

Resistance to new computer systems by new users is a problem frequently encountered by software engineers [Barden], often with little sympathy. But we as software engineers also find it difficult to accept new ideas, particularly from the soft sciences.

Reasons why the software engineering community has not seemed to accept the need for cross-disciplinary fertilisation in the past in this area, was proposed by Bjørn-Anderson as three-fold: first, we take a narrow engineering approach to software systems and in particular to the human-computer interface of our systems, second, an instrumental approach to communication (without adequate reference to human needs in communication), and third, the naive assumption that our technology is neutral, both in the workplace and in society. [Bjørn-Anderson].

The trends of decreasing hardware costs and increasing software costs have led to the increasing importance of software engineering techniques in the development of software systems. The current upsurge of interest in software quality may lead to an increasing demand for systems which satisfy cognitive ergonomic demands of future system users and purchasers. The next "wave" may be "orgware" [Bjørn-Anderson] [Eason & Harker] [Tyldesley]. A recent book, "Peopleware", destined to become a classic in software engineering ergonomics, deals with the requirements of human individuality, political factors, office environments, and software development teams. [DeMarco & Lister]

2.1.4 Cognitive Models and Design Methods and Tools

Kitchenham and Carn point out that design methods need to provide three facilities: guidelines for design creation, notations for design recording, and procedures for design verification. Mathematical, i.e. formal methods, while supporting the recording and verification of design, do not provide much to support design creation. Structured methods, such as entity-relationship modelling, data flow analysis, data structure methods, and object-oriented design, while providing varying support for design creation and recording, are weak in verifying designs. [Kitchenham & Carn]

2.2. Opportunism and Planning

Before discussing the implications of cognitive ideas on some software engineering areas, a recent study is described to give an example of a cognitive research result by Visser [Visser].

2.2.1. Functional design specification: a study

The results of a study of the cognitive aspects of specification are given in a study done by having the researcher "shadow" an engineer during a three-week period while he wrote a functional specification for the computerised control of an automated tool installation. The only difference from normal working for the engineer was that he was asked to verbalise his thoughts as much as possible about what he was doing.

The most important finding of this study was that the description given by the engineer both before the specification task began and after it had finished did not correspond to his actual actions.

2.2.2. Planned versus actual activities

Before beginning the design specification activity, the engineer constructed a top-down depth-first hierarchic plan.

During the specification process, the engineer followed the plan only as long as he did not perceive any more opportune actions. He did not follow a different hierarchic plan, nor was his work disorganised. His actual work was organised opportunistically rather than hierarchically.

After the design had been completed, the engineer was asked to describe what he had done. He replied that he had followed the hierarchic plan in carrying out out his activities.

When challenged by the data recorded by the researcher concerning his actual activities, he was unconcerned about the discrepancies. He had "more or less" followed the plan; according to the engineer, the deviations didn't matter.

2.2.3. Cognitive analysis of plan deviations

The deviations from the plan were actually taken on the basis of cognitive cost and importance.

An example of cognitive cost: after the initialisation routine for the first function had been done, the initialisation for the other functions was done before going on to specifying the rest of the first function. The cognitive cost of repeating the initialisation activity was lower now than it would be later.

The importance of an action is related to the type of action, e.g. fixing the omission of an operation which had been forgotten in the plan was important enough to cause a deviation from the plan. Deviations were also related to the importance of the object of the action, e.g. the duration of a real-time operation is verified, but not its identifier.

2.2.4. Cognitive causes of plan deviations

Cognitive processes which lead to plan deviation actions can be due to several causes.

Activation of other component.
First, a component's mental representation could activate another component's representation. This can occur in a number of ways:

- By analogy: defining one function may "remind" the engineer that he has forgotten to define or has incompletely defined a similar function in another part of the system.

- The recognition of a prerequisite for the function which is currently being defined; the current work is interrupted to define the prerequisite function before being resumed.

- The perception of the interaction between two different functions, leading to corrections to the finishing state of an interfacing function with reference to the start state of the current function.

- Opposites: the omission of the opposite or reverse of the current function is brought to mind.

Same aspect of other component
Defining an object leads to a local plan for defining the same aspects of other components.

Different point of view
Processing information from different points of view, e.g. safety, reliability, mechanical.

Available information
Taking advantage of available information, e.g. when new information is presented to the designer, a requirement is modified, or specialist views from an information source or expert are consulted.

Drifting
Drifting, or involuntary attention switching, occurs during the most difficult activities. This may lead to postponement of some planned activities.

2.2.5. Conclusions

There are two important conclusions for software engineers:

First, the engineer was not aware of his own actions in the deviations from the plan. He not only believed that he would follow the hierarchic plan, but that he had followed it, when in fact he had not.

Second, he did not consider the actual deviations from the plan to be important or significant.

Note that other studies have also supported these findings: [Green-77] [Sime et al] [Arblaster et al] [Vessey & Weber] [Green-89] [Green-90].

Although a study of only one engineer, these results could be significant for the way in which work is done in specifying systems, and in the design of software tools to support system specification, as discussed below.

2.3. Implications for Requirements Specification

2.3.1. Accuracy of requirements capture

If the capture of requirements is based only on the analysis of current work practices, the requirements which are specified may depend only on the way people think they work, rather than on how they actually work. A good requirements capture methodology will include observation techniques as well as interview techniques (as existing methodologies do already).

However, no matter how accurate the capture of requirements for a proposed system, when that system is ultimately installed, the system itself will have an effect on the way that people work, often to such a degree that the existing system is not what is actually required. This cycle of specify, construct, use, re-specify usually comes as a surprise to software engineers, yet is an inevitable consequence of the use of the system, as is shown by cognitive research.

2.3.2. Implications for Software Development Methodology

Models of learning [Wærn] show that for procedural knowledge (how to do things) rather than declarative knowledge (facts), it is more important to be actively involved in using the relevant procedures. In specifying how a proposed system should work, it may well not be possible for users/customers to describe what they want until they have had the opportunity to use it. The use of a prototype as a "living" specification has been found to be successful because of this effect. [Gomaa & Scott]; this also explains why an incremental development approach rather than a monolithic development cycle is more likely to be successful at implementing users' real needs. [Graham-90] [Floyd et al] [Harker] [Agresti]

In some cases, the attitude of the system specifiers may be "we don't know what we want, but we'll know it when we see it", which at least brings out into the open the fact that the ideal future system cannot be known in advance. In other cases, the specifiers believe that they can pre-specify the "correct" ideal future system in advance without any hands-on use of a partial system or prototype; this belief persists despite little evidence to support it and much evidence to contradict it. [Gilb] [Graham-89]

2.3.3. *Mental models*

When users work with a system, they form a mental model of the task they are performing, which represents their understanding of the system. [Wærn] If it were possible for the system designer to take the users' mental models into consideration in the specification and design of the system, it would be more likely to provide adequate information for the users at relevant times. Research into user models for games is given in [Neal-89]

2.4. Implications for Software Design

2.4.1. *User Interface Design Principles*

The principles of user interface design are reasonably well-established in the cognitive sciences. A good summary is given in [Wærn]. Guidelines are also given in other sources. [Schneiderman] [Rubin] [Carey] [Dumas] [Sutcliffe] [Gardner & McKenzie] A fascinating exercise, which can be used as a self-awareness test, is given by [Molich & Nielsen]

User interface design is concerned with the following aspects:

Division of labour between hardware and software

An important aspect of the specification and design of a system is the decision as to which tasks should be automated and which should be left under manual control. Software engineers may be tempted to automate as much as possible, but this is often far from the best design of the system, for reasons discussed below.

If user tasks are completely de-skilled, then any skill which users currently hold, and which may be needed in an emergency when the computer system fails and manual procedures are needed, will be lost through lack of use. [Wærn]

In addition, the de-skilling of a task is often perceived as a de-valuing of the individual performing that task, which can lead to lower morale and performance. The system should perform any sub-tasks which are tedious, difficult or impossible to do by hand, while the creative sub-tasks are left to the human operators. Allowing human operators to exercise their judgement and skills leads to less stress and better performance of tasks. A feeling of achievement is enjoyed when the tasks are under the control of the operator, reasonably complex, and contain a wide variety of activities. [Bainbridge]

Software engineering design should be concerned with the eventual system in its operational environment and the effect which the system will have on that environment, including the working lives of the users. Traditional software engineering approaches have often been guilty of mistaking the means (the system) for the end (more effective work), so that the means becomes an end in itself. [Gilb]

Communication Style

The decision as to which user communication style should be used depends on various factors such as level of expertise of users, the tasks to be performed, and the purpose of performing it; a mixture of styles may be appropriate. Novice and expert users may want different styles for the same tasks. The design of error messages can also benefit from user interface design principles.

Possible options are menu selection (permanent or temporary, topic groupings, menu levels), form fill-in, command language, natural language, and direct manipulation. Details of keyboard input guidelines are given in [Gilb & Weinberg]. Guidelines for communication are also given in [Molich & Neilsen]

Experts tend to prefer command language to menu selection, but direct manipulation of objects seems to give more cognitive satisfaction to users. Direct manipulation is best for intermittent users, but is not suitable for some complex applications. [Wærn]

The consistency or coherence of the interface is important for system usability. Interface consistency is concerned with the aspects of the system which conform to the rules which the user perceives about the system's structure and behaviour, i.e. the system behaves in the was the user expects it to behave based in previous experience of the system. [Cahour et al]

Physical Communication

The physical devices used for communication with software systems include keyboards, number pads, a mouse, display units, printers, auditory output, e.g. warning signals, synthesized speech. Physical devices need to take the physical properties of human beings into account, e.g. flicker on screens, comfortable keyboards, and the limitation of warning messages to a number which can be handled by a human operator (see short-term memory below).

Response times for repetitive tasks should be consistent; consistency is more important than speed for many tasks. In problem-solving tasks, fast response time is important for processes which would otherwise interrupt the flow of thought in the task. [Wærn]

Meta-Communication

Meta-communication is concerned with activities to do with communication about the conceptual model underlying the design of the system. Meta-communication includes user documentation, help messages, design documentation, information about the present state of the system, and the means to alter the state of the system.

Aspects to consider for meta-communication include the location of information (inside or outside the system), printed or "live" information (expert), and explanation of errors made by the user.

Other user design considerations

Other types of user interface design, also described in [Wærn] include database design, the design of expert systems, and the design of computer-aided design systems(CAD).

2.4.2. Knowledge Transfer Effects

In a new learning situation, adult learners will try to rely as far as possible on prior knowledge. This effect is called knowledge transfer, as existing knowledge is applied (transferred) to a new situation. Transfer can be an intentional strategy, but is also applied unintentionally, when implicit assumptions about the new situation are made which are not objectively warranted. In addition, transfer often occurs in the learning of a new procedural task, when automatic learned schemas "take over" in a new situation. For example, using commands from the word processor you know, when you are trying to learn a new one.

Transfer effects can be positive or negative. Positive transfer occurs when the existing knowledge is helpful to the new task; negative transfer occurs when the existing knowledge is detrimental to the new task. Learning a new procedure requires the formation of new "production rules" (procedure for what procedure to follow under certain conditions) according to psychological formulas. The quantitative effects of transfer depend on the number of production rules with similar conditions and the strength of the relation between condition and action. The qualitative effects depend on the similarity of the resulting actions to the desired actions. [Wærn]

2.4.3. Investigation of Claimed Benefits

New techniques in software engineering seem to become "bandwagons", often without any empirical research to back up ergonomic claims, for ease of use, for example. In some cases, the benefits claimed may result from factors other than those assumed.

For example, when structured programming was widely adopted, it was considered to be more understandable because of the hierarchical structures used in design. However, a cognitive study showed that the hierarchical approach was not significantly better than other structuring approaches such as decision tables, or representations of information using visual cues, including indentation. [Sime et al] [Arblaster et al] [Vessey & Weber] [Green-77] More recent studies of program understanding have been done by the Ergonomics Psychology Project at INRIA [INRIA] [Détienne-86] [Détienne-89] [Détienne & Soloway], where studies of knowledge elicitation for expert systems is also studied.

One of the arguments currently advanced for the superiority of object-oriented approaches is that they are more "natural", i.e. they make the design process easier. A recent cognitive study found that problems of negative transfer were encountered by programmers who were experienced in other languages, so that the object-oriented approach was not as natural as had been assumed. [Détienne-90] There are a few other studies of object-oriented approaches. [Pierret-Golbreich-89] [Pierret-Golbreich et al]

Studies in the human-computer interface of expert systems have also been carried out by INRIA [Falzon & Visser] [Pierret-Golbreich-88] [Visser & Hoc] The problems of knowledge elicitation from experts have also received attention. [Visser & Falzon-88] [Visser & Falzon-89] [Visser & Morais]

The use of an expert system to model cognitive activity is an example of cross-disciplinary fertilisation from software engineering to cognitive studies. [Barnard et al]

2.4.4. *Islands of Certainty*

When designing something new, designers tend to latch on to what they know, and build the rest of the system around their existing knowledge, i.e. first get to the island where your knowledge is more certain, and then proceed into the unknown. This is also called "encystment" [Dörner] or "functional fixedness" [Smyth et al]. This is particularly prevalent in inexperienced designers, whose knowledge of design alternatives is limited.

2.5. Implications for Software Tools

2.5.1. *Tool Design*

All of the considerations for system design and user interface design apply to the development of software tools for the use in software engineering.

2.5.2. *Flexibility of Working*

If tools are developed monolithically from specifications, the tool may be designed for a top-down rational approach which is the one which is both planned and is stated to be followed by software engineers. However, in actually performing the tasks supported by the software tool, deviations from the plan may occur. If the tool does not support the way software engineers actually work, as opposed to the way that they believe they [should] work, then the tool will not offer adequate support to the software development process in actual practice.

For example, some syntax-directed editors were found to be unsuccessful in actual use because they were too restraining on the way people actually wrote programs. [Neal-87]

2.5.3. *Assistance to Working Memory*

Tools should provide specific assistance to help to overcome the limitations of short-term memory (see below). Some suggested ways of providing this are parallel presentation of intra- or inter-level information, presentation of all constraints on the solution order, or maintaining a trace of postponed subproblems needing backtracking. [Visser & Hoc]

2.5.4. *Adaptability*

The tool interface should be adaptable to changing circumstances and for different users. The feasibility of using cognitive characteristics in providing adaptability has been studied. [Benyon & Murray]

2.6. Implications for Software Engineering Training

2.6.1. *Awareness of HCI*

An important aspect of the training of software engineers, whether in academic courses of study or in continuous on-the-job training in industry, is the awareness of Human Computer Interaction principles wherever it impacts the software development process, e.g. requirements analysis, design, testing.

2.6.2. *Standards*

Software engineering standards should include reference and guidelines to HCI. For example, The IEEE standard glossary of software engineering terms contains no definition of HCI (or MMI), ergonomics, or cognitive, although "egoless programming" and "user documentation" are included [ANSI/IEEE Std 729-1983]. Brief mention of user interface considerations is made in design and requirements standards, however. [ANSI-IEEE Std 1016-1987] [ANSI-IEEE Std 830-1984, Section 6.3.1.5.1].

2.6.3. Learning New Methods or Tools

Transference Effects

When planning the training programme for new methodologies, methods, practices, or tools, the possible transference effects should be taken into account.

In choosing a software tool, one which corresponds to the way in which people already work will be integrated into working practices much more easily and quickly because of positive transference effects. This has been noted for the adoption of IPSE's [Le Quesne]

Recommendations concerning the learning needs for designers adopting an object-oriented approach includes the use of examples of known applications in the new approach, to enable the necessary mental connections to be made between the known and the new. Novices to OOP did not have the problems of negative transfer, but they did not develop adequate concepts of data flow or control flow which the experienced programmers had developed through using procedural languages. [Détienne-90]

Similar negative transference effects have been found in the study of programmers new to parallel architectures [Neal-90], in changing from procedural to declarative languages [Siddiqi & Khazaei].

2.6.4. Methods of study

The wide differences between novice and expert behaviour in solving problems may be an argument for trying to institute some form of apprenticeship training, where novices observe an expert at work. Some cross-training effects can be achieved by the use of formal review meetings, such as Fagan's Inspection. [Fagan]

Training in meta-learning may be effective; e.g. pointing out the learning strategies which are being used and informing about alternative learning strategies. Encouraging designers to extend their solution space to actively look for alternative designs (lateral thinking) can provide more effective design solutions. [Gilb-mss] [Kitchenham & Carn]

3. THE RELEVANCE OF COGNITIVE CONCEPTS TO SOFTWARE TESTING

3.1. Test is a four-letter word

Software testing has suffered from negative connotations for some time. When software developers are asked to name the most exciting and/or glamorous areas of software engineering, testing is seldom if ever top of the list. (It's usually second to bottom, just above documentation.) It has not helped that there has been a tendency in industry to assign the testing activity to those considered least able, or that in an academic environment, products are not generally required to attain the standards of working products in the same sense as industrial software, e.g. adequate user interface, proof against misuse by users, leading to either little emphasis on good testing or the restriction of testing to technical aspects.

Because of the damage done by those who advocate that it should be possible to write software without making any errors, errors have come to be associated with sinfulness. I believe that software engineers are reluctant to think about software testing because of its association with errors and therefore with the possibilities of their own individual technical inadequacy, but this association is incorrect. The current interest in quality in software development deals with many of the same issues, but "quality" is a word with positive rather than negative connotations. Nonetheless, effective testing (testing in the broadest sense) is the only way to assess software quality, and one of the most effective ways to achieve it.

This section describes some cognitive concepts which the author has found to be helpful in training and consultancy in software testing. The general effect of the cognitive ideas is to free testers from some of the negative connotations of testing in order to become more productive and effective test designers and test managers.

3.2. Short-term Working Memory

3.2.1. Size Limitations

The term "short-term memory" was used to describe experiments in retention of random objects. It is now called "working memory"; the ideas are described in many sources [Smyth et al] [Wærn] [Lindsay & Norman] [Curtis]. The short-term memory is of limited size (7 ± 2), and items are retained for a limited time. Thus the problem often is not that an item has been forgotten, but that the knowledge of the existence of the forgotten item has disappeared. Memory lapses are related to attentional limitations [Smyth et al] [Curtis], and are exasperated by time delays and interference from other tasks. Memory is best at the beginning and end of a sequence of items, called the primacy and recency effects [Smyth et al].

The specific relevance to software testing is that most errors which are trivial to make are caused by short-term memory overflow; however, errors which are trivial to make can have serious non-trivial effects in software.

3.2.2. Chunking

Memory is improved if items are organised into related groups or "chunks" of information. It may be that the ability to chunk information is the distinguishing characteristic between novices and experts [Curtis]. Limitations of memory may contribute to poor decision-making [Lindsay & Norman]. Writing down lists and using symbols can improve short-term memory [Lindsay & Norman].

The use of check-lists for verification and validation reviews or for checking test cases is one of the most effective ways of overcoming short-term memory limitations in VV&T by chunking related items.

3.3. Incompatibility

3.3.1. Differences between computers and people

The software engineer deals with implementing ideas in a uniquely intolerant environment. A computer is a machine which is fast, accurate and consistent. Software consists of lists of precise, detailed, and explicit discrete instructions; every bit has some effect. In working with any physical medium, some deviation within given tolerances is acceptable; this is not the case for software.

The software engineer shares with other members of humanity the characteristics of being inconsistent, inaccurate, and ambiguous; i.e. highly creative, original and imaginative. These are characteristics which are diametrically opposed to the characteristics of software systems.

3.3.2. Creativity

Creativity is the ability to bring into existence something which has not existed before within the individual's experience. Creativity in software engineering results in some highly successful innovations and others which are not. A by-product of creativity in the intolerant and incompatible software environment is that errors are made, many of them "trivial" (easy to make).

3.3.3. Wrong-ness

There is a tendency to imply that the making of errors is wrong; this is not surprising, since the making of errors would hardly be described as correct procedure! However, the word "wrong" has several meanings, including "incorrect" and "bad or immoral". Of course the making of an error is an incorrect action, but it is not evil, because it is not intentional. It can be argued that no intentional action is in fact wrong, because the person believed that he or she was doing the right thing at the time, based on current perception and knowledge.

In software engineering, however, there are some who argue that if only we were doing software development right, we would not make any errors. Some of the rationale for the use of formal methods also depends on this premise. Nevertheless, this is contrary to cognitive research and may well be counter-productive to software development. It is interesting to note that the well-publicised successes of software development using formal methods have not claimed that they have succeeded in preventing all errors; on the contrary they are combined with effective means of removing errors, such as Fagan's Inspection.

Removal of guilt for making errors can free the software engineer to direct their creative energy towards the development and testing process, thus resulting in a higher quality software product.

3.4. Cognitive Effort

The effect of encystment or functional fixedness, mentioned above, where people tend to latch onto known ideas, or islands of certainty, has an effect in testing and debugging. For example, known methods of test case design may continue to be used without a search for new types of errors. Another example is often seen in debugging: once a hypothesis for an observed error has been formulated, the evidence of the fault which is gathered tends to be that which supports the existing hypothesis rather than gathering evidence objectively.

When cognitive effort is expended in problem solving activities, tension is created which is released when a solution is thought of; this is perceived as a positive cognitive experience. The desire for further such positive experiences leads to a short-circuiting of the analysis processes in problem-solving, for example, fixing a software error before fully understanding the nature of the fault.

If cognitive effort is put into a given mental task, there is a tendency to try and preserve that effort, even if it becomes clear that it was actually in error; this is known as cognitive consistency or vested interest.

3.5. Long-term Memory Aspects

3.5.1. World View

Long-term memory is organised into rich networks and patterns, with each individual having their own unique pattern of knowledge and schemas. In order for new information to be incorporated into long-term memory, it needs to be integrated into the existing pattern, and this will be difficult if the new item is dissonant with the existing body of knowledge. The resistance which needs to be overcome in order to incorporate dissonant information into existing cognitive memory is called the "cognitive dissonance barrier". [Lindsay & Norman]

The effect is that individuals who have been exposed to similar sources of knowledge tend to have similar patterns which form their collective "world view". This has an impact on the choice of personnel to be involved in testing. The software engineer, with a technical or mathematical education, will bring a technical bias or prejudice to the selection of test cases which will be good for finding some types of errors, but not good at finding other types of errors. A user will be able to find the types of errors which are least likely to be found by developers because of the differences in their long-term memory prejudices. Similar arguments can be advanced for the use of independent test teams, quality assurance personnel, novices, students, or outside consultants in the testing process.

3.5.2. Recognition versus Recall

Another aspect of the long-term memory is the drastic superiority of recognition to recall [Wærn]. Although only a limited number of items can be committed to memory sufficiently to be recalled, a brief exposure to large number of items can often enable them to be recognised as having been present. This is another reason why check-lists are effective.

3.6. Effectiveness of Test Strategies

Finding errors in one's own work is very difficult; when proof-reading a document, you tend to see what you meant, not what is actually there. For software, a figure of only 25% - 30% of your own errors can be detected [Myers] [Beizer]. Effective testing can find 55% of errors [Hetzel], and some verification and validation techniques are even more effective. Fagan's Inspection, a manual technique, can find up to 80% of errors [Gilb]. Automated V&V tools can find 100% of some types of errors, but cannot find all types of errors.

3.7. Dilemmas of Testing

The best definition of testing for software engineers during the development life cycle is that given by Myers [Myers]: looking for errors rather than showing that it works. In spite of convincing intellectual arguments justifying this approach to testing, it is very difficult to put it into practice consistently because of cognitive issues. There is a strong bias in favour of verifying hypotheses rather than in trying to falsify them, even when falsification is more effective. [Wærn]

Another fundamental problem of testing is that the scope is usually infinite; there are always more test cases that could be devised. Testing is therefore never finished, only stopped; the devising of test stopping criteria is important but difficult.

The best strategy for devising test cases is to devise those which most quickly find the errors. However, the errors which are most difficult to find are often due to a combination of subtle interactions between aspects which are not surmised to be connected. Diversity is the best way to find the greatest variety of errors, and thinking of unexpected things; these are ways of thinking which are contrary to the human tendency to prefer a known way of working and to repeat known actions on new data (as in islands of certainty above).

The automation of testing is now beginning to be possible. Automation can be of great assistance in software testing, mainly by extending the search for some types of errors more rigourously. However, there will still be errors which are not found and which cannot be found by automated testing tools. Since human beings put the errors in, only creative manual testing will be able to find them.

4. SUMMARY

This paper has looked at some concepts of cognitive psychology, to illustrate the relevance of that discipline to software engineering.

The study of the human-computer interface, although depending to some extent on the "soft" sciences, is a legitimate and valid area of study, and one which has an impact on software engineering in two ways: the design of the user interface for any system, and the ways in which software engineers carry out the mental processes involved in producing software systems.

The relevance of cognitive concepts to software engineering in general were illustrated by recent cognitive research into the way an engineer carried out the design of a functional specification; it was found that although the engineer stated that he intended and in fact had followed his hierarchic top-down plan, the HCI observer found that he had actually followed an opportunistic strategy. This has a direct bearing on the specification and design of software systems and software development tools.

The impact of cognitive ideas on requirements analysis, design (with indications of human-computer interface design principles), and the implications for software tools and software engineering training were examined.

Finally, the relevance of cognitive concepts in the area of software testing were examined, and those which have been found to be helpful in training and consultancy by the author were outlined.

5. REFERENCES

NOTE: This reference list includes books on HCI which are not referenced directly in the text of the paper, but are included for completeness.

J. A. Adams, <u>Human Factors Engineering</u>, Collier Macmillan, 1989.

[Agresti] W. W. Agresti, editor, <u>Tutorial: New Paradigms for Software Development</u>, IEEE Computer Society Press, 1986.

[ANSI/IEEE Std 729-1983] American National Standards Institute, IEEE Standard Glossary of Software Engineering Terminology, Std 729-1983.

[ANSI/IEEE Std 830-1984] American National Standards Institute, IEEE Guide to Software Requirements Specifications, Std 830-1984.

[ANSI/IEEE Std 1016-1987] American National Standards Institute, IEEE Recommended Practice for Software Design Descriptions, Std 1016-1987.

[Arblaster et al] A. T. Arblaster, M. E. Sime, and T. R. G. Green, "Jumping to some purpose", <u>The Computer Journal</u>, Vol. 22, pp. 105 - 109.

[Baber]   R. L. Baber, The Spine of Software, Designing Provably Correct Software, Theory and Practice, John Wiley & Sons, 1987.

[Bainbridge]   L. Bainbridge, "Ironies of Automation", in J. Rasmussen, K. Duncan, and J. Leplat, eds, New Technology and Human Error, John Wiley and Sons, 1987, pp. 271 - 283.

[Barden]   V. E. Barden, "Resistance to Computers", IT Circle Technical Report, The National Computing Centre, 1989.

                  P. Barker, Basic Principles of Human-Computer Interface Design, Hutchinson, 1989.

[Barnard et al]   P. Barnard, M. Wilson, and A. Maclean, "Approximate modelling of cognitive activity with an expert system: a theory-based strategy for developing and interactive design tool", The Computer Journal, Vol. 31, No. 5, Oct. 1988, pp. 445 - 456.

[Beizer]   B. Beizer, Software Testing Techniques, Van Nostrand Reinhold, 1983.

[Benyon & Murray] D. Benyon and D. Murray, "Experience with Adaptive Interfaces", The Computer Journal, Vol. 31, No. 5, Oct. 1988, pp. 465 - 473.

[Bjørn-Anderson] N. Bjørn-Anderson, "Are 'Human Factors' human?", The Computer Journal, Vol. 31, No. 5, Oct. 1988, pp. 386 - 390.

[Boehm]   B. W. Boehm, "Software Risk Management", ESEC '89, edited by C. Ghezzi and J. A. McDermid, in Lecture Notes in Computer Science, G. Goos and J. Hartmanis, series editors, No. 387, Springer-Verlag, 1989, pp. 1 - 19.

                  P. Booth, An Introduction to HCI, Lawrence Erlbaum Associates, 1989.

                  J. R. Brown and S. Cunningham, Programming the User Interface, Wiley, 1989.

[Cahour et al]   B. Cahour, P. Falzon and J.-M. Robert, "Interface consistency and text coherence: a psycholinguistic approach", presented at Work with Display Units '89, Montreal, Canada, Sept. 11 - 14, 1989.

[Carey]   J. Carey, <u>Human Factors in Management Information Systems</u>, Ablex, 1988.

[Curtis]   B. Curtis, <u>Tutorial: Human Factors in Software Development</u>, 2nd edition, IEEE Computer Society, 1985.

[Damodaran]   L. Damodaran, editor, Special Issue on Human-Computer Interaction, <u>The Computer Journal</u>, The British Computer Society, Cambridge University Press, Vol. 31, No. 5, October, 1988.

[DeMarco & Lister]   T. DeMarco and T. Lister, <u>Peopleware: Productive Projects and Teams</u>, Dorset House, 1987.

[Détienne-86]   F. Détienne, "Program understanding and knowledge organization: the influence of acquired schemata", <u>Proceedings of Third European Conference on Cognitive Ergonomics, 1986</u> (to be published in P. Falzon (ed.), <u>Cognitive Ergonomics: understanding and learning human-computer interaction</u>, John Wiley & Son, in press).

[Détienne-89]   F. Détienne, "Program understanding activity: a schema-based approach", in D. Gilmore, T. R. G. Green, J.-M. Hoc, and R. Samurçay (eds.), <u>Psychology of Programming</u>, Academic Press, People and Computer series, in press, 1989.

[Détienne-90]   F. Détienne, "Difficulties in designing with an object-oriented language: an empirical study", presented at the 2nd workshop of the Psychology of Programming Interest Group, Wolverhampton Polytechnic (Walsall), 4 - 6 Jan. 1990.

[Détienne & Soloway]   F. Détienne and E. Soloway, "An empirically-derived control structure for the process of program understanding", INRIA report no. 886, 1988.

[Dörner] D. Dörner, "On the difficulties people have in dealing with complexity", in J. Rasmussen, K. Duncan, and J. Leplat, (eds.), <u>New Technology and Human Error</u>, John Wiley and Sons, 1987, pp. 97 - 110.

[Dumas] J. S. Dumas, <u>Designing User Interfaces for Software</u>, Prentice Hall, 1988.

[Eason & Harker] K. D. Eason and S. Harker, "The Supplier's Role in the Design of Products for Organisations", <u>The Computer Journal</u>, Vol. 31, No. 5, Oct. 1988, pp. 426 - 430.

[Fagan] M. E. Fagan, "Design and code inspections to reduce errors in program development", <u>IBM Systems Journal</u>, Vol. 15, No. 3, 1976, pp 182 - 211.

[Falzon & Visser] P. Falzon and W. Visser, "Variations in expertise: implications for the design of assistance systems", in G. Salvendy and M. Smith (eds.), <u>Designing and using human-computer interfaces and knowledge based systems</u>, Elsevier, 1989.

[Floyd et al] C. Floyd, F.-M. Reisin, and G. Schmidt, "STEPS to Software Development with Users", <u>ESEC '89</u>, edited by C. Ghezzi and J. A. McDermid, in Lecture Notes in Computer Science, G. Goos and J. Hartmanis, series editors, No. 387, Springer-Verlag, 1989, pp. 48 - 64.

[Gardner & McKenzie] A. Gardner and J. McKenzie, Human Factor Guidelines for the Design of Computer-Based Systems, HUSAT Research Centre, Ministry of Defence Procurement Executive and The Department of Trade and Industry, HMSO, 1988. (6 volumes)

[Gilb] T. Gilb, <u>Principles of Software Engineering Management</u>, Addison-Wesley, 1988.

[Gilb-mss] T. Gilb, <u>Software Engineering Design</u>, manuscript.

[Gilb & Weinberg] T. Gilb and G. M. Weinberg, <u>Humanized Input: Techniques for Reliable Keyed Input</u>, QED, 1977.

[Gomaa & Scott]   H. Gomaa and D. G. H. Scott, "Prototyping as a Tool in the Specification of User Requirements", in W. W. Agresti, ed., <u>Tutorial: New Paradigms for Software Development</u>, IEEE Computer Society Press, 1986.

[Graham-90]   D. R. Graham, "Incremental Development and Delivery for Large Software Systems", Proceedings of <u>CSR: Sixth Annual Conference on Large Software Systems</u>, Elsevier, 1990.

[Graham-89]   D. R. Graham, "Incremental Development: a review of nonmonolithic life-cycle development models", <u>Information and Software Technology</u>, Vol. 31, No. 1, Jan/Feb 1989, pp. 7 - 20.

[Green-89]   T. R. G. Green, "Cognitive dimensions of notations", in A. Sutcliffe and L. Macaulay (eds.), <u>People and Computers</u>, Cambridge University Press, 1989.

[Green-77]   T. R. G. Green, "Conditional program statements and their comprehensibility to professional programmers, <u>Journal of Occupational Psychology</u>, Vol 50, 1977, pp. 93 - 109.

[Green-90]   T. R. G. Green, "Programming Languages as Information Structures", manuscript from the author, 1990.

[Harker]   S. Harker, "The Use of Prototyping and Simulation in the Development of Large-Scale Applications", <u>The Computer Journal</u>, Vol. 31, No. 5, Oct. 1988, pp. 420 - 425.

[Hetzel]   B. Hetzel, <u>The Complete Guide to Software Testing</u>, QED, 1988.

[HICOM]   HICOM, Communications and Information for the HCI Community, Contact: Ceri Hopkins, HICOM New User Coordinator, Dept. of Computer Science, The University of Birmingham, PO Box 363, Birmingham, B15 2TT U.K., Phone 021-414-3708, Email: hopkinsCA@uk.ac.bham.cs

[Hirschheim & Newman]	R. Hirschheim and M. Newman, Information Systems and User Resistance: Theory and Practice, The Computer Journal, Vol. 31, No. 5, Oct. 1988, pp. 398 - 408.
[INRIA]	INRIA: Institut National de Recherche en Informatique et an Automatique, Domaine de Voluceau, Rocquencourt, B. P. 105, 78153 Le Chesnay Cedex, France. Tel. (1) 39 63 5511.
[Jagodzinski & Clarke]	A. P. Jagodzinski and D. D. Clarke, "A Multidimensional Approach to the Measurement of Human-computer Performance", The Computer Journal, Vol. 31, No. 5, Oct. 1988, pp. 409 - 419.
[Kitchenham & Carn]	B. Kitchenham and R. Carn, "Research and Practice: Software design methods and tools", Chapter 5.2, in D. Gilmore, T. R. G. Green, J.-M. Hoc, and R. Samurçay (eds.), Psychology of Programming, Academic Press, People and Computer series, in press.Psychology of programming, draft, version 4.0, Feb. 1989.
[Lequesne]	P. N. Lequesne, "Individual and Organisational Factors and the Design of IPSE's", The Computer Journal, Vol. 31, No. 5, Oct. 1988, pp. 391 - 397.
[Lindsay & Norman]	P. H. Lindsay and D. A. Norman, Human Information Processing, An Introduction to Psychology, Academic Press, 1977.
[Mayfield & Wells]	T. F. Mayfield and J. C. Wells, "User-Centred Design of a Computer-Based Control and Surveillance System for Nuclear Power Plant", Computers and Safety, A first International Conference on the use of programmable electronic systems in safety related applications, IEE Conference Publication No. 314, 1989.
[Molich & Nielsen]	R. Molich and J. Nielsen, "Improving a Human-Computer Dialogue", Communications of the ACM, Vol. 33, No. 3, March 1990, pp. 338-348.
[Myers]	G. J. Myers, The Art of Software Testing, John Wiley and Sons, 1979.

[Neal-87] L. Neal, "Cognition-Sensitive Design and User Modeling for Syntax-Directed Editors", Proceedings of CHI+GI'87 Conference on Human Factors in Computing Systems and Graphics Interface (Toronto April 5 - 9), ACM, New York, 1987a, pp. 99-102.

[Neal-89] L. Neal, "The Role of User Models in Systems Design", TR-18-89, doctoral thesis, Harvard University, Cambridge, Mass, Oct. 1989.

[Neal-90] L. Neal and D. Littman, "Empirical studies of parallel problem solving", presented at the <u>Second annual workshop of the Psychology of Programming Interest Group</u>, Wolverhampton Polytechnic (Walsall), 4 - 6 Jan. 1990.

[Pierret-Golbreich-88] C. Pierret-Golbreich, "A computer aided modelling system using an object-centered representation", in J. M. David, R. Huber, J. P. Krivine, and C. Kulikowski (eds.), <u>IMACS Transactions on Scientific Computing-'88, Vol 2: AI and Expert systems in scientific computing,</u> Baltzer A. G., Scientific publishing company, Basel, Switzerland, 1988.

[Pierret-Golbreich-89] C. Pierret-Golbreich, "The role of object-representations for transfer and modeling of expertise", <u>IA en Simulation Numérique et Symbolique, SCS Europe,</u> Lyon, France, March 22 - 24, 1989.

[Pierret-Golbreich et al] C. Pierret-Golbreich, I. Delouis, and D. L. Scapin, "An object-based tool for tasks acquisition and representation", research report, Rocquencourt, INRIA, 1989.

[PPIG] PPIG: Psychology of Programming Interest Group, Co-ordinator: Dr. David Gilmore, Psychology Dept, University of Nottingham, Nottingham NG7 2RD, UK, Tel. 0602-484848 Ext. 3724.

J. Rasmussen, K. Duncan, and J. Leplat, editors, <u>New Technology and Human Error</u>, John Wiley and Sons, 1987.

[Rubin]	T. Rubin, <u>User Interface Design</u>, Ellis Horwood, distributed by John Wiley & Sons, 1988.
[Shneiderman]	B. Shneiderman, <u>Designing the User Interface</u>, Addison-Wesley, 1987.
[Siddiqi & Khazaei]	J. Siddiqi and B. Khazaei, "What are the 'carry over effects' in changing from a Procedural to a Declarative approach?", <u>Proceedings of the Second annual workshop of the Psychology of Programming Interest Group</u>, Wolverhampton Polytechnic (Walsall), 4 - 6 Jan. 1990.
[Sime et al]	M. E. Sime, T. R. G. Green, and D. J. Guest, "Scope marking in computer conditionals - psychological evaluation", <u>Int. Journal of Man-Machine Studies</u>, Vol. 9, pp. 107 - 118.
[Smyth et al]	M. M. Smyth, P. E. Morris, P. Levy, and A. W. Ellis, <u>Cognition in Action</u>, Lawrence Erlbaum Associates, 1987.
[Sutcliffe]	A. G. Sutcliffe, <u>Human/Computer Interface Design</u>, Macmillan, 1988.
	H. Thimbleby, <u>The User Interface Handbook</u>, Addison-Wesley, 1989.
[Tyldesley]	D. A. Tyldesley, "Employing Usability Engineering in the Development of Office Products", <u>The Computer Journal</u>, Vol. 31, No. 5, Oct. 1988, pp. 431 - 436.
[Vessey & Weber]	I. Vessey and R. Weber, "Conditional statements and program coding: an experimental evaluation", <u>Int. Journal of Man-Machine Studies</u>, Vol. 21, pp. 161 - 190.
[Visser]	W. Visser, "More or Less Following a Plan During Design: Opportunistic Deviations in Specification", INRIA, June, 1989.
[Visser & Falzon-88]	W. Visser and P. Falzon, "Eliciting expert knowledge in a design activity: some methodological issues", research report No. 906, Rocquencourt, INRIA, 1988.

[Visser & Falzon-89]   W. Visser and P. Falzon, "Eliciting the knowledge of a design expert, abridged proceedings, poster sessions of HCI International '89 - Third International Conference on Human-Computer Interaction, Boston, Massachusetts, U.S.A., 18 - 22 Sept. 1989.

[Visser & Hoc]   W. Visser and J. M. Hoc, "Expert software design strategies", in J. M. Hoc, T. Green, R. Samurçay, and D. Gilmore (eds.), Psychology of Programming, Academic Press, in press.

[Visser & Morais]   W. Visser and A. Morais, "Concurrent use of different expertise elicitation methods applied to the study of the programming activity", Rocquencourt, INRIA, 1989.

[Wærn]   Y. Wærn, Cognitive Aspects of Computer Supported Tasks, John Wiley & Sons, 1989.

Software Verification and Testing Tools: Availability and Uptake

D. R. Graham

Independent Software Engineering Consultant
Grove Consultants, Grove House
40 Ryles Park Road, Macclesfield,
Cheshire SK11 8AH England
Tel. 0625 - 616279

1 VERIFICATION, VALIDATION, AND TESTING

1.1 Verification and Validation and Tool Support

1.1.1 VV&T

Software Verification, Validation, and Testing activities are concerned with the assessment and enhancement of the quality of software systems. Verification and Validation are often used interchangeably (or together as V&V) to refer to those activities which are done throughout software development to ensure that the output of each phase of the development life cycle is a correct transformation of the input to that phase; for example, that a high-level design is correctly derived from requirements, or that a low-level design is correctly derived from the high-level design. Testing of software systems is generally regarded as those activities to do with the execution of code and the examination of the output of code. A broader definition of testing could include all V&V activities, and some definitions of V&V include all testing activities. The definitions used in this paper are given below.

1.1.2 Verification

Verification is the checking of any life cycle product for correctness, either with respect to some other product or independently, summed up by Boehm's informal definition, "Are we building the product right?". Verification can be done by manual methods, such as design reviews (e.g. Fagan's Inspection), or by software tools for static analysis. Verification tools assist in checking the software for consistency, conformance to programming standards, and in providing information to assist manual verification (such as proving).

1.1.3 Validation

Validation of software is concerned with ensuring that the software system is correct with respect to the expectations of the system instigators or eventual users. The requirements for the system can be expressed in formalised specifications, semi-formally or informally. Validation ("are we building the right product" [Boehm]) is an evaluation process, comparing the system with the user or customer expectations for that system. It is my contention that validation is not and cannot be automated to any significant degree, since it relies on human perception, understanding, and awareness for evaluation criteria. Software tools can assist in the evaluation of a software system against its <u>expressed</u> requirements, which I would define as a form of verification. Software tools can assist in the evaluation of <u>intended</u> requirements by prototyping (with or without 4GL's), simulation (e.g. of screens), and animation of requirements, but this is the extent of tool support for validation. It is the realisation in software (the system), of the actual needed or desired requirements, rather than the expressed or intended requirements, which is true validation, and cannot be tool-supported. Although the tools in this area support only verification and testing and not validation, they are often informally referred to as "VV&T" tools.

1.2 Definition of Testing

Testing is the dynamic execution of a software unit under certain conditions, for the purpose of evaluating the software. The Software Under Test (SUT) can be of any size, from a module or procedure, a program, an integrated set of modules, up to a complete system. Tests can be either scripted, i.e. details of exactly what to input and what output is expected, or unscripted, i.e. time is allocated for the SUT to be exercised without planning in advance exactly what will be input. Extending the definition given by [Goodenough], the conditions necessary for a dynamic execution to be considered a test are:

1.2.1 Controlled Conditions

The test must be run under controlled or closely observed conditions. In order to demonstrate that a software error has been removed, it is necessary to perform three activities: first, demonstrate the occurrence of the error using a test set, second, alter the software to remove the error, and third, use exactly the same test set under the same controlled conditions to demonstrate that the error is no longer there. This third step cannot be achieved unless the test conditions, as well as the test input, are reproducible. In some real-time systems, it may not be possible to reproduce exact operational conditions; in this case the environment must be closely observed and a number of test sets run, in order to achieve a matching of "before" and "after" environmental conditions, to demonstrate the removal of an error. In unscripted testing, faults which occur can be difficult to reproduce.

1.2.2 Sample Input

The dynamic execution of software, in contrast to symbolic execution [Carre], involves the choice of input values as test cases from the input domain space of the software under test (SUT). Because of the combinatorial explosion effects of a large number of input values and input domains, both valid and invalid, it is never possible to test all values. Testing therefore consists of choosing individual or sample input values from the domain according to the test strategies or test techniques being utilised. The problem is not usually finding some test cases to input, but selecting the best test cases out of thousands of possibilities.

1.2.3 Predicted Output

The purpose of executing a test of software is to evaluate it objectively against some criteria. In order to evaluate, it is essential that those criteria are defined, so that the testing process is as objective as possible. For scripted testing, the test output associated with each sample test input must be predicted in advance of the test itself being run. For unscripted testing, the tester or test observer must be able to recognise when perceived output of the SUT is correct and when it is incorrect. The "test output" in this context includes not only output produced directly by the software (on a screen or printer), but also the absence of output, error messages, changes to data structures such as files, and internal communication to modules other than the SUT; these outputs may not be immediately visible when the SUT is run, thus requiring verification of these effects by other means, either during or after the test itself. For scripted tests, these effects must also be predicted.

1.2.4 Analysed Results

The final essential aspect of testing is that the actual output of the dynamic execution be analysed with respect to the output which was predicted. Without this analysis, there can be no evaluation, which is the purpose of the test. There is no point in running any test if there will be no evaluation of results. Therefore, if you have no resources to examine the test output, don't waste time performing the tests at all.

A dynamic execution of software which meets these four conditions can be considered to be a test of that software. A test configuration for a scripted test therefore consists of the software under test (SUT), a set of input cases to the SUT, the expected outputs for the specified inputs, and the actual output produced by the SUT. In addition, test plans, procedures, designs, etc. should be specified as part of the management of the testing process; unscripted tests should be included in the test plans and allocated time in the test schedule.

1.3 Test techniques and publications

Test techniques are normally distinguished between functional (also called black box or closed box) techniques and structural (also called white box, glass box or open box) techniques. In addition, structural analysis is used to evaluate the effectiveness of test input by analysing the structural coverage, and is best used in combination with functional techniques for the derivation of test input cases.

There are a number of books and articles on testing techniques. [Myers] is still probably the best single book on testing. [Hetzel] is a good one for managers. [Beizer] is the best for detailed structural techniques. [Kaner] is a very practical book for testers, with a wonderful appendix of hundreds of error examples to look for. [DeMillo] has U.S. military standards and approaches, a very comprehensive test bibliography. A recent book by [Roper and Parrington] is a good introduction to testing, containing an on-going case study. The author has written a Technical Report for NCC's Software Engineering Circle [Graham, NCC] on test and debug techniques and tools.

2 MANUAL VERSUS AUTOMATED TESTING

Testing can be performed manually or with help from software tools. Without tool support, manual involvement is needed in preparing the test input cases, running the tests, preparing the expected results from the Requirements Specification, comparing the test output with the expected results to evaluate the correctness of the SUT (including visible output and other effects of the software being run), and removing the errors found, i.e. debugging. Tool support can be given to many of these areas, but more successfully to some aspects of testing than to others.

Manual testing is capable of finding examples of all types of errors, and theoretically of finding all errors. In practice, however, dynamic execution is not very effective at finding errors. Typically, dynamic execution testing can find 50%-60% of errors ever found. A software tool can find all occurrences of some types of error, but cannot find all types of error, only the types which it is capable of looking for. Most tools currently available offer assistance in detecting only syntactic errors, not semantic errors. For comparison, the rigourous application of Fagan's Inspection, a manual verification and validation technique, can find up to 80% of errors. [Gilb]

The errors which are often the most difficult to reproduce, identify and remove, occur as the combination of circumstances which testing rarely achieves, but which software tools are even less likely to achieve. The application of software tools to verification and testing can be cost-effective, but it is not a panacea. It has been found that a combination of test techniques is more effective than single techniques [Selby]; the same is likely to be true for tool-supported testing.

It is important to note that no matter how carefully manual testing is done, it will not find all errors, because the manual testing process is also an error-prone activity. It is important to note that no matter how much automated testing is done, it will not find all errors, because the automated testing process will find only "systematic" errors, i.e. those which can be found be applying a rule-based strategy. Many of the most elusive errors are found only by human inspiration and ingenuity.

3 SOFTWARE VV&T TOOL CLASSIFICATION

3.1 Other Tool Classifications

A number of tool classifications have been put forward; a good summary is given in [Pressman], and descriptions of some early tools are given in [Miller & Howden], [Saib], [Deutsch]. The only published book which lists tool information is [DeMillo], which lists tools in the U.S. A total of 218 tools are named, and 37 have data sheets from the suppliers (a number of the tools listed are not commercial products). Tool information in the U.S. is also available as the "Testing Tools Reference Guide" and "Tools Guide Update" from Software Quality Engineering [SQE]. The National Computing Centre produced an early survey of eight tools [Abbott, 1985], and a recent survey of 25 tools was written for NCC by the author [NCC, 1989]; this paper is based on the classification scheme introduced in that report. A more comprehensive survey of 30+ tools will be produced by Unicom Seminars in 1990/91, called "Software Testing Tools Report" [Graham, Unicom]

3.2 Support from other software tools

There are a number of software tools which provide support for testing and particularly verification activities as part of a comprehensive development support tool. For example, requirements analysis tools provide consistency checking, which is a verification activity. This paper is concerned only with tools which provide support exclusively to verification and testing activities as stand-alone tools, and not with the facilities provided by other tools whose main functionality is outside VV&T.

3.3 The Tool Classification Categories

Software VV&T tools are here classified into the categories listed below, based on the types of facilities offered. These classifications are intended for general guidance only; in many cases, it is not clear-cut which classification a tool should belong in. Many tools will actually come under more than one classification. The tool classifications are discussed in depth in the following section. The tool classifications are:

- Capture/Playback
- Comparator
- Input Generation
- Verification (Static Analysis)
- Simulator
- Test Harness/Test Driver
- Test Coverage Measurement
- Debugging

4. Tool Information

The tools which have been included in this survey include only those which are commercially available in the U.K., i.e. are actively supported and marketed. The tools chosen are applicable to "reasonable" sized systems, i.e. tools applicable to stand-alone PC working are excluded. It includes only those tool which are specifically and exclusively directed towards verification and testing activities.

For each tool classification listed, a functional description of the generic type of tool in the classification is given, and the tools which are commercially available in the U.K. at the time of writing are listed at the end of each section. It should be noted that this area is one which is currently undergoing rapid change, so the information herein published will be out of date, at least with regard to the tool information itself. The latest information for a particular tool can be obtained from the tool vendor. The author does not suppose that this is a complete list of all tools in this category, and would welcome information concerning those which should have been included and were not. Tools which were discovered after this paper was completed are listed at the end of the Appendix: List of Suppliers.

4.1 Capture Playback Tools

Capture and Playback tools provide the capability to record and replay a test input script. Although they do not save time the first time test data is input to the software under test, they have three advantages. First, they enable any test script recorded by the tool to be replayed exactly. This enables the correction of faults to be demonstrated with confidence that the input was exactly the same. Secondly, the tests can be replayed without supervision, so a great deal of testers' time can be saved on subsequent testing, i.e. during regression testing. A third advantage is that most capture playback tools also allow the recorded test scripts to be edited; this enables the test script to be changed as needed for error corrections or new fields added to input scripts, for example. The expected output can sometimes also be edited. An extension to the editing facility is the provision of a "test language", which enables the test scripts to be typed in rather than recording an actual input.

A capture playback system can be either intrusive or non-intrusive. An intrusive system resides on the same machine as the software under test; a non-intrusive system resides on a separate machine. The non-intrusive system should not affect the timing of the software being tested, but it does require the purchase of special test hardware (e.g. a PC).

One of the uses of a capture playback system is for capturing those elusive errors which users seem to be so good at making, and which developers just can't seem to reproduce. People are not very good at remembering with total exactness precisely what keystrokes they performed, in what order, and at what time intervals. Attaching a capture playback tool to a remote terminal can enable the data recorded when the strange error does occur to be observed and reproduced.

Commercial Capture/Playback Tools:

The tool name, environment in which the tool runs, the supplier name, and the approximate cost are given below:

Tool:	Envirm't	Supplier	Cost
CICS PLAYBACK	IBM	Compuware	£8K
EVALUATOR	IBM PC	QA Training	£3K
TESTA	IBM PC +	John Bell	£4K+
VAX DEC/TEST MANAGER	VAX	DEC	£1-30K

4.2 Comparator Tools

A comparator tool allows two files to be compared with one another, with only the differences between the two being output from the comparator. If two files are exactly the same, the tool's discrepancy report may say "no differences found" for example.

A file comparator is a general tool, not necessarily restricted to software testing, but is a very useful tool for software testing. One of the most important tasks in the testing process is to compare the output of the software under test with the expected output for that module. However, the comparison of long lists of numbers or symbols is the sort of task which is difficult for people to do accurately but which is ideal for computers to do.

The comparator can be used to compare actual output with expected output, but it can also be used to compare the output this time with the output last time, i.e. for regression testing. This enables the mundane task (checking that things are exactly the same) to be automated, while the non-routine tasks (analysing what is different this time, which is not easily automated) to be done manually, thus getting the most effective mix of human and automated analysis.

There are two problems with the design of a comparison tool. First, there will be some output data which is different for every test run but which doesn't matter, for example time and/or date. A comparator tool should allow "masking" of these "don't matter" fields, so that they are not compared.

A second problem is of the two files being compared getting out of step. A new input item added to the software requires both a new test input and a new output. A straight comparison of the new output file with the old will produce agreement until the new output item, but everything after that will disagree, although it will be obvious by looking at it that each item is off by one. A comparator tool should therefore be able to get itself back in step, either automatically, or with specific instructions from the tester when the comparator is run.

Comparator tools are often combined with capture playback tools. In fact, a capture playback tool enables so much more output to be generated by replaying tests, that a comparator is probably an essential adjunct to successful use of a capture playback tool.

Some comparator tools enable the comparison of screen output as well as printed output. Used in conjunction with capture playback tools, screens can be saved at intervals (snapshots) to be compared with the same screen in a subsequent test run. Screen areas can be selectively masked for "don't matter" items of data.

A comparator is probably the easiest software testing tool to produce in-house, although the commercial tools may well turn out to be cheaper in the long run.

Commercial Comparator Tools:

The tool name, environment in which the tool runs, the supplier name, and the approximate cost are given below:

Tool:	Envirm't	Supplier	Cost
CICS PLAYBACK	IBM	Compuware	£8K
EVALUATOR	IBM PC	QA Training	£3K
SOFTEST	not IBM,ICL	IPL	£7K+
SOFTORG	IBM	Densitron	£10K
TESTMANAGER	IBM	MSP	£18K
TESTA	IBM PC +	John Bell	£4K+
VAX DEC/TEST MANAGER	VAX	DEC	£1-30K

4.3   Input Generation Tools

The selection of the input cases for testing is generally done manually, following some of the accepted test techniques such as equivalence partitioning, boundary value analysis, cause-effect graphing or path analysis. However, test input cases can be generated automatically for some types of tests.

For large volumes of test data to test performance under heavy load, i.e. stress testing, it is the quantity of test data which is needed rather the quality of the individual test inputs. (One assumes that volume testing comes after the thorough individual testing.) A single test script can be replayed over and over, possibly at a higher speed than it was originally recorded. Test input can be generated or modified by using a pseudo-random number generator to give some variety to the input data items. The modification of data items can also be done for data files, to give a large volume. This type of input generation can be done by a capture/playback tool or by a special purpose tool for particular applications; no commercial tools exist specifically for this type of volume application.

Another type of input generation tool can be used when the requirements for the module being tested are recorded in a formal way. A "finite-state" system such as an automated bank till can be tested by sequences of test cases derived from a system specification by an input generation tool.

Commercial Input Generation Tools:

The tool name, environment in which the tool runs, the supplier name, and the approximate cost are given below:

Tool:	Envirm't	Supplier	Cost
TESTGEN	DEC	Gerrard S/W	£8K+

4.4 Verification / Static Analysis Tools

Many of the errors which are made in software development are "trivial", i.e. they are very easy for human developers to make. However, such errors often have severe and non-trivial effects on the software. A misspelled word in a printed output is a mere annoyance, but using the wrong variable name to compute how much oxygen to give a chemical reaction can have an explosive effect.

Compilers are the first type of static analysis tool, and can find misspellings if variables are pre-declared, for example. However, there are a number of other things which a compiler does not detect: for example, whether you have forgotten to assign a value to a variable before using it, or if a declared procedure is never actually called.

Static analysis tools can find a number of errors in software without dynamically executing it, hence their classification as verification tools rather than testing tools. They can find all occurrences of some types of error, so they are 100% accurate for some things. They are not a substitute for testing, however, as there are other errors which are not found by static analysis (the software might perfectly perform the wrong function).

Static analysis tools perform several types of analysis, as detailed below. Not all tools perform all of the functions listed; a selection of types of facilities is given.

Complexity analysis computes the cyclomatic complexity, related to the number of decisions in the module, and may also compute other complexity measures. Static analysis tools can also give a measure of the "structuredness" of the code, and check conformance to programming standards for structure.

Data flow analysis detects errors and anomalies of variable usage. For example, if a variable is used in an expression before a value has been assigned to it, or if it is assigned a value which is then never used.

Control flow analysis detects logic errors, such as program code which is never executed, or loops which cannot be exited (infinite loops).

Information flow analysis examines the relationship of input to output variables, and can tell which input values affect a given output value, or which output values are affected by a given input value. This can be used to verify (manually) that the correct dependencies between input and output values have been achieved. A partial program can be extracted, listing only the statements which use or are affected by given variables.

Static analysis tools may also provide other functions to support formal verification techniques such as correctness proving, e.g. symbolic interpreters, verification condition generation, primitive proof checking, semantic analysis, and compliance analysis either to programming standards or to the specification of the software.

Using statis analysis tools on incomplete systems may result in a large number of spurious errors being detected, e.g. when variable uses have not yet been included or occur in a different module.

Commercial Verification/Static Analysis Tools:

The tool name, environment in which the tool runs, the supplier name, and the approximate cost are given below:

Tool:	Envirm't	Supplier	Cost
LOGISCOPE	Ap, DEC, IBM, SUN,+	Verilog	£10K+
MALPAS	DEC	Rex Thompson	£14K+
PATHVU	IBM, ICL, +	XA	£25K
PRO-QUEST	DEC, IBM PC	John Bell	£4K+
SOFTORG	IBM	Densitron	£10K
SPADE	DEC	PVL	£19K+
TESTBED	not IBM PC	PA	£8K+

4.5 Simulator Tools

Simulator or emulator tools are used to simulate some aspect of the real world in order to test software which cannot be tested directly in its final environment, because it is too dangerous, too expensive, or inappropriate; for example, aircraft guidance software, nuclear power station control, chemical process control, or financial institutions.

The simulator tool feeds input to the software under test as though that input was coming from its intended environment, and also receives the program output in a similar way, e.g. by intercepting control signals which are intended for special hardware devices.

Simulators are often specific to a particular environment and so are usually bespoke developments in their own right. Before a simulator can be relied upon for testing, it is important that the simulator software itself be tested rigourously.

No matter how good the simulation is, the real world will always be different, so simulation testing is not a substitute for real-world testing, but can be a useful predecessor.

Commercial Simulator Tools:

The tool name, environment in which the tool runs, the supplier name, and the approximate cost are given below:

Tool:	Envirm't	Supplier	Cost
SOFTPROBE II	DEC, IBM PC, +	Warren Point	£3K+
TESTA	IBM PC +	John Bell	£4K+
XRAY	not IBM or ICL	Microtec	£2K+

4.6 Test Harness/Test Driver Tools

Test harness (or test driver) tools enable a set of tests to be run automatically. A series of test inputs are fed to the software under test, and the outputs are collected. A comparator tool can be part of the test harness, so that the eventual output of the set of tests is a set of discrepancy reports.

Test harness tools may also perform configuration management tasks for the test documentation, keeping track of when tests were run, with what version of the software and test input, who initiated the test, where the output results are stored, etc.

The use of a test harness tool enables large quantities of tests to be run unattended, for example overnight or at weekends. Combined with a comparator tool, it can provide the facility for true regression testing after software changes have been made, by actually re-running all previous tests each time a change is made.

Commercial Test Harness/Test Driver Tools:

The tool name, environment in which the tool runs, the supplier name, and the approximate cost are given below:

Tool:	Envirm't	Supplier	Cost
EVALUATOR	IBM PC	QA Training	£3K
SOFTEST	most	IPL	£7.5K+
SOFTORG	IBM	Densitron	£10K
TESTMANAGER	IBM	MSP	£18K
TESTA	IBM PC +	John Bell	£4K+
VAX DEC/TEST MANAGER	VAX	DEC	£1-30K

4.7 Coverage Analysis Tools

Coverage analysis tools provide a measure of how much of the structure of a module or system has been exercised by a given set of tests. There are no commercial tools to measure functional coverage.

System level coverage measures how many of the component parts of the system have been called by a test set. Code coverage measures the percentage of statements, branches, or LCSAJ's (Linear Code Sequence and Jumps) exercised by a test set. The measurement of condition coverage (all conditions in decisions) is not yet automated by any known tools available in the U.K. Decision-use coverage is likewise not known to be automated as yet. Some debugging tools can measure statement coverage.

In order to measure coverage, the code must first be instrumented, i.e. code must be inserted to count the number of times a structure is used. This is done automatically by the tool, but it does require an additional compilation-type step, and the resulting instrumented code will be of increased size and decreased performance to the original code. Instrumentation must therefore be removed before measuring performance, which may affect the timescale for testing.

Once the code is instrumented, the test sets (most effectively derived by functional techniques) are executed. The results are the percentage measurements achieved in whatever structure is being measured (statements, branches, etc.). This information can then be used by the testers to devise new test input cases which will exercise those parts of the software which have not yet been reached. When those test cases have been run, a cumulative total of structures exercised is given by the tool.

Good structural coverage does not imply good testing. If all statements are exercised by a test, for example, this is certainly a better and more thorough test than one which leaves some statements untested. However, just because a program structure has been exercised at least once, it does not mean that that code has been tested well. Structural coverage can measure the "width" of the testing, but not the "depth". Software which has been well covered by structural tests can still contain serious software errors.

Any coverage analysis tool can also be used for performance analysis. Since the number of statements (for example) exercised can be detected, the test input need not be the test case script, but could be a realistic sample of real data. The coverage of real data gives the number of times each statement is used; those which are used a large number of times are the performance "hot spots", i.e. those parts of the code which are the most used. If performance needs to be improved, the greatest gains can be made by optimising the "hot spots", since the improvements will be multiplied by the number of times the code is used.

Commercial Test Coverage Tools:

The tool name, environment in which the tool runs, the supplier name, and the approximate cost are given below, with the structural coverage level(s) assessed given in brackets (1 = statement, 2 = branch, 3 = LCSAJ):

Tool:	Envirm't	Supplier	Cost
LOGISCOPE(1,2)	Ap,DEC,IBM,SUN,+	Verilog	£10K+
OLIVER(1)	IBM	APT	£17K+
SIMON(1)	IBM	APT	£13K+
PRO-QUEST(2)	DEC, IBM PC	John Bell	£4K+
SOFTORG(1,2)	IBM	Densitron	£10K
SOFTPROBE II(1)	DEC, IBM PC,+	Warren Point	£3K+
SAW(1)	many	Instrumatic	£29K
TESTBED(1,2,3)	not IBM PC	PA	£8K+
VAX PCA(1)	DEC	DEC	£1-27K
XPEDITER(1)	IBM	Topdata	£50K
XPF(1)	IBM	Pansophic	£30K+

4.8 Test Database Tools

A test database is used when the software being tested either uses or affects data which is stored, i.e. where the test output is insufficient to assess the entirety of the software's effects. A test database is usually an example of the database which the software manipulates. It should contain at least one example of every type of record, field and index.

A comparator tool can be used to examine the effect of the software under test on the database, by comparing the "before" and "after" states of the database.

A test database is often special-purpose, as it needs to be tailored to the particular application.

Commercial Test Database Tools:

The tool name, environment in which the tool runs, the supplier name, and the approximate cost are given below:

Tool:	Envirm't	Supplier	Cost
FILE-AID	IBM	Compuware	£7K
SOFTEST	most	IPL	£7.5K+
SOFTORG	IBM	Densitron	£10K

4.9 Debug Tools

Although any software development system will include some kind of debug facilities as part of the compilation package, there are other stand-alone debug tools which can be purchased to provide facilities over and above those provided in standard compiler packages. This report concerns itself only with the latter type of debug tool.

Debug tools enable software errors to be identified and isolated so that they can be corrected. They also allow software fixes to be tried out to some extent, to verify that the fault has been correctly identified. Debug tools generally work on only one program or module, and allow observation and manipulation of program data and logic control flow, by setting up interruptions to the normal program execution. The debug tool is like a harness for the program under test; the program is run under the control of the debug tool.

Debug tools can operate at different levels. Machine level tools allow access only by hardware or assembler level addresses. Mnemonic level tools allow names to be used for variables and procedures, although breakpoints still need to be set with reference to assembly level. Source level tools allow all interaction with the tool to take place with reference to the source code (3GL). Screen-based tools allow "animation" of control flow, i.e. highlighting the statements in the order of execution, with data items monitored so that changes can be seen on the screen as they occur. Debug tools can also be integrated with editors and compilers, or with configuration management tools.

Some debug tools can perform coverage analysis for statement coverage, and therefore also can also do performance analysis. Some can also record and playback input scripts.

Debug tools are usually specific to a particular hardware and software environment.

Commercial Debug Tools:

The tool name, environment in which the tool runs, the supplier name, and the approximate cost are given below:

Tool:	Envirm't	Supplier	Cost
ABEND-AID	IBM	Compuware	£7K
CICS DBUG-AID	IBM	Compuware	£8K
OLIVER	IBM	APT	£17K+
SIMON	IBM	APT	£13K+
SOFTPROBE II	DEC, IBM PC,+	Warren Point	£3K+
SAW	many	Instrumatic	£29K
XPEDITER(1)	IBM	Topdata	£50K
XPF(1)	IBM	Pansophic	£30K+
XRAY	not IBM, ICL	Microtec	£2K+

5 TOOL INFORMATION SUMMARY TABLES

The attached Tables summarise the tool information for software testing and verification tools available in the U.K. Table 1 contains the tool list with the functionality class given; Table 2 gives the tool environments. Both lists contain an indication of relative cost and give the tool supplier name. The cost indications were obtained from tool vendors in the summer of 1989. Some tools can be purchased outright; others are sold as site licenses. For current price and detailed information see the tool vendor.

5.1   Table 1. Tool Classifications

The information on which the Table 1 is based is drawn from the study of information supplied by tool vendors. In some cases quite detailed information was supplied; in others only "glossies" with very little technical content were supplied. The tool information should therefore be taken as a consistent view of a number of tools, but should not be regarded as authoritative concerning any one particular tool.   The categories listed are those given above:

    Cap: Capture and Playback
    Com: Comparator
    In : Input Generation
    Ver: Verification, i.e. Static Analysis
    Sim: Simulator
    Har: Test Harness or Driver
    Cov: Test Coverage Analyser
    Dbg: Debug
    DB: Test Database

5.2   Table 2. Tool Environments

The hardware environments in which the tools surveyed will operate are given in the Table 2. The categories are:

        Ap: Apollo
        Dec: Digital Equipment Corporation
        HP: Hewlett Packard
        IBM: IBM Mainframes
        pc: IBM or compatible PC
        ICL: ICL
        Sun: SUN workstation
        oth: other environment

For more detailed information about particular tools, see NCC's free VV&T Tool Leaflet, or tool vendors. A list of vendor's addresses and telephone numbers is given in the Appendix.

6   TOOL UPTAKE

6.1   Tool Survey Limitations

The usage of the tools surveyed is shown in Table 3 (U.K. Usage of Surveyed Tools) and Table 4 (Worldwide Usage of Surveyed Tools). The figures for tool usage were given by the tool vendors in July 1989, and may well have changed significantly since that time.

The tools for this survey were collected from software tool fairs (in particular the Software Tools Exhibition and Conference at Wembley in June 1989), and also from the list of tools on the software tools database of the National Computing Centre.

The figures given in Table 3 for U.K. usage should reflect the state of tool usage in the U.K. reasonably accurately, provided that all relevant tools have been included in this survey.

Table 4, Worldwide Usage of Surveyed Tools, does not accurately reflect the usage of VV&T tools worldwide, however; it only gives the worldwide usage of tools which are commercially available in the U.K. There are a large number of VV&T tools available in the U.S.A., for example, which have not been included in this survey because they are not generally commercially available in the U.K. (e.g. no U.K. support).

The figures in the tables are also distorted by the fact that some of the tool vendors declined to give tool usage figures. For example, DEC either does not have tool usage information available or is not willing to divulge that information.

6.2   Tool Usage Comparison, U.K. and Worldwide

A comparison of tool usage of UK-available tools in the U.K. and worldwide is shown in Table 5 below.

The worldwide usage of UK-available VV&T tools is mainly in debugging tools (41% of tool users), and coverage measurement tools (35%). However, the number of users of coverage analysis tools is somewhat misleading, as 2600 of the 3070 users (85%) actually get their coverage analysis facilities from a debug tool (and hence can measure statement coverage only). Omitting those, the figure should actually be 15% (470 coverage tools: 400 use LOGISCOPE, 50 use TESTBED, and 20 others).

The major usage of VV&T tools within the U.K. is in coverage analysis (37%), again including those with statement coverage only, for example using a debug tool. The percentage using branch coverage is 8.2% (90 users).

Table 5. Tool Usage Comparison, Worldwide and U.K. (for UK-available tools)

Tool Name	Cap	Com	In	Ver	Sim	Har	Cov	Dbg	DB
Worldwide	165	210	3	640	540	85	3070	3525	469
Percentage	2%	3%	0%	7%	6%	1%	35%	41%	5%
U.K.	40	43	3	143	100	43	405	315	0
Percentage	4%	4%	0%	13%	9%	4%	37%	29%	0%

6.3 Tool Usage Conclusions

The areas where tool usage is more intensive in the U.K. than in the rest of the world is most significantly in Static Analysis/Verification tools. The U.K. also has a slightly higher usage of Capture/Playback tools, Comparator tools, Simulators, and Test Harness/Test Drivers.

The areas where tool usage is less intensive in the U.K. than in the rest of the world is in debugging and test database tools.

One conclusion which is reinforced by this data is the emphasis in the U.K. on the "front end" of software development; even in software testing, which is a "back end" activity, the emphasis is on "front end" activities, i.e. static analysis rather than debugging. It is to be hoped that this emphasis has and will result in increased quality of developed software in the U.K. However, "back end" activities still require attention; tools which address the very real problems, particularly during maintenance, will still be needed. In fact, they may become even more cost-effective as the earlier stages of the life cycle become more controlled; that may simply be "increasing the size of the input pipe" to the back end [Peter Sedgewick].

It would appear that little use is made in the U.K. of independent debugging tools, compared to their use worldwide. The rest of the world may have found this type of tool to be the most cost-effective in software development, yet U.K. software developers do not seem to offer these facilities to their development staff. It may be that these figures simply reflect the greater use of "home-grown" tools for debugging in the U.K., or it could be indicative of a lack of awareness of what tools are available, the additional facilities offered, and their cost-effectiveness.

One final conclusion is that the overall uptake of VV&T tools is very low at present. With the current growing concern with the production of quality software, the application of verification and testing tools will be an important growth area over the next five to ten years. The influence of Def. Stan. 00-55 will also have an effect in the increased use of static analysis tools. I believe that the pressure for increased use of such tools will probably come from purchasers and users of software systems, who will demand greater quality.

7. FUTURE DIRECTIONS IN VV&T TOOLS DEVELOPMENT

7.1 Test Management

Existing commercial tools do not yet address all of the specific problems of the management of the testing process, although many of them do offer support to some aspects of test management. Test management activities include configuration management and project management activities.

7.1.1 Configuration Management

Existing tools do offer help in configuration management of test documentation, input cases, expected output files, test outputs, discrepancy reports, etc. Of course, existing configuration management tools could also be used to keep track of test information as well as other system documentation. The author would be interested to know if any organisations use a standard CM tool mainly for test information, and if so, how well it works. An additional configuration management problem with test data is the identification of what re-tests are needed when a particular section of code is changed, i.e. what regression tests are linked to which fault reports/fixes.

Managing the progress of required regression tests is a very complex process, which is addressed by some existing tools. Are there any particular problems here, or will configuration management tools, whether specifically designed for testing or not, cope with the problems?

7.1.2 Project Management

There are as yet no commercially available tools which address the problems of planning, estimating, resourcing, scheduling, and monitoring the testing process. Perhaps existing project management tools can be used for this purpose; again, the author would like to hear from anyone who is using a PM tool for the management of the testing process. One of the fundamental problems in managing the testing process is deciding how much testing should be done; it is difficult to estimate how long a job will take if that job is not of a determined size. It may be that the testing process must first be controlled before true test management can occur. Standard models of the testing process, with roles and responsibilities clearly defined are needed first.

Managing the testing of very large systems is an area which has had very little attention paid to it, particularly the testing of large real-time systems. Are the problems of testing large systems adequately catered for by other types of test management tools? Perhaps the reason why developers of safety-critical systems are keen on static analysis tools is because they suspect that such systems are untestable within realistic constraints of timescale and budget. Static analysis is no substitute for testing, however, particularly in the system's final operating environment, if testing is possible there (which is not the case for weapons, nuclear power and chemical plants, etc.)

7.2 Individual Test Running Tools

7.2.1 Existing Tools

There seems to be good tool support for the running of individual tests, and for the linking of individual tests together to form larger test sets, by tools described as test harnesses or test drivers, although these are generally aimed at text input. Capture/playback and comparator tools help in the running and evaluation of results of individual tests, and input generators, test databases and simulators help in setting up a test environment.

7.2.2 WIMP Interface Testing

Testing the user facilities of a mouse-driven graphical interface is significantly different to testing text-based input and output. No commercially available tools are known to the author which provide capture playback or comparator facilities for such systems.

7.2.3 Real Time Test Drivers

Another area where there is no tool support known to the author as yet is in the driving of real-time individual tests of low-level modules. The major problem in testing real-time systems is that a test result is often indeterminate; because random timing can affect the order in which "parallel" processes are executed, which can give a different result every time. Locating errors in real-time software is particularly difficult when the exact conditions of a fault cannot be reproduced at will. Although simulator tools do address this problem to some extent by observing real-time events (SAW allows the tracing of timing in two processors, for example), is it possible to produce a tool that would give a pre-determined real-time test ordering, which could then be varied in a systematic way, to produce a determinate rather than indeterminate real-time testing environment?

7.2.4 Input Generation

Test input can be generated from two sources: the specification of the system (functional approach), i.e. the problem to be solved, and from the system code (structural approach), i.e. the solution to the problem. The only commercial input generation tool derives test input cases from a reasonably rigourous functional specification of the system. A prototype to derive test cases from a functional specification in narrative form is described in [Roper], but is far from being a commercial tool. There are no tools known to the author which derive input test cases based on the structure of the code. In fact, deciding which values will cause a path to be executed (also referred to as "sensitizing the path") is difficult to do manually. (But see Mutation Analysis below.) An approach based on program traces is described in [Hoffman and Brealey]. Analysis and Design (CASE) tools may be able to provide data constraints for test data based on control flow structure.

7.2.5 Debug tools for 4GL's

Are there any enhanced facility debug tools for fourth generation languages, as there are for third generation languages?

7.2.6 Selective Regression Testing

Is it possible to automate the selection of regressions tests which should be run if software is changed? This may be part of the configuration management activity for the tests, i.e. keeping track of what modules would be affected by changes in other modules.

7.2.7 Knowledge-based Testing Tools

There is as yet no known expert system which deals with software verification, validation, or testing activities, but possibilities for capturing the knowledge of the "best" testers should prove interesting.

7.3 Test Quality Evaluation Tools

Evaluating the quality of the testing process and the test input data used is an area which is addressed by existing tools but only in one area, that of structural coverage. Other types of coverage would give additional confidence that the testing of the system was adequate.

7.3.1 Structural Coverage

Measurement of the percentage of coverage of statements, branches, and LCSAJ's (Linear Code Sequence and Jump) are done by existing tools, and measure the "goodness" of the test data by how much of the control flow structure has been exercised. Although this does give some relative idea of the width of the testing, it is far from sufficient. A test set which covers all of the control structure does not necessarily exercise the software adequately.

7.3.2 Functional Coverage

It is possible to measure some types of functional coverage, which would give another dimension in which to look at test adequacy. One possible coverage measure might be the percentage of boundary value conditions exercised by a test set. No commercial tools are known to the author which measure functional coverage, although a research prototype has been developed by Marc Roper of Strath-Clyde University [Roper].

7.3.3 Data Coverage

Recent research from the U.S. indicates that measuring the coverage of data definition-use pairs may be an effective coverage measurement. [Rapps and Weyuker], [Bieman and Schultz]. No existing tools are known to the author.

7.3.4 Mutation Testing

A Mutation testing tool (Mothra) has been developed in the U.S. [DeMillo et al] but is not a commercially available tool. The prototype includes input generation, comparison and debugging facilities, and gives the prospect of the whole of the testing process being completely automated (except when errors or deficiencies of the test data or live mutants are found). The mutation testing tool has been used to test 1000 line of code within a week. Perhaps this machine-intensive technique will become feasible in the future.

7.4 Conclusions

Software testing is an area of software development which has not received a great deal of attention from software engineers in the past, in spite of the fact that often nearly half of the development cost will be spent on testing. Testing has often been perceived as a tedious activity, yet it is seldom adequately tool-supported.

The growing interest in producing quality software products will lead to an increasing interest in and use of verification and testing tools. There is great scope for new tools in existing tool classifications, and also for new types of verification and testing tools.

8. Acknowledgements

Thanks to Blenheim Online for permission to reproduce this paper for SE90. The work on which this paper is based was partially funded by the National Computing Centre and Unicom Seminars. Thanks also to Jon Craton of IPL and Ray Lewis of British Telecom for helpful comments and suggestions.

9. REFERENCES

Abbott, Joe. Software Test Aids, A State of the Art Report, The National Computing Centre, 1985.

Beizer, Boris. Software Testing Techniques. Van Nostrand Reinhold, 1983.

Bieman, James M. and Schultz, Janet L., "Estimating the Number of Test Cases Required to Satisfy the All-du-paths Testing Criterion", Proceedings of the ACM SIGSOFT '90 Third Symposium on Software Testing, Analysis, and Verification (TAV3), Software Engineering Notes, Vol 14, No. 8, Dec. 89, Ed. Richard A. Kemmerer, ACM Press, 1989, pp. 179 - 186.

Boehm, Barry W. Software Engineering Economics, Prentice-Hall, 1981.

Carre, B. A. Validation Techniques, in Software Engineering for Microprocessor Systems, ed. P. Depledge. Peter Peregrinns, 1984.

Deutsch, Michael S. Software Verification and Validation: Realistic Project Approaches. Prentice-Hall, 1982.

DeMillo, Richard A., Krauser, E. W., Martin, R. J., Offutt, A. J. and Spafford, E. H., "The Mothra Tools Set", SERC-TR-23-P, Software Engineering Research Center, Purdue University, W. Lafayette, Indiana, U.S. A. 47907, June, 1988.

DeMillo, Richard A., McCracken, W. Michael, Martin, R. J., and Passafiume, John F. Software Testing and Evaluation. Benjamin/Cummings, 1987.

Gilb, Tom. Principles of Software Engineering Management. Addison-Wesley, 1988.

Gilb, Tom. Software Engineering Design. manuscript, 1989.

Goodenough, John B., "A Survey of Program Testing Issues", in Research Directions in Software Technology, ed. Peter Wegner, Massachusetts Institute of Technology, 1979.

Graham, Dorothy R. Software Test and Debug: Techniques and Tools, Technical Report for the Software Engineering Circle, The National Computing Centre, 1989/90.

Graham, Dorothy R., principal researcher: "Software Testing Tools Report", Unicom Seminars, to be published 1990/91.

Hetzel, Bill. The Complete Guide to Software Testing. QED, 1988.

Hoffman, Daniel and Brealey, Christopher, "Module Test Case Generation", Proceedings of the ACM SIGSOFT '90 Third Symposium on Software Testing, Analysis, and Verification (TAV3), Software Engineering Notes, Vol 14, No. 8, Dec. 89, Ed. Richard A. Kemmerer, ACM Press, 1989, pp. 97 - 102.

Kaner, Cem. Testing Computer Software. Tab Books, 1988.

Miller, Edward and Howden, William E. Tutorial: Software Testing and Validation Techniques, IEEE Computer Society, 1978.

Myers, Glenford J. The Art of Software Testing. John Wiley & Sons, 1979.

The National Computing Centre, "Software Tools for Verification, Validation and Testing", 1989.

Pressman, Roger S. Software Engineering: A Practitioner's Approach. McGraw-Hill, 1987.

Parrington, Norman and Roper, Marc. Understanding Software Testing. Ellis Horwood, 1990.

Rapps, S. and Weyuker, E. J., "Selecting software test data using data flow information", IEEE Trans. Software Engineering, SE-11, Vol 4, pp 367 - 375, April, 1985.

Roper, Marc, "The Automatic Generation of Test Cases", Testing Large Software Systems, Seminar Series on New Directions in Software Development, Wolverhampton Polytechnic, March, 1990.

Software Quality Engineering, "Testing Tools Reference Guide", SQE, 3000-2 Harley Road, Jacksonville, FL 32257 U.S.A., 1990.

Saib, Sabine H. RXVP - Today and Tomorrow, in Software Validation, ed. Hans-Ludwig Hausen. North-Holland, 1984.

Selby, Richard W. , Combining Software Testing Strategies; An Empirical Evaluation, Proceedings of the Workshop on Software Testing, IEEE Computer Society, July 1986, pp 82 - 90.

Table 1. Tool Classification Table

Tool Name	Cap	Com	In	Ver	Sim	Har	Cov	Dbg	DB	Cost	Supplier
ABEND-AID								x		£7K	Compuware
CICS DBUG-AID								x		£8K	Compuware
CICS PLAYBACK	x	x								£8K	Compuware
EVALUATOR	x	x			x					£3K	QA Training
FILE-AID									x	£7K	Compuware
LOGISCOPE			x			x				£10K+	Verilog
MALPAS				x						£14K+	Rex Thompson
OLIVER						x	x			£17K+	APT
PATHVU			x							£25K	XA Systems
PRO-QUEST			x			x				£4K+	John Bell
SIMON						x	x			£13K+	APT
SOFTEST		x			x					£7.5K+	IPL
SOFTORG		x	x		x	x			x	£10K	Densitron
SOFTPROBE II				x		x	x			£3K+	Warren Point
SAW						x	x			£29K	Instrumatic
SPADE			x							£19K+	PVL
TESTA	x			x						£4K+	John Bell
TESTBED			x			x				£8K+	Program Analysers
TESTGEN			x							£13K	Gerrard S/W
TEST MANAGER		x			x					£18K	MSP
VAX DTM	x	x			x					£1-30K	DEC
VAX PCA						x				£1-27K	DEC
XPEDITER						x	x			£50K	Topdata
XPF						x	x			£30K+	Pansophic
XRAY				x				x		£2K+	Microtec
Tool Name	Cap	Com	In	Ver	Sim	Har	Cov	Dbg	DB	Cost	Supplier

Table 2. Tool Environment Table.

Tool Name	Ap	Dec	HP	IBM	pc	ICL	Sun	oth	Cost	Supplier
ABEND-AID				x					£7K	Compuware
CICS DBUG-AID				x					£8K	Compuware
CICS PLAYBACK				x					£8K	Compuware
EVALUATOR					x				£3K	QA Training
FILE-AID				x					£7K	Compuware
LOGISCOPE	x	x		x			x	x	£10K+	Verilog
MALPAS		x							£14K+	Rex Thompson
OLIVER				x					£17K+	APT
PATHVU				x		x		x	£25K	XA Systems
PRO-QUEST		x			x				£4K+	John Bell
SIMON				x					£13K+	APT
SOFTEST	x	x	x		x		x	x	£7K+	IPL
SOFTORG				x					£10K	Densitron
SOFTPROBE II		x			x			x	£3K+	Warren Point
SAW								x	£29K	Instrumatic
SPADE		x							£19K+	PVL
TESTA					x			x	£4K+	John Bell
TESTBED	x	x	x	x		x	x	x	£8K+	Program Analysers
TESTGEN		x							£13K	Gerrard S/W
TEST MANAGER				x					£18K	MSP
VAX DTM		x							£1-30K	DEC
VAX PCA		x							£1-27K	DEC
XPEDITER				x					£50K	Topdata
XPF				x					£30K+	Pansophic
XRAY	x	x	x		x		x		£2K+	Microtec
Tool Name	Ap	Dec	HP	IBM	pc	ICL	Sun	oth	Cost	Supplier

Appendix: List of Supplier Names and Addresses for VV&T Tools,
Products included in this paper's analysis:

Dr. Duncan Clutterbuck,
Program Validation Ltd,
26 Queens Terrace,
Southampton, Hampshire SO1 1BQ
Product: SPADE
Telephone: 0703 - 330001

Mr. Alan Barker,
Program Analysers Ltd,
56 Northbrook Street,
Newbury, Berkshire RG13 1AN
Product: TESTBED
Telephone: 0635 - 528828

Mr. Chris Gerrard,
Gerrard Software Ltd,
Venture House,
Cross Street,
Macclesfield Cheshire SK11 7PG,
Product: TESTGEN
Telephone: 0625 - 612846

Mr. John Annis,
Manager Software Products Ltd,
4th floor Thames Tower,
99 Burleys Way, Leicester LE1 3TT
Product: TESTMANAGER
Telephone: 0553 - 537999

Software Technical Support,
Digital Equipment Co Ltd,
Queen's House,
Forbury Road,
Reading Berks RG1 3JJ
Products: VAX DEC/TEST MANAGER and VAX PERFORMANCE & COVERAGE ANALYZER
Telephone: 0734 - 393200

Appendix: List of Supplier Names and Addresses for VV&T Tools,
Products included in this paper's analysis:

Mr. David Alexander,
Topdata Software UK Ltd,
Barbican House,
26/34 Old Street, London EC1V 9HL
Product: XPEDITER
Telephone: 01 - 250 - 1774

Mr. Graham Williams,
Pansophic Systems UK Ltd,
Pansophic House, No. 1 York Road,
Uxbridge Middlesex UK8 1RN
Product: XPF
Telephone: 0895 - 72501

Mr. Robert Day,
Microtec Research Ltd,
Ringway House,
Bell Road
Daneshill, Basingstoke RG24 0FB
Product: XRAY
Telephone: 0256 - 57551

Products not included in this paper's analysis:

Ms. Dee Collins,
MicroFocus Europe Ltd.,
26 West Street,
Newbury, Berkshire RG13 1JT
Product: ANIMATOR
Telephone: 0635 - 32646/32595

Mr. Stuart Morrice,
Direct Technology Ltd.,
Grove House
551 London Road,
Isleworth, Middlesex TW7 4DS
Product: AUTOMATOR/mi
Telephone: 01 - 847 - 1611/3911

Appendix: List of Supplier Names and Addresses for VV&T Tools,
Products not included in this paper's analysis:

Mr. Diarmuid MacDonald,
Sterling Software International (U.K.) Ltd.,
64 - 78 Kingsway,
London, WC2B 6AL
Products: AUTOTEST and COMPAREX
Telephone: 01 - 528 - 8333

Mr. Graham Oliver,
C.A. Computer Associates Ltd.,
Computer Associates House
183/187 Bath Road,
Slough, Berks. SL1 4AA
Products: CA-DATAMACS/II, CA-EZTEST/CICS, CA-OPTIMIZER
Telephone: 0753 - 777333

Ms. Caroline Tee
On-Line Software International Ltd
Tenterden House,
3, Tenterden Street
Hanover Square
London W1R 9AH
Products: DATAVANTAGE, INTERTEST, SIMDUMP, and VERIFY
Telephone: 01 - 631 - 3696

Mr. Dennis Foreman
Programming Research Ltd.,
Kings Avenue House,
King's Avenue,
New Malden, Surrey KT3 4BY
Product: FLINT
Telephone: 01 - 942 - 9242

Defect Removal Models: Theory and Practice

MICHAEL COLEMAN, JOHN ALLAN

Product Assurance Laboratory
IBM United Kingdom Laboratories Ltd
Hursley Park
Winchester SO21 2JN
U.K.

1 ABSTRACT

The paper describes the use of a Defect Removal Model (DRM) within the software development life-cycle.

It covers both the basic theory of DRMs - their design and content - and the practical aspects of their use as predictors of software quality. Throughout the paper we endeavour to provide an objective commentary as to the usefulness of defect removal modelling within a software engineering environment. In this respect, and with an eye to the gradual maturing of CASE tools, the importance of automating all aspects of the modelling process is emphasised.

2 INTRODUCTION

Curious as it may seem, a major unit of measure for the quality of a software product is that of the defect. A defect - a failure of the software to meet its specification in some way - is a necessary evil; a by-product of a creative process. It is in this inevitability that the seeker of software quality finds a virtue. The guarantee that defects will be present in some number is a common point of reference between and within software products. The challenge is to use that commonality to good effect.

And it IS a challenge. For the finding of large numbers of defects could be an indicator of highly efficient testing and, thus, of high quality software. But it could also, of course, be an indicator that many have been found because many exist, and that the software is of appalling quality. The challenge is in determining which case applies.

The requirement, therefore, is for some sort of modelling technique based on the recognition of defects and which lends itself to unambiguous interpretation. In the first half of this paper we describe such an approach - the Defect Removal Model (DRM) - and the principles upon which it is based; in the second part of the paper we examine the extent to which, in practice, the use of a DRM is able to satisfy such a requirement.

3 THEORY: DEFECT REMOVAL MODELS

The form of a Defect Removal Model is that of a two-dimensional matrix. Figure 1 illustrates a simple DRM.

```
'Simple' Defect Removal Model

            Defects  Defects  Total    Removal  Defects  Defects  Fix
            Brought  Added    Defects  Effic'y  Out      Left     Inject
            Forward                    %                          Rate
            -----------------------------------------------------------
            Calc     Est      Calc     Est      Calc     Calc     Est
            -----------------------------------------------------------
PreDesign   0.00     9.00     9.00     60.00    5.40     3.60
Design      3.60     18.00    21.60    55.00    11.88    9.72
Code        9.72     9.00     18.72    20.00    3.74     14.98
Unit Test   14.98    1.87     16.85    35.00    5.90     10.95    0.13
FV Test     10.95    1.37     12.32    85.00    10.47    1.85     0.13
System Test 1.85     0.23     2.08     65.00    1.35     0.73     0.13

            -----------------------------------------------------------
Total Product                                            0.73
            -----------------------------------------------------------
```

Figure 1. Example of 'Simple' Defect Removal Model

In general terms, each row of the model represents a phase of the development and testing process in use, typically ranging from Pre-Design through to System Test. The columns of the matrix reflect the passage of defects (in terms of errors/thousand lines of code) during any phase as follows:

- **Defects Brought Forward** - Defects remaining from the previous phase. Note that the PreDesign phase need not always be zero! A follow-up release of an existing product would 'bring forward' the earlier release's final 'defects left' value.

- **Defects Added** - An estimate of the number of defects that will be added during this phase.

- **Total Defects** - Sum of the previous two elements, giving a total number of defects moving into the removal process.

- **Removal Efficiency** - An estimate of the percentage of defects being removed for this phase.

- **Defects Out** - Computation of actual numbers of defects being removed per KLoc, given the estimated removal efficiency.

- **Defects Left** - Defects remaining, either to be taken forward to the next phase or - the bottom line - remaining in the final product.

- **Fix Inject Rate** - A feedback value, for the test phases, reflecting the number of defects introduced in fixing other defects! The value in the example represents 1 new defect for every 8 fixed.

In summary: defects are brought forward from the previous stage of the process; augmented by further defects generated by new development work; and a proportion subsequently removed, according to some removal efficiency figure, to give both estimates of defects resolved during the phase and of defects which survive to pass on to the subsequent phase.

Those defects left after the final phase (System Test in our example) are a measure of the product's code quality.

The simple model, however, assumes that all code will be developed by means of the same development process - in our example, a classic 'waterfall' process. This will not always be so. Different development processes might quite validly be applied to different major sections of the code. This will quite properly be the case where a large part of the code is ported from a previous release. Less validly, but perhaps more realistically, some parts of the development process will be ignored when the pressure is on - design reviews of emergency design changes, for instance, have a habit of being omitted.

Thus the simple model of Figure 1 will invariably be extended into the more complex form illustrated by the example given in Figure 2.

```
'Complex' Defect Removal Model

Note - Figures are Errors/Kloc
            Defects  Defects   Total   Removal  Defects  Defects    Fix
            Brought  Added    Defects  Effic'y    Out     Left    Inject
            Forward                       %                        Rate
            ----------------------------------------------------------
             Calc    Est      Calc     Est      Calc    Calc      Est
            ----------------------------------------------------------
Code Development Process 1 (9.05 KLoc) :
  PreDesign    0.00   10.00    10.00    60.00    6.00    4.00
  Design/Code  4.00   34.00    38.00    60.00   22.80   15.20
  Unit Test   15.20    1.23    16.43    60.00    9.86    6.57     0.13
  Build Ver'n  6.57    0.04     6.61     5.00    0.33    6.28     0.13
  FV Test      6.28    0.60     6.89    70.00    4.82    2.07     0.13

Code Development Process 2 (4.64 KLoc) :
  PreDesign    0.00   10.00    10.00    60.00    6.00    4.00
  HLD          4.00   15.00    19.00    60.00   11.40    7.60
  LLD          7.60   18.00    25.60    60.00   15.36   10.24
  Code        10.24   20.00    30.24    60.00   18.14   12.10
  Unit Test   12.10    0.98    13.08    60.00    7.85    5.23     0.13
  Build Ver'n  5.23    0.03     5.26     5.00    0.26    5.00     0.13
  FV Test      5.00    0.48     5.48    70.00    3.84    1.64     0.13

Code Ported (262.00 KLoc) :
  Build Ver'n  0.82    0.01     0.83     5.00    0.04    0.78     0.13
  FV Test      0.78    0.01     0.79    10.00    0.08    0.71     0.13

System Test (35.81 New/Changed & 262.00 Ported KLoc) :
  New & Chg    1.84    0.16     2.01    65.00    1.31    0.70     0.13
  Ported       0.71    0.01     0.72    10.00    0.07    0.65     0.13

            ----------------------------------------------------------
Total Product                                            0.66
            ----------------------------------------------------------
```

Figure 2. Example of 'Complex' Defect Removal Model

Here, two different development process sections, and a ported code section each generate a 'defects left' value (2.07, 1.64, 0.71 defects/KLoc respectively) following the completion of Functional Verification testing. The procedure now is simply to combine these values into a weighted average 'defects brought forward' value (of 1.84) to take into the System Test phase.

Although the numbers of identifiably different processes are likely to be few, there is no reason why this approach could not be adopted for any number of development processes. Whether or not this is advisable is a matter for judgement. The best yardstick to apply is: does the process generate a significant percentage of the final code (and, by implication, a significant number of the total defects)? If so, then it is worth creating a separate section of the DRM to reflect that process.

4 THEORY: THE DRM AS A (POTENTIAL) PREDICTIVE TOOL

In theory, a DRM delivers information which is widely applicable to meeting both project schedule and code quality targets.

'Defects Out' figures, and the bottom line 'defects remaining in the product' provide an estimate both of what should be achieved during inspection and test phases and what remains to be achieved after the product has been shipped. This enables various assessments to be made:

- how much effort will be involved in finding the expected number of defects? (bearing in mind that the model refers to valid defects only, and that to this figure has to be added the invalid defect reports which are an inevitable by-product of the testing process)

- for a fixed level of resource, how long will any particular testing phase have to last in order that the required number of defects be found?

- Given the defects/KLoc remaining in the product, what level of service activity needs to be catered for?

In addition, the outputs from the model provide a yardstick by which likely code quality can be assessed, for an acceptable matching of predicted defects against actual defects for any development phase is a useful indicator that the developed product is on track to meet its quality goal. A particular phase which proves to be deficient in the number of defects found should trigger an investigation since it may mean that corrective action of some form will be needed. This need not be the case, since good design by an experienced team would also be expected to lead to fewer inspection errors being detected; the important thing is that deviation from the model is seen as a warning of potential trouble and that the reasons for the deviation need to be understood. If the deviation is not indicative of goodness appropriate corrective action may then be taken.

For instance, should fewer defects than anticipated have been found during the high-level design phase then some of the options to consider would include:

- additional design reviews

- revised plans for additional testing (with all the schedule implications which that holds)

- acceptance - perish the thought! - of a higher number of defects left on the bottom line.

At the end of the project, a comparison of the numbers of defects actually found against the numbers predicted by the model will suggest those phases of the process which were delinquent and which should be improved next time round.

5 PRACTICE: THE DYNAMICS OF A DRM

The astute reader will have spotted a certain amount of chicken-and-eggedness about what has been presented so far. The outputs from a DRM depend on the 'inputs': for each phase, estimates of how many defects will be added, and how efficiently they will be removed. But where do these estimates come from? The answer, of course, is from previously successful DRMs.

Generating the primeval DRM is something of a problem, therefore. In the absence of any information from previous projects, estimates of defect removal efficiencies and errors added are going to be highly dependent on which way the wind is blowing.

But what if data is available? Even then, the DRM 'inputs' are going to be estimates and nothing more. Products, even follow-on releases of a product, are not going to follow the same development pattern as their predecessors. For one thing, even though the development process might be the same, the developers might not.

Consider some of the factors that might increase/decrease the DRM 'defects added' estimate during the code phase:

- experience of coder
- coder's familiarity with programming language
- programming language being used
- program development tools being used
- etc .....

Similarly, what might increase/decrease the 'defect removal efficiency' for a design phase:

- number of review meetings
- experience of reviewers
- experience of designers
- design tools being used
- etc .....

Practical point number one, therefore, is that a DRM is not a precision instrument (in spite of the fact that it uses numbers to two places of decimals). It is an indicator, a tool which provides information from which assessments can be made and corrective actions triggered. Assuming, that is, that the model bears some resemblance to reality: that it is a valid indicator of what is actually happening.

For this to be the case, practical point number two is that DRMs cannot be regarded as static. The initial model, generated as part of the product's quality plan, has to be regarded as just that: an initial estimate. As the development process proceeds, and actual figures become available, the DRM must be refined in the light of investigations into an understanding of why any deviations have occurred. Deviations may be signs of goodness or badness; what is important is that the DRM reflects them.

6 PRACTICE: A DRM'S RING OF CONFIDENCE

6.1 Monitoring and Validating

The message of the previous section is that devising a DRM is not enough. To such models must be allied approaches which continually monitor, and ultimately verify, the results obtained; only in this way can one attain a sufficiently high level of confidence in the interpretations of quality derived from the model.

In this section we outline three such approaches as representative of what needs to be done throughout the development cycle: statistical quality control of design inspections; test tracking - during the functional verification phase - of actual defects found against the predictions of a DRM; and removal efficiency pairing analyses.

6.2 Statistical Quality Control

The objective of a Statistical Quality Control (SQC) tecnique is two-fold:

- To track the total number of problems (as defects/KLoc) actually found for an inspection stage against the number the DRM is predicting.

- To ensure that consistency is being achieved across the set of inspections conducted during any phase.

In practice, a project is split into a number of components. These generally represent different functional areas of the product and are allocated to different groups of people. The process applied to the inspections is the same, but the inspections are carried out by different people. The use of Control Charts establishes confidence that the process is being applied equitably by all groups. If this is so, then results should indicate comparable defect rates being found by the different inspection groups.

A Control Chart is a time-series graph of a quality measurement plotted against time, with the addition of Action and Warning lines to provide reference values for interpretation: that is, for a first level application of statistical inference.

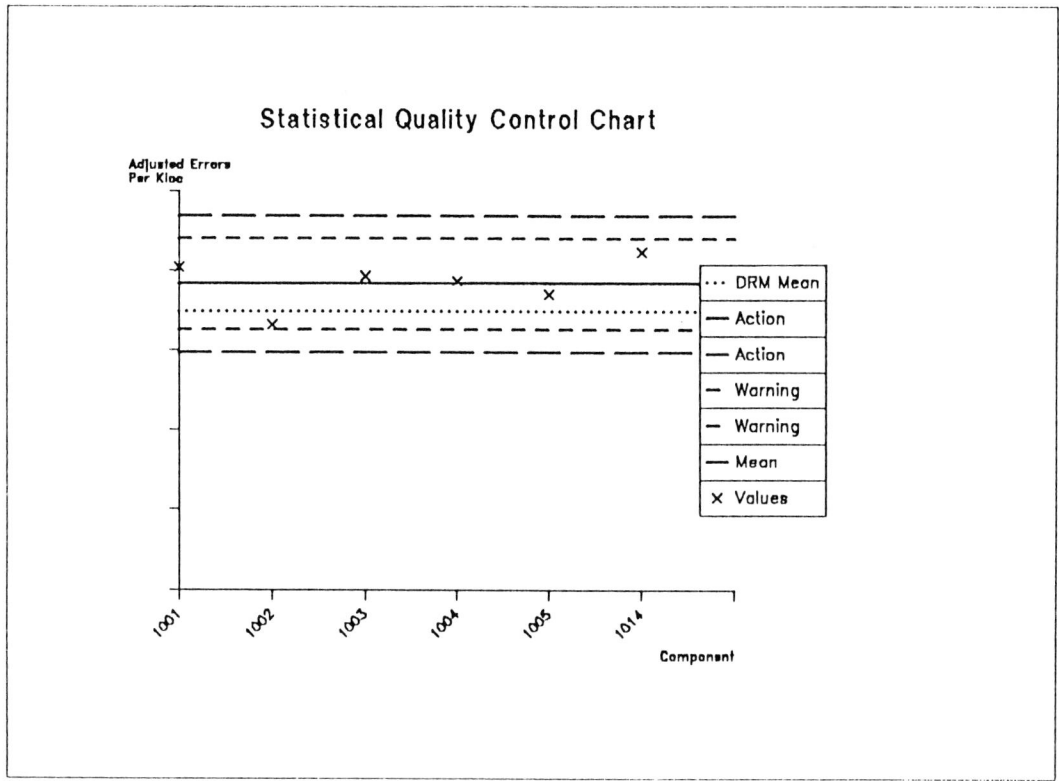

Figure 3. Statistical Quality Control Chart

To compensate for the fact that inspections are being conducted on components of different 'sizes', an algorithm is employed which uses the normal computed mean as the basis for computing an 'adjusted' errors per KLoc value. In this way the adjusted error for each inspection takes into account sample size, so that smaller components have less weight accorded to their 'defects found' counts.

An example of the final chart is shown as Figure 3.

Normally, it would be expected that :

- the observed mean is consistent with the DRM mean
- all data points would lie within the boundaries defined by the Warning lines.

Deviation from either would result in some action being taken. Typical actions might be :

- Observed Mean inconsistent with DRM Mean

Understand why! Analyse the DRM assumptions and why the process does not match them. Use information to reset remainder of DRM and for future DRMs.

- Data point outside Warning line

    Check the component to see if similar results were obtained on previous stages. If they were, analyse the component for complexity. If this is unique, place emphasis on tracking the component through later stages.

- Data point outside Action line

    Needs immediate investigation and possible re-inspection. Work to understand the reason for that number of problems.

6.3 Test Tracking

It is self-evident that a DRM generates defect totals : the total number of defects expected to be discovered during the Functional Verification (FV) testing phase, for instance. Thus the comparison of defects predicted against defects actually found can only truly be made at the end of the phase. Given a good correlation between predicted and actual defects this is no problem. Less acceptable though, is the converse - of discovering a serious imbalance at or near phase end.

Testing, moreover, tends not to be a process to which SQC methods can be readily applied since the individual test cases would normally each be generating small numbers of defects.

The task of tracking defects found during a testing phase, therefore, assumes considerable importance. The technique must give an indication of the progress of the test phase, bearing in mind that not all of the code may have been tested (or even written!) as yet. As an example, consider the problem of tracking Functional Verification (FV) testing.

The delivery of code into FV is phased, additional function being delivered into FV through a series of 'drivers': subset versions of the final product. This process if defined by a Driver Plan, which details the constitution of each and every driver in terms of its functional elements (new code, ported code, code developed following design change requests, or whatever) and the dates upon which those drivers will be available for FV testing. It will also, again for each functional element, define its KLoc size, initially as an estimated figure but ultimately the delivered number of Locs.

From this information, and the DRM values for expected defects/KLoc found by the FV phases of each development process, a composite plot can be produced showing the anticipated progress of defect detection throughout the duration of the FV phase. This is illustrated by the solid line of Figure 4.

Note that the plot exhibits an implied assumption, namely that all defects relating to any one driver will be detected during the life-span of that driver; in other words, by the time the next driver is delivered into FV. This is something of a simplification, of course, but not unacceptable; testing will tend to focus on the new function being delivered in a driver, if only because other tests are held up awaiting fixes, and thus the defect removal curve would reasonably be expected to follow the shape of the projected defects curve.

(As a small digression, note that throughout this paper we have only considered DRM examples which exhibit 'certainty' defect removal, ie defects will be removed with an x% efficiency. An extension currently being explored is that of DRM's which incorporate 'uncertainty' by allowing, for instance, defect removal efficiencies to be defined as lying between some upper and lower bounds. In the context of the example of Figure 4, three plots - upper, median and lower - would be produced for projected defects found).

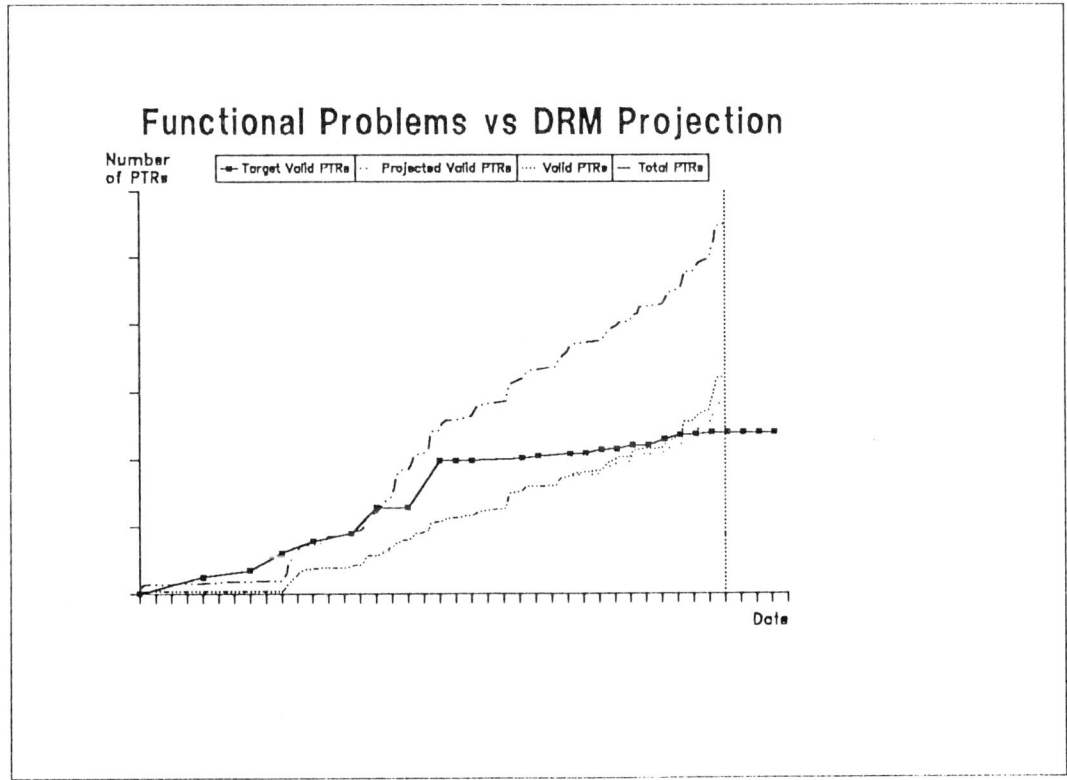

Figure 4. Tracking FV Test against a DRM

In brief, we now plot on the same axes curves showing actual numbers of defects found (total and valids only) together with a projection as to the final number of valid defects expected, given the number found so far. The outcome is a chart which indicates very clearly the progress of FV testing against the DRM. The principle could, of course, be extended to cover any test phase in the same way.

6.4 Defect Removal Efficiency Pairing
Further confidence can be gained for the DRM overall by conducting verification tests on the 'defect removal efficiencies' of any pair of phases. Most commonly this would be carried out for the final two phases - Functional Verification (FV) and System Test (ST).

In brief, the technique involves estimating the probability distribution of each defect removal efficiency (DRE) and operates as follows.

Knowing the actual number of defects, x, removed during the FV test phase, a range of DRE values is used so as to compute a corresponding range of values for 'defects carried forward' into the ST phase. With this range of values, and using a second range of DRE values for the ST phase, it is now possible to compute a range of 'defects left' values for the product as a whole. This information is plotted on a chart such as Figure 5.

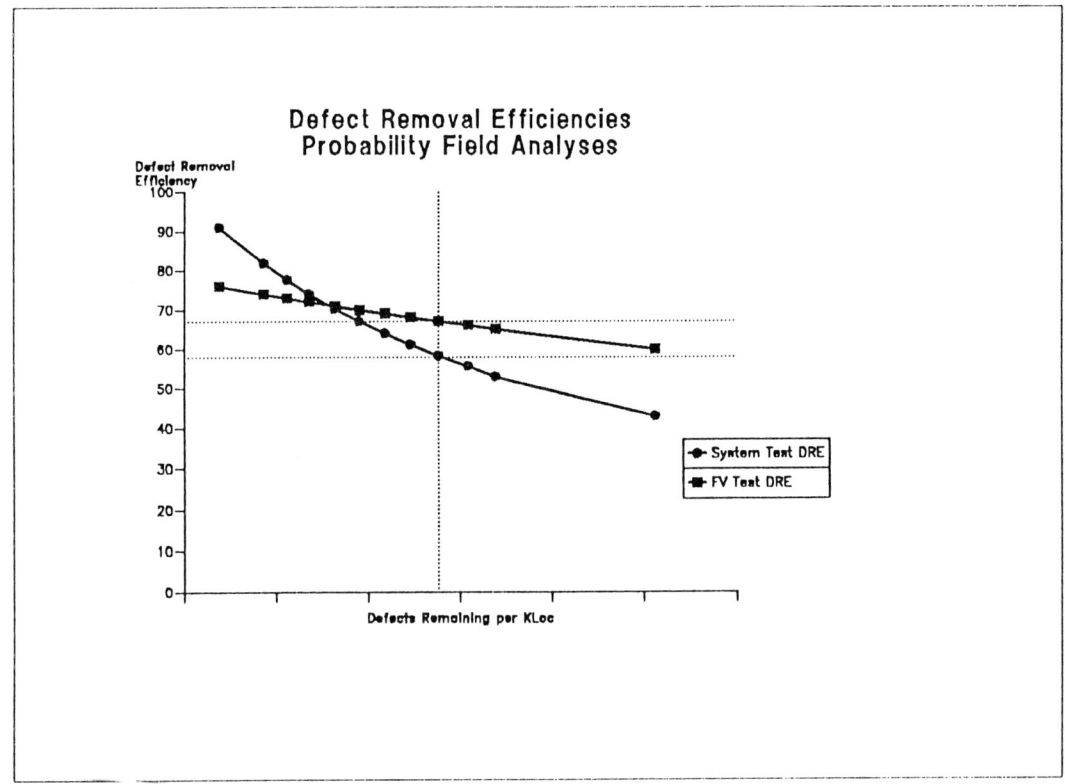

Figure 5. Probability Analyses of FV/ST Defect Removal Efficiencies

The important fact to note is that the points on the two curves are tied; it is not possible to choose the best possible DRE for FV testing, for instance, without justifiably being able to accept the tied DRE value for ST (in the example given, over 90% - not an easy justification to make!)

Selecting, therefore, the tied pair of efficiencies which are most in concert with the results obtained from the other DRMd tracking techniques, the perpendicular dropping down to the X-axis indicates the 'defects remaining' value which is most likely. (Or, alternatively the most likely bounds for defects remaining if two perpendiculars are dropped from the two most likely tied pairs of DRE values.

This is a technique that can be applied throughout the DRM to tie successive phases together and give clear confidence ranges for the 'defects left' values being passed on to subsequent phases. As with the other techniques, however, it is no more than an indicator, a confidence builder in the integrity of the DRM as a whole; it is still dependent upon the experience of the user.

7 FUTURE PRACTICE: AUTOMATED DEFECT REMOVAL MODELLING

The stress laid in this paper on the dynamicism of the DRM has an implication both now and, as CASE tools mature, in the future. In the first respect, monitoring and verification of a DRM needs to be a continual process. Much calculation is required - both as regards the DRM itself and in capturing and analysing defect data. This suggests, since tedium is a powerful disincentive, that the techniques employed must be capable of automation.

Perhaps more importantly, there are the implications for the future of such modelling in the CASE environment. To whatever extent the development process becomes automated, parallel automation of quality tracking must follow. CASE tools will claim to improve quality - but unless they can maintain and process quality assessment and tracking data how can the claim be proved?

Experience with the techniques outlined above suggests that the incorporation of an automated quality model such as a DRM within a CASE environment should present no insuperable problem. Much of what has been described has been automated through stand-alone systems. The fundamental requirements are:

- A means of storing and manipulating the DRM itself (equivalent to a spreadsheet capability), together with the means of exporting selected elements such as 'defects out' predictions.

- A statistics package - nothing spectacular, simply capable of computing such basics as probabilities, standard deviations and the like.

- A directory of the product's component parts, with such information as component size and composition.

- A support database in which can be recorded the results of design reviews - defects found, cause, valid/invalid etc.

- A driver plan for phased testing processes, containing details of components being delivered into test, their size, and the type of development process used (relating to the DRM).

- A defect reports database, with each defect recorded in terms of its source, the date on which it was opened, its current status, cause when known, valid/invalid etc.

- A chart generation utility - capable of importing data from various sources and presenting it in the form of line graphs/histograms/pie charts as required.

Many of these - component directory, reviews/defect reports databases for instance, would be central to the CASE environment anyway; what is not so certain, unless stipulated at the outset, is that the facilities will be able to support product quality tracking as well as product development.

8 SUMMARY

A Defect Removal Model is a valuable tool for both prognosing the volumes of defects to be found during a product's development life-cycle, and for providing a measure of final code quality at the end of that cycle. It is an indicator, however, not a precision instrument.

A DRM is only as good as the data upon which it is based. Whether or not previous experience data is incorporated into the DRM, a continual process of evaluation and validation needs to be conducted throughout the development life-cycle. The DRM is to be regarded as a dynamic model, with actual defect data being used to refine the model at all stages. Validation promotes confidence.

Automation of the DRM and its associated processes is highly desirable. Continuous assessment is extremely difficult unless a degree of automation is present; timeliness is impossibly difficult unless the extraction of actual, as well as predicted, defects is not automated.

9 ACKNOWLEDGEMENT

Thanks are due to Alex Down, of the Product Assurance Laboratory, IBM United Kingdom Laboratories Ltd, Hursley, for details of the probability-field method for assessing defect removal efficiency pairs.

Analysis and Design

Designing Systems with Objects, Processes and Modules, B. Kirk
The Synthesis of Object-Oriented Designs from the Products of Structured Analysis, P. Sully & D. Ince

Designing Systems with Objects, Processes and Modules

B. R. KIRK MSc, MBCS

Robinson Associates, Red Lion House, St Mary's Street,
Painswick, Glos GL6 6QR, United Kingdom

ABSTRACT

This paper is concerned with the fundamental problem of how to make the design of large systems intellectually manageable. The literature is littered with methodologies which favour this or that approach to the problem. Nearly always they reflect the rather narrow interests of their sponsors. The situation is now acute as well as chronic as we try to design larger and more reliable systems in a shorter time. An approach that has proved successul for creating large real time and database based products is described.

1 OBJECTS, PROCESSES AND MODULES

The approach we describe for resolving the dilemma is pragmatic. It is based on a cocktail of concepts which have already been proved to be effective. Our only contribution is to point out how they can be used together productively.

Figure 1 is an adaption of Grady Boochs [1] excellent picture of 'what programming is about'. Really programming is all about modelling a solution to a problem, using the processor(s) to activate some precise description of the solution. In the Figure the problem contains objects which have various relations with each other, they all have experiences as time passes and/or events occur. This leads to the state of the objects changing.

Systems and software engineering is all about how we choose to **represent** these real objects (be they aeroplanes or humble invoices) within a modelled world. We have to choose representations for each object's information, state, behaviour and its relations with the other objects. As all designers know the choices of representation should be formed by the functionality of the problem; in practice the constraints usually cause a lot of design distortion (programming a real time system in FORTRAN for example).

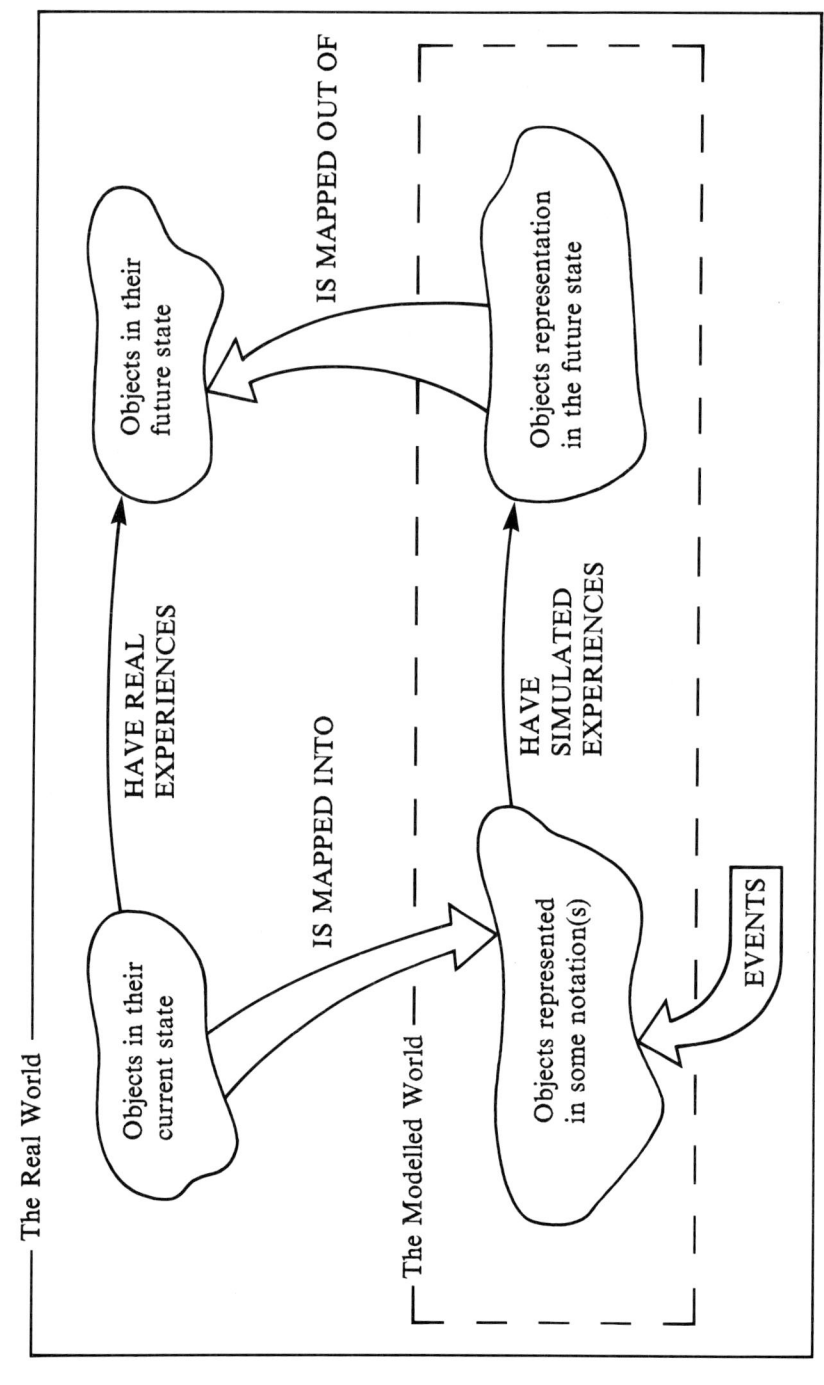

Figure 1 "What programming is all about"

The diagram below shows our dilemma ...

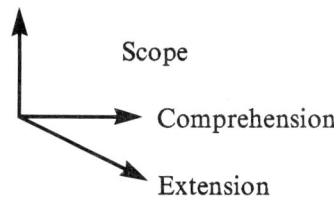

The **scope** of what is requested seems only to be limited by what can be imagined. Somehow as designers we must gain **comprehension** of all the implications of the whole system in all its states. And most taxing of all we must provide accurate solutions that support **extensions** to match the requirements as they evolve.

1.1 Using Relevant Abstractions

Engineers analyse problems using concepts and then synthesize their solution by organising some physical form, in this case the software part of the system. The diagram shows the main criteria ...

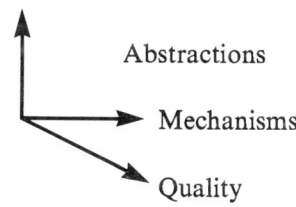

The **abstractions** we use to analyse and model the problem have evolved over the past 40 years of computing, these include

Machine Codes	- numbers representing instructions, data and locations
Names	- for instructions, data and locations
Macros	- to encapsulate and reuse the text of sequences of instructions or data
Procedures	- to envapsulate and reuse sequences of instructions at run time
Control Structures	- to encapsulate the flow of control

Classes	- to encapsulate evolutionary definitions in a reusable and extensible way
Modules	- to encapsulate whole components, hiding information and/or ownership
Extensible Modules	- to encapsulate objects which have statically related definitions
Delegating Objects	- to encapsulate objects which are dynamically related and extensible. An object which cannot provide a requested method delegates it to another object which can.

Languages provide a means to express solutions to problems in terms of these abstractions, for example, Assembler, Algol, Simula, Modula-2, Oberon, Ada, Delegate. **The trend in abstraction is towards an object oriented approach because this minimises the conceptual distance between the problem and its programmed solution:**

"the solution is a simulation of the problem"

The **mechanisms** are simply ways of achieving something [2]. For example modules M1 and M2 provide an interface between various tasks in two processors. Typically module M1 might provide a clean interface to some old software that has become fossilised. This makes it possible to reuse the vast majority of the original software with minimal changes. Of course M2 completely hides the details of the interface from all the new software. By using modules on each side to encapsulate the mechanisms it becomes possible to change the mechanism separately from the rest of the system. We have found that a good test for the quality of a module's interface is to consider how much it would need to change if the mechanism it encapsulates had to change, but not necessarily the functionality.

The **quality** of the implementation is the third main factor. Engineers differ from computer scientists in that they are faced with many practical constraints and exceptions yet their solution must be effective in actual use. For example a machine can cut diamonds and diamonds are valuable. The clients are not impressed by large diamonds that unfortunately have the wrong shape due to software errors. Accordingly about 15% of the modules we write are 'test harness' modules which either exercise the modules under test or act as dummy modules for uncompleted parts of the system. Sometimes we write modules to provide rough prototypes of parts of the system that were poorly specified or particularly difficult to achieve.

By isolating these areas adequate solutions can be found quickly and the risk to the whole system minimised and its quality optimised..

Sometimes the structure or quality of existing software is too risky to incorporate into the system. In these cases we usually **'reverse engineer'** the software. This involves analysing the code to discover what the intended requirements were, we then make the requirements self-consistent. The software is then redesigned in line with the system model and its objects, processes and modules. This concept provides clean maintainable software rather than horribly bodged incongruous coding - it also takes less effort.

In all cases we construct systems as 'piles of machines' implemented as modules. Always striving to verify that the partially complete system has 100% correct functionality within itself. This policy of **stepwise construction** of the system provides visibility of progress, a practical means to assess quality and confidence for our Clients [3, 4].

2 CRITERIA FOR SYSTEM PARTITIONING

The main reason that we partition systems into objects, processes and modules is to encapsulate our comprehension and thus extend our capabilities. This is achieved by using abstraction to separate out distinct parts of the problem. These abstractions are then implemented by building logical machines which provide the required behaviour on top of physical ones to realise the abstraction in a form and at a cost which is appropriate to the user [5]. In the past the criteria for modularisation were influenced by the 'everything is a hierarchy' view of programming, latterly the use of 'information hiding' as a criterion has been much more useful.

What is really needed is a set of criteria that maximise the separation of

> the representation of the objects in the problem
> their static and dynamic relationships
> particular ways of implementing (mechanisms)

At the same time we wish to optimise

> ease of comprehension
> ease of development by teams
> ease of extension possibilities

Perhaps the fundamental criterion is that each separate part, be it an active object or a component module, should be *testable*.

If it is not certain that something can be tested before it is built then there is little point in building it because there is no possibility for quality assessment or control.

2.1 Analysis and Design with Objects

When faced with the analysis and design of a large system the difficulty is often to know where to start. At the 'top' level we have found it very beneficial to consider the system as a set of cooperating objects. In this way the system requirements are analysed to produce a non-hierarchical logical model of the system in terms of objects. Each objects behaviour is defined by a set of request messages that it would have to receive in order to fulfill its role in providing the required system behaviour. In general each object in the analysis model corresponds directly to a physical (or abstract) object in the requirement, see Figure 1.

Creating a concurrent-object-information-flow-diagram as the 'top' level of the analysis and design process gives a clear overview of the whole system. It is the equivalent of the hardware engineers 'system block diagram' and the architects initial building design sketches, nothing really new.

2.2 Documenting Objects and Interactions

To document this model the conventional dataflow diagram (actually an information flow diagram) can be used with each bubble representing an object and each flow arrow representing information messages flowing dynamically between objects. The great advantage of this notation for analysis is that it does *not* impose any decisions about the concurrency of the subsequent implementation. To complete the analysis at this level a description of each object is needed, this is summarised in Figure 2. Each object has an interface through which it is subjected to a sequence of request messages. Inside the object is a set of operations which provide the required behaviour when activated by the incoming messages and which operate on a set of private state variables, this structure can also be viewed as an Abstract Data Type. The lifespan of each object can also be described in terms of its coming into existence, initialisation, the ordered sequence of operations on it and ultimately its final demise. Note that some objects may have to apparently persist even though the system is not continuously operational.

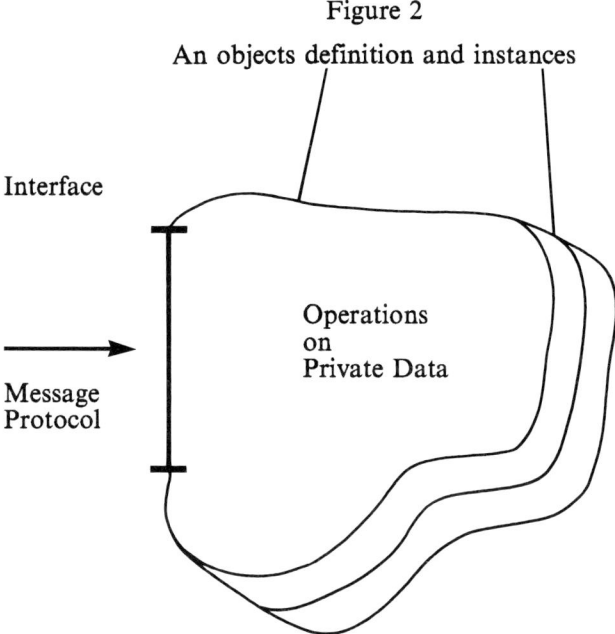

Figure 2
An objects definition and instances

The system is activated by objects reacting to the message traffic sent to them by other objects. The traffic can be represented as *conversations* using standard communication protocol flow diagrams, see Figure 3. It is analysed to specify all the message types and logically separate message transaction sequences. Great care needs to be taken to recognise objects which have multiple clients and in particular transactions which occur simultaneously (or quasi simultaneously) in time. When each object is implemented a key aspect of its internal design is based on whether it can only serve a conversation of sequential transactions with a single client or whether it can serve conversations with concurrent, 'overlapping' transactions with multiply client objects.

The system could of course be analysed recursively with each object being partitioned internally in terms of lower level objects. Languages such as SmallTalk force this approach all the way down to the finest grain of the most primitive operations. In practice we have found one level of object analysis is adequate for most purposes but in principle there is no reason why further object partitioning should not be used. We make use of delegation of functionality between objects at runtime rather than class based inheritance defined at compile time [6].

Figure 3

Part of a conversation between objects

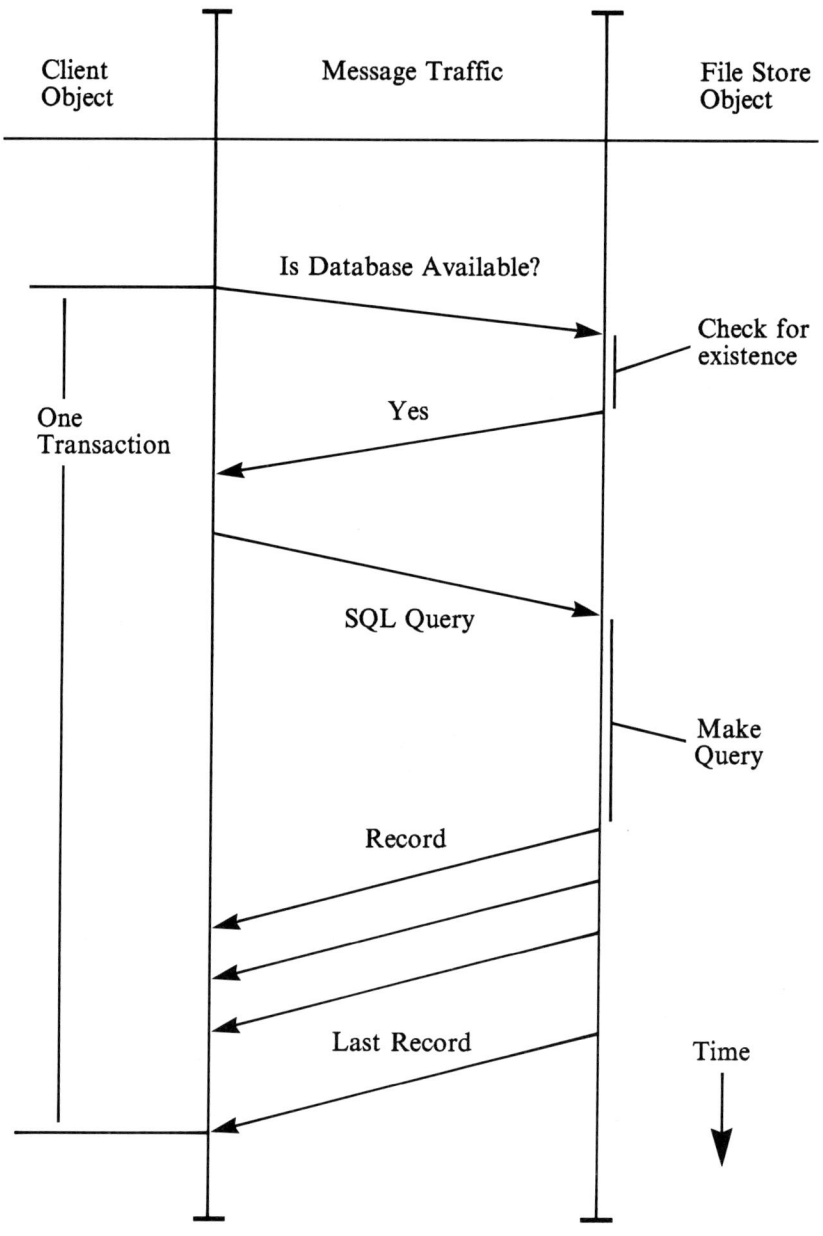

2.3 Designing the Objects

Design is all about making decisions on how best to represent and activate the model of the system in order for it to have the required behaviour and performance. In general 'form should follow function' in any good design however several factors conspire to distort the ideal implementation and because of this the solution is never exactly a simulation of the problem.

The major factors are the design constraints, such as using existing languages, inappropriate operating systems, existing computers, reusing existing software, compatibility with existing protocols etc etc. In practice these are nearly always unavoidable so we must use engineering techniques to preserve as much of the ideal system structure as possible and also to minimise the impact of the constraints. In this case the main design issues are

1   how to implement the objects and their message traffic in terms of processes and modules

2   deciding appropriate mechanisms to provide the required behaviour with adequate performance given the constraints

3   how to package the mechanisms in modules inside objects so that they can be easily changed or extended

4   deciding the mass of appropriate representation for the information inside the system

5   how to construct the system in separate testable pieces with the available tools and runtime environment

3 ENGINEERING THE OBJECTS

Engineering is all about using ingenuity and experience to convert materials into something useful and reliable. The conventional tools for engineering software objects such as SmallTalk and C++ are often inadequate [7, 8]. They are based on the assumption that objects are analysed recursively into a hierarchy of classes (a class is an abstract data *type* which defines some data and the operations on it).

Other assumptions are that there is only a single process on a single processor for activating the system, and that the software is a single monothic lump. Whilst well suited to academic, experimental and prototyping work such languages are poorly suited to the task of constructing large reliable systems. It is an interesting observation about computer languages that the more popular they are the less appropriate they seem to be to their actual use.

When engineering objects we need to cater for the inate concurrency of the system being constructed and the inherent limitations of ourselves as human beings who are building it. Accordingly the most important factors are

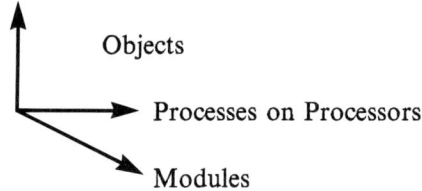

By mapping objects onto processes on one or more processors it becomes possible to provide the best simulation of concurrency with the least conceptual effort. By mapping objects onto modules it becomes possible to break the programs up into parts which can be individually comprehended and separately build and tested by a single person [9].

3.1 Objects and Processes

Ideally it would be convenient to map each object onto a processor and in effect activate the dataflow diagram on a one to one basis. Usually this is neither practical nor affordable and so a more flexible approach is to map each object onto a process. The processes can now be mapped onto one or more processors that effectively partitions the objects of the system across the processors. Of course objects which share a processor are likely to be able to communicate with each other more quickly than with objects on separate processors. Sometimes it is more appropriate to have several objects sharing a single process, for example many file objects which are managed by a filing system object. Occasionally, for performance reasons, an object may require two or more processors. Typically there might be an object, say a protocol driver, which transfers execution from its software process to a hardware based process, say a serial communications UART.

When the UART has completed the hardware processing then execution is transferred back to the original process. This style of sharing of processes between objects is often called interrupt driven programming, an unfortunate and misleading misnomer.

When making design decisions as to how best to map objects onto processes the crucial issues are

1　　the number of processors available

2　　the number of processes desirable and practical

3　　the mechanisms for passing messages between objects residing on the same or different processors (they should look the same to the objects!)

4　　the bandwidth of dynamic message traffic between the objects

5　　the amount and relative importance of processing within each object

6　　the value and resolution of any timing constraints that must be met by the object

7　　whether each object has multiple simultaneous clients

As always the art of designing is an impossible balancing act involving creative compromise.

3.2 Objects and Modules

To make project management possible and to keep programmers sane it is important to partition the system into modules which can be specified, understood built and tested by a single person. The relationship between objects and modules obviously cannot be on a one to one basis. In practice there are several relationships shown in Figure 4, these are

1　　modules which belong **exclusively to an object**, such as a data buffer module in a protocol driver object

2   modules which are **shared between objects**, such as a module for sending information between objects

3   modules that are **duplicated between objects**

The latter case is interesting, an example being a file system. On a recent system programmed in Modula-2 a non-reentrant file module was duplicated in several objects in different concurrent programs on the same system. The normal consistency checking between modules at compile time and link time available in Modula-2 (and Ada) had to be augmented with a configuration management package to cover this eventuality.

Figure 4

Objects and Modules

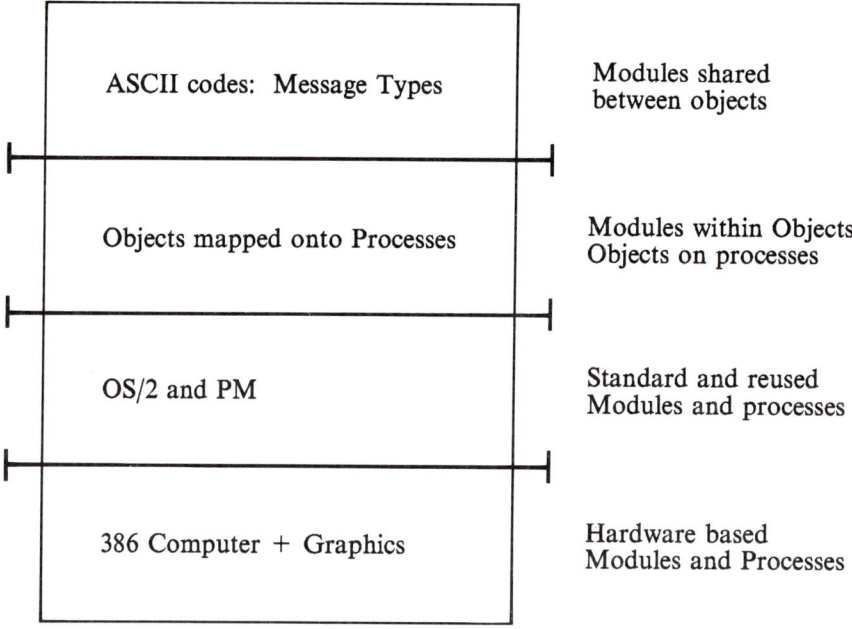

3.3 Practical Implementation

Several systems have been built based on these concepts. In each case the software was written in Modula-2 with a minimum amount of 'C' to provide interfaces in order to reuse existing software packages. The operating systems were as follows:

1. DOS+ from Digital Research with GEM

2. Concurrent DOS from Digital Research with GEM

3. OS/2 with Presentation Manager from Microsoft

The first implementation was the most tortuous because of the 640K address space limitation of DOS. The second was much easier because the objects could be mapped onto CDOS processes in multiple DOS address spaces of 640K each. By far the most suitable environment is OS/2 with Presentation Manager because it removes the address space limitation, has an appropriate multitasking model and, most important, the whole underlying architecture is based on the object viewpoint. As an added bonus Presentation Manager includes facilities for monitoring the message traffic between objects and so can provide a trace of system activity. This can be a great aid to understanding the nature of actual system behaviour.

4 CRITERIA FOR MODULARISATION

Of course the prime criteria for modularisation are that the resulting modules should be easily comprehended by a single person and should be testable separately from the rest of the system. However, looking back on our projects we can now see the actual criteria that have been most effective when designing modules [10]. They include the encapsulation of reuse, adaption, concurrency, consistency, mechanisms and instrumentation.

4.1 Reuse

It is a fact of life that reuse of what already exists is often essential. Usually the reason is short-term economic optimisation (but in retrospect this is rarely justified in practice!) but sometimes it is just not possible to reimplement old parts of a new system because there is not enough time or the knowledge is no longer available. In any case if a product is still 'alive' it certainly will need to be extended to match its behaviour and performance to the evolving needs of its users. This needs to be done with minimal modification of existing parts but the aim is to inherit the functionality and system model from the existing system. Unfortunately the mistakes and constraints are also inherited, the main disadvantages of standardization.

A practical example of such a module is one that provides an interface to an existing file system.

4.2 Adaption

When creating large systems it always pays to make the software part as portable as possible. Conventionally this is done by providing 'device driver' modules which abstract away particular physical characteristics at the lowest level and offer a clean logical software interface instead. The bulk of the software then uses the clean interface so making it portable and also improving the flexibility for hardware machine choice. Typically these modules are hidden in the operating system but any new devices can have their drivers written in a high level language such as Modula-2.
A practical example of such a module is a module which adapts the standard DOS keyboard driver so that it can provide a Russian style keyboard layout.

4.3 Concurrency

The instruction by instruction execution of programs by CPUs has unfortunately led generations of programmers to presume that concurrency does not exist. They inherently try to coerce the concurrency of the problem into a single stream of CPU instructions. For many years poor Van Newman has been given the blame for this because his architecture is inherently sequential. Of course this assertion is nonsense if we accept that the solution is a simulation of the problem. The machine that the solution runs on may constrain the resulting performance but certainly should not determine the structure of the solution.

The liberation from this mental straight jacket came with data flow diagrams which show the flow of information between processing activities. Their use has broken the curse of the flowchart which deems its users to think only in terms of sequential control flow. In a similar way the Entity Relation diagram and Entity Life History have liberated the design of information structures.

We have found it more useful to consider the flow of information between naturally concurrent objects in the system, be they logical or physical objects. By initially analysing the problem in terms of the concurrent objects it contains we get some very clear benefits

1   the implementation can be a simulation of the problem

2   the processor(s) can be allocated to and shared between the objects depending on their individual performance needs of throughput and response time

3   once the shared modules and interfaces between objects are defined and designed the implementation of the objects can be developed separately by members of a team

4   synchronisation and communication between objects can be optimised separately to suit the needs of the objects

5   the system can be constructed incrementally by providing dummy objects as 'stubs'

A practical example of such a module is a module which provides an interface to a concurrent operating system or perhaps pipes which provide an information conduit between processes.

4.4 Consistency

The possibility for automating consistency checking is perhaps the greatest benefit of using non-permissive languages (we consider 'C' and Assembler to be permissive!). Pascal introduced strong data type checking. Modula-2 has introduced the possibility of explicit control of visibility of module contents combined with an environment which automates inter-module consistency checking at both compile time and run-time. New languages like Object Oberon offer the possibilities of representing object classes whilst retaining modularity [9]. Even greater support is needed when modules are shared between separately compiled programs because a change mode to satisfy one program may have nasty knock on effects which are inconsistent for the other programs. We tackled this problem by extending the PVCS Version Control system using batch command files to automate the consistent updating of modules shared between programs.

A practical example of such a module is one that defines the message types for sets of communicating objects in the system.

4.5 Ownership and Mechanisms

Perhaps the most powerful criteria is that of ownership. Here the concept is that the module owns a mechanism such as how a filing system is structured or how a particular protocol works. The interface, or external visibility, of the mechanism is minimised. Its clients are only informed of its information and services on a 'need to know' basis. When trying to partition a system, an object or a program into modules, it is important to encapsulate the ownership of mechanisms and/or information but also to guarantee that its behaviour and performance can be verified. If modules are well designed in this way then the mechanisms can evolve to meet the requirements with minimal changes to the client modules. The underlying architecture of objects, programs and module relationships should be resilient to particular choices of mechanisms chosen for an implementation.

A practical example of such a module is one which contains and hides a communications protocol as perhaps either a state machine or a conventional structured program.

4.6 Instrumentation

Often it is useful to hide instrumentation facilities behind module interfaces. For example if we are sending messages between objects it is useful to have a log of all messages sent. This makes it possible to perform an audit trail of the systems activity either on-line or as a post mortem if the system dies. It can be convenient to replace the instrumented modules with plain vanilla ones when the system is released. In fact we never remove the instrumentation facilities - for two reaons. Firstly it might upset some delicately balanced relations between sets of interacting objects. Secondly we have found that systems always seem to prefer to fail when they have the minimum capability to inform you of the reason for the failure.

A practical example of such a module is a 'dummy' module which provides an interface to an existing piece of software but which also reports on its pattern of usage. Perhaps saving usage statistics in memory for later analysis.

5 CONCLUSIONS

In this paper we have tried to show how large systems can be designed using well established concepts and yet remain intellectually manageable. The main lessons that we have learned from the implementation of several large systems are ...

1. Viewing a required system as a set of cooperating objects leads to a clean analysis model.

2. Designing the new system based on objects processes and modules preserves the original system structures and makes engineering easier.

3. Implementing systems using objects processes and modules is easily and naturally achieved using current languages and operating systems such as Modula-2, OS/2 and Presentation Manager.

4. The most useful criteria for modularisation are reuse, adaption, concurrency, consistency, ownership and instrumentation.

5. The most important properties of objects and modules are whether they can be understood by a single person, other than their author, and developed and tested separately from the rest of the system.

6. Specialised languages such as SmallTalk and C++ would have been inappropriate for all the applications considered.

7. Designing and implementing systems as a set of cooperating objects provides for great productivity, flexibility and portability.

REFERENCES

1. Booch G, Feb 1986
    "Object Oriented Development"
    IEEE Trans Software Engineering, SE12 No 2

2. Dijkstra E W, May 1968
    "The structure of the THE multiprogramming system"
    Comm of the ACM, N5, Vol 11.

3   Wirth N, April 1971
    "Program Development by Stepwise Refinement"
    Comm of the ACM, Vol 14, No 4

4   Kirk B, October 1989
    "Stepwise Refinement and Modula-2 for Perestroika and 1992"
    Prac. Conf. on Modula-2, Polytechnic South West, Plymouth,
    England

5   Maruichi, Uchiki and Tomoro, 1987
    "Behavioural Simulation based on Knowledge Objects"
    Dept Electrical Engineering, Keio University, 3-14-1
    Hiyoshi, Yokohama 223, Japan.

6   Stein L A, Liebermann H, Ungar D, 1989
    "A shared view of sharing: The Treaty of Orlando"
    Object Oriented Concepts ... ISBN 0-201-14410-7 Addison Wesley

7   Goldberg A, et al, 1983
    "SmallTalk 80: The language and its implementation"
    ISBN 0-201-11371-6 Addison Wesley

8   Sakkinen M, August 1988
    "On the Darker Side of C++"
    Proceedings of ECOOP '88, Oslo, Norway

9   Mossenbock H, Templ J, April 1989
    "Object Oberon - A Modest Object Oriented Language"
    Structured Programming, Vol 10, No 4

10 Parnas D L, December 1972
    "On the criteria to be used in Decomposing Systems
    into Modules"
    Comm of the ACM, Vol 15, No 12

The Synthesis of Object-Oriented Designs from the Products of Structured Analysis

P. D. SULLY
Yourdon International, London, UK

D.C. INCE
Faculty of Mathematics, Open University, Milton Keynes.

Abstract

Essential systems analysis is an established structured analysis method which has received widespread acceptance from both software developers and customers. Object oriented systems development is a highly promising new technique for analysis and design which, at first sight, seems antithetical to conventional structured analysis. However, this paper puts forward the thesis that the two approaches are complementary. First, an object development notation is introduced. This notation has been designed in order that an object-oriented design can be derived from the notations used in structured analysis. Second, heuristics are described which can be used for transforming a system expressed in a structured analysis notation into the object-oriented notation. Finally, a small example of the transformation is described.

1. INTRODUCTION — STRUCTURED ANALYSIS

The aim of this section is to describe the current form of analysis which forms part of the Yourdon Structured Development Methodology [McMe84], [Ward85]. Using this methodology a system specification can be expressed using three major components, each of which describe the transformation, structure and time/sequence behaviour of a system. Each of these components are described by a separate and distinct graphical notation. Figure 1 shows examples of these notations. Transformations are described by data flow diagrams; the structure of a system's stored data is represented by an entity-relation diagram; and the time/sequence behaviour is expressed as a state transition diagram, which in essence is a finite state automaton.

The data flow diagram expresses the transformations in a system. It is important because it represents useful work that is to be performed by a system. The process symbol, usually written as a bubble, expresses a logical unit of work. The flow of data between processes is represented by a directed arc.

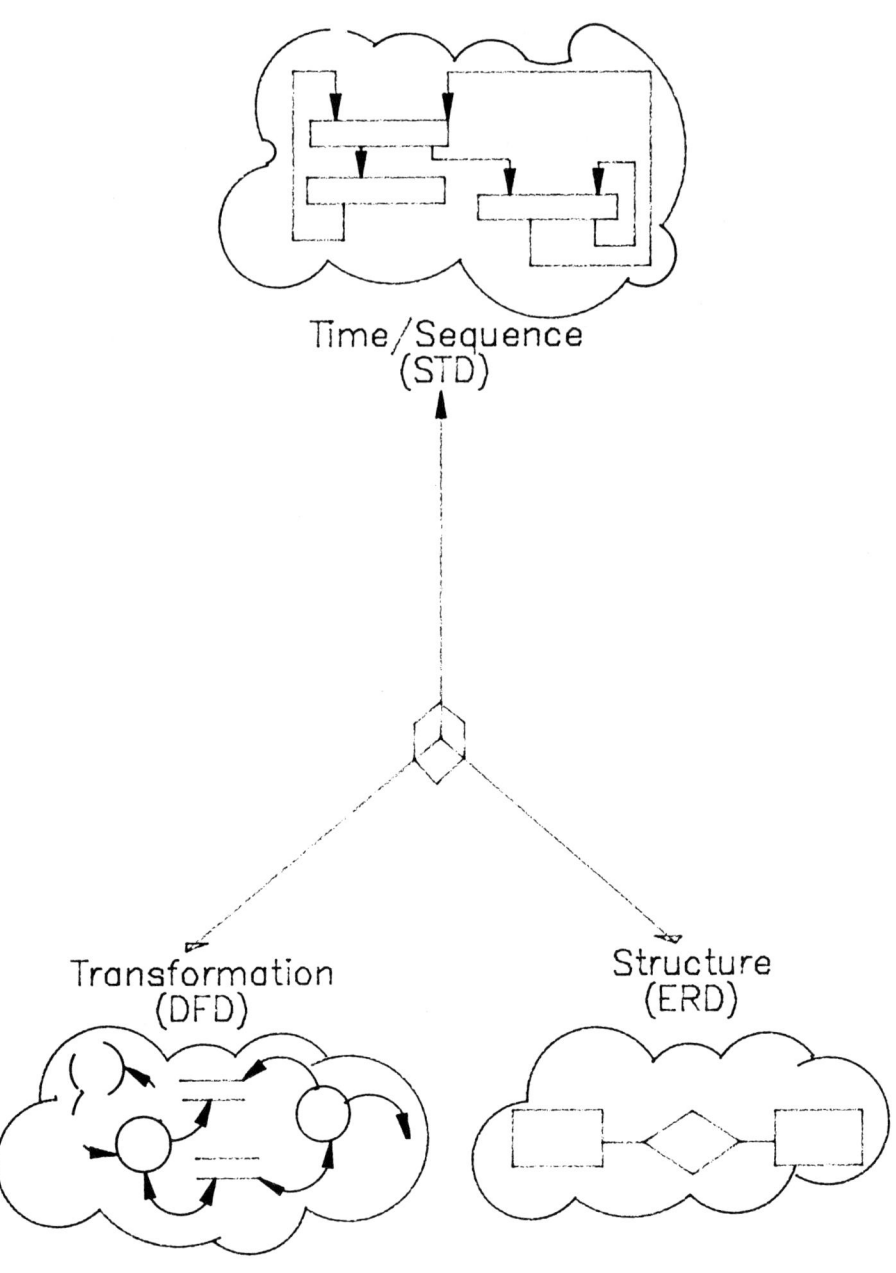

Figure 1

There are three types of flow that may be represented: information, control and material. There are also two modes of flow: discrete, represented by a single headed arrow and continuous, represented by a double headed arrow

The store symbol, represented by two parallel lines, describes a flow that has been stored for subsequent use. The last symbol in this group is a terminator. This symbol marks the edge of the system. Data flow diagrams will be levelled: processes will be expressed in terms of other data flow diagrams in order to control complexity. The Yourdon structured methodology, like many other methodologies, contains many heuristics which encourage well constructed diagrams. Many CASE tools have a number of these heuristics embedded within them.

The entity relationship diagram is a means of expressing how entities are related. A number of symbols are used for these diagrams. The two major symbols are a rectangle and a diamond. A rectangle represents a concrete entity, for example, an account, a product or an employee. The diamond represents a connection or relation between entities. The entity-relation diagram is used to formulate a schema before its subsequent implementation as a data base.

The state transition diagram is a means of expressing finite state behaviour. This notation comprises four symbols. The state is represented by a long thin rectangle with an appropriate name. The transition between states is represented by a directed arc connecting state symbols. Associated with a transition is a condition/action pair. The condition is the logical condition that gives rise to a transition, the action represents the set of processing actions that occur when a transition occurs.

For all of the diagram types the symbols are easy to draw freehand. Moreover, the reader of diagrams does not easily become confused between the diagram types. The diagrams are supported by text which takes the form of a data dictionary: a catalogue or repository of all the data items in the system, together with process specifications: descriptions of the behaviour of each lowest level data flow diagram process.

The Yourdon view of the development cycle is that of splitting the development phases into two major models: the logical model and the physical model. The logical model is often referred to as the essential model. It is the essential model that is used as a vehicle for checking with the customer that the representation matches user requirements. The physical model is called the implementation model in the Yourdon Structured Development Method, because it refers to physical implementation units which may be processors, tasks or modules.

The essential and implementation models link to become the Yourdon view of the development cycle. The stages beyond implementation (code, unit test, integration, system test, acceptance test and maintenance) are considered to be guided by local developer standards. Each model consists of a complete set of diagrams .There is traceability through the model so that for example, a system function can be traced to the modules that implement the function. Also the project manager may easily partition the units of the models into useful work breakdown structures for project planning purposes.

2. OBJECT ORIENTED DEVELOPMENT

The life cycle outlined in the previous section was developed for an orthodox development style where the requirements were expressed in an essential model that the user/client and the developer could comprehend. The various subsequent models allowed access to the various stages, with a new layer of technical dependence, in a controlled manner. The projected object-oriented life cycle described in this section is different from that presented in the previous section in two major ways: first, the life cycle itself is different and, second, the development infrastructure is recognised.

Objects should represent concepts, and be a self-contained capsule of data, operations and state behaviour . An object should selectively hide details from its users who should be able to simply communicate by sending messages to the object.

2.1 An Object Oriented Notation

A new set of symbols are required to express the concept of an object and the various ways that it is useful for the developer and the customer to view it. The object symbol should have the characteristic of being able to introduce the object and show externally the operations that it may provide. This is useful when complimented by an internal view that would almost certainly be produced by the developer. Additionally, there is the need to depict how a set of objects is arranged for use for in application.

To satisfy these aims the metaphor that we have used is that of a perfect machine which, to an external observer, behaves like a vending machine, i.e. it is box shaped and has a set of buttons which depicts the services that it provides.

Additionally there is the need for the developer's staff to be aware of the full internals of the machine. This is depicted in an analogous fashion by removing the front panel. In the notation each service (function/operation) corresponds to a process symbol representing the work which the machine is capable of.

External view of an Object

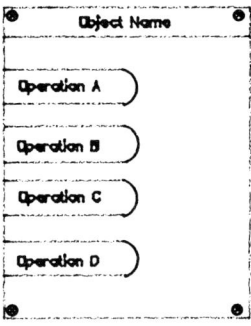

Internal view of the same Object

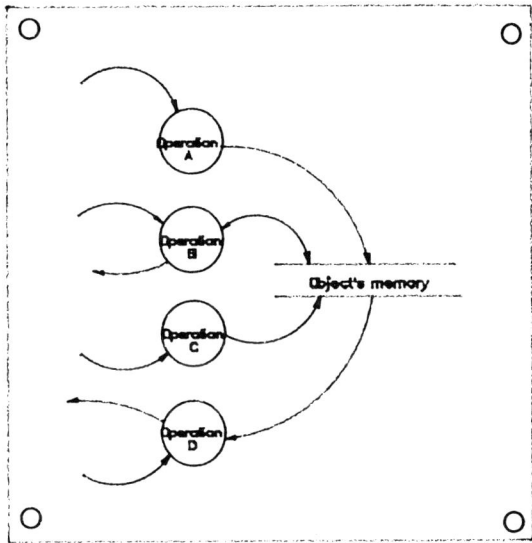

Figure 2

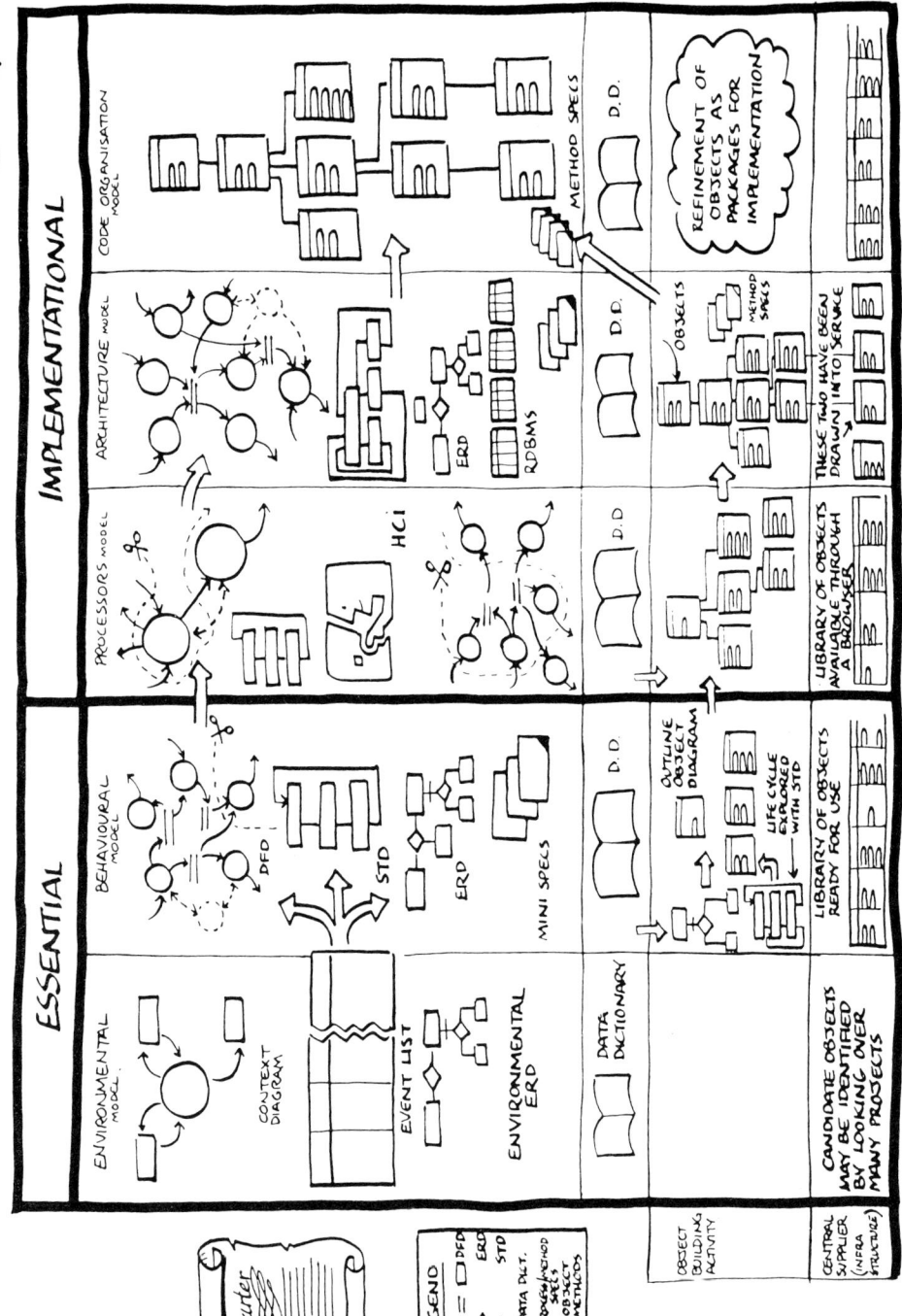

Figure 3

Each machine will also have some set of data that must persist, and where memory is depicted by the store symbol. Our machine may also have some degree of discrete control (time/sequence behaviour) which is depicted in the internal view by a control process, with its detailed behaviour expressed by a state transition diagram Within the object (our "machine") the services (operations) may use additional objects in the role of servers, and these too may be connected by flows from the process symbol to a diminutive object symbol's operation button as shown in figure 2.

How does the machine metaphor for an object stand up? We believe it faithfully represents the object paradigm. Our object machine shows an external view with buttons to operate the machine. The Internal view of the object machine shows the operations as processes. Messages are actually flows to an operation. The operations in an object machine can call upon services from a server object. This is equivalent to a message from the operation to the server object's specific operation. The relationships between machines can be depicted in an organisation chart, akin to a structure chart, which shows objects and their relationship as suppliers and clients. A directed arc depicts the situation of a client sending a message to the supplier object. These organisation charts are shown in figure 3 as part of the object building activity.

2.2. The Life Cycle Extensions

In order to cope with object-oriented design the orthodox development cycle described in the previous section needs to be changed in a number of ways. First, the environmental model, which describes the top-level of a system, needs to have an entity relationship diagram included which identifies any candidate objects. The behavioural model is the same. However, the entity-relation diagram associated with this model will have been constructed according to a more rigourous procedure than would be normally employed — this part of the development being optimised for clear expression of the requirements. At this stage the user/client is not expected to be conscious of the object nature of the system under view. The systems analyst and the technical designers may well want to be aware of the object character of the system to be built, the subsequent phases being optimised for designers to build the product.

The implementation models, like the processor and task models are the first models that recognise the specifics of the technology to be applied, and it is the task model which is inspected and developed for objects to be developed. It is this model that requires the heuristics for the recognition of various object diagram configurations which may be developed into viable packages.

The subsequent model: the code organisation model is radically different from its use with conventional Yourdon development. It is object packages that are being arranged, and there will be heuristic rules appropriate to this activity. It is intended that many objects may well be common to the system and other systems which have been developed. In order to obtain a greater level of reusability there has to be some form of infrastructural activity to support this.

2.3. Integration

It is apparent that at this stage there must be rules (or heuristics) to facilitate development of objects at the various stages of development. Specifically, as objects are organised around data the entity-relation diagram has an augmented role both in the product's development cycle and for the enterprise model.

The enterprise model serves as a base to build services that are likely to be required over many systems development projects. The economy comes in the form of components that may be usefully be re-incorporated into evolving developments. This principle is already known as incremental development. Object-oriented construction takes this incrementalist approach an order of magnitude further.

3. HEURISTICS

In order for there to be a systematic way of constructing objects from the products of the Yourdon development cycle into a form such as that described in [Meye89] there has to be a set of rules or heuristics. Such rules are applied to structured graphic notations in order to develop an object-oriented design.

3.1. The Types of Heuristics Needed

To assist in the object oriented systems development activity it is necessary for a set of heuristics to facilitate construction, and to give a frame of reference for working practices. These rules have been developed and can be placed into a number of categories:

- Construction rules from entity-relation diagram objects to object-oriented analysis objects
- Development rules from the structured life cycle state transition diagrams to object-oriented analysis objects and object-oriented design objects.
- Rules which transform data flow diagrams to operations on objects.
- Rules which transform data flow diagram mini spec pre/post specifications to operations.
- Rules for relating control centred data flow diagrams to object positioning.
- Rules for the refinement of objects and their re-classification for inheritance.
- Rules for recognition of objects in roles (objects such as sensors, actuators, controllers and transducers).
- Rules for threading a "transaction" through a pathway.

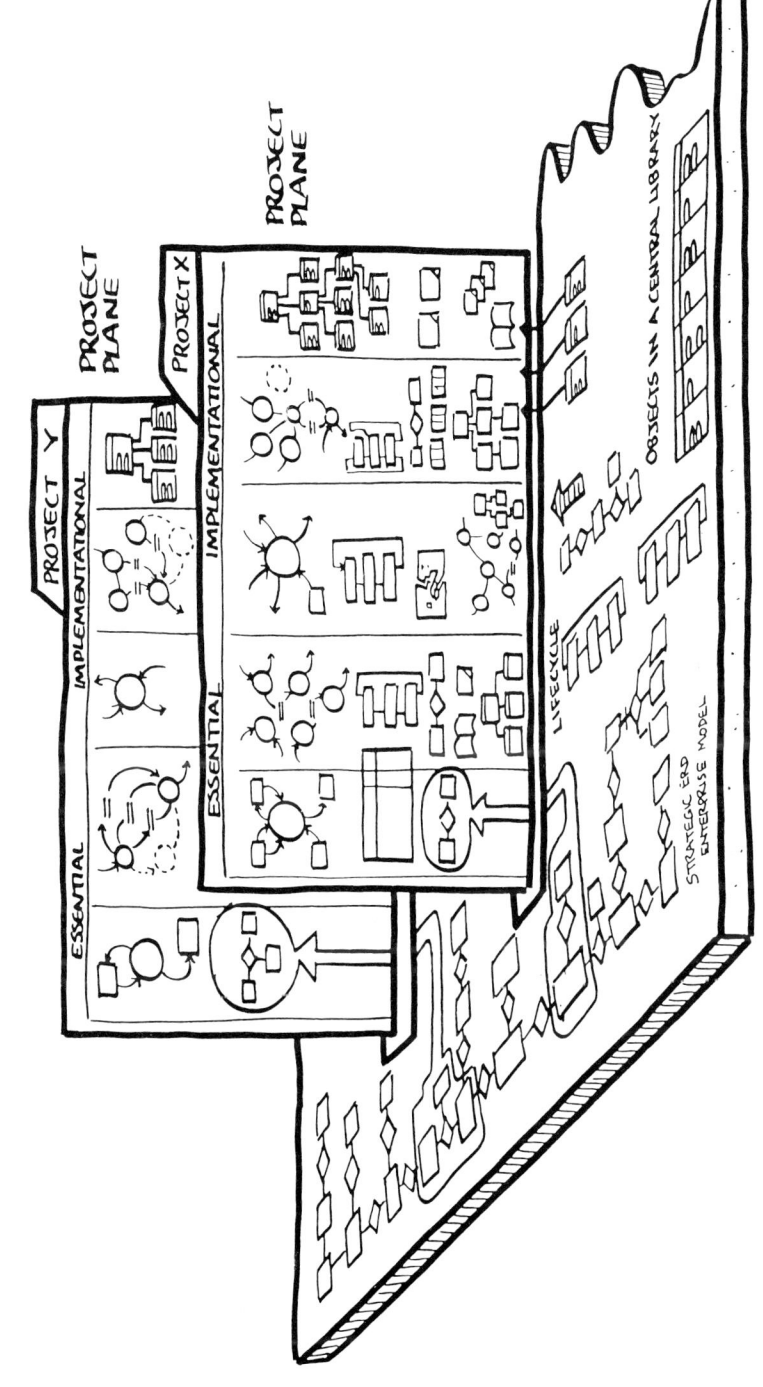

Figure 4

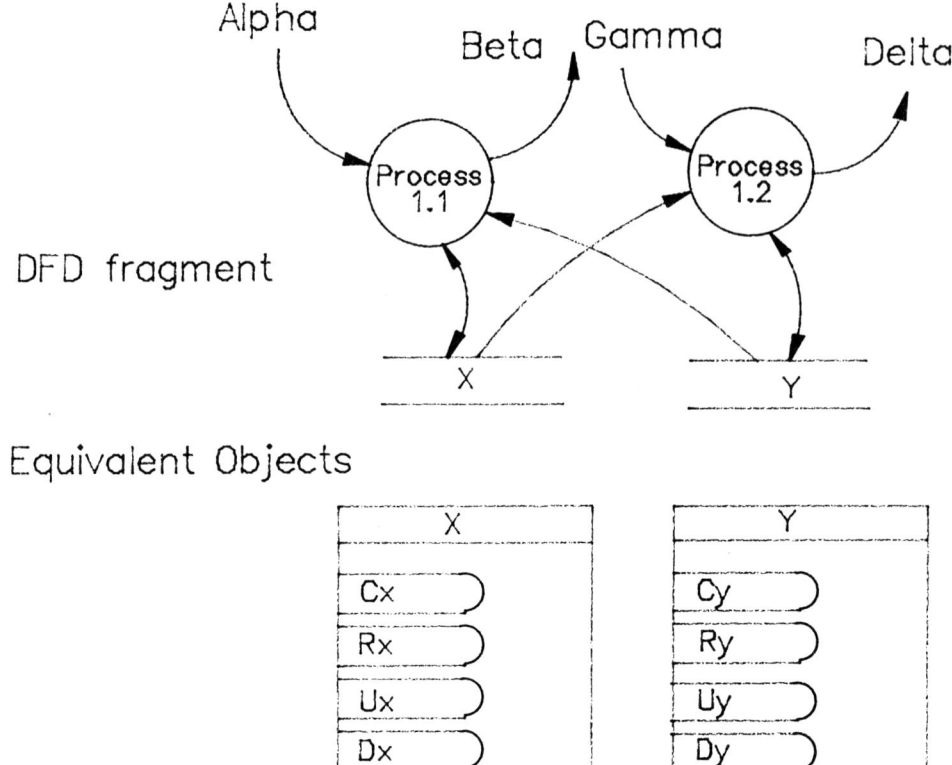

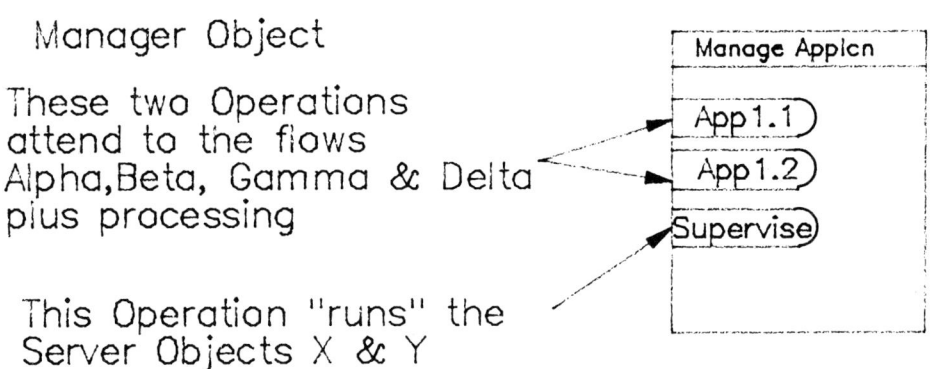

Figure 5

- Rules for the conservation of pre/post conditions specifications.

3.2. Specific Heuristics

The purpose of this section is to describe. in outline. the heuristics that we have developed for transforming the products of structured analysis into an object representation.

[1] Data flow diagrams, if decomposed into their most primitive form (one flow input, one flow output and a store access) may correspond directly to a operation for that store reincarnated as an object.

[2] Data flow diagrams usually do more than just access one store, whereupon the process becomes fragmented into a number of methods. This principle is best illustrated by looking at figure 5. Processes 1.1 and 1.2 may be depicted as using two stores X and Y. Objects are organised around data so X and Y in turn become objects. The processing that was undertaken by 1.1 and 1.2 now becomes distributed as the object's operations (methods) some of which will be in the form of custodial activities and application specific activities. There will be processing that has to attend to the external flows and application specific activities. This is posted to a created manager object.

[3] Data flow diagrams in a processor model, for an asymmetric distribution of the essential model to n processors (n>=2), tend to exhibit inherent distortion of the original requirement. To preserve the essence of the requirement the cut must be a minimum weight cut across essential flows.

[4] Process specifications written in pre and post-condition specification form are rearranged as object operations.

[5] Each entity-relation diagram entity is a candidate object. Supertype and subtype entities are candidate representations for inheritance. Entity relation diagram associative objects are dynamic sets of information.

[6] Entity-relation diagrams may be derived directly from an event list provided it is formatted as a frame with slots for: agent, action and subject area with an optional instrument.

[7] As a provider of entity-relation diagram services it is necessary to cut the entity-relation diagram for each processing region. There shall be a major portion of processing and a minor portion of processing:

[i] Cuts are made across relationships.

[ii] Each cut will cause a "Ghost" entity to remain on the major portion of the entity-relation diagram and a reduced entity on the minor portion entity-relation diagram.

An organisation chart of the Objects.
The further details related to the internals of an Object may
seen by looking inside, see rightmost diagram.

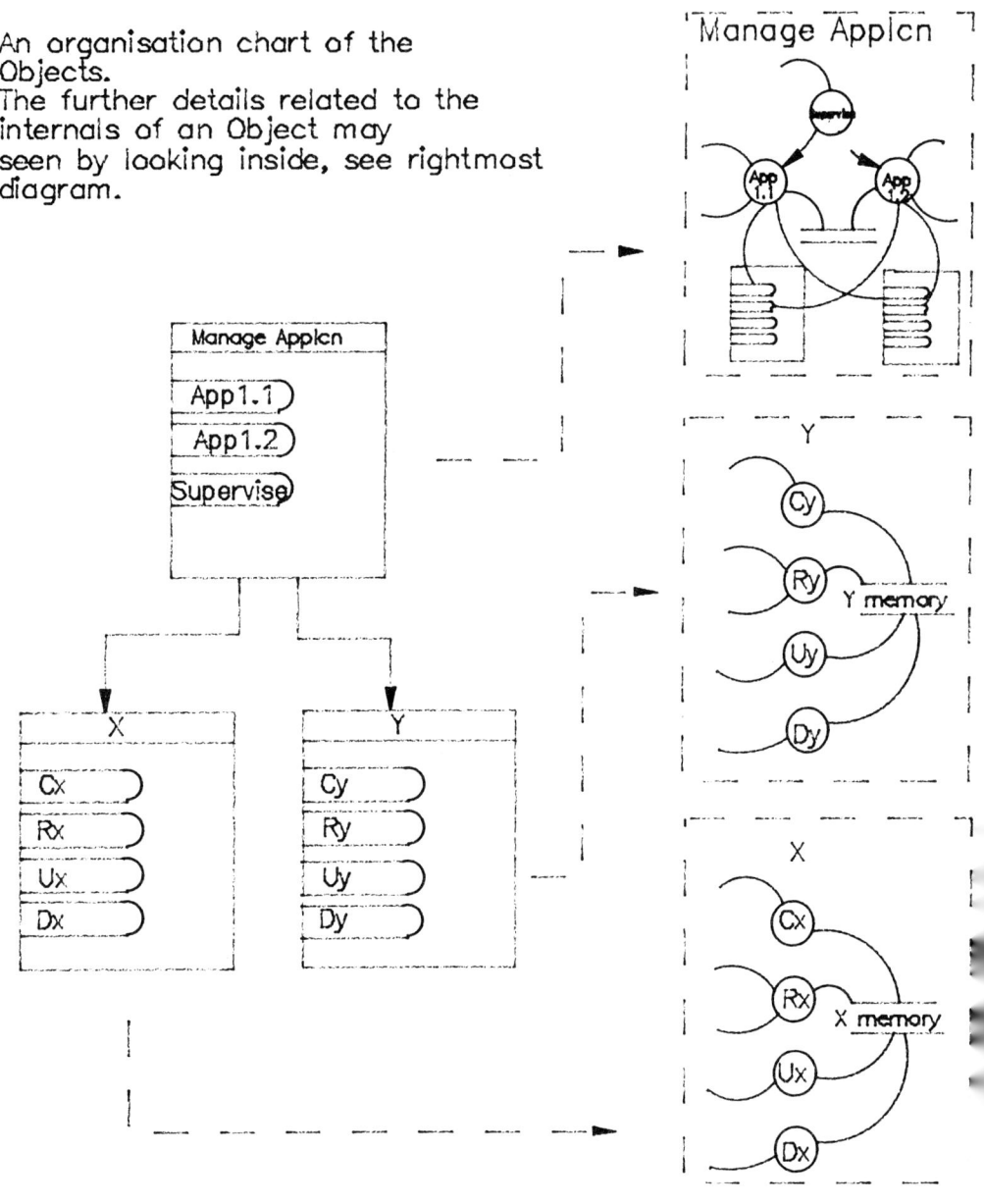

Figure 6

[iii] The service provider shall perceive a compressed entity that migrates from the major processing portion to the minor portion periodically.

[8] The life cycle for an entity is expressed by an state transition diagram. For a full life cycle the actions associated with each transition condition become the methods for that entity. The source for the life cycle is the event list formatted according to a frame with the following slots: agent action, subject, area and, optionally, instrument.

[9] A process specification in its essential form shall have an incarnation in the operation (method) specification for the same subject area. There should be conservation of pre and post condition specifications fragments (i.e every essential assertion must have an equivalent Object/Operation assertion).

[10] A state transition diagram is a representation of time and sequence behaviour (discrete control). For a translation of an essential state transition to its corresponding object representation: states are preserved in a controlling object, transitions remain, conditions will be the same, actions however have different constituents (viz: using N object.services instead of M processes) to accomplish the same time sequence behaviour. The state transition diagram is used also as a vehicle for exploring the life cycle of an entity, the diagram type being called the entity state transition diagram. The conditions that give rise to alterations of entity state correspond with real world events and the actions correspond with the set of operations that the object will have to cater.

[11] In the case of asymmetric distributed processing (processors >= 2), one should think of a virtual observer who is familiar with the essential required behaviour and his/her view should remain the same. Therefore, there will be a service object which shall provide operations (methods) which preserve the virtual observer's viewpoint.

[12] Refinement may be said to have taken place when an adjustment increases the ratio of $P_l/(M_l-M_c)$ from the previous iteration. Where P_l is the number of essential process description lines, M_l is the number of operation (method) prescription lines for the application, M_c is the operation (method) prescription lines held centrally, for example, a library. There is a shrinkage in the specification lines because there are repeated common functions, with an essential mini spec this is shown in figures 5 and 6 where processes 1.1 and 1.2 will have the same access specification specified for access to X.

[13] There are a number of quality rules relating to traceability:

[i] An object model shall perform the same end-end transaction threading as the original data flow diagram.

Environmental Model

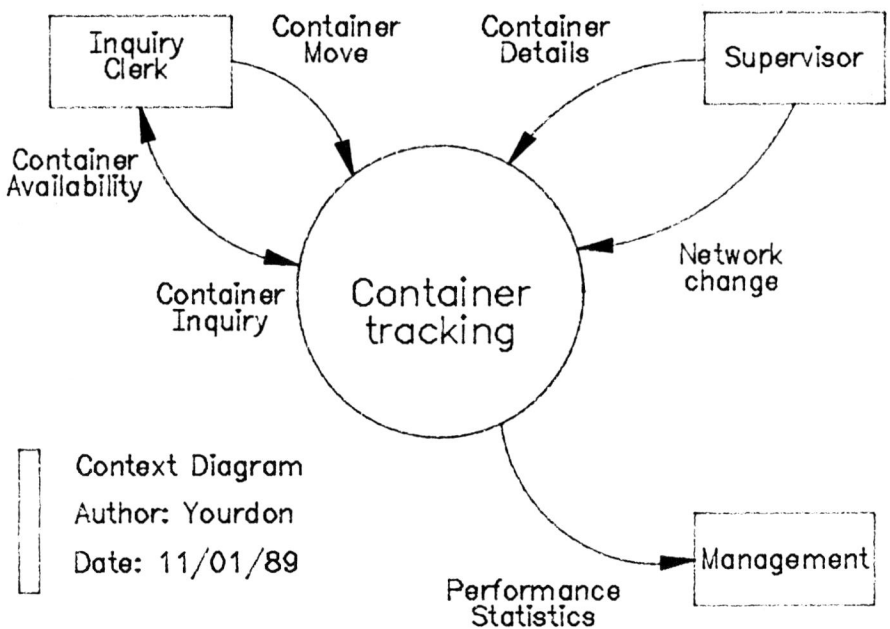

Events:

Clerk updates Container Status/location
Clerk inquires into Container Availability
Supervisor maintains Containers
Supervisor maintains Network
Time to produce Performance Statistics

Figure 7

Behavioural DFD

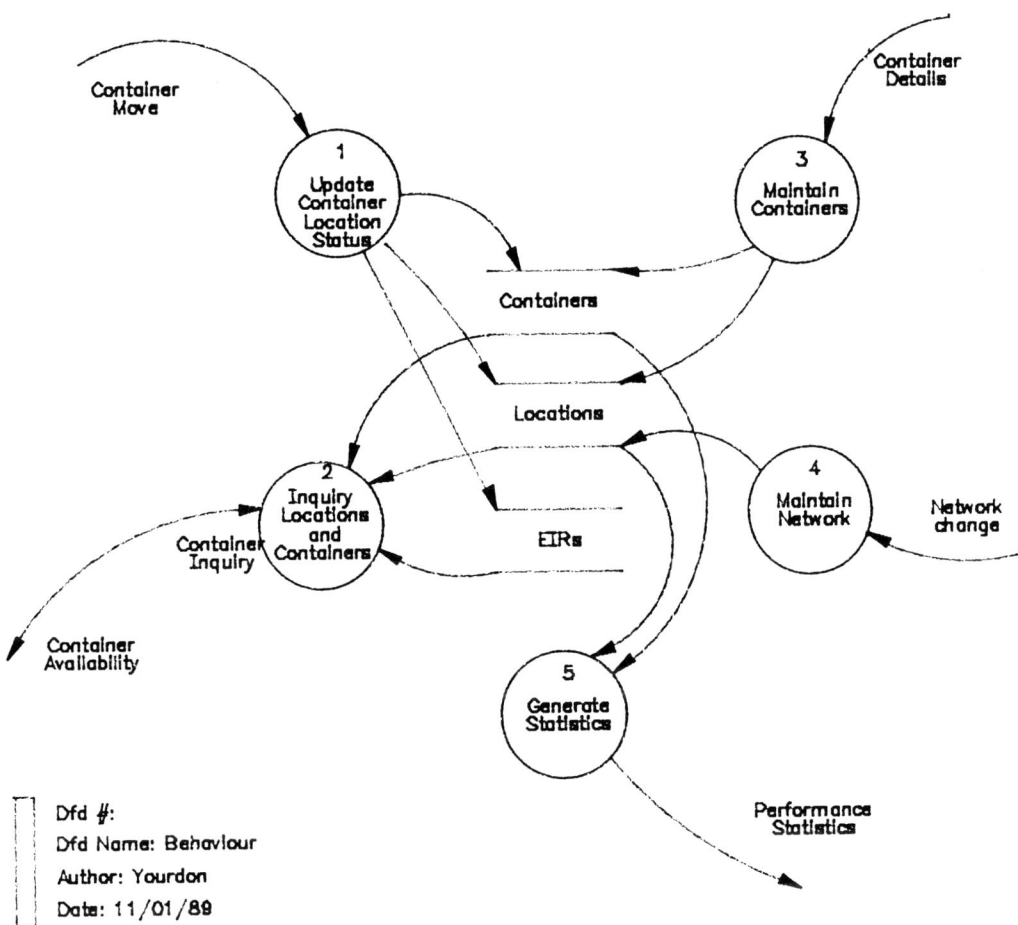

Figure 8

Behavioural ERD

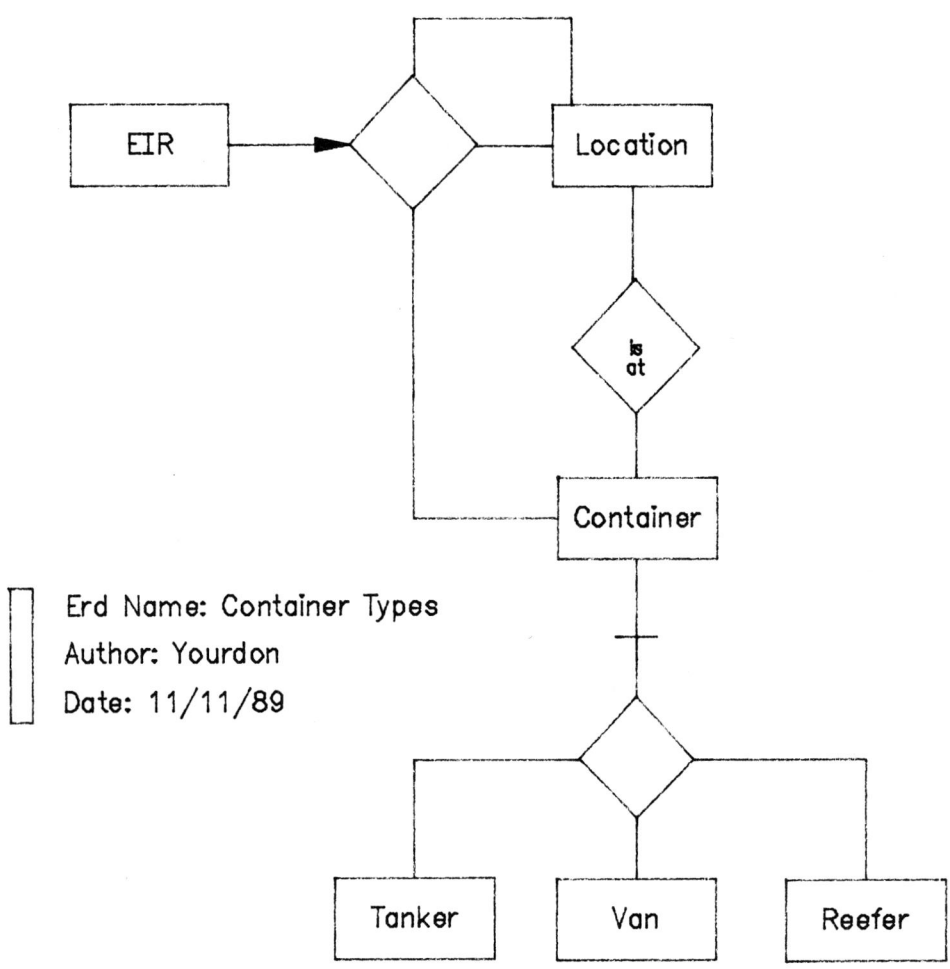

Figure 9

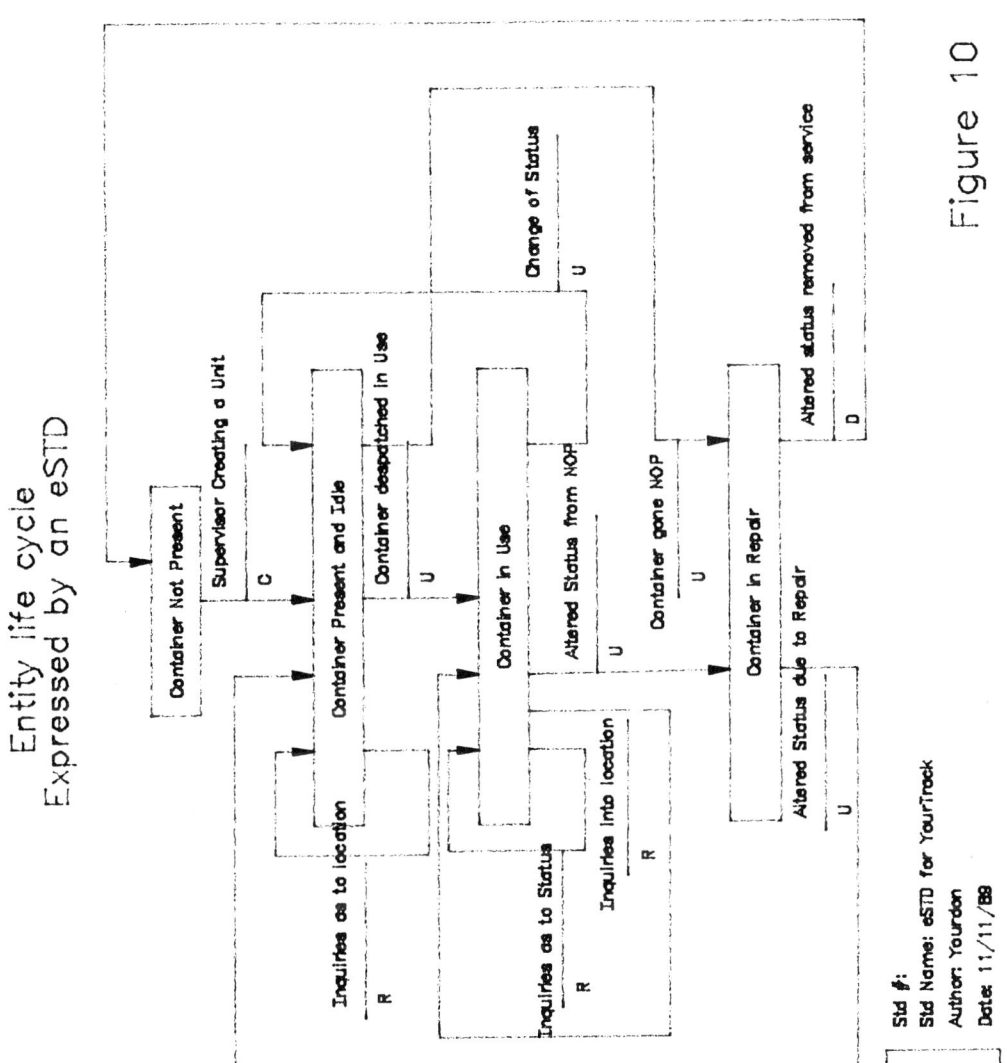

Figure 10

[ii] Each essential process specification fragment shall be posted to a operation (method) specification. Unposted fragments from the essential model shall be considered an omission (or incipient distortion).

[iii] Every entity-relation diagram entity shall have, as a minimum, a life cycle e.g. (create, change, use and delete). The lack of any one of these shall be considered suspect.

[14] Object Specification rules.

[i] The "inside" view of an object is the graphic basis of it's definition.

[ii] Each externally visible operation must be accountable in the "inside" view of the object.

[iii] There may be extra processes that only become visible when seeing the "inside" of the object, such as control.

[iv] The object's memory is depicted by the store symbol.

[v] Communications from an operation to another object's operation is depicted by a dialogue flow from the operation symbol to the specific object operation.

[vi] Expression of the full discrete control behaviour is accomplished by an state transition diagram as an auxiliary diagram using the same construction rules.

[15] Classes of abstract roles may be identified from the essential models such as: sensors (passive, active and intelligent), actuators (slave, dynamic and intelligent, controllers and transducers). This activity allows identification of potentially re-usable units.

4. AN ILLUSTRATIVE EXAMPLE

The example is taken from a container tracking application where we have simplified as much as possible to show the principles involved.

The essential specification yields an environmental model that has a context diagram and an event list which is used to establish the scope of the system with the end user; this is shown in figure 7. The behavioural model provides a basis for an expression of the work to be accomplished; this is shown as the data flow diagram in figure 8, the structure expressed as the entity-relation diagram shown in figure 9 and the time/sequence detailed as the state transition diagram shown as figure 10. All this becomes source material for the objects which are derived.

Objects are derived from entities depicted on the entity-relation diagram. The main entity for our system is the container, and its life cycle is described by the state transition diagram shown in figure 10. The actions will be related to operations that the container object will need.

The object dependency diagram detailed in figure 11 shows how the objects are to be organised for the container tracking application. The object specification diagrams (figures 12, 13, 14) are a detailed expansion of the inside of objects *container*, *tracking* and *container*. The object *location* uses server objects called *net* (which is already on the "stocks"). This, in turn, uses server objects *node*, *network* and, *window* as shown in figures 15 and 16.

The object dependency diagram, along with the object specification diagrams and the associated project dictionary is the reference source for building the solution. Additionally it is essential that an organisation which develops a solution must have a comprehensive object/class browser to allow reuse across projects. The object *net* is a redefinition of an already existing object *location* because of class resources already existing which service generalised networks and network nodes. This is an important resource for an organisation. Reuse of centrally held objects means the prototyping activity may be facilitated. This is illustrated in figures 17 and 18, where one application *SalesCom* may be metamorphosed into another *YourTrack* with greater ease because of reuse at a higher level.

A question which might be asked is why have two styles of development? The essential structured analysis approach has the advantage of providing the user/client with the means of participating actively in the systems development activity. The essential model allows the participation to its fullest by preservation of functional visibility. The object representation is not an easily conveyable to the client/ user. It is not easily understood by users/clients. It is the recognition of this phenomenon that leads us to view the two approaches as complimentary.

5. Conclusions

It is our belief that the essential systems analysis activity can greatly contribute to the synthesis of object oriented designs. Indeed the employer of one of the authors (Sully) already offers a course on object-oriented development [OOSD91]. An object representation may easily be derived from the essential model part of the Yourdon structured development method without undue distortion of requirements while, at the same time, providing traceability. The heuristics assisting with that aim will no doubt be modified as a result of practice. However, early experience has indicated that this change should be minimal. The approach outlined in this paper allows the integration of structured development and object oriented development and fills a major gap in object-oriented development: the elicitation and specification of requirements.

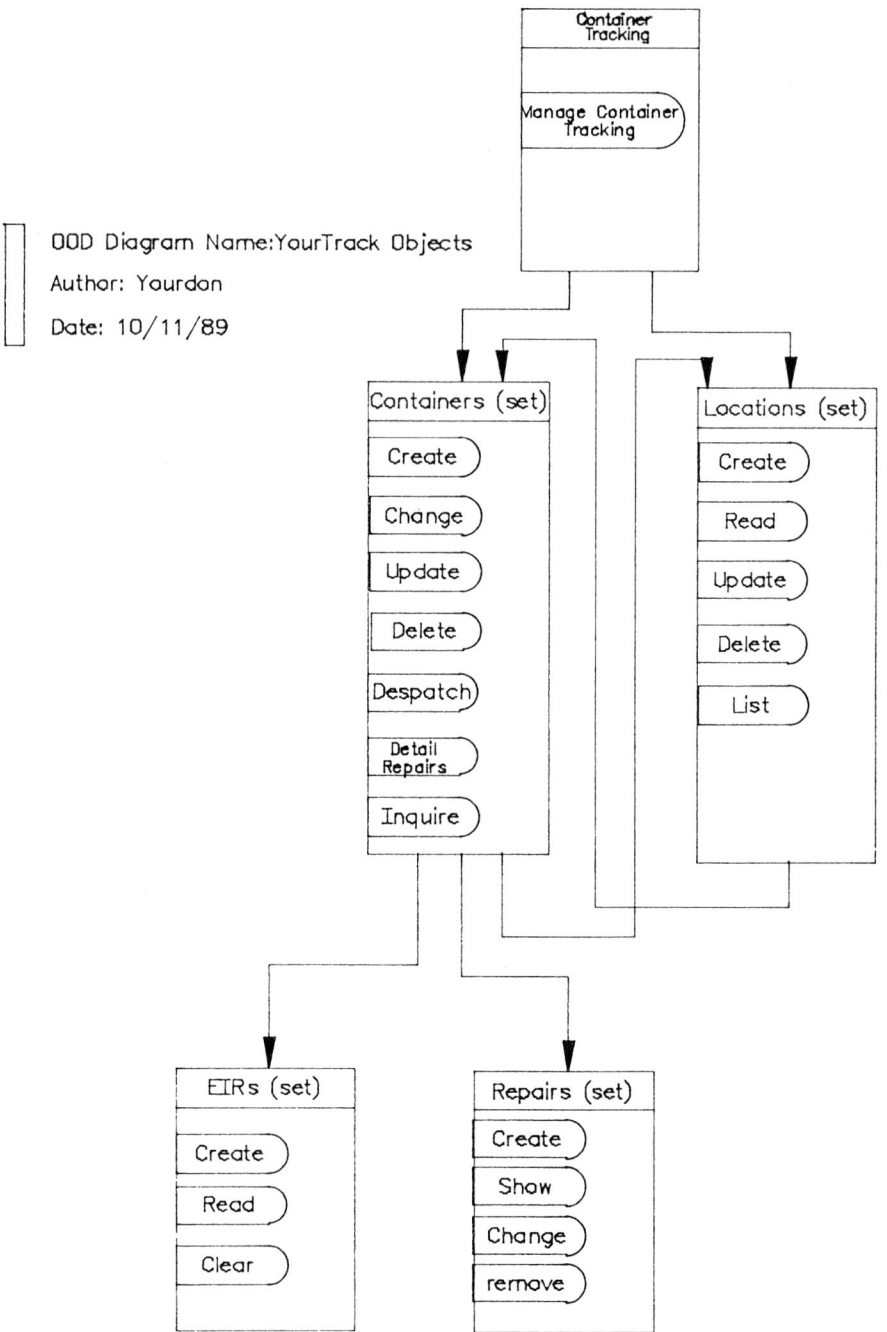

Figure 11

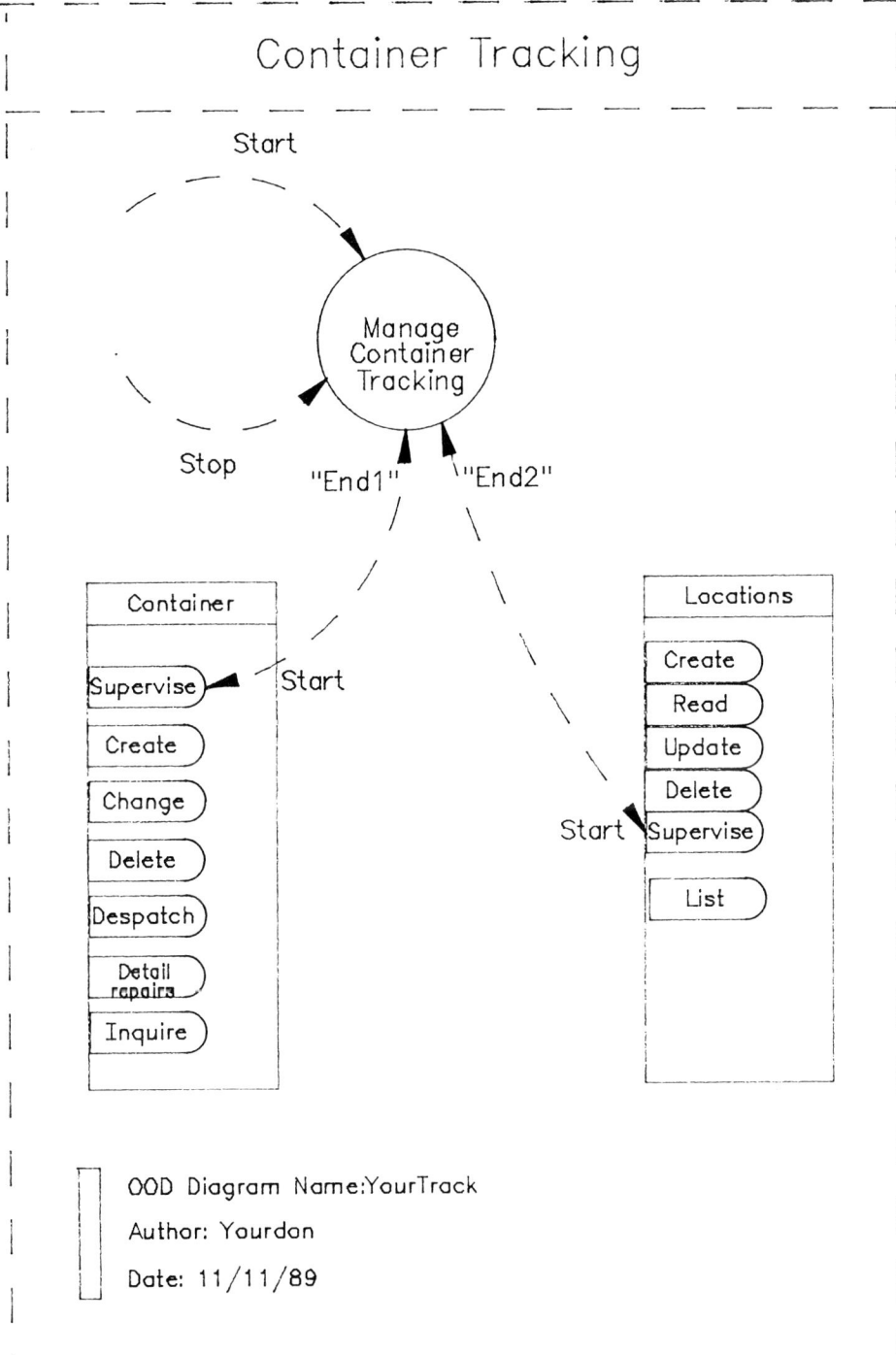

Figure 12

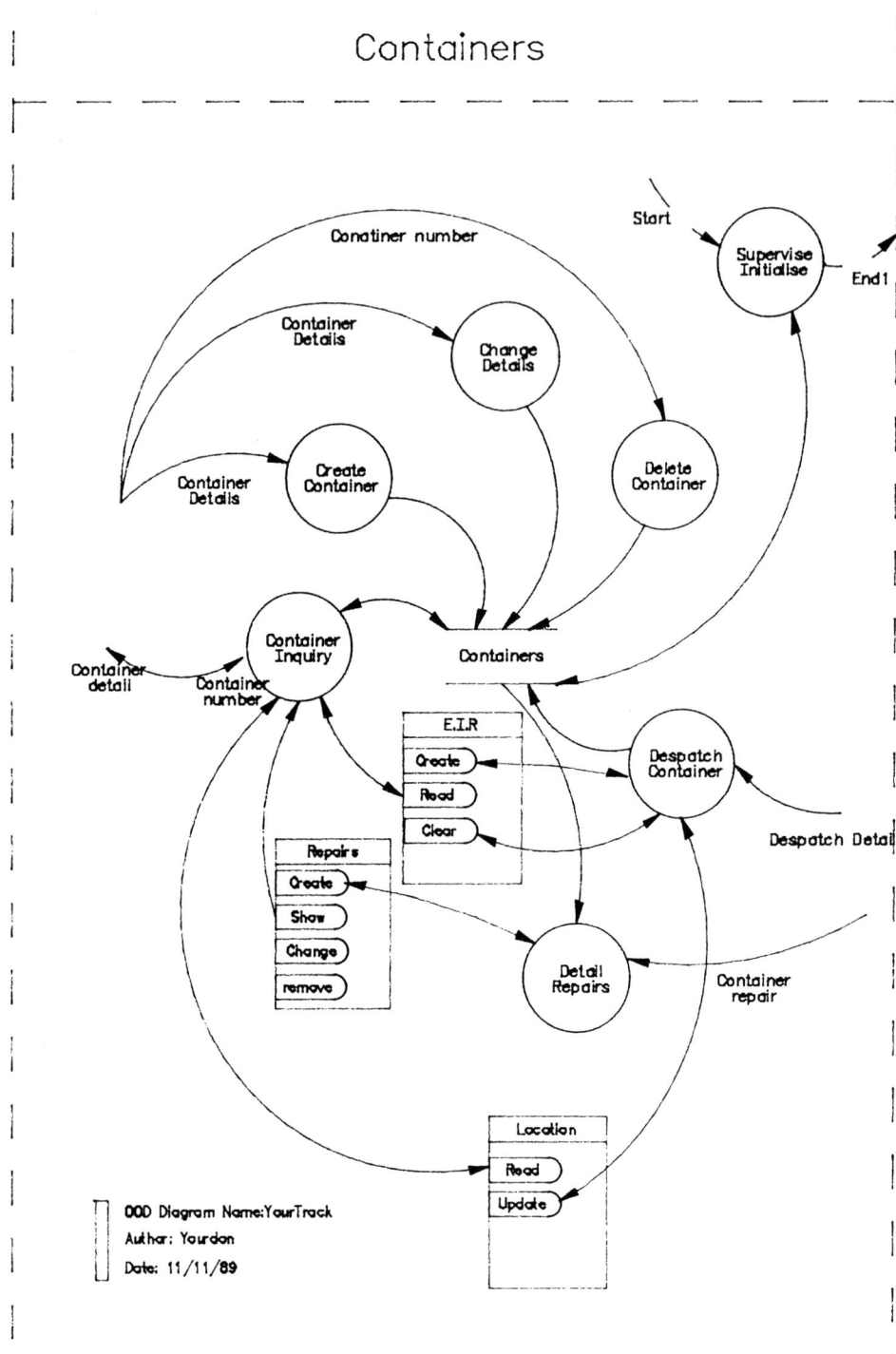

Figure 13

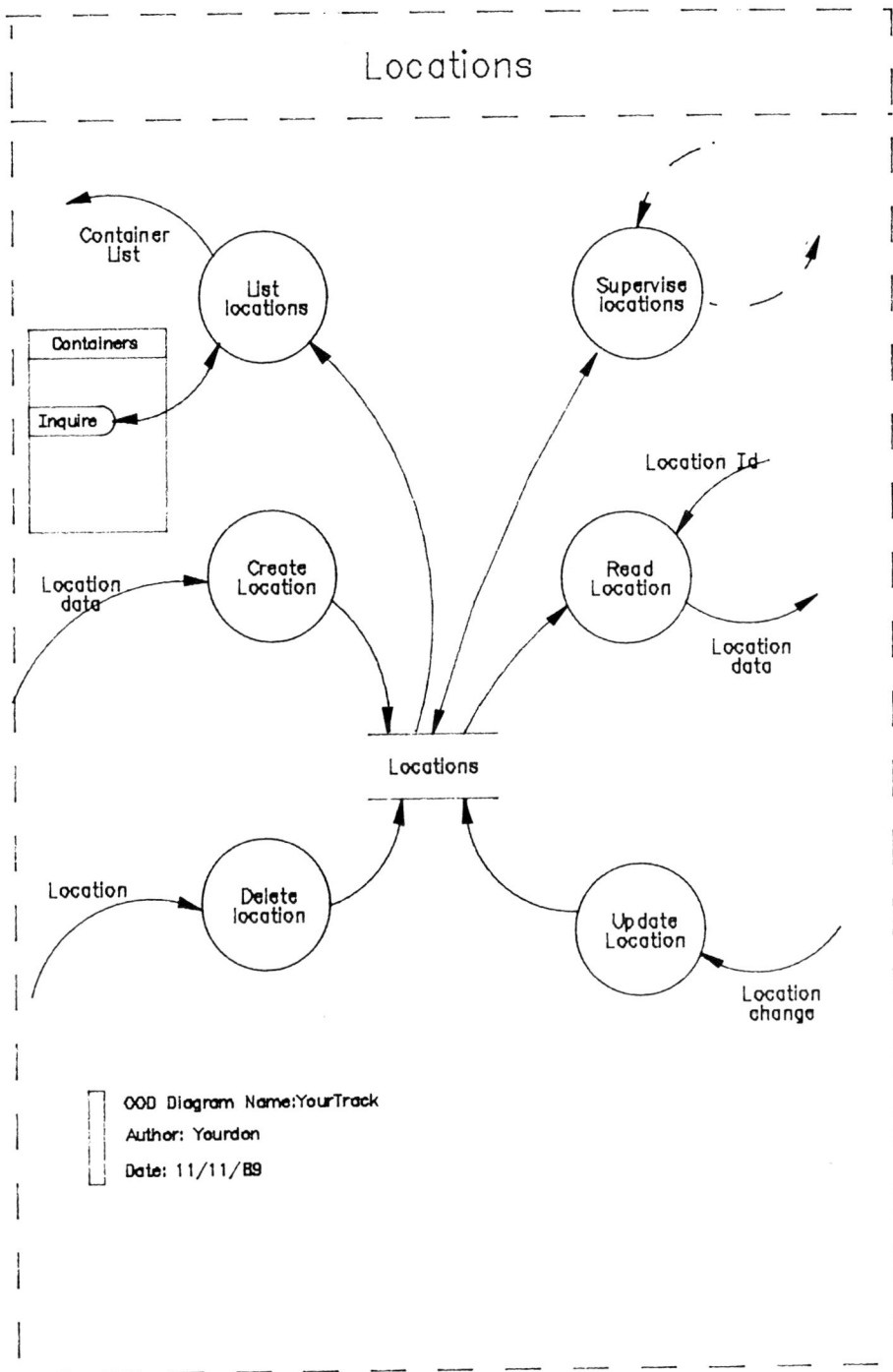

Figure 14

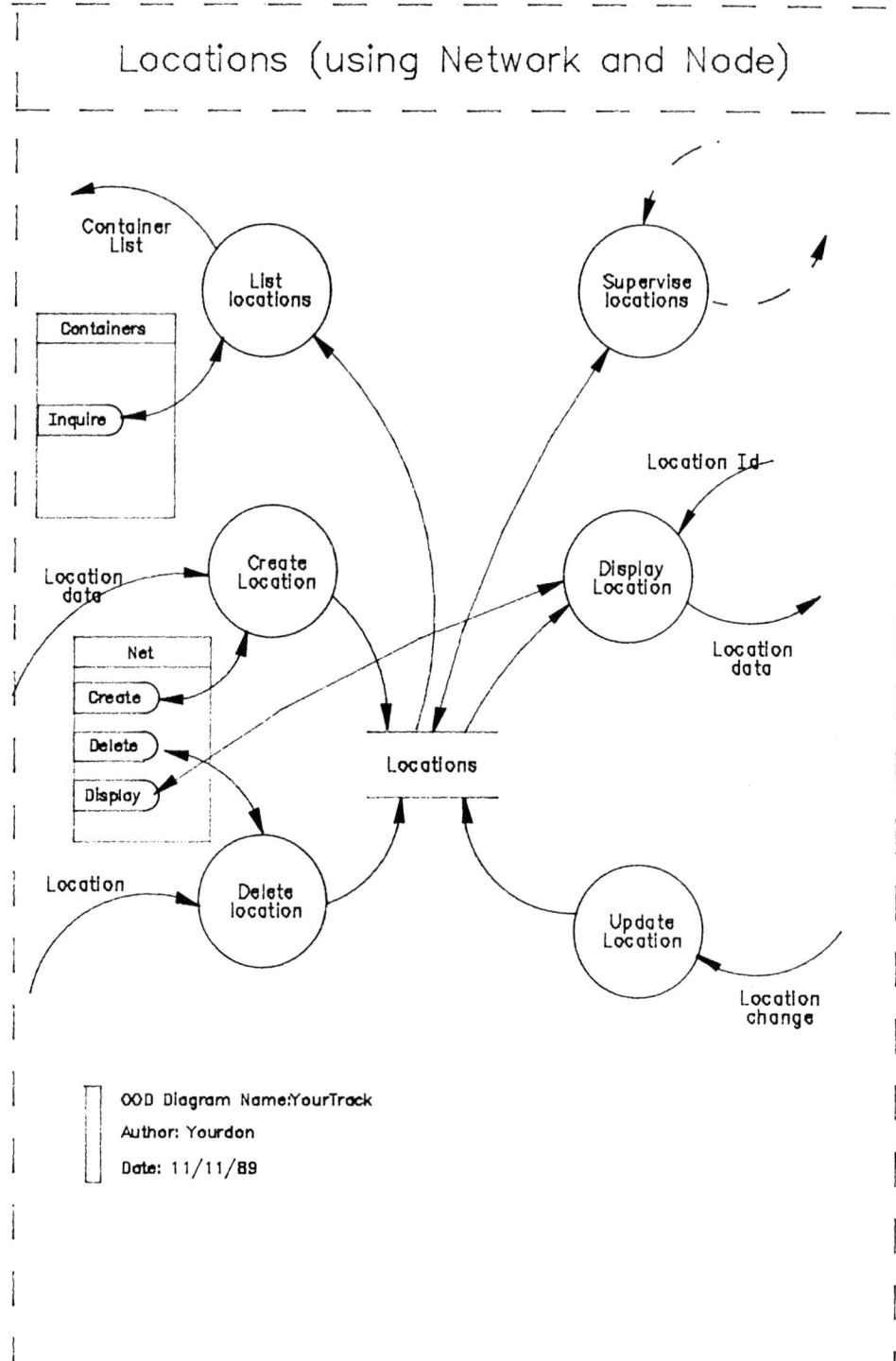

Figure 15

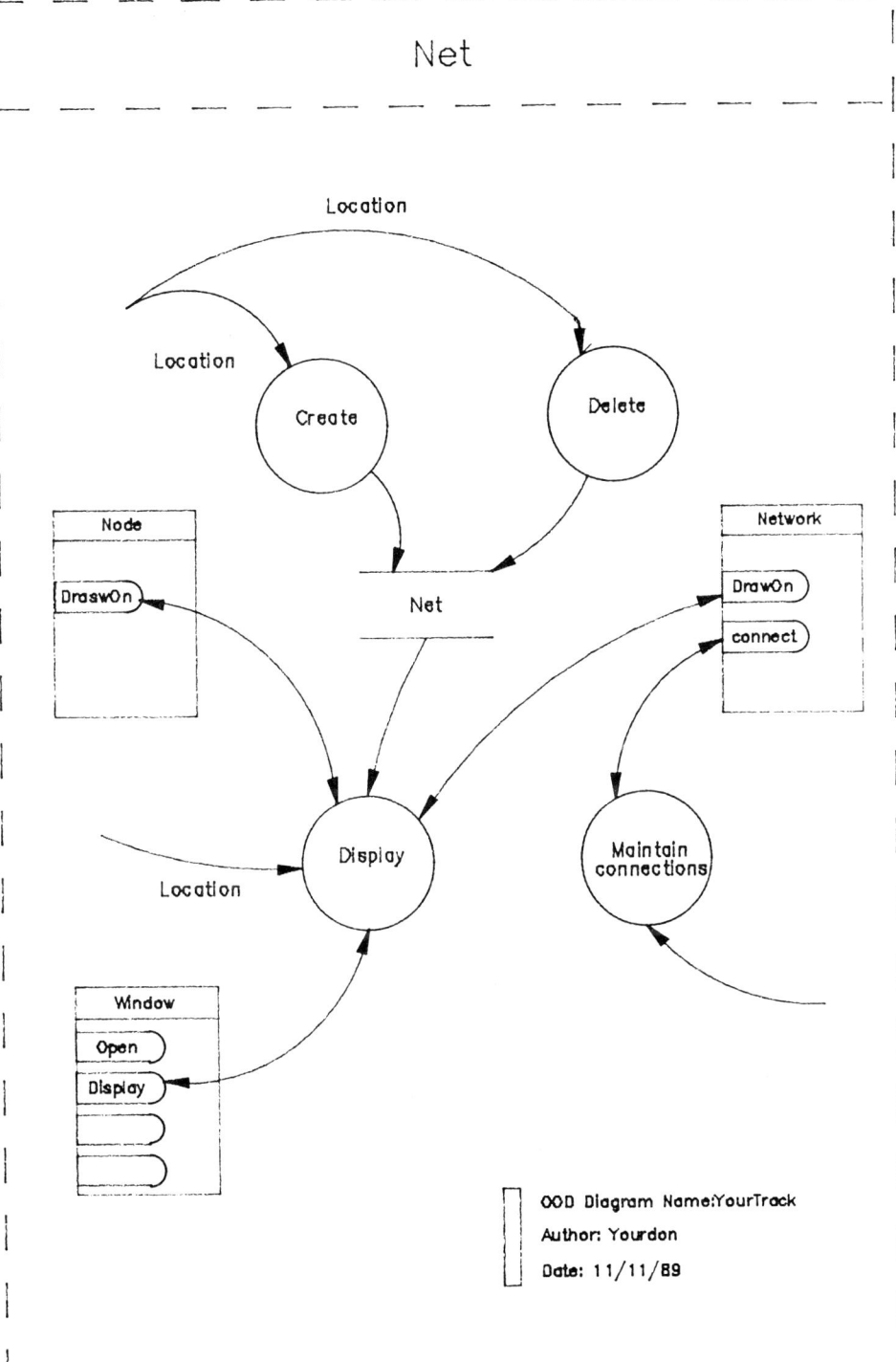

Figure 16

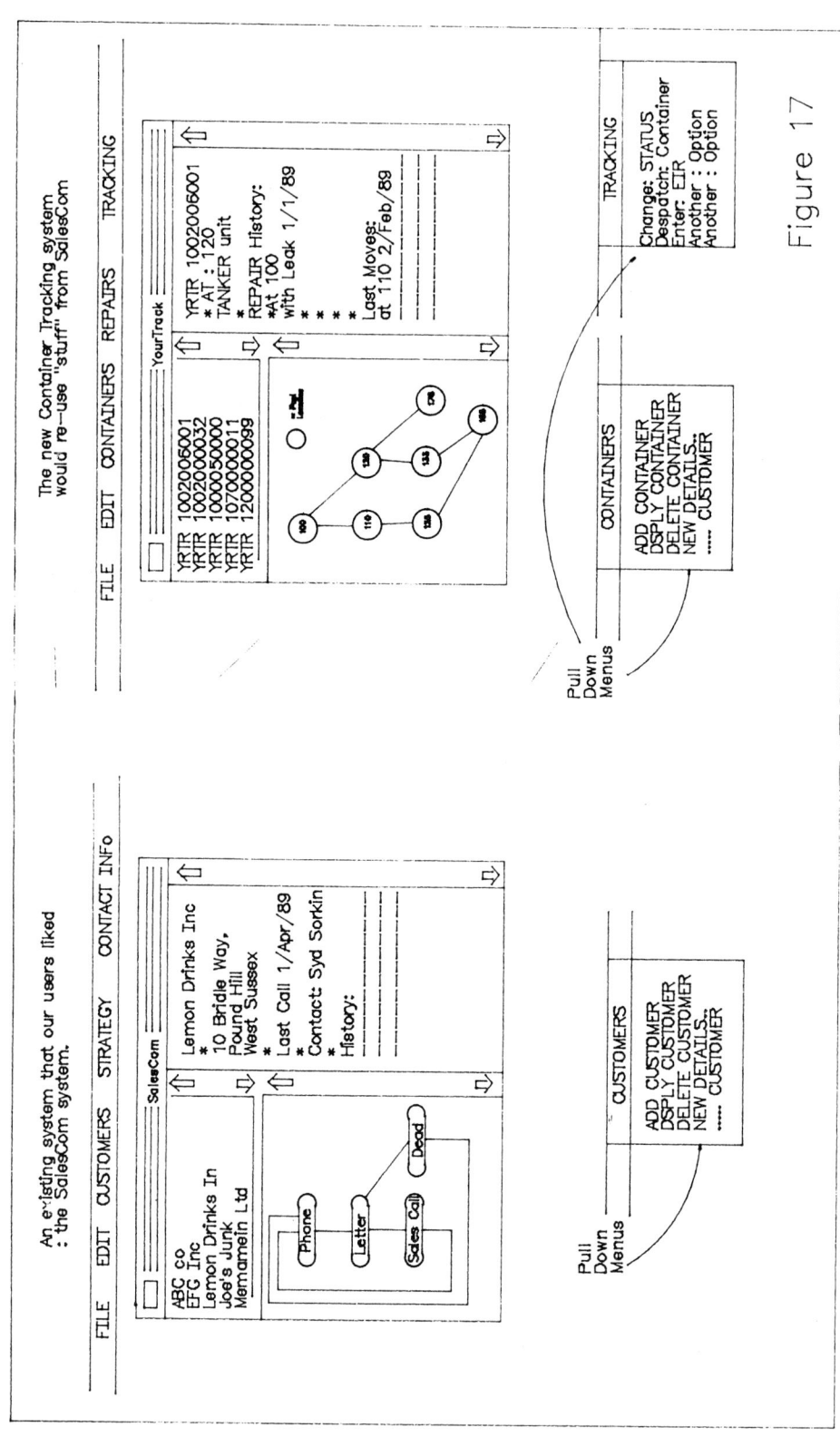

Figure 17

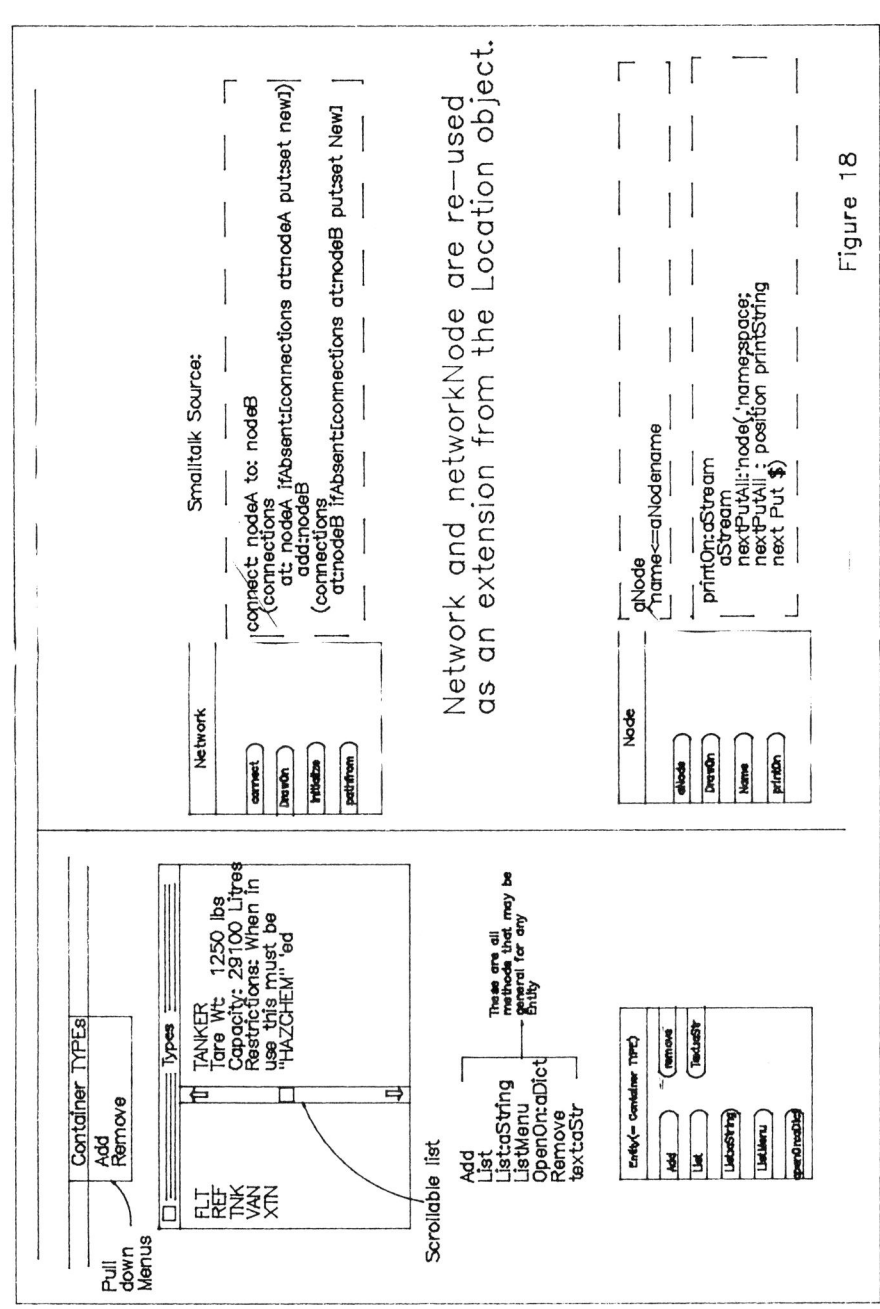

Figure 18

BIBLIOGRAPHY

[McMe84] McMenamin, S. and Palmer, J. *Essential Systems Analysis..* Yourdon Press. 1984.

[Ward85] Ward, P and Mellor, S. *Structured Development for Real Time Systems.* Yourdon Press. 1985.

[Meye89] Meyer, B. *Object Oriented Software Construction.* Prentice-Hall. 1989.

[OOSD91] *Object-oriented Development.* Yourdon International Course.

Resources

Managing Key Resources During Systems Engineering, R. Barker
Implications of Assessing Software as a Financial Asset, P. Rigby and M. Norris

Managing Key Resources During Systems Engineering

RICHARD BARKER

Vice President
CASE and Business Applications
ORACLE EUROPE

1 INTRODUCTION

It is often thought that during the 1990s high-quality systems will be engineered by using good CASE tools, fourth-generation languages, database management systems and other techniques that can be brought to bear. In reality, this is only part of the story. Engineering quality systems is predominantly about the deployment of key resources in an effective manner, and utilizing the most appropriate methods and techniques for the job in hand. This paper discusses some of the key resources that must be understood and managed, and looks at the problems and issues that have to be addressed.

The most important key resource is the human resource – people – the top developers. But one must not forget the other areas like financial, physical and other, less tangible resources, such as the skills of management, ideas, technologies, techniques and methods, which need to be harnessed towards a common goal.

The basic techniques of project control are well known and consist of standard approaches such as setting aims and objectives, performing work breakdown, defining deliverables, identifying dependencies, and so on. When considering key resource management, however, the critical aspect is that of allocating and scheduling those key resources in what is often a highly complex environment across multiple projects, taking into consideration conflicting priorities, objectives and aspirations. This process of managing key resources is addressed in detail in this paper, on the basis that a problem understood is often a problem that can be solved. The paper then deals with the approach and type of technology needed to make this form of management easier, that is, to computer assist this complex but highly beneficial task. The computer aid required not only covers the more obvious hardware and software capabilities, but how the facilities required can be integrated with other technologies such as life-cycle CASE tools, electronic mail and other packages that may be available in the development environment.

At the end of the day, success (which may be measured by timeliness, quality, meeting budgetary requirements, having motivated staff or whatever) is dependent upon managing key resources in the most effective manner.

2 TYPICAL PROBLEMS

Project management and control may be approached in different ways. When we look around the computer industry we find a small set of common, recurring themes.

There are those large establishments with complex projects spanning many years of work, where sophisticated project management and control techniques are being used to manage large teams. Such environments often suffer from the fact that the people on the project do not know **why** they are doing what they are doing, do not know the scope, do not know the impact of any decisions that they make, and generally treat their work as a nine-to-five job. Often, such development environments are not following a life-cycle methodology to guide them through the entire process. They may be using old technology that is slow and cumbersome, which therefore focuses people on the mechanisms they are using, as opposed to the objectives they are trying to achieve.

At the other end of the spectrum there is the small, dynamic, start-up company, where three or four people work together with a common goal. Their success is dependent purely upon the ability of their leader to encompass the whole and react rapidly when things go wrong against the model he has in his head. Such organizations have different problems. They may well achieve their initial objectives and produce innovative ideas, 'whizzy' interfaces or some other unique capability to support them on the road to success. Unfortunately, these projects often suffer from the lack of infrastructure to enable them to take their early products forward into the future. Business success can also result in a high rate of growth, and it is not long before that leader is now managing teams of teams and his personal influence is diluted – at which point it is vital to recruit like-minded people or to apply relevant, structured methods to fulfil the same need.

A third, typical environment is where some particular technique is used as the dominant way of running projects. This might be data modelling, prototyping, dataflow modelling, or function analysis. This will often tend to result in systems that are heavily skewed towards one particular dominant technology.

A fourth approach is the discrete, non-overlapping project technique – islands of people – independent business units. Each of these may be so focused on a single objective that wheels are continuously being re-invented, skilled people wasted on tactical rather than strategic issues and vast amounts of resource squandered unnecessarily. The use of **multiple** methods, tools, enabling technologies and management styles is often exhibited across such groups.

The truly successful companies, which have managed to master the complex task of engineering high-quality systems, are those which have learnt how to use appropriate techniques and methods, focus their different resources and get a sensible balance of emphasis in a cost-effective and timely manner. How do they do this and what are the methods and technologies that systems engineers have available today?

3 AVAILABLE METHODS

During the last few years we have seen the advance and adoption of some important new methods and technologies. In the methodology arena two important technologies have been brought to bear. One of these is the life-cycle methodology, which takes the concept of building a system from conception through to final implementation.

Figure 1
The Waterfall Method

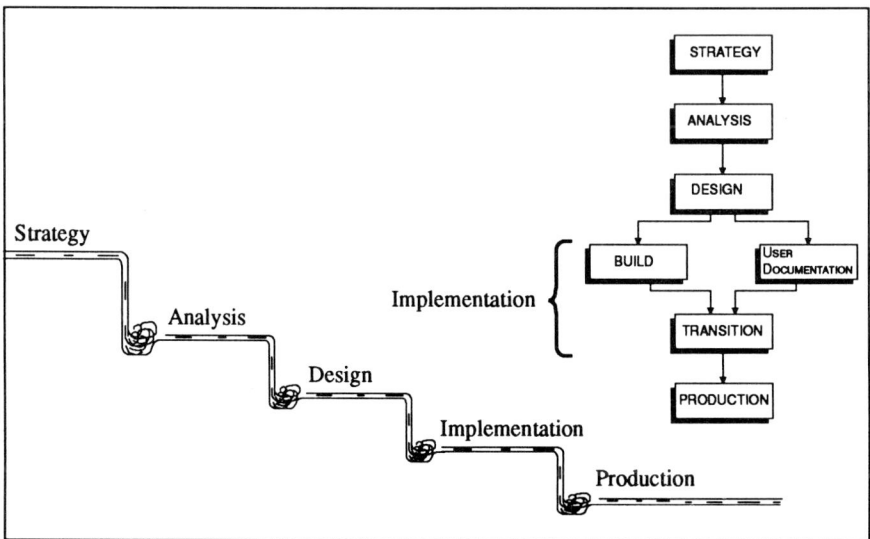

Life-cycle approaches tend to be structured methodologies, such as Information Engineering (IE), Structured Systems Analysis and Design Method (SSADM) and Merise. Most of these fall into the classification of waterfall methods, whereby they follow a stage by stage, relatively linear approach of producing deliverables in one stage which then go over the waterfall to be delivered to the next stage and so on. In reality, these stages have a high degree of overlap and many of the tasks are highly iterative.

Other methods have grown out of fourth-generation languages and expert systems technologies to give us the ability to build complete systems using some form of prototyping mechanism. In both cases, strong emphasis is placed upon user interaction to ensure quality.

**Figure 2
Prototyping**

Both approaches have their problems. With the waterfall technique, extended timescales and badly-met expectations are often encountered; whereas with prototyping, early deliverables but a lack of quality are regularly found. A major bank, for example, prototyped a 200+ screen personnel system which had severe performance, usability and duplicate data problems. The end-user backlash cast severe doubt on the data processing department's capability and the applicability of the software tools being used. The situation was saved by a focused and quick reverse engineering exercise, the production of a top-down framework and rapid corrective action based on this new combined insight.

The second major set of methods available in the market deals with project management and control. In this case we are talking about systems that control tasks, deliverables, dependencies and critical paths for an individual project.

It is these project control systems that need to be thoroughly understood if we are to manage our key resources during the life-cycle methodologies we may have to adopt. But the status of of the available project control tools is such that they may **cause**, rather than solve, problems!

Most readily-available project management systems today are single-user, personal-computer-based systems. This technology immediately gives us problems such as:

- queueing up of people to use the facility
- the scale of projects that can be handled within the capacity of the device
- poor usability due to resolution of screens, memory capability and lack of integration with a development environment
- a product facility level that only addresses low-level task and dependency control.

When these tools are analyzed in detail, the facilities to address the issue of helping **members** of a project team are rarely found. Most of the facilities are targeted at either the project leader or, through producing aggregate information, at his manager. Where such tools have been slavishly used, there are many recorded instances of the tool requiring twenty percent of the resources of the whole team, for questionable benefit.

So what are the key issues that need to be addressed? And what sort of project control life-cycle do we need to go through? What technologies can be brought to bear to provide really effective help in this complex task?

4 KEY ISSUES

Undoubtedly the old maxim of over-delivery (slight), on time, within budget must still apply. If, however, we stand above an individual project and look at its success within the scope of an area of our business, does its success actually cause problems in other areas? Have we got the balance right? Was project B actually more important than delivering project A on time? Were we using our resources correctly?

As a provocative thought, maybe the long-term success of a company is when it can maximize the effective use of its key resources towards assured **future** prosperity, whilst doing the minimum adequate to satisfy short-term goals.

During the past two years I have asked the question, 'How many people in your organization are **really** critical to its success?' at over one hundred companies. The answer has ranged from around one in five to a perhaps more realistic figure of one in fifty. An alternative way of thinking about this is to consider how long it would take to replace someone. If less than three months, they were hardly critical in most situations. Those people identified as critical are key resources. Their time must be balanced between the day-to-day operational aspects of running the business and strategically developing new products, services or better ways of running the organization to give a competitive edge, increase market share, or achieve whatever other corporate objective is desired.

Surely, someone who is a top-class designer and wants to do that task should be rewarded and recognized for that value, and encouraged to help the organization in the manner to which he or she is best suited. How often do we find that such people feel forced to enter management or do some other job as the only way of progressing their careers?

5 SO WHAT ARE THESE KEY RESOURCES?

5.1 Financial Resouces

In large projects the focus is frequently on the project budget – the financial resource. Understanding this, the money side of any project, is certainly very important. 'What is my total budget?' may be the only question we need to ask, but in large projects success can be determined by a thorough understanding of when that money can be made available over time.

Is the money available instantly at the beginning of the project?

Does it come on stream on a month-by-month basis?

Can it be used to acquire capital goods or is it there purely to support the ongoing expenditure of staff and their consumables?

Can any amount be redistributed to use for purposes such as employing contractors or consultants; and if so are there limits or rates that must apply, or policies on fixed price contracts?

At the beginning of a project it is normally relatively straightforward to cost it out completely. In key resource management terms, however, some important aspects need to be considered.

i) **Tolerance** – once the budget has been signed off, are we allowed to overspend, and if so by how much? Can monies be brought forward if a project has to be rescheduled?

ii) **Specials** – a project rarely goes through without some unforeseen expenditure arising. This will often fall into two categories – expenditure that we should have thought of in the first place or that we estimated incorrectly, and expenditure that has arisen through no fault of our own (or perhaps opportunities that need to be addressed have occurred).

Does the project leader have the flexibility to change the budget allocations, acquire cash set aside for other purposes, to deploy resources on a cross-project basis to maximize return on investment, and maybe to acquire new technologies or individuals early and thus reduce the cost of doing subsequent tasks?

This management of the financial aspects can have many knock-on effects. If new technologies are acquired, typically with a cost justification, has the learning curve actually been considered along with the aptitude of the staff who may need to use this technology? These hidden start-up costs quite often negate the value of the otherwise apparently sensible deployment of financial resources.

Control of the financial resource is reasonably well understood in most establishments. The trappings of control are normally found in the form of the ongoing budgetary spreadsheets, monitoring of orders and commitments, and comparison of actual versus budget. But controlling the other key resources can often have a more dramatic, positive or even negative effect.

5.2 Physical Resources

Many a project has failed because of an inability to manage the comparatively simple task of controlling the physical resources or environment within which the project is to be run. What sort of physical resources are we talking about?

The most obvious of these is office space. Most people work in a far more effective manner if they have a sensible amount of personal space made available to them. Such space needs to be available in sufficient time for a project team to set up a sensible working environment. As the project expands, more space may become necessary to accommodate new team members or perhaps the users who are getting involved to ensure the quality of the system. One major application development team in Oracle suffered badly from the lack of available space, to such an extent that it was easily measurable by timesheet analysis and numbers of bugs in the product; and less quantifiable but still obvious was the fall in morale. Growth cannot always be matched by the availability of new premises. After this near crisis period of six months, a move to new, spacious accommodation resulted in a trend the opposite way to higher productivity and much improved quality.

The availability of space needs to be balanced by the continuity of working from the same environment over a protracted period of time. Any form of change to the work environment causes a disproportionate amount of disruption and waste of time compared with any other form of change. It may even be better to leave people in relatively cramped conditions for longer, rather than switch them to constantly changing locations. Part of the reason for this problem is that of familiarity with the working environment. People get used to being able to turn to the left to talk to their project leader; to being able to turn round in the opposite direction to talk to the technical leader of the team; and to being able to reach down and acquire the files that they put there the day before. Constant change may be compared with the problem of driving. If every time you got into a car you found the steering wheel and pedals in different places, how well would you drive until you got used to the new positions? A less than perfect **stable** working environment can be more acceptable than constant flux whilst striving for the perfect balance.

Other critical physical resources are to do with the tools for the job. In the software engineering industry these include the right-sized desk (big enough to work on large-scale diagrams and take a computer terminal or workstation), templates or CASE tools for producing neat, accurate diagrams, electronic whiteboards and meeting rooms for efficient group discussions.

For the development teams in Oracle Corporation (where the growth rate is sixty to eighty percent per year) the critical physical resources are workstations, connection to the computer network, the availability of three million instructions per second (3MIPs) of power and five hundred Megabytes of disk space and electronic mail connectivity for all new developers. However, it is often the small things that cause delay and frustration. How many of your designers use memo-stickers, and what would happen if they were suddenly no longer available? What happens if you run out of overhead projector foils or the pens to write on them, or the marker pens for your whiteboard? What happens when your last remaining meeting room gets taken over by the auditors for two months at the end of the year?

The successful management of physical resources requires a thorough understanding of which tools of the trade and which physical resources are absolutely required to give maximum productivity within the project team, with minimum disruption. When development staff continually complain about the availability of terminals, poor response time, running out of consumables, and unavailability of meeting rooms there is a failure in managing these resources. Project leaders should ensure that their team members have the necessary tools of their trade when they need them; this is not a menial task.

5.3 Special Key Resources

Two companies or two projects may apparently have essentially the same financial, human and physical resources available. What is it that makes the difference between the success of one and the failure of another? Management of the human resource is undoubtedly the most significant aspect, but awareness of the intangible resources that must be deployed should not be overlooked.

Perhaps the most important of these are the **techniques** that have been found to be of value within the organization. It is of immense value to be able to look back on similar or other activities to see how they succeeded and what techniques they used. A cost-effective way of harnessing this resource is by means of a short, sharp, post-implementation review. A recent review of a development project that overran its timescales identified interesting inhibitors to its success. These included 'secrecy culture', where groups kept important decisions to themselves, invalid short-cuts and the expected problems with communication channels and environmental issues.

A familiar method for delivering techniques is through standards, which should cover such concepts as good practice and guidelines. Techniques can be disseminated informally through cross-fertilization by people from similar projects, and the use of peer-group check and review procedures to communicate ideas, as well as improving the quality of the project under review.

Techniques to be adopted have to be carefully considered. Whilst it is obviously important that they are relevant to the task in hand, it is also important that they are accepted by the people who must use them; that they are liked; that they are fun to use; and that they give that intangible benefit of aiding communication between colleagues and with the user fraternity. These techniques must fit together coherently, and it must be clear when each technique should be used and how they interrelate. The use of **inappropriate** techniques can increase the cost and timescales by fifty percent. But it is difficult to quantify the effect of different techniques.

A major retail company attempted to measure the applicability of two alternative life-cycle methods. At each interview or information gathering exercise there were four analysts, an expert and a newly trained analyst for each method. Modelling and requirement definition were then carried out separately, and comparisons made on the basis of time spent, quantity and quality of deliverables agreed and the judgement of the applicability to the current and future business.

One interesting result was that one method produced a data model with only thirty percent of the number of entities and relationships identified by the other method, and yet it was capable of reflecting the information needs of far more of the business. This more generic model also enabled subsequent stages of the life-cycle to be replanned with proportionately fewer tasks and shorter timescales. This proved to be a most useful exercise to help select an approach that would fit the business and culture of the data processing department.

Associated with techniques are the technologies to support them. Within the systems engineering discipline we will undoubtedly be looking at the use of sophisticated diagrammatic techniques, such as entity relationship modelling, dataflow diagramming, state transition diagrams, and so on, as appropriate, to support the relevant life-cycle method that has been adopted. There are, however, many more technologies available to us which can be used as key resources.

Computer hardware technology is changing at an awesome rate. Ten years ago it was rare for development staff in software companies to have their own terminal – now it is not uncommon to find development environments set up for team working with each team member having a terminal or workstation connected into a network. In Oracle, for example, in the mid 1980s the development team members each had a character mode terminal and an average of 0.200 MIPs each on a shared computer. Today each team member would have a three or even ten MIP workstation and perhaps another 3MIPs on a networked server computer. The staff responsible for porting the code even have two or three such workstations from different manufacturers networked into minis and mainframes from up to forty different manufacturers. Commodity Unix boxes are becoming available with massive parallel-processing architectures delivering over one hundred million instructions per second for around a hundred thousand dollars. The software explosion is no less daunting, with portable, application development tools, CASE tools, fourth-generation languages, artificial intelligence, application generators and so on.

When considering these powerful key resources we have to remember the negative effect of adopting such technology too fast. Have we the time to learn how to exploit these new facilities? Can we afford the learning curve? Are there experts to whom we can turn to get advice and guidance? Have we added the disruption and learning costs to that of the hardware or software licences? Are we adopting too many technologies too fast? The key here is to thoroughly understand what we are trying to achieve, the way in which we need to achieve it, and use these clearly understood guidelines to help us select the appropriate high-quality tools, to adopt them in a controlled manner, and to ensure that the people who will be subjected to their introduction are motivated towards their use in the successful delivery of our projects. Adopting new technology and methods is a disruptive and problem-fraught task. The only successful way to do so is to treat the adoption process as a project in its own right.

Perhaps the least tangible of our key resources is that of attitude. The most talented collection of people will not be able to succeed unless they are backed up by positive, well-informed management. The most successful projects have always encouraged the close participation of users or clients with the people delivering the project. A positive attitude is required to encourage the use of good techniques, to praise good practice and crack down on poor quality. People need to have available the techniques most appropriate to them and to the job they are trying to do. These techniques help them focus on the production of high-quality work and good communications. If a project team, along with the users and management, is encouraged to think clearly and objectively about what they are trying to achieve, to stand above their local problems, and see the broader picture, they will tend to be far more successful than if they are closeted with some isolated objective to achieve.

5.4 Human Resources and Their Deployment

The final, and probably, most important resource that must be managed well on any systems engineering project is the team members, consultants, contractors, managers, users and anyone else who can help towards the success of the project. Allocation of the right people to the job is at the heart of good management of people on projects. The starting point is the allocation of a really skilled person or small team to define and plan the project. In this case there is no substitute for simply knowing someone who can be trusted, has a proven track record and who has the appropriate enquiring mind and ability to home in on the salient details in a well-structured and thorough way. An early important deliverable is the resource-unlimited plan, which tells us in detail what has to be done, the deliverables, dependencies, possible parallelism, estimates and the optimum type of resources that have been assumed in this estimating procedure. Ideally, task definitions will also be available, along with comments on specific resource notes that might apply (e.g. Andy Brown should get involved in this design because of his experience on the XYZ project last year).

Now we are at the highly-creative and iterative stage of allocation. How do we do it? Well, in simple terms we can just look at the team that is going to be responsible for this project and allocate the people according to their experience and skill. Once allocated, we construct a detailed project schedule, add in contingency for holidays and sickness, shuffle the work to minimize gaps and optimize timescales, and call it a day. This is a very common approach, which is often very successful on small projects. It typically succeeds when there is no **really urgent** deadline for delivery, and when the human resources are constrained to the allotted team and sufficient for the job. In more complex circumstances allocation is a skilful balance of many conflicting factors. A good balance can only be achieved by a thorough understanding of all the important factors and alternatives open to us. So how can we find out?

One of the most important skills in managing key resources and allocating them to a project is the analytical skill of finding out the relevant facts and the synthesis skill of putting down a coherent model of the project and plan of campaign. A well-established way of doing this is to have a brief period of divergent, then convergent, modelling; a technique that has been used during strategy, product design and problem solving within Oracle Corporation, ICL and many other organizations for many years. This is to extend our understanding and knowledge to encompass all possible relevant information; and to classify and model it by various means and then against a set of objectives to produce a simpler, more generic set of models and plans that define the way forward. Both sets of models must be tested. Divergent models must be checked for completeness, relevance and accuracy. Convergent models must also be checked for feasibility, impact on conflicting priorities, and used to predict the effect on time, money, quality and acceptability.

Some useful techniques for gaining thorough, wide understanding are as follows:

- interviewing key players
- brainstorming sessions and lateral thinking
- mind-mapping or spider diagrams
- role playing users, operations staff and other roles in or on the receiving end of the project
- categorization and classification, often thought of as simple lists under sensible headings.

Some of the headings under which any of these techniques should seek out information are shown below:

Project   aims and objectives
           priorities and constraints (financial, physical, human, ethical, ...)
           critical success factors
           key deliverables
           key dates (e.g. demonstrable to sponsor by 1st April)
           potential conflicts of interests
           dependencies
           potential alternative suppliers
           acceptance criteria
           tolerances on dates and quality
           expected working practice and standards
           tools to be used
           and so on, not forgetting a category for **good ideas**.

But for people, we also need to know their specific availability. What does their diary look like? What is their work pattern? Does anyone work shifts or unusual hours? Is having transport important or being willing to work away from home? Have we considered public and personal holidays, pressures at home (such as an imminent childbirth or house move), health or other factors, which could affect availability.

It is also useful to know what people would **really** like to do. We will get twice the work out of well-motivated people than out of those who grudgingly do some uninteresting (to them) task. A well-tried technique to help here is the use of personal reviews or planning sessions, which can result in a clear understanding of **personal** objectives, aims, priorities, preferences and so on which can then be considered during project allocation. Knowledge of what else people are doing is vital – their forward load. Key people tend to work on more than one project at a time, often have special management or technical roles to play and will tend to be the people who have to look at new ideas or fight fires. These details **must** be known. We also need to ascertain who has the knowledge and authority to sort out any conflicts of priorities.

Now the task of allocation really can start properly. Ideally this is done by a small team comprising the project leader, a top technical person and someone who has a broader picture (perhaps a manager). The process is a simple one of allocate, predict the effect, test against project and other criteria, iterate until a satisfactory solution is found.

Figure 3
Iterative Resource Allocation

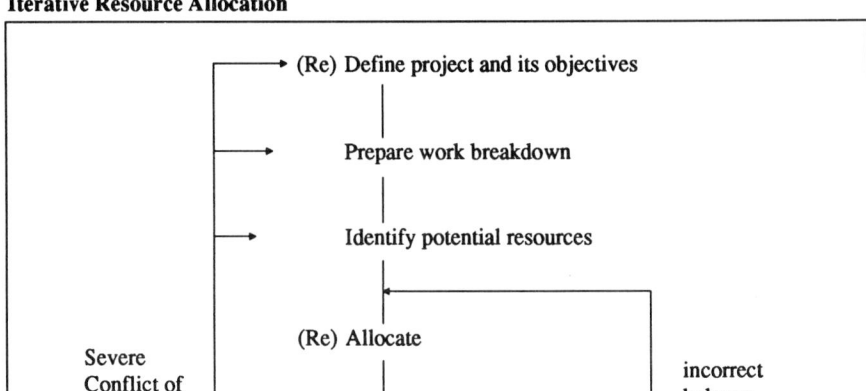

When unacceptable estimates are found, the top technicians should be deployed to find alternative ways of doing the job. Failing that, perhaps a guru on the subject should be used, as sometimes a real expert can produce difficult deliverables in a few days whilst a mere mortal might take weeks, or possibly waste effort without even achieving the desired result.

The prediction of the effect, or **'what-if'** playing, has to consider the obvious aspects like impact on timescales and money. Equally important is the effect any trade-offs can have on the quality, list of deliverables and attitude of the staff or users. Personal impact must be considered – has everyone got something they will enjoy doing? Will morale be OK? Are careers being pushed forward or put at risk? Can training be done on the job?

Conflicts of priorities will occur. These conflicts must be considered from a wide perspective: the impact on development cost versus the impact to the business of not having the system; short-cuts today versus high maintenance costs later; delays to the user versus overstretched development staff. When such conflicts occur they must be resolved quickly, and ideally by consensus. People's preferences need to be considered, peers approached for ideas and advice, affected people involved (users, managers, customers, suppliers, team members, ...) and quality groups consulted. And in the end, the procedure may need to be escalated for decision and sign-off.

Unfortunately this allocation process is **not** a one-off exercise. Priorities change, timescales slip, dependencies are not met, allocated staff find jobs difficult or impossible, people are needed on other more critical projects, and so on. Regular reviews and monitoring of project timescales, working practice, quality, morale and anything else that affects the project must be carried out and reallocations/new schedules drawn up using the same approach.

6 Computer-aided Key Resource Management

The process outlined above is difficult, error prone and can involve a lot of resource to do it effectively. There is no substitute to using top-class people who understand such issues and have the skill and determination to do an excellent job. However, there is ample opportunity to provide focused computer support.

The most effective hardware solutions that can be brought to bear include networked computers shared by all members of the project team. But why limit it there? When projects commonly overlap, and resources are often deployed on multiple projects, the network should cover all overlapping projects and be available to all development and other affected staff. Given such an environment, we now have the opportunity to deploy electronic mail, common diary systems and ensure a standard set of software tools is made available.

Where the teams are separated geographically, electronic mail and shared repositories for information are very useful, **but must not be relied upon**. Experience in many countries has shown that electronic mail can not only obstruct communication, but can cause severe conflicts between different groups. The problem arises when people get so much mail it is answered in a rush, online, and without proper thought, so that the response is often accidentally tense, emotive and antagonistic. This must be understood and compensated for by well-written mail and occasional telephone conversations and meetings. There is **no** substitute for face-to-face meetings.

Multi-user repositories are a key factor − or put another way, the use of database technology by development staff. If everything necessary is recorded once and cross-referenced so that we always have access to the most up-to-date copy, life gets a lot easier. Access control and version control are necessary to protect the data and cater for evolution.

Workstation technology provides a mixture of improved productivity and quality. By a workstation, we mean a high-resolution screen, keypad and mouse, connected to a powerful desktop computer with its own memory and disk. To be really effective, these are connected onto the network and provide multi-tasking capability through some industry-standard window-management facility. Productivity comes from the raw power and from the ability to multi-task. Quality tends to come from being able to view multiple, related windows at the same time, thus aiding the decision process.

Now how would a computerized project management and control system use such technology and what else might it provide in the way of facilities?

The first thing to do would be to have a multi-user repository for all the data required to control overlapping projects. The repository would hold all the project-related data such as work breakdown, task definition, deliverables and so on. A database is an ideal tool by which we can control complex interrelated data, such as dependencies and deliverable flow. Knowledge about all the key resources available could be held. Such knowledge would take the form of computerized diaries, forward loads and, subsequently, resources used on any task or activity.

That a single system could be used for complete diary management, time recording and cross-project allocation is obviously very useful. If we add cross-project scheduling to that we have a very powerful capability. We need facilities to enable us to say things like:

- Reschedule projects A, B and C but leave D and E as they are.
- Allocate resources to hit the deadlines, and tell me what extra resources would be necessary.

Automatic schedulers need to be very sophisticated if they are to be really useful. They should cater for allocation of resources on the basis of one hundred percent of the time from a given point, using any free time, on specific dates, on specific periodic dates (e.g. every Monday), weighted towards the start or finish of a task, evenly spread, 'n' days before the end of a task or milestone and so on, as applicable. Algorithms should be capable of bias towards a 'just in time' scenario, to ensure milestones are hit, rate of financial spend, against a profile to maximize on the degree of parallelism, to achieve optimum use of key resources or any combination. Consideration should also be taken of resource availability and the predefined profile of how the resource should be used.

For example, a top designer could have a predefined profile of:

- two days a week on project A
- no more than four days a month on project B
- half a day a week on management
- a four-day course on the second week of every month
- two half days per week set aside for fire-fighting, which can be reallocated the day before if no fires appear
- peer-group checks of one or two days' duration, as available, on projects C and D.

Schedules should be able to take these factors into consideration, albeit with the necessary degree of specific authorized overrides, so that the ongoing actual required allocation can take precedence over the profile agreed at the person's last planning session.

'What-if' planning would need to predict possible outcomes and define **how** they would be achieved. High-performance what-if analysis is imperative to allow a good selection of alternative scenarios to be considered. A special case of what-if planning is by the use of synchronized displays. If we image a high-resolution screen on which we have windows on to a diary system for our top designer, task definitions, bar charts, critical-path-analysis network charts for both project A and B, as we change the allocation of two days of time of the designer from project A to B, **all** the windows change in synchronization to reflect the intended alteration. If not satisfactory, the system could undo or re-do the steps until a satisfactory conclusion is reached.

Integration of software systems can then play a part. Let us say that the conclusion of the above reallocation was to give a new task to the designer. There is no reason why the system should not send an electronic mail message to advise him of this change. On completion of the task, which perhaps uses some CASE diagrammer, the system could implicitly 'know' the completion event, send the resultant diagram electronically to the person who is going to check it, update the schedules and trigger a financial transaction to the accounting system. This degree of cross-project resource management and integrated software development environment is achievable now, as soon as the vendors choose to bring together the components as a coherent whole.

The essence of a useful computer-aided key resource management is summed up by the ability to define a key resource and its preferred profile of use; to use a multi-user, multi-project, highly flexible scheduling capability, which knows about project objectives, and then integrates all the systems that may be being used by that key resource into a comprehensible development environment. The advent of repository managers from IBM, Digital, Oracle and other companies will enable system integraters to bring together such capability. Oracle Corporation is, for example, bringing out a multi-user, repository-based project management and control system that integrates with personal diaries, CASE tools, electronic mail and various application packages such as general ledger (for budgeting) and personnel (for employees, roles and organization structures). Finally, such environments must be fun to use, unobtrusive, highly efficient and must obviously add value to team members and project leaders alike.

Over the years, project management and control systems have been perceived as necessary evils, which require weekly feeding of timesheets in return for which management occasionally notice some slips in timescales and comes down upon the perpetrator with all the wrath that can be mustered. These new environments must not only add value, but **be seen** to be adding value, and perhaps an outcome should be the occasional congratulations from management following strategic deployment of their key resources.

References and Further Reading

Barker W.R. et al	CASE*Method Tasks and Deliverables	Addison Wesley 1990
de Bono E.	de Bono's Thinking Course	BBC 1984
Jones J.C.	Design Methods	Wiley
Ohmae, K.	The Mind of the Strategist	Penguin 1988
Russell, P.	The Brain Book	Routledge 1989

Implications Of Assessing Software as a Financial Asset

P J Rigby & M T Norris

British Telecom Research Laboratories,
Systems and Software Engineering Division
Martlesham Heath, IPSWICH IP5 7RE

Abstract
Over the last ten years, software has grown to be one of the most important assets both financially and operationally that many companies possess. This importance is at odds with the fact that software is rarely shown as an asset on a company balance sheet. The implication of this is that it is not audited, costed and depreciated like other assets and is therefore not budgeted to be replaced when it is no longer fit for purpose. This paper illustrates how these issues can be tackled by developing a cost model for software. The paper builds on an existing cash flow prediction technique, which uses development, maintenance and quality cost as drivers, by addressing the prerequisite issues of software auditing and assessment.

1. INTRODUCTION
The difficulties involved in the creation of complex software based systems are now well documented and have given rise to a wide range of design tools and techniques [1]. Despite this, the practicing software engineer still works in a discipline without any strong scientific foundation. There are, as yet, few established theories or rigorous models to guide and assist in the construction of software systems. Without these, the software engineer is placed more in the position of the craftsman than the engineer [2].

Although it is widely recognised as a problem facing the engineer, there are other issues arising from this situation that pose problems for the manager and for the user. Rather than being technical problems of how to develop software, these are commercial questions such as what the software is worth and when should it be replaced.

The root cause is the nebulous nature of software - the whole product is documentation (it could be a single text), some of it purely explanatory, some for the benefit of the user and some to support the installer. The 'working' part of a software product (i.e the high level code) is also text only distinguished by the fact that it is written in a sufficiently formal way that it can be used to command a machine to perform specific functions.

One of the consequences of this situation is that software, despite it's importance [3] is rarely treated as a key company asset. A systematic method for determining how the financial viability of a software system should be assessed and when it should be retired from use has been proposed [4] . The basic idea introduced in this method is that of the 'software *death* cycle' which contrasts with the conventional 'software lifecycle' [5, 6] in that the focus is on the cost of keeping a system rather than the economics of developing a new one. In effect, this approach is a first step in planning the evolution of software systems on the same commercial basis as that which exists (and has done for many years) with hardware systems.It is far from an answer, however, and the implications of trying to assess software as a financial asset are considerable

This paper discusses some of these implications with reference to practical experience of having tackled them. In the next section, we briefly review the process by which the software base to be costed is established: the software audit. Subsequent sections describe how this basic data can be turned into a form suitable for planning how a piece of software should be managed over its lifetime.

2 AUDITING SOFTWARE

The obvious first step in assessing software as a financial asset is to determine exactly what software needs to be assessed. The implication of this is that a clear picture of what is under consideration has to be drawn and this can only be achieved if a thorough software audit is conducted. This is not a straighforward matter. Technical issues such as identification of program versions and variants have to be dealt with as well as contractual and legal issues of licensing etc.

In practice the conduct of a software audit need to address the following:

• Listing which programs are held on the computers within the department being audited and all of the locations where they are held. This is not as straightforward as it may seem, for instance naming conventions are rarely sufficiently standardised enough to help in identifying which programs are related to one another or indeed when two programs are identical.

• Finding out the relevant details of each program. This aspect extends well beyond what the program actually does. The support documentation associated with the program (if any) has to be identified and the support environment for the program has to be defined (e.g the version of operating system required for it to run)

- Checking against purchase orders and other external documentation to to see what software is licensed (and how many licenses are current), what software has been developed and where it has been issued etc.

- Checking the software against local records for history and use. Essentially this part of the audit seeks to identify software, documentation etc that is either superseded or is no longer used. An effective configuration management scheme makes this relatively easy to check.

This is by no means an exhaustive list. Conducting a software audit - even for a fairly small unit - can be a time consuming and expensive exercise. Exactly how much effort is involved obviously depends on how thorough the audit is. Nonetheless, by the end of the exercise important and useful information should have been recorded

- What is there and what status it has (Licensed, used, how many copies etc)

- What is redundant (this goes as much for documentation as for code) and can be thrown away to release space - both physical and electronic.

- What is redundant (but still required) and should be archived

The software audit is an important part of quality control as it generates a baseline record of the current situation and a checklist for future audits. In addition to this, there are a number of other benefits that accrue. Firstly, the <u>actual</u> software base is recorded. This enables software usage to be planned on the basis of what really exists rather than what is supposed to be available. Secondly, a known software base can be isolated. New software can be quarantined before being included on the asset register.

A final benefit of compiling a list of the software held within an organisation is that some of the costs of ownership can be estimated. For instance, given the known maintenance cost and estimated storage costs for the software held, an objective picture of how much it costs to keep the existing systems can be built up. This provides a basis for determining the software asset base. The next section looks at the next step in this process- that of assigning a value to the software.

3 ASSESSING VALUE
Knowing what software is being used is one thing, putting a value on that software is quite another. Although a number of factors can be suggested, the value of software will inevitably be dependent on the perception of the person assigning the value.

Rather than try to put absolute figures on the value of a piece of software, this section outlines some of the key factors that should be considered. These range from straightforward financial factors such as the income generated by a particular program in royalties or sales revenue, through to very nebulous factors such as the goodwill earned by a tried and trusted utility program [7]. These examples typify two extremes:

• commercial software, that is either paid for in order that a job can be done or developed so that it can be sold. The value of software in this category is relatively straightforward to asses as it either earns or costs money. This does not, however, enable a complete assessment as other factors such as development costs [8] and likely maintenance expenditure are difficult to determine precisely [9].

• strategic software, that performs an essential function within an organisation. The value of such software often bears little relation to the cost of its development or its potential market value. As such, the assessment of software in this category is usually highly subjective.

Other categories could be added to the above list but the inherent difficulties in putting a value on software are adequately illustrated. Even then, assigning a value to a program is not the end of the story. This value is not generally static: that which is priceless today may be worthless in a couple of years and vica versa. To complete the picture, some notion of the predicted value of a piece of software must be added

It is helpful to put the above in context by considering very briefly the life and death of an anonymous (but typical) software system. The original specification for this system was produced in 1969 in the form of typewritten paper document. Although somewhat dogeared this document is still available today; it still has some value. The software produced from the specification was produced in the form of a FORTRAN program which was stored as a set of machine readable punched cards. The recent request to add a new facility to the software has run into some problems

• There is no card reader on the computer - the last one was seen in the Science museum a few years ago.

• There is no FORTRAN compiler which handles the dialect in which the program was written.

These two problems, to which others could be added, are symptoms of the lack of stability of the support environment for any piece of software. The situation may not be too bad in this case - the function of card readers can be recreated and

FORTRAN compilers still exist. The predicted value of the software in this instance would depend on the viability of resurrecting the code. It is worth noting that the complexity of modern support environments (e.g. pixel based graphic workstations, sophisticated text preparation packages such as Latex) is making this sort of problem worse, not better. It is suggested that key software systems will, in future, need to be identified so that their useful life can be extended as may be required for them to recoup the cost of their initial purchase or development.

If all of the above factors can be quantified and put together it is possible, in principle, to derive a picture of the cost/benefit of the software from its inception to its death. Only then could it be claimed that the software is managed as an asset and that it is acquired, used and, eventually, retired on a commercial basis

The basis upon which these phases are determined has been described previously in the software death cycle model described in [4]. The basic premise underlying the model is that that maintenance to a given standard of quality costs money and has to be offset against the benefits that accrue from that software [10]. At some point, the cost of ownership begins to outweigh the benefit of its continued existence and this is the point at which net income goes negative. This is the point at which the software should be retired from use. The scaling of the cost curves in the model is determined through software audit and assessment. A typical example of the application of this approach - abstracted from a real situation - is shown in Figure 1.

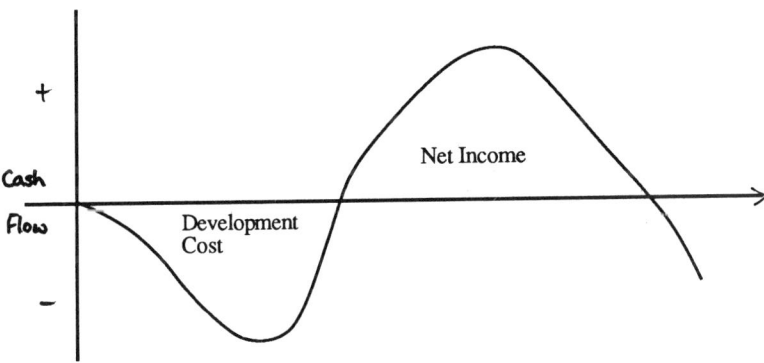

Figure 1 A cash flow model of software ownership

The above figure is based on a program that was developed, marketed and sold commercially. The initial cost of development is shown as pure expenditure (i.e. time and money taken to produce the product with no income) and the net earnings from the product are assessed from direct sales income minus the cost of supporting the product. In practice, the situation can be fairly complex: factors such as the number copies in use, the build and distribution costs, the implementation cost and the sales and maintenance income all had to be assessed before the overall picture of cashflow for this particular piece of software could be drawn up.

In this instance, a well documented set of income and expenditure figures were available. As discussed above, this is not always the case. Nonetheless, a similar cashflow prediction can be drawn up for software that is bought in or indeed for program written purely for local use once some value can be placed on the software. Ultimately, the overall value of an organisations software can be assessed over time by merging the cashflow predictions of all programs identified.

4 ESTABLISHING A VALUE SYSTEM

Once a piece of software has been identified and a value has been assigned to it, a rational plan of what to do with it can be drawn up. A mechanism for such planning is illustrated in figure 2, below with reference to a number of examples that have been assessed within the authors environment.

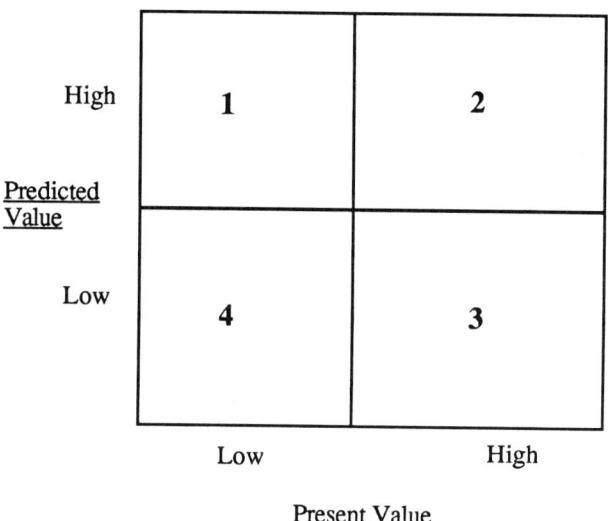

Figure 2   A value system for assessing software

The format of figure 2 is similar to the 'Boston matrix' developed for product marketing strategy purposes [11]. The terms and ideas that have evolved in this area are used here to enable comparisons and parallels to be drawn

For the purposes of this application, two key drivers are relevant - present and predicted value. Both of these values have to be assessed within the owners terms of reference as described in the previous section The point of considering these two values is that they have a direct bearing on what should be done with a particular piece of software. This is best explained by describing the details of each of the points shown in the diagram.

1. A prototype ('Rising star')

This software embodies a powerful new approach to some problem. At present the approach has only limited application but this is likely to change with advances in technology. The software is therefore of little current use but has the potential to become very valuable.

The strategy adopted for software falling into this category is to build on the potential of the software by investing in its development. This implies careful control over the variants of the software which evolve so that options are not closed prematurely.

2. A build system for a commercial product ('Star')

This program is vitally important now and is likely to remain so for the foreseeable future. The characteristics of this sort of program are that it is essential to the support of the business using it and that it cannot be readily replaced.

The strategy adopted for programs falling into this category is to ensure that the software is regularly backed up and that all changes are kept under strict configuration control. In other words, it must be tended with just sufficient effort to hold it in place.

3. A general purpose application program. ('Milk cow')

The current value of this program is high as it is currently used to support an important function. This category is exemplified by a spreadsheet that holds the current budget figures for the department. In the longer term another spreadsheet would do the job just as well, so the long term value of the program is low.

The strategy adopted for programs falling into this category is to harvest the benefits of its use. Little effort would be spent on improvement as its usefulness must be milked for all it is worth before it is superseded.

4. A non standard screen editor ('Dog')

The program has no particular value at present. It has been put on the system just to see what it does. It is unlikely that it will have any long term value as, even if functionally sound, it is unlikely to supersede the standard screen editor that is currently used in the unit.

The strategy adopted for software falling into this category is to remove it!

The development of a control strategy such as is described above is, in effect, the final part of treating software as an important asset. The extent to which other marketing concepts (e.g.techniques for moving between the areas in figure 2) can be applied to software ownership remains for further study [12].

5 CONCLUSIONS

Software is now one of the most important assets that many companies possess. Given this, it is vital that it is accounted for on the same basis as other assets [13]. This paper has addressed the issue by describing how the software base of an organisation can be assessed. From this, a basis for putting a value on that software and for how its viable commercial life can be determined are both proposed

At present, there is little evidence that software is being accounted for in this way. The introduction of quality management systems is a first step in bringing together the technical and financial management of software [14]. An inevitable aspect of this convergence is that software will have to be measurable in financial terms.

In explicitly modelling the cost aspects of software over its whole lifetime, concepts such as its depreciation become apparent. Given the ever increasing reliance on software within high technology industries, this will surely become a commercial necessity as software develops as an engineering rather than a craft discipline.

Acknowledgements

The authors of this paper would like to thank the Director of Communication Systems Technology, British Telecom Research Laboratories for permission to publish this paper. Thanks are also due to the many friends and colleagues in the System and Software Engineering Division who contributed to this work, in particular Alan Stoddart and Mick Morley for their valuable observations and comments.

References

1) National Computer Centre/Dept Trade &Industry   "The STARTS guide - a guide to software methods and tools" pp44-59
2) Jackson L A , "Software system design methods and the engineering approach"

BT Tech J vol4 no3 (1986)

3) UK Cabinet Office report   "Software - A vital key to UK competitiveness" (HMSO books) ISBN 011 630829 X

4) Rigby P J & Norris M T "The software death cycle" Proc UK IT 90 Conference (March 1990)

5) Kerola P & Freeman P,   "A Comparison of Life Cycle Models" Proc 5th Int Conf on Software Engineering (San Diego, 1981)

6) Agostoni G et al   "Managing software quality during the complete lifecycle" 1st European seminar on software quality (Brussels, 1988)

7) Boehm B, "Software Engineering Economics" (Prentice Hall 1988)

8) Galorath D "Software cost estimating" Proc 6th Conference of the society for cost analysis and forecasting (London, 1989)

9) Foster J "Priority control in software maintenance" Proc 7th Int SETSS Conference (Bournmouth, 1989)

10) Leintz B & Swanson B "Software Maintenance Management" (Addison Wesley 1988)

11) Helday B   "Strategy and business portfolio" (Pergamon press 1977)

12) Wind Y & Robertson T   "Marketing strategy: new direction for theory and research" Journal of Marketing, Spring 1983

13) Monk P, "Technological change in the information economy" pgs 122-125 (Pinter publishers) ISBN 0-86187-713-6

14) Rigby P, Stoddart A & Norris M   "Assuring quality in software - practical experience of attaining ISO 9001" BT Engineering Journal vol 8 part 4

HCI / Reuse

User Centred Design: Experience from a Commercial Project, D. Browne, H. Mylam & A. Woods

Specification Reusability: Why Tutorial Suport is Necessary, A. Sutcliffe & N. Maiden

USER CENTRED DESIGN: Experiences from a Commercial Project

Dermot P. Browne,

Data Logic Ltd, Queens House, Greenhill Way, Harrow, Middx.

Helen Mylam,

Andy Woods,

Scientific Research and Development Branch, Home Office, Horseferry House, Dean Ryle Street, London.

ABSTRACT

The Home Office Large Major Enquiry System (HOLMES) is used by all UK police forces for the investigation of serious crimes. However, the first systems were delivered in mid-1985, which means that they will be life expired in 1992/1993, and planning for their replacement has already begun.

In designing HOLMES2 it is intended that advantage will be taken of developments in technology that have taken place since the first system was specified; also that lessons learned in using HOLMES will be reflected in the new system. As a result a detailed design phase is now underway. As part of this work a demonstrator is being built to determine the facilities which could be included in the next generation system, HOLMES2.

This paper reports the experiences gained during the building of this demonstrator system, particularly our reactions to conducting a project in a user-centred manner.

1 HISTORY OF THE HOLMES SYSTEM.

The Yorkshire Ripper enquiry conducted between 1975 and 1981 was one of the main catalysts for the development of what is now known as HOLMES (Home Office Large Major Enquiry System). As a consequence of this enquiry the Byford review was set-up, the results of which were published in 1981. One of the main points of the review was the need for improved, standardised means for dealing with the massive amount of data that can be generated during a large investigation. It had been suggested that the Yorkshire Ripper could have been brought to justice sooner had the Police had better facilities for storing, collating and cross-referencing information. The result was standardised administrative procedures and the utilisation of computer technology.

Between 1980 and 1984 a pilot system known as MIRIAM was developed by the Home Office and evaluated by the Essex constabulary. During the same period interim arrangements were developed centrally to enable forces to enjoy the benefits of computer support for the investigation of major crimes whilst a purpose built system was being developed. These arrangements were based upon a commercially available package known as AUOTINDEX. A bespoke system known as MICA was developed in collaboration with the West Yorkshire Police during this period and was also adopted by a number of forces. In August 1984 the Scientific Research and Development Branch of the Home Office issued a specification for the present HOLMES system, which was based on the experience gained from operating its experimental MIRIAM system in Essex and from the use of MICA in other forces. The first HOLMES system went operational in May 1985 and by the end of 1988 almost every British constabulary had access to the system.

In mid-1988 SRDB began research in preparation for the production of HOLMES2. Among the issues addressed by this research are means by which the system could be rendered more productive, whether its use could be extended to small incidents, and whether it could be improved from an information analysis perspective. It is hoped that this and other initiatives will result in a specification for HOLMES2 being issued in the early 1990s.

Figure 1. shows the main milestones in the history of HOLMES.

2 OVERVIEW OF HOLMES

HOLMES is the computer support to the standard procedures for the conducting of an enquiry. In particular, HOLMES supports the storage and retrieval of information and manages the flow of documentation in an incident room.

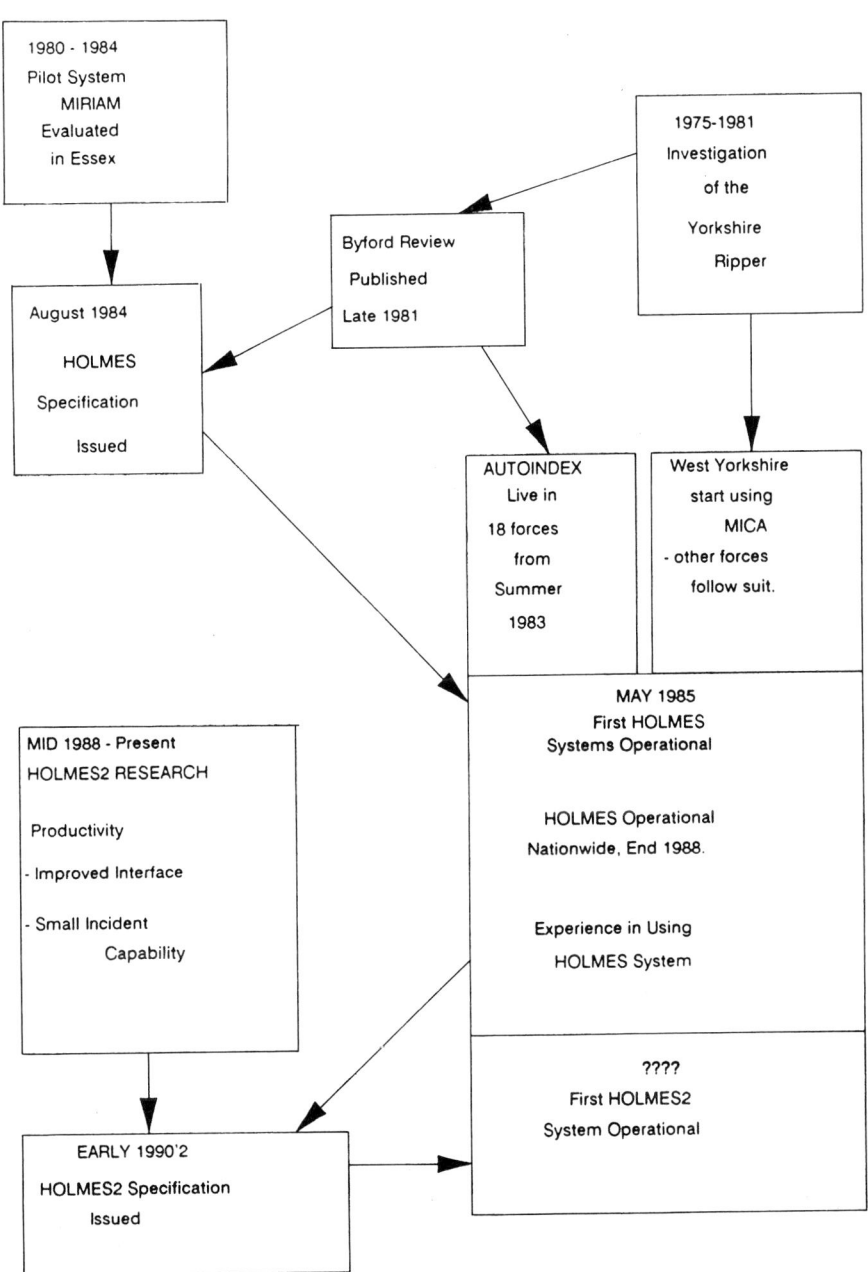

Figure 1. History of HOLMES

This study has concerned itself with the information storage and retrieval aspects of HOLMES. In this context there are three roles performed by personnel in an incident room which are of interest; Statement Reading, Indexer and Researcher.

At present statement reading involves the manual annotation of statements in order to highlight the information of relevance to the enquiry. Annotation also includes notes on how the information is to be entered into the system (indexed) and detailing any actions to be carried out as a result of that information. The task is usually carried out by an experienced detective. In this way statement readers gain a thorough overview of the enquiry.

The HOLMES database is structured into a number of indexes. The Nominal index, for storing details pertaining to people, the Vehicle, Telephone and Address indexes, as one would expect. The Category index contains information of particular relevance to the enquiry which is not covered by the other indexes, eg details of weapons, exhibits or premises. The Sequence Of Events(SOE) index contains time dependent lists of events relating to certain aspects of the crime. For instance, there might be one sequence detailing the movements of the victim and another detailing events at the scene during the material times.

It is the job of indexers to transpose the information contained within documents relating to an enquiry into the format expected by HOLMES according to the annotation supplied by the Statement Reader. This requires them to read, research and record the information in a manner whereby it may easily be retrieved by another user and no information is duplicated.

The quality of information held on a HOLMES system is dependent on the quality of the statement reading and indexing processes.

Actions to be raised and progressed as a result of information received are also entered onto HOLMES. Examples of Actions include the taking of a statement from a known individual or the tracing of an as yet unidentified person.

Related information must also be cross-referenced. For instance, a nominal record might be cross-referenced to a vehicle record and an address record to indicate where that person lives and the car that they own. Two nominals might be cross-referenced if they are known to be friends.

The third major role is that of Researcher. While Statement Readers and Indexers must research the database as a necessary part of their job, ie in order that indexing does not create duplicate information, researching may also be a dedicated job in some incident rooms. The purpose of the job is investigative, so that information can be pieced together and the enquiry progressed.

2.1 Holmes User Interface.

The HOLMES user interface is page based with a standard QWERTY keyboard for all input. While the dialogue is highly context sensitive the onus is on the user to remember the context. All documents such as Statements, Personal Description Forms, and Phone messages are held off-line.

A four week training course is provided for all would be HOLMES users. There is a handbook of rules and conventions for use with HOLMES. This includes listings of the short codes that are prolific throughout the dialogue. The handbook also covers many procedural directives that are essential to effective HOLMES usage. The conventions help ensure that all indexing is performed in the same way both within an incident room and across forces. This reduces the opportunity for data to be missed when searching the database. In addition, it reduces the likelihood for data to be duplicated.

3 BACKGROUND TO THE HOLMES DEMONSTRATOR PROJECT.

3.1 Feasibility Study.

As part of SRDB's research in preparation for HOLMES2 a feasibility study was conducted in order to assess the utility of providing an automatic indexing facility for major crime enquiries. The general objectives of such a system were seen to be:

° to increase the rate at which information contained in documents was indexed

° to ensure that important information was not being missed by improving its accuracy and presentation

° to improve the usefulness of the information to the enquiry by helping to ensure that the indexes were being kept up to date, and that they were easy to research

The feasibility study included a survey of HOLMES incident rooms, the construction of a demonstration program, consultation with a knowledge engineer, discussions amongst the Major Incident Project team, the HOLMES support group and police officers with experience at all levels of incident rooms.

3.2 Incident Room Survey.

This was conducted under the direction of SRDB with support from the Police Requirements Support Unit (PRSU) of the Home Office. It was the first survey to attempt to establish how the HOLMES system is working in practice. Eight incident rooms in different forces were visited. The objective of the visits was to gather statistics about the amount of time taken to index documents and to find out from indexers how they were using HOLMES. An important point to come out of this survey was that indexing is a bottleneck in all incident rooms.

3.3 Demonstration Program.

A demonstration program was designed and written for operation on a Xerox workstation. The aim of this exercise was to show how some of the ideas for automating part of the indexing process could manifest themselves. An additional aim was to show how some of the state-of-the-art User Interfacing techniques offered by a workstation could be employed.

It was found that having a demonstration program improved discussion of ideas for automatic indexing and intelligent front-ending. In addition difficulties likely to arise in the construction of a working prototype could be realised, more easily understood, and planned for.

3.4 Knowledge Engineering Consultant

Requirements for a detailed design study and recommendations on the technical feasibility of various ideas were provided by a Knowledge Engineer. Included in these recommendations was that development be progressed incrementally and that the software be structured in a manner similar to that often cited (Green, 1986) for User Interface Management Systems(UIMS). For instance, software for the Presentation and input of data be separate from the Dialogue Control component and Database access components.

3.5 Overview of Findings.

Whilst users are generally satisfied with the facilities which the HOLMES system provides, there are some problems with its use, the most common complaint being that HOLMES is 'manpower intensive'. The input of information requires considerable effort from trained indexers. In the high pressure atmosphere of a murder enquiry incident room there may be insufficient time and manpower to carry out thorough research on the information in the system.

The feasibility study also highlighted the possibility that by emphasising the use of new technology to provide an enhanced Human-Computer Interface (HCI), rather than the application of pure artificial intelligence techniques to this area of research, significant benefits in the reduction of time spent indexing could be achieved.

As part of a larger design study for HOLMES2 a demonstrator system is being built to progress the findings from the feasibility study.

The objectives of this are:

- to test various techniques and principles, such as electronic annotation of documents versus pen and paper annotation.
- establish where and how graphics can be provided to assist with indexing and representation of information.
- provide a basis for the specification of an operational prototype.
- provide valuable information for the specification of HOLMES2.

4 PROJECT OVERVIEW.

Given these objectives a number of principles were adopted. Firstly, the design of the demonstrator, of necessity, be conducted in a user-centred manner giving continual opportunity for critique. A specification technique that could be reviewed by designer and user alike would be adopted. A productive development environment supporting the use of graphics was essential, and a formal evaluation would be conducted.

The project avoided some of the usual distinctions between client and contractor. Members of the Home Office and Data Logic were assigned roles within a team framework for the purposes of the demonstrator's design. Three Home Office personnel and two Data Logic personnel worked very closely on the design of the user interface. An experienced indexer from the Metropolitan police was also seconded to the project to offer first hand experience.

The project was divided into four phases.

4.1 Design Phase.

This began with a short familiarisation phase during which Data Logic consultants visited incident rooms accompanied by the secondee. On each visit Statement Readers and Indexers were interviewed using ready prepared questions. The topics covered included 'problem areas', and 'desirable improvements'. Where possible Statement Readers and Indexers were asked to perform their job while being observed.

Working on the well established principle (Jorgensen, 1984) that good user interfaces should manifest consistent behaviours and not spring surprises on their users, a style document was created. This covered issues such as the maximum number of items to appear on a menu, how to determine whether an option be implemented as a radio button or a menu item and how on-line help should be made available.

The main deliverable from the design phase was a document containing a Statechart based specification of the User Interface with example screen layouts demonstrating dialogue sequences.

Statecharts (Harel, 1988) were developed originally for the Israeli aerospace industry and are now being adopted for applications as diverse as interactive computer systems and process control systems. They are an extension of the conventional medium of state-transition diagrams (Woods, 1970), to include features that support the description of large interactive systems without suffering the problem of small extensions leading to exponential growth in the number of states and transitions. An example Statechart is shown in figure 2. This diagram is by necessity monochrome but the actual notation makes a lot of use of colour. In this example:

- System states are represented by rectangles. The name of the state is given in the top left hand corner (eg WAIT, DETAIL, Menu Select).

- Transitions are represented by arrows. The action causing a change of state is shown by the side of the arrow (eg LM (pressing the left-mouse button), LM Accept (selected), LM Cancel (selected), where Accept and Cancel are options within a dialogue box).

- Conditions may be imposed on such actions (eg in the expanded state DETAIL, pressing the left mouse button on any selection will cause a change from substate 'Disabled' to substate 'Enabled' only if the selection is other than A which is a substate offering the Help, Accept and Cancel options).

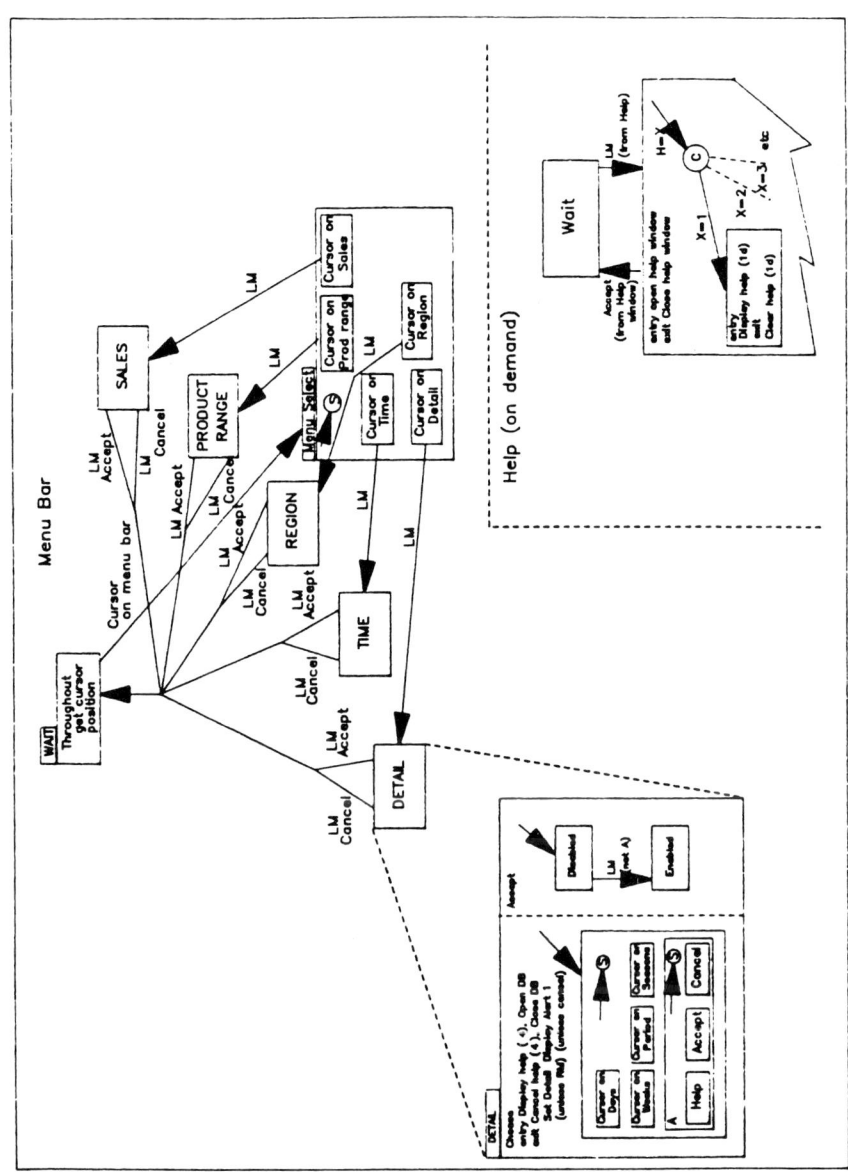

Figure 2. Example Statechart Specification

- The dotted line represents a form of broadcast (eg a selection made within the left hand side (Choose) can cause an action on the right hand side (Accept) without having to draw interlinking lines). An example of this would be the user Choosing 'Days', 'Weeks', 'Period', or 'Season' would Enable the Accept Button.
- Within any state, the default substate is shown by having a short arrow pointing to it.
- Actions can be triggered when entering a state (eg display help within 'DETAIL'), on leaving a state (eg cancel help within DETAIL), and throughout the existence of a state (eg get cursor position within WAIT).
- States which can be called globally (eg help) need only be specified once and thereafter accommodated by simply including a help option at appropriate points in the specification. No interlinking lines are necessary.
- The default substate can be conditional on a user selection (represented by a letter 'S' within a circle eg within 'Menu Select'), or on some conditions (represented by a letter 'C' within a circle eg. within help).

The reader is referred to Harel(1988) for a full account of the Statechart notation.

Large complex interactive systems are difficult to specify because:

- they are event driven having to continuously react to external and internal stimuli.
- it is difficult if not impossible, to predict user or system behaviour for all possible conditions in advance.
- a vast amount of cross-referencing and interlinking is required within a user interface specification

To surmount these difficulties it is necessary for a user interface specification method to:

- cluster states. eg "in all dialogue states, selecting the help icon will result in the display of full page context dependent help."
- show independence or orthogonality. eg "a database enquiry is independent of system state."
- allow global transitions. eg "whenever an icon is selected, change to the required mode."

- allow refinement of states. eg "the display mode consists of a text window, graphics and icons."

The statechart notation supports these requirements. It was felt that they would provide a basis for critique from all of the design team members, be an unambiguous specification from which implementation could progress, and act as the specification for an operational prototype at the end of the project.

It was realised that Statecharts would still not permit the documenting of the presentational component of the user interface, only its behaviour. To fill this gap the project resorted to example screen layouts. These were generated using Analyst(TM)*, a document preparation system written in Smalltalk 80(TM)*.

4.2 Implementation Phase.
Smalltalk-80 in conjunction with the Analyst tool were chosen as the development environment. Smalltalk-80 is an object-oriented development environment which is well suited to the rapid development of sophisticated interactive applications. The Analyst tool is an integrated set of special application packages implemented in Smalltalk-80. Although it is primarily a document preparation system, being object-oriented it supports the re-use of existing code. Packages provide the basis for form generation, graphics and menu production to name but a few.

Together, Smalltalk-80 and Analyst, it was felt, could fulfil the project's requirements for:

- Productivity- The Demonstrator needed to be developed in a short timescale by a small team of programmers.
- Performance- The user interface needed to offer reasonable response times.
- Robustness- The software needed to be robust to the point where it could be used without supervision.

The chosen delivery vehicle was a Macintosh IIx with development taking place on a Sun 3/160 as well.

---

*Smalltalk-80 is a trademark of Parc Place Systems. Analyst is a trademark of Xerox Special Information Systems.

4.3 Testing.

In the spirit of User-Centred design, testing and review was a continual process. As design took place it was reviewed and amended. The design document was released as seven different versions. Each version included modifications requested by and agreed by the design team.

As implementation progressed hands-on testing was encouraged and modifications implemented subsequently.

4.4 Evaluation.

Case study material generated from a real enquiry, with names and details amended to ensure anonymity, was utilised as a basis for a comparative evaluation. Pilot studies were conducted on both the HOLMES system and the Demonstrator loaded with the case study. This was followed by the collection of experimental data from users performing pre-determined tasks on the two systems. This data included timing information, error data and subjective data as collected via questionnaires. At the time of writing the evaluation results are not yet available.

5 CRITIQUE OF THE PROJECT.

The following is a retrospective and candid view of the project, paying particular attention to the merits of User-Centred design and the value of using Statecharts as a specification notation.

5.1 Design Phase.

The initial short familiarisation exercise was found to be essential. Only by spending time with Holmes users was it possible to gain an overview of the whole process of running a major enquiry. One of the problems encountered on short Demonstration type projects such as this, can be that not enough time is allocated to understanding the problem domain. While it was not feasible for Data Logic staff to spend as much time in incident rooms as might have been desirable, the inclusion in the design team of experienced Holmes users certainly compensated for the lack of first hand experience. There is no replacement for the experience of actual users of a system. This became clear when they pointed out that some design decisions were inappropriate. Without such involvement early in the project, mistakes would have propogated through the development cycle and have been much more expensive to rectify (Mantei & Teorey, 1988).

The production of a style document was a worthwhile undertaking. Given that an object-oriented development environment was utilised, styles could be set-up and re-used throughout the system. An example of this was the setting up of a Model for the radio buttons to appear on data input forms.

Statecharts were a mixed success. Their use in combination with a User-centred approach caused a major overhead in terms of specification maintenance. A tool is commercially available for the generation and maintenance of Statecharts but was not available for use by this project. In terms of providing a basis for agreement between project members they were also of mixed value. While it was thought that all of the project team would come to use the Statecharts as the basis for design revision this was not found to be the case. The main reason for this was probably that it was easier to comment on the example screen layouts. Programmers found them of value and did on many occasions question the correctness of the specifications where they thought the required behaviour of the interface was not reflected in the specification. Although Statecharts were of limited value, there is little doubt in the minds of the specification generators that with appropriate tool support they would be a boon to the design of highly interactive systems. They are economical in terms of space. The whole of the demonstrator was specified on approximately twenty sides of A3 paper. They encourage consistency in the design of a system's behaviour and they are semantically powerful. Statecharts are felt to be the most viable notation for the generation of user interface specifications, presently available. It remains to be seen whether the Statecharts will be valuable as a hardcopy specification beyond the life of this project.

Example screens were found invaluable in conveying both how the user interface would look and to a more limited extent how it should behave. The latter was achieved by generating sequences of screens representing a dialogue between system and user. Such a sequence is shown in figures 3-5. Figure 3 contains two windows. The leftmost one contains the text of a Statement from a witness with associated annotations as created by a Statement Reader. The righthand window shows in graphical form different records identified from the statement. The icons on this graphic represent the different types of index and the boxes below the icons represent specific records. The lines from the central icon represent cross-reference links. In figure 4 it can be seen that more windows have overlayed those shown in figure 3. From right to left these represent an enquiry window, the content of a particular record from the telephone index and on the left a listing of cross-references to that telephone record. Figure 5 shows the display as it would look following the invocation of

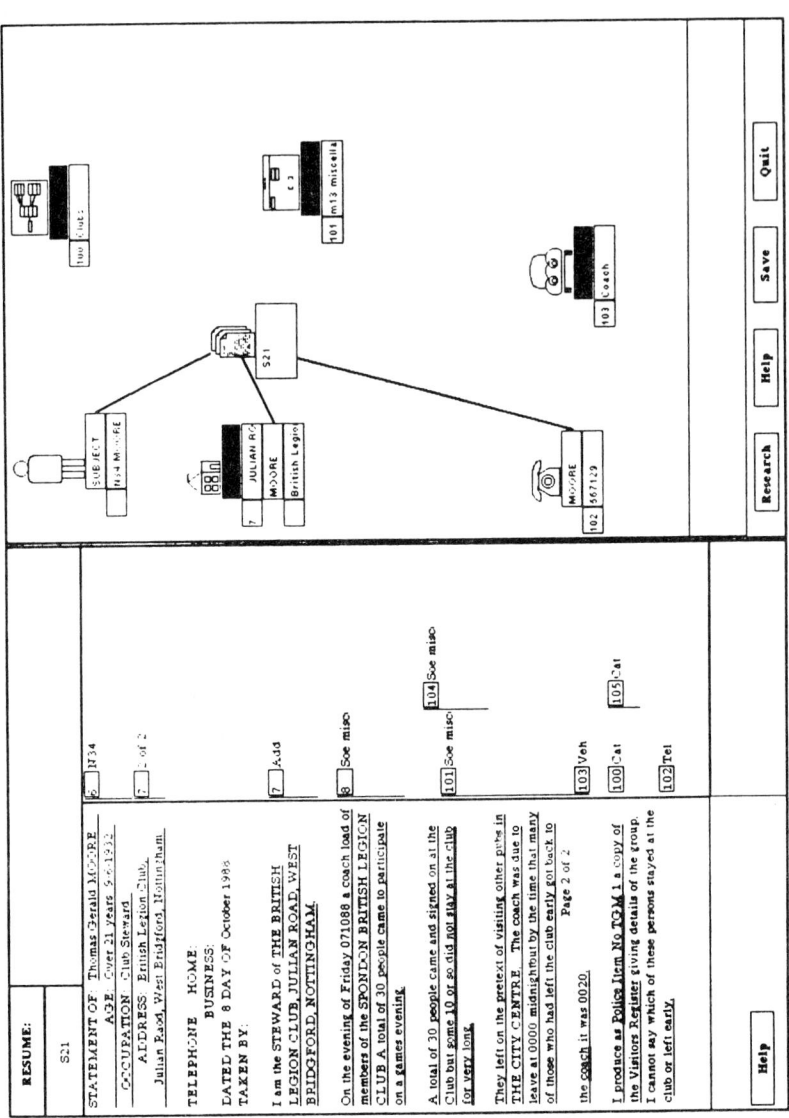

Figure 3. Example Screen Layout

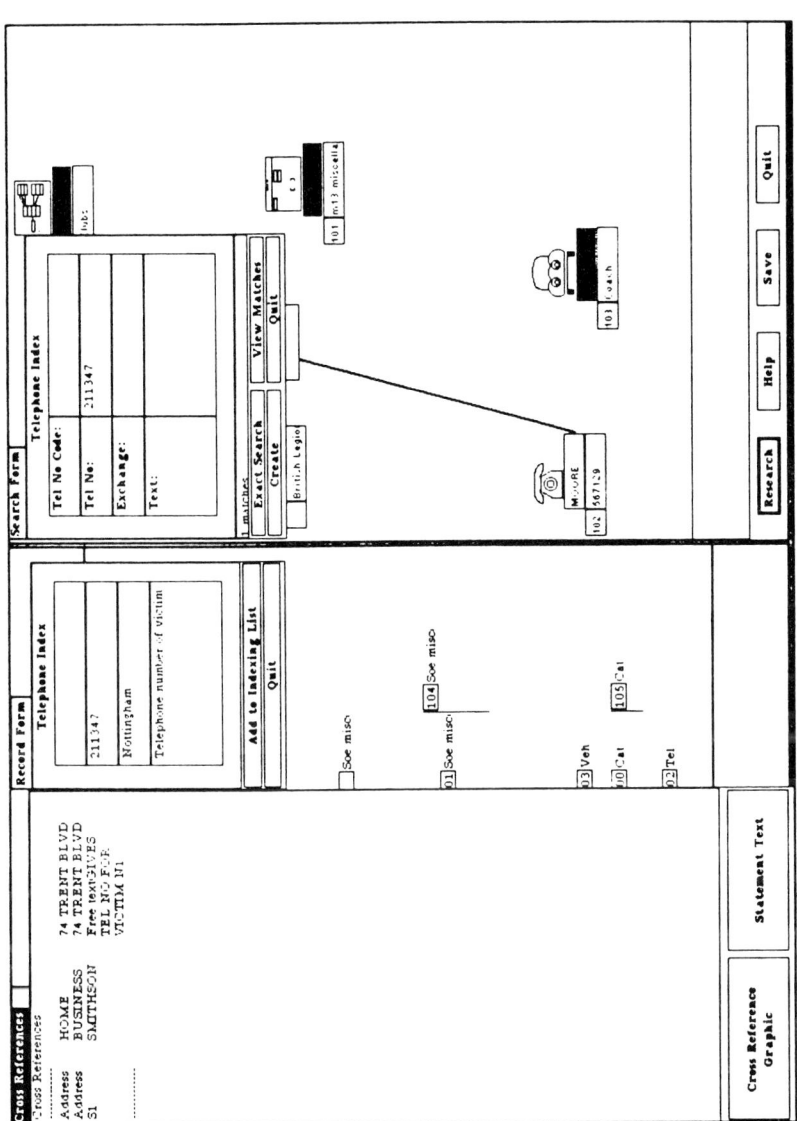

Figure 4. Example Screen Layout

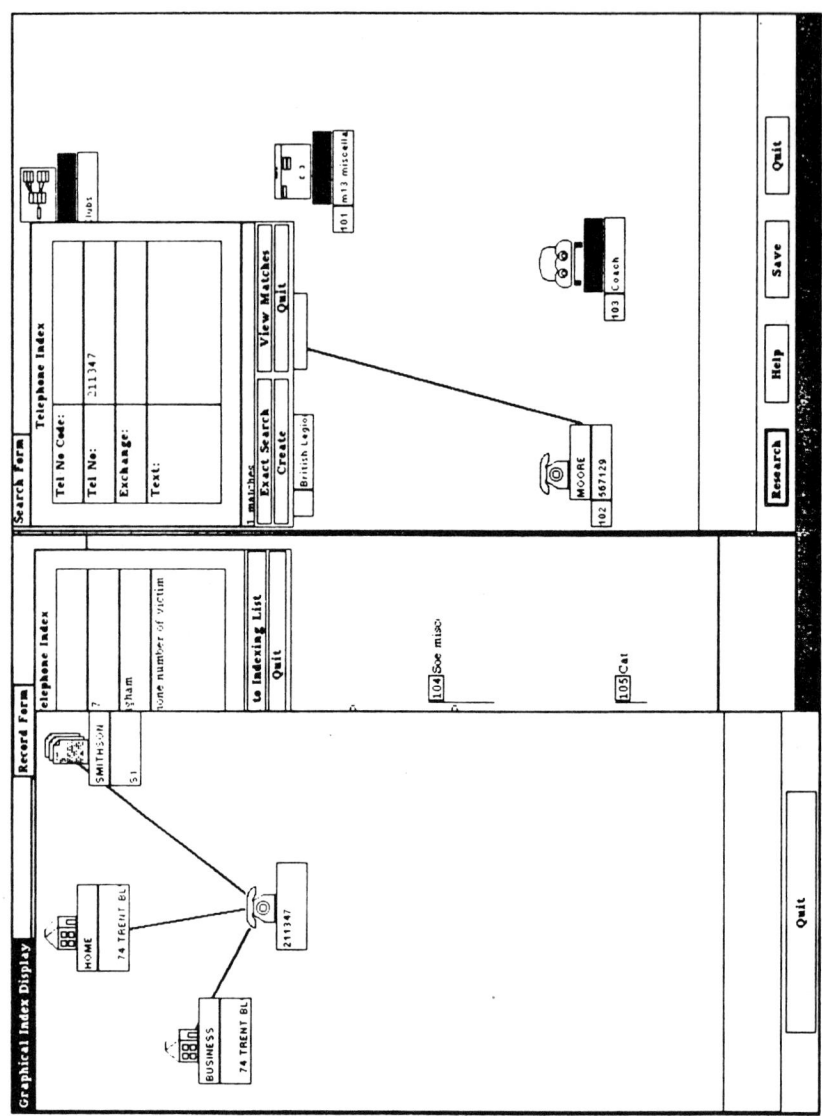

Figure 5. Example Screen Layout

the radio button labelled 'Cross Reference Graphic'. Rather than a list of cross references, a graphic containing the original telephone record is shown as the central icon.

Of the order of seventy example screens were produced and made available as soon as possible to the whole project. Each time the design document was released many changes were suggested. In total this necessitated seven versions of the document to be released before the design team were happy with its contents. For completeness the design document also contained the task hierarchy diagrams as generated from the incident room visits and what were referred to as dialogue maps. An example of the latter is shown in figure 6. Dialogue maps show how menus, radio buttons, and forms relate one to another for a particular piece of dialogue. They were found useful for purposes of identifying the appropriateness of groupings of options on menus and the sequencing of the dialogue. In addition they generated comment on the actual terminology used in the dialogue.

5.2 Implementation Phase.
A team of two programmers was assigned to the project. Early developments concentrated on the building of foundation software to support database searching and the production of the different indexes and documenting management software. Following this, work began on the user interface software for Statement Reading and then Indexing and Database Researching in parallel.

In general it was found that the combination of Smalltalk-80 and Analyst permitted the rapid production of the windows, menus, radio buttons, forms etc. required to support the user interface design. The object-oriented paradigm certainly permitted the re-use of software. For instance, software for the functionality of an UNDO/REDO facility was easily incorporated into the demonstrator with only minor modifications. Code from Analyst was also utilised such as that available for the production of forms.

Drawbacks were also found with this choice of development environment which caused the project some serious setbacks. Most important among these was the apparent flawed nature of the file handling software provided with Analyst. Once the immensity of the problems this was causing were identified it was decided that the software be re-written so that the file handling be performed by standard Smalltalk software. In addition, incompatibilities were found between the versions of Analyst running on our two development machines.

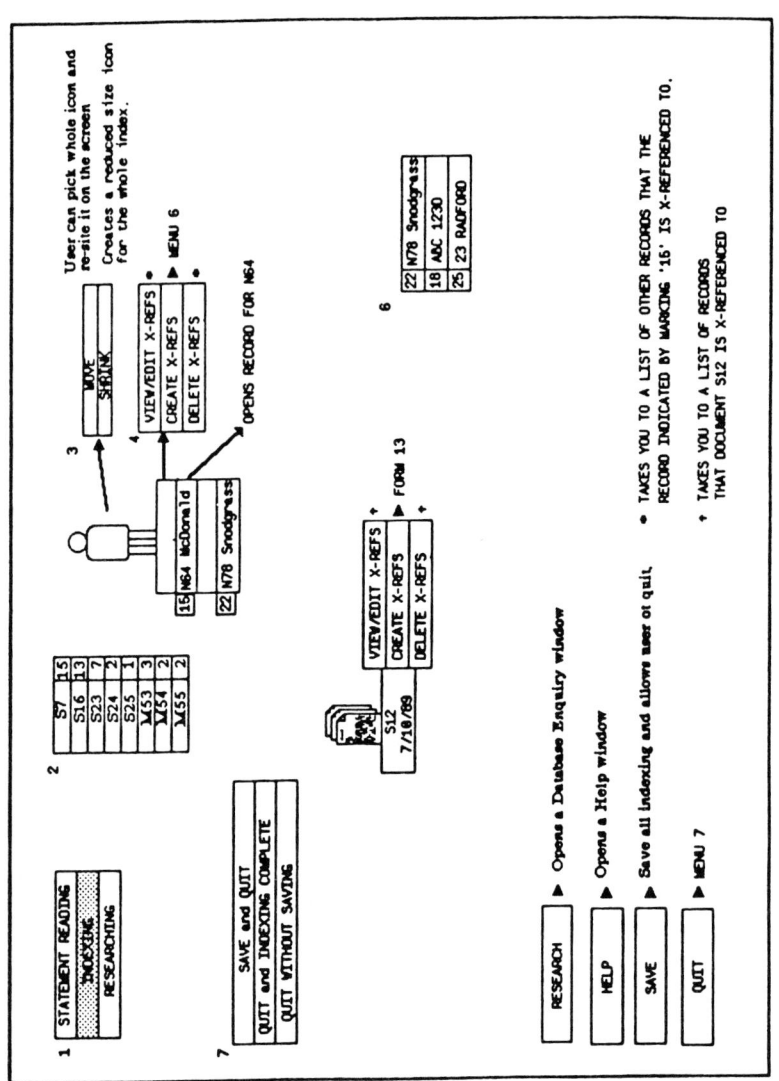

Figure 6. Example Dialogue Map

This caused problems when transferring files of software changes between the two machines.

With regard to system response times, again our experiences were mixed. While it was possible to quickly produce parts of the system so that they were operational, it was often the case that the software had to be modified in order to achieve sufficiently quick response times.

5.3 Testing.
As the software was being produced, hands-on interaction with the system was encouraged. This permitted early evaluation by the design team, including experienced Holmes users, in order to identify any design flaws and any implementation bugs. This approach was taken because it was acknowledged that however complete a design document may appear to be there is always opportunity for errors to be introduced during coding or inadequacies to be overlooked. The best method of assessing the adequacy of a design is by hands-on interaction. This had been realised by SRDB during their feasibility study and was carried through into this Demonstrator project. The changes requested ranged from modifications to the labels for options on menus to the behaviour of particular indexes.

Without doubt this User-Centred approach to system development benefited the usability of the final deliverable. On the negative side it made the project rather difficult to manage. The main reason was that the design documentation was difficult to keep up to date. Given that all of the example screen layouts were produced as static graphics and were used to represent sequences of interaction, even a small change to one aspect of the design necessitated a major re-draft of the design documentation. Alavi (1984) in a survey of prototyping projects noted similar problems. To quote: "Planning and control of prototyping projects are more difficult because the form of the evolving system, the number of revisions to the prototype, and some of the user requirements are not known at the outset."

5.4 Evaluation.
Few conclusions can be made at present from the evaluation as it has not been completed. Nonetheless initial findings from the pilot evaluations are interesting.

Many of the users were not familiar with using a mouse for interaction. It was found that some users took a considerable length of time (hours) to become fluent in its use. Difficulties were most apparent where the dialogue required the user to choose from what are referred to as walking menus or tree menus. These are menus that start as a single menu but grow in width as the user settles over an option, second and possibly subsequent menus can then be chosen from. Such menus require a significant amount of dexterity but have the advantage that very specific options can be chosen with a single mouse click and without the user being overwhelmed with options.

Having an interface that utilises a mix of radio buttons and pop-up menus might be thought to cause problems but was found to be acceptable. The decision whether to offer an option as a radio button or on a menu was made using a simple rule. If the option's effect was global to the window in which it would be invoked then it was provided as a radio button, otherwise it was provided as a menu option. Applying this rule meant that options such as 'SAVE', 'QUIT', and 'HELP' always appeared as radio buttons.

It was also decided that users should not be made responsible for the manipulation of windows. That is, all windows were automatically sized and positioned on the screen. Closing of windows was also performed automatically usually as a side-effect of operations such as a QUIT, or the opening of another window.

In general the response from users is positive. They quickly become accustomed to the style of the interface and can perform effectively within a few hours. The advantages of using a window based interface seem to be accepted. The graphics that are provided particularly for the presentation of cross-references seem to be well founded and are appreciated by users as an improvement on purely textual listings.

The full results of the evaluation of the demonstrator's usability will include data on subjective opinions and comparative data on speed of interaction.

6 THOUGHTS FROM THE PROJECT

Without doubt there is merit in taking a User-Centred approach to user interface design. By involving users at every stage of development it was found that improvements could be made and the final product did not require major user interface changes. Nonetheless, such an approach creates its own problems which are not well supported by tools and techniques.

The use of example screen layouts were invaluable for eliciting comment on the user interface design early in the project, but again created a major overhead in terms of maintenance. Tool support in the form of a Visual programming tool that allowed menus, windows, buttons etc. to be linked together would have been a boon. Such tools are now beginning to become available.

The developers do not regret using the chosen object-oriented programming environment. This paradigm surely has a major role to play in the future of Information Technology procurement. Nonetheless, caution needs to be shown with regard to the robustness of the available tools. The re-usability offered by this paradigm enhanced the project's productivity.

The Statechart notation while having advantages over alternative notations does require tool support. This does exist in the form of Statemate (Harel et al. 1988). This tool supports the production of a prototype interface directly from the specification. This would have been of little value to this project because of the chosen hardware and software configurations. Nonetheless the editing facilities available in Statemate would have eased the overhead of maintaining the specifications.

7 CONCLUSION.

With up to 60 per cent of the code for an interactive system being devoted to providing its user interface, and a large percentage of post implementation maintenance often being required for user interface changes, it is surely time that better tools, techniques and approaches were made available for user interface design and implementation. The project described above, adopted what it felt were the best available offerings. If this project were repeated tomorrow, there would be some changes to our approach but few better options are actually available.

The Object-Oriented Programming paradigm was probably a good choice although our increased awareness of the shortcomings of the specific development environments might lead us to investigate alternatives. We do not believe that a viable alternative to Statecharts exists but their use is significantly impaired if not supported by adequate editors. Example screen layouts were very useful but again they are difficult to maintain when undertaking a project that encourages review and modification. In an ideal world an executable specification technique that produced re-usable object-oriented code would exist. Such a technique with supporting tool set would enable designers to specify an interactive system's behaviour, and be able to present this to end-user representatives for review. Both hardcopy of the specification and the screens produced could then stand as the design documentation.

8 REFERENCES.

Alavi, M. "An Assessment of the Prototyping Approach to Information Systems Development." Communications of the ACM. V.27 (6) pp. 556-563, June 1984.

Green, M. "A Survey of Three Dialogue Models." ACM Transactions on Graphics V.5(3) pp. 244-275. July 1986.

Harel, D. "On Visual Formalism," Communications of the ACM. V.31 (5) pp. 514-531, May 1988.

Harel, D., Lachover, H., Naamad, A., Pneuli, A., Politi, M., Sherman, R., and Shtul-Trauring, A. "STATEMATE: A Working Environment for the Development of Complex Reactive Systems." IEEE 10th International Conference on Software Engineering. pp. 396-406, April 13-15, 1988.

Jorgensen, A. H., "On the Psychology of Prototyping" In "Approaches to Prototyping", ed. R. Buddhe et al. pp. 278-289, Springer Verlag, 1984.

Mantei, M. M., and Teorey, T. J., "Cost/Benefit Analysis for Incorporating Human Factors in the Software Lifecycle." Communications of the ACM. V31(4). pp. 428-439. 1988.

Woods, W. A. "Transition Network Grammars for Natural Language Analysis." Communications of the ACM. V.13(10). pp. 591-606. 1970.

Specification Reusability: Why Tutorial Support is Necessary

Alistair Sutcliffe and Neil Maiden

Department of Business Systems Analysis,
City University,
Northampton Square,
London EC1V 0HB,
U.K.,
Phone: +44-1-253-4399 ext 3420,
E Mail: sf328@uk.ac.city (JANET).

1. INTRODUCTION

Specification-level reuse can take advantage of CASE technology, hence improving software productivity and quality during requirements analysis. Specification reuse poses two equally-important problems: retrieval of a reusable specification, and customisation of that specification to a new domain. The problems involved in customising software are poorly understood, hence our aim is to investigate the process of customisation during software reuse, with a look towards developing appropriate tool support.

Customising a retrieved specification is a knowledge-intensive task, hence it requires human involvement. Tool-driven customisation would require extensive elicitation of knowledge about the reusable and problem domains, however recognised limitations of domain analysis suggest this may be an unattainable dream. Successful reuse requires the software engineer to understand the functionality of a reusable specification, and the context in which it was originally developed. However investigation of program debugging tasks suggests understanding unfamiliar software can be difficult and time-consuming. Expert programmers required considerable time and mental effort to debug unfamiliar programs whilst novice programmers failed to understand either the program functions or structure (Holt et al. 1987). Indeed, novices tended to adopt strategies which hindered understanding (Nanja & Cook 1987). Little is known about how software engineers actually reuse software components, hence the design of tools supporting reusability has little sound theoretical or empirical basis (e.g. Fischer 1987, Adams 1989). Novice software engineers stand to benefit most from specification reuse, so our objective was to investigate how novice software engineers understand and reuse specifications.

Abstract templates specifying general classes of systems (e.g. *library* systems) have been proposed as an alternative method of delivering specification-level reuse (Reubenstein 1986, Rich, Waters and Reubenstein 1987). However novices appear to understand programs in concrete terms (e.g. Adelson 1984), whilst abstraction in software engineering is representative of expert performance. This study investigated the effectiveness on analyst performance of both abstract and concrete specification reuse.

'Black box' reuse has purposely hidden the functionality and original context of reusable software. However 'white box' reuse appears necessary if software engineers are to fully understand reusable components. Specification reuse requires the software engineer to identify corresponding objects in both the problem and reusable domains: these mappings can only be made if the software engineer understands the role and context of each object in the structure of the system. Intuitively successful reuse between two systems requires a consistent mapping of the knowledge structure of the two systems, so that reuse between corresponding objects can take place. The existence of such higher-order relations between objects in two domains suggests these domains are analogous (Gentner 1983, Gentner and Gentner 1983), hence software engineers might be expected to reason analogously during specification reuse.The role of analogy in problem solving has received extensive research (e.g. Carbonell 1985, Kedar-Cabelli 1988, Hall 1989, Mostow 1989): although no agreed theory of analogy exists a consensus view is that successful analogous reasoning is difficult to achieve. This study set out to investigate the processes and extent of analogous reasoning exhibited by software engineers during specification reuse.

2. METHODS

The 30 (23 male, 7 female) subjects were full-time MSc students in Business Systems Analysis and Design. They had knowledge of several structured analysis and Jackson (JSD) techniques (Jackson 1983). All but 6 of the subjects had previous systems development experience. The subjects, whose age ranged from 21 to 36 years, volunteered their services, for which they received practice and supplementary tuition on JSD techniques.

2.1 Experimental Material

Subjects were asked to develop a JSD process structure diagram for a scheduling function in a video hiring company. The problem built upon domain knowledge already acquired by the subjects from a case study. The case study involved analysis of a system for hiring videos to hotel chains for internal use. Subjects were instructed to develop a JSD function process to describe the allocation of video tapes to hotels and to note any assumptions they made. An expert solution to this problem is described in Appendix A.

Two analogies with the video hiring problem were purposely constructed. The concrete analogy was with a production planning system allocating manufacturing machines to production jobs. The abstract analogy described a scheduling function allocating resources to tasks which had to be fulfilled. The main analogical concept was the functional requirement to allocate a resource within certain constraints. This was manifest as scheduling a resource, (or video copies in the concrete domain) within constraints (e.g. time, hotel preference, etc.). The reusable specifications were represented using JSD notation.

2.2 Experimental Design

The experimental procedure was as follows:

(i) Pre-test questionnaire to capture prior experience.

(ii) A between subjects, two conditions experiment:

> Control group-   10 subjects were given the problem (video-hiring) narrative alone.
>
> Experimental-   Abstract Analogy (Group AA): 10 subjects were provided with the problem narrative and the abstract JSD template of a scheduling problem.
>
> Experimental-   Concrete Analogy (Group CA): 10 subjects were given the problem narrative and the JSD specification of the real production planning application.

The groups were balanced with respect to subjects' experience. Both reusable specifications were similar in size and complexity to the solution described in Appendix A. Details of the reusable specifications are given in Maiden and Sutcliffe (1989). At the end of the experiment all subjects were expected to have developed a solution to the video-hiring problem.

(iii) Retrospective questioning and structured interviews to capture problem solving strategies and specification reuse, immediately following the experiment.

(iv) Post-test questionnaire to capture subjects' attitude to reuse: the questionnaire was given immediately after completion of the retrospective questioning.

The hypothesis was that both the supplementary analogical specifications would promote reuse and improve specification completeness and accuracy. Measurable dependent variables included solution completeness and errors. For further details of experimental materials and procedure see Sutcliffe and Maiden (1989b).

During the experiment, Groups CA and AA subjects were requested to verbalise or think aloud about: (i) similarities between the reusable specification and the problem, and; (ii) how these similarities were used to solve the problem. Guidelines on protocol analysis and retrospective probing, as outlined by Ericsson and Simon (1984) were followed. To encourage reuse, subjects were instructed verbally and in writing that 'the reusable components should provide you with a considerable amount of help in tackling the new problem'.

Subsequent retrospective questioning probed subject's general problem-solving strategies by asking them to describe how they achieved their solutions. Questions were directed at subject's understanding of the reusable specification, the problem domain and the analogy. Subjects were also asked whether they recognised analogical links between the reusable and problem domains.

2.3 Analysis

The protocols were analysed for the identification and exploitation of analogy. Identification of analogical mappings depended on verbalising the names of major components (entities, functions, procedures) within each problem domain. The supplementary reusable specifications given to the experimental groups contained several associations with the problem task. Analogous reasoning is considered to be based on the recognition and exploitation of three types of mapping, referred to as Literal Similarity, True Analogous and False Analogous mappings (Gentner 1983, Gentner & Toupin 1986). The problem included a number of potential mappings, each of which could be used to construct the analogy. Literal similarity implied a mapping with similar surface components. Analogous mappings occurred between components with different surface features, for example in the CA prompt the Machine entity mapped analogously to Video Tape.

recognition of the analogy, whilst understanding the concrete specification may have been more successful. Novices were forced to reason with and hence understand the concrete specification, whilst the generally-applicable descriptions of the template tend to encourage copying. In addition our experience suggests the derivation of general and useful templates is difficult, for example the scheduling template reused in this experiment cannot form the basis of a solution for all scheduling problems, hence limiting the payoff from any one template. On the other hand CASE technology can ensure a good supply of evaluated concrete specifications.

Specification copying proved effective with the deliberately-manufactured scheduling analogy, however real-world reuse is likely to require more customisation. Strong tool-based support to encourage understanding is required. An explanantory approach drawing on a domain knowledge base (e.g. Flynn et al. 1986) may not be successful, since eliciting and replaying domain knowledge is time-consuming and difficult to achieve (e.g. Neighbors 1980, Mostow 1989). Rather software engineers should be encouraged to infer explanations behind reusable specifications, which can then be used as a basis to justify reuse and customise correctly. Computer-aided learning, and more recently intelligent tutoring (e.g. Ohlsson 1986, Wenger 1987, Polson and Richardson 1988) suggest environments and techniques with which software engineers can be helped to understand specifications. The intelligence of these tutors is derived from knowledge of how novice software engineers do and should reuse specifications. Implications for such an intelligent tutor are three-fold: first the tutor must incorporate knowledge to model novice software engineers during reuse, so that the most appropriate support can be given. The model of reuse presented here provides a basis for such a diagnostic component, however further empirical work is required to identify individual reuse strategies and a catalogue of misconceptions made by novices.

Second strategies to encourage learning must be developed and implemented. Understanding the reusable specification is analogous to learning to use new applications. Here strategies which encourage learning by experience and partial exposure to the full functionally (i.e. less than the whole problem domain) have been found to be effective (Carroll and Carrithers 1984, Carroll et al 1988). Studies of errors during learning (Lewis and Anderson 1985, Miyake 1986, Burstein 1988, Jansweijer et al. 1989) suggest an iterative approach promotes more effective problem understanding. A didactic dialogue could encourage understanding by focusing the reuser's attention on key aspects of the analogy. Furthermore partial exposure of the analogy inhibits specification copying, hence discouraging mental laziness. A possible strategy for reusability may be to help the software engineer structure the problem, by providing analogous specifications and promoting iterative learning with techniques for gradual exposure of analogical links between knowledge structures in the two domains. Process models of analogous reasoning strategies used by expert software engineers, which build upon a theory of the knowledge structure of software engineering analogies, may provide a theoretical basis for these tutorial strategies.

Third the intelligent tutor will require analogical reasoning capabilities to support learning strategies and provide feedback on software engineer's solutions and analogical models. Existing computational models of analogical and case-based reasoning (e.g. Alterman 1986, Hammond 1986, Hall 1989, Schank and Leake 1989) suggest several approaches for the development of this analogy engine.

Successful specification reuse can help to overcome considerable difficulties experienced by novice analysts in previous studies (Sutcliffe and Maiden 1989a). As Young (1983) and Sein (1988) have reported, model formation can be error-prone and hard, in addition Sutcliffe and Maiden (1989a) found that initial problem scoping was important in determining success for novice analysts: reusable specifications provide integrated models of a domain which both the scope and structure of the problem. As a result specifications of analogous applications could reduce the analyst's mental load during model formation. Evaluating candidate designs in new scenarios is a key element in successful software development (Adelson and Soloway 1985, Fickas 1987, Guindon et al. 1987, Guindon and Curtis 1988), hence analogy could help development of alternative scenarios.

Finally successful reuse can also enrich the software engineer's own knowledge base, providing experience necessary to solve similar problems or explain further analogous reusable specifications. Viewing CASE environments as both problem solving and learning tools may ease the skills shortage, providing more experienced software engineers without taking them away from their work place.

5 ACKNOWLEDGEMENTS

We wish to thank the students on the MSc in Business Systems Analysis and Design who participated in this study. N. Maiden is supported by SERC post graduate studentship number 88803006.

6 REFERENCES

Adams R., 1989, The Structure of a Reuse Support System, Proceedings of Reuse Workshop, SERC, Utrecht, Netherlands, November 1989.

Adelson, B., 1984, When Novices Surpass Experts: the Difficulty of a Task can increase with Expertise, Journal of Experimental Psychology: Learning, Memory and Cognition, 9(4), pp 422 - 433.

Adelson B. and Soloway E., 1985, The Role of Domain Experience in Software Design, IEEE Trans. on Software Engineering, SE-11, No 11, November 1985, pp 1351 - 1360.

Alterman R., 1986, An Adaptive Planner, Proceeding of AAAI-86, 5th National Conference on Artificial Intelligence, Philadelphia, pp 65 - 69.

Burstein M.H., 1988, Incremental Learning from Multiple Analogies, in Analogica (Research Notes on Artificial Intelligence), ed. A.E. Prieditis, Pitman, London, pp 37 - 62.

Carbonell J.G., 1985, Derivational Analogy: A Theory of Reconstructive Problem Solving and Expertise Acquisition, Technical Report CMU-CS-85-115, Computer Science Department, Carnegie-Mellon University, March 1985.

Carroll J.M. and Carrithers C., 1984, Blocking learner errors in a training wheels system, Human Factors, 26, pp 377-389.

Carroll J.M., Smith-Kerker P.A., Ford J.R. and Mazur-Rimetz S.A., 1988, The Minimal Manual, Human Computer Interaction, 3, pp 123-133.

Chi M.T.H., Glaser R. & Rees E., 1982, Expertise in Problem Solving, in Advances in the Psychology of Human Intelligence, ed. R. Sternberg, Lawrence Erlbaum Associates, pp 7 - 75.

Ericcson E. & Simon H., 1984, Protocol Analysis, MIT Press.

Fickas S., 1987, Automating the Specification Process, Technical Report CIS-TR-87-04, Department of Information and Computer Science, University of Oregon, January 1988.

Fischer G., 1987, Cognitive View of Reuse and Redesign, IEEE Software, July 1987, pp 60 - 72.

Flynn D.J., Layzell P.J. and Loucopoulos P., 1986, Assisting the Analyst: aims and approaches of the Analyst Assist project, in Software Engineering-86, ed. Barnes D. and Brown P., pp 19 - 26, Peter Peregrinus/BCS.

Gentner D., 1983, Structure-Mapping: A Theoretical Framework for Analogy,

Cognitive Science 7, pp 155 170

Gentner D., and Gentner D.R., 1983, Flowing Waters or Teeming Crowds: Mental Models of Electricity, in Mental Models, Lawrence Erlbaum Associates, ed. D. Gentner and A.L. Stevens, pp 99 - 130.

Gentner D. and Stevens A.L., 1983, Mental Models, Lawrence Erlbaum Associates.

Gentner D. and Toupin C., 1986, Systematicity and Surface Similarity in the Development of Analogy, Cognitive Science, 10, pp 277 - 300.

Gilmore D.J. and Green T.R.G., 1988, Programming plans and programming experience, The Quarterly Journal of Experimental Psychology, 40A, pp 423-442.

Guindon R., Curtis B. & Krasner H., 1987, A Model of Cognitive Processes in Software Design: Analysis of Breakdowns in Early Design Activities by Individuals, MCC Technical Report STP-283-87, August 1987.

Guindon R. & Curtis B., 1988, Control of Cognitive Processes During Software Design: What Tools are Needed ?, Proceedings of CHI '88 conference: Human Factors in Computer Systems, ed. E. Soloway, D. Frye and S.B. Sheppard, pp 263 - 269, ACM Press.

Hall R.P., 1989, Computational Approaches to Analogical Reasoning: A Comparative Analysis, Artificial Intelligence, 39, pp 39 - 120.

Hayes J., 1980, Cognitive Psychology and Interaction, in Methodology of Interaction, ed. by Guedj et al., North-Holland.

Hammond K.J., 1986, CHEF: A Model of Case-based Planning, Proceedings of AAAI-86, 5th National Conference on Artificial Intelligence, Philadelphia, pp 267 - 271.

Holt R.W., Boehm-Davis D.A. and Shultz A.C., 1987, Mental Representations of Programs for Student and Professional Programmers, in Empirical Studies cf Programmers: Second Workshop, ed. G.M. Olson, S. Sheppard & E. Soloway, Ablex, pp 33 - 46.

Jackson M.J., 1983, Systems Development, Prentice-Hall International.

Jansweiller W., Elshout J.J., and Wielinga B.J., 1989, On the Multiplicity of Learning to Solve Problems, in Learning and Instruction. European Research in an International Context. Vol II & III, ed. H. Mandel, E. de Corte, N. Bennet and H.F. Friedrich, Oxford: Pergamon.

Johnson-Laird P.N., 1983, Mental Models, Cambridge MA, Harvard-University Press.

Kedar-Cabelli S., 1988, Toward a Computational Model of Purpose-Directed Analogy, in Analogica (Research Notes on Artificial Intelligence), ed. A.E. Prieditis, Pitman, London, pp 89 - 106.

Lewis M.W. and Anderson J.R., 1985, Discrimination of Operator Schemata in Problem Solvers, Journal of Experimental Psychology: Learning, Memory and Cognition, 8, No 5, pp 484 - 494.

Maiden N.A.M. and Sutcliffe A.G., 1989, Specification Reusability: Why Tutorial Support is Necessary, Technical Report, Department of Business Systems Analysis, City University, June 1989.

Miyake N, 1986, Constructive Interaction and the Iterative Process of Understanding, Cognitive Science, 10, pp 151 - 177.

Mostow J., 1989, Design by Derivational Analogy: Issues in the Automated Replay of Design Plans, Artificial Intelligence, 40, pp 119 - 184.

Nanja M. and Cook R.C., 1987, An Analysis of the Online Debugging Process, in Empirical Studies of Programmers: Second Workshop, ed. G.M. Olson, S. Sheppard & E. Soloway, Ablex, pp 172 - 184.

Neighbors J.M., 1980, Software Construction Using Components, Ph.D. Thesis, Technical Report 160, Department of Information and Computer Science, University of California, at Irvine.

Novick L.R., 1988, Analogical Transfer, Problem Similarity and Expertise, Journal of Experimental Psychology: Learning, Memory and Cognition, 14, No 3, pp 510 - 520.

Ohlsson S., 1986, Some Principles of Intelligent Tutoring Systems, Instructional Science, 14, pp 293 326.

Pennington N., 1987a, Comprehension Strategies in Programming, in Empirical Studies of Programmers: Second Workshop, ed. G.M. Olson, S. Sheppard & E. Soloway, Ablex Publishing, pp 100 - 113.

Pennington N., 1987b, Stimulus Structures and Mental Representations in Expert Comprehension of Computer Programs, Cognitive Psychology, 19, pp 295 341.

Polson M.C. and Richarson J.J., 1988, Foundations of Intelligent Tutoring Systems, Lawrence Erlbaum Associates, Hillsdale, NJ.

Reubenstein H.B., 1986, A Requirements Analyst Apprentice: A Proposal, MIT Artificial Intelligence Laboratory, Working Paper No. 290, September 1986.

Rich C., Waters R.C. & Reubenstein H.B., 1987, Towards a Requirements Apprentice, MIT Artificial Intelligence Laboratory, August 1987.

Schank R.C. and Leake D.B., 1989, Creativity and Learning in a Case-based Explainer, Artificial Intelligence, 40, pp 353 - 385.

Schoenfeld A.H. & Herrman D.H., 1982, Problem Perception and Knowledge Structure in Expert and Novice Mathematical Problem Solvers, Journal of Experimental Psychology: Learning, Memory and Cognition, 8, pp 484 - 494.

Sein M.W., 1988, Conceptual Models in Training Novice Users of Computer Systems: Effectiveness of Abstract Vs Analogical Models and Influence of Individual Differences, Ph. D. Thesis, School of Business, Indiana University, January 1988.

Sutcliffe A.G. & Maiden N.A.M., 1989a, Analysing the Analyst: Investigation of Cognitive Models in Software Engineering, submitted for publication.

Sutcliffe A.G. & Maiden N.A.M., 1989b, Cognitive Studies of Software Reusability: An Experimental Evaluation of Analogy, Dept of Business Systems Analysis Report, 89/2.

Wenger E., 1987, Artificial Intelligence and Tutoring Systems: Computational Approaches to the Communication of Knowledge, Los Atlos, Morgan Kauffman.

Young R.M., 1983, Surrogates and Mappings: Two Kinds of Conceptual Mappings for Interactive Devices, in Mental Models, ed. D. Gentner and A.L. Stevens, Lawrence Erlbaum Associates, pp 35 - 52.

Sutcliffe & Maiden: Specification reusability 509

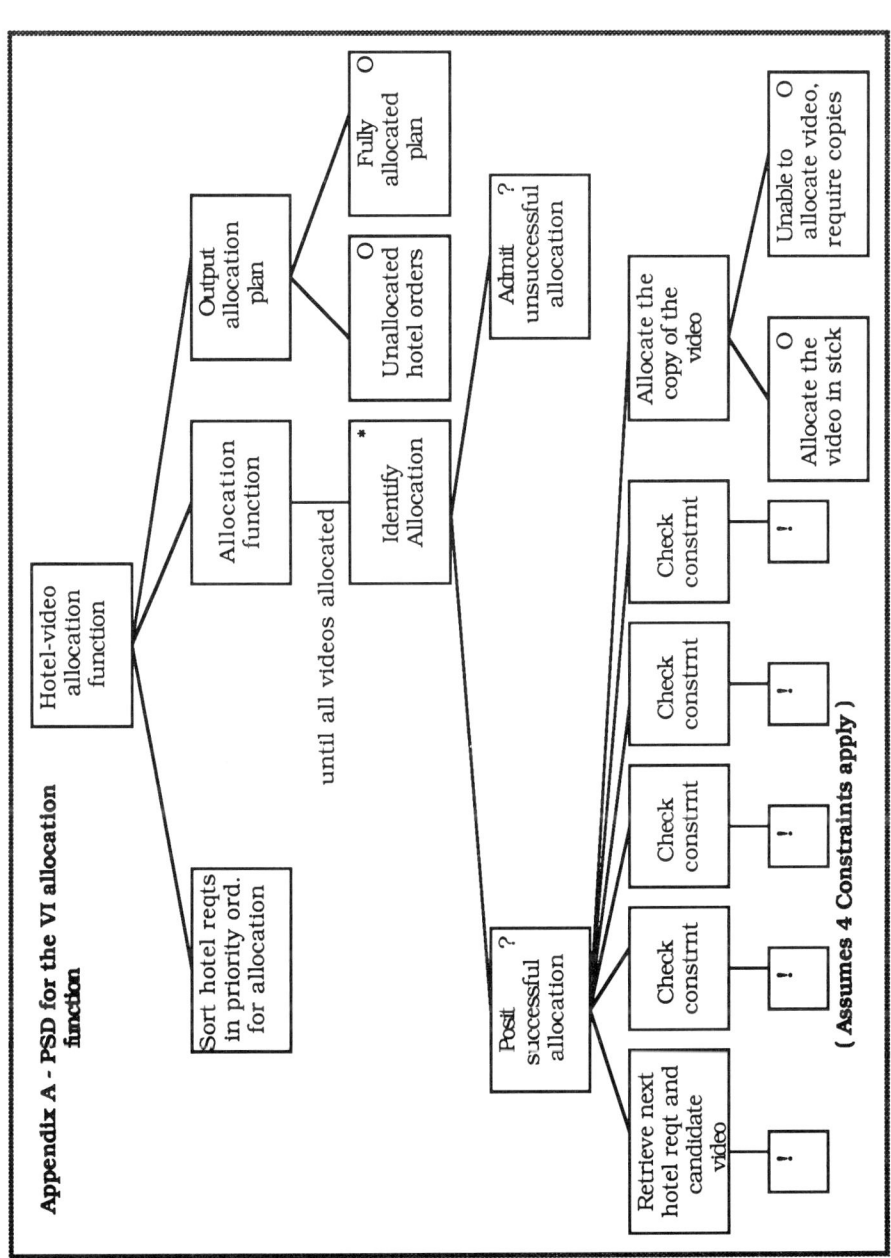

Appendix A - PSD for the VI allocation function

Technical Futures

The Systems Engineering approach within British Telecom, A. Fawthrop
Technology Prediction in Software Engineering, R. Higham, M. Norris and H. Chapman

SYSTEMS ENGINEERING 1990

BRIGHTON

24-27th JULY 1990

"The Systems Engineering approach within BRITISH TELECOM".

ANDY FAWTHROP

Systems Engineering Development Manager,
BRITISH TELECOM

copyright British Telecommunications, 1990

"The Systems Engineering approach within BRITISH TELECOM"

BACKGROUND

Information Technology (IT) has come to play an increasingly large role in the operations and the future business strategy of many large corporations over recent years. Whereas a certain level of support for financial and administrative functions has been commonplace for some time, there are many progressive companies who have come to depend upon computerised functions for survival in their day-to-day business, and several who have begun to use IT as a pro-active, competitive weapon. British Telecom, recently privatised and de-monopolised, has been obliged to undergo a learning process faster than most in order to grow through these increasing levels of IT maturity. The company is a prime example of the need for computerised information systems to provide support for its key business objectives - the provision of quality communications services and products to its customers.

This paper describes the major initiative which has been undertaken in Systems Engineering in order to improve the quality of BT's information systems products, and to improve the productivity of the process which plans, builds and operates those systems.

THE COMPANY

British Telecom operates the world's sixth largest telecommunications network, providing service to 23 million customers and handling 70 million calls a day. It is the largest company in the UK and the second largest in Europe, by market capitalisation. In the last full financial year (1988/9) its turnover exceeded £10 billion, its profits were almost £2.3 billion and its capital investment programme ran close to £2.4 billion. It employs 237,000 staff.

The company operates as a Group of separate operating Divisions. The largest Division by far is British Telecom UK (BTUK) which employs 200,000 staff. This Division operates all local and long distance networks within the United Kingdom and provides associated products and services to UK residential and business customers. It is organised into three geographical Territories, comprising 28 local Districts each of which provide the main point of day-to-day customer contact through such functions as sales, billing, fault-repair, order-handling and so on.

THE COMPUTING ORGANISATION

BTUK is provided with its information services by an in-house organisation known as the Computing and Information Services Directorate (CIS). The CIS organisation is responsible for:

o   developing computing plans and the technical structure to support BTUK business systems;

o   developing and maintaining those systems;

o   providing computer operations, technical services and communications

copyright British Telecommunications, 1990

facilities to support the systems;

o developing and implementing corporate (ie beyond BTUK) office automation, speech communication and data communication facilities;

o providing computer training throughout British Telecom.

It employs approximately 2,400 staff centrally and a further 2,700 in local Districts in order to handle these responsibilities. It operates about 60 large mainframe computers sourced primarily from IBM, Amdahl and ICL with a combined raw power of approximately 1,700 mips. In addition it supports several hundred mini-computers from a range of suppliers, particularly DEC, and literally thousands of personal computers and workstations.

INFORMATION SYSTEMS

Information Systems are vital to the successful operation of British Telecom. This is recognised from the highest level within BT and one of the five strategic objectives within BTUK refers directly to computing - the need to provide high quality, integrated information systems and related business procedures. Indeed the mission of the CIS development organisation reflects this - it is required to develop and maintain high quality, integrated information systems in direct support of business objectives. These demands are in addition to the normal requirements of 'within time and within budget'. In today's business climate, these demands are viewed as being only reasonable and CIS is expected to be fully responsive to such needs.

The Systems Development organisation employs around 1,600 development staff on over 200 concurrent projects. In addition some 300 significant application systems are currently implemented and require continuing enhancement and maintenance. The prime production environments are IBM/MVS, ICL/VME and DEC/VMS.

PROBLEMS IN SOFTWARE DEVELOPMENT

Before discussing Systems Engineering as a discipline within BT, it is well to be clear about the sort of problems which it attempts to solve. This can be summarised as that of the increasing 'maturity' of the industry. This maturity is the cause of the following symptoms:

o Complexity

Many applications within the organisation have now passed through the relatively straightforward stage of implementing base functions. Batch systems have gone on-line, central systems are becoming distributed, the end-user expects greater functionality and responsiveness, networks have increased in speed and size and so on. The net result of these changes is the need to build much larger, more complex systems which involve very large numbers of software components and large teams of software builders. The versions, configurations and inter-relations of these components are becoming too complex for manual techniques to cope with. There is a need for methods and tools to assist in this process.

o Criticality

Increasingly we, and other organisations, are building software systems upon which the Business depends for its actual operation and profitability. Security, quality and legal/regulatory requirements mean that software must not only be seen to be accurate, but failures in our

copyright British Telecommunications, 1990

stores handling, works management and fault-handling systems upon which our engineers depend, means financial penalties in our customer and supplier relationships. We must therefore be able to build reliable, available, checkable and accurate software to a tighter specification than ever before. Existing methods and tools are often inadequate for this purpose.

o   Cost and Timescale

Despite over thirty years 'practice', it is still apparently difficult to deliver accurate software systems which meet Business needs and sponsors' expectations reliably to cost and timescale. The advent of customer-supplier analyses, fixed-price contracts and (as far as commercial activity is concerned) increasing competition mean that this is an increasingly untenable state of affairs. Project managers need better support for the planning, estimating, organising and control of software projects, as well as more control over the whole requirements process.

o   Maintenance

The major drain on costs and resources today is that of maintaining the vast array of systems and interfaces which already exist. There have been various studies which have indicated a general industry pattern of maintenance occupying over two-thirds of the lifespan of software. Whilst this appears to limit the resource available for new developments, it is often the case that existing systems contain the data and functionality needed in new requirements. However, we rarely have the documentation, tools and techniques with which to utilise this enormous asset, in order to apply adaptive maintenance and re-engineering approaches. As a consequence we re-develop new systems and the backlogs increase.

o   IT Skills Shortage

The skills shortage in critical areas has been with us for some time and there is now a good body of evidence to show that demand of these skills will continue to outstrip supply. The only real solution is to make better use of the resources we currently have. We need software tools which will allow:

- simpler, faster creation of quality software;

- optimisation of the value in existing software by being able to re-use it;

- automated support for a total elimination of all laborious, slow, error prone tasks in the software process;

- greater mobility and flexibility of technical staff;

In other words we need software to help people become more productive. Further, a good technical environment is likely to be a key factor in the future for attracting and retaining the most highly-skilled staff.

copyright British Telecommunications, 1990

o   Meeting Requirements

The time has long since passed when we could afford to build systems which do not exactly meet the needs of the Business. Individual systems which do not deliver the function originally required are a drain on resources by causing rework, by providing inefficient operation, and by allowing missed opportunity. Equally, systems which cannot work together through poor interfaces, function gaps, function overlaps, data overlaps and inconsistencies mean that the Business is not being adequately supported by the I.S. infrastructure. The costs of these failures are not acceptable in today's quality environment and need to be reduced by the adoption of a coherent approach.

o   Commercial Advantage

Whilst most software constructed in BTUK/CIS is for internal consumption, there are many parts of BT, engaged in competitive tendering for the supply of applications or system software to external customers. CIS itself however is increasingly likely to be involved in the provision of software components which are part of a larger systems integration bid, or where internal software is sold-on (directly or in adapted form) to other PTTs. The need to build well-structured, designed and packaged applications reliably and cheaply will make the difference between success and failure in a competitive situation. The ability to hold generic components which can be tailored and configured to address a wide range of applications to meet customer needs would be an enormous commercial advantage.

o   Control

An organisation which wants to gain control of its software development and quality costs needs to have an agreed set of methods and tools. In this way it can minimise staff (re-)training costs, implement a coherent set of measures of the process and audit compliance to the process. The existing diverse range of mostly manual methods is not adequate for this purpose.

o   Conformance

There is an increasing requirement to demonstrate conformance to a particular method of software development for certain customers. In the USA the Department of Defence mandates conformance to its standard STD-2167 for all its suppliers in the defence and aerospace sectors concerned with "mission-critical" systems. In the UK the situation is not as strictly defined although the CCTA has made it increasingly difficult, if not impossible, for BT and other bidders to secure contracts for Government work unless the supplier can demonstrate that software will be developed with the use of SSADM. In a further recent development CCTA have mandated use of Defence Standard 00-55 for the completion of military MOD work. This includes the requirement for the use of formal specification methods. The US market for software tools which enforce STD-2167 is very strong and the UK market for SSADM support is growing.

THE COMPETITIVE ENVIRONMENT

Organisations and technology are changing rapidly. Companies like Boeing, McDonnell Douglas, DuPont, BMW, Fiat and Pacific Bell are among the leaders in recognising that the internal efficiency of their own organisation, and the

copyright British Telecommunications, 1990

Information Technology which supports it, is a vital ingredient in the struggle for future survival and competitive edge. BT however is not merely involved in the modern business world in the UK. It is a very large organisation, with increased international interests, seeking further diversification and involved in some of the fastest moving technology markets - telecommunications and a vast range of value added services and products. If BT is to survive and prosper it will need to have a technology-led Business Strategy so that the challenges can be met head on. This has been recognised by the Board for some time and a number of initiatives have been fired off to support this strategy. Systems Engineering represents one of those initiatives and will make a major contribution to our Business goals.

SOLUTIONS

British Telecom has chosen to tackle these types or problems by focussing on all the aspects which impinge upon system quality. A thorough-going review has been completed which has identified the following key components:

o organisation;
o management;
o business culture;
o training;
o standards
o methods and procedures;
o tools and techniques.

Various projects and initiatives are in place to pursue each of these components. The last three components have come to be grouped together under the title Systems Engineering.

Systems Engineering is a top-down approach to the management of the entire software process. Its constituents are:

o organisation and automation of the entire software development lifecycle from the capture of new requirements through to the eventual retirement of software;

o definition and analysis of information related to strategic business plans;

o modelling Business data and processes for the entire organisation;

o analysis, design, construction, testing, validation and documentation for new systems;

o maintenance and evolution of existing systems;

o key activities concerned with the management of the process and the deliverables within that process.

The approach is significantly different from the varied and traditional approaches of the past. Systems Engineering is an architected, structured, defined approach which is as much about organisational/ management change as it is about technical change. It involves a fundamental recasting of the view that software development is a slow, manual, expensive and undisciplined craft, to the expectation that it is a rapid, automated, predictable, controlled, and quality-assured engineering discipline. The analogy with engineering has been picked up from its earlier use in CAE/CAD/CAM and is

copyright British Telecommunications, 1990

appropriate, since engineering is a 'clean' discipline. It is defined. It has components which progress through a factory and are built by the use of tools. The components progress according to a pre-defined process. They are modules within a larger configuration which are brought together when the final assembly is built. The pieces fit together because their interfaces were planned and designed in advance. The components can often be used in other assemblies because they provide common functions. The aim of Systems Engineering is to follow a similar, disciplined process in the construction of software assemblies. Software tools are used to build applications in the Software Factory.

SYSTEMS ENGINEERING

Systems Engineering in British Telecom means:

o developing an approach, a strategy, to improve the quality and productivity of the software process;

o choosing methods and tools to support the strategy;

o designing, creating and customising the environment;

o developing a strategy to promote, implement and support the environment;

o integrating the training required;

o researching new techniques and tools;

o introducing quality and productivity metrics to monitor the effectiveness of the environment;

o producing a programme for the continuous improvement of the environment.

The structure of the programme consists of a three-layer architecture - methods, automation and support and education. These are

o TELSTAR II, the software methodology, is the vehicle by which the procedures for how we run our business will be defined. It will provide a complete and coherent framework for all activities, defining a common direction for all computing staff. Continuously reviewed and enhanced, it will be able to support a Systems Engineering approach. It will provide the baseline system against which the implementation of business policies for quality can be judged. The content, architecture and development of TELSTAR II are described in more detail below.

o MAESTRO is the IPSE-based software platform which will be used to automate, implement and enforce the TELSTAR II software methodology. It provides the technical capability to achieve this and to satisfy requirements in the future. It offers a dedicated hardware and software environment for the development process, allowing the integration of control and management facilities. The components, architecture and development of MAESTRO are described in more detail below.

o Education and Support. The introduction of new methods and tools requires a thorough, integrated training programme to be developed. If all staff are to be able to carry out the roles and technical activities ascribed to them within a Systems Engineering environment, then they must be given the appropriate courses and workshops at the right time, in the

copyright British Telecommunications, 1990

right volume and at the right quality. Without adequate training and re-education neither methods nor tools will be employed effectively or consistently. Experience both within BT and outside has shown that any major revision to working practices is unlikely to succeed without a competent and professional support network. Earlier attempts to standardise practices on an even less comprehensive basis than that now envisioned have met with failure when support has not been available. The Systems Engineering programme in CIS will provide both central and local support to all line-units involved.

INTEGRATED METHODS

The basic purpose of TELSTAR II is to provide an agreed, documented reference-point for how we plan, develop, operate and maintain Business-led Information Systems. The objectives of TELSTAR II are:

o   to describe integrated procedures and techniques for a number of technical and managerial areas (these are described below under Scope);

o   to bring together both theoretical soundness and practical good experience;

o   to provide the basic specification for a comprehensive automation programme;

o   to provide a documented process as the basis for the introduction of quality systems and the award of BS5750/ISO9000 registration;

o   to create a single framework for all software activities in the Business, incorporating rigorous discipline and preventing all failures across interfaces;

o   to incorporate a documentation and support structure which allows continuous improvement.

The keynote of TELSTAR is integration - integration of method and technique into a work structure that will support the integration of IT products and services into the Business. The approach to development of TELSTAR has been one of top-down refinement to produce a logical model. This has given a framework into which the best of current, proven working method has been integrated. The top-end logical model covers twelve areas, known as modules, which are described below.

o   Strategic Planning describes the process of defining the Information Systems and technical architecture which will support long-term Business objectives. It includes high-level data- and process-modelling techniques which produce a 'pure' future view of the IS strategy. It considers a timescale of up to five years and beyond.

o   Planning describes the production of shorter-term development plans over the 12-18 month horizon. It takes as its inputs the strategic plans produced above, together with a realistic view of current systems, architectures, priorities and resources.

o   Architecture describes the processes needed to maintain accurate descriptions of current and proposed applications and data architectures. It assists the Planning and Development activities to support Business objectives, and is the technical focus for systems integration. It is

copyright British Telecommunications, 1990

particularly useful in helping to define the ownership of cross-functional systems, and in resolving a wide range of duplication and interface problems.

o   Requirements Management describes the organisational processes of eliciting, assessing, prioritising, authorising and progressing a wide range of 'requirements' inputs. It oversees the execution of authorised activity in pursuit of the Business's strategic needs, and ensures the correct development of the large integrated environment required in BT. It includes the preparation of a formal Business Case.

o   Systems Development describes the System Development Life Cycle (SDLC), from the triggering of activity based on user-driven or strategic requirements through analysis, design and construction to the implementation and maintenance of the software. It covers the technical processes required to create the necessary deliverables of a system (code, JCL, documentation).

o   Testing covers those activities concerned with the rigorous planning, execution and measurement of the software testing process.

o   Computer Installation Management describes the full range of Operations and Technical Services activities required to support a large, complex set of applications systems across multiple, networked mainframes. Applicable to both central support services as well as to computer centres, this module is decomposed into sub-modules covering:

- capacity planning;
- change management;
- contingency planning;
- customer service management;
- data centre administration;
- machine room operations;
- network planning;
- network support;
- problem management;
- production control;
- security management;
- service level management;
- storage management;
- technical support.

o   Data Management describes how data is managed across the Business in accordance with the Corporate Data Policy. It includes both Data (Dictionary) Administration and Database Administration processes. It ensures the compatibility of Strategic, Development and Operational data models, by the provision of a three-level dictionary architecture, surmounted by the Corporate Data Dictionary (CDD).

o   Project Management describes the activities necessary to ensure that all technical processes within TELSTAR are effectively managed at the 'project' level to timescale and cost targets.

o   Quality Management provides a focal point for the mechanisms needed to manage quality in all other modules. Each of the other modules contains in-line activities for defect prevention, quality appraisals and controls and defect correction. The module states the policy and principles from which these mechanisms were determined. It identifies the quality roles

copyright British Telecommunications, 1990

and support functions which are needed to manage quality within a Business unit, and sets out a system which can be used to obtain registration under appropriate international standards (currently ISO9000).

o   Office Automation describes the evaluation, installation, testing and development processes associated with the provision of Office Automation facilities.

o   Security provides a central point of reference for all modules to ensure that security requirements are observed in the design and operation of software.

The physical structure of TELSTAR consists of:

o   Frameworks, which provide a basic outline of each module;

o   Procedures which describe the procedural steps that may need to be carried out to complete tasks to produce end-products. They contain the guidance necessary to determine which tasks are required in a number of possible situations. These are the 'methods' part of TELSTAR and concentrate on 'what to do';

o   Techniques, which describe the particular techniques and notations necessary to carry out the procedural steps. They are referred to, or 'called', by Procedures, and they cover 'how to do it'.

o   Documents are a specialised form of technique and consist of descriptions of documents that need to be produced as the output or by-product of procedures and techniques.

o   Forms consist of form-types or 'formats' together with a description of how/where used and how to fill them in.

o   Training Specifications, which provide guidance on 'what needs to be taught';

o   Automation Specifications, which provide instructions of sufficient detail to allow automation to be provided for the relevant techniques and documents.

THE NEED FOR AUTOMATION

The description of TELSTAR II conveys something of its scale and scope. The comprehensive and integrated nature of the product is intentional but requires extensive automation if it is not to collapse under a weight of paper. The system has been designed with automation in mind from the outset.

The benefits sought from automation are simply those to be derived from having the system on-line, instantly available and able to provide pro-active guidance to all users, not simply passive 'support'. In turn it is expected that automation should provide:

o   speeding of the development process;
o   reduction in software costs;
o   automated generation of documentation;
o   automated generation of code;
o   standard and thorough error checking;

copyright British Telecommunications, 1990

- consistency and completeness checking;
- enforcement of standards, structure and discipline;
- formalisation and standardisation of code and documentation;
- machine processable specifications;
- version control and configuration management;
- greater control of the process;
- support for maintenance tasks;
- support for management tasks;
- creation of application catalogues to promote software reusability;
- improved software portability;
- single point of reference and integrity;

Improved productivity is derived from the elimination of many tasks, the re-use of existing components and the speeding-up of remaining tasks. Communication of information (requirements, ideas, designs) between analysts and users is simplified and speeded. The developer or maintainer spends less actual time to achieve the quantity of functional output. Improved quality is derived from the elimination of error-prone tasks, such as the transformation of information from one format or notation to another, and by the rigorous and thorough application of error checking. Thus errors are both more easily prevented from occurring in the first place, and also more quickly detected when they do occur.

In approaching our automation programme, we realised that there were two possible solutions:

(a) a software vendor would choose to develop such a system which exactly reflected our requirements, or;

(b) we, as a user, would have to link together a number of different tools to achieve our objectives.

The first option was very unlikely to happen since no company had the resources likely to be needed, no one vendor was likely to understand the diverse needs of a company like BT, nor likely to service such a large individual requirement at the expense of other potential customers. Complete solutions were very unlikely, with any one vendor offering only a subset of the total requirements. Commercial concerns would also ensure that a vendor could probably only afford to support tools for a specific host environment e.g. IBM/CICS/DB2. Vendors would therefore concentrate on generics - either a 'platform' product or individual CASE tools. Since neither the market nor the technology is mature yet, this policy was probably correct. However, this left BTUK with the only other option, which was to build its own environment. This meant that we had the following basic requirements:

- a 'plug-board' or 'platform' product to act as our basic start point;

- clear designs and interfaces from all vendors in order that we could determine both the functionality and the 'pluggability' of individual products;

- industry standards to be agreed quickly so that we could develop common interfaces, be able to mix-and-match with confidence, and be able to work within a multi-vendor environment;

- the technology, and the research efforts which were driving it, to mature quickly to give us the best possible components from which to built our environment;

copyright British Telecommunications, 1990

o   software capable of interfacing to an open range of target host environments;

o   software which possessed the following characteristics:

   o   able to support all elements of the methodology;
   o   able to support the size and complexity of projects commonly developed in BT;
   o   built to provide team-working facilities, within a secure environment;
   o   uses a common user interface and common data repository mechanism;
   o   is able to interface to a wide range of communication systems and target hardware/software environments (an open system);
   o   has published designs and interfaces to allow customisation and adaptation;
   o   provides support for maintenance tasks as well as development tasks;
   o   allows integration of management and control tasks;
   o   permits migration from existing tools and repositories;
   o   can provide a dedicated development environment with sub-second response-times;
   o   incorporates the collection of metrics data within the supported process;
   o   is consistent with emerging international standards, and is therefore portable in nature;
   o   is designed by and supported by a vendor with adequate market credibility, R&D funding and an appropriate technical vision for the future;
   o   can be made to run on BT hardware under UNIX.

AUTOMATION

Without a clear strategy and a clear set of requirements as outlined above, several units within BT's systems development department had already drifted into the piecemeal use of a number of products. Those products were, and still are, very useful and productive tools in their own right, but generally speaking did not address the long-range strategic goals which we had set ourselves. Generally speaking these products were either single-user, or else were methodology-specific and non-tailorable or else were not target-software independent. We have used IEW, IEF, Automate, DELTA and Excelerator amongst others.

Using our chosen approach we selected an Integrated Project Support Environment (IPSE) based on Softlab's MAESTRO product, rather than use CASE or I-CASE solutions. We feel that this offers a better long-term approach because of the ability to offer:

o   full team-working;
o   customised support for specifics within our methods/technique set;
o   integration of management and control activities.

Logically the architecture of MAESTRO is a three-tier approach:
o   a workstation connected to...
o   a minicomputer server connected to...
o   communications with a mainframe, (the host or 'target' environment).

The workstation is used to support software which requires the power and flexibility of a PC e.g. graphics-based functions, local storage, etc. The user produces individual products (designs, documents, code etc.) and

copyright British Telecommunications, 1990

transfers them to the mini computer for central storage, and for communication with other team-members. The server provides team-based functions (configuration management, version control, communication facilities, OA services, central storage etc.). The workstation can thus be seen to hold a local Design Database, whereas the server holds the shareable Design Database and the Project Database. Components which have been produced, checked, assembled, configured etc. can then be uploaded to the mainframe environment (of any manufacturer) for use of host services e.g. TP monitors, DBMS etc. Additionally the workstation can be used to emulate the host's own terminal types.

Physically the system is distributed. Each server and its cluster of terminals can be networked together to form a larger logical system. The servers can be linked directly via their own communications ports or, as we have chosen to do in UK/CIS, the LANs can be networked via a WAN, in this case our internal backbone communications network known as INTERNET. Terminals on one system, security permitting, can access objects on other servers.

The main characteristic of MAESTRO is that of an Open Software Development Platform. This means that it provides basic software components e.g. operating system, database, communications which enable other applications and facilities to be provided.

The components of the software are used to build what we have called a Composite Task Structure (CTS). The CTS enables us to:

o   associate tasks from different TELSTAR modules into a procedural stream;
o   hold task-breakdowns and compositions within the structure;
o   relate documents to tasks;
o   relate roles/responsibilities to tasks;
o   automatically generate certain outputs;
o   accept external inputs.

A short, stylised example of this is included in copies of the visuals.

The main successes of this approach have been:

o   presentation of a coherent structure to the user;
o   enforcement of certain techniques, notations and controls (where necessary);
o   integration of technical and management disciplines.

The main problems and failures have been:

o   the sheer size and complexity of the task structure which needs to be built to automate TELSTAR;

o   maintenance of that structure;

o   the need to navigate different paths and short-cuts eg for smaller projects is difficult as the structure is inflexible;

o   some shortcomings in the capabilities of current software (it is not yet object-oriented);

o   the depth and scarcity of skills required to carry out this type of programming.

copyright British Telecommunications, 1990

TIMETABLE

An overall view of our timetable is given in the visuals. To date we have produced the first three releases (out of four) of the TELSTAR methods and produced one working, experimental IPSE known as TELSTAR TOOLBOX. Future plans include the intention to publish part four of TELSTAR in Autumn 1990, together with a second version of the TOOLBOX for further evaluation. Large scale roll-out of methods and techniques has already begun through our training and support organisations, but the large-scale roll-out of the IPSE is still some way off.

EXPERIENCES TO DATE

When we embarked upon our ambitious programme we were acutely aware of general experiences in other companies, and we spent some time in exploring critical success factors. To date we have been able to confirm most of our original intended precepts with direct experience. For example, we understood very early on that what we were doing was not about technical innovation. This initiative is really about the management of change, and is as much concerned with organisational and managerial issues as it is about technical issues. We knew that the technology had to be workable in its own right, but that the management of its introduction and the subsequent support for it would be even more critical. This has been borne out in our experience. There have been several examples of where units in our company have readily accepted both new methods and new tools, but where major problems have been encountered in trying to agree about who should carry out particular roles and responsibilities. In other words, the 'what' and the 'how' were easy in comparison to the 'who'. Whilst this may be a reflection of our organisation, we note similar experiences from elsewhere.

A second major experience relates to the layers of the programme. We have particularly noticed that the methods/techniques layer is absolutely crucial. Without a commonly agreed and implemented 'process', even to the extent of employing common definitions and terms, it is impossible to implement a convincing set of tools, or a convincing regime of metrics to measure the effectiveness of the process. We long suspected, and we now know, that the significant early gains are to be found in the comprehensive introduction of common methods, even in 'manual' form, rather than in tools. Automation speeds the process up and contributes towards product quality, but is a misdirected investment unless it is in direct support of an agreed process.

FUTURES

The future holds a virtually infinite range of possibilities. Within that however is the possibility of choosing to establish an environment for software which is very different to today's environment. Traditional development with its emphasis on coding and testing, paper-based imprecise specifications, manual production of code and documentation and a severe lack of techniques for rigorous testing and effective maintenance must slowly disappear. The new world will have an emphasis on more of the front-end activities of requirements and analysis. Design will relate itself not only to provably meeting functional requirements but also to the inclusion of "non-functional" elements - testability, maintainability, reuseability and reconfigurability. With the automatic generation of design, code and documentation the possibility of maintaining systems at the requirements specification level will be realised. Code and other implementation-dependent paraphanalia will become disposable commodities.

copyright British Telecommunications, 1990

Looking further ahead we can see the use of expert systems and artificial intelligence to gather requirements and to reconcile their views against existing data and process structures. The generation of formal specifications which are then machine processable will allow the very process of construction and testing to be fully automated. The traditional lifecycle will be firstly improved and then almost entirely removed.

We might think of the future as consisting of three environments:

o   the Development Environment consisting of the methods and tools referred to in this paper. Developers, users and user management would interact with this environment to create, specify and develop the Information Systems required to support the Business;

o   the Execution Environment or 'production' scene consisting of the hardware, software and communications necessary to support the systems produced by the Development Environment. Operations personnel, their management and the end-users would interact with this environment to deliver the Business benefits and competitive advantage inherent in the systems' functionality.

o   the Data Environment consisting of the databases, dictionaries and data management necessary too support the previous two environments. Establishment of a Corporate description, administration and storage of the infrastructure data needed to support the Business will allow the Development Environment to create and re-create the functional processes needed to respond to ever-changing requirements, as well as providing the stability necessary for a dependable Execution Environment.

    Between these three environments, or perhaps created by them will be global software 'Network'. This network in its widest sense will be the living, dynamic IT lifeblood of the organisation. All developments, whether they are in the hardware, the software, the communications, the applications or the Business procedures themselves will be 'changes' to this Network. These changes will require testing, controlling and management of an order unprecedented. Like the heart in the human body, the Network will need to function continuously because the life of the organisation will depend upon it. It is within this type of environment that Systems Engineering will play a vital role - by being the manager of change.

COMMENTS

Our experiences have given us some insight into the rather over-hyped CASE market-place. Cutting through the jargon and products and applying the technology to a Business like our has led to a number of observations. These are:

o   the lack of agreed standards (and the plethora of draft standards) is not helping either the vendor or the customer. The volatility in this area is giving rise to jargon, to hype and to a lot of promises. Vendors are having a hard time selling to a market which wants to 'wait and see', and customers are finding it difficult to understand how, where and when conformance to standards will be achieved;

o   customers should choose their vendors carefully. There is a great deal of volatility amongst the start-ups and a great deal of difference in the R&D and the support which they are able to put into products;

copyright British Telecommunications, 1990

o products are being badly over-sold. We have our own experiences to know that products often fail to live up to the sales-pitch. The best advice is <u>either</u> - be prepared to try things, then build round them and/or throw them away <u>or</u> - be clear about your requirements and evaluate the products ruthlessly against your criteria. Either way, do not bet the Business just yet;

o most products we have looked at do <u>not</u>

- provide team-working;
- allow customisation;
- enforce security, version control and/or configuration management;
- work in an open-systems, open-target environment;
- support very large-scale developments;
- provide any management control or quality metrics;
- integrate properly with other products.

o there are no 'silver bullets' or 'gold bricks' so do not think you can buy one;

o the overall market is very volatile, with new products, functions and technologies emerging constantly. It is difficult to keep up and differentiate.

<u>CONCLUSIONS</u>

We believe that we have taken a long-term view of the problems facing our Business today and that we are correctly adopting a Systems Engineering approach towards driving up quality and productivity and driving down costs. The top-down approach, covering every technical and managerial aspect has led us to invest very strongly in our three-layer architecture of methods, automation and support. The methods are integrated, the automation is provided directly in support of those methods and the support programme is vital to ensure the successful adoption of both methods and automation.

Our programme has come a long way over the past two years but we perceive we have very much further to go in order to achieve our long-term objectives. A large amount of resource has already been invested - which provides both a lesson and a warning to others. The lesson is that these things do not happen overnight and it requires time to effect a major cultural change of the type we are contemplating.

The warning is two fold. Firstly, we would not have got this far without strong and continuous senior management commitment to what we are doing. We have this because we have clear Business goals and a visible long-term strategy, and it can be seen that Systems Engineering contributes directly to both. Secondly, if you have not started yet within your Company - then you have some catching up to do! BT is very serious about its commitment to expansion and the use of IT as a competitive weapon. Systems Engineering is a key initiative in that strategy.

Consequently, we believe that it is worthwhile investing in Systems Engineering. This type of approach will provide strong support to our key business objectives - the provision of quality communications products and services to our customers.

END

copyright British Telecommunications, 1990

Technology Prediction in Software Engineering

R C Higham, M T Norris & H Chapman

Systems and Software Engineering Division
British Telecom Research Laboratories
Ipswich IP5 7RE, England

Abstract
One of the most important and difficult aspects of software engineering is the prediction of future trends in both base technology and in best practice. The need for such forward planning is made more acute by the ever increasing importance of software as an enabling technology. This paper describes an exercise in generating a view of the future of software engineering which draws on the consensus views of a wide range of software users, developers and researchers. The aim has been to identify a shared vision of the key technologies and practices fifteen years hence. The main stages involved in the creation of the vision statement are described below along with an outline of its scope.

1. INTRODUCTION

Software, or rather the ability to produce it, has become an increasingly important part of the high technology business over recent years [1]. Competitiveness in this field depends critically upon leading edge technology, for outdated techniques are an anathema and the pace of change is rapid indeed. To remain at the forefront requires a stream of innovative products and ideas which meet the needs of the customer. But there are two key problems which have to be faced before this can be effected. Firstly, there is a limited supply of engineers to generate the new ideas [2] and secondly, the sheer complexity of the current systems and technology [3] make it difficult to know where best to focus effort. Given this situation, it is of vital importance to have a clear understanding of where the limited resources available in this area should be targeted.

A considerable amount of effort has been expended over the last few years in ensuring that UK industry is using the most up to date software engineering tools and techniques [4]. Predicting future developments in the area has, however, received less attention, although it has been recognised as one of the prime concerns in a number of other countries [5]: a major theme at a recent software engineering conference in the US addressed 'Software in the Year 2001' [6]. The published findings from these sources are a useful start and they give some interesting pointers. There is, however, some way to go before a useable 'vision' of the way ahead emerges. To achieve this, the vision has to be specialised for the particular purpose for which it is intended and it has to be carefully checked for both viability and practicality. These objectives imply that its creation should be a carefully controlled exercise which draws on as much local expertise and opinion as possible.

This paper describes how this has been achieved within the British Telecom Systems and Software Engineering Research unit. The next section explain how the initial preparation and scope of the vision was determined. Section 3 outlines the polling technique adopted in this project to achieve the required validation and breadth of analysis of the initial vision. Subsequent sections report on the results of the exercise and, briefly, the interpretation and use of the findings.

2. INITIAL SCENARIO

The first step in preparing a vision of future technology was to analyse the commercial environment in which it would exist. This proved to be a relatively straightforward exercise, as a clear statement of aims and objectives were available to set this context [7]. The outcome of this stage was a definition of exactly what the vision should provide: a view of the practice of systems and software engineering 15 years hence which clarifies the steps that need to be taken now to ensure that the key aspects of software enabling technology are developed.

Given this focus, the next step was to collate published material in the relevant technical areas. This phase was fairly easy as one of the prime concerns in the authors environment is awareness of current research across a wide range of software technology, such as project management [8], requirements capture [9], formal specification [10], software maintenance [11] and testing [12]. The technical data gathered in this phase was supplemented with more general publications on technology trends and predictions [13]. By the end of this step, a large amount of interesting but largely unstructured data had been assembled. The next phase was concerned with forging this into a single coherent document.

This was initiated by forming a small group which analysed the data collected, proposed a structure into which it could be fitted and compared the result against current output from local centres of specific technical expertise. This process was completed within a period of two weeks and produced the initial vision statement.

Although useful, the initial vision statement was by no means the end of the exercise. The importance of the task being addressed made it essential that the final vision should reflect a wide range of informed opinion from software users, developers, managers, maintainers and researchers. A further phase of analysis was, therefore, required before the document could be used to provide a valid and credible basis for refinement into a broadly based evolution plan to guide software technology development. A workshop format was considered for this purpose but was rejected due to the difficulties of arranging meetings with a large number of people and of objectively weighting the differing views expressed in open forum. Eventually, a polling approach was selected, the main advantage being that it caters for the required number of people but avoids the effects of 'groupthink' [14] and other biases which can readily surface in workshop like situations.

A delphi poll [15] was conducted as the final stage in generating the vision. This technique, which has been successfully applied in similar areas [16] involved about 30% of the staff in the 150 strong software engineering research unit, including at least one representative from each technology area and a mix of engineers, managers and users. The construction and operation of the poll are described in the next section

3. SCOPE AND OPERATION OF THE POLL

The poll, which was conducted over a period of three months, consisted of a twenty three proposals, each addressing an aspect of the future, which were derived directly from the initial vision statement. The objective was to run the poll until a consensus view was reached across a significant number of the proposals. An example of the type of proposal used in the poll would be:

"The increasing maturity of software engineering will be reflected in specialisation of roles for engineers - Software librarians, component engineers, project consultants etc"

Additional proposals could be added by respondents at any point during the poll. In this exercise, only one extra proposal was identified, although several of the original ones had to be recast for clarification. In all, the poll made proposals in a number of distinct areas. These areas are listed below, along with examples of the issues raised in each:

• the future environment in which software engineering will be placed (e.g will useful standards be in place, will user expectations be raised, will software become easier to modify and update)

• the main problem areas to be addressed (e.g will the physical distribution of systems increase, will the sheer volume of information being generated necessitate machine assistance based on artificial intelligence)

• the key technical requirements (e.g. will software components provide functional building blocks for systems, will theoretical approaches to software construction be developed)

• candidate technologies (will object oriented design provide a basis for reuseability, will formal methods enable a more scientific approach to system development)

• social aspects (will the roles, responsibilities and skill required of software engineers change and separate according to specific functions and roles)

In addition to the above, questions on the perceived value of prophecy were included in the poll as some form of check on its value/credibility. In each case, rather than a straighforward rating for level of concurrence, the question required the respondent to assess the proposal against a number of criteria:

• The probability of its implementation
• Personal confidence level in the implementation estimate made
• Significance of the proposal were it to come to fruition
• Desirability of the proposal

The questionnaire used in the poll required a rating for each proposal (on a five point scale) to be given for each of these criteria. At the end of each round of the poll the complete set of answers (in the form of histograms - see figure 1) was fed back (anonymously) to all participants to show the range of answers in that round of the poll. In subsequent runs, respondents were invited to reassess their ratings given that any rating outside of the 'normal' response' (i.e. more than one point away from the current mean rating) would be designated as an 'outlier' and that justification of that particular answer would be required. These justifications could be fed back (again, anonymously) to the respondents in the next round: this was not required in this exercise as only two rounds of the poll were necessary. The poll was run until there were no significant changes of opinion between one round and the next. In this exercise the chosen level of convergence was that the standard deviation in scores should be less than 1 for 95% of the proposals.

4. RESULTS

The initial run of the poll, which drew a 95% response rate, indicated that there was a large measure of agreement on many of the issues raised: about 80% of the proposals converged on a particular rating (plus or minus one point) for each of the criteria used. Two runs of the poll were, however, required before the predetermined level of convergence was achieved across the proposals. The second round drew a 75% response rate, although it was determined that the majority of those who dropped out at this stage did so because they had no further comments to make. The detailed results and their interpretation are discussed below.

4.1 Specific findings

The complete analysis of results from the poll entails ranking all of the proposals according to the ratings given (primarily by mean rating with standard deviation as secondary driver). Since four separate criteria have been used in this case, four such rankings are required before an objective assessment of results can be made. There are a number of ways in which the data can be interpreted. For the purposes of this paper, the scores for 'probability' are taken as the main driver, with significance a secondary factor. The same data could be interpreted on a different basis for another application (e.g. 'desirability' would be key if the objective was to establish which technologies motivate staff). The raw data generated for all of the proposals against the four criteria used in this exercise is not included here as it runs to some 25 pages: details may be requested from the authors. Some of the more striking findings of the poll are highlighted below. At least one proposal from each of the the broad areas of the initial vision statement is covered.

Future Environment

The distribution of answers to the proposal that "useful standards will emerge in the areas of operating systems, databases, system architecture and design notation" is shown in the histogram in figure 1.

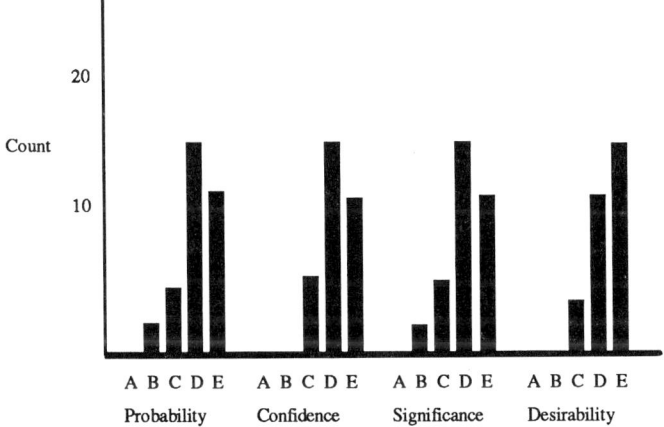

Figure 1 - Distribution of rating for the four criteria for Environment, proposal 8

As well as being highly desirable, this proposal was seen as being very significant. The ratings for probability and confidence are high (in fact, this proposal received the top rating in this category for all 4 criteria). This would, therefore, seem to be one area where considerable advance is likely over the next fifteen years. The remaining proposals in this category yielded fairly mixed results. Even so, a number of interesting factors were apparent - the proposal that software would be easier to update was seen as very significant and desirable but scored second from bottom on probability. In contrast, a rise in customer expectations of software systems was seen as very likely but not so desirable!

Main Problem Areas

This category also produced one proposal that stood out from the rest - "It will become increasingly important to provide high integrity, high reliability and high levels of security in future (networked) systems." The distribution of responses to this proposal is shown in the histogram of figure 2.

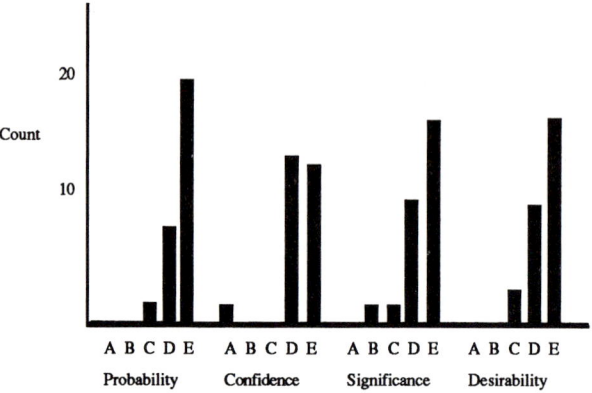

Figure 2 - Distribution of rating for the four criteria for Main Problem Area, proposal 4

This proposal came closer than any other to being viewed as a certainty. The majority of respondents in this case were very confident that this proposal would prove valid. Furthermore all of the other scores for this proposal were the highest in the category, indicating that it is likely to prove the major problem that system suppliers will have to face up to in the provision of future systems.

Key Technical Issues
As this category contained a wide range of proposals, three of the more notable ones have been chosen to illustrate a broad view of the responses received. Firstly, two proposals that stand out in terms of their likelihood are:

"The complexity of systems will require engineers to think and design at a more abstract level"
and
"Sophisticated techniques and tools will be needed to manage the building and testing of systems"

The histograms for these proposals are shown in figures 3 and 4 respectively.

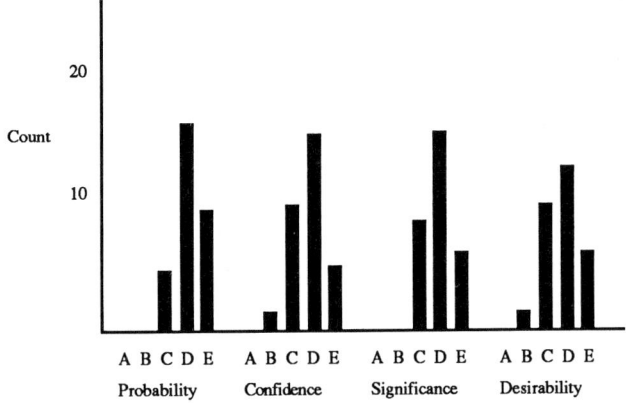

Figure 3 - Distribution of rating for the four criteria for Key Technical Issue, proposal 2

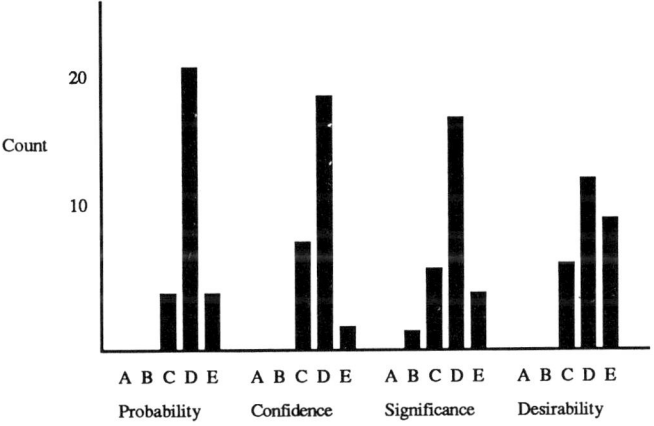

Figure 4 - Distribution of rating for the four criteria for Key Technical Issue, proposal 9

By way of contrast, one proposal was viewed as unlikely to come about (for all its desirability) was "Suitable theoretical approaches to the construction of and analysis of distributed and concurrent systems will be developed. These theories will be stable and enduring, not application specific". The response pattern for this proposal is shown in Figure 5.

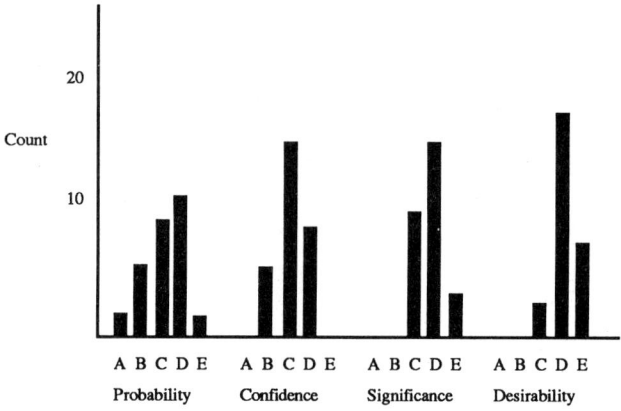

Figure 5 - Distribution of rating for the four criteria for Key Technical Issue, proposal 3

The above examples are typical of the views expressed in this category. Technical issues of formality, accuracy and validity were consistently rated as being less probable (but more desirable) than those concerned with software components and automatic system build/test. The implications of this apparent trend are discussed later.

Candidate Technology

The responses in this category match very closely with those for the key technical areas. The proposal that formal notations could provide a sound basis for system construction was rather lowly rated (see Figure 6) across all of the criteria, whereas the ratings for artificial intelligence as a means of enabling engineering information to be handled were consistently high (see Figure 7).

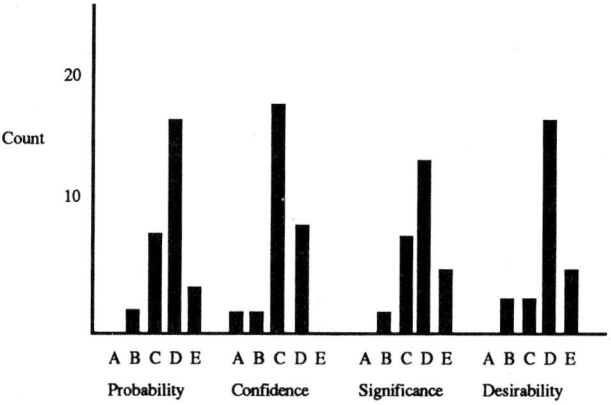

Figure 6 - Distribution of rating for the four criteria for Candidate Technology, proposal 3

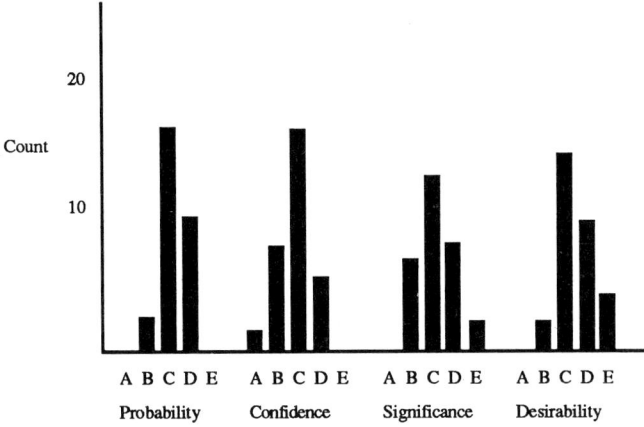

Figure 7 - Distribution of rating for the four criteria for Candidate Technology, proposal 2

Other results

The remaining categories included in the poll - social aspects and value of prophesy - proved fairly inconclusive, much to the disappointment of the authors. The former did indicate that people rather than technology are likely to be the critical element in commercial success, although the scores were considerably lower than those for the other categories. The value of prophesy was also seen as marginal, given the fact that breakthroughs in many areas of science and technology are often unpredictable [17]

4.2 Review of Data

In retrospect, the polling technique described here has provided a considerable amount of useful data. After two runs, the initial aim of generating consensus across a wide range of software engineering issues has been met. In addition to this, the comments received in the course of the poll have lead to considerable clarification of issues and broadening of scope.

There are a number of clear trends that have emerged from the analysis of the poll results. Firstly, there is the identification of the definition and manipulation of software components as the major technical issue. This emerges as a strongly held belief, the fulfilment of which will have significant impact. Secondly, the perception that standards will emerge implies that it will be feasible to identify and create a range of generally applicable software modules. This paves the way to the provision of reliable components. Finally, there is the perception that high security and reliability will be the dominant requirement in future software systems. Putting these trends together seems to indicate that software engineering is likely to move ever closer to existing hardware technology in that it will consist of a cycle of construction from modular units, locating faults on a module basis, identifying a suitable replacement and finally testing the rebuilt system

The final part of this exercise has been to rewrite the initial vision document to reflect the findings from the poll. This updated version is considerably more complete than the initial draft as the rationale behind each of the statements in it can be justified by reference to the relevant supporting information from the poll. The final vision document [18] which serves as one of the business planning documents for BTs Systems and Software Engineering research unit.

5. CONCLUSION

This paper has described an exercise in predicting software technology fifteen years hence based on the consensus views of a range of experts in the field. Specifically a delphi polling technique has been used to rate the likely future significance, desirability, probability and confidence of an initial set of proposed technologies and situations based on published information and local knowledge. Analysis of this poll has both extended the scope and revealed the level of agreement on various aspects of the overall question.

Given limited resources and the wide scope of software engineering, it is important to focus attention on the key aspects. The initial impetus for the work described here was to gain a stable view of what these key aspects are likely to be over the next fifteen years. On the wider front, the finer aspects of desirability of specific advances have emerged from the exercise. In this respect the poll has not only generated a sound basis for technical planning but has also established useful data which can be used in other planning and forecasting applications. The overall picture of the future of software engineering that emerges from this work is that it is likely to mature over the next fifteen years more in terms of techniques to regularise the construction of systems than in rigorous principles for design and evolution.

Acknowledgements

The authors of this paper would like to thank the Director of Communication Systems Technology, British Telecom Research Laboratories for permission to publish this paper. Thanks are also due to the many friends and colleagues in the System and Software Engineering Division who contributed to this work, especially Mike Tilley and Charles Jackson whose personal vision provided an excellent start and to John Foster who suggested the use of a poll.

References

1. *Software - A vital key to UK competitiveness* UK Cabinet Office report (HMSO books) ISBN 011 630829 X (1986)

2. Cohen B *The education of the information systems engineer* Electronics and Power pp203-5, March 1987

3. Jackson L A *Software system design methods and the engineering approach* BT Tech J vol4 no3 (1986)

4. *The STARTS Guide (- a guide to good software practice)* prepared by UK Industry, the DTI and NCC, published by the Dept of Trade and Industry (1987)

5. *International Computer Opinion Survey* Price Waterhouse(June 1988)

6. *Software Engineering in the Year 2001* 11th International Conference on Software Engineering (Panel Session 4)

7. Rigby P, Stoddart A & Norris M *Assuring quality in software - practical experience of attaining ISO 9001* BT Engineering Journal vol 8 part 4

8. Stoddart A G & Dell P W *Project management and control requirements* BT Technology Journal vol 4 no 3 (1986)

9. Bustard, D W , Norris M T & Van Toen B *Capturing and analysing user problems: separating the 'why' from the 'what'* Software Engineering '90 Conference (Brighton, July 1990)

10. Norris M T *The application of formal methods in system design* BT Technology Journal vol 3 no 4 (1986)

11. Foster J R, Jolly A E P & Norris M T *An overview of software maintenance* B T Technology Journal vol 7 no 4 (Oct 1989)

12. Lewis R, Beck D & Hartmann J *Assay - a tool to support regression testing* 2nd European Software Engineering Conf (Warwick, Sept 1989)

13. Naisbitt J *Megatrends* McDonald Press (1982)

14. Janis I *Victims of Groupthink* (Houghton Mifflin) 1972

15. Linstone H & Turoff M *The Delphi method - techniques and application* (Addison Wesley) 1975

16. Higham R C *Software maintenance: motivation & productivity* BT Research & Technology Technical Memorandum RT31/005/89

17. Galbraith S *Answers to our ills may be just around the corner - but prediction is the hard bit* Glasgow Herald, Jan 2nd 1990, pg12

18. Systems and Software Engineering Division *A 15 year vision of software engineering* Internal business planning document BSP2

Reuse

Towards a generic and extensible reuse environment,. Th. Moineau, J. Abadir & E. Rames

PRACTITIONER: Pragmatic Support for the Reuse of Concepts in Existing Software, C. Boldyreff, P. Elzer, P. Hall, U. Kaaber, J. Keilmann & J. Witt

Towards a Generic and Extensible Reuse Environment

Th. MOINEAU
SEMA GROUP,
16 Rue Barbès, 92126 MONTROUGE (France)

J. ABADIR, E. RAMES
MATRA ESPACE,
31-32, Rue de Cosmonautes, Z.I. du Palays, 31077 TOULOUSE Cedex (France)

Abstract: This paper presents part of the work that has been carried out in the ESF-ROSE project, whose main goal is to develop an environment for software reuse: the ESF-ROSE System. The major innovative aspects of the ESF-ROSE System are genericity, extensibility and full integration into the software development environment. A comprehensive description of the conceptual model of the system is given. The system's main functionalities and logical architecture are also described.
Key-words: Software Reuse, Software Factory, Generic System, Software Classification

List of abbreviations:

CSM : Component and System Model.
ESF : Eureka Software Factory.
FSE : Factory Support Environment.
LA : Library Administrator.
LS : Library System.
RE : Reusable Element.
ROSE : Reuse Of SoftwarE.
RTK : Reuse Tool Kit.

1 INTRODUCTION.

ESF-ROSE[1] is a subproject of the ESF (Eureka Software Factory) project which is a European research effort funded under the EUREKA program. ESF started in September 1986 and is intended to last for 10 years.

The ESF project aims at providing a Factory Support Environment (FSE), that is a software production environment which particularly supports a more industrialized production of software. This is based on concepts such as support for all production related activities, including technical, managerial and organizational

---

[1] The ESF-ROSE project must not be confused with another project on reusability which is also called ROSE [Lub87]

tasks and the integration of the activities of people and computers according to well defined process models [ESF89a]. The FSE aimed at by ESF is capable both of being configured for specific industries and of evolving with the innovations which arise from worldwide research and development teams.

Currently, there are 17 subprojects in ESF, covering areas from architectural support for building ESF software factories, to specific tools for different activities of software production. The ESF-ROSE subproject provides in particular the means to reuse software components.

The aim of ESF-ROSE is:
- to analyze and to define in a comprehensive way the concept of reuse of software elements (here software element means any kind of information produced within a FSE),
- to develop an environment (the ESF-ROSE System) for the reuse of software elements within a FSE,
- open up new research and to go beyond the state of the art with more theoretical work.

Reusability is today a topic of primary practical importance. Yet the concept of reuse is quite old: since 1949 for some authors [Tra87] and at least since McIlroy envisaged its reality in 1969 [McI69]. But we had to wait until 1983 to see the first real work on the subject (ITT Workshop on Reusability in programming [BPC83]). Currently reusability is becoming one of the most popular topics of the computing literature and is foreseen to be as important during the 90s as were expert systems during the 80s [Tra88]. The reason for this interest is evident: reusability is the key for improving software development productivity and quality.

The various approaches to reusability can be classified into two basic groups [BR87]: the composition approach and the generation approach.

In the composition approach, the components being reused (the building blocks) are stored in a library and are combined according to well-defined rules to form more complex systems. This idea was already mentioned by McIlroy in 1969, and has been applied for a long time in some well known libraries of mathematical procedures. A lot of current work follows this approach, as for instance RSL [BAB*87], STARS [DRR83], etc. Two main problems are encountered in this approach: the first is the specification or the description of the component so as to allow easy retrieval and so that the user can understand it properly for future adaptation. The second problem is the definition of the composition principles by which components are combined into target systems. Several approaches exist for the description of a component. The use of keywords [EW87] is a well known method. More innovative methods involve partially interpreted schemes [KRK87]. For the composition of components, one can cite the use of Module Interconnection Languages [PN86], message passing and inheritance in object-oriented approaches [Mey84] or artificial intelligence techniques, e.g. problem solving algorithms [MR88]. More formal methods like algebraic specifications are also used for both the description and the composition [Gog84, EW86, GM88]

In the approach by generation, the final program is generated from its specification. This "specification" can be written in a Very High Level Language (or in a Problem Oriented Language) as for instance MODEL [CLP84], or can be written in a more formal specification language such as CDL [Gau87]. The final product can be generated either directly or by means of successive transformations [Che84]. This approach has been used for a long time for compiler-compilers, report writers and man-machine interface generators for instance. The DRACO system [Nei84] is one of the most advanced system in this domain: it can create a problem oriented language (and all the associated tools: compiler, pretty-printer and so on) from a description of the application domain.

Both of the above approaches have their advantages and drawbacks and there is no agreement upon a unique approach to reusability. Viewpoints differ as to which approach offers the best opportunity for payoff. The ESF-ROSE project has chosen the composition approach, mainly because of the partners' background and of the adequacy of this approach to the needs of their respective companies.

This paper is organized into six parts. The first part describes the requirements for the ESF-ROSE subproject. An abstract reuse process model is outlined in the second part. The third part gives a comprehensive description of the conceptual model of the ESF-ROSE System. The fourth and the fifth parts describe the main functionalities and the logical architecture of the ESF-ROSE System and of its current mockup. The last part presents the time scale of the ESF-ROSE project.

2 REQUIREMENTS FOR ESF-ROSE

The motivation for the ESF-ROSE subproject result from the following facts:

- There is currently no common agreement on reusability: reusability is still a research topic, many approaches are proposed and only prototypes exist.

- Current work considers the reuse process as a stand-alone activity and do not integrate it into the software development process. As a consequence, reuse systems are not actually integrated into the software development environments.

- Most current systems are specific to the reuse of one kind of software element, mainly reuse of code, and they consider a specific language such as Ada (STAR [DRR83], ASR [Con87]) or Eiffel [Mey84].

This leads to the following requirements for ESF-ROSE:

1. **The ESF-ROSE System must be fully integrated into the FSE.**

   This means that a FSE user must be able to consult ESF-ROSE System so as to reuse any kind of software element he needs and this without leaving his development environment. This integration into the FSE will be achieved on two levels:
   - on the conceptual level, by integrating the reuse process into the software development process, and
   - on the technical level, through the integration mechanisms provided by the ESF kernel (cf. [ESF89a]).

2. **The ESF-ROSE System must be a generic system.**

   The ESF-ROSE System must be a generic system that can be instantiated for different situations, e.g. different kinds of software elements such as pieces of specification, design or code but also documentation (project management plan, user manual), different development methods, various application domains, etc. So, the end-user will actually use a customized instance of the ESF-ROSE system. Genericity is mainly supported in ESF-ROSE by its generic conceptual model.

3. **The ESF-ROSE System must be an extensible system.**

   This is necessary on the one hand to be able to evolve with the future innovation arising from the research community and on the other hand because total coverage of the reuse process requires a large number of tools that cannot be developed in one step.

   The extensibility concept is achieved in ESF-ROSE through its logical architecture. It is composed of two main parts:
   - a *kernel* implementing the basic well-established mechanisms, and
   - a *set of tools* supporting the various activities involved in the reuse process.

   Thanks to the integration mechanisms developed within ESF, new tools can be included as they become available.

4. **The ESF-ROSE subproject must have a pragmatic approach.**

   Genericity is a powerful paradigm, but has a lot of drawbacks. It is difficult to achieve; also generic systems are useless until they are instantiated and the instantiation process is usually long and difficult. To overcome these drawbacks, we are building several instantiations of ESF-ROSE System (by instantiating the kernel and the generic tools and/or implementing new specific tools).

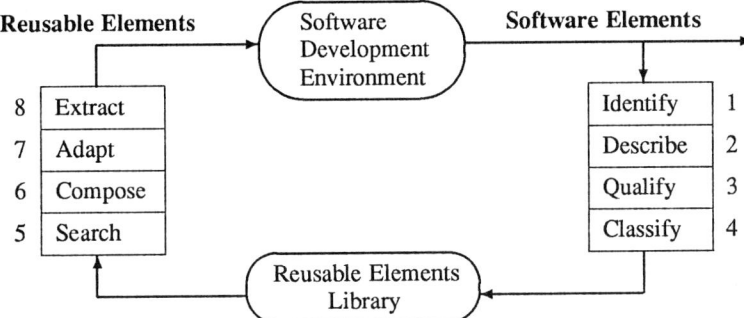

Figure 1: A *a posteriori* reuse process.

3 THE REUSE PROCESS MODEL.

The activities involved during the reuse process are depicted in figure 1. Due to the genericity requirement for ESF-ROSE, this process is a generic one that has to be customized according to the specificities of the FSE into which the reuse system is integrated. It is a very abstract representation that is currently enhanced by considering research work on process modeling[2] and various existing reuse processes (as for instance [Moi88]). In addition, we do not represent in figure 1 the dynamic aspects of the reuse process, i.e. the ordering and the interactions between the various activities.

This process reveals eight different activities concerning two main phases: populating the library (activities 1 to 4) and using the library (activities 5 to 8). Note that activities 1 to 4 are distinct activities in the *a posteriori* reuse process (illustrated in figure 1), which can be used today in the industrial framework; we hope that they will simply become part of the development process in the near future.

- **activity 1**: Software elements to be entered in the library must be identified. This identification is based on domain analysis. Candidate software elements can be checked against their interest for the users of the library (relevance to the library, reusability features and potential, etc.).

- **activity 2**: Software elements to be entered in the library have to be described so as to enable their later reuse. This means that all the information needed for their retrieval (e.g. key-words, etc.), their understanding (e.g. informal description, etc.) and their composition have to be added.

- **activity 3**: Software elements to be entered in the library have to be qualified. Indeed software reuse can become effective if and only if the reuser

---

[2]For this task we cooperate closely with the SPECIMEN ESF subproject devoted to process modeling within a Factory Support Environment.

can can have all the information about the quality level of the piece of software he is willing to reuse, so as to become confident of it; otherwise the well-known *Not Invented Here Syndrome* will inhibit software reuse.

- **activity 4**: Software elements to be entered in the library have to be classified to ease their later retrieval. Software elements entered in the library are called reusable elements.

- **activity 5**: Users must be able to select reusable elements corresponding to their needs. Note that retrieval is possible only if provision has been made when entering the software elements into the library (cf. activities 2 and 4).

- **activity 6**: Users must be able to compose the selected reusable elements so as to form more complex systems.

- **activity 7**: The retrieved reusable elements are adapted so as to conform to the formalism used in the development environment.

- **activity 8**: The adapted reusable elements are extracted from the reuse environment and sent to the software development environment. If necessary they can be modified[3] and then integrated in the new application.

4 A CONCEPTUAL MODEL FOR ESF-ROSE.

As explained above, the conceptual model of ESF-ROSE is a generic model. In this paper, we will not present the complete ESF-ROSE conceptual model, rather we will concentrate on two main parts of it:
- the **Component and System Model** which is devoted to describing the structure and the composition mechanisms of reusable element kinds, and
- the **Classification Model**, which is devoted to describing the classification scheme to be used in the instances of the ESF-ROSE System.

The Component and System Model and the Classification Model are two quite independent parts of the Conceptual Model: their only interface is the concept of reusable elements. Hence the modularity paradigm has been followed even in the conceptual model of ESF-ROSE : it is possible to enhance independently the Component and System Model or the Classification Model.

---

[3] Note that after a modification, the reusable element has to be tested and qualified again. Hence even minor modifications have, as far as possible, to be avoided.

4.1 A Component and System Model for ESF-ROSE.

The Component and System Model (CSM) provides a framework for describing the structure of software elements in a way that enables their reuse. The genericity we want to achieve in ESF-ROSE requires that we base our work on three levels of generalization: model, type, occurrence:

- A **model** is a set of rules to which a type must conform. It is a formalism to describe the types, and hence the occurrences.
- A **type** of something is a thing constructed according to the specifications of the model.
- An **occurrence** of something corresponds to the physical existence of a thing corresponding to a type T. It is possible to have many occurrences of the same type.

Hence a type describes the common structure and properties of all its possible occurrences. In the CSM point of view, types correspond to particular kinds of software components, as for instance ADA package, HOOD objects, SADT diagram, and so on. An occurrence is the description of a software element corresponding to a certain type, as for instance, the ADA module "Stack-management", the HOOD object "Clock", the SADT diagram "Install-library", the software requirements document "esf/rose/srd/v1", and so on. The aim of ROSE is to enable the reuse of occurrences[4].

We will give here a brief introduction to the CSM; a more complete description of the CSM can be found in [ESF89b]. We will first give an example to motivate the major concepts of the CSM, then we will describe the occurrence level and the type level.

But, let us first emphasize the fact that the following examples is only intended to illustrate the concepts of the CSM. We have chosen this examples among a number of possible candidates for its pedagogical value: *they are definitively neither good examples for practical use nor the only ones that can be defined by means of the CSM.*

The Ada-Module example.

Suppose that we want to reuse Ada[5] packages. The information to be reused is the Ada code, but we have to add further information for its retrieval such as an informal description, a formal specification of the code, some information related to performance aspects and so on. All these informations are not independant: the code for instance must be a correct implementation of the specification.

ESF-ROSE is not only meant to reuse basic packages (such as stack or queue management), but is also meant to enable reuse of set of interconnected packages

---

[4]A type is an abstract concept and is not an information; thus a type cannot be reused. However a type description is an information occurrence (of type *type*) and can thus be reused in order to define new type descriptions.

[5]Ada is a trade mark of the US Department of Defence

```
with LIST;                              generic type Item is private;
generic type Item is private;           package LIST is
package STACK is                          type List is limited private;
  type Stack is limited private;          function empty returns List;
  function empty returns Stack;           procedure add-head
  procedure push                                  (c : in Item; l : in out List);
          (c : in Item; st : in out Stack);  function head (l : List) returns Item;
  function top (st : Stack) returns Item;    procedure delete-head (l : in out List);
  procedure pop (st : in out Stack);         empty-list : exception;
  empty-stack : exception;                private
  private                                   type List is access List-elem;
    type Stack is access List;              type List-elem is ... ;
end STACK;                              end LIST ;
```

Figure 2: STACK Ada module: the STACK and LIST package interfaces.

(i.e. systems or configuration). It is important to support reuse of systems as well, because a system or a configuration is not only the union of its constituent parts: the whole is more than the sum of its parts. Hence the CSM should enable the description of the **composition mechanisms** that are used to build systems. To illustrate this, consider the Ada Module STACK of figure 2. This module implement stacks by means of lists. Hence this module needs a LIST module whose package interface is given in figure 2. Suppose now that we also have another Ada module implementing the lists, as for instance the module SIMPLE-LIST of figure 3. We may want to put these two modules together so as to get a more complete module for management of stacks. Unfortunately, this is not directly possible, because the type and operation names in STACK and in SIMPLE-LIST do not correspond: *empty* is called *nil*, *add-head* is called *cons* etc.

There are various way to handle this problem. One can for instance add some renaming clauses and renames some type and package names in the SIMPLE-LIST package so as to make the names compatible . The resulting LIST package interface of the STACK+LIST module is shown in figure 4; the differences between this package interface and the SIMPLE-LIST package have been underlined.

We would like to emphasize here on the need for a renaming. Indeed the modules that are composed together will usually not have been designed to work together (e.g. when they have been developped within different projects), hence the names are likely to be often not compatible.

The occurrence level.

The main concept of the CSM is the concept of **Reusable Element** (RE): RE is the quantum of reusability, i.e. this is the smallest quantity of information that

```
with NATURAL;
generic type Item is private;
package SIMPLE-LIST is
    type List is private ;
    function nil returns List ;
    procedure cons (c : in Item; l : in out List) ;
    function car (l : List) returns Item;
    procedure cdr (l : in out List) ;
    function length (l : List) returns Natural ;
    function nullp (l : List) returns Boolean ;
    empty-list : exception ;
    private
        type List is access List-cell ;
        type List-cell is ... ;
end SIMPLE-LIST ;
```

Figure 3: SIMPLE-LIST Ada module: the package interface.

can be reused. Hence REs must be **self contained**, i.e. a RE must contain all the information necessary for its reuse. Thus a RE can correspond to several software elements. For instance if two pieces of code are so closely related that they cannot be used independently, then they must be gathered into one unique RE.

According to the well-known principle of *separation of concerns*, a RE is not a monolithic piece of information: each RE is specified by several separate partial descriptions, called **views**, which describe different characteristics of the RE. The superposition of all views for one RE forms its complete and consistent description, provided that the semantic relationships between the views are observed. These relationships between views are expressed by means of so called **connections**.

Views and connections can be **aggregated**. Aggregated views are composed of sub-views and of connections between these sub-views. Aggregated connections are composed of sub-connections and of sub-views. Non-aggregated views or connections are called **basic**.

For instance, an Ada-module as described above can be constituted of the following views:
- an informal description;
- a formal specification;
- a plug which is a set of Ada package interfaces and which describes the resources exported by the modules;
- a code which is a set of Ada packages interfaces and bodies;

```
with NATURAL;
generic type Item is private;
package LIST is
     type List is private;

     function empty returns List renames nil;
     procedure add-head (c : in Item, l : in out List) renames cons;
     function head (l : List) returns Item renames car;
     procedure delete-head (l : in out List) renames cdr;
     function is-empty (l : List) returns Boolean renames nullp;

     function nil returns List;
     procedure cons (c : in Item, l : in out List);
     function car (l : List) returns List;
     procedure cdr (l : in out List)
     function length (l : List) returns Natural;
     function nullp (l : List) returns Boolean;
     empty-list : exception;
private
     type List is access List-elem;
     type List-elem is ... ;
end LIST;
```

Figure 4: STACK+LIST Ada module: the LIST package interface (inferred from the SIMPLE-LIST package interface).

- zero or more sockets which are sets of Ada package interfaces and which describe the resources imported by the modules.

The code itself can be further decomposed into two sub-views: one containing the package bodies and one containing the package interfaces. It is possible to add a connection between the code and the specification to express that the code is a correct implementation of the specification.

As explained above, the CSM has thus to provide a means to describe composition mechanisms, including the description of the way views of a complex RE can be build by means of the views of its constituents. This is achieved by the concepts of **inferred view** and of **inference connection**.

An inference connection builds the content of an inferred view (its output view) by means of the content of other views (its input views). Hence there is two kinds of views: the plain views whose content has to be stored, and the inferred views whose content is inferred and is not necessarily stored. There is also two kinds of connections: the plain connections which express a semantic property among the views that they connect together, and the inference connections which also build the content of an inferred view. Note that inferred view can participate in plain connections and can be input of inference connections (but cycles are of course forbidden).

For instance the code of the Ada module STACK+LIST is an inferred view and STACK+LIST should contain an inference connection with the codes of STACK and of SIMPLE-LIST as input and the code of STACK+LIST as output. This aggregated inference connection is further decomposed into two basic inference connections: one which deals with the package interfaces and the other one which deals with the package bodies. Furthermore this aggregated connection contains a basic view whose content is the renaming needed between STACK and SIMPLE-LIST.

Note that the view or connection occurrences do not make any sense when taken apart their belonging RE. Hence view or connection occurrences only exist within a RE and cannot be shared by several REs.

The type level.

In the CSM a **type** is associated with each object. A type describes the common structure and properties of all its possible occurrences.

In this paragraph, we will roughly describe how to define types. Note that the definition of a type must include some additional information that are used by the Library System. These information are described in the next section.

Defining an **RE type** consists in giving the type and the number of view, connection and RE occurrences that can be contained in an occurrence of this RE type, together with the role that these occurrences play within the RE occurrence.

For instance, an occurrence of the aforementioned RE type *Basic-Ada-Module* must have:
- one view of type *Text* playing the role *informal-description*,
- one view of type *Interface* playing the role *plug*,
- one view of type *Ada-code* playing the role *code*,
- zero or more views of type *Interface* playing the role *socket*.

An occurrence of the RE type *Complex-Ada-Module* must have:
- one *informal* description, one *plug*, one *code* and zero or more *sockets* as for an occurrence of the type *Basic-Ada-Module*,
- one RE of type *Basic-Ada-Module* or *Complex-Ada-Module* playing the role *client*,
- one RE of type *Basic-Ada-Module* or *Complex-Ada-Module* playing the role *server* (the server is plugged into the client),
- one inference connection of type *Make-Code* between the *socket* of the *client* and the *plug* of the *server* (to state in which sockets the server is plugged) and the *code* views of the *client* and of the *server*,
- and so on.

Let us discuss a little bit further about the concept of role. The roles are needed as reference to a constituent. The type of the constituent is not sufficient for that purpose, as illustrated by the *plug* and the *socket* of a *Basic-Ada-Module* which have the same type (namely *Ada-Interface*). If we draw a parallel with the Relational Model for database [Cod70], the constituents corresponds to (non atomic) attributes, their type corresponds to attributes domains and their roles correspond to attributes names.

Defining an **aggregated view type** (both plain or inferred) consists in defining the type and the number of view and connection occurrences that can be contained in an occurrence of this aggregated view type, together with the role that these occurrences play within the view occurrence. Defining a **basic view type** (both plain or inferred) consists in giving its content type. Note that an inferred view type is not tight to an inference connection type, i.e. the content of an inferred view can be inferred by any inference connection whose output view is of the good type. For instance an occurrence of the aggregated view type *Ada-Code* must contain:
- one view of type *Ada-Interface* playing the role *interface*, and
- one view of type *Ada-Body* playing the role *body*

Defining a **plain basic connection type** consists in giving, the type and the number of views that can be input views of an occurrence of that connection type together with the role that these occurrences play for the connection occurrence. To define an **inference connection type**, one has to give also the type of the output view, the way this output view is inferred and a precondition to state whether the input views are correct or not. Defining an **aggregated connection type** consists also in defining the type and the number of connection occurrences that can be contained in an occurrence of this aggregated connection type, together with the role that these occurrences play within the connection occurrence.

For instance an occurrence of the aggregated inference connection type *Make-Code* has as input:
- one view of type *Plug* playing the role *server-plug*,
- one view of type *Socket* playing the role *client-socket*,
- one view of type *Ada-Code* playing the role *server-code*, and
- one view of type *Ada-Code* playing the role *client-code*.

The first two views are used by the precondition of the connection to check that all resources required in the socket are actually exported by the plug. The last two views are used to infer the output view which is of type *Ada-Code*. Moreover this connection type is aggregated and contains:
- one view of type *Renaming* playing the role *renaming*,
- one basic inference of type *Merge-Ada-Bodies* playing the role *make-body*, whose inputs are the *renaming* and the *body* sub-views of the *server-code* and *client-code*, and whose output is the *body* sub-view of its output view.
- one basic inference of type *Merge-Ada-Interfaces* playing the role *make-interface*, whose inputs are the *renaming* and the *interface* sub-views of the *server-code* and *client-code*, and whose output is the *interface* sub-view of

its output view.

Up to now, we have not defined precisely the **inference mechanism**. The actual inference mechanism is still under experiment. We will nevertheless try to give a rough idea on this mechanism. Each **content type** is described by an attributed grammar in BNF notation. When a view is created, its content is parsed according to this grammar and the content is not stored as entered, but it is rather stored as an abstract syntax tree, where some nodes are annotated according to the attributes specified in the grammar.

The inference mechanism consists then in:
- extracting specified sub-trees from the input views,
- modifying these sub-trees and
- building the inferred content by putting together these sub-trees.

The precondition mechanism for connections consists in checking some properties of the attributes of the abstract syntax tree corresponding to the content of the input views.

Such an inference mechanism may seem a little bit complicate, but the cases we have to cope with require such a powerful mechanism. For instance the "merge" of two Ada code modulo a renaming is just not possible if we manipulate only text files: we have to manipulate abstract syntax trees to avoid scoping clashes for example.

Other inference mechanisms can be defined. For instance the above mechanism does not deal with semantics (even static semantics), nor is it able to cope with informal text. We will refine this mechanism later on, so as to get a trade-of between power (to deals with static semantics or with natural language), efficiency and facility of use.

In the above description of the RE type *Complex-Ada-Module*, we have said that an occurrence of that type must have one *server* of type *Basic-Ada-Module* or *Complex-Ada-Module*. Indeed it does not matter if the module to be plugged is either basic or complex. Thus we need a notion of **generalization**. This is achieved in the CSM by means of the notion of sub-type/super-type. We can say for instance that *Basic-Ada-Module* and *Complex-Ada-Module* are sub-types of the more general type *Ada-Module*; then any occurrence of type *Basic-Ada-Module* or *Complex-Ada-Module* can appear instead of an occurrence of the type *Ada-Module*, and thus when defining the type *Complex-Ada-Module* one has only to say that the *server* must be of type *Ada-Module*. This notion of generalization is useful for the view types and for the connection types as well.

An inheritance mechanism is associated with the notion of sub-type. Indeed while describing the RE types *Basic-Ada-Module* and *Complex-Ada-Module*, we have seen that both types contain a plug, a code and zero or more sockets; thus it is interesting to state that an *Ada-Module* must have a plug, a code and zero or more sockets and then the description of *Basic-Ada-Module* and *Complex-Ada-Module* will inherit these roles and the corresponding types from *Ada-Module*.

An inherited role in a RE type can be restricted to be a sub-type of the type corresponding to the role in the super-type. This inheritance mechanism allows to reuse type descriptions.

Note that such no generalization concept exists on the occurrence level; the inheritance mechanism used in the object oriented languages is in fact one particular composition mechanism that can be modeled by means of the CSM.

As ESF-ROSE is a generic system, **manipulation** of occurrences are different according to their types. For instance the generic Consultation Tool of the RTK does not display Ada packages and SADT diagrams the same way. Hence with each type is associated the way to perform given actions on its occurrences (such as for instance "display"). This description contains the name of the procedure to call (by means of the mechanisms of the ESF kernel) together with the required parameters. The list of action names is not limited and can be extended as needed.

Remark.

The difference between the concept of RE and the concept of view is twofold:
- These two concepts have different semantics: a RE is required to be self-contained whereas a view is not.
- These two concepts have different behaviours: a view cannot be shared by several REs, whereas a RE can be shared by several complex REs; REs can be composed together so as to form complex REs; a RE can be reused alone, whereas a view cannot; and the attributes of REs and of views in the library are different (cf. for instance the reuse reports below).

Other concepts of the CSM to support reuse.

A RE must contain all the information needed for its reuse. There are a lot of such information as for instance quality results, design history, environments requirements and so on (see for instance [FN87] for a list of such information in the case of code reuse). Among these information, some must be handled by the ESF-ROSE kernel and are called attributes. The others are to be modeled as views of the corresponding REs. Note that the distinction between view and attribute is not based on the importance of the information, but on the fact that only the kernel of ESF-ROSE can handle them. We will describe below the most significant attributes of the CSM.

Reuse guidelines: Developing a software element for its later reuse is a difficult task. For that reason guidelines are associated with each type in ESF-ROSE. The developers can consult them so as to develop software elements that are more likely to be reused. Examples of such guidelines for the Ada language can be found for instance in [Den87]. The software elements that do not follow the guidelines will usually not be accepted in the library.

Quality results: As it has been mentioned before, software reuse can become effective if and only if the reuser can be confident in the piece of software he will reuse. Thus a reuser must be able to determine the quality level of a RE. Otherwise the well-known *Not Invented Here Syndrome* will inhibit software reuse. The results of the qualification phase are stored within the reusable element in the library, so that the reuser can consult them.

The qualification procedure depends on the type of the software element: qualification criteria for an Ada package and for a specification document are likely to be different. Hence with each type (i.e. RE, view or connection type) is associated with a set of quality criteria and a set of procedures to check these criteria. These procedures can be applied on the occurrences by means of the communication mechanism of the ESF kernel [ESF89a] (thus the procedures must be known within the FSE) and the results is automatically stored within the occurrence.

Note that a RE can be stored in ROSE even if it does not fullfil the quality criteria associated with its type, or if some of the criteria has not been checked. Indeed, even low quality level REs can be reused for instance during a prototyping phase; but the user must be aware of that and can choose to reuse this REs or not.

Reuse reports: Another way to avoid the *Not Invented Here Syndrome* is to associate a reuse history with each RE. A reuse history is the collection of the reuse reports of the RE (i.e. who has reused it, when, in which context, what were the difficulties, what was the gain and so on). Indeed a RE which has been successively reused a lot of times is a RE which gives confidence and thus a RE which will inhibit the *not invented here* syndrome.

Reuse reports are useful also in order to explain how to reuse a given RE. Indeed reuse reports can contain statements like: "I have reused this RE in this environment with the following tunings and it works fine ...". Then other users can benefit from this experience when reusing this RE.

Bug reports are special cases of reuse reports: they report about a bug found in some reusable element. Bug reports have also a special behaviour: when a bug report is received, all the users that have reused this reusable element are immediately alerted, and the reuse of the corresponding RE can be forbidden.

4.2 A Classification Model for ESF-ROSE.

One of the essential problems in reusing software elements is locating and retrieving them from a large collection. Within ROSE, we propose a classification system as a basis for organizing the collection of REs and as a support for an efficient and simple retrieval mechanism.

We will first give the requirements we had for the classification model of ESF-ROSE, after that we will describe the chosen approach and then the classification model, lastly we briefly explain how to build a new classification scheme.

The requirements for the classification in ESF-ROSE.

For the classification and retrieval of REs, we can make the following observations which are based on real industrial needs:
- The collection (the set of REs) is continuously expanding.
- We can have several software elements semantically equivalent, but having different environments, implementation details and coming from different application domains.
- The users do not know the exact content of the collection, nor do they know the internal structure of the software elements and have some difficulty in formulating a valid query.
- The users have different backgrounds and profiles.

Hence the classification system must be:
- *extensible* for supporting growing collection of reusable elements,
- *powerful* for capturing the differences between semantically equivalent REs,
- *adaptable* to be used in different FSEs devoted to different application domains and to fullfil the needs of a large numbers of users with different viewpoints and skills, and
- *efficient* to enable the user to find easily the REs that meet his requirements.

The classification approach in ESF-ROSE.

Classification approaches can be divided into two basic groups: enumerated approach and faceted approach [PF87]. The enumerated (or traditional) method postulates a universe of knowledge divided into successively narrower classes that include all the possible classes. These classes are then arranged to display their hierarchical relationships. The faceted approach relies not on the breakdown of a universe, but on building up or synthesizing from the subject statements or the vocabulary of particular objects to be classified.

Each approach has its own advantages and drawbacks but the faceted approach seems to meet the requirements previously stated i.e. a classification must be easy to change and customize according to different users' viewpoints. However, the main drawback of the faceted classification is that each facet is characterized by a "flat" list of terms in natural language. This lack of structure in a facet causes increased search time.

The classification approach in ESF-ROSE is an adaptation of the faceted classification presented in [PF87]. The main difference is that, in ESF-ROSE, a facet is structured into several levels of abstraction.

A first introduction to the Classification Model.

We describe here the main concepts of the Classification Model. This section is illustrated by the classification scheme of figure 5, which is an example taken from the aerospace domain.

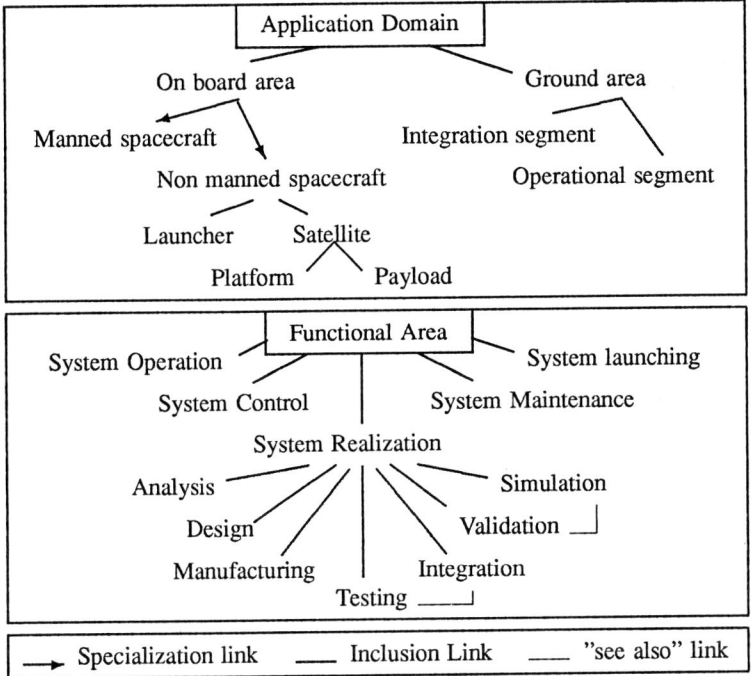

Figure 5: Example of classification scheme (aerospace context)

The Classification Model. It is a set of rules to which a classification scheme must conform. It means a formalism to describe, create and manage classification schemes.

The Classification Scheme. It is the set of entities describing a domain of discourse along with information describing their interrelationships and management. A library of reusable elements contains one classification scheme: it reflects the differences that can arise between various reusable elements.

The Classification Criteria. Within a scheme, several classification criteria can be defined. (criterion and facet are synonymous) A classification criterion is considered as a particular view on a reusable element. For instance, we can observe a RE according to a domain view, a conceptual view or an architectural view.

To exemplify the previous definition, we can imagine a classification scheme with two classification criteria: the functional area criterion and the application domain criterion (cf. figure 5). The functional area criterion allows the classification of all the REs according to the main activities performed by the application they are part of. The application domain criterion allows the classification of all the REs according to where the application is exercised. To meet the extensibility requirement, the classification scheme can be enriched with new criteria so as to keep track of the evolution of the REs collection.

The Classes. A classification criterion contains a set of classes. A class is a group of elements and must not be confused with the term "class" as used within the object-oriented language terminology. A class describes a concept of the universe of discourse. All the members of a class share at least one characteristic that members of other classes do not. In classifying a RE, a reference link is created between the RE and the class that best describes that RE for a given criterion. Note that a RE will usually belong to several classes within different classification criteria, so as to reflect its various aspects (facets). Hence using a classification schema consists in selecting the classes of interest within the various criteria, so as to get the REs that belong to the intersection of these classes.

Roughly speaking, a class can be considered as a decomposition into several sub-classes, a subclass into sub-sub-classes and so on (see the link concept below). Hence our approach is actually a merge of the faceted approach and of the enumerated approach.

A class is described by a list of characteristics such as:
- the name of the class,
- an informal description stating briefly the semantics of the class,
- a list of synonyms; these are terms used within different projects, but referring to the same concept defined by the class
- a list of properties; a property is a couple $< attribute, value >$ and describes invariant features of a class. For example, the class *Communicate*, gathering all the REs which transfer information between two points, can be characterized by the properties: origin, destination, communication support.

The Links. A class can be connected to other classes by means of links. There are two kinds of links:
- The **hierarchical links** such as **specialization** and **inclusion**. For instance, in the *application domain* criterion, the classes *Manned spacecraft* and *Non manned spacecraft* are a specialization of the class *On board area*, and the classes *Analysis* and *Testing* of the *Functional area* criterion are both part of the class *System Realization*.
  This sort of link allows to bind classes to sub-classes.
- Other semantic links, such as the *see also* link. For instance, the classes *System testing* and *System integration* of the *Functional area* criterion are related by a *see also* link.

Some link types are predefined (such as specialization, inclusion or *see also*) but it is always possible to define new types of link.

The Weights. Weights can be associated with links between the REs and their classes. These weights can represent the matching degree between the REs features and the properties of a class. The weights are used to help the user when navigating in a classification scheme.

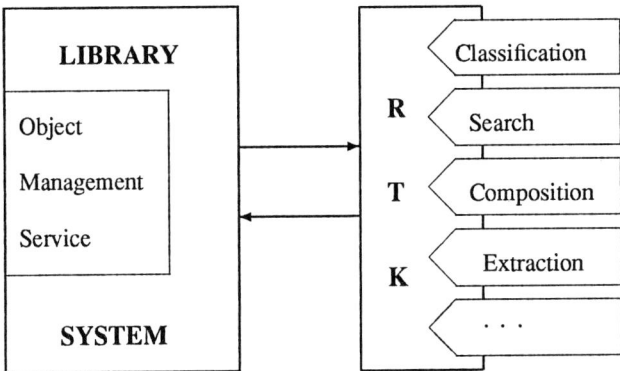

Figure 6: Logical architecture of the ESF-ROSE System

Building a classification scheme.

It is important to organize the RE collection in ways that reflect the user's mental model of the domain. So, to build a classification scheme, we have to analyze the domain to which the REs belong (domain analysis). This activity not only allows the identification of elements that are potentially reusable but also their characteristics, relationships and a meaningful vocabulary that end users can understand. The Domain Analysis approach allows the collection of REs to evolve without major modification of the classification scheme.

The classification scheme is built according to a bottom-up approach. First, a domain analysis is performed on a representative sample of software elements. Significant terms that describe concepts are selected; the terms which belong to the same semantic category are grouped together and allow the definition of a classification criteria (e.g. all the terms which express an action or a function are grouped in a classification criteria named *function*). Then, closely related terms within each criterion (those which express the same idea) are abstracted into a class (e.g. all the terms dealing with the "input" notion). This abstraction process is repeated on the classes just defined. Finally, we obtain a hierarchy of classes for each classification criterion.

5 THE ESF-ROSE SYSTEM.

The ESF-ROSE System supports the different activities of the reuse process. Due to the extensibility requirement explained in chapter 2, the ESF-ROSE System is divided into two parts: the kernel and a set of tools. The logical architecture of the ESF-ROSE System is shown in the figure 6.

The kernel supports the basic mechanisms for the storage, the classification and the retrieval of reusable elements. It can be seen as providing the services to be used by all of the tools. Thus the kernel is referred to as the **Library System** (LS).

The tools provide more advanced functionalities. They act as an interface between the user and the Library System. The set of tools is called the **Reuse Tool Kit** (RTK). The RTK is extensible and it is possible to add new tools provided that they conform to the LS interface and to the integration mechanism of ESF. The ESF-ROSE subproject will develop only a subset of the tools that can exist in the Reuse Tool Kit.

We will describe hereafter the functionalities of the LS and of the tools that we intends to develop within the ESF-ROSE subproject.

5.1 The Library System.

The Library System is meant to manage a set of libraries, which are mainly devoted to storing, classifying and retrieving the reusable elements. For this purpose, it encapsulates a Data Management System. Each library is administrated by a Library Administrator (LA) who is in charge of the configuration and the management of his library.

The main functionalities of the LS are listed below. Note that they are only low level functionalities and a user should not interact directly with them: the RTK should act as an interface between the user and the LS.

REs management. It includes mainly the following functionalities:
- Creation/modification/deletion of types and occurrences: For all these actions, the LS ensures the coherence of the library, by checking that:
    - each type description conforms to the ESF-ROSE Component and System Model;
    - each occurrence conforms to its type;
    - when a type is deleted, all its occurrences and all the types referring to it have been deleted previously;
    - when a RE occurrence is deleted, all the REs containing this occurrence have been deleted before.

  Moreover the LS manages the successive versions of the types and of the RE occurrences.
- Retrieval of types and occurrences: This functionality is very low-level and should not be confused with the functionality of the search tools in the RTK. The supported requests are of the form: "retrieve the type description of the type X", "retrieve the RE occurrence named Y", "retrieve the RE occurrences of the type X", "retrieve the occurrences of the class C", etc.

Classification scheme management. It is mainly:
- Creation/modification/deletion of classification scheme, including the criteria, the classes and the links.

- Classification of a RE occurrence: it is simply the creation of a reference link between a class and the RE. More sophisticated functionalities are provided by the Classification Tool of the RTK.

Users management. It includes mainly:
- Subscription/discontinuance of a user.
- Management of the users' profiles: a user's profile contains all the information about the user: his identity (name, E-mail address, etc.), his access rights (see access rights management below), his logbook (which RE he has reused, the connection time, ...), etc. A part of this information is used by the LS, the rest is used by the tools of the RTK which can modify it dynamically.

Policies management. As the LS is as generic as possible, a lot of policies are not defined (or more precisely, they are predefined but can be customized as needed). Among these policies, one can cite:
- The access rights policy: Each action on an ESF-ROSE object (type, occurrence, classification scheme etc.) can be restricted to a given category of users. A user who does not belong to an authorized category (or to one of its super-categories) will not be allowed to perform the action. The predefined actions are: create, consult, modify, delete and so on. It is possible to define new actions and the Library Administrator can define categories of users and can assign a user to a given category.
- Commercial policy: one may want to have a commercial policy for a library. This can include subscription fees, usage fees (corresponding to the time the library has been used by the user), reuse fees (i.e. each RE has a price to pay when one wants to reuse it) and so on. The Library Administrator is in charge of defining the commercial policy to be used for his library (if he wants such a commercial policy).

Qualification results management. As explained above, each occurrence is associated with information that allows the end-user to get a precise evaluation of the quality level of the REs he is willing to reuse. On request, the LS applies the procedures defined in the type description and automatically stores the results within the occurrence. The LS ensures that the results are actually the ones produced by the specified procedures and that these results cannot be modified by a human intervention.

Note that it is not necessary to check all the qualification criteria when entering a reusable element in a library. Indeed checking a quality criterion can be very (machine-)time consuming, and the LA will perhaps not have the time to check some very high level quality criteria (which are perhaps needed only by few people). Hence checking these criteria is up to the user who actually need them. Anyway, the results are stored so that other users can benefit from them.

Reports management. Reports are used for the communication between the LS

and the LA on the one hand and the users of the FSE on the other hand. Among these reports, one can cite:
- The reuse reports: As explained before, a reuse report is prepared by the reuser of an occurrence and is stored within the corresponding occurrence. It is clear that the user will usually not fill in these reports spontaneously. It is up to the staff management and to the LA to insist on the importance of the reuse reports.
- The bug reports: An RE should not have bugs, but *errare humanum est* and bugs are likely to be found in some REs. Each time a reuser finds a bug, he is invited to send back a bug report. The bug reports are stored within the occurrence and an action can be taken by the LA, such as forbidding further reuse of the RE, notifying the users who have already reused this RE and so on.
- The "Not Found" reports: Each time a user of the ESF-ROSE System does not find a RE he needs, he can send a "Not Found" report to the LA. When reading such a report, the LA can either store the report in the "Not Found" list (so as to remember that it should be of interest to enter a corresponding RE in the library) or he can reply to the user (to say where to find the RE for instance).

The form of these reports is predefined, but most of them can be customized.

5.2 The Reuse Tool Kit

We will briefly describe here the tools that are planned to be developed within ESF-ROSE. Due to the spiral approach chosen for the development of the ESF-ROSE System, the functionality of the tools cited here are likely to be improved, and new tools are likely to be added later on if we feel the need for them.

The Insertion Tool. This tool is meant to translate the software element into the ESF-ROSE formalism. Hence this tool can be considered as a reverse engineering tool. We do not intend to build a generic version of this tool, we rather intend to develop several insertion tools devoted to specific types of software elements (e.g HOOD, Ada, ...).

The Qualification Tool. As explained above, each occurrence is qualified according to its type. But we feel that some quality criteria are quite general, such as modularity, consistency and so on. Hence, we plan to study these criteria and to implement a tool devoted to checking them. Of course these criteria can be tuned according to the required quality level of each library. The results of this global qualification will be stored in the qualification part of the occurrences.

The Classification Tool. The classification tool provides high level functionalities for the management of classification schemes. In addition, it helps in classifying a new RE into the classification scheme of a given library.

This tool have two main functionalities:

- Creation of a classification scheme, i.e helping the Library Administrator in creating a classification scheme.
- Classification of a reusable element, i.e supporting the Library Administrator in finding the "best" location in the classification scheme (classes) to put the reusable element.

The Search Tool. The Search Tool is not really a tool, it is rather a collection of tools that help retrieval of REs. This collection currently includes the Classification Navigation Tool, the Consultation Tool and the Sieve Tool described below. We intend to complete this collection by tools using artificial intelligence techniques, and by search tools specific to some instances (for example a search tool for modular code with algebraic specifications is foreseen).

The Classification Navigation Tool. This tool assist the ESF-ROSE user in finding a RE that corresponds to his needs, by means of the classification criteria and of the class properties. Search criteria are of two types:
- a combination of class identifiers, each belonging to one classification criterion,
- a combination of class properties which reflect the RE features covered by the classification scheme.

Retrieval is done by navigating through the scheme and intersecting the set of REs provided by the selection of classes in each criterion.

The Consultation Tool. This tools allow examination of the various views and connections of the REs, but also consultation of the qualification results and of the various reports associated with the REs (reuse reports, bug reports, etc). This tool will use the "display" manipulation attribute of the types in order to display the occurrences.

The Sieve Tool. Sieves are used to eliminate candidates which do not have some required characteristics. One can for instance eliminate all the candidates which are not implemented in Ada, or the candidate with unsatisfactory performances. A sieve is composed of a reference value, a comparison procedure, a RE type name and a role name. An RE will go through a sieve if and only if it is of the specified type and if the comparison procedure applied on the reference value and on the contents of the view playing the specified role yields true. Sieves can be interconnected by means of the usual logical operators (and, or, not) so as to build complex sieves. The complex sieves built by the user can be stored in his profile for later reuse.

The goal of the sieves is to check properties that are not covered by the classification scheme (such as for instance precise performance characteristics).

The Composition Tool. This tool will use the composition mechanisms expressed by the type descriptions in order to assist the user in building complex REs out of REs from the library. We plan to build both a generic composition tool (this tool builds a template that the user has to fill) and a set of specific composition tools (e.g for Ada modules, for HOOD objects, ...).

The Adaptation Tool. This tool is meant to translate the REs the user has selected or created (by composition) into the formalism used in the software development environment. We intend to develop several adaptation tools devoted to specific types of software elements.

The Extraction Tool. This tool is devoted to the transfer of selected REs from the ROSE System to the software development environment of the user.

It is clearly difficult to build a fully generic extraction tool, because it depends both on the type of the RE to extract and on the current software development environment. Hence we intend to develop several extraction tool devoted to specific reusable element types and to specific software development environments (for instance configuration management tools, Ada compiler libraries, project databases, etc).

The Library Administration Tool. This tool is meant to help the Library Administrator in configuring and managing his library: establishing policies (e.g. access rights policy or commercial policy), customizing reports, adding and removing users, adding new REs, managing the reports, etc.

The ROSE Administration Tool. This tool is mainly dedicated to the monitoring of the different tools available in the ESF-ROSE system. Hence this tool is the process control engine of ESF-ROSE: it controls that the ROSE System is used in a way that is compatible with the reuse process model.

6 THE ESF-ROSE MOCKUP.

A mockup of the ROSE-System has been developed (a first version was completed in October 89). This mockup conforms to the architecture described above: it consists of a Library System and of a Reuse Tool Kit. It is implemented using Y3 (an object oriented environment on top of Le-Lisp) and runs on SUN workstations under X11. The inference mechanism is implemented with Centaur [BCD*87].

This mock-up has been instantiated for reuse of HOOD objects and of Ada modules (which corresponds to the Ada instance used to illustrate the Component and System Model in section 4.1). The HOOD instance is currently assessed with a real-scale case study from the aerospace domain; we plan to assess the Ada instance the same way.

This mockup support all the functionalities of the Library System (except the policies management). Its RTK include the tools listed below.

HOOD Insertion Tool. This tool is meant to translate automatically HOOD object descriptions into the ESF-ROSE formalism.

Classification Tool. The current classification tool has two main functionalities:
- Creation of a classification scheme.
  This part enables the Library Administrator to create criterion and hierarchy of classes with a graphical and user-friendly interface. The user can create/delete criteria, and, within each criterion, create and delete classes. The domain analysis process is currently not supported.
- Classification of a reusable element.
  This part support the Library Administrator in finding the "best" location in the classification scheme (classes) to put the reusable element. This process is decomposed into two steps:
    - Analysis step: the RE is examined so as to extract the features useful for classification purposes. For instance, the analysis of the informal description view of a RE (if any) provides a list of keywords needed for the next step. They can be extracted either automatically (using syntactical or linguistic analysis after removal of the non-significant words) or by manual inspection.
    - Comparison step: each classification criterion of the scheme is scanned so as to find the classes whose concepts are the closest to the features of the RE. For each class, the system checks whether the class identifier (or one of its synonyms) and its properties match (at least partially) the features of the RE.

  It is to be noted that each step can be performed both manually and automatically: the system provides preliminary results that can be enhanced and confirmed by the library administrator.

Search Tool. The current Search Tool consist in three tools : the Classification Navigation Tool, the Sieve Tool and the Consultation Tool. It implements a search strategy based on the following three steps (but each step is optional and the user can skip any one of them):
- Search on classification criteria and class properties (the Classification Navigation Tool).
  The search can be conducted in two ways:
    - The user is not able to specify exactly the requirements by a keyword based query. He navigates in the classification scheme and obtains an idea about the available REs. This navigation is supported by a graphical and user-friendly interface. The user marks the classes of interest within the various criteria. The system computes the REs that belong to the intersection of these classes and puts them in a set for further processing.
    - The user has a good idea about the library content and knows the exact characteristics of the RE he needs. So, he directly formulates an accurate query by providing the search criteria. In future, we plan

to optimize the search by using the user profile and weights: this procedure will first propose criteria that are most relevant to a given user and elements that best fit the user requirements.
- Search on RE features not covered by the classification scheme (the Sieve Tool).

Sieves are used to eliminate candidates which do not have some required characteristics. This tool enables to define basic and complex sieves, to apply them on a set of REs, and to store them for later reuse.

Several sieve types have been implemented:
  - the performance sieve type, which allow to select only the REs which have better performances than a specified treshold.
  - the key word sieve type, which allow to select only the REs which have the specified key-words in one view whose content is a text.
  - the signature sieve type, which allow to select only the Ada-module REs whose plug corresponds (modulo a renaming) to a given package interface.

Other sieve types are currently under implementation.
- Examination of reusable elements (the Consultation Tool).

This tool enables to examine the remaining candidates so as to select the most suitable one. This tool alows to examine the various views and connections of a RE, but also to consult the qualification results and the various reports associated with a RE.

Composition Tool. Two composition tools are currently implemented:
- A generic composition tool.

This tool builds a template that the user has to fill. The holes in the template (e.g. the content of the views, ...) are represented by meta-variables. The list of the meta-variables in the template is displayed to the user, who can select one of these meta-variables to specify its actual value; the tool replace each occurrence of the meta-variable by this value.
- A composition tool specific to the Ada instance.

The user only has to specify the name of the client, of the server and of the socket to fill with the server, together with the correct renaming; the tool automatically create the corresponding complex Ada module.

This tool is currently integrated with the above signature sieve type, so that the user no more have to write down the renaming to be use: this tool finds alone all the possible renamings, the user only has to select the most convenient one.

Extraction Tool. Two versions of this tool have been developed:
- A generic extraction tool, which creates a directory whose name is the name of the extracted RE, and which store the content of selected views of this RE in a file within this directory.
- An extraction tool specific to the Ada instance, which create a directory

whose name is the name of the extracted RE, and which split the code view of this Ada module into several files, one file for each package. Moreover the file names are compatible with the convention used by our Ada compiler.

Library Administration Tool. The current version of this tool is mainly a graphical and user-friendly interface of the corresponding primitives of the Library System.

ROSE Administration Tool. No such tool have been implemented for the ESF-ROSE mockup: the monitoring of the various tools is done by the overall user-interface. But we intend to build such a tool in the next version of ESF-ROSE.

7 TIME SCALE AND FUTURE WORK.

The ESF-ROSE subproject began in September 1988 and is planned to end in June 1992. The ESF-ROSE System is developed according to the spiral approach [Boe88]. It was thus planned to develop successively a mock-up, a prototype and the final system which will be integrated into real FSEs (one for real-time applications and the other for business applications).

The experience gained in the development and evaluation of the mock-up served as a basis for the development of the prototype and has been used to enhance the model and the functionalities of the system. The ESF-ROSE System will be incrementally build from the prototype, by enhancing the Library System and by building new tools (we intend to study more over the artificial intelligence techniques and the use of formal methods).

The mockup was completed in October 1989. The prototype is planned for beginning 1991; it will include the Ada and the HOOD instances of the mockup. We also plan to develop instances that are devoted to:
- reuse of code by means of algebraic specification (cf. [GM-88] and [GDS-89]),
- reuse of documents (such as users' manuals),
- reuse of widgets for X Window System[6],
- business applications with the MERISE methodology [TRC83],
- ...

The prototype will be assessed on real-scale projects.

The final ESF-ROSE System will be integrated in the two FSEs currently built within the ESF project : PEBA for business applications and FERESA for real time applications.

---

[6]X Window System is a trademark of the Massachusetts Institute of Technology

ACKNOWLEDGMENTS.

The ESF-ROSE project is a collaborative research and development project between Matra, Sema Group and the University of Dortmund. Hence this paper is a synthesis of the work done by the members of the project, mainly J. Abadir, N. Badaro, J. Cramer, B. Durin, V. Dzuba, H. Hünnekens, Th. Moineau, B. Mouton, E. Rames, W. Schäfer, F. Villeneuve and S. Wolf.

We would like to express our sincere appreciation to Bruno Hirsch for his useful criticisms and suggestions about earlier versions of this article since they contribute greatly to improving its readability and clarity. We also thank Claude Chrisment and Steve Common whose comments have made this a better publication than originally planned.

References

[BAB*87] B.A. Burton, R.W. Aragon, S.A. Bailey, K.D. Koehler, and L.A. Mayes. The reusable software library. *IEEE Software*, 1987.

[BCD*87] P. Borras, D. Clement, Th. Despeyroux, J. Incerpi, G. Kahn, B. Lang, and V. Pascual. *Centaur the system*. Technical Report 777, INRIA, France, 1987.

[Boe88] B.W. Boehm. A spiral model for software development and enhancement. *Computer*, May 1988.

[BPC83] T. Biggerstaff, A. Perlis, and T.E. Cheatham, editors. *Workshop on Reusability in Programming*, ITT Programming Technology Center, 1983.

[BR87] T. Biggerstaff and Ch. Richter. Reusability framework, assessment and directions. In *Proc. 20th Annual Hawaii Int. Conf. on System Sciences*, 1987.

[Che84] T.E. Cheatman. Reusability through program transformation. *IEEE Transaction on Software Engineering*, SE-10(5), 1984.

[CLP84] T.T. Cheng, E.D. Lock, and N.S. Prywes. Use of very high level languages and program generation by management professionals. *IEEE Transaction on Software Engineering*, SE-10(5), 1984.

[Cod70] E.F. Codd. A relational model of data for large shared data banks. *CACM*, 13(6), 1970.

[Con87] R. Conn. The Ada software repository and software reusability. In *Proc. 5th Annual Joint Conf. on Ada Technology and Washinton Ada Symposium*, 1987.

[Den87] R.J. St. Dennis. Reusable Ada software guideline. In *Proc. 20th Annual Hawaii Int. Conf. on System Sciences*, 1987.

[DRR83] L.E. Druffel, S.T. Redwine, and W.E. Riddle. The STAR program : overview and rationale. *Computer*, Nov. 1983.

[ESF89a] ESF Technical Design Group. *ESF Technical Reference Guide*. Technical Report, ESF Consortium, Berlin, Germany, 1989.

[ESF89b] ESF-ROSE Consortium. *Specification of a Component and System Model*. Technical Report, ESF Consortium, Berlin, Germany, Apr. 1989.

[EW86]   H. Ehrig and H. Weber. Programming in the large with algebraic module specifications. In *Proc. 4th Int. Conf. on Very Large Data Bases*, 1986.

[EW87]   D.W. Embley and S.N. Woodfield. A knowledge structure for reusing abstract data types. In *Proc. 9th Int. Conf. Software Eng.*, 1987.

[FN87]   W.E. Frakes and B.A. Nejmeh. An information system for software reuse. In *proc. 10th Minnowbrook Workshop for Software Reuse*, 1987.

[Gau87] R. Gautier. A component description langage. *ACM Sigsoft Software Engineering Notes*, 12(1), 1987.

[GM88]   M.-C. Gaudel and Th. Moineau. A theory of software reusability. In *proc. ESOP'88*, Springer-Verlag LNCS 300, 1988. See also *LRI Report N° 565*, March 1990 (revised version).

[Gog84] J.A. Goguen. Reusing and interconnecting software components. *IEEE Software*, Feb. 1984.

[KRK87] S. Katz, C.A. Richter, and T. Khe-Sing. PARIS : a system for reusing partially interpreted schemas. In *Proc. 9th Int. Conf. Software Eng.*, 1987.

[Lub87] M. D. Lubars. Wide spectrum support for software reusability. In *Proc. Workshop on Software Reusability and Maintainability*, Oct. 1987.

[McI69] M.D. McIlroy. Mass produced software components. In P.Naur and B. Randell, editors, *software Ingineering*, pages 138–155, NATO Sci. Committee, Garmisch, Germany, 1969.

[Mey84] B. Meyer. Reusability : the case for object-oriented design. *IEEE Software*, March 1984.

[Moi88] Th. Moineau. Réutilisation de logiciels : vers une réhabilitation de la réutilisation du code lors de la phase de conception. In *Proc. CGL4*, Oct. 1988.

[MR88]   B. Meijer and E. Rames. Software reuse : from theory to practice. In *Proc. Int. Workshop On Software Engineering & its Applications*, Dec. 1988.

[Nei84] J.M. Neighbors. The DRACO approach to constructing software from reusable components. *IEEE Transaction on Software Engineering*, SE-10(5), 1984.

[PF87]   R. Prieto-Diaz and P. Freeman. Classifying software for reusability. *IEEE Software*, 5(1), Jan. 1987.

[PN86]   R. Prieto-Diaz and J. M. Neighbors. Modules interconnection languages. *Journal of System and Software*, 6(4), Nov. 1986.

[Tra87] W. Tracz. Software reuse : motivators and inhibitors. In *Proc. COMPCON S'87*, 1987.

[Tra88] W. Tracz. Software reuse maxims. *ACM Sigsoft Software Engineering Notes*, 13(4), Aug. 1988.

[TRC83] H. Tardieu, A. Rochfeld, and R. Colletti. *La méthode MERISE : principes et outils*. Les éditions d'organisation, Paris, France, 1983.

PRACTITIONER: Pragmatic Support for the Reuse of Concepts in Existing Software

C. BOLDYREFF, P. ELZER, P. HALL, U. KAABER,
J. KEILMANN and J. WITT

The Practitioner Consortium - ESPRIT Project P1094

1. INTRODUCTION AND RATIONALE

Software reuse has become recognised as a vitally important method for reducing software costs and enhancing software quality. Practitioner has its own particular approach to software reuse:
- reuse of concepts rather than code
- working with existing software, rather than prescribing practices which will lead to the development of new software which is reusable.

1.1. Cost of Software Production

With the advances in computing technology, we are tackling ever larger software projects. The new faster hardware enables us to tackle problems that would have been infeasible a few years earlier. However, the cost of software is not simply proportional to the size of the software; it increases non-linearly with size and complexity. We want to produce more software systems: how can we do it?

During the thirty or so years that computing systems have been in use, we have developed a growing understanding of how software should be developed: there are very many text books addressing *software engineering*, and very many companies selling software development *methods* and *tools*. Yet in spite of this there have been no significant increases in software productivity. If we measure productivity in terms of lines of code produced per day, then we still only produce 10 to 20 lines per day when all ancillary activities are also taken into account. While we may have roughly doubled our rate for the same problem, we have then halved it again because we are tackling harder problems. We could in principle continue as before - for more software, employ more people. But demand grows faster than our educational systems can produce suitable graduates.

Something must be done. We must achieve the same capability within our computer systems, but produce less code and require fewer people to do it. One way to do this is to program in ever higher levels of language, to move towards specifications from which automatic programming takes over. But another way to do this is to attempt to recover the capital investment in existing software and to build upon the know-how that has gone into previous designs and implementations. A lot of software development produces systems similar to ones that have been produced before: perhaps new capabilities are required, some technological advance is to be accommodated, but essentially the system will be the same as some previous system. Yet we are unable to reuse the previous software. Many seemingly small factors, like the difficulty in understanding the existing implementation or the need to move to some new language, cause us to start again.

We must be able to recover the investment in existing software: to do so is one way to break the productivity barrier. How we can do this is the focus of the Practitioner project.

Frequently the issue in software development may not be the cost of development, but the timescale: a new system must be available before some critical date, and cost may be irrelevant. This concern is closely related to the productivity concern discussed above. Any solution to the productivity problem would be a solution to the timescale problem. One solution is the reuse of software.

1.2. Quality of Software Produced

The inadequate quality of software has long been a source of irritation to users of software, and a source of embarrassment to the producers of software. The newer methods, with their more disciplined approach to development, place less reliance on individual software engineers, and have made possible significant improvements in quality.

But our ambitions work against this trend:
- As systems become larger and more complex, they become very significantly more difficult to understand and get right. Smaller systems with larger functionality are what we want. We could understand them and thereby ensure their correctness and fitness for purpose.
- Larger systems have more software to go wrong, and with increased complexity there are more ways for them to go wrong.
- With software becoming all pervasive, it now controls systems which, if they failed, could lead to loss of life or loss of large amounts of money. These high integrity systems have to be very reliable.

The reuse of software concepts and components provides one solution. Software concepts and components that have been in service for many years will have been proven in use. Defects of both design and coding will have been removed, through the uncovering of these defects by constant use: the residual defect rate will be significantly less than for new software. Software put together from reusable parts will then itself be inherently more reliable. Of course the new system will contain some new software, if only the specification of the interconnections between the parts: but this new software will be comparatively small and therefore tractable.

The quality problem is associated with the productivity problem: many quality problems arise through constraints on cost and timescale, if we were more productive then we could take more care in the development of software and apply the many well-known methods for assuring quality.

1.3. Qualification of Personnel

System development by the reuse of domain concepts, along with many of the high-level languages and application generators being advocated, moves the software development activity towards the end-user. Increasingly software development organizations are finding that they need to acquire application skills, either through the involvement of end-users, or through the specialist training of their technical personnel.

On the one hand this appears to give benefit, it leads to systems which are more likely to fulfil the requirements of the users, and exploits people from other disciplines thus relieving the skills shortages. On the other hand it increases training costs for computing staff, and requires a kind of generalist that may itself be in short supply.

1.4. Cost of Reuse

In discussing the above problems, it has been argued that one solution is the reuse of software concepts and components, with a particular emphasis on the recovery of investment in existing software. We have argued for benefits in productivity, timescale, quality, and personnel requirements. But all this requires some investment.

To be able to reuse software we need to identify the concepts and components that are reusable, and describe these in a manner that helps in their reuse. We need to store these and assist engineers find the concepts of concern to them. And we need to help engineers deploy the concepts within the solution to some new development problem. All this requires investment, in the methods and tools to support reuse, and in the particular concepts that will be reused. While the former will need to be amortised over several years, the cost of an individual concept will need to be amortised over several uses: simple economic models suggest that very few reuses would be sufficient.

1.5. The Practitioner Approach to Reuse

With its emphasis on reusing concepts realised in existing software, the project has developed and refined a working definition of such *concepts*, and means of their capture: a questionnaire. To guide the application and exploitation of the questionnaire, the project has developed a metamodel of reuse, investigated various forms of representation appropriate for software concepts, and initiated a programme of research applying the techniques and tools of Linguistics to the Natural Language descriptions of software concepts. Existing software has been analysed; and work has begun on the development of a prototype Reuse Support System.

2. METHODOLOGY

2.1. The *Concept*

In *everyday language* it seems to be quite self-evident what is meant by the term *concept*, but it has turned out to be rather difficult to arrive at a proper definition of this term in the framework of Computer Science. Interestingly though, it appears in literature in various places with approximately the same meaning as it has been used in the Practitioner project. So, for example, as far back as 1968, at the famous Software Engineering Conference in Garmisch, Wirth remarked:

> *I believe that the art of computer programming is based on a relatively small number of fundamental concepts. It became clear during the development of Pascal that most of these concepts are already present in mathematics in some form, usually surrounded by a terminology different from the one used by programmers. It is necessary to demonstrate this duality in the expression of concepts* ... [WIR 68].

The view that programming languages can be regarded as highly formalized collections of programming concepts that have been completely understood at the time of the development of the language, is becoming accepted and has proven very useful for teaching and understanding of such languages [HOR 84, ELZ 84].

The term *concept* has been used more frequently in A.I. and in Cognitive Science [SCH 75, BRO 84]. The way it is used there, e.g. as *conceptual modelling*, corresponds with the intentions of the Practitioner project. On the basis of that understanding, the authors have propounded the following definition [PRA 87]:

> *A* **concept** *is an abstract task, described by its purpose (and/or goal), the related objects, related tasks and/or the functional principles of the underlying mechanism (which will be typically, but not necessarily, of an algorithmic nature).*

Examples of such concepts are (in order of increasing complexity):
- Simple arithmetic and logic operations on simple data types (one might also call these: *atomic concepts*)
- Stacks and their respective operations, operations on composite data types, save/restore sets of registers, synchronization mechanisms, etc.
- Schedulers, clock-handlers, disk-drivers, buffering mechanisms, etc.

Finally, in the application domains of the Practitioner project, some rather complex concepts have been identified, such as:
- Processing of production orders in a control program, adaptive control algorithms, monitoring of material flow, etc.

This *Cognitive Science view* of the concept has proved to be a viable working definition. It seems to describe adequately the abstraction process that goes on in the mind of any designer, i.e. the proper *clustering* of details into some comprehensible compound - the concept - that helps a human brain to handle otherwise unmanageable masses of details. The related thought processes were first classified by Rasmussen [RAS 76] for the task of the operator of complex industrial processes, but were later extended to include the designer's task [RAS 85, ROU 84].

2.2. The Questionnaire

Rationale
Very early in the project, a *questionnaire* was designed [ELZ 87] to serve as a standard template for the capture of concepts. This was intended to be flexible

with respect to the particular detailed design descriptions used, and both textual and graphical descriptions have been used, conforming to a variety of *methods*.

The questionnaire requires three *views* of the concept to be documented. An application oriented view records how the concept is used (or is intended to be used) within other higher level concepts. A functional view specifies the concept in terms of its input and output data, control flows, errors, and the functions performed on these. The structural view describes the concept in terms of the composition of subconcepts, thus enabling us to capture multilayered concepts, with high-level concepts described with respect to immediate constituents which are themselves concepts, and so on.

Other Uses of the Questionnaire

While the questionnaire was initially designed as a vehicle for knowledge acquisition, it has also found general use within Practitioner in other ways.

It provides a standard form for the documentation of new software, and it is intended that software produced within the project should have its design documented using the questionnaire. The similarity between the questionnaire and the IEEE Standard 1016 on Design Descriptions [BAR 86, IEEE 87] has been noted.

For software that is being captured from diverse sources, the questionnaire provides a standard format for concepts, a canonical form, which enables these concepts to be brought together.

The questionnaire also provides a common vehicle for the capturing of requirements for new systems which will be built from the concepts in our library. It is possible that the requirements questionnaire may be matched against the library to retrieve one or more library concepts that would satisfy the requirements. More generally, the need for other concepts will need to be deduced from the requirements questionnaire, and these searched for in the library.

Experience with Use

The questionnaire has now been used by a variety of people across Practitioner, and we have accumulated a considerable experience in its use. Filling in the questionnaire has required a searching analysis of what it is that is being described; when existing software is being described, the documentation and code has had to be analysed. Filling in the questionnaire has sometimes proved to be a difficult and tedious job, and there is a clear need for tools to help in this process.

There have been variations in the interpretation concerning what should be included under the various headings, and in one case where there was sound existing documentation very close to the questionnaire, this similarity was only observed after some considerable time.

In use it has been discovered that the description of versions is inadequate, and the questionnaire will need to be extended in this area. Similarly, no facility has been provided in the questionnaire for the description of generic concepts, and extension for this will also be needed. The studies reported below provide guidance in both these areas.

2.3. A Metamodel

Given the experience with the questionnaire, and the many discussions within the project and with our reviewers, we have abstracted a metamodel of reuse [HAL 89]. There are two focusses of the metamodel - the data of reuse, and the process of reuse.

For the data of reuse, we have described the questionnaire using an entity-relationship model, which naturally emphasises the cross-referencing between questionnaires within the parts hierarchy. We have made a number of simplifications and extensions, drawing upon more general understanding about the software development process as manifest for example in IPSEs. This has led us to characterise the interaction between concepts via a single entity, the *interface*, which embraces the data, control, and error or exception handling parts of the questionnaire. This use of interfaces also shows the relationship between the questionnaire and object-oriented descriptions of software.

An important addition has been the acknowledgement that concepts will in general be generic (or even parameterised), with their use as parts of other concepts being instances of the concept where some or all of the parameters are fixed. Initially concepts would be expected to be specific, with this genericity being abstracted later from a number of specific concepts.

The questionnaire and its developments described in the metamodel form the central data for reuse. This data is created and used within the reuse life cycle and described in the metamodel through dataflow diagrams. There are four principal activities within this cycle:

- identification, selection, and abstraction of concepts for reuse
- classification and storage of concepts
- search for and retrieval of concepts
- design of new systems from reusable concepts.

The new systems are recycled through the reuse process to capture new concepts to be stored in the library, and so the cycle is closed.

In the design of new systems, the metamodel acknowledges the idea of design frameworks, high level concepts that fall between requirements and component concepts aligned with the implementation.

2.4. Representation of a Software Concept

The metamodel of the data of reuse provides a data model for the basic reusable element within Practitioner, the software concept. This model along with the complementary model of the process of reuse has guided the specification of the prototype Reuse Support System (RSS). The concerns investigated here have been related to developing an operational view of software concepts based on Object Oriented Descriptive methods. The various representations have been considered with the intention of providing the groundwork for a common base representation of the software concepts descriptions derived from the questionnaire to inform designers of the RSS prototype and associated tools.

This study has been motivated in part from a problem early on in the project [PRA 87]: What knowledge structures are appropriate within the RSS to reflect the possible interrelations between software concepts in order to advise the designer with regard to technically reasonable combinations? As a result of investigations undertaken, it is now recognised that a common canonical form is required to represent software concepts and their interrelations not only to provide an appropriate representation of knowledge captured via the questionnaire to support the designer in the reuse of concepts, but also to facilitate the integration of tools within the RSS. Such a common representation of software concepts will enable separately developed tools within the RSS which manipulate concepts to be successfully integrated.

2.5. Program Linguistics

This research has focussed on following topics:
- Classification methodology and Retrieval Strategies
- Terminology Analysis

Classification Methods and Retrieval Strategies

We need to classify the concepts. Various classification methods were considered: classical enumerative, controlled index terms, facetted, and thesaurus based. Two of these have been used in the classification of software [TAJ 84, PRI 85]. On Practitioner, we combine the facetted method with the thesaurus based method. We are constructing thesauri using the relevant ISO standards [ISO 85, ISO 86]; and terms held in each thesaurus are grouped under facets.

What we want to retrieve are software concepts described by questionnaires. The questionnaire is a highly structured document, something which is characteristic of software documentation in general. It is tempting to use the fields of the questionnaire as database keys, and this can work for some of the fields e.g. *name of concept, version*; but obviously this does not work for the textual descriptions of the questionnaire. This leaves a problem of how to retrieve concepts in questionnaires which are possible reuse candidates, when the user can not provide a precise query formulation. Relating terms used in a query through a thesaurus to those used to describe known concepts provides a basis for such retrieval. Construction of, and semi- or fully automatic updating of knowledge based thesaurus to support retrieval are tasks we are currently tackling.

Terminology Analysis

A prerequisite for the construction of such knowledge based thesaurus is terminology analysis, and we have already developed two strategies for acquisition of terminology knowledge:

1) one based on automatic extraction of index words from a natural language text, reducing this list by means of a stop word list, specifically produced for the software domain. This gives us a list of the crucial terms (concepts) from the material analyzed.

2) The other method that we have used is interviews with experts, in order to capture expert terminology and knowledge. Doing knowledge acquisition by

means of interviews has turned out to be a quite demanding process, because the interviewer has to be quite an expert himself in order to evaluate and understand 'expert knowledge'.

This work has included automatic and expert analysis of terminology. By automatic analysis of the software documentation and questionnaires, we have extracted the following:

- Lexically Ordered List of Terminology
  This list provides us with total description of the vocabulary.
- Frequency Ordered List
  This provides a basis for the construction of a stop list; the strategy is that words which occur with a high frequency should be put into a stop list, as they do not support precision in retrieval.
- Stop Lists
  We have extracted two kinds of stop lists: *common words* and *meaningless words*.

Through analysing interviews with programmers, we collected synonyms and alternative terms for the concepts found in existing software from various application domains.

3. EXISTING SOFTWARE DOMAINS ANALYSED

The project has carried out major investigations of real-time applications software within two domains: steel production and building automation. A small pilot study of our techniques and tools was made on the UNIX software tools.

3.1. Steel Production

The Application Problem

One of the two business units of ABB that participate in the Practitioner project is concerned with the design and implementation of large control systems for the steel industry. The application problem is characterized by the fact that over a period of ten years more than fifty control systems have been developed and that substantial know-how exists in the department, but that design know-how is mostly transferred to new projects in informal ways (*by word of mouth*), and that existing programs are hardly ever reused.

The reason for this is that all applications seem to be different from each other. In addition to this, there are usually major (sometimes drastic) changes of the technological basis (hardware and system software) during the typical project duration of several years. It also occurs that, due to the various customer requirements, several hardware families have to be supported in parallel.

On the other hand, it had long been known within the department that underlying common concepts existed in the seemingly different solutions. But experiments with conventional software technology (module libraries, data dictionaries, documentation standards, software development systems) did not result in a satisfactory degree of reuse, despite some partial successes. An analysis of the situation indicated that the reuse problem in such an environment could only be solved on a higher level of abstraction, the concept level.

Analysis of Existing Material

The questionnaire was used as a guideline and checklist for the identification, description and structuring of those design concepts that appeared repetitively in the existing material.

In order to be able to handle the mass of material the analysed application domain had to be narrowed down to four areas:

- continuous casting
- strip processing
- tube rolling
- section rolling

This comprised approximately 2200 pages of documentation of two levels:
- requirements specification
- design documentation.

It represented approximately fifty man-years of development effort. The bulk of it consisted of typewritten text containing drawings where appropriate. The analysis was done by one person who could draw upon the advice and part-time assistance of other members of the department. The task consisted mainly of reading the design descriptions of a number of projects and trying to identify common patterns, i.e. concepts. These were then described using the questionnaire. Twelve questionnaires were completed in total.

The work was very tedious and time consuming, but turned out to be highly successful in the sense that it yielded insights that had been partially expected beforehand. The main results are:

- One cannot properly reuse detailed design concepts without a sufficiently clear idea of the overall system framework in which they are to be used. This led to the definition of a standard structure for control software systems in steel production which is explained more deeply in section on The Standard Structure and its Use.

- The software life cycle has to be extended by the procurement phase. Strong correlations exist between the preparation of offers and preliminary system design (cf. also The Standard Structure and its Use).

- Terminology (and taxonomies) play a much more important role in the design and reuse process than any of the contributing engineers had expected beforehand. To others this might not look surprising; it reveals the importance of communication in a planning and design process. It was discovered that the various people involved in the design process use different terminologies and that in discussions and documents these are mostly intermixed. This results in poor comprehensibility of texts and obscuring of design ideas.

The Separation of Terminologies

An attempt was made to separate these different terminologies. A first simple approach was to organize the terms in a three-dimensional scheme. Each coordinate was thought to correspond to one particular terminology. Each individual term was to stand for one concept. It was further imagined that the plane, spanned by two coordinates, could be filled e.g. by a matrix, mapping the terms on one to another. The axes were:

- An Application Axis, containing those terms that are used by engineers with expertise in steel production and overall control system design and which stand for functions typically found in this class of applications. Examples are: Coil Management, Roll Program Handling, Roll Administration, Secondary Spray Cooling.
- An Organizational Axis, comprising terms that stand for functions typically found in the analyzed design descriptions. This terminology is mainly used by engineers who do concrete system design and development and who have knowledge in the organisation of production processes. Examples are: Order Management, Material Management, Data Table Management, System Communication.
- A Data Processing Axis, on which terms can be found that describe concepts typical for the implementation of DP-systems, like Buffer Administration, Task Communication, etc. This is the usual terminology of the implementation specialist and programmer.

At first work concentrated on the organizational axis, because this was the most readily available expertise within the responsible department. It soon turned out that the terms on this axis corresponded very well with the functionality of the usual building blocks (=design concepts for subsystems) out of which the system designs were composed. Therefore these terms were collected and ordered. It turned out that their number was relatively small and that they could be arranged in two levels of detail. Work is still continuing with respect to the next lower level, which will considerably increase the number of established terms.

No work was invested with respect to the data processing axis because similar aspects are dealt with elsewhere in the Practitioner project (e.g. in connection with the UNIX terminology), and because it was found that there existed already a rich literature on data processing terminologies and taxonomies, see e.g. the Computing Reviews classification.

But as soon as it was tried to arrange the application oriented terms in a similar way as the *organization terms*, the picture became more complicated. The terms identified clearly belonged into the same overall category, i.e. metal production and processing, but they could (at least until now) not be ordered into a structure of comparable simplicity as in the case of the organizational axis. There were *narrower terms* and *broader terms* that could be arranged into a tree-like structure, but there were also synonyms and *semi-synonyms*, i.e. terms that partially meant one component, subsystem or action, but also included aspects of another. Worst of all, it turned out that many customers used private terminologies that had to be interpreted by the designers during offer writing.

As far as the mapping of the coordinates onto each other is concerned, a matrix had appeared to be sufficient in most cases. But after the discovery of very complex relations within the application oriented terminology, other mechanisms had to be discussed. This holds in particular for the implementation of application concepts by means of *organizational concepts*. The mapping of the organisation related terms onto the DP-oriented terms still seems to be fairly straightforward, i.e. the higher level concepts on the *organizational-axis* can be implemented using the *lower-level* concepts of the *DP-axis*. However, recent discussions have shown, that, depending on the overall implementation technique used, the mapping of the application concepts onto the organisational concepts can follow quite different rules than the ones described earlier.

The simple three-dimensional model had therefore to be abandoned and will be replaced by a more refined model after a more detailed analysis of the application oriented terminology. Nevertheless, it has helped to understand several observations that had been made during the analysis phase. One of these is described in the following section.

The Missing Layer

After some concepts had been extracted from an implemented system, an attempt was made to identify them in other existing software systems as well in order to verify their validity. This attempt was successful on the uppermost descriptive level, but on the level of detailed design all similarities seemed to have disappeared.

Upon investigation, it was found that in nearly all accessible system designs one descriptive level was missing and that the detailed design had been greatly influenced by the peculiarities of the underlying system software and even hardware. Figure 1 illustrates this discovery.

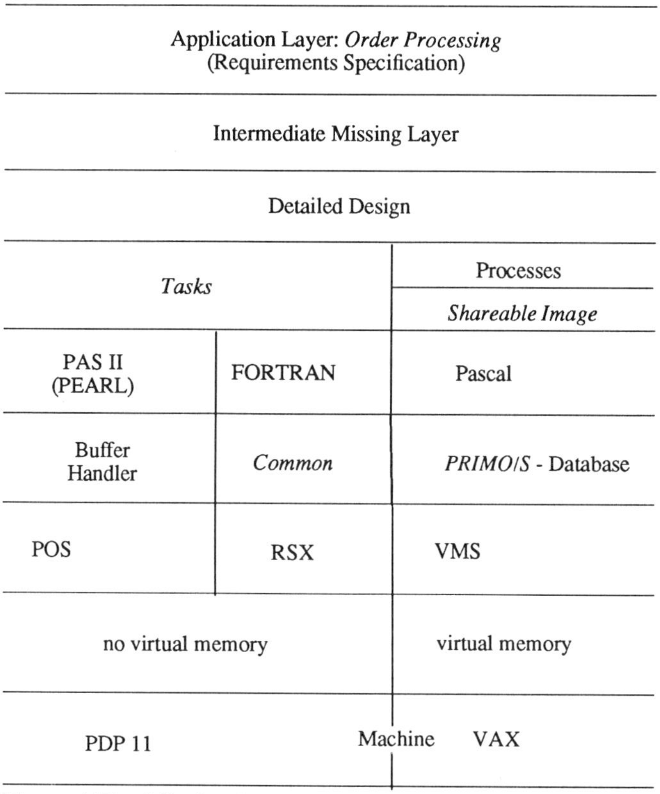

Application Layer: *Order Processing* (Requirements Specification)		
Intermediate Missing Layer		
Detailed Design		
Tasks		Processes
		Shareable Image
PAS II (PEARL)	FORTRAN	Pascal
Buffer Handler	*Common*	*PRIMO/S* - Database
POS	RSX	VMS
no virtual memory		virtual memory
PDP 11	Machine	VAX

Figure 1 The Missing Layer

At first there did not seem to be a correlation between the three dimensions of a description and the discovery of this *missing layer*. However, following consultations with experienced design engineers, it was observed that there was indeed a correspondence between the descriptive dimensions and the levels of design in the phase model. It appeared that the various *dimensions* corresponded very well with the following design levels:

    Application Axis   - Requirements Analysis,
                              Overall System Design

    Organizational Axis   - Structural and Functional Specification,
                              Overall Software Design

    Data Processing Axis   - Detailed Software Design,
                              Implementation

This observation also explains a phenomenon commonly observed in the use of software specification and description methods: Stepwise refinement (or decomposition) of a design in one particular method (e.g. SADT) usually only works over a limited number of levels. Then a *rupture* is observed and the method seems to be no longer applicable. This is usually the point where developers abandon the method and resort to their *personal intuition*, because of lack of a clear idea how to handle the transition in a controlled way.

The *multi-dimensional model of design* has shown that these ruptures can be understood as *transition points* from one terminology into another and a more complex mapping function has to be applied than just refinement. In most cases, however, a matrix still appears to be sufficient. As this explanation was regarded as plausible by all developers involved, it has been kept as a *working hypothesis* for the Practitioner project.

The Standard Structure and its Use

After several concepts on the overall software design level had been identified and provisionally described, an attempt was made to combine them into a global prototypical system design. It turned out to be very difficult to draw stable border lines between the concepts. Therefore, a generalized system structure was developed and described on its two uppermost design levels, using the method given in the questionnaire. The respective graphic representations used familiar system design symbols. Two diagrams, one showing *Uppermost Level of General System Structure* and the other showing *First Level of Detail of General System Structure*, were distributed within the department and their use recommended as a basis for the preparation of offers. This was an immediate success. The engineers felt that they could understand the texts of the calls for tender better than before and were able to detect similarities in the seemingly different customer requirements that before had been obscured by slightly different terminologies and implicit assumptions of certain system structures.

After this highly successful first experiment the engineers were encouraged to use the standard structure for the overall design of systems to be built for successful bids. However, difficulties arose. It seemed to be no longer possible to map a more precise interpretation of the customer requirements onto a refinement of the proposed general system structure. It has not yet been possible to work out a solution for this new problem, but the current results suggest the following:

Work on terminologies has to be intensified.

It appears that there are more subtle differences in the use of the various terms by the individual customer than originally expected. This makes it very difficult for the development engineer to map the meaning of these terms onto a more precise idea (= concept) of a solution (cf. also The Separation of Terminologies). Therefore work has been started to develop a thesaurus (= standard terminology) of those application terms that have come to the knowledge of the most experienced development engineers in the department, to describe the meaning of these terms as well as known synonyms, and to make this material available to the engineer in a computer based form. This appears to be a classical case of knowledge acquisition, concentrating on the taxonomy part of a knowledge base. This corresponds extremely well to other researchers' discoveries, e.g. Prieto-Diaz in [PRI 87].

Aspects of Cognitive Science come into play.

Regarded from a Cognitive Science viewpoint, the above observations seem to be completely plausible. The creation of a suitable model (i.e. a collection of one or more software concepts in the sense of Practitioner) of the system to be developed - the standard structure - suddenly facilitated the interpretation of the representation of another person's - the one writing the call for tenders - mental model by the design engineer. The degree of correspondence between these two models was entirely sufficient for purposes of offer preparation, but insufficient for matching more detailed models, i.e. the details of the application and the next refinement level of the design. Therefore work has to be invested in a better description of the lower levels in order to support the design engineer in doing this matching.

The Software Life Cycle has to be extended.

If the above observations hold - and there is evidence that suggests they will - it seems to be reasonable to include the process of offer preparation in the software life cycle model. This is not new from a theoretical point of view, because it can be subsumed under requirements specification, but has not been done so far in any well established way in practical applications to the knowledge of the authors.

Experience with the Questionnaire in this domain

In general the questionnaire has turned out to be a very good tool for the work described in the above sections. Nevertheless some deficiencies were detected and will lead to a modification of this document:

- The questionnaire does not contain means to describe and discriminate versions of a design concept
- The mechanisms for describing data in the questionnaire are clumsy and cannot be readily understood
- The separation of the descriptions of the functionality of a concept on various design levels in one questionnaire has to be better defined and explained.
- The handling of keywords by underlining them has been critizised by most users.

Novices usually have to be trained in the use of the questionnaire just like any other program description method. This seems to be quite reasonable, when compared other nontrival means of knowledge acquisition.

However, the central idea of the questionnaire, the decomposition of a design into discrete functional levels by the rule that one questionnaire can only contain one level of *Immediate Parts*, has proven its value.

3.2. Building Automation

The Application Problem

The application problem in the second business unit of ABB involved in the Practitioner project was completely different. In that department, which provides control software for building automation purposes, a very successful reconfigurable software package had been developed and adapted to over seventy specific installations worldwide. The reconfiguration process was supported by an interactive program system that allowed the development engineer to configure the special version needed on the basis of application parameters like *number of inputs*, *control algorithms wanted*, etc. It was hoped that the analysis of this package by the Practitioner project would yield guidelines on how software modules could be parameterized, how configuration management could be improved, etc.

The starting point for that analysis was that the system had to be ported to a new hardware generation. As it had been very well structured from the beginning (e.g. SADT had been used for the specification, a data model of the system had been kept stable over several years, and documentation guidelines together with a well managed and coherent team had kept management visibility at a high level) no serious technical problems were expected. It was rather hoped that some of its successful features could be incorporated into the Practitioner Reuse Support System. As the work progressed, other issues turned out to be more important.

A central problem was that the original system had been designed as a centralized architecture for a particular computer, and that it had to be ported to a decentralized system of another vendor. In order to justify the effort it was decided to redesign it in such a way that it could be more readily adapted to other hardware families, if this should be necessary in the future.

This automatically led to a decomposition of the system design into more separable concepts and it was felt that one day it might be necessary to administer a collection of loosely related software concepts in the way that had been foreseen by the Practitioner project. To gain experience with that technique, we undertook an experiment with a *pre-prototype* of a retrieval system for software concepts. In contrast to the work described in 3.1., these concepts already existed in a detailed design and partially in code. The experiment was therefore judged as a valuable complement to the work described above.

Results to Date

The results of the experiment turned out to be very interesting:

- It is possible to extract concepts and software modules from existing documentation automatically by means of a software tool, if this documentation conforms to a consistent practice.
- The relevance of the multi-dimensional model of description was confirmed. For the mapping of the organizational axis on the data-processing oriented axis similar considerations hold as for the mapping of the other two axes onto each other.
- The strict separation between the various levels of implementation, which is maintained by the questionnaire, can help considerably to increase the reusability of software concepts at a detailed level as well.

From the beginning of the experiment a significant similarity between the existing documentation guidelines and the structure of the questionnaire was observed. It was therefore deemed possible to write a software tool that could extract the necessary information from the existing documentation and reformat it according to the categories of the questionnaire. At first this appeared not to be a success at all because the resulting documents were clumsy and did not show a technically meaningful structure.

But a subsequent analysis produced two very encouraging results:
- The unsatisfactory results were mainly due to problems of interpretation of the structure of the questionnaire on the side of the developers of the transformation tool. After gaining a better understanding of this structure and its objectives, they were able to modify the tool and extract documents very close to the questionnaire structure. Of course this confirms the observation made above, that the use of the questionnaire requires training.
- It was confirmed that the mapping of the organizational axis onto the data-processing axis can also be done according to the principles described in the section on The Separation of Terminologies. This resulted from an analysis of the questionnaires produced automatically, which, below a certain level of detail, did not seem to reflect program structure any more. It produced groupings of modules according to pure implementation requirements. At the same time the terminology for the description of the subconcepts changed into purely data-processing oriented terms.

Seen in the overall framework of the Practitioner project, the latter result appears to be very encouraging from a methodological point of view. It confirms the usefulness of the separation of terminologies and the significance of terminology changes as an indicator for major transitions in the design process.

Experience with the Questionnaire in this domain

The questionnaire was tested in interaction with existing documentation. Two important recommendations resulted:
- The questionnaire is not completely clear yet in its lower levels. So e.g. the representation of *atomic concepts* was not understood, and the references to existing code have to be better specified. As a basis for version control, the questionnaire in its current form is inadequate.
- The structure of the questionnaire has to be made generic, because users cannot be expected to redocument their entire base of existing software in order to reuse it within the Practitioner Reuse Support System.

On the other hand it turned out that some traditional shortcomings of (even good) existing documentation have to (and can) be remedied in order to improve reusability of software. Interestingly enough the most important one of these is again connected with terminology, its use and its context; it was observed that the main problems with the reuse of an (otherwise excellently documented) software package could be traced back to the fact that its original designers had obviously taken for granted the special properties of the underlying operating system and hardware to such an extent that they usually did not document at all where they had used them! The questionnaire, often criticised as overly rigid or too detailed, would have prevented this by providing information such as *functions used*, *control input* and *control output*, etc.

4. CONCLUSION

The main result so far is that the ideas underlying the Practitioner approach could be consolidated and its feasibility firmly established. In particular the intense and sometimes controversial discussions with potential users have resulted in a mutual understanding of the problems of the users by the tool designers and, in turn, of the possibilities and limitations of tools on the side of the users.

A metamodel has been proposed that consists of a *reuse life cycle* and a data model of the questionnaire. The near future will show its viability. The idea of *program linguistics* has turned out to be more stable and fruitful than originally expected. The significance of *terminologies for the design process* has been shown and thereby a deeper understanding of the various phases in the software life cycle gained. The role of taxonomies as part of the knowledge base has been confirmed and connections to Cognitive Science detected.

A broad base of material has been established and provided a sound basis for the design and development of the prototype RSS. It comprises taxonomies as well as filled in questionnaires with descriptions of program concepts. This holds both for the UNIX and for the Real Time *cultures*. Last but not least: potential test users have been identified and motivated. It is important to establish reuse as an idea in both the managers of software development and in the development teams. Reuse must be seen as help and not as an additional requirement to the developer, imposed by management and seen as impairing the developer's *productivity*. This can only be achieved if the RSS is able to provide enough meaningful material to the user and if its concept-base can be easily expanded by the inclusion of new information.

5. ACKNOWLEDGEMENTS

The work described in this paper has been carried out with the support of the CEC under the ESPRIT project P1094. The collaborators in this project are Asea Brown Boveri AG, Computer Resources International, PCS Computer Systeme GmbH and Brunel University. In addition to the authors, individuals from all of these orgainisations have made contributions to the work reported here.

6. REFERENCES

[BAR 86] H Jack Barnard, Robert F Mertz, and Arthur L Price, *A Recommended Practice for Describing Software Designs: IEEE Standards Project 1016*, IEEE Transactions on Software Engineering, Vol SE-12, No 2, February 1986.

[BRO 84] Brodie, Mylopoulos, Schmidt (Editors); **On Conceptual Modelling**, Springer-Verlag, 1984.

[ELZ 84] Elzer, P.F.; *Software Project Management*, Proceedings of the 4th IFAC/IFIP Symposium on Software for Computer Councel, Graz, Austria, May 1984, pp.1-12, Pergamon Press.

[ELZ 87] Elzer, P.F. *et al*; *Recommendations on the Use of Descriptive Methods*, Practitioner P1094-WPA1.2-CRI-007, April 1987.

[HAL 89] Hall, P.A.V.; *A METAMODEL for Software Components and Reuse*, Practitioner P1094-BrU-PH-WPB1-Working Paper, 12 January 1989.

[HOR 84] Horowitz, E.; **Fundamentals of Programming Languages**, Springer-Verlag, 1987.

[IEEE 87] **IEEE Recommended Practice for Software Design Descriptions**, ANSI/IEEE Std 1016-1987, The Institute of Electrical and Electronic Engineers, Inc., 1987.

[ISO 85] ISO 5964-1985; Documentation - Guidelines for establishment and development of multilingual thesauri.

[ISO 86] ISO 2788-1986; Documentation - Guidelines for establishment and development of monolingual thesauri.

[PRA 87] Practitioner Consortium, ESPRIT Project P1094 -PRACTITIONER: A Support System for Pragmatic Reuse of Software Concepts, Technical Annex, Version 3, 25 May 1987.

[PRI 85] Prieto-Diaz, R.; A Software Classification Scheme, Doctoral Dissertation, University of California: Department of Information and Computer Science, 1985.

[PRI 87] Prieto-Diaz, R,; *Domain Analysis for Reusability*, COMPSAC87 Conference, Tokyo, Japan, October 7-9, 1987.

[RAS 76] Rasmussen, J.; Outlines of a Hybrid Model of the Process Plant Operator, from: Monitoring Behaviour and Supervisory Control, T. Sheridan and Johansen (eds.), Plenum Press, 1976

[RAS 85] Rasmussen, J., Goldstein, L.P.; *Decision Support in Supervisory Control*, Proceedings of the 2nd IF AC/IFIP/IFOFS/IEA Conference on Analysis, Design and Evaluation of Man-Machine-Systems, Varese, Italy, Sept. 1985, Pergamon Press.

[ROU 84] Rouse, W.B., Hunt, R.M.; Human Problems Solving in fault Diagnoses tasks, in: W.B. Rouse (Editor), Advances in Man-Machine Systems Research, Vol 1, JAI Press, Greenwich, Conn., 1984.

[SCH 75] Schank, R.C., ed.; **Conceptual Information Processing**, Amsterdam, North Holland, 1975.

[TAJ 84] Tajima, D. and Matsubara, T.; 1984, *Inside the Japanese Software Industry*, IEEE Computer, (17):3, 1984.

[WIR 68] Wirth, N.; *The programming language PASCAL and its design criteria*, in: Buxton, Randell (eds.): Software Engineering Techniques; Report on NATO Conference, Rome, April 1970, Kynoch Press, Birmingham, 1970.

Authors' Addresses

Cornelia Boldyreff and Professor Pat Hall, Department of Computer Science, Brunel University, Uxbridge UB8 3PH, United Kingdom.

Dr.-Ing. Peter Elzer, ABB Asea Brown Boveri, CRH/L2, Eppelheimer Str. 82, 6900 Heidelberg, Federal Republic of Germany.

Ulla Kaaber, CRI Computer Resources International A/S, CPE, Bregnerodvej 144, 3460 Birkerod, Denmark.

Dipl.-Ing.(FH) Johannes Keilmann, ABB Asea Brown Boveri, ME/TC2, Kafertaler Str. 258, 6800 Mannheim 1, Federal Republic of Germany.

Dr. Jan Witt, PCS Computer Systeme GmbH, Pfalzer-Wald-Strasse 36, D-8000 Munchen 90, Federal Republic of Germany.

FEB 7 1991